POLISH CINEMA

POLISH CINEMA

A HISTORY

SECOND, UPDATED EDITION

Marek Haltof

First published in 2002 by
Berghahn Books
www.berghahnbooks.com

© 2002, 2019 Marek Haltof

Second, updated edition published in 2019

All rights reserved. Except for the quotation of short passages for the purposes of criticism and review, no part of this book may be reproduced in any form or by any means, electronic or mechanical, including photocopying, recording, or any information storage and retrieval system now known or to be invented, without written permission of the publisher.

Library of Congress Cataloging-in-Publication Data
A C.I.P. cataloging record is available from the Library of Congress

Library of Congress Cataloging in Publication Control Number: 2018040179

British Library Cataloguing in Publication Data
A catalogue record for this book is available from the British Library

ISBN 978-1-78533-972-1 hardback
ISBN 978-1-78533-974-5 paperback
ISBN 978-1-78533-973-8 ebook

Contents

List of Illustrations	vii
Acknowledgements	xi
Introduction	1
1 Polish Silent Cinema (1896–1929)	9
2 The Sound Period of the 1930s: Adaptations, Patriotic Melodramas, and Films in Yiddish	41
3 Cinema, World War II, and the Postwar Construction of National Identity (1939–1948)	69
4 Screen Stalinism: Socialist Realist Films (1949–1954)	96
5 Ashes and Diamonds: The Polish School (1955–1963)	115
6 Adaptations, Personal Style, and Popular Cinema (1964–1975)	170
7 Camouflage and Rough Treatment: The "Cinema of Distrust" (1976–1981)	220
8 The Cinema of Martial Law and Afterward (1982–1988)	254
9 A Fistful of Dollars: Polish Cinema after the Wall Came Down (1989–1998)	274
10 Adapting the National Literary Canon and Reclaiming the Past (1999–2004)	341
11 The Transforming Years (2005–)	370

Appendices	427
Selected Filmography	431
Selected Bibliography	445
Index of Names	471
Index of Film Titles	486

Illustrations

Fig. 1.1   Kazimierz Junosza-Stępowski. Publicity still. Public domain
           (www.polona.pl).   10
Fig. 1.2   Pola Negri. Publicity still. Courtesy of Filmoteka Narodowa.   18
Fig. 1.3   Jadwiga Smosarska (left) in *The Leper* (1926), directed by Edward
           Puchalski and Józef Węgrzyn. Public domain (www.polona.pl).   19
Fig. 1.4   Gregori Chmara and Maria Majdrowicz in *A Strong Man* (1929),
           directed by Henryk Szaro. Courtesy of Filmoteka Narodowa.   25
Fig. 2.1   Maria Bogda and Adam Brodzisz in *The Baltic Rhapsody* (1935),
           directed by Leonard Buczkowski. Narodowe Archiwum Cyfrowe.
           Narodowe Archiwum Cyfrowe. Public domain (Wikimedia
           Commons).   48
Fig. 2.2   Helena Grossówna (center) in *Forgotten Melody* (1938), directed by
           Konrad Tom and Jan Fethke. Courtesy of Filmoteka Narodowa.   53
Fig. 2.3   Józef Węgrzyn and Hanna Karwowska in *The Ghosts* (1938), directed
           by Eugeniusz Cękalski and Karol Szołowski. Courtesy of Filmoteka
           Narodowa.   60
Fig. 2.4   Lili Liliana as Leah in *The Dybbuk* (1937), directed by Michał
           Waszyński. Public domain. Author's collection.   62
Fig. 2.5   Molly Picon (left) and Symcha Fostel in *Yiddle with His Fiddle* (1936),
           directed by Joseph Green and Jan Nowina-Przybylski. Courtesy of
           Filmoteka Narodowa.   63
Fig. 3.1   (From the left) Jadwiga Andrzejewska, Renata Bogdańska, and Albin
           Ossowski in Michał Waszyński's *The Long Road* (1946). Photograph
           from the collection of Anna Maria Anders. Courtesy of Filmoteka
           Narodowa.   73
Fig. 3.2   (From the left) Maria Kaniewska (*Raportführerin*), Edward
           Dziewoński (SS doctor), Wanda Jakubowska, Janina Marisówna
           (*Aufseherin*), and Aleksandra Śląska (*Oberaufseherin*) on the set of

	Jakubowska's *The Last Stage* (1948). Photograph from Edward Dziewoński's archive. Courtesy of Roman Dziewoński.	86
Fig. 4.1	Kazimierz Opaliński in Andrzej Munk's *Man on the Tracks* (1957). Courtesy of Filmoteka Narodowa.	108
Fig. 5.1	Zbigniew Cybulski as Maciek (left) and Adam Pawlikowski in Andrzej Wajda's *Ashes and Diamonds* (1958). Courtesy of Filmoteka Narodowa.	133
Fig. 5.2	Henryk Boukołowski and Zofia Marcinkowska in Kazimierz Kutz's *Nobody Is Calling* (1960). Courtesy of Filmoteka Narodowa.	137
Fig. 5.3	(From the left) Krzysztof Komeda, Tadeusz Łomnicki, and Roman Polański in Andrzej Wajda's *Innocent Sorcerers* (1960). Screenshot by the author.	153
Fig. 6.1	(a) A scene from Jerzy Kawalerowicz's *Pharaoh* (1966); (b) Jerzy Zelnik as the young pharaoh (left) and Leszek Herdegen as a priest. Screenshots by the author.	176
Fig. 6.2	(From the left) Andrzej Seweryn as Max Baum, Daniel Olbrychski as Karol Borowiecki, and Wojciech Pszoniak as Moryc Welt in Andrzej Wajda's *The Promised Land* (1975). Photograph by Renata Pajchel. Courtesy of Film Studio Zebra.	184
Fig. 6.3	Franciszek Pieczka as Matthew, Małgorzata Braunek (left), and Maria Janiec (right) in Witold Leszczyński's *The Life of Matthew* (1968). Photograph by Jacek Mierosławski. Courtesy of Film Studio Zebra.	198
Fig. 6.4	Jadwiga Jankowska-Cieślak as Magda and Władysław Kowalski in Janusz Morgenstern's *Kill That Love* (1972). Photograph by Renata Pajchel. Courtesy of Film Studio Zebra.	202
Fig. 6.5	(From the right) Jerzy Bińczycki, Olgierd Łukaszewicz, Jan Englert, and Jerzy Cnota in Kazimierz Kutz's *Salt of the Black Earth* (1970). Courtesy of Filmoteka Narodowa.	205
Fig. 7.1	Jerzy Stuhr in Krzysztof Kieślowski's *Camera Buff* (1979). Courtesy of Filmoteka Narodowa.	226
Fig. 7.2	Jerzy Radziwiłowicz in Andrzej Wajda's *Man of Marble* (1977). Photograph by Renata Pajchel. Courtesy of Film Studio Zebra.	228
Fig. 7.3	Krystyna Janda as Antonina Dziwisz (right) and Adam Ferency as one of the interrogating officers in Ryszard Bugajski's *Interrogation* (1982/1989). Photograph by Renata Pajchel. Courtesy of Film Studio Zebra.	243

Fig. 8.1	Scott Wilson and Maja Komorowska in Krzysztof Zanussi's *Year of the Quiet Sun* (1985). Courtesy of Filmoteka Narodowa.	258
Fig. 8.2	Mirosław Baka (Jacek) and Jan Tesarz (taxi driver) in Krzysztof Kieślowski's *A Short Film about Killing* (1988). Courtesy of Filmoteka Narodowa.	269
Fig. 9.1	Jerzy Stuhr as an American gangster on the Odessa Steps in 1925 in Juliusz Machulski's *Déjà Vu* (1989). Courtesy of Film Studio Zebra.	308
Fig. 9.2	Bogusław Linda as Franz Maurer (left) and Cezary Pazura in Władysław Pasikowski's *The Pigs* (1992). Courtesy of Film Studio Zebra.	312
Fig. 9.3	Irène Jacob in Krzysztof Kieślowski's *The Double Life of Veronique* (1991). Screenshot by the author.	326
Fig. 10.1	Adrien Brody as Szpilman (center) and his family in Roman Polański's *The Pianist* (2002). Screenshots by the author.	351
Fig. 10.2	Marek Kondrat as Adam Miauczyński (near the window) in Marek Koterski's *The Day of the Wacko* (2002). Screenshot by the author.	361
Fig. 10.3	Rutger Hauer in Lech Majewski's *The Mill and the Cross* (2011). © Lech Majewski, 2010. Published with permission.	364
Fig. 11.1	Artur Żmijewski (left) and Andrzej Chyra as Polish officers in Andrzej Wajda's *Katyń* (2007). Screenshot by the author.	373
Fig. 11.2	Itay Tiran (center) in Marcin Wrona's *Demon* (2015). Photograph by Marta Gostkiewicz for Magnet Man Film. Courtesy of Kino Świat.	382
Fig. 11.3	Agata Trzebuchowska as Ida (left) and Agata Kulesza in Paweł Pawlikowski's *Ida* (2013). Screenshot by the author.	384
Fig. 11.4	(From the left) Dawid Ogrodnik (Tomasz Beksiński), Aleksandra Konieczna (Zofia Beksińska), and Andrzej Seweryn (Zdzisław Beksiński) in Jan P. Matuszyński's *The Last Family* (2016). Photograph by Hubert Komerski for Aurum Film. Courtesy of Kino Świat.	394
Fig. 11.5	Mirosław Haniszewski (standing) as a militia lieutenant in Maciej Pieprzyca's *I'm a Killer* (2016). Courtesy of Renata Czarnkowska-Listoś and RE Studio.	395
Fig. 11.6	(From the left) Marta Mazurek (Silver), Kinga Preis (Krysia), and Michalina Olszańska (Golden) in Agnieszka Smoczyńska's *The Lure* (2015). Screenshot by the author.	400

Fig. 11.7   Marian Dziędziel (center) as the father of the bride, Tamara Arciuch (bride), and Bartłomiej Topa (groom) in Wojciech Smarzowski's *The Wedding* (2004). Courtesy of Film It/Krzysztof Wiktor.   406

Fig. 11.8   Michalina Łabacz (center) as Zosia Głowacka in Wojciech Smarzowski's *Volhynia* (aka *Hatred*, 2016). Courtesy of Film It/Krzysztof Wiktor.   410

Acknowledgements

I received a great deal of support during the preliminary planning and researching of this project. I would like to thank the Polish Scientific Research Committee (Komitet Badań Naukowych) for supporting the first edition of this work with a generous grant. I gratefully acknowledge the help of Northern Michigan University in Marquette for supporting my research and this work with a faculty grant.

I am thankful to the staff of the Filmoteka Narodowa (National Film Archives) in Warsaw, Poland—Adam Wyżyński, Grzegorz Balski, Krzysztof Berłowski, and Robert Mazurkiewicz—for their generous research assistance. Also, special thanks go to Roman Dziewoński, Renata Czarnkowska-Listoś, Kino Świat, Film It, and the Film Studio Zebra in Warsaw for their help with secondary sources.

Special thanks go to my colleague at NMU, David Boe, for his unvarying support regarding the complexities of the English language. In addition, I would like to thank several scholars who assisted in the preparation of this book in various ways: Andrzej Gwóźdź, Alicja Helman, Jolanta Lemann, Jan F. Lewandowski, Edward Możejko, Bohdan Y. Nebesio, Ewelina Nurczyńska-Fidelska, Wacław M. Osadnik, Michał Oleszczyk, Mirosław Przylipiak, Grażyna Stachówna, and Piotr Zwierzchowski. In addition, my thanks go to Allan Boss and Shawn Kendrick for offering editorial comments concerning the first edition, and Greg Beamish and Alex Clark for their editorial suggestions regarding the second edition.

In addition, my sincere thanks go Paul Coates, Kris Van Heuckelom, and Annette Insdorf—three readers for Berghahn Books. I also extend my sincere gratitude to Chris Chappell, senior editor at Berghahn Books.

Introduction

I am pleased to have this opportunity to update and expand my 2002 book, *Polish National Cinema*. Its new title, *Polish Cinema: A History* emphasizes that this is a revised and enlarged chronological account of the development of Polish cinema from 1896 to 2017.[1] Since 2002, more than five hundred new films have been released alongside dozens of old films, once considered lost, that have reemerged from archives. In addition, several significant studies have been published (in Polish as well as in English) on various aspects of the Polish film industry.

The present book deals not only with films themselves but also with their characteristic features and elements, recognized locally and internationally as distinctively Polish—what one might call a recognizable "national accent." The focus is on full-length narrative films, although the book occasionally offers commentary on major Polish television films, documentaries, and animated films.

Polish cinema has made considerable progress in recent years and, arguably, has become better known outside of Poland. This publication follows the largest presentation of Polish films outside of Poland: the touring twenty-one-film retrospective "Martin Scorsese Presents: Masterpieces of Polish Cinema," which premiered at the Film Society of Lincoln Center in New York on 5 February 2014. It also follows Polish cinema's first Oscar in 2015, the Best Foreign Language Film category for *Ida* (Poland-Denmark) directed by Paweł Pawlikowski.

Throughout its history, the Polish film industry has been able to produce a diverse corpus of work. Several representatives of Polish cinema have enjoyed international fame; some are even generally regarded as masters of cinema. Almost every film history textbook contains a chapter discussing the emergence and importance of the Polish School phenomenon. The names of Poland's best-known directors, such as Andrzej Wajda, Roman Polański, and Krzysztof Kieślowski, are mentioned among the world's most important filmmakers. In many books, the Łódź Film School serves as a model for successful film education.

* * *

Any writer dealing with the development of Polish cinema must take into account the complexity of Poland's history. Changing political situations typically defined the development of local cinema. Polish films thus reflect the history of a land in which national insurrections resulted in military defeat, a presence of occupying forces, and the suppression of Polish culture. It is feasible to distinguish films made in the Polish territories during the absence of the Polish state (before 1918), the cinema of interwar Poland (1918–1939), the cinema of communist Poland (1945–1989), and the films made after the return of democracy in 1989.

It is also necessary to take into account Poland's borders, which have changed throughout history. After the three partitions (in 1772, 1793, and 1795), Poland was wiped off the map in 1795 and divided among its three powerful neighbors—Russia, Austria, and Prussia—until the end of World War I. The partitions of Poland, including the one in 1939 between Soviet Russia and Nazi Germany, defined the character of Polish nationalism: its pro-Catholic stance and antiauthoritarianism, and its largely romantic vision of history.

Because of this "burden of history," Polish cinema and other arts often had to perform specific political, cultural, and social duties. Without a state, without an official language, the partitioned Polish territories were unified by the Roman Catholic religion, a common heritage and culture, as well as a spoken language. Before 1918, Polish territories were on the peripheries of the three European superpowers. Their economy remained poor and underdeveloped; its population had a high illiteracy rate, especially in the biggest Russian-controlled sector.[2] Consequently, it was not the press but the cinema that performed an educational role for a number of people because this art form spoke to the literate and the illiterate.

Polish history provided an abundance of themes for the screen, and local audiences always seemed to prefer films narrating local history and referring to local culture. As a result, a large number of Polish filmmakers were preoccupied with local issues that were, sometimes, difficult for outsiders to comprehend. In addition, during the communist period, Polish films were often seen in the West as works depicting the "political other." Politically minded Western critics, as well as Polish critics, often overlooked their value as works of art.

Given this uneasy background, before the return of democracy in 1989, Polish filmmakers were often expected to perform various educational and nation-building duties. While they also produced entertainment films, the filmmakers saw themselves primarily as guardians of national culture and propagators of the national literary canon. During Poland's communist period, local filmmakers were perfectly aware of their role within the nationalized film industry as educators, entertainers, social activists, and political leaders. Filmmakers were at the foreground of Polish life, accustomed to a situation in which their voices and their works were carefully watched by both authorities and general Polish audiences.

The transition to democracy altered the relationship between filmmakers and their audiences. In the late 1990s, Polish filmmakers began winning back their audiences with popular adaptations of the national literary canon. The foundation of the Polish Film Institute (PISF) in 2005 continued this work by stimulating the film production and increasing popularity of Polish cinema in Poland, as well as abroad.

To write about Polish cinema before 1939, in particular, is a difficult task because little is known about Polish films produced in the early twentieth century. In fact, most early Polish films have been lost. A number of films and documents related to film production before World War II in Poland were destroyed, especially during the Warsaw Uprising of 1944. Because of the absence of several primary sources (films), a researcher must reconstruct the picture of Polish cinema before 1939 through miraculously preserved artifacts—fragments of films, articles, reviews, still photographs, film posters—most of which are archived at the Polish Filmoteka Narodowa (National Film Archives) in Warsaw. An expert on early Polish cinema, Małgorzata Hendrykowska, stressed this arduous investigative task by titling her book on the origins of cinema in Poland *Śladami tamtych cieni (Following Those Shadows)*.[3]

Before the fall of communism in 1989, little had been written about early Polish cinema. The communist authorities preferred to promote the picture of prewar "bourgeois Poland" as a land of commercial cinema and disrespect for art films. They also did not want to mention several prewar films that were anti-Russian and anti-Soviet; these films were neither released nor discussed in the People's Republic of Poland. One faces similar difficulties when dealing with the communist period. Polish sources published before 1989 often suffer from restrictions that had been imposed by the oppressive communist ideology. Frequently, they testify more about the nature of "cultural politics" in Poland than about the aesthetic or political impact of these films or their true popularity.

Polish cinema familiarized local and international audiences with its unique political context. This context and the relationship between film and politics in

Poland had been so self-evident that they frequently served as a preconceived methodological approach. In film criticism, Polish cinema often existed mostly as an expression of Polish history and of political and social tensions, and rarely as a discipline in its own right. The distinguished Polish filmmaker Kazimierz Kutz wrote bitterly in 1996: "Polish cinema in years past, propelled by anticommunism of the West, benefited from the permanent discrediting, because the theme had been always more important than the style. It never had to compete intellectually; we were allowed to enter salons in dirty boots to describe communism, which the public wished a quick death."[4]

For Western viewers, Polish film frequently served as an introduction to communist politics, to the nature of the totalitarian state, to censorship and its repercussions—an Aesopian reading. Nowadays, more and more critics and audiences, not tainted by perspective of the previous system, see films as films, not as political statements playing some role in the demolition of the communist system. By perceiving films merely as political tools, willingly or not, some critics, including me, often situated them among other remnants of the past. Milan Kundera's comment is appropriate in this respect: "If you cannot view the art that comes to you from Prague, Budapest, or Warsaw in any other way than by means of this wretched political code, you murder it, no less brutally than the worst of the Stalinist dogmatists. And you are quite unable to hear its true voice."[5]

* * *

Randall Halle in his book *The Europeanization of Cinema* stresses several of the problems film historians face while debating the early stages of cinema, chiefly the difficulty of distinguishing the difference of the national and the international (film as an international medium and a national product).[6] Halle is right that film historians, including me in *Polish National Cinema*, often tend "to nationalize this prenational cinema."[7] Because of the lack of a Polish state, the Polish territories becoming peripheries of the partitioning superpowers, and the extraterritorial and international nature of early cinema, several Polish filmmakers moved to neighboring state capitals (Moscow, Berlin, and Vienna) where they contributed greatly to cinemas of Russian, German, and Austro-Hungarian empires. Their ethnicity was often overlooked. For example, in his pioneering study about films made on Polish territories during World War I, Mariusz Guzek lists thirty-one films directed by the Polish director Edward Puchalski in Russia from 1915 to 1917, several of them comedies starring the Polish actor Antoni Fertner as Antosza (Antoś). He also lists fourteen films made in Russia with the significant participation of Polish artists from 1915 to 1918, and he provides a list of thirty-two documentaries shot by the Russian military film units on Polish territories.[8] To complicate this issue, one should also take into account filmmakers and film inventors born in foreign capitals to Polish parents who became pioneering figures within other national cinemas. For example, the first Polish animator Władysław Starewicz (Ladislas Starewitch, 1882–1965), the world-known pioneer of puppet films, was born in Moscow, made his first films in Kaunas (today Lithuania) and Moscow, and after 1918 continued his career in France.

For practical reasons, in this book I consider only those Polish filmmakers who either started their careers in Poland (or the Polish territories) or significantly contributed to the development of the Polish film industry. In addition to creating its own national industry, however, Poland has been greatly contributing to world cinema through its émigrés. Most of them are representatives of what in Poland is called "Polonia" (a term referring to Polish émigrés). Most of them are not discussed here, since their artistic biographies are now a part of other national cinemas. For example, I do not discuss extensively Polish diasporic filmmakers, that is, directors, cinematographers, and actors working outside of Poland. For example, not present in this book is a discussion of films directed outside of Poland by Paweł Pawlikowski. He was born in 1957 in Warsaw, but was educated and made most of his films in England, with the exception of the aforementioned Academy Award–winning *Ida*. Also absent in this text are the achievements of a group of prominent Polish cinematographers working in the United States, such as Andrzej Bartkowiak (1950–), Adam Holender (1937–), Janusz Kamiński (1959–), Andrzej Sekuła (1954–), and Dariusz Wolski (1956–). This book also does not include Polish actors whose careers developed abroad, such as Joanna Pacuła and Gosia Dobrowolska. Several film directors, for example, Roman Polański and Jerzy Skolimowski, are considered as essentially Polish artists despite the fact that they left Poland during the early stages of their careers. Their films made in Poland are discussed in this book in more detail, whereas their international careers are covered only briefly.[9]

* * *

Since the mid-1980s, the concept of national cinema has been much debated in film and cultural studies. Many writers have theorized the idea of a nation, nationalism, and national identity, most often returning to the much-quoted book by Benedict Anderson, *Imagined Communities*.[10] National cinema as a multidimensional theoretical construct appears in Thomas Elsaesser's book on German, Susan Hayward's on French, Andrew Higson's on English, and Tom O'Regan's on Australian national cinemas, to name just a few classic examples.[11] More recently, several studies have addressed the issue of transnational cinema concerning Polish film.[12] Apart from the understandable transnational aspect of Polish cinema before 1918 (films made during the last years of the partition period and during World War I), Poland produced films in both Polish and Yiddish during the interwar, so language alone cannot be used as the defining feature of Polish cinema. In recent years, the Polish Film Institute has funded several international productions, including minority projects. Frequently, these borderline films disappear from cinema history books, since they are claimed by different historiographies.

While I am cognizant of the theoretical complexities of the issues involving writing a history of a national film industry, for the purpose of this book I have adopted a simple and functional definition of Polish cinema. I examine films that fulfill at least two of the following criteria: works that were made in Poland (or on the Polish territories before 1918), in the Polish language, and by Polish filmmakers (filmmakers living in Poland, regardless of their nationality). Furthermore, I consider the transnational aspect of Polish films: I examine international coproductions with significant Polish contribution (director and part of the crew), as was the case of Kieślowski's *Three Colours* trilogy (1993–1994). Rather than provide close textual analysis of select films that have already been seen outside of Poland at international film festivals and discussed by scholars, I prefer to present an extensive factual survey of Polish film in general. Less familiar films and names are included to show the richness of Polish cinema and to build a more complete, balanced picture.

The book is divided into eleven chapters. Unlike *Polish National Cinema*, which included three topical chapters covering the representation of the Stalinist years, the representation of Jewish-Polish relations and the Holocaust, and the new action cinema, this revised edition employs a chronological framework—this periodization largely mirrors the political changes that occurred in Poland. The data provided for the films include the year of theatrical release instead of the year of production. During the communist period, the authorities shelved and delayed several films; in such cases, I provide both dates. The Polish title is listed first, followed by the English title in parentheses. All subsequent references employ the English title.

Notes

1. *Polish National Cinema* was the first comprehensive study of Polish cinema in English. It was translated into Polish in 2004 (it was the first single-volume monograph on the history of Polish cinema) and into Japanese in 2006.
2. In 1897, 69.9 percent of the population was illiterate. Małgorzata Hendrykowska, "Was the Cinema Fairground Entertainment? The Birth and Role of Popular Cinema in the Polish Territories up to 1908," in *Popular European Cinema*, ed. Richard Dyer and Ginette Vincendeau (London, New York: Routledge, 1992), 118.
3. Małgorzata Hendrykowska, *Śladami tamtych cieni: Film w kulturze polskiej przełomu stuleci 1895-1914* (Poznań: Oficyna Wydawnicza Book Service, 1993). All translations of non-English works and quotations in this book are my own unless otherwise indicated.
4. Kazimierz Kutz, "Swojski pejzaż," *Kino* 9 (1996): 54.
5. Peter Hames, *The Czechoslovak New Wave* (Berkeley: University of California Press, 1985), 142.
6. Randall Halle, *The Europeanization of Cinema: Interzones and Imaginative Communities* (Champaign: University of Illinois Press, 2014).
7. Ibid., 61.
8. Mariusz Guzek, *Co wspólnego z wojną ma kinematograf? Kultura filmowa na ziemiach polskich w latach 1914-1918* (Bydgoszcz: Wydawnictwo Uniwersytetu Kazimierza Wielkiego, 2014), 570-73 and 560-62.
9. For more, see Marek Haltof, *Historical Dictionary of Polish Cinema* 2nd ed. (Lanham, MD: Rowman & Littlefield, 2015), 8-9.
10. Benedict Anderson, *Imagined Communities: Reflections on the Origin and Spread of Nationalism* (London: Verso, 1983).
11. Thomas Elsaesser, *New German Cinema: A History* (London: British Film Institute, 1989); Susan Hayward, *French National Cinema* (London: Routledge, 1993); Andrew Higson, *Waving the Flag: Constructing a National Cinema in Britain* (Oxford: Oxford University Press, 1995); and Tom O'Regan, *Australian National Cinema* (London: Routledge, 1996).
12. Sebastian Jagielski and Magdalena Podsiadło, eds., *Kino polskie jako kino transnarodowe* (Kraków: Universitas, 2017); Ewa Mazierska and Michael Goddard, eds., *Polish Cinema in a Transnational Context* (Rochester, NY: University of Rochester Press, 2014).

CHAPTER 1
Polish Silent Cinema (1896–1929)

Watching films made then, one may think that authentic life withered in front of the gates of film production companies. Consequently, cinema became the only-of-its-kind reserve of local stereotypes, obsessions, and phantasms.
—*Alina Madej,* Mitologie i konwencje

Polish cinema has a history essentially as long as cinemas elsewhere. The first screening in the Polish territories with the Lumière brothers' camera, Cinématographe, took place on 14 November 1896 in Kraków's municipal theater. The program consisted of some of the films from the first Lumière screening in Paris on 28 December 1895.[1] Nevertheless, the public was already familiar with moving images before this screening organized by the Lumières' representative. As early as mid-1895, Thomas Edison's Kinetoscopes had been introduced in several major Polish cities, so Poles credited cinema's discovery to Edison.[2]

In the early twentieth century in the Polish partitioned territories, as elsewhere, films were shown during public fairs among other wonders of nature. A typical program consisted of documentaries, news, and historical reenactments.[3] Films performed vital educational and nation-building functions for Polish audiences. In the absence of the Polish state, these films portrayed images of other Polish cities (now part of different states) and covered important national events such as mass gatherings at funerals of great Polish artists (for example, the memorial services of writers Stanisław Wyspiański in 1907, Eliza Orzeszkowa in 1910, and Bolesław Prus in 1912). Films also recorded the celebrations of significant national moments in history, such as the 1910 Kraków commemorations of the 1410 Battle of Grunwald against the Teutonic Knights, won by the combined Polish and Lithuanian forces.

Like other nations, Poland had its own cinematic inventors such as Jan Szczepanik and Bolesław Matuszewski. Piotr Lebiedziński and the Popławski brothers (Jan and Józef) collaborated on the construction of an apparatus that

Figure 1.1 Kazimierz Junosza-Stępowski. Publicity still. Public domain (www.polona.pl).

recorded and projected pictures, which they called "Zooskop Uniwersalny." With the help of "Zooskop," the Popławski brothers recorded a number of short scenes on glass plates in 1893. In 1896, another Polish scientist and inventor, Kazimierz Prószyński (1875–1945), created his own camera, called—like his studio—Pleograf (Pleograph).[4] In 1902, the perfected Pleograph was employed by Prószyński to produce the first Polish narrative film, a simple, single-shot feature, *Powrót birbanta* (*The Return of a Merry Fellow*), which introduced one of the most important prewar actors, Kazimierz Junosza-Stępowski (1882–1943). From 1901 to 1903, Prószyński also produced and screened several short documentaries and scenes capturing images of Warsaw.

Regular film production in the partitioned Polish territories started, however, some years later with adaptations of the national literary canon, commercially oriented melodramas, and comedies. In 1908, a short comedy, *Antoś pierwszy raz w Warszawie* (*Antoś for the First Time in Warsaw*, directed by Jerzy Meyer; real name: Joseph-Louis Mundwiller), produced by the owner of a Warsaw cinema called Oaza, introduced another actor, Antoni Fertner (1874–1959). On the screen, he created a fun-loving, chubby character from the provinces, Antoś, an extension of his own popular theatrical and cabaret performances in Warsaw. After being seen in several comedies as Antoś, Fertner became the first recognizable "star" of Polish cinema. From 1915 to 1918, during World War I, he continued his career in Russia working for, among others, Alexandr Khanzhonkov's studio.[5] Fertner appeared in more than thirty Russian films, earning the nickname "the Russian Max Linder." He reemerged in Polish cinema in the 1920s. His favorite brand of comedy was farce; coupled with musical comedy, farce flourished in the 1930s, again with Fertner, though now in strong supporting roles.

In 1908, a film called *Pruska kultura* (*Prussian Culture*, Mordechai Towbin)—the oldest preserved Polish film—introduced a new genre of prewar Polish cinema: "patriotic pictures."[6] The term applies to films set predominantly in recent history that show struggles against Poland's powerful neighbors and efforts to preserve Polish culture and language in the absence of the Polish state. The prototypical patriotic picture, *Prussian Culture* depicts the Prussian Poles suffering under the process of Germanization at the turn of the century and portrays their struggles to preserve their national heritage and to stop German colonization.

A great number of patriotic pictures were produced during World War I and directed against the most oppressive of the occupiers—the Russian tsarist regime.[7] These melodramatic versions of "patriotic kitsch"—such as *Ochrana warszawska i jej tajemnice* (*The Secrets of the Warsaw Police*, 1916) and *Carat i jego sługi* (*The Tsarist Regime and Its Servants*, 1917), both made by the Jewish-Polish producer/director Aleksander Hertz and his studio Sfinks (Sphinks) in Warsaw—laid the foundations for future national art and became an important part of Polish culture. One of the main accusations that had been raised against early Polish film producers was the lack (or decline) of patriotic themes in locally made films. Other allegations dealt with the decline of public morality and the endangered physical health of the youth.

Following the tradition of the French *film d'art*, theatrical actors began to appear in Polish films to give the new medium a much-desired aura of artistic status. In Polish territories, however, theater was not only the domain of high art but also the respected guardian of national values. Artists were called on to play the roles of educators of the masses and defenders and propagators of national culture. Such a task proved extremely difficult to combine with the requirements of popular culture. Despite that, a surprisingly large number of well-known Polish writers had been either writing specifically for cinema (e.g., Gabriela Zapolska) or allowing their works to be adapted for the screen (e.g., Henryk Sienkiewicz, Eliza Orzeszkowa, and Stefan Żeromski).

Adaptations of works published in the early twentieth century created another significant trend in Polish cinema. The year 1911 marks the production of several films adapted from recently published, much-discussed works by Polish authors: *Dzieje grzechu* (*The Story of Sin*, Antoni Bednarczyk), based on Stefan Żeromski's novel; *Meir Ezofowicz* (Józef Ostoja-Sulnicki), based on Eliza Orzeszkowa's work; and *Sąd Boży* (*God's Trial*, Stanisław Knake-Zawadzki), based on Stanisław Wyspiański's drama *Sędziowie* (*The Judges*). Since only fragments of *Meir Ezofowicz* are preserved today at the National Film Archives in Warsaw, and the only source of knowledge about these adaptations remains a few press reports and reviews, it is difficult to discuss their merit as films. We know that they were box office successes, effectively competing with imported films. Although they touched on such problems as the assimilation of Jews (*Meir Ezofowicz*), they attracted viewers primarily with their sensational, "forbidden" topics (*The Story of Sin*) and the exoticism of the portrayed community (*God's Trial*).[8] The historian Sheila Skaff in the only English-language book devoted exclusively to Polish cinema before World War II, *The Law of the Looking Glass, Cinema in Poland, 1896–1939*, writes the following about *Meir Ezofowicz*:

The seemingly bizarre choices made in filming Meir Ezofowicz *may have arisen from Herz's insistence on offering a little something for everyone—for Polish speakers, a Polish novel; for Yiddish speakers, a Yiddish title; for multiculturalists, a story of positive intercultural relations; and for anti-Semites, an anti-Semitic director. Finally, scandal-seekers chitchatted about the fact that a prominent Jewish producer had hired the enemy to direct his films.*[9]

Polish filmmakers were eager to popularize the national literary canon and looked for stage-tested scripts that, apart from signs of high art, contained melodramatic and sensational plots. Their choices had been dictated by the preferences of the Polish viewers. With the exception of the 1912 adaptation of Sienkiewicz's *Szkice węglem* (*Charcoal Sketches*), produced as *Krwawa dola* (*Bloody Fate*, Władysław Paliński), other films were adapted from previously popular stage plays or operas. All of them were closely linked with the Polish historical and cultural contexts. Unlike *film d'art* in France, in Polish productions, "costume was not an indication of theater, a peculiar reference to 'genuine art,' but the sign of the presence of Polish culture."[10] This may explain the popularity of the faithful adaptation of *Halka* (1913, Karol Wojciechowski) from the Polish national opera by Stanisław Moniuszko. Another popular film, adapted from a celebrated play by Władysław Ludwik Anczyc, *Kościuszko pod Racławicami* (*Kościuszko at Racławice*, 1913, Orland), was an epic production with thousands of extras that portrayed the defeat of the Tadeusz Kościuszko Insurrection of 1794 by a combined Russian and Prussian army. This film had also been screened for Polish emigrants in the United States and Canada.[11]

Both domestic and foreign films that had Polish themes, or were based on Polish literary classic works, proved to be box office successes in the Polish territories. One of them was a lavish Italian spectacular *Quo Vadis?* (1913) by Enrico Guazzoni, adapted from Henryk Sienkiewicz's classic 1895 novel of the same title and set in Rome under Emperor Nero. The preference of Polish audiences for films narrating their history or referring to Polish culture had been often exploited by film distributors, who did not hesitate to alter titles or intertitles to find an audience.[12] "The history of cinema in Poland is, in large part, a history of people alternately participating in and negotiating ways to avoid the linguistic and class tensions with which they lived on a daily basis," writes Skaff.[13] She also emphasizes that although cinema from its origins supported the cause of Polish nationalism, it also "exacerbated existing conflicts between speakers of different languages under the partitions."[14] Several recently published regional histories of Polish cinema stress the complexity of the language issue on the Polish territories that were multinational, multilingual, and part of different powerful states.[15]

The most significant single influence on early Polish films was exercised by Danish melodramas, which were widely distributed in Poland, especially contemporary "decadent" melodramas starring Asta Nielsen and directed by Urban Gad. Polish filmmakers imitated their sensational and tragic stories. They also attempted to portray formerly forbidden topics: sexuality, prostitution, and the world of crime. For example, in *Wykolejeni* (aka *Aszantka, Human Wrecks / The Led Astray*, 1913, Kazimierz Kamiński and Aleksander Hertz), one finds the familiar story, also exploited in later Polish films, of a young girl from the province who comes to a big city and is corrupted by its excess and lack of moral principles. The influence of Danish films began to wane during World War I; gradually, German films, including expressionist films, started to dominate the Polish market.

The Beginning of Yiddish Cinema in Poland

A significant number of early films made in the Polish territories were productions in Yiddish, the language of more than ten million Jews living in Eastern Europe and in Jewish Diasporas in the United States.[16] Interwar Poland was a multinational state, with national minorities (Jewish, Ukrainian, Belarusian, German, etc.) comprising more than 30 percent of the total population. The census based on language, conducted in 1931, shows that Poles accounted for less than 70 percent of the population. The Jewish minority (speaking Yiddish as the first language) comprised 8.7 percent and was behind the Ukrainian-speaking minority of 14 percent.[17] In the capital city of Warsaw (the center of Polish film production), Jews accounted for about 38 percent of the population in 1914, as much as 50 percent in 1917, 26.9 percent in 1921, and 28.4 percent in 1931.[18]

The first Yiddish films known to have been produced in Poland appeared in 1911, such as *Der Wilder Foter* (*The Savage Father*, Marek Arnsztejn [Arnshteyn]). In 1913, six out of sixteen films were productions in Yiddish based mostly on popular plays by Jacob (Jakub) Gordin, such as *Der Unbekanter* (*Stranger*, Nachum Lipowski) and *Gots Sztrof* (*God's Punishment*, aka *God's Orchard*, Izak Kamiński).[19] Warsaw became the center of Yiddish cinema during World War I with such production companies as Kantor Zjednoczonych Kinematografów—branded as "Siła" (Power)—founded by Mordechai (Mordka) Towbin, and Kosmofilm, headed by Samuel (Shmuel) Ginzberg and Henryk Finkelstein, both companies established in 1913. Films in Yiddish had been popular in the 1920s, especially works produced by Leo Forbert's studio, Leo-Film, and photographed by Forbert's cousin, Seweryn Steinwurzel, who quickly gained the reputation as arguably the best prewar cinematographer working on both Yiddish and Polish films. Forbert's production *Tkies Kaf* (*The Vow*, aka *The Handshake*, 1924, Zygmunt Turkow), starring the famous Ester-Rokhl Kamińska ("the Jewish Eleonora Duse") and her daughter Ida Kamińska (Turkow's wife), was lauded by, among others, a Polish critic, Andrzej Włast, who praised its on-location scenes, commenting that they were done "with a great feeling of photogeneity."[20] In his book on Yiddish film, J. Hoberman comments that *The Vow* "confidently drew on folk tradition—the various misalliances and deceptions resolved through divine intervention—and this supernaturalism was certainly part of its appeal."[21]

Jewish films and themes were appreciated by Poles and other nationalities living in prewar Poland, who enjoyed their exoticism, reliance on metaphysics, and social themes, such as the Jewish participation in Polish history and the problem of assimilation. Among these films is *In di Poylishe Velder* (*In Polish Woods*, 1929, Jonas Turkow), an adaptation of Joseph Opatoshu's novel published in 1921, which employs well-known Jewish and Polish actors to tell a story about Polish-Jewish unity during the January Uprising of 1863 against tsarist Russia.[22]

Studio Sfinks (Sphinx)

Film production in the Polish territories before World War I remained the domain of economically feeble, ephemeral studios. This situation continued even after the World War I. For example, 321 feature films produced in interwar Poland (1919–1939) were made by as many as 146 film production companies. Ninety of them shut down after making their first picture, and only twenty-five were able to make more than three films.[23]

The studio Sfinks, established in 1909 and headed by Aleksander Hertz (1879–1928), dominated the film landscape in prewar Poland.[24] In 1915, Hertz merged with another studio, Kosmofilm, which also owned a film laboratory in Warsaw.[25] With the outbreak of World War I, when other film studios went bankrupt, Hertz established international contacts first with Russian and then with German companies. These connections helped him to survive on the market and to broaden his sphere of influence. The number of films made in the Polish territories increased during the war. The new Sfinks production and distribution company, headed by Hertz with Henryk Finkelstein as his deputy, established a virtual monopoly. During the German occupation of Warsaw (from August 1915 to November 1918), Sfinks produced, among others, several "patriotic anti-Russian pictures" that reflected the spirit of the times, such as the aforementioned *The Secrets of the Tsarist Warsaw Police* and *The Tsarist Regime and Its Servants*.[26]

Before the end of the war, the studio, which relied heavily on its own version of the star system, was immersed in a crisis. It had lost its two biggest stars, Pola Negri and Mia Mara (Aleksandra Gudowiczówna, later known as Lya Mara), who moved to Germany in 1917. Because of the lack of Polish statehood and a solid film industry, it was common for Polish artists to be active outside of the Polish territories, especially in Berlin, Moscow, and, to a lesser degree, Vienna. Moscow attracted several Polish actors and filmmakers, including Ryszard Bolesławski, Edward Puchalski, and pioneer of puppet cinema Władysław Starewicz (aka Ladislas Starevich, 1892–1965). Born in a Polish family in Moscow, Starewicz received acclaim for his stop motion animation films with insects and dolls, such as *The Beautiful Lukanida* (1910), *The Battle of the Stag Beetles* (1910), *The Ant and the Grasshopper* (1911), and numerous others made at Aleksandr Khanzhonkov's studio. After 1919, he continued his career in France. Opportunities for Polish artists were not confined to the neighboring capitals; for example, Helena Makowska and Soava Gallone (Stanisława Winawerówna) had successful acting careers in Italy.

Despite the growing competition on the Polish market, the early 1920s belonged to Hertz's Sfinks and its continuing strategy, which recognized the commercial appeal of stars. Hertz was also responsible for launching the career of his new star, Jadwiga Smosarska. In the early 1920s, he produced a series of melodramas, known as the "Sfinks golden series," with Smosarska as the lead. These were films like *Tajemnica przystanku tramwajowego* (*The Tram Stop Mystery*, 1922) and *Niewolnica miłości* (*The Slave of Love*, 1923), both directed by Jan Kucharski. Portraying the dangers facing young women, these moralizing films exploited sensational themes under the umbrella of "educational films."

Sfinks dominated mainstream Polish cinema with its combination of patriotic and melodramatic features: the use of national themes and mythologies, the exploitation of "educational" topics, and borrowings from Hollywood (sensationalism, dynamic action, stars). One of Hertz's films produced in 1926, *O czym się nie myśli* (*The Unthinkable*, Edward Puchalski), contains almost all of the aforementioned features: the sensational title, love that goes beyond class borders (a successful musician from a wealthy family gets involved with a worker's daughter), and "the girl with the past," who (to make it worse) is suffering from a venereal disease (the film was intended to campaign against sexually transmitted diseases). Finally, it has love and betrayal mixed with the necessary patriotic theme (the protagonist takes part in the Polish–Soviet War of 1919–1920).[27] Although the studio lasted until 1936, Hertz's premature death in 1928, at the age of forty-nine, marked the end of the first period of Polish cinema.

Polish Film Stars: Pola Negri and Jadwiga Smosarska

Hertz's biggest discovery certainly was Pola Negri (Barbara Apolonia Chałupiec, 1897–1987), a "Polish Asta Nielsen"—a young, photogenic, and energetic star with a modest background in dancing and theater. In a series of unsophisticated but popular melodramas, starting with her debut, *Niewolnica zmysłów* (*Slave of Sin*, aka *Love and Passion* and *Slave to Her Senses*, 1914, Jan Pawłowski),[28] she created a Polish femme fatale who attracts and then destroys her lovers. The eight melodramas that Negri made for Sfinks are frequently set in the exotic Warsaw underworld, and peopled with streetwise characters and outlaws—those driven by passionate love and suffering from its destructive power.

In the only surviving film out of eight melodramas made for Sfinks, *Bestia* (aka *Kochanka Apasza; The Polish Dancer*, 1917, Aleksander Hertz), as well as in *Slave of Sin*, the character played by Negri is killed by her jealous former lover. Another film, *Żona* (*Wife*, 1915, Jan Pawłowski), is described by a reviewer in 1915 as "the tragedy of a wife who loves her husband but, after a long internal struggle, must accept a disgraceful proposition from her husband's supervisor because she is afraid that he may lose his job. She confesses her mistake to her husband and then takes her life."[29] Negri sealed her popularity with a series of films made by Sfinks in 1917 known as *Tajemnice Warszawy* (*The Mysteries of Warsaw*), which referred to real-life Warsaw criminal activity and erotic affairs.[30]

The Sfinks origins of Negri's stardom, as well as the beginnings of her career in Germany, are less well known than her career in the United States. Thanks to her

Figure 1.2 Pola Negri. Publicity still. Courtesy of Filmoteka Narodowa.

role in the pantomime *Sumurun*, produced in 1913 by Ryszard Ordyński (1878–1953) for a Warsaw theater, Negri moved in 1917 to Berlin to play the same character in Max Reinhardt's stage production.[31] From 1917 to 1922, she starred in approximately twenty German films. Her career, however, accelerated after she met Ernst Lubitsch, who directed her in internationally famous films, such as *The Eyes of the Mummy Ma* (*The Augen der Mumie Ma*, 1918), *Carmen* (1918), *Madame DuBarry* (*Passion*, 1919), and *Sumurun* (aka *One Arabian Night*, 1920), which enabled her to move with him to Hollywood in 1922.[32]

After Negri's departure for Germany, Jadwiga Smosarska (1898–1971) became Sfinks's leading star in the 1920s, and she remained one of Poland's major stars into the 1930s.[33] Unlike Negri's aggressive, caricatured women, Smosarska specialized in characters who embodied a number of clichéd female Polish virtues. Her protagonists were patriotically minded, romantic, well bred, and beautiful, yet they suffered the pangs of unhappy, often tragic, love. She started her career by playing supporting roles in propagandist "patriotic pictures" dealing with the Polish–Soviet War, such as *Cud nad Wisłą* (*Miracle on the Vistula*, 1921), directed by Ryszard Bolesławski, an actor, screenwriter, and director trained at the famous Moscow Art Theatre, who moved to Hollywood in 1922.[34]

Characters played by Smosarska in patriotic pictures are in line with the Polish romantic female stereotype, which was, and still is, present in many Polish films. In Polish iconography, originated during Poland's partition (1795–1918), a female character stands for suffering, pain, and subordination—the symbol of the suffering country.[35] This iconography also stresses that women are responsible for preserving national heritage, since the public sphere, usually the domain of men, is taken by the occupiers. The symbolic Polish woman represents a peculiar form of Polish patriotism, which is a combination of the martyrological (she sacrifices her own welfare for the country—images of numerous mothers sending their sons

Figure 1.3 Jadwiga Smosarska (left) in *The Leper* (1926), directed by Edward Puchalski and Józef Węgrzyn. Public domain (www.polona.pl).

to meet their death and glory in a series of national uprisings) and the religious (she is reminiscent of Mary suffering after Christ's crucifixion). The mythologization of a female character in Polish culture, the stress on her dignity, often leads to her monumentalization and one-dimensional representation, because, "while making choices, she always takes into account the interest of the country, and even the simplest household duty gains exceptional importance as being part of a sacred service for the enslaved country."[36]

Smosarska achieved fame later when she appeared in several melodramas produced by Sfinks, such as *The Tram Stop Mystery* and *The Slave of Love*. Polish critics compared her no longer with Asta Nielsen (which, at that time, was the highest compliment a Polish actress could get)[37] but rather with less theatrical and increasingly popular American actresses, chiefly Lillian Gish. For instance, in *Iwonka* (1925, Emil Chaberski), she plays an innocent Gish-like character in love with a handsome uhlan (light cavalry) lieutenant, her savior. In this and other works, Sfinks succeeded in creating a mélange of patriotic and melodramatic films that reinforced clichés dealing with Polishness. The setting of the action of *Iwonka* in so-called Kresy (Borderlands, Polish Eastern Provinces) and images of noble young girls from country manors who parade with their good-looking uhlans are present in many subsequent films.

The peak of Smosarska's career is certainly the box office hit of the 1920s—*Trędowata* (*The Leper*, 1926), directed by Edward Puchalski and Józef Węgrzyn, and adapted from the best-selling novel by Helena Mniszkówna. (Mniszkówna's popular romance had almost no competition in Polish literature, which was then highly didactic and obsessed with history.) The film offers an unsophisticated love story that goes beyond class borders and is free from the political and social responsibilities that restrained "serious" Polish literature. The title of the film refers to the protagonist, Stefcia Rudecka (Smosarska), a young teacher in mutual love with the nobleman Waldemar Michorowski (Bolesław Mierzejewski). Under Stefcia's civilizing influence, Waldemar leaves his life of revelry and becomes a responsible man. Stefcia is, however, rejected by his family and his class, and treated like a leper. Because of the intrigues instigated by Waldemar's circle, Stefcia becomes ill and dies before their scheduled wedding. As one Polish critic noticed about this narrative: "[Mniszkówna] employed the pattern so simplified and categories so general that apparent banality had been changed into mythology."[38] The apparent lack of originality and the fact that the action takes place among the Polish rich and famous made the film attractive to "ordinary" viewers. This may explain many subsequent imitations of Mniszkówna's writing, as well as many adaptations for the screen of her other works.[39]

Film Industry after 1918

The restoration of the Polish state in 1918 created conditions for the development of national art. After the war, however, there was practically no film industry in Poland. The postwar period was affected by the presence of economically feeble Warsaw-based studios, a few outdated films, high tariffs and taxes, and ineffectual distributors based in former partition territories. In 1921, twenty-seven million inhabitants lived in Poland, 69.2 percent of whom were Poles. Cinemas numbered around four hundred.[40] During the interwar period, the ratio of cinemas to inhabitants situated Poland at the very low end of the scale in Europe, above only Albania and Yugoslavia. In Poland, there was one cinema for every 46,400 inhabitants, compared to 12,000 inhabitants in Germany and 9,500 in Czechoslovakia.[41] The situation had moderately improved toward the end of the 1920s with 727 cinemas in operation.[42] Undoubtedly, the economic backwardness, due to the period of partition, and the unstable postwar political and economic reality that Poland experienced after 123 years of nonexistence contributed greatly to this situation.[43]

The poor Polish economy, inflation, and huge differences in the economic development of various parts of the country contributed to the imposition of heavy taxes on the owners of cinemas. The municipal tax on movie passes was at 50 percent in Warsaw in 1919 and as much as 100 percent in 1920. Such measures led to the decline of attendance, to the sporadic closing of cinemas, and, finally, to an unusual protest strike by cinema owners in 1923. Taxes were lowered in 1926 to 75 percent, and again in 1931, when they oscillated between 10 and 60 percent, depending on the film.[44] Taxes had been reduced on Polish "patriotic pictures," which may partly explain the popularity and rate of recurrence of such pictures in prewar Poland.

American films entered the Polish market after the war and became hugely popular. D. W. Griffith's films were screened in Warsaw for the first time in 1920 (*Judith of Bethulia*, 1914, and *Intolerance*, 1915), but the name of the "father of American cinema" was barely mentioned in press reviews. Everything changed in 1922 after the Polish premiere of Griffith's *Orphans of the Storm* (1921). Critics started talking about the American school of filmmaking, associating it no longer with sensationalist action cinema but rather with art films.⁴⁵ According to Kristin Thompson, American films dominated the Polish market and contributed 39.4 percent of all screened films in 1924, 52.9 percent in 1925, and as much as 70.6 percent in 1926.⁴⁶ Flooded by American films, Polish authorities tried to impose a ten-to-one contingent plan (ten imported films for every Polish production), which did not materialize because of the pressure Hollywood placed on the Polish minister of foreign affairs and the minister of the interior.⁴⁷

Although numerous American films were screened in Poland after 1922, immediately after World War I (1918–1921), critics and viewers in Poland preferred European (chiefly German) films to American products.⁴⁸ Occasionally, American films (including films by Griffith) had been promoted as or compared to German films to find viewers in Poland. Later, films by Griffith, Cecil B. DeMille, and Charlie Chaplin and some American genre films (thrillers and William S. Hart's Westerns) took the Polish screens by storm. In 1925, some American studios, including the Fox Film Corporation and Universal, established their distribution offices in Poland.⁴⁹

The mid-1920s also marked the return of French films, including critically acclaimed impressionist films. In 1925, French films held 20 percent of the Polish market, and German films 15 percent.⁵⁰ Despite the geographical closeness, the number of Soviet films on the Polish market was extremely small because of political censorship in Poland.⁵¹ Postwar Poland was a country traditionally suspicious of ideas coming from its communist neighbor, so it is not surprising to note that in 1925 Soviet films had only 0.4 percent of the Polish market; *Battleship Potemkin* (1925, Sergei Eisenstein) and *Mother* (1926, Vsevolod Pudovkin) had problems being released on Polish screens.⁵² However, Russian films made before the Russian Revolution of 1917 and films made by Russian directors who emigrated from Imperial Russia to France were imported to Poland, mostly by Sfinks. From 1918 to 1921, approximately forty such films premiered on Warsaw screens, including pictures starring the Russian émigré actors Ivan Mozzhukhin and Vera Kholodnaya.⁵³

Genre: Patriotic Pictures

Immediately after World War I, "patriotic pictures" became a staple of Polish cinema. Heavily promoted by the new Polish state, these films referred to recent wartime experiences and emphasized the role of the Polish Legions and their commandant, Marshal Józef Piłsudski, in regaining independence.[54] The historic fear of Russia was expressed in several films dealing with the 1920 Polish–Soviet War, such as *Miracle on the Vistula, Bohaterstwo polskiego skauta* (*The Heroism of a Polish Boy Scout*, 1920, Ryszard Bolesławski), and *Dla Ciebie, Polsko* (*For You, Poland*, 1920, Antoni Bednarczyk). The 1918–1919 battle with the Ukrainian forces for Lvov (today Lviv in Western Ukraine) was portrayed in *Tamara* (aka *Obrońcy Lwowa, The Defenders of Lvov*, 1919), made by the first and only female Polish director working during the silent period—Nina Niovilla.[55] Films confronting recent Polish-German history were scarce but did exist. For example, the turbulent modern history of industrial Upper Silesia, with its series of risings against German rule, was the topic of the propagandist *Nie damy ziemi skąd nasz ród* (*We Will not Give up Our Land*, 1920, Władysław Lenczewski). Another film, the well-received *Bartek zwycięzca* (*Bartek, the Victor*, 1923, Edward Puchalski), was adapted from Sienkiewicz's novella about the struggles to preserve Polishness under the German rule, and it starred the famous Polish wrestler Władysław Pytlasiński.

In the mid-1920s, Polish patriotic pictures had been evolving in two directions: political melodrama and historical reconstruction. The first group, including films such as *Miłość przez ogień i krew* (*Love Through Fire and Blood*, 1924, Jan Kucharski), has been aptly summarized as follows: "In search of an attractive script, the producers were ready to reach for whatever themes, ideas, programs, atmosphere, political news; they treated them in the manner of cheap pulp fiction."[56] Historical reconstructions include films made chiefly after Marshal Piłsudski's coup d'état in May 1926, during the so-called *Sanacja* (literally, period of moral purification). These films mythologized Piłsudski, his Polish Legions, and the patriotic tradition they represented. Frequently, they dealt with the January Uprising (*powstanie styczniowe*) of 1863 against tsarist Russia or with the 1905 revolution in the Russian-controlled part of Poland. The ideology of the 1863 and 1905 heroic struggles served the newly emerging mythology of Marshal Piłsudski's Polish Legions well. The regaining of independence in 1918 was portrayed in Polish historiography as a result of the earlier efforts by the young and desperate patriots.[57]

The former assistant of Robert Wiene, Józef Lejtes (1901–1983), directed one of the best examples of patriotic pictures, *Huragan* (*The Hurricane*, 1928, Polish-Austrian production). Its story of suffering and intrepid struggle is told through tableaux-like compositions, modeled on Artur Grottger's series of sketches titled *Polonia* (1863) and *Lithuania* (1864–1866). Grottger's powerful visions of the uprising—stressing its heroic and tragic dimension, patriotic fervor, and the pain of the defeat—virtually replaced the factual knowledge about the 1863 insurrection. Grottger and the painter Jan Matejko are often credited as being responsible for influencing Polish national imagery. Grottger's works frequently overshadowed and emulated later literary attempts to retell the events of 1863. In the interwar period, Polish films followed Grottger's version of the events and his manner of portraying patriotism, pathos, and religious and patriotic symbols. As Alina Madej rightly points out, Grottger's imagery—as seen in its theatricalization of mise-en-scène, actors' poses, and lighting—had overtaken the film. In so doing, the director Lejtes follows the long Polish tradition of staging "live paintings," usually allegories of abstract concepts (such as "Poland," "freedom"), or the "apotheosis" of important historical figures.[58]

References to Polish painting tradition aside, the martyrological national drama by Lejtes also contains elements of Griffith's dynamic editing techniques and melodrama. The love story between a young insurgent, Tadeusz Orda (Zbigniew Sawan), and a proud noblewoman, Helena Zawiszanka (Renata Renée), is set against the backdrop of the 1863 January Uprising. Rather than following the unwritten rules of melodrama, *The Hurricane* ends tragically, as do many Polish historical dramas: after learning about his lover's death at the hands of the Russians, the insurgent dies a heroic death, attacking the enemy with a group of his compatriots. The final call to arms and the suicidal charge, however, bring some hope. They symbolically link the events of 1863 with the year 1918, creating a connection with another group of insurgents: the victorious Piłsudski's legionnaires.

A combination of the patriotic and the melodramatic is also present in many other films that tell the story of the 1863 uprising. Some of them are literary adaptations, for example, *Rok 1863* (*Year 1863*, 1922, Edward Puchalski), based on Stefan Żeromski's novel *Wierna rzeka* (*Faithful River*).[59] The blend of melodrama and history, with the addition of the assimilationist discourse, is also discernible in a group of Yiddish films, addressed primarily to Jewish audiences: *In Polish Woods* and Henryk Szaro's debut in Yiddish, *Der Lamedvovnik* (*One of the Thirty-Six*, 1925). Furthermore, the return of recent history is also seen in a small group of films about "Piłsudski's road to Poland," such as *Mogiła nieznanego żołnierza* (*The Tomb of the Unknown Soldier*, 1927) by Ryszard Ordyński and *Szaleńcy* (*Daredevils*, 1928, rereleased in 1934 in the sound version) by Leonard Buczkowski (1900–1967).

The Tomb of the Unknown Soldier contains many elements of another group of Polish films: dramas inspired by metempirical phenomena, such as metempsychosis and telepathy, and peopled by demonic characters (and by mediums and ghosts).

German influences, sometimes described in Poland pejoratively as *mabuzeria* (inferior imitations of Fritz Lang and early Paul Wegener dramas),[60] are apparent in several films: *Blanc et noir* (1919, Eugeniusz Modzelewski, written by Dimitri Buchowetzki, who also played the leading role), *Syn szatana* (*Satan's Son*, 1923, Bruno Bredschneider), *Orlę* (*Young Eagle*, 1927, Wiktor Biegański), and *Mocny człowiek* (*A Strong Man*, 1929, Henryk Szaro). The latter, an adaptation of Stanisław Przybyszewski's novel published in 1913, received critical acclaim—the leading role was played by the Ukrainian-born actor Gregori Chmara, who had earlier appeared in classic German films such as *Raskolnikow* (*Crime and Punishment*, 1923, Robert Wiene) and *Die freudlose Gasse* (*The Joyless Street*, 1925, Georg Wilhelm Pabst).

German *Kammerspielfilm* influences, chiefly Pabst's films, are noticeable in *Kropka nad i* (*The Final Touch*, 1928) and *Policmajster Tagiejew* (*The Police Chief Tagiejew*, 1929), both films directed by Juliusz Gardan (Gradstein, 1901–1944). The latter was based on Gabriela Zapolska's novel and produced by Leo-Film, which

Figure 1.4 Gregori Chmara and Maria Majdrowicz in *A Strong Man* (1929), directed by Henryk Szaro. Courtesy of Filmoteka Narodowa.

emerged as the strongest film studio after Sfinks. Toward the end of the 1920s, however, Polish films were not being compared to German cinema; now the comparison was to American film. For instance, *Czerwony błazen* (*Red Jester*, 1926, Henryk Szaro) was praised by the critic Leon Bruno, who noted that this fine film bears "the signs of the good American school, assimilated by the clever and talented disciple." The much-praised beginning of Buczkowski's debut *Daredevils* was "indeed American" for one of the reviewers.[61]

Adaptations and Personal Style

Polish cinema has been known for its close bonds with national literature. In the early twentieth century, literature provided an abundance of patriotic and social themes not only for the stateless nation but also for the emerging national cinema. It also gave Polish cinema some respectability among audiences and helped to grant cinema the stature of art. Adaptations of the national canon remained very popular in the second half of the 1920s. Literary works by, among others, Stefan Żeromski, Józef Ignacy Kraszewski, Adam Mickiewicz, and the Nobel laureates Władysław Stanisław Reymont and Henryk Sienkiewicz had been written by notable contemporary writers and adapted for the screen.

The most prestigious productions include *Ziemia obiecana* (*The Promised Land*, 1927, Aleksander Hertz and Zbigniew Gniazdowski) and *Pan Tadeusz* (1928, Ryszard Ordyński). The former, adapted from Reymont's novel of the same title, commemorated the twentieth anniversary of Hertz's work as a film producer. The latter, *Pan Tadeusz*, adapted from Mickiewicz's national book-length poem, became the focal point of the celebrations of the tenth anniversary of Polish independence. Although very popular among the audiences for their faithfulness to the esteemed literary sources, these films were rarely praised by contemporary critics, who frequently faulted the trivialization of the original, the literariness of the film, the lack of originality, and, usually, the lack of professionalism.

The 1920s also marked the appearance of the first directors with recognizable personal style. Probably the most interesting of them was the actor-writer-director-producer Wiktor Biegański (1892–1974), who started his career in 1913 with *Dramat Wieży Mariackiej* (*The Drama of the St. Mary's Church Tower*, unreleased). In 1921, he co-established a film cooperative, Kinostudio. He became the founder of the Warsaw Film Institute in 1924, which produced several prominent prewar Polish stars such as Nora Ney, Adam Brodzisz, and Maria Bogda. Biegański was also responsible for launching the career of his assistants, future leading Polish directors, including Michał Waszyński and Leonard Buczkowski.

Biegański is primarily known for a series of melodramas that usually deal with the themes of betrayed love, rape, and, eventually, the revenge of the deceived.[62] He is also known for his innovative use of locations that perform an important dramatic role in some of his films, for example, in his works set in the Tatra Mountains, such as *Otchłań pokuty* (*The Abyss of Repentance*, 1922) and *Bożyszcze* (*The Idol*, 1923). Unlike other producers, Biegański tried to pursue personal, independent projects and paid a heavy price for it. Situated on the periphery of the mainstream cinema, his films were well received by critics but ignored by audiences and attacked by the government for their lack of "patriotic" and nationalistic themes. Critics praised his works for their dynamic montage, painterly mise-en-scène, and ability to tell a story visually. They also commented that Biegański had been influenced by the German expressionist and the French impressionist cinema.[63]

Another important influence discernible in Biegański's works comes from prerevolutionary Russian cinema, chiefly films produced by Alexandr Khanzhonkov's company. This influence, present in particular in Biegański's most popular film, *Wampiry Warszawy* (*The Vampires of Warsaw*, 1925), is apparent in his films' rich mise-en-scène, slow pace, tragic denouements, and stress on psychologization—traits that are characteristic of films made by Yevgeni Bauer for Khanzhonkov. Biegański's later films, made before the advent of sound—for instance, *Kobieta, która grzechu pragnie* (*The Woman Who Desires Sin*, aka *When a Wife Cuckolds Her Husband*, 1929)—were less popular with critics.

Toward the end of the 1920s, a new group of directors emerged, including Józef Lejtes, Leonard Buczkowski, Henryk Szaro, Michał Waszyński, and Juliusz Gardan. They dominated Polish filmmaking in the 1930s by producing some of the best examples of prewar Polish cinema. For example, the prolific Michał Waszyński (Moshe Waks, 1904–1965), who made as many as thirty-nine films from his 1929 debut, *Pod banderą miłości* (*Under the Banner of Love*), to 1939's *Włóczęgi* (*The Tramps*), is responsible for films that are considered the most representative of Polish films (including films in Yiddish) of the 1930s.[64] The change of guard also indicates the origins of a new sensibility and a novel, more professional, approach to cinema.

Early Polish Film Theory and Criticism

In interwar Poland, film theory and criticism formed an original and interesting domain of thought, not limited to incorporating ideas from abroad, but instead proposing its own concepts. In contrast to the first Western European theorists, who tried to define the specificity of cinema, Polish authors were more interested in film's place in society and its cultural role.

Although the film industry was economically weak, film theory and criticism flourished during the first years of independence. According to Marcin Giżycki, the mediocrity of film production in prewar Poland provided the impetus to campaign for artistic cinema. Between the two world wars, Polish intellectuals and artists went through a peculiar "film fever,"[65] as Giżycki calls it, which was quite incompatible with the current stage of development of local cinema. The result of this "creative fever" deserves more careful examination.

The first texts written by a Pole on cinema appeared as early as 1898: Bolesław Matuszewski's two studies published in Paris, "Une nouvelle source de l'Histoire" (A new source of history) and "La Photographie animée" (Animated photography).[66] These were pioneer texts, arguably on a world scale, that aimed at presenting the practical possibilities of film to the world of science and government institutions. Though now almost forgotten, these works were well received and debated in many French journals.[67]

Matuszewski (1856–1943?), a well-known Warsaw photographer and camera operator, worked for the Lumière brothers in Poland, France, and Russia, where, in 1897, Tsar Nicholas II awarded him the title of court cinematographer. As a camera operator traveling across Europe, Matuszewski was interested primarily in the recording function of film as an eyewitness to history. Film, according to Matuszewski, provides new research methods for the science of history by supplying it with "direct vision." In his studies, he considers "living photographs" capable of truthful documentation of reality. Unlike traditional photography, which is capable of distortions and falsifications, "living photographs" can present only "absolute truth."[68] Matuszewski grounds this opinion, interestingly, on the technical impossibility of altering thousands of pictures (frames).

Matuszewski, regarded in Poland as the pioneer of scientific cinema, in his studies stresses cinema's educational and cultural role in bringing nations together. He postulates the creation of film archives, a "storehouse of historical cinematography," functioning as a "new source of history." He also calls for the publication of a professional film journal devoted to technical and cultural aspects of cinema. Given his practical and theoretical interest in documenting rather than reproducing reality, Matuszewski marginalizes, as might be expected, the narrative opportunities of cinema. He follows the Lumières' line of the development of cinema, namely, of those who "believe in reality."

After Polish independence was regained, the social and cultural implications of cinema became of prime importance. The lack of a strong film industry probably explains the interest in cultural rather than purely cinematic issues. Most writers on cinema, while agreeing on the medium's entertainment role, stressed the complexity of the filmic phenomenon and noted its documentary, cultural, and educational functions. Like other "silent theorists," Polish writers compared cinema with other arts in order to elevate cinema to the status of art. They also stressed those properties of cinema that were unique to the new medium.

Unlike in France and the Soviet Union, where cinema was mostly discussed by practitioners associated with the film industry (in other words, by people interested in aesthetic issues), in Poland film attracted primarily the interest of critics who were not professionally involved in film production and evaluation. These were mainly writers, literary and art critics, art historians, and educators. Most critics were not academic teachers or scholars per se, as was the case with many German film theorists. We may partly attribute the lack of serious discussions of the formal aspects of cinema to critics' social and educational interests and to their ignorance of cinema's aesthetic problems.

An important influence and a continuous point of reference for early Polish writers on cinema were provided by the German theoretical legacy. Not only did the German language occupy the position of a principal language of Central Europe, but Germany, "the land of theory," as Walter Bloem writes (without exaggeration),[69] also provided stimuli for theoretical debates and engaged Polish critics and writers with its polemics. In the 1920s, Polish writers and literary critics started to be more interested in cinema's aesthetic issues, and French influences became more discernible, especially the impact of avant-garde concepts. The assimilation of ideas from the French impressionist cinema movement of the 1920s enabled the actor turned critic and then filmmaker Leon Trystan (1899-1941), to develop his own concept, which focuses on the specificity of film. Although Trystan did not produce a theoretical book on cinema, he attempted to develop a coherent film theory in his articles.

Trystan popularized the French impressionist avant-garde theory of Louis Delluc and Jean Epstein.[70] In his works published from 1922 to 1924, Trystan propagates poetic cinema: cinema that is avant-garde, "photogenic," influenced by the concept of "film as music."[71] The concept of *photogénie (filmowość)*, part of "pure cinema" consisting of movement alone, occupies a central position in Trystan's writings. He pronounces that "a theorist dealing with film aesthetics should consider a movement itself, a movement as a movement, with the exception of 'content' ... he should deal only with formal values of cinema."[72] When compared with other Polish theorists of that time, Trystan is more preoccupied with aesthetic issues, which is why he was attacked by other, more culturally inclined critics, including Karol Irzykowski. Trystan made seven feature films from 1926 to 1938. In the first two, made in 1927, *Kochanka Szamoty (Szamota's Lover)* and *Bunt krwi i żelaza (The Mutiny of Blood and Iron)*, he tried to follow his theoretical premises; he combined melodrama with "photogenic" scenes that enhanced the atmosphere and created suspense. The later films were commercial undertakings. His last film, *A Brivele der Mamen (A Little Letter to Mother*, 1938, codirected with Joseph Green), was made in Yiddish and premiered in the United States after the war.

The first original work and the crowning accomplishment of prewar Polish film theory was Karol Irzykowski's *X Muza: Zagadnienia estetyczne kina (The tenth muse: Aesthetic problems of cinema)*, published first in 1924.[73] Well known in Poland, but still limited to readers of Polish, this book could have played an important role in the development of classical film theory if it had been translated.

Karol Irzykowski (1873–1944), a literary critic and writer and one of the most important figures on the Polish literary scene, followed other early film theorists and tried to overcome some prejudices against cinema. As early as 1913, Irzykowski was already writing, in a manner reminiscent of Emilie Altenloh, the German author of the first serious sociological study on cinema,[74] that "a contemporary European goes to the cinema but is ashamed of it."[75] Even though Irzykowski proudly states that he does not quote others because cinema is still "the field untouched by thinkers" and therefore he is "the source,"[76] his theoretical study is partly influenced by the German theoretical tradition. He refers primarily to works by Konrad Lange, Hermann Häfker (the author of probably the first monograph on film aesthetics),[77] and Rudolf Holzapfel. Irzykowski also debates the concept of *photogénie* expressed by Delluc and Epstein and propagated in Poland beginning in 1922 by Trystan. In addition, Irzykowski references prominent Polish critics and theorists such as Leon Belmont, Stanisław Brzozowski, and Tadeusz Peiper.

According to many film scholars, Irzykowski's study belongs to the most important works of film theory produced in the 1920s.[78] Paul Coates interprets *The Tenth Muse*'s obscure status outside Poland as being the consequence of its "accidental" formulation in Polish, which resulted in "its exclusion from the ranks of the world's imperially disseminated languages" because of "the fierce jealousy with which Poles hug their national culture to themselves." Yet. this cannot be the sole reason. The aphoristic writing of Irzykowski, so different from the academic works of German theorists, contributed to his work's lack of popularity. Coates aptly compares Irzykowski's style to that of Jean-Luc Godard. Furthermore, Coates implies that there is, in fact, "no 'Irzykowski line' on cinema"; instead, one finds a labyrinth of "interlocking lines the reader is invited to extend beyond the confines of the book."[79]

The fact that *The Tenth Muse* was written concurrently with the development of cinema (the volume's first chapter was finished in 1913) gives it a personal flavor; the book resembles an intellectual diary. Irzykowski is aware of all the problems an innovative theory has to face. In the introduction, he writes that he has purposely left many questions unanswered and is not afraid of contradictions because his intention is not to "transform theory into a system."[80] The personal character of *The Tenth Muse* is probably one of the main reasons why Irzykowski's work never received the wide acclaim and readership as did, for instance, the systematic study by Béla Balázs[81] published in the same year.

Unlike many of his contemporaries, Irzykowski focuses on the artistic possibilities of film rather than on its present, imperfect stage of development. When compared with the other arts, states Irzykowski, cinema's unique feature is the visibility of movement of material forms, illustrating man's struggle with matter. In the very first paragraph of the introduction, he defines film as "the visible association of man with matter."[82] This laconic and complex pronouncement, the nucleus of his theory, already appeared in 1913. Developing the man-matter dichotomy, he writes: "The 'man and matter' formula, in any case, simply corresponds to the optical relations between things in a film: in a film, matter is generally an immobile part, an inert background, whilst it is man who triggers movement, change and unrest."[83]

Irzykowski believes that by capturing reality that has not been processed artistically ("naked nature, not covered by a network of human concepts"),[84] film allows the viewer to uncover the world free from misrepresentation of concepts and words. In line with the German theorists influenced by Gestalt psychology (e.g., Hugo Münsterberg), Irzykowski stresses the roles of memory, conscience, and imagination, which enable cinema to penetrate our inner world. As Jadwiga Bocheńska appropriately points out, Irzykowski, as early as 1903, was already paying a great deal of attention to the mystifying role played by both conscious and subconscious processes in his experimental antinovel *Pałuba*. Echoing Bergson, Irzykowski claims that cinema imitates the mechanism of human perception and, furthermore, simulates human memory, imagination, and conscience. In this context, film is viewed as being capable of reproducing with equal adequacy external reality and internal processes, even without the direct participation of an artist.[85]

Taking into account Irzykowski's emphasis on the uniqueness of the cinematic medium, it comes somewhat as a surprise to find that he places it outside contemporary aesthetics. Despite his sympathy for cinema, and the lack of any intellectual prejudice against cinema, the reason for situating cinema outside of the domain of aesthetics is quite pragmatic: by employing concepts of traditional aesthetics, chiefly works by Rudolf Holzapfel, Irzykowski cannot prove that film is truly an art form. Instead, he claims that, from the point of view of contemporary aesthetics, film belongs to "inauthentic" arts, which work with the given materials of nature, such as gardening, the art of the actor, or pedagogy. The decisive factor, however, that contributed to Irzykowski's stand was most likely the influence of Konrad Lange, a German authority who refused film the status of art. Lange asserted that the moving picture is only a mechanical reproduction of reality, a nonartistic illusion.[86]

Irzykowski claims, however, that film does not necessarily have to be considered art to perform its function as "a filter of reality." Its main task is to register the world around us. The only instance, Irzykowski believes, in which film may be considered an art form, in line with contemporary aesthetics, is the case of cartoons, which belong to the realms of both painting and film. In cartoon, a metaphor of reality, an artist has full control over the entire creative process.[87] Yet, the author of *The Tenth Muse* discusses mainstream narrative films, not cartoons.

Irzykowski's study, like many other once innovative, now historically important works, remains unknown to the English reader already familiar with great systematizers like Balázs or Rudolf Arnheim and famous filmmakers and theoreticians such as Eisenstein or Pudovkin. Irzykowski's motivation in producing his theoretical study was to influence the course of Polish cinema. Yet, despite his importance and broad readership in Poland (there were numerous reprints after the war), Irzykowski's ideas had only limited influence on cinematic practice and on the dominant mode of theorizing and film criticism.[88]

Notes

1. Małgorzata Hendrykowska, *Śladami tamtych cieni: Film w kulturze polskiej przełomu stuleci 1895–1914* (Poznań: Oficyna Wydawnicza Book Service, 1993), 115; Władysław Banaszkiewicz and Witold Witczak, *Historia filmu polskiego 1895–1929*, vol. 1 (Warsaw: Wydawnictwa Artystyczne i Filmowe, 1989), 34.
2. Małgorzata Hendrykowska, "100 lat kina w Polsce: 1896–1918," *Kino* 12 (1997): 45.
3. Discussed extensively in Małgorzata Hendrykowska, "Was the Cinema Fairground Entertainment? The Birth and Role of Popular Cinema in the Polish Territories up to 1908," in *Popular European Cinema*, ed. Richard Dyer and Ginette Vincendeau (London: Routledge, 1992), 112–26.
4. For more information in English on Kazimierz Prószyński, see Marek Hendrykowski, "Kazimierz Prószyński and the Origins of Polish cinematography," in *Celebrating 1895: The Centenary of Cinema*, ed. John Fullerton (London: John Libbey, 1998), 13–18. Details concerning technical aspects of pleograph can be found in Banaszkiewicz and Witczak, *Historia filmu polskiego*, 48–50. Prószyński is also credited (with Matuszewski) as the father of Polish documentary cinema. From 1901 to 1903, he produced several short films in his Pleograf Company (Towarzystwo Udziałowe Pleograf). Before 1918, he lived mostly in France and England where he patented the Aeroscope camera in 1910. In prewar Poland, he continued his career inventing (albeit without commercial success) new types of camera and reading machines for the blind, among others. See also Sheila Skaff, *The Law of the Looking Glass: Cinema in Poland, 1896–1939* (Athens: Ohio University Press, 2008), 26–32.
5. Jerzy Maśnicki and Kamil Stepan, *Pleograf: Słownik biograficzny filmu polskiego 1896–1939* (Kraków: Staromiejska Oficyna Wydawnicza, 1996), entry "Fertner." Fertner's memoirs, *Podróże komiczne* [Comic journeys] (Kraków: Wydawnictwo Literackie, 1960) were published one year after his death.
6. *Prussian Culture* was considered lost until 2000. This eight-minute film was uncovered in a Parisian archive (where it was titled *Les Martyrs de la Pologne*) by Polish scholars Małgorzata Hendrykowska and Marek Hendrykowski. See Małgorzata Hendrykowska and Marek Hendrykowski, "Pierwszy polski film fabularny: *Les Martyrs de la Pologne / Pruska kultura* (1908)," *Kwartalnik Filmowy* 67–68 (2009): 212–29; published in English as "The First Polish Feature Film: *Les Martyrs de la Pologne / The Prussian Culture* (1908)," *Images* 6, nos. 11–12 (2008): 5–25.

7. The role of cinema on the Polish territories during the complex situation of World War I is discussed insightfully and extensively (630 pages!) by Mariusz Guzek, *Co wspólnego z wojną ma kinematograf? Kultura filmowa na ziemiach polskich w latach 1914-1918* (Bydgoszcz: Wydawnictwo Uniwersytetu Kazimierza Wielkiego, 2014).
8. Hendrykowska, *Śladami tamtych cieni*, 183-200. J. Hoberman describes *Meir Ezofowicz* as the story of "an idealistic young Jew [who] revolts against clerical constraints to join the struggle for Polish freedom." J. Hoberman, *Bridge of Light: Yiddish Film between Two Worlds* (New York: Museum of Modern Art and Schocken Books, 1991), 17.
9. Skaff, *The Law of the Looking Glass*, 41. Discussing Hertz's career, Skaff stresses rightly that coming from a Jewish family, Hertz "took care that the last names of even the camera operators and technicians sounded Polish" (42).
10. Hendrykowska, *Śladami tamtych cieni*, 206.
11. Ibid., 205; Banaszkiewicz and Witczak, *Historia filmu polskiego*, 72.
12. Hendrykowska, *Śladami tamtych cieni*, 137 and 164-66; Banaszkiewicz and Witczak, *Historia filmu polskiego*, 91-92. Polish intertitles appeared on imported films since 1908.
13. Skaff, *The Law of the Looking Glass*, 47.
14. Ibid., 48.
15. See, e.g., monographs on the history of cinema in Gdańsk/Danzig by Marek Andrzejewski, *Z dziejów kina w Gdańsku 1896-1945* (Gdańsk: Wydawnictwo Uniwersytetu Gdańskiego, 2013); Lwów/Lemberg/Lviv by Barbara Gierszewska, *Kino i film we Lwowie do 1939 roku* (Kielce: Wydawnictwo Akademii Świętokrzyskiej, 2006); Bydgoszcz/Bromberg by Mariusz Guzek, *Filmowa Bydgoszcz 1896-1939* (Toruń: Dom Wydawniczy Duet, 2004); Poznań/Posen and Greater Poland / Province of Posen by Małgorzata Hendrykowska and Marek Hendrykowski, *Film w Poznaniu i Wielkopolsce 1896-1996* (Poznań: Ars Nova, 1997). Polish scholars paid particular attention to the history of cinema in Upper Silesia (Górny Śląsk in Polish). See esp. Urszula Biel, *Śląskie kina między wojnami, czyli przyjemność upolityczniona* (Katowice: Śląsk, 2002); Jan F. Lewandowski, *Kino na pograniczu: Wędrówki po dziejach filmu na Górnym Śląsku* (Katowice: Wydawnictwo Naukowe Śląsk, 1998); and several anthologies edited by Andrzej Gwóźdź, *Filmowcy i kiniarze: Z dziejów X muzy na Górnym Śląsku* (Kraków: Rabid, 2004), *Filmowe światy: Z dziejów X muzy na Górnym Śląsku* (Katowice: Śląsk, 1998), *Historie celuloidem podszyte: Z dziejów X muzy na Górnym Śląsku i w Zagłębiu Dąbrowskim* (Kraków: Rabid, 2005), *Kina i okolice: Z dziejów X muzy na Śląsku* (Katowice: Wydawnictwo Naukowe Śląsk, 2008), *Odkrywanie prowincji: Z dziejów X muzy na Górnym Śląsku* (Kraków: Rabid, 2002).
16. Marek Hendrykowski and Małgorzata Hendrykowska, "Yiddish Cinema in Europe," in *The Oxford History of World Cinema*, ed. Geoffrey Nowell-Smith (Oxford: Oxford University Press, 1996), 174-75. In interwar Poland, approximately 170 Jewish dailies and journals were published in Yiddish and Hebrew, the language spoken by 85

percent of the Polish Jews. Natan Gross, *Film żydowski w Polsce* (Kraków: Rabid, 2002), 18.
17. Neal Ascherson, *The Struggles for Poland* (London: Michael Joseph, 1987), 59.
18. Edward D. Wynot Jr., *Warsaw between the World Wars: Profile of the Capital City in a Developing Land, 1918–1939* (New York: Columbia University Press, 1983), 106 and 108.
19. Stanisław Janicki, *Polskie filmy fabularne 1902–1988* (Warsaw: Wydawnictwa Artystyczne i Filmowe, 1990), 14–18. Małgorzata Hendrykowska provides different numbers: nineteen films, including eight in Yiddish. Hendrykowska, *Śladami tamtych cieni*, 206.
20. Eric A. Goldman, *Visions, Images, and Dreams: Yiddish Film Past and Present* (Ann Arbor, MI: UMI Research Press, 1983), 20. The 1924 version of *The Vow* is lost. The Polish National Film Archives in Warsaw has the sound version of *The Vow* released in 1937, directed by Henryk Szaro, and with Zygmunt Turkow in the leading role. This version was released in the United States as *A Vilna Legend*. Western viewers chiefly know Ida Kamińska for her role in the Oscar-winning Czechoslovak film *The Shop on Main Street* (1965, Ján Kadár and Elmar Klos).
21. Hoberman, *Bridge of Light*, 80.
22. Ibid., 143–49.
23. Edward Zajiček, *Poza ekranem: Kinematografia polska 1918–1991* (Warsaw: Filmoteka Narodowa and Wydawnictwa Artystyczne i Filmowe, 1992), 10. See also Edward Zajiček, *Zarys historii gospodarczej kinematografii polskiej: Tom I—Kinematografia wolnorynkowa 1896–1939* (Łódź: Państwowa Wyższa Szkoła Filmowa, Telewizyjna i Teatralna, 2015).
24. In her memoirs, Pola Negri writes, "Of the several small companies in Warsaw, Sphinx was the only one approximating any artistic standards." Pola Negri, *Memoirs of a Star* (New York: Doubleday, 1970), 113.
25. Guzek, *Co wspólnego z wojną ma kinematograf?* 328.
26. Anti-Russian films produced in the last years of World War I by Sfinks, including *The Secrets of the Tsarist Warsaw Police*, which was well received by Polish audiences in the former Russian partition territory, are discussed at length by Guzek in his detailed monograph. Ibid., 400–30. He also devotes a lengthy subchapter to Sfinks's activities at the beginning of the war (1914–1915). Ibid., 344–65.
27. Since this film is lost like many others, I owe its plot summary to Banaszkiewicz and Witczak, *Historia filmu polskiego*, 190–91.
28. Some Polish sources list Negri's Polish films as directed by the leading Sfinks director, Jan Pawłowski. Other sources indicate the producer, Aleksander Hertz, as responsible for all the films. Władysław Banaszkiewicz, "Pola Negri: Początki kariery i legendy," *Kwartalnik Filmowy* 1 (1960): 37–80.
29. Originally published in *Nowa Gazeta* 450 (1915): 3, quoted in Banaszkiewicz and Witczak, *Historia filmu polskiego*, 121.
30. *Tajemnica Alei Ujazdowskich* (*The Mystery of Ujazdowskie Avenue*), *Arabella*, and *Pokój nr 13* (*Room No. 13*).

31. Jan F. Lewandowski, "Zagadkowa Pola Negri," *Kino* 7–8 (1997): 24. Lewandowski notes that Negri's role in Ordyński's *Sumurun* was a turning point that helped to establish her career in Berlin; it proved to be more important than her films. Negri also stresses the importance of Ordyński's pantomime in her autobiography. Negri, *Memoirs of a Star*, 119–29. It must be noted, however, that Sfinks's films featuring Negri were distributed in Germany. Ryszard Ordyński (Dawid Blumenfeld) was a respected theater and film director, as well as a well-traveled theater reviewer. He worked as Max Reinhardt's assistant in Berlin and directed plays for the Deutsches Theater. In 1915, he moved to the United States, where he worked as a stage director at the Metropolitan Opera (credited as Richard Ordynski). After collaborating with major American studios as a screenwriter, actor, and director, he returned to Poland in 1920, making his first film in 1927.
32. Negri starred in several Hollywood films directed by, among others, Ernst Lubitsch (*Forbidden Paradise*, 1924), Raoul Walsh (*East of Suez*, 1925), Dimitri Buchowetzki (*Lily of the Dust*, 1924, *The Crown of Lies*, 1926), Mauritz Stiller (*Hotel Imperial*, 1927; *The Woman on Trial*, 1927), and Rowland V. Lee (*Three Sinners*, 1928; *Loves of an Actress*, 1928). In the early 1930s, after appearing in her first sound film, *A Woman Commands* (1932, Paul L. Stein), Negri moved back to Germany, where she starred in films such as *Mazurka* (1935, Willi Forst) and *Madame Bovary* (1937, Gerhard Lamprecht). In 1941, Negri returned to America. In 1964, she appeared in her last film, *The Moon Spinners*, directed by James Neilson. Details from Negri's life can be found in her 1970 autobiographical book, *Memoirs of a Star*, and in Mariusz Kotowski's monograph, *Pola Negri: Hollywood's First Femme Fatale* (Lexington: University of Kentucky Press, 2014). For Negri's early career with Sfinks, see Guzek, *Co wspólnego z wojną ma kinematograf?* 365–400.
33. Details concerning Jadwiga Smosarska's life and career can be found in Małgorzata Hendrykowska, *Smosarska* (Poznań: Wydawnictwo Naukowe Uniwersytetu im. Adama Mickiewicza, 2007).
34. Ryszard Bolesławski (Srzednicki, aka Richard Boleslawski, 1889–1937) in 1923 created the American Laboratory Theatre in New York in order to promote Stanislavski's method acting. Later, after the advent of sound, he became a successful Hollywood director with such films as *Rasputin and the Empress* (1933), *The Painted Veil* (1934), and *The Garden of Allah* (1936), working with some of Hollywood's biggest stars, including Greta Garbo, Marlene Dietrich, Lionel Barrymore, and Charles Laughton. Bolesławski's career is discussed in Marek Kulesza *Ryszard Bolesławski: Umrzeć w Hollywood* (Warsaw: Państwowy Instytut Wydawniczy, 1989).
35. Discussed extensively in Elżbieta Ostrowska, "Obraz Matki Polki w kinie polskim: mit czy stereotyp?" *Kwartalnik Filmowy* 17 (1997): 131–40; Elżbieta Ostrowska "Filmic Representations of the 'Polish Mother' in Post–Second World War Polish Cinema," *European Journal of Women Studies* 5 (1998): 419–35.
36. Ostrowska, "Obraz Matki Polki," 133.

37. Halina Bruczówna, one of the leading stars of Sfinks, recalls that most actresses considered "the most perfect model to be Asta Nielsen." Banaszkiewicz and Witczak, *Historia filmu polskiego*, 122.
38. Tadeusz Walas, quoted in Alina Madej, *Mitologie i konwencje: O polskim kinie fabularnym dwudziestolecia międzywojennego* (Kraków: Universitas, 1994), 38.
39. Helena Mniszek's novels were adapted by Juliusz Gardan in 1936 (*The Leper*), by Henryk Szaro in 1937, *Ordynat Michorowski (Duke Michorowski)*, by Michał Waszyński in 1938, *Gehenna (A Nightmare)*, and later, after the war, by Jerzy Hoffman in 1976, *Trędowata (The Leper)*. The 1927 version with Smosarska is lost.
40. Banaszkiewicz and Witczak, *Historia filmu polskiego*, 136 and 140.
41. Ewa Gębicka, "Sieć i rozpowszechnianie filmów," in *Encyklopedia kultury polskiej XX wieku*, ed. Edward Zajiček (Warsaw: Instytut Kultury and Komitet Kinematografii, 1994), 420.
42. Banaszkiewicz and Witczak, *Historia filmu polskiego*, 216.
43. The violently disputed borders with Polish neighbors were finally settled at the Riga Treaty, signed in March 1921, which ended the war between Soviet Russia and Poland (1919–1921). The defeat of the Soviet army, led by General Mikhail Tukhachevsky, at Warsaw, known as the *Cud nad Wisłą* (Miracle on the Vistula), occupies a place of prominence in Polish mythology and, consequently, in Polish film.
44. Wynot, *Warsaw between the World Wars*, 282.
45. Wojciech Świdziński, *Co było grane? Film zagraniczny w Polsce w latach 1918–1929 na przykładzie Warszawy* (Warsaw: Instytut Sztuki PAN, 2015), 126–28.
46. Kristin Thompson, *Exporting Entertainment: America and the World Film Market, 1907–1934* (London: British Film Institute, 1985), 136.
47. Kerry Segrave, *American Films Abroad: Hollywood's Domination of the World's Movie Screens from the 1890s to the Present* (Jefferson, NC: McFarland, 1997), 46–47.
48. Świdziński, *Co było grane?* 59–82.
49. Banaszkiewicz and Witczak, *Historia filmu polskiego*, 141 and 177.
50. Jerzy Płażewski, "Film zagraniczny w Polsce," in Zajiček, *Encyklopedia kultury polskiej XX wieku*, 328.
51. For details concerning censorship during the interwar period, see Małgorzata Hendrykowska, "Meandry i paradoksy międzywojennej cenzury filmowej w Polsce," *Images* 18, no. 27 (2016): 63–86.
52. Ibid. Contrary to popular opinion, Soviet cinema had some admirers in Poland. One of the leading prewar Polish critics, Stefania Zahorska, was known as a promoter of films in which imaginative form matches "humanistic content," the ideal of which she found in the montage cinema of the Soviets, especially that of Eisenstein. Her stand was far from common, given the situation in Poland after the Polish–Soviet War. According to Sheila Skaff, *Battleship Potemkin* was released in Poland in 1927. Skaff, *The Law of the Looking Glass*, 85.
53. Świdziński, *Co było grane?* 100–101.

54. When Polish independence was proclaimed on 11 November 1918, Józef Piłsudski became the commander in chief of the Polish armed forces and the provisional head of state.
55. Nina Niovilla (Antonina Elżbieta Petrykiewicz, 1874–1966) began her directorial career in 1918 in Germany. In addition to *Tamara*, she directed six films, including *Czaty* (*The Guards*, 1920), an adaptation of Adam Mickiewicz's ballad, and another patriotic picture, *Idziem do ciebie Polsko, matko nasza* (*We Come to You, Poland, Our Mother*, 1921). She also wrote screenplays, produced one film, and acted in other directors' films. See the pioneering text on female Polish filmmakers by Grażyna Stachówna, "A Wormwood Wreath: Polish Women's Cinema," in *The New Polish Cinema*, ed. Janina Falkowska and Marek Haltof (London: Flicks Books, 2003), 99.
56. Banaszkiewicz and Witczak, *Historia filmu polskiego*, 185.
57. Madej, *Mitologie i konwencje*, 148–49.
58. Ibid., 140–41.
59. Leonard Buczkowski remade *Year 1863* in 1936 as *Wierna rzeka* (*Faithful River*, 1936). Tadeusz Chmielewski produced the third version in 1983, but because of political restrictions (the unfavorable portrayal of Polish-Russian history), it was not released until 1987.
60. Tadeusz Lubelski, "Film fabularny," in Zajiček, *Encyklopedia kultury polskiej XX wieku*, 120. The term *mabuzeria* refers to Fritz Lang's *Dr. Mabuse, der Spieler* (*Dr. Mabuse, the Gambler*, 1922).
61. Jerzy Maśnicki and Kamil Stepan, "100 lat kina w Polsce: 1921–1928," *Kino* 1 (1998): 53.
62. Since all of Biegański's films are lost, the only source of information remains critics' reception of his works. See Maśnicki and Stepan, *Pleograf*, entry "Biegański"; Maśnicki and Stepan, "100 lat kina w Polsce," 51.
63. Maśnicki and Stepan, "100 lat kina w Polsce," 51.
64. Before his debut film, Waszyński received high-quality training in Russia, Poland, and Germany where he worked as an assistant to F. W. Murnau. This background, in addition to Waszyński's indisputable talent and organizational skills, was apparent in several of his films from different genres. See the biography by Samuel Blumenfeld, *L'homme qui voulait être prince: Les vies imaginaires de Michal Waszinski* (Paris: Grasset & Fasquelle, 2006).
65. Marcin Giżycki, *Walka o film artystyczny w międzywojennej Polsce* (Warsaw: Państwowe Wydawnictwo Naukowe, 1989), 15. For an insightful discussion, see Kamila Kuc, *Visions of Avant-Garde Film: Polish Cinematic Experiments from Expressionism to Constructivism* (Bloomington: Indiana University Press, 2016).
66. Bolesław Matuszewski's "Une nouvelle source de l'Histoire (Création d'un dépôt de Cinématographie historique)" (twelve pages) and "La Photographie animée, ce qu'elle est, ce qu'elle doit être" (eighty-eight pages) were both published by Matuszewski in Paris in 1898. They were first published in book form in 1995 by the National Film Archives in Warsaw: Bolesław Matuszewski, *Nowe źródło historii: Ożywiona fotografia, czym jest, czym być powinna* (Warsaw: Filmoteka Narodowa,

1995). This edition of Matuszewski (in Polish and in French) has the following on its cover: "Pierwsze w świecie traktaty o filmie" [First in the world treatises on film].
67. Reviews are included in the 1995 Polish edition of Matuszewski's works, appendix 3.
68. Matuszewski, Nowe źródło historii, 57.
69. Walter Bloem, Seele des Lichtspiels: Ein Bekenntnis zum Film (Leipzig-Zurich: Grethlein, 1922); trans. Allen W. Porterfield as The Soul of the Moving Picture (New York: E. P. Dutton & Co., 1924), xiii.
70. Louis Delluc, Photogénie (Paris: Éditions de Brunoff, 1920); Jean Epstein, Bonjour cinéma (Paris: Éditions de la Sirène, 1921).
71. E.g., Leon Trystan, "Fotogeniczność," Ekran i Scena 10–11 (1923); "Kino jako muzyka wzrokowa," Film Polski 2–3 (1923).
72. Leon Trystan, "Rytmizacja ruchu w kinie," Almanach Nowej Sztuki 2 (1924): 57, quoted in Banaszkiewicz and Witczak, Historia filmu polskiego, 253.
73. Karol Irzykowski, X Muza: Zagadnienia estetyczne kina (Kraków: Krakowska Spółka Wydawnicza, 1924). Quotes from the fourth edition prepared by Jadwiga Bocheńska (Warsaw: Wydawnictwa Artystyczne i Filmowe, 1977). Fragment in English translation by Paul Coates, "The Tenth Muse (Excerpts)," New German Critique 42 (1987): 116–27. The phrase "the tenth muse," propagated by Irzykowski, was, and still is, broadly employed in Poland to address cinema.
74. Emilie Altenloh, Zur Soziologie des Kinos: Die Kino-Unternehmung und die sozialen Schichten ihrer Besucher (Jena 1913), 96. Reference made by Andrzej Gwóźdź, Niemiecka myśl filmowa (Kielce: Szumacher, 1992), 30.
75. Karol Irzykowski, "Śmierć kinematografu," Świat 21 (1913). Later included as the opening chapter in his The Tenth Muse (1977), 35.
76. Irzykowski, X Muza, 26 and 28.
77. Hermann Häfker, Kino und Kunst (Munich: Volksvereins-Verlag, 1913).
78. E.g., Paul Coates, "Karol Irzykowski: Apologist of the Inauthentic Art," New German Critique 42 (1987): 114; Alicja Helman, "Polish Film Theory," in The Jagiellonian University Film Studies, ed. Wiesław Godzic (Kraków: Universitas, 1996), 11; Zbigniew Czeczot-Gawrak, Zarys dziejów teorii filmu pierwszego pięćdziesięciolecia 1895–1945 (Wrocław: Ossolineum, 1977), 150.
79. Coates, "Karol Irzykowski," 114.
80. Irzykowski, X Muza, 27.
81. Béla Balázs, Der sichtbare Mensch, oder Die Kultur des Films (Vienna: Deutsch-Österreichischer Verlag, 1924).
82. Irzykowski, X Muza, 26.
83. Ibid., quoted in Coates, "Karol Irzykowski," 118.
84. Irzykowski, X Muza, 40.
85. Jadwiga Bocheńska, Polska myśl filmowa do roku 1939 (Wrocław: Ossolineum, 1974), 105–7.

86. Konrad Lange, *Das Wesen der Kunst: Grundzüge einer realistischen Kunstlehre* (Berlin: Grote, 1901). The same comments about film being a nonartistic illusion were repeated in Lange's studies published several years later.
87. Irzykowski, *X Muza*, 248–54.
88. Irzykowski's importance and relevance to contemporary Polish film practice can be seen in the 1981 creation of the new experimental production collective, the Karol Irzykowski Film Studio in Łódź.

CHAPTER 2
The Sound Period of the 1930s
Adaptations, Patriotic Melodramas, and Films in Yiddish

Many European nations perceived the introduction of sound in film and the disintegration of the existing international film market as an opportunity to break the hegemony of Hollywood. The demand for pictures in national languages was enormous, and some Central European countries quickly took advantage of it. There was, however, no immediate national film production renaissance in Poland; the sluggish economy, worsened by the global economic depression, proved to be an obstacle. Although the first sound film was screened in Poland in 1929 (*The Singing Fool*, Lloyd Bacon, starring Al Jolson), the period of transition was slow and difficult. Since Poland did not introduce any protectionist measures, as did neighboring Czechoslovakia, Germany, and Hungary, most pictures released in Poland were in foreign languages, predominantly English. This gradually alienated the Polish viewer, and, consequently, cinema attendance dropped drastically in the early 1930s; by 1932, it had decreased 30 percent when compared to 1929 and 1930.[1]

The advent of sound had been treated with suspicion in Poland, as well as in other parts of the world. In the early 1930s, most Polish cinemas were not adapted to screening sound films. Excessive taxes did not encourage theater owners to invest in converting their theaters to play sound. Local films were thus produced in both silent and sound versions. The government later tried to intervene, issuing a regulation in 1936 that established lower taxes and preferential treatment for locally produced films.[2] Nevertheless, as late as 1938, eighteen silent cinemas remained in operation. For the approximately thirty-five million inhabitants of Poland, the number of cinemas was low at 807 (compared to, for example, 1,834 in Czechoslovakia, 8,049 in Italy, and 8,900 in Germany).[3]

Polish audiences favored Polish films, so in the early 1930s, there were attempts to disguise Hollywood films as national products. Paramount's studios in Joinville near Paris began to produce multilingual films, including films in

Polish, in 1930 and 1931. The leading Polish theatrical and film director, Ryszard Ordyński, and a group of distinguished Polish actors, such as Kazimierz Junosza-Stępowski, Bogusław Samborski, and Aleksander Żabczyński, became involved in the production of several films that later had little resonance in Poland. They included *Tajemnica lekarza* (*The Mystery of a Doctor*, 1930) and *Głos serca* (*Voice from the Heart*, 1931). The mechanical method of producing multilingual films and the lack of the Polish context, landscape, and theme contributed to the box office failure of and lukewarm critical response to these films. The problem was not solved by the introduction of the dubbing technique. Hollywood films dubbed in Polish and produced by, among others, the newly established dubbing center in Joinville encountered mixed response in Poland. Given the heritage of the partition period (the high illiteracy rate), dubbing could have served as a solution. On the other hand, the high costs of dubbing and nationalist concerns, expressed by many Polish intellectuals, made subtitling more popular. After the initial period of sound cinema, characterized by the predominance of dubbed films, Polish viewers came to favor subtitled foreign-language films—a preference that remains unchanged today.[4]

The problems with imported films created a niche for the national cinema: films set in the Polish landscape, focusing on Polish history and mythology, and spoken in the national idiom. In the latter half of the 1930s, Polish films generated four times more viewers than foreign films did.[5] However, the first Polish sound picture was truly an international endeavor. *Moralność pani Dulskiej* (*The Morality of Mrs. Dulska*), which premiered on 29 March 1930, was based on a Polish drama by Gabriela Zapolska, was directed by a Russian director working in Vienna (Bolesław Newolin), was produced by Austrian and Polish Jews (Bolesław Land and Maurycy Herszfinkel), and starred Marta Flanz (Land's wife) and Dela Lipińska (Newolin's wife). Both actresses, who did not speak Polish, were dubbed. To make the picture complete, the Italian Giovanni Vitrotti did the cinematography and the Czech Emil Štepánek designed the set. The Polish press harshly criticized the poor quality of the sound-on-disc, recorded at the Syrena Record in Warsaw, and its imperfect synchronization.[6]

The first 100 percent Polish talking picture (with sound also recorded on disc) premiered in October 1930. Michał Waszyński's melodrama *Niebezpieczny romans* (*A Dangerous Love Affair*) was produced in four languages—French, English, German, and Polish—and starred one of the most popular prewar actors, Bogusław Samborski, known as "the Emil Jannings of Polish film."[7] Several early Polish sound films proved to be critical and popular successes, for example, *Kult ciała* (*The Cult of the Body*), Waszyński's Polish-Austrian coproduction that premiered as a silent film on 18 January 1930, with sound added later in Vienna. *Każdemu wolno kochać* (*Anybody Can Love*, Mieczysław Krawicz and Janusz Warnecki), a musical comedy released in February 1933, is generally considered the first Polish film with sound-on-film (optical soundtrack).

Before World War II, the Polish film industry centered in Warsaw. As many as 63 out of the 67 films made before 1918, and 258 of the 267 full-length films completed during the interwar period, were made in the Polish capital.[8] Warsaw possessed not only a vibrant artistic community but also a group of entrepreneurs, mostly of Jewish origin, who were willing to risk their money and invest in the erratic film business. In the 1930s, the most important (though still small by Western standards) film companies were mostly in Jewish hands: Sfinks (since Aleksander Hertz's death in 1928 run by the former Kosmofilm cofounder and later Sfinks's deputy director Henryk Finkelstein), Leo-Film (owned by Maria Hirszbejn), Blok-Muza-Film (Henryk Gleisner, Leopold Gleisner, and Emil Kac), Rex-Film (Józef Rosen), Feniks (Felicja and Leon Fenigstein), and Libkow-Film (Marek Libkow). The only significant Polish-owned company remained Urania-Film, which was controlled by one of the best-known prewar Polish actors, Eugeniusz Bodo (1899–1943), for many a symbol of commercial Polish cinema in the 1930s.[9] The producer Maria Hirszbejn (1889–1942?) belongs among the most powerful women in the history of the Polish film industry. She controlled Forbert-Film, changed its name to Leo-Film in 1926, and was responsible for several films in Polish and Yiddish directed by Zygmunt Turkow, Henryk Szaro, Juliusz Gardan, and others. Unlike Hertz, who enjoyed the limelight, Hirszbejn never became a public figure. As Sheila Skaff explains:

> *Hirszbejn and Hertz almost seem to have lived in different societies. Citing public opinion, Hertz avoided placing Jews (with the exception of himself) in visible positions in his company; Hirszbejn actively recruited religious and secular Jews to work on all her films. Hertz's heavy hand and role in his scandal-prone company are legendary; Hirszbejn remained entirely behind the scenes and claimed the title of executive producer as often as that of producer.*[10]

The economically weak studios tried to promote their own stars, yet they generally relied on the established theatrical actors. Since the industry was based in

Warsaw, a city with an abundance of theaters and cabarets, trained actors were readily at hand. The theatrical actors brought to the screen personae that they had already formed on stage; they rarely ventured beyond their established image. The producers routinely cast a small group of Warsaw artists in a clichéd manner; furthermore, they expected the artists to flesh out the narrative with their theatrical/cabaret signatures—songs, dances, and comic dialogues. As a result, many Polish actors reappeared in several films, delivering predictable lines that verge on self-parody. For instance, the comic actor Stanisław Sielański appeared in strong supporting roles as a sly dog, a servant, and a provincial hillbilly; one of the most popular prewar actresses, Mieczysława Ćwiklińska, who, after her film debut at age fifty-four, appeared in thirty-five films within six years, specialized in upper-class matrons and mothers; and Antoni Fertner played good-natured, well-to-do fathers.[11]

The popular melodrama *O czym się nie mówi* (*What You Do Not Talk About*, aka *The Unspeakable*, 1939, Mieczysław Krawicz), based on a 1909 novel by Gabriela Zapolska about prostitution, serves as a good example of typecasting. In this film, several actors bring previous theatrical and filmic roles to the screen: the Polish femme fatale Ina Benita stars as a prostitute; the cabaret actor Ludwik Sempoliński appears as a fun-loving character; one of the best prewar dramatic actresses, Stanisława Wysocka, plays a poor yet decent widow; Stanisław Sielański repeats his stunt as a provincial bumpkin in Warsaw; Mieczysław Cybulski and Stanisława Angel-Engelówna once again appear as leading characters—honest yet tested by tragic circumstances.

Unquestionably, the Polish version of the star system reflected the state of the Polish film industry. Although the Warsaw stars became the center of attention for audiences and numerous film magazines, stardom as a film institution never fully developed in Poland because of the instability of the local film industry and the necessity to rely on theatrical actors. The reliance on theatrical actors subjected prewar Polish cinema to excessive theatricalization that was evident not only in the performances but also in the prevalence of the verbal over the visual, as well as the predominance of long and medium shots that were often executed with an immobile camera.[12]

Warsaw was crucial for Polish cinema for another reason: even though it had only 10 percent of all movie theaters in Poland, the city generated as much as 33 percent of total box office sales.[13] This figure is reflected in the choice of filmic themes related to Warsaw, in the settings, and in the type of humor popular in

Warsaw cabarets and revue theaters. It is fair to say that interwar Polish filmmaking clearly became a Warsaw societal affair.

It was uncommon for films to be produced outside of Warsaw, but the results were often promising. One example is *Biały ślad* (*White Trail*, 1932), a silent film set in the Polish Tatra Mountains that was directed and filmed by Adam Krzeptowski (1898–1961). With its romantic plot played out against the backdrop of beautiful yet dangerous mountains, *White Trail* clearly resembles *Bergfilme* (mountain films) by Arnold Fanck. The movie narrates an uncomplicated story about unrequited love, relying entirely on quasi-documentary footage of the mountains. The protagonist of *White Trail*, a young mountaineer, falls in love with a girl who has just returned from her schooling in the city. She, however, loves another man, a handsome mountain climber. The film's climax occurs when tragedy strikes: an avalanche nearly kills two of the protagonists. More important than the frail story, however, are the film's dynamic images of skiing competitions, the constant use of moving (skiing) camera, and the narrative relevance of the panoramic mountain scenes. The story is told visually—a rarity in old Polish cinema.

Krzeptowski's film was very well received at the first Venice Film Festival in 1932, where it competed not only with several now classic American films (*Dr. Jekyll and Mr. Hyde* and *Frankenstein*, among others), but also with a classic *Bergfilm*, Leni Riefenstahl's *Das blaue Licht* (*The Blue Light*, 1932). Polish critics generally praised *White Trail* but also considered it amateurish (this was Krzeptowski's feature debut, with a cast of nonprofessional actors). From todays' perspective, however, this "amateurish" quality makes *White Trail* a unique Polish production. Its cinematography and visual style in general make it very different from the photographed stage plays that predominated at the time. Krzeptowski's next (and last) film set in the Tatra Mountains, *Zamarłe echo* (*Dead Echo*, 1934), disappointed critics: although they praised the visual aspects of the film, they harshly criticized its melodramatic story.[14]

Another film set outside of Warsaw offers an almost ethnographic experience. Set in the southeastern part of prewar Poland (today in the southwest Ukrainian Carpathian Mountains), in the Hutsul region, *Przybłęda* (*The Vagabond*, 1933, Jan Nowina-Przybylski) provides a glimpse of exotic local culture. The story tells of an attractive outsider, Maryjka (Ina Benita), who is chased by the local men and almost lynched by the villagers for hiding a man, another outsider. Although *The Vagabond* undeniably delivers an outside view of Hutsul culture, with its stylization and superficial folklore (villagers are portrayed parading in their Sunday best), it nevertheless offers a refreshing experience in the context of prewar Polish cinema. It leaves behind the pretentious salons of Warsaw and the cabaret milieu of many Polish films to search for new photogenic settings rarely seen before on the screen. The best parts of *The Vagabond* consist of documentary-like scenes, the work of one of the most talented prewar Polish cinematographers, Albert Wywerka (1894–1945), who photographed approximately sixty-five films, among them several classic examples of interwar Polish cinema. This film also elevated to stardom one of the most interesting actresses of prewar Polish cinema, the blond femme fatale Ina Benita (1912–1943). The character she played in her next film, *Hanka* (aka *Oczy czarne*, *Dark Eyes*, 1934, Jerzy Dal), was nearly the same as the one she played in *The Vagabond*. Benita is, however, better known for her films made in the late 1930s: *Gehenna* (*A Nightmare*) and *Serce matki* (*Mother's Heart*), both directed by Michał Waszyński in 1938, and *What You Do Not Talk About*. Arguably, her best screen performance is the role of a river barge captain's daughter in *Ludzie Wisły* (*The People of the Vistula*, 1938, Aleksander Ford and Jerzy Zarzycki), which will be discussed later in this chapter.

Patriotic Pictures

In the 1930s, "patriotic pictures" still featured significantly in the Polish repertoire. The events of 1905, the January Uprising of 1863, and the formation of the Polish Legions remained popular themes on Polish screens. As in the 1920s, a typical patriotic picture referred to the atrocities committed by the Russians before and during World War I. Its melodramatic plot, usually revolving around the theme of love suffering because of the intrusion of politics, was commonly coupled with an unsophisticated version of history. The purpose of stereotyped characterization of "them" (Russian bureaucrats, officers, and the like) was to offer an evil background against which the impossible love played out. In films such as *The Police Chief Tagiejew* and *Serce na ulicy* (*A Heart on the Street*, 1931), both directed by Juliusz Gardan, the "them" intervened like the elements in disaster films. Despite forced happy endings (a requisite of the melodramatic formula), patriotic pictures taught that personal life and love had to be sacrificed "at the nation's altar"; individual yearnings had to be silenced for the common good. The stories told in patriotic pictures are an idealized take on Polish patriotism. According to Mariusz Guzek, who discusses references to heroic death as a marketing strategy during interwar Poland, these films often feature images of "monumental, heroic, and patriotic dying" as if to illustrate the Latin maxim "Dulce et decorum est pro patria mori" ("It is sweet and glorious to die for one's country").[15]

An early Polish attempt to produce talking pictures, *Na Sybir* (*To Siberia*, 1930, Henryk Szaro), is a typical example of the "patriotic genre." Partly a sound film (with sound sequences recorded in Berlin), it offers a "patriotic love story" set during the turbulent period of 1905 and afterward. *To Siberia* tells the story of a young student turned freedom fighter, Ryszard Prawdzic, alias Sęp (Adam Brodzisz), who hides outside of Warsaw after a successful attempt on the Russian governor-general's life. While working as a private teacher in a country manor, he meets an equally patriotically minded woman, Rena Czarska (Jadwiga Smosarska).[16] When Prawdzic unexpectedly returns to Warsaw, Czarska follows him, and they meet by chance at the moment of his arrest. She then follows him to Siberia and organizes his successful escape.

To Siberia closely emulates silent filmic examples of patriotic (anti-Russian) works. This is evident in the portrayal of the principal antagonist, Colonel Sierov, played by Bogusław Samborski (who specialized in such roles), and in the film's didactic overtones. This is also apparent in the film's episodic structure, being an illustration of patriotic tales combined with images of the peaceful Polish countryside. Jadwiga Smosarska plays a stereotypical Polish noblewoman whose actions are motivated equally by patriotic feelings and by her love for Prawdzic. The framing scenes heighten *To Siberia*'s edifying premise. The film opens with a brief introductory lecture that stresses the importance of the 1905 revolutionary events in Polish history and ends with Prawdzic's father-in-law (Mieczysław Frenkiel) reminding two grandchildren that they can live in a free Poland thanks to the bravery of their father. Because of its popularity among audiences, *To Siberia* was later imitated by many films, whose reliance on clichéd, almost cartoonish images and situations sometimes borders on the comedic.

The star of *To Siberia*, Adam Brodzisz, often appeared in other patriotic pictures in the early 1930s. Since his debut in *Z dnia na dzień* (*From Day to Day*, 1929, Józef Lejtes), this popular and photogenic actor[17] starred in, among others, *Uroda życia* (*The Beauty of Life*, 1930, Juliusz Gardan), *Dziesięciu z Pawiaka* (*The Ten from the Pawiak Prison*, 1931, Ryszard Ordyński), and *Młody las* (*The Young Forest*, 1934, Józef Lejtes). He specialized in good-natured, good-looking, and patriotically minded lovers.

Most "patriotic pictures" are trapped by their own conventions and clichés. For instance, Ordyński in *The Ten from the Pawiak Prison* refers to actual events that took place in 1906, but alters them to fulfill the demands of patriotic melodrama. The film tells the story of the attempts of the PPS (Polish Socialist Party) to free its ten members who were arrested and kept in the infamous Pawiak prison in Warsaw. This film propagates the official version of patriotism, popular among audiences and the ruling elite, and changes the historical facts to make the film more appealing to the public, as well as to please Marshal Józef Piłsudski and his government.[18]

In several other films, the historical events are modified as well, not only to accommodate the melodramatic love story but also to suit the current political situation. For instance, *Bohaterowie Sybiru* (*The Heroes of Siberia*, 1936, Michał Waszyński) narrates the story of Polish POWs and exiles in Siberia in 1918. On

Figure 2.1 Maria Bogda and Adam Brodzisz in *The Baltic Rhapsody* (1935), directed by Leonard Buczkowski. Narodowe Archiwum Cyfrowe. Public domain (Wikimedia Commons).

hearing about the formation of Polish military forces, they travel through war-torn Russia. One of the Polish officers makes a comment that could be stolen from Marshal Piłsudski's political speech: "A strong army is the decisive factor securing the welfare of a citizen, the development of education and arts. Herein lies the sense of the state." Such observations, using history to comment on the current state of affairs, are frequent in Polish cinema and are not limited to the "patriotic genre."

The national pride that developed from the newly regained freedom and from the interwar economic development is featured in many Polish films. In *Rapsodia Bałtyku* (*The Baltic Rhapsody*, 1935, Leonard Buczkowski), two young navy officers on a warship (Adam Brodzisz and Mieczysław Cybulski) look with pride at the newly built Baltic port in Gdynia near Gdańsk (Danzig). While the camera cuts between the medium shot of the two officers and long shots of distant Gdynia, the following conversation takes place:

> "Our shore! Look! What power comes from this Gdynia."
> "And do you remember what it looked like fifteen years ago!?"
> "And now ..."
> "The profound effort of our nation made this miracle. You know ... I feel somehow strangely moved when I look at this, our only gateway to the world. And I think that the same happens in the heart of every Pole."[19]

Prewar Polish films are not afraid of using pathos to express martyrological events from the past or to present current achievements; they also portray the euphoria resulting from reclaimed freedom. Nevertheless, the events of 1905, the battlefields of World War I, and the Polish–Soviet War often serve merely as backdrops for action films or melodramas. This is the case, for instance, with *Krwawy Wschód* (*Bloody East*, 1931, Jan Nowina-Przybylski), which was advertised as the first epic war film with sound. In this film, the Polish–Soviet War serves as a background for a familiar love triangle: in the trenches, an officer confesses to his friend that, while recuperating in a hospital, he and a nurse fell in love. He shows her picture to his friend, who recognizes the nurse as his own wife. The husband volunteers for a difficult mission and dies securing the happiness of his friend.

Another brand of "patriotic pictures" features films set in distant times that promote popular and nationalistic versions of Poland's history. Frequently, these films refer to popular paintings or sketches and mythologized stories. In the Polish context, these were safe choices. Polish audiences had (and still have) a predilection for stylized, safe history, as if it were an illustration of common historical knowledge. This version of history, which reinforced rather than questioned national myths, was well received by audiences but generally attacked by critics for these very reasons. Polish history, mythology, and the landscape seemed to be enough to attract Polish viewers regularly exposed to Western (mostly Hollywood) films. *Przeor Kordecki: Obrońca Częstochowy* (*Abbot Kordecki: The Defender of Częstochowa*, 1934, Edward Puchalski) may serve as a good example. This film refers to the Polish–Swedish war (known as the "Swedish Deluge") that took place from 1655 to 1660 and was mythologized in popular historical accounts, chiefly by Henryk Sienkiewicz in his epic novel *The Deluge*.[20] During the Swedish Deluge, the monastery at Częstochowa, led by Abbot Augustyn Kordecki, successfully defended itself against the Swedish troops. Alina Madej writes that the film had been constructed so that its "every element refers to the commonly known national *universum*. The defense of the monastery at Jasna Góra supports the myth that the country has the highest sacred value. This myth is expressed by ostentatious religious-patriotic imagery, and the love story motif developed in a mawkish-lyrical tone."[21] Several other films had similar strong religious overtones, including Jan Nowina-Przybylski's suspense drama *Ty, co w Ostrej świecisz Bramie* (*Thou, Who Shines in the Gate*, aka *Hail Mary, Full of Grace*, 1937).

In the early 1930s, Józef Lejtes, arguably the best Polish director of the interwar era, quickly gained a reputation for his cinematic treatment of recent Polish history and his take on the "patriotic genre." In *Dzikie pola* (*Wild Fields*, 1932), he deals with the fate of Polish soldiers trying to return to their country from Russia after the end of World War I. Another critically acclaimed film, *Córka generała Pankratowa* (*General Pankratov's Daughter*, 1934), officially directed by Mieczysław Znamierowski but in actual practice by Lejtes,[22] refers to the political unrest in 1905. With its superb cast (Nora Ney, Franciszek Brodniewicz, and Kazimierz Junosza-Stępowski), Seweryn Steinwurzel's camera, Henryk Wars's score, and Lejtes's adroit use of the conventions of melodrama applied to the events of 1905, it became one of the best-known examples of patriotic Polish cinema of the mid-1930s.

The events of 1905 also provided the setting for two other well-received films by Lejtes: *The Young Forest* and *Róża* (*The Rose*, aka *Red Rose*, 1936). The former, the best film of 1934, according to the readers of the weekly magazine *Kino*,[23] deals with the conflict between Polish students and their Russian teachers. The latter, an adaptation of Stefan Żeromski's novel, focuses on the story of the PPS members and their fight against the tsarist regime. Unlike other directors of patriotic pictures, Lejtes does not let the films' romantic subplot overtake the story. He avoids national stereotyping, provides a more complex characterization of the Russians, and in *The Young Forest* illustrates the Polish-Russian solidarity against the tsarist regime.

Lejtes was not interested solely in recent Polish history; some of his other films refer to mythologized events in more distant Polish history. His *Barbara Radziwiłłówna (Love or a Kingdom,* 1936), with Jadwiga Smosarska in the leading role, portrays the love story between the king of Poland, Zygmunt August, and Barbara from the noble family of Radziwiłł. Another historical epic, *Kościuszko pod Racławicami (Kościuszko at Racławice,* 1938), deals with an event that has a permanent place in Polish mythology: the 1794 national insurrection led by Tadeusz Kościuszko.

Comedy

Very few of the 117 feature films produced in Poland in the 1920s can be classified as comedies.[24] Patriotically oriented melodramas dominated in the 1920s, but the mid-1930s belonged to comedy. Popular Polish cinema began to be controlled by people associated with Warsaw musical theaters and cabarets. From that milieu came popular actors such as Adolf Dymsza and Eugeniusz Bodo; composers, including Henryk Wars; and directors, for example, Konrad Tom, who was also an actor. The use of the same group of actors, mostly coming from popular Warsaw cabarets Qui pro Quo and Banda (The Band), and similar backgrounds sometimes gives the audience a sense of déjà vu. Actors such as Kazimierz Krukowski, Tola Mankiewiczówna, Zula Pogorzelska, and Aleksander Żabczyński are put in clichéd situations taken from musical theater and frequently perform their well-known cabaret numbers on-screen. The targets of Polish comedies remain the "terrible middle class" and the provincial hillbillies. The comedies frequently verge on caricature in their use of grotesque characters and names. The theatrical roots of many films resulted in an emphasis on dialogue and music at the expense of the composition of frame and editing, for these were mostly musical comedies consisting of hit songs composed by the popular Henryk Wars.[25]

Essentially, Polish comedies employed the structure of musical theater, farce, and Viennese operetta, or they imitated German comedies. A typical unsophisticated narrative centers on two attractive lovers who, with the help of secondary characters (mostly played by comic actors), overcome difficulties and are united in the finale. Other types of narratives use the Cinderella story and the theme of mistaken identity. The poor are disguised as the rich in *Jego ekscelencja subiekt* (*His Excellency, the Shop Assistant*, 1933), and the rich are veiled as the poor in *Jaśnie pan szofer* (*His Excellency, the Chauffeur*, 1935), both directed by Michał Waszyński and both starring Ina Benita and Eugeniusz Bodo. The case of mistaken identity is also prominent in comedies about women masquerading as men, for example, *Czy Lucyna to dziewczyna?* (*Is Lucyna a Girl?* 1934), directed by Juliusz Gardan, with Jadwiga Smosarska and Eugeniusz Bodo in the leading roles.

For many Polish viewers, Adolf Dymsza (Bagiński, 1900–1975) functions as the symbol of prewar Polish comedy.[26] At the beginning of his career, Dymsza appeared in several supporting roles that were well received by both the public and critics. He was usually cast as a working-class or streetwise character who could outwit anybody. This character, a Warsaw sly dog named Dodek, was the continuation of Dymsza's earlier cabaret performances.

After a series of memorable supporting roles, for example, in one of the biggest financial successes of 1933, *Anybody Can Love*, Dymsza's later films were typical star vehicles, written specifically for him and accommodating his type of humor and screen persona. Sometimes he was paired with other well-known comic actors, for example, Vlasta Burian, the "Czech Groucho Marx,"[27] in a Polish-Czech coproduction, *Dwanaście krzeseł* (*Twelve Chairs*, 1933, Michał Waszyński and Martin Frič). The protagonists of this film (loosely based on a Russian novel by Ilya Ilf and Yevgeni Petrov) search for twelve used chairs because $100,000 is hidden in one of them. The differences in comic style and situational and verbal humor caused by the language barrier are the film's prime sources of humor.

The stock situations and characters from Polish "patriotic pictures" returned in the mid-1930s as parodies in two comedies starring Dymsza: *Antek Policmajster* (*Antek the Police Chief*, 1935) and *Dodek na froncie* (*Dodek at the Front*, 1936), both directed by Michał Waszyński. Frequently voted the best prewar Polish comedy, *Antek, the Police Chief* is set around 1905 and deals with a Warsaw character, Antek Król (Dymsza), who is chased by the tsarist Russian police for a trivial crime. Escaping by train, he finds himself in the compartment of a drunken and sleeping Russian police chief, who is traveling to his new post in one of the provincial towns. Antek steals the police chief's uniform, takes on his identity, and performs his role in the tradition of Nikolai Gogol's best short stories. Even when Antek's identity is revealed, he is let free by the governor (Antoni Fertner) who is afraid of disgracing

THE SOUND PERIOD OF THE 1930s · 53

himself. The situational humor, the mockery of the martyrological dimensions of earlier patriotic pictures, and the presence of known actors in supporting roles (Maria Bogda, Mieczysława Ćwiklińska, and Konrad Tom) made the film a success with audiences. Other films featuring Dymsza, such as *ABC miłości* (*ABC of Love*, 1935), *Wacuś* (1935), and *Bolek i Lolek* (*Bolek and Lolek*, 1936), all directed by Michał Waszyński, although box office successes, were never as popular as *Antek, the Police Chief*. The weak scripts of these films, built around unsophisticated cabaret numbers, did not enable Dymsza to develop his screen personality.[28]

The crowning achievement of prewar Polish musical comedy remains *Zapomniana melodia* (*Forgotten Melody*, 1938, Konrad Tom and Jan Fethke). This comedy of errors offers a fresh and unpretentious filmic experience. The well-executed script by Fethke, Ludwik Starski, and Napoleon Sądek introduces a lively and logically developed plot. Stefan (Aleksander Żabczyński), who is in love with Helenka (Helena Grossówna), is mistaken for the son of a cosmetic firm owner

Figure 2.2 Helena Grossówna (center) in *Forgotten Melody* (1938), directed by Konrad Tom and Jan Fethke. Courtesy of Filmoteka Narodowa.

who competes with the company owned by Helenka's father (Antoni Fertner). Helenka's father, afraid of the competition, destroys the recipe for his new product, but first memorizes it with the help of a melody that he later forgets. In the film's climax, he recalls the forgotten melody while listening to Stefan's song to his beloved Helenka.

Forgotten Melody was cast with an ensemble of popular actors, including Grossówna, Żabczyński, Fertner, Jadwiga Andrzejewska, Michał Znicz, and Stanisław Sielański. It neither relies on a star performance nor resembles popular cabaret sketches—the Achilles' heel of many prewar Polish comedies. The prewar Polish reviewers aptly noted a similarity to American musicals, mainly to the well-received films featuring Universal Studios's star, Deanna Durbin.[29] Today, this film is chiefly remembered in Poland for its musical pieces composed by Henryk Wars to the lyrics of Ludwik Starski. The success of *Forgotten Melody* prompted later codirector Fethke to write and direct a similar musical comedy, *Przez łzy do szczęścia* (*To Happiness through Tears*). Produced before the war in 1939, the film was released by Germany in the occupied Polish territories in October 1943.[30]

Melodrama

In Poland, as well as in other countries, melodramas continued to be popular because of their sensationalism that dealt with "forbidden" aspects of life. For example, the theme of prostitution and "white slavery" appears in *Uwiedziona* (*A Seduced Woman*, 1931, Michał Waszyński), drug addiction in *Biała trucizna* (*White Poison*, 1932, Alfred Niemirski), alcoholism in *Dusze w niewoli* (*Souls in Slavery*, 1930, Leon Trystan, with the legend of Polish theater Ludwik Solski), and sexuality in *Dzieje grzechu* (*The Story of Sin*, 1933, Henryk Szaro). Generally, these films recycle the cautionary story about the dangers that young women face when they try to follow their dreams to earn money and have a career overseas. A separate group of now forgotten films consists of works labeled by Małgorzata Hendrykowska as "exotic kitsch."[31] *Głos pustyni* (*The Sound of the Desert*, 1932) and *Czarna perła* (*The Black Pearl*, 1934), both directed by Michał Waszyński, are set in North Africa and Hawaii, respectively, and are abundant with clichéd narratives concerning brave and intelligent Poles and backward locals.

The treatment of women in Polish melodramas oscillates between presenting them as femme fatales in the tradition of Pola Negri's silent features made for the

Sfinks studio, and as vulnerable figures at the mercy of the social and political circumstances. The former representation, which is not very popular in Polish cinema, can be seen in *Zabawka* (*The Toy*, 1933, Michał Waszyński). The title refers to the protagonist Lulu (Alma Kar), a Warsaw cabaret star, who is invited to a country manor by a wealthy landowner. The landowner's son and a local Don Juan both fall in love with Lulu and pay for it. The name of the protagonist and the theme of the film suggest G. W. Pabst's influence (Louise Brooks as Lulu in *Pandora's Box*, 1929), and this inspiration had been emphasized by Andrzej Łomakowski, one of two screenwriters of the film.[32]

The destructive role of the city woman is a common filmic theme that is present in one of the most successful early sound films, *Cham* (*The Boor*, 1931), directed by Jan Nowina-Przybylski, photographed by Albert Wywerka, and based on Eliza Orzeszkowa's novel. This melodrama, set in rural Poland, draws on the familiar clash between the corrupt city and the pastoral country. As in *Sunrise* (1927), the classic by F. W. Murnau, the woman from the city seduces a village man (this time an unmarried man). *The Boor* narrates a love story between a former prostitute, Franka (Krystyna Ankwicz), and a good-natured fisherman, Paweł (Mieczysław Cybulski). Paweł forgives Franka not only for her past but also for her marital affairs and her attempt to poison him. He also defends her against the angry villagers. Franka despises him as *cham* (the boor), cannot stand his good-hearted nature, and drowns herself, leaving him alone with her daughter.

Much praised by Polish critics, *Wyrok życia* (*Life Sentence*, 1933, Juliusz Gardan)[33] portrays its protagonist, Hanna (Jadwiga Andrzejewska), as a victim of hostile circumstances. While in prison, after being convicted of killing her child and sentenced to death, she relates episodes from her life to her defense lawyer, Krystyna (Irena Eichlerówna). From Hanna's stories, we learn of her lonely childhood, brief and unhappy love, and harsh economic conditions. Poverty forces her to abandon her child (who drowns), in hopes that it will be found and taken care of by somebody else. When Hanna's lawyer manages to get her out of prison and invites her home, it appears that Krystyna's husband is the father of Hanna's child. When Hanna learns that he really loves Krystyna, she leaves their house.

Stylistically, *Life Sentence* uses many elements of expressionist cinema and the poetics of silent cinema. For Polish filmmakers who were more ambitious at that time, this was "a kind of defense against the abuse of words in standard talkies."[34] The opening sequence, for example, juxtaposes the prosecutor's uplifting words about children with images of a father punishing his child. What follows are the scenes of the jurors returning to their daily business, the neon lights announcing "the evening of laughter," and the paper with the news about the trial disappearing into a gutter. Despite this opening sequence, with the film moving toward social drama, the melodramatic conventions quickly overtake the story and convey that Hanna's lack of social skills and her own immaturity, not social and economic conditions, are to blame for her misfortune.

One of the biggest box office hits of the decade was the religious melodrama *Pod Twoją obronę* (*Under Your Protection*, 1933), written and directed by the experienced Edward Puchalski. The film was practically directed by Józef Lejtes, but, because of his Jewish origins, his name had to be removed from the credits in order to please the Roman Catholic Church, the patron of this "Christian film."[35] It narrates a story about a Polish pilot, Jan Polaski (Adam Brodzisz), who is working on an invention that has caught the interest of foreign spies. In mysterious circumstances, his plane crashes the day before his wedding to Maryla (Maria Bogda).[36] Paralyzed but cared for by his faithful fiancée, he travels to the holy picture of the Black Madonna in Częstochowa, where he is miraculously cured. The combination of a simple melodramatic plot and strong religious content (the choice of Częstochowa) proved to be an enormous success with audiences. *Under Your Protection* played for twenty-one continuous weeks in one of the biggest Warsaw cinemas, the Apollo. This was an unprecedented story. At the climax of the film, the miracle at Częstochowa, many viewers knelt and prayed.[37]

Several popular films in the 1930s were adaptations of well-known literary works—classics of literature and pulp fiction alike. An early sound film by Ryszard Ordyński was loosely adapted from Henryk Sienkiewicz's novella *Janko Muzykant* (*Johnny the Musician*, 1930). Sidestepping Sienkiewicz's stress on social injustice, Ordyński produced a formulaic film about a career against all odds. A young shepherd boy, Johnny, himself a talented musician, steals a fiddle from a country manor, is caught, and is sent to a juvenile detention center. Later, with the help of his inmates, who support his talent, he breaks out and in Warsaw finds success as a musician.

Józef Lejtes is known for his clever adaptations of celebrated contemporary novels: *Dziewczęta z Nowolipek* (*The Girls of Nowolipki*, 1937) and *Granica* (*The Line*, 1938), based on the novels by Pola Gojawiczyńska and Zofia Nałkowska, respectively. *The Girls of Nowolipki* portrays the dramatic stories of four young women: Bronka (Elżbieta Barszczewska), Franka (Jadwiga Andrzejewska), Amelka

(Tamara Wiszniewska), and Kwiryna (Hanna Jaraczówna), who live in the same working-class Warsaw building. The multiplicity of realistic details, the complex psychological pictures of four women, and the portrayal of their aspirations, which are verified by the reality of life, made this film not only a box office success but also a cultural event.[38]

The Line offers a fatalistic story of a man, Zenon Ziembiewicz (Jerzy Pichelski), torn between two women: Justyna (Lena Żelichowska), with whom he has had an ongoing affair, and his wife, Elżbieta (Elżbieta Barszczewska). Lejtes is more interested in the tragic dimensions of the triangle than in the social issues permeating Nałkowska's novel (Justyna is a simple woman from the village, Elżbieta a sophisticated one from the big city). Żelichowska's performance as Justyna stresses the tragic aspect of her character and makes her an intricate persona, vulgar and tender at the same time, suffering from the extremes of love and hate for the man with whom she has had a continuous affair.

The melodramatic conventions and sentimental narrative are also present in adaptations of pulp fiction, box office successes based on the novels of Helena Mniszkówna, Tadeusz Dołęga-Mostowicz, and Maria Rodziewiczówna. Dołęga-Mostowicz's books in particular became extremely popular in the late 1930s. One of his adaptations, *Znachor* (*The Quack*, 1937, Michał Waszyński), remains for many the symbol of popular Polish cinema in the 1930s. The story concerns a well-known surgeon, Rafał Wilczur (Kazimierz Junosza-Stępowski), who loses his memory, and lives as a tramp for many years. He eventually settles in a village and helps the locals as a quack. Later, because of some happy coincidences, he regains his memory, as well as his previous social standing and material status. Junosza-Stępowski, a respected theatrical actor who during his long career appeared in fifty-seven films (twenty-two of which were silent), is chiefly remembered for his portrayal of the noble surgeon, Professor Wilczur.

The popularity of this film helped to produce two sequels, *Profesor Wilczur* (*Professor Wilczur*, 1938), again directed by Waszyński, and *Testament Profesora Wilczura* (*Professor Wilczur's Last Will*, Leonard Buczkowski), which was made before the war but not released by the Germans until 1942. Equally popular were melodramas based on Mniszkówna's writings—the new version of *Trędowata* (*The Leper*, 1936) and an adaptation of Rodziewiczówna's novel, *Wrzos* (*Heather*, 1938), both directed by Juliusz Gardan. *The Leper* introduced a new pair of popular screen lovers, Elżbieta Barszczewska and Franciszek Brodniewicz, while *Heather* introduced Stanisława Angel-Engelówna.

A New Sensibility: The START Group

In 1930, the Society for the Promotion of Film Art (START)[39] was established in Warsaw, an important part of the Polish critical, and later filmmaking, scene. Founded by, among others, Jerzy Toeplitz, who became a famous film historian, and the notable Polish filmmakers Wanda Jakubowska, Eugeniusz Cękalski, Jerzy Zarzycki, Aleksander Ford, Jerzy Bossak, and Stanisław Wohl, this dynamic cine-club promoted ambitious, artistic cinema through screenings, lectures, and seminars, as well as articles published in almost all of the major Polish journals. The young members of START were primarily cultural educators who were interested in changing the landscape of film production in Poland. In an article published in Warsaw in 1932, the board of the society explicitly points out that the main task of the group is to "popularize and propagate a few valuable films, to discredit and boycott worthless cultural productions, and to awaken interest in film as a first-class educational component."[40]

The START members began their careers by attacking commercial Polish productions while promoting art cinema. Regarding cinema—and for that matter, all arts—as more than just entertainment, they were united by "the struggle for films for the public good," which was the START slogan from 1932. Under the influence of Soviet filmmakers, the START activists considered film a socially useful art. In an extensive press campaign, the START members raised fundamental problems concerning Polish cinema. They believed that the only chance to have an artistic cinema was to have an enlightened audience. By educating the public, they hoped to limit the production of mediocre films and to create audiences ready to accept truly creative, even experimental, cinematic works.

The only member of START with some film experience was Aleksander Ford (1908–1980). His much-praised debut, *Legion ulicy* (*The Legion of the Street*, 1932), was one of the first films to show a realistic picture of everyday life coupled with elements of social commentary. Ford's film, which focused on Warsaw street boys who sell newspapers, was well narrated and devoid of the stereotypical sentimental features that permeated Polish narratives. An attempt to reflect the atmosphere of the street was more important for Ford than the story itself. The realistic aspect of *The Legion of the Street*, enhanced by the casting of young, nonprofessional actors, certainly presages Ford's documentary beginnings. The young director, then only twenty-four, was hailed, particularly by the leftist press (he was a known communist), as the most promising Polish director. Ford's film, like many others, is now lost. Stills, publicity materials, reviews, and articles held by the Polish National Film Archives prove that this film was well received by most reviewers. It was voted the best film of the year by *Kino* readers. One critic commented: "Among domestic productions, this film is a kind of curiosity. It is neither an illustration of a novel nor photographed theater, but a genuine film, born out of cinematographic elements such as movement, visual approach to phenomena, riveting photography, editing, etc."[41]

Ford also made two films in Yiddish about Jewish life: *Sabra* (1933) and *Mir kumen on*, also known as *Droga młodych* (*Children Must Laugh*, aka *The Road of the Youth*, 1936). The quasi-documentary *Sabra* was made on location in Palestine and portrayed the harsh living conditions of Jewish settlers and their struggles with hostile Arabs. Initially planned by Ford as a warning against the politics of resettling in Palestine, the final version of the film included optimistic, poster-like images of the emerging Jewish state. *Children Must Laugh*, a film financed by the Jüdischer Arbeiter Bund and produced by Saul Goskind, dealt with the Medem Sanatorium for children with tuberculosis in Miedzeszyn. The film encountered problems with the censor for allegedly spreading communist propaganda and was never released theatrically (it was only shown at small private gatherings).[42] Ford's other ventures into mainstream cinema were less successful, and it has been noted that the combination of the conventions of traditional cinema and communist messages produced a "pretentious style" that was "anachronistic in its modernist avant-gardism."[43]

After the disintegration of START in 1935, its former members attempted to make films that reflected their interest in socially committed cinema. In 1937, some of the START members, including Ford, Cękalski, and Wohl, established the Cooperative of Film Authors (Spółdzielnia Autorów Filmowych). Their two productions, *Strachy* (*The Ghosts*, 1938, Eugeniusz Cękalski and Karol Szołowski) and *The People of the Vistula* (Aleksander Ford and Jerzy Zarzycki), are among the finest achievements in prewar Polish cinema.

The Ghosts, an adaptation of Maria Ukniewska's semiautobiographical novel, is set in the Warsaw world of cabarets and musical theaters. The film's dialogue was cowritten by the well-known Polish poets Konstanty Ildefons Gałczyński and Władysław Broniewski, and the cast included, with the exception of the newcomer dancer Hanna Karwowska, some of the finest prewar actors: Eugeniusz Bodo, Józef Węgrzyn, Jacek Woszczerowicz, and Mieczysława Ćwiklińska. The safe choice of two legends of Polish theater, Węgrzyn and Woszczerowicz, to play

Figure 2.3 Józef Węgrzyn and Hanna Karwowska in *The Ghosts* (1938), directed by Eugeniusz Cękalski and Karol Szołowski. Courtesy of Filmoteka Narodowa.

supporting roles proved to be a success. The old bombastic and alcoholic Russian dancer Dubenko (Węgrzyn), who dies during the film, and the mysterious illusionist Srobosz (Woszczerowicz) remain the film's strongest characters.

The story of *The Ghosts* deals with two young female friends who work in a chorus line for a second-rate revue theater. The more pragmatic Teresa (Hanka Karwowska) has an affair with the star of the show, Zygmunt Modecki (Eugeniusz Bodo). The sentimental and vulnerable Lilka (Jadwiga Andrzejewska) cannot bear the pressures and intrigues surrounding her and, in an act of desperation, commits suicide. The specific nature of the portrayed world and the aura of scandal that accompanied the publication of Ukniewska's novel undeniably attracted Cękalski and Szołowski. Despite their avant-garde backgrounds and leftist convictions, their approach to cinema can be best described as mainstream with a tendency to experiment.

The theme of *The Ghosts* has little to do with the lofty ideals of START, yet the film's visualization contains traces of the group's search for the new language of film. With its tendency toward symbolism and melancholy, as well as a dark visual style (due to nighttime settings), Stanisław Wohl and Adolf Forbert's cinematography reflects the strong influences of French poetic realism. *The Ghosts* also exhibits several slightly old-fashioned avant-garde devices: rapid, sometimes rough montage; superimposed images to portray dream sequences; and voice-over narration to comment on the state of the protagonist's mind. The film is distinguished by its feeling of authenticity and by very well-choreographed and well-executed dance numbers, a rarity in Polish cinema.[44]

The second production of the Cooperative of Film Authors, *The People of the Vistula*, based on Helena Boguszewska and Jerzy Kornacki's realistic novel *Wisła (The Vistula)*, is known for its realistic portrayal of marginalized groups of society. The melodramatic aspect of this film focuses on Anna (Ina Benita), the daughter of a barge owner on the Vistula River, who is in love with a handsome petty thief from the shore, Aleksy (Jerzy Pichelski). The true heroine of the film, however, is Matyjaska, the tragic, struggling owner of another barge, who is played by a leading prewar theatrical actress, Stanisława Wysocka.

This film is set in the milieu of Jean Vigo's *L'Atalante* (1934) and bears some features of Vigo's masterpiece: glimpses of social conditions, a love story on a river barge, and the life on the shore that is contrasted with that on the barge. Like Vigo, the makers of *The People of the Vistula* employ many traveling shots, evoke the beauty of life on the river, and show sympathy for the portrayed community. Stanisław Lipiński's cinematography commands attention from this film's dynamic opening sequence: the low-angle shots against the sky, the moving camera, and the portrayal of river life in the manner of a folk ballad. The realistic depiction is somewhat compromised by the intrusion of the staged "bar scenes," which were forced on Ford and Zarzycki by the film producers.[45]

Films in Yiddish

The richness and uniqueness of prewar Jewish culture in Poland is reflected in the thriving Yiddish cinema of the 1930s. Films in Yiddish were made in Poland but were primarily fashioned for the American market. In the 1930s, they became an important part of the Polish film scene. However, the first sound film in Yiddish,

Al Chet (*For the Sin*, aka *I Have Sinned*), directed by Aleksander Marten (Marek Tennenbaum), a former student of Max Reinhardt,[46] was made as late as 1936, six years after the first sound film in Polish.

One of the best-known examples of the flourishing Yiddish cinema in Poland is the Yiddish classic *Der Dibuk* (*The Dybbuk*, 1937), directed by Michał Waszyński, photographed by Albert Wywerka, made with the participation of the accomplished prewar set designers Jacek Rotmil and Stefan Norris, and scored by Henoch Kon. The film is adapted from a popular play by S. An-sky (Shloyme Zanvil Rappoport) of the same title. Deeply rooted in Jewish folklore and mysticism, and heavily influenced by German expressionist theater, this film about unfulfilled love is frequently listed as a masterpiece of prewar European cinema.[47] *The Dybbuk* portrays the world of nineteenth-century Eastern European Hasidim—the world of traditional metaphysics—and couples it with a melodramatic story about doomed lovers. It offers a metaphysical tragedy in the spirit of *Romeo and Juliet*.

A Polish-born Jewish American, Joseph Green (Józef Grinberg, 1900–1996), is known for some of the best-known examples of Yiddish cinema produced in Poland, which depict Jewish life in Eastern Europe. Educated in Berlin, he toured Europe with the Vilna Troupe. In 1924, he moved to New York and then to Hollywood, where he became interested in cinema. His career started with the

Figure 2.4   Lili Liliana as Leah in *The Dybbuk* (1937), directed by Michał Waszyński. Public domain. Author's collection.

Figure 2.5 Molly Picon (left) and Symcha Fostel in *Yiddle with His Fiddle* (1936), directed by Joseph Green and Jan Nowina-Przybylski. Courtesy of Filmoteka Narodowa.

distribution of American-made Yiddish films in Poland. Later, he invested his talent into Yiddish films made on location in Poland, with the participation of Polish-Jewish talent, as well as Polish filmmakers. From 1936 to 1939, Green produced four films, beginning with a well-received musical comedy *Yidl mitn Fidl* (*Yiddle with His Fiddle*, 1936), starring the Jewish American actress Molly Picon, based on Konrad Tom's script and codirected by Green and a Polish director, Jan Nowina-Przybylski. It tells the story of a girl (Picon), dressed as a boy fiddler, and three other *klezmorim* (musicians) touring the Jewish quarters of small Polish towns. When the girl falls in love with one of the musicians, Troim (Leon Liebgold), she has to reveal her identity. The film was shot mostly on location in Kazimierz Dolny, a picturesque, historic town with well-preserved architecture and a sizable Jewish population. This was the place—as J. Hoberman writes—that "had somewhat the same importance for Yiddish cinema as Monument Valley for John Ford."[48] This film is today chiefly remembered for its music, written by the American Abraham Ellstein.

The list of Joseph Green's successful productions also include *Der Purimshpiler* (*The Purim Player*, aka *The Jester*, 1937), codirected with Jan Nowina-Przybylski, and *A Little Letter to Mother* (1938), codirected with Leon Trystan. Ten films in Yiddish were made in Poland from 1936 to 1939. Although they frequently employed the familiar features of musical comedy and melodrama, their strength lies in their reliance on Jewish folklore and metaphysics, and on the flair of authenticity in their portrayal of the Jewish shtetl life in Poland. As Eric Goldman writes, these films "left us a legacy for centuries to come and a record of a life that would be no more."[49]

Notes

1. Barbara Armatys, Leszek Armatys, and Wiesław Stradomski, *Historia filmu polskiego 1930–1939*, vol. 2 (Warsaw: Wydawnictwa Artystyczne i Filmowe, 1988), 15.
2. Taxes for Polish films were as low as 5 percent in Warsaw and 3 percent outside the capital, compared with 60 and 35 percent, respectively, for foreign films. Furthermore, cinema owners had a chance to benefit from an additional 25 percent reduction of taxes on foreign films if their screening time of Polish feature films was more than 10 percent. Ibid., 16 and 42.
3. Edward Zajiček, *Zarys historii gospodarczej kinematografii polskiej: Tom I—Kinematografia wolnorynkowa 1896-1939* (Łódź: Państwowa Wyższa Szkoła Filmowa, Telewizyjna i Teatralna, 2015), 170–71.

4. Subtitling is a common practice in modern Poland, especially in cinemas. On television, subtitles are often replaced by the voice of a reader over the original dialogues so that the viewer can also hear the original language version.
5. Edward Zajiček, *Poza ekranem: Kinematografia polska, 1918–1991* (Warsaw: Filmoteka Narodowa and Wydawnictwa Artystyczne i Filmowe, 1992), 17. In the 1930s, however, Hollywood clearly dominated the Polish market, comprising 77 percent of all foreign films in 1934 and 61 percent in 1938. The remaining films mostly came from Germany, France, and Austria (Viennese comedies). See also Jerzy Płażewski, "Film zagraniczny w Polsce," in *Encyklopedia kultury polskiej XX wieku: Film i kinematografia*, ed. Edward Zajiček (Warsaw: Instytut Kultury and Komitet Kinematografii, 1994), 329.
6. Discussed by Jerzy Maśnicki and Kamil Stepan, "100 lat kina w Polsce: 1930–1933," *Kino* 2 (1998): 47–48. For a detailed discussion about the transition from silent to sound film in Poland, see Sheila Skaff, *The Law of the Looking Glass: Cinema in Poland, 1896–1939* (Athens: Ohio University Press, 2008), 103–36.
7. Armatys, Armatys, and Stradomski, *Historia filmu polskiego*, 239.
8. Figures from Edward D. Wynot Jr., *Warsaw between the World Wars: Profile of the Capital City in a Developing Land, 1918–1939* (New York: Columbia University Press, 1983), 280–81.
9. Edward Zajiček, "Kinematografia," in Zajiček, *Encyklopedia kultury polskiej XX wieku*, 53. Eugeniusz Bodo—producer, actor, director, and singer of Swiss origin—started his career in Warsaw theaters in 1919. Because of his ability to sing and dance, his career flourished after the introduction of sound. Although he was a versatile actor, he is chiefly remembered for his roles in musical comedies. He sang several prewar Polish hits in films directed by Juliusz Gardan and Michał Waszyński, among others.
10. Skaff, *The Law of the Looking Glass*, 84.
11. Mieczysława Ćwiklińska (Trapszo, 1879–1972), also an acclaimed singer, specialized in comedy and farce. After the war, she appeared on the screen only once, playing a strong supporting role in Aleksander Ford's classic Holocaust drama, *Border Street* (1949). She remained active onstage until her death at age ninety-three. Another symbol of early Polish cinema, Antoni Fertner, never appeared in postwar films.
12. Alina Madej, *Mitologie i konwencje: O polskim kinie fabularnym dwudziestolecia międzywojennego* (Kraków: Universitas, 1994), 60.
13. Wynot, *Warsaw between the World Wars*, 281.
14. Jerzy Maśnicki and Kamil Stepan, *Pleograf: Słownik biograficzny filmu polskiego 1896–1939* (Kraków: Staromiejska Oficyna Wydawnicza, 1996), entry "Krzeptowski."
15. Mariusz Guzek, "Umieranie jako strategia repertuarowa polskiego kina dwudziestolecia międzywojennego," in *Kino polskie wobec umierania i śmierci*, ed. Piotr Zwierzchowski and Daria Mazur (Bydgoszcz: Wydawnictwo Akademii Bydgoskiej im. Kazimierza Wielkiego, 2005), 14–15.
16. The symbolic meaning of several Polish screen names may escape the attention of a non-Polish-speaking viewer. They not only display the nationality or class background of a protagonist, but also frequently signal the features of the protagonist's personality.

For example, the name "Prawdzic" designates somebody who believes in truth, who can be trusted (*prawda* = truth). Another name, "Czarska," is close to "charm" (*czar* in Polish).

17. Adam Brodzisz (1906–1986) graduated from Wiktor Biegański's Warsaw Film Institute in 1927 and received his first acting opportunity in 1929 after winning "the contest of the photogenic" organized by the *Warsaw Evening* newspaper. In 1931, together with Eugeniusz Bodo and Michał Waszyński, he cofounded the film studio B-W-B.
18. *The Ten from the Pawiak Prison* was based on the account of Colonel Jan Jur-Gorzechowski, the chief organizer of the 1906 action. Ferdynand Goetel's script, however, focuses on the melodramatic story of a young freedom fighter (played by Adam Brodzisz) and changes historical events. For example, to make their deed more heroic, the ten patriots in this film are arrested for the terrorist act against the military police general, not for participating in anti-Russian demonstrations. The premiere of Ordyński's film was attended by Polish officials, including Marshal Piłsudski.
19. *The Baltic Rhapsody* belongs to a popular group of "sea movies" (*filmy morskie*) such as *Pod banderą miłości* (*Under the Banner of Love*, 1929, Michał Waszyński), and *Wiatr of morza* (*The Wind from the Sea*, 1930, Kazimierz Czyński). The newly gained access to the Baltic Sea after World War I gave rise to this group of films.
20. Henryk Sienkiewicz's *Potop* (*The Deluge*) forms his well-known historical trilogy with *Pan Wołodyjowski* (*Pan Michael*, aka *Colonel Wołodyjowski*) and *Ogniem i mieczem* (*With Fire and Sword*). Jerzy Hoffman adapted this trilogy for the screen in 1969 (*Pan Michael*), 1974 (*The Deluge*), and 1999 (*With Fire and Sword*). These works will be discussed later in the book.
21. Madej, *Mitologie i konwencje*, 118. The monastery at Częstochowa, the Polish holy sanctuary, houses the icon of the Black Madonna (the Virgin Mary). The term *Jasna Góra* (literally, Bright Mountain) refers to the monastery.
22. Józef Lejtes was hired to direct *General Pankratov's Daughter*. Mieczysław Znamierowski acted as an assistant director and as a producer. To be credited as a director, he gave up his salary. Jerzy Maśnicki and Kamil Stepan, "100 lat kina w Polsce: 1934–1937," *Kino* 3 (1998): 47.
23. Armatys, Armatys, and Stradomski, *Historia filmu polskiego*, 257.
24. Stanisław Janicki, *Polskie filmy fabularne 1902–1988* (Warsaw: Wydawnictwa Artystyczne i Filmowe, 1990), 28–67.
25. Born into a Jewish musical family, Henryk Wars (Warszawski, 1902–1977) scored as many as forty-three films from 1932 to 1939. His numerous prewar hits include one of the best-loved songs "Miłość ci wszystko wybaczy" (Love will forgive you everything), performed in a 1933 film, *Szpieg w masce* (*The Masked Spy*, Mieczysław Krawicz), by Hanka Ordonówna, and "Już nie zapomnisz mnie" (Now, you will remember me), sung by Aleksander Żabczyński in *Forgotten Melody* (1938). Prewar film music was also produced by such popular composers as Jerzy Petersburski, Władysław Daniłowski (Dan), Władysław Szpilman, Roman Palester, and Jan Maklakiewicz.

26. An excellent overview of Adolf Dymsza's career is provided by Roman Dziewoński, *Dodek Dymsza* (Warsaw: LTW, 2011).
27. Josef Škvorecký, *All the Bright Young Men and Women: A Personal History of the Czech Cinema*, trans. Michael Schonberg (Toronto: Take One Film Book, 1971), 22.
28. Dymsza continued his career after World War II, starring in popular films such as *Skarb* (*The Treasure*, 1948, Leonard Buczkowski); *Sprawa do załatwienia* (*A Matter to Settle*, 1953, Jan Rybkowski and Jan Fethke), where he appeared in a total of eight parts; and *Nikodem Dyzma* (1956, Jan Rybkowski). In 1970, Jan Łomnicki directed *Pan Dodek* (*Mr. Dodek*), a tribute to Dymsza's prewar comic achievements that incorporates scenes from ten of his twenty-six prewar films.
29. Armatys, Armatys, and Stradomski, *Historia filmu polskiego*, 304.
30. Jan Fethke (1903–1980) was a Polish-German screenwriter and director born in Upper Silesia. He worked for the German studio UFA in the 1920s, where he cowrote *Mother Krause's Journey to Happiness* (1929, Piel Jutzi), and in the mid-1930s moved to Warsaw. During the war, he worked for German film studios. After 1945, he continued his career in Poland, cowriting, among others, Aleksander Ford's classic Holocaust drama, *Border Street*, in 1949 (credited, because of his wartime activities, as Jean Forge—the same pseudonym he used in the 1920s when he published novels in Esperanto).
31. Małgorzata Hendrykowska, "Polak walczy z dzikusami: Kicz egzotyczny w polskim kinie międzywojennym," *Kino* 9 (1996): 22–23 and 31.
32. Armatys, Armatys, and Stradomski, *Historia filmu polskiego*, 234–35.
33. *Life Sentence* was voted the best film of the 1933–1934 season. Ibid., 226.
34. Ibid., 28.
35. Ibid., 244–45.
36. Maria Bogda and Adam Brodzisz, popular prewar actors, were an actual offscreen couple (married in 1930).
37. Armatys, Armatys, and Stradomski, *Historia filmu polskiego*, 244–45.
38. The reviewers praised the composition of the film and the harmony of the narration, and stressed that in Polish cinema *The Girls of Nowolipki* became the first "stylistic directorial success." Zbigniew Pitera, "Twórcy sztuki filmowej," *Srebrny Ekran* 12 (1937), quoted in Armatys, Armatys, and Stradomski, *Historia filmu polskiego*, 286.
39. Stowarzyszenie Propagandy Filmu Artystycznego Start. From 1931, officially known as Stowarzyszenie Miłośników Filmu Artystycznego START.
40. "Film polski na bezdrożach," *Głos Stolicy* 87 (1932): 5, quoted in Jadwiga Bocheńska, *Polska myśl filmowa do roku 1939* (Wrocław: Ossolineum, 1974), 174.
41. Stefania Heymanowa, quoted in Maśnicki and Stepan, "100 lat kina w Polsce: 1934–1937," 50.
42. See Marek Haltof, *Polish Film and the Holocaust: Politics and Memory* (New York: Berghahn Books, 2012), 53–55. *Sabra* also experienced problems with censorship, this time with the British censor who treated Ford's film as "propagandist, anti-Arab, leftist, and dangerous." See also J. Hoberman, *Bridge of Light: Yiddish Film*

between Two Worlds (New York: Museum of Modern Art and Schocken Books, 1991), 227.
43. Armatys, Armatys, and Stradomski, *Historia filmu polskiego*, 226.
44. In 1979, Stanisław Lenartowicz made a television series (four episodes), *Strachy (The Ghosts)*, also based on Maria Ukniewska's novel.
45. The producers were afraid that Ford and Zarzycki intended to make an uneventful, realistic film about the life of "simple people." Boycotted by the owners of cinemas, who despised Ford and his political convictions, the producers decided to shorten the documentary-like scenes, which created the ballad-like atmosphere of this film at the expense of staged "bar scenes." Armatys, Armatys, and Stradomski, *Historia filmu polskiego*, 270.
46. Maśnicki and Stepan, "100 lat kina w Polsce: 1934–1937," 49.
47. E.g., Parker Tyler, *Classics of the Foreign Film: A Pictorial Treasury* (Secaucus, NJ: Citadel Press, 1962). For some insightful comments, see Ira Konigsberg, "The Only 'I' in the World: Religion, Psychoanalysis and the Dybbuk," *Cinema Journal* 35, no. 4 (1997): 22–42. According to Konigsberg, the restored version of *The Dybbuk* premiered in New York in September 1989: "The dead were returned to life, and a culture long vanished, wiped out by the Holocaust, was resurrected on the screen" (23). See also Daria Mazur', *Waszyński's The Dybbuk*, trans. Maciej Smoczynski (Poznań: Wydawnictwo Naukowe Uniwersytetu im. Adama Mickiewicza, 2009).
48. Hoberman, *Bridge of Light*, 283. See also an insightful discussion in Joshua S. Walden, "Leaving Kazimierz: Comedy and Realism in the Yiddish Film Musical *Yidl mitn Fidl*," *Music, Sound, and the Moving Image* 3, no. 2 (2009): 159–93.
49. Eric A. Goldman, *Visions, Images, and Dreams: Yiddish Films Past and Present* (Ann Arbor, MI: UMI Research Press, 1983), 109.

CHAPTER 3
Cinema, World War II, and the Postwar Construction of National Identity (1939–1948)

The development of Polish cinema was brutally halted in 1939 when the Polish state ceased to exist. Nazi Germany attacked on 1 September, and then Soviet armies invaded from the east on 17 September, thus completing another partition of Poland. During the war, Poland lost more than six million citizens, almost 22 percent of the entire population. That number includes about three million Polish Jews, approximately 90 percent of Polish Jewry.[1]

Like other European countries, Poland was subsequently able to rebuild its economy and to redevelop its culture. The disappearance of the Jewish culture in Poland, however, was almost complete. Today, there are probably no more than ten thousand Jews living in Poland, compared with 3.3 million before the war. With the war, as Eric Goldman writes, "Poland ceased to be one of the great centers of Yiddish life and culture; instead it became its burial ground."[2] Unlike many other countries affected by the war, whose film production was maintained at the prewar level or even increased in the early 1940s, Poland had no feature film production during the occupation.

World War II

The Germans maintained the cinemas in occupied Polish territories after September 1939 for profit, as well as for propagandist reasons. Their repertoire included prewar Polish comedies, some features that were made but did not premiere before the war, and a handful of films finished after the outbreak of war, such as *To Happiness through Tears* (1943, Jan Fethke) and *Żołnierz królowej Madagaskaru* (*The Soldier of the Queen of Madagascar*, 1940, Jerzy Zarzycki), the latter now lost. Also lost is a prewar adaptation of Eliza Orzeszkowa's canonical novel *Nad*

Niemnem (*On the Niemen River*, aka *On the Banks of the Niemen*) that was finished shortly before the war. It never had its premiere, which had been scheduled for 5 September 1939. The film was produced by the leading prewar Polish studio Falanga and codirected by Wanda Jakubowska and Karol Szołowski. Jakubowska explained in several interviews that, during the occupation, she learned from Stefan Dękierowski—a cofounder of Falanga in 1923 who was still in charge of its laboratory during the war and active in the Polish underground resistance—that the Germans had decided to reedit the film as a picture about German settlers in the East who were persecuted by their Polish neighbors. Afraid that their film might be used for propaganda purposes, Jakubowska and Szołowski decided to hide the film's negative. Their friends removed the prints of *On the Niemen River* from the Falanga laboratory and hid them in two different locations. To minimize the dangers in case of being interrogated, the filmmakers were not informed of the hiding places. Unfortunately, Szołowski and Jakubowska's friends perished without a trace during the war; the copies of the film never resurfaced and most likely were destroyed.[3]

German films and a small number of Spanish and Italian films dominated the market in the occupied Polish territories. Propagandist films did not constitute most films screened in the *Generalgouvernement* (General Government), yet their presence prompted the Polish resistance movement to encourage a boycott of movie theaters. What began with the slogan "tylko świnie siedzą w kinie" (only pigs go to the cinema), was followed by actions, such as the use of stink bombs, to discourage Poles from going to movies and, indirectly, to support the German war effort. Despite such actions, the call to boycott cinemas was unsuccessful. In 1941, films screened in the General Government had twenty million viewers (including fourteen million Polish viewers) and were shown in 124 cinemas: 18 for Germans only, 62 with separate screenings for Poles and Germans, and 44 for Poles only.[4]

The Polish underground not only attempted to discourage people from visiting movie theaters, but also punished filmmakers and actors who collaborated with the Germans during the war. For instance, the Polish underground resistance executed Igo Sym, a popular prewar actor of Austrian origin, because he worked closely with the Gestapo, acted in the anti-Polish propaganda film *Heimkehr* (*Return Home*, 1941, Gustav Ucicky), and recruited Polish actors to appear in this film.[5] In retaliation, the German authorities sent a group of distinguished Polish actors, including Leon Schiller and Stefan Jaracz, to Auschwitz. Another tragic story involves arguably the best prewar Polish actor, Kazimierz Junosza-Stępowski, who was killed in 1943 by members of the Polish Home Army (Armia Krajowa, AK) while trying to protect his wife, a drug addict and Gestapo informer.[6]

War Losses

The deaths of several film icons testify to the harsh realities of the war. The actor Eugeniusz Bodo (Bogdan Junod), born in Switzerland (with a Swiss passport) and a symbol of commercial Polish cinema of the 1930s, was arrested by the Soviet secret police in 1941 in Lwów (now Lviv) and killed in a Soviet concentration camp in 1943.[7] The scientist and inventor Kazimierz Prószyński was arrested during the Warsaw Uprising in August 1944 and died in the Mauthausen-Gusen concentration camp on 13 March 1945. The list of extensive losses also includes film people killed in concentration camps, for example, the actor Witold Zacharewicz (1914–1943) who was murdered in Auschwitz, and those killed in action or shot by the Germans, such as the director Mieczysław Krawicz and the actors Tadeusz Frenkiel and Franciszek Brodniewicz.

The losses were particularly high among Polish filmmakers of Jewish origin. Henryk Szaro (Szapiro), a leading prewar director, was killed in the Warsaw Ghetto in June 1942. He shared his fate in the ghetto with, among others, the film producer Maria Hirszbejn, the actor, producer, and director of Polish and German films Danny Kaden (Daniel Kirschenfinkel, 1884–1942), and the popular composer and author of musical scores for Polish films Szymon Kataszek (1898–1943). The Gestapo killed several Jewish Polish filmmakers, among them the producer of many classic Polish films Józef Rosen (1902–1942) and the most accomplished prewar set designer Jacek Rotmil (1888–1944), who was arrested and killed at the Pawiak prison in Warsaw. The list of victims also includes actors such as Michał Znicz (Feiertag (1888–1943) and Ajzyk Samberg (Samborek, 1889–1943); directors such as Aleksander Marten (Marek Tennenbaum, 1898–1942) and Aleksander Reich (1887–1942); writers and screenwriters such as Jadwiga Migowa (pseudonym Kamil Norden, 1890–1942), Andrzej Marek (Marek Arnsztejn, 1878–1943), and Alter Kacyzne (1885–1941); and directors who died in the Soviet Union, such as Leon Trystan (Chaim Lejb Wagman, 1899–1941) and Juliusz Gardan (Gradstein, 1912–1944).[8]

The war also interrupted Ina Benita's (Janina Ferow-Bułhak) burgeoning acting career. Benita, who had Jewish roots, was accused of *Rassenschande*, the crime against racial purity. Since 1943, she had an affair with an Austrian Wehrmacht officer. When the authorities discovered their relationship, the officer was sent to the Eastern Front and the pregnant Benita was imprisoned. The blond femme fatale of prewar Polish cinema died in 1944 during the Warsaw Uprising, most probably in the city's underground sewers, while trying to escape the fighting with her baby son who was born four months earlier at the Pawiak prison.[9]

Polish Filmmakers during the War

Although some filmmakers survived the occupation in Poland, including the screenwriter Ludwik Starski, the director Leonard Buczkowski, and the actor Adolf Dymsza, the majority left after September 1939. Some of the best film professionals, including the directors Michał Waszyński and Józef Lejtes, the cinematographers Seweryn Steinwurzel and Stanisław Lipiński, the screenwriter-director Konrad Tom, and the composer Henryk Wars, among others, found themselves on the territories occupied by the Soviet Union and later served in General Władysław Anders's Polish II Corps (*Drugi Korpus Wojska Polskiego*). Others survived the war in the West and returned to Poland after 1945, but were unable to find employment in the nationalized postwar Polish film industry.[10]

A small group of filmmakers was active in well-organized film units that had been created by the Polish army in the West. The director Michał Waszyński's war activities may be considered typical for many prewar film professionals. He documented the route of the Polish II Corps and its battles against the German troops, for example, the Battle of Monte Cassino (Italy) at the beginning of 1944. Waszyński was also responsible for the only Polish feature film produced during the war, *Wielka droga* (*The Long Road,* aka *The Great Road,* 1945), which premiered in Rome in 1946 (in Poland in 1991). The film was written by Tom, photographed by Lipiński and Steinwurzel, and scored by Wars, and it starred Jadwiga Andrzejewska and Renata Bogdańska (who married General Anders in 1948). The narrative of *The Long Road* follows the melodramatic story of two lovers separated by war. The film combines location shooting with documentary war footage of the Battle of Monte Cassino, which is the film's real strength. The film opens with scenes in prewar Lwów, portrays the September 1939 aggression on Poland by Nazi Germany and Soviet Russia, the deportations of Poles to Siberia, the

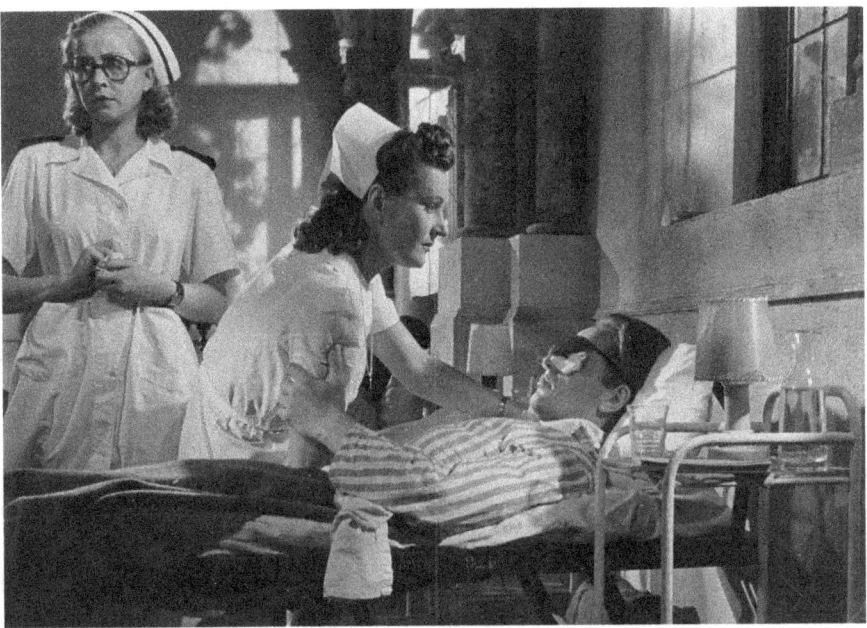

Figure 3.1 (From the left) Jadwiga Andrzejewska, Renata Bogdańska, and Albin Ossowski in Michał Waszyński's *The Long Road* (1946). Photograph from the collection of Anna Maria Anders. Courtesy of Filmoteka Narodowa.

formation of a Polish army in the Soviet Union, and the long road of Polish soldiers in Anders' Army from the Soviet Union via Iran, Palestine, and Egypt to Italy.

After the war, Waszyński settled in Italy and later in Spain. He directed two feature films in Italy and acted as an assistant director on *Othello* (1952, Orson Welles). He also worked as an art director on *Roman Holiday* (1953, William Wyler) and as an associate producer on two films directed by Anthony Mann (*El Cid*, 1961, and *The Fall of the Roman Empire*, 1964) and Joseph L. Mankiewicz (*The Barefoot Contessa*, 1954, and *The Quiet American*, 1958).[11] Like Waszyński, other makers of *The Long Road* remained in the West, not risking the return to the Soviet-occupied Poland. For example, Seweryn Steinwurzel, cinematographer praised by critics for his technical expertise and artistic leanings, settled in Brazil, where he worked in the film industry as a constructor and technologist. He moved to Israel in 1975, where he spent the last years of his life. Another cinematographer, Stanisław Lipiński, first moved to England and then, after 1956, to Canada where he worked for television. Henryk Wars settled in the United States after the war where, credited as Henry Vars, he composed music for several Hollywood films from 1951 to 1971. Exceptional is the case of Jadwiga Andrzejewska (1915–1977), a leading prewar actress specializing in comedy and melodrama, who returned to Poland in 1947. Although she frequently appeared in postwar Polish films, these were mostly episodic (sometimes uncredited) roles.

Polish filmmakers living in England during the war documented the struggles for Poland and created anti-Nazi propagandist works. For instance, Eugeniusz Cękalski made compilation propagandist films in England, some of them narrated by known British actors such as Leslie Howard (*The White Eagle*, aka *A Nation in Exile*, 1941) and John Gielgud (*Unfinished Journey*, 1943).[12] An experimental antifascist propaganda work by Franciszka and Stefan Themerson, *Calling Mr. Smith* (1943), also received some critical attention.[13]

Several filmmakers who associated with prewar leftist groups survived the war in the Soviet Union and created a military film unit Czołówka (Vanguard) within the Polish 1st Tadeusz Kościuszko Infantry Division, which fought alongside the Red Army. Aleksander Ford, Jerzy Bossak, Stanisław Wohl, and Ludwik Perski, all prewar START members or followers, returned with the Red Army as officers in the Kościuszko Division.

Geopolitics

After 1945, the new political system forcefully imposed onto the Polish organism replaced one dreaded system with another. Traditionally disliked and feared, Poland's eastern neighbor and its communist ideology started to leave their mark on Polish life. This led to the gradual Sovietization: the subjection of Poles to the rules of the communist minority operating under the umbrella of the Soviet Union, and the rejection of any links with the prewar "bourgeois Poland."

In addition, the Polish borders changed dramatically. Poland moved to the west, at least geographically, and lost its eastern territories, Kresy Wschodnie (Eastern Borderlands), places immortalized in patriotic tales by, among others, Henryk Sienkiewicz in his epic historical novels. As compensation, Poland gained new territories in the west and the north, with new borders set on the Odra (Oder) and Nysa Łużycka (Neisse) rivers, the so-called Ziemie Odzyskane (Recovered Territories, literally Regained Lands). Because of the migration from the east to the west, from villages to cities, Polish people required incredible mobility. The migration, the changed borders, and the losses caused by the war visibly altered the Polish landscape. After the war, Poland became an almost ethnically homogeneous society. The Polish Jews had been murdered, the defeated Germans were forced to resettle behind the Odra/Nysa line, the Ukrainians and other nationals who populated eastern provinces were now part of the Soviet Union or were deported there, and the Poles from the east were forced to move to regained Polish western provinces. Consequently, Poland started to become an ethnic and religious monolith, with most of the population being Roman Catholic. Before the war, Poland had been a multinational society, with Poles comprising 68.9 percent of the total population in 1931.[14]

Before the war, and throughout history in general, the Polish identity had been created by interactions with Poland's powerful neighbors and with many national minorities living within Poland. This important aspect of national self-definition had been lost. Instead, Poles were deprived of contacts with other nationalities because of political isolation, poverty, communist propaganda, and travel restrictions.[15] Furthermore, they were also isolated within the Soviet Bloc, similar to other Central European nations.

Efforts to create a new national identity began with the rewriting of Polish history from the communist (Marxist-Leninist) perspective. This became a history that stressed the "progressive" tendencies in the Polish past and presented the new, politically correct version of troubled Polish-Russian relations. Despite attempts to erase traces of traditional Polish identity and to reinterpret Polish history, certain aspects, important for the national identity, remained. Arguably, the most important one continued to be the role of the Roman Catholic Church in preserving Polishness, especially during Poland's partition (1795–1918). Catholicism played a significant role in defining and strengthening the Polish character. Throughout the ages, Poles fought with numerous enemies representing different religions, from Islamic Turks to Orthodox Russians. Polish nationalism, identified with the Roman Catholic Church, always focused on national freedom being paramount, to be defended at all costs; it demanded personal sacrifice for national causes. In trying to change the nature of Polish nationalism, communist authorities fought a losing battle. They failed to replace nationalism with internationalism, religion with ideology, and Polish romanticism with revolutionary spirit.

Loss of Continuity: Film Industry

In the new geopolitical situation after the war, numerous filmmakers chose permanent emigration rather than return to the Soviet-dominated Poland. As mentioned earlier, some of the established prewar figures continued their careers in the West, such as the composers Bronisław Kaper and Henryk Wars, the directors Michał Waszyński and Józef Lejtes, and the experimental filmmakers the Themersons.[16] Because of their decision to remain abroad, their postwar careers were rarely mentioned in Poland.[17]

Some filmmakers from the West tried to return to Poland after the war. For example, the actor Aleksander Żabczyński fought as a lieutenant during the September campaign of 1939 and then, until the end of the war, in the Polish army in the West (he was wounded in the Battle of Monte Cassino). He returned to Poland in 1947 and became associated with Warsaw theaters but, like several others, never appeared on-screen in postwar films.

The authorities infrequently addressed the issue of collaboration of Polish artists after the war. For example, actors like Adolf Dymsza, who performed in Warsaw's theaters during the war, underwent verifications and, sometimes, symbolic punishment. The director Leonard Buczkowski, for example, is credited in his first postwar film, *Zakazane piosenki* (*Forbidden Songs*, 1947/1948), as Marian Leonard, punishment for making several short films for German companies during the war. The penalty was in effect after *Forbidden Songs* and lasted three years.[18] Although several Polish filmmakers who collaborated with Nazi Germany were chastised by the Polish underground during the war, and punished by the communist film authorities after 1945 for obvious political reasons, the issue of collaboration with the Soviet occupier was never mentioned in postwar Poland.[19] For example, after the 1939 September campaign, several (mostly left-leaning) filmmakers who moved to the Soviet-occupied part of Poland offered their services to the Soviet film authorities and worked on Soviet political propaganda films. Aleksander Ford, Stanisław Wohl, the Forbert brothers, and several other filmmakers gathered toward the end of 1939 in Lwów and later in Kiev, where they found work in Soviet cinema. They contributed to several Soviet films that were clearly of anti-Polish nature.[20]

Postwar Poland, renamed the Polish People's Republic (PRL), started its existence by gradually erasing links with prewar Poland.[21] Reliable information about the prewar national period had virtually disappeared from school curricula and was replaced by accounts of the class struggle and the larger-than-life communist movement. The silence over certain nationally sensitive and important issues and the harsh criticism of others created a conviction that everything was to begin anew in a social and cultural void.

The same applied to Polish cinema. Although the leading postwar filmmakers started their careers before the war, they attacked the prewar film industry and the dominant film culture of that period. Jerzy Bossak, the editor of the Polish biweekly *Film* magazine, stated in 1946: "In prewar Poland there were no good films, not just because there was no difference between the maker of films and the maker of artificial jewelry, but also because we did not know how to make films and look at them. ... Today we must create conditions in which Polish film can flourish."[22] Buczkowski became the only established prewar film director to be able to make films in communist Poland. Contrary to Bossak's claim, some of the first and most popular postwar films were made by the prewar professionals who had associated with the *filmowa branża* (film trade), much criticized by START members.

The negation of prewar achievements paralleled the mythologization of certain marginal, yet politically more fitting, trends, in particular the role of START. Some START members, headed by Aleksander Ford, entered Poland with the Polish army from the Soviet Union and immediately seized political power. Ford and his START colleagues controlled the nationalized post-1945 Polish film industry, both as decision makers and filmmakers.

There was only one Polish film organization in existence immediately after the war, the Wytwórnia Filmowa Wojska Polskiego (Polish Army Film Unit), and it was attached to the army's political department. Its tasks had been not only to document war activities (frequently biased and unreliable), but also to capture film equipment and film stock left by the Germans and to take care of the surviving movie theaters.[23] Polish filmmakers who affiliated themselves with the Polish army coming from the East were able to take some advantage of technical supplies belonging to the German film company UFA in Babelsberg and Lower Silesia, where the Germans had stored their film equipment. The equipment and confiscated films enabled the establishment of a film studio in Łódź (the only Polish city with an infrastructure intact).[24] Before the end of 1945, the studio in Łódź was ready to produce films.

The film industry was nationalized on 13 November 1945. Film Polski ("Polish Film," the National Board of Polish Film) was established as the sole body that was producing, distributing, and exhibiting films in Poland. From 1945 to 1947,

Aleksander Ford was the head of the organization. He accumulated power and ran the board in an almost dictatorial manner.

The damaged and outdated infrastructure remained the biggest problem for the nationalized film industry. In 1945, only approximately 230 cinemas were functional, and by 1947, that number had risen to 599. The first three years after the war were considerably liberal as far as the repertoire of Polish cinemas is concerned, despite the growing domination of Soviet war films such as *Raduga* (*The Rainbow*, 1944, Mark Donskoi). Although some Soviet films were genuinely popular in Poland, such as the musical comedy *Volga-Volga* (1937, Grigori Alexandrov), Polish audiences frequently reacted with hostility to the presence of Soviet films, especially overtly propagandist pictures that idolized Stalin.[25] In 1946, 158 films remained in distribution, including fifty-three prewar Polish, eighty-four Soviet, sixteen English, and five French films.[26] In 1948, there were ninety-nine films on Polish screens: thirty-three American, twenty-three Soviet, eighteen French, sixteen English, seven Czechoslovak, and two Italian films.[27] Some of the best films of the decade were screened in Poland, including *Citizen Kane* (1941, Orson Welles), *Alexander Nevsky* (1938, Sergei Eisenstein), and *Rome, Open City* (1945, Roberto Rossellini).

Following the Soviet example, the Polish communist government paid particular attention to the "cinefication" (*kinofikacja*) of rural areas by building new cinemas and by creating mobile cinemas (*kina objazdowe*). The number of permanent cinemas climbed rapidly from 762 in 1949 to 2,033 in 1952, but, interestingly, the number of viewers remained virtually the same.[28]

In addition to the infrastructure, other big problems facing the Polish film industry were the shortage of filmmakers and the lack of skilled professionals due to war losses and emigration. To change that, the Young Filmmakers Workshop (Warsztat Filmowy Młodych) was founded in Kraków, a city virtually untouched by the war. Its first graduates included the future prominent filmmakers Jerzy Kawalerowicz (1922–2007) and Wojciech J. Has (1924–2000). The crucial step, however, was establishing in 1948 the later famous Łódź Film School, which began to dominate the Polish film industry in the mid-1950s with such talented graduates as Andrzej Wajda (1926–2016), Andrzej Munk (1921–1961), Kazimierz Kutz (1929–), and Janusz Morgenstern (1922–2011). In 1955, as many as 158 graduates of the Łódź Film School worked in the national film industry, with the total number of active film professionals being 228.[29]

In postwar Poland, it was extremely difficult to produce a politically acceptable script. The ambitions of the communist government and Film Polski were very high, yet very few feature films were made within the first ten years after the war: two in 1947, two in 1948, three in 1949, four in 1950, two in 1951, four in 1952, three in 1953, ten in 1954, and eight in 1955.[30] No feature film was released in 1945 and 1946, largely because of censorship and the impossibility of dealing with certain sensitive issues, including Polish-Jewish relations during the war, the 1944 Warsaw Uprising, and the role of the underground Home Army.[31] Many scripts were subjected to severe criticism on political grounds and endless rewrites. Others were produced and immediately shelved. For example, Dr. Janusz Korczak's (Henryk Goldszmit, 1878–1942) biography belongs to one of the oldest and the most prestigious projects in postwar Polish cinema. Ludwik Starski (1903–1984) submitted his first script proposal about Korczak's story on 14 September 1945, but, because of various political circumstances, it was postponed for more than four decades.[32]

Sometimes films were released in mutilated versions, as happened to *Miasto nieujarzmione* (*The Unvanquished City*, 1950, Jerzy Zarzycki). The powerful yet laconic and understated story of survival written by the Jewish Polish pianist and composer Władysław Szpilman (1911–2000) inspired one of the earliest projects in the history of postwar Polish cinema. The first draft of the script, then titled *The Warsaw Robinson*, links the story of one man's survival amid the ruins of Warsaw with Daniel Defoe's novel *Robinson Crusoe*. The draft was written by Czesław Miłosz and Jerzy Andrzejewski in the spring of 1945 and was based on their conversations with Szpilman. The project was discussed on 24 June 1945, at the meeting of the Committee for Evaluating Film Scripts. The committee, chaired by Aleksander Ford, decided to shelve the project until 1948 because of its alleged apolitical stand; they recommended several revisions to overcome the main character's "passivity," and postulated grounding the story within the proper (communist) ideological and political framework.[33]

Robinson warszawski (*The Warsaw Robinson*) was shown in November 1949 at the congress of filmmakers in Wisła, during which the doctrine of socialist realism was officially enforced in Poland. Attacked for its lack of "revolutionary spirit," Zarzycki's film underwent further modifications (such a highlighting the role of the Soviet Army in liberating Warsaw and the addition of a Soviet soldier amid the ruins) and was released in December 1950 under the more politically acceptable title *The Unvanquished City* (*Miasto nieujarzmione*).[34] The final cut serves as a travesty of Szpilman's memoirs. It serves the communist ideology by viciously attacking the nationalist forces represented by the Home Army. It also bluntly accuses the AK leadership of destroying the city hand in hand with the Germans and follows not a surviving Jewish man (Szpilman) but rather a working-class Polish character, Rafalski, who witnesses the destruction of Warsaw. The casting of a Jewish protagonist in order to remain true to the spirit of Szpilman's memoirs was never considered. His story of survival had to wait for more than fifty years to be faithfully adapted for the screen by Roman Polański in *The Pianist* (*Pianista*, 2002).

First Postwar Films

The war remained the main subject of most projects. The postwar Polish viewers were eager to see their wartime experiences on-screen. According to a poll conducted in mid-November 1946 by *Film*, 36 percent out of ten thousand responders opted for broadly understood war movies, some dealing with topics silenced by the communist authorities after the war, such as the 1944 Warsaw Uprising.[35] One of the first postwar films, *Dwie godziny* (*Two Hours*, Stanisław Wohl and Józef Wyszomirski), was made in 1946 but not premiered until 1957.[36] The film offers a panoramic view of the traumatized and demoralized postwar Polish society. It opens with a scene on a train traveling from Germany to Poland with several ex-prisoners, some still wearing striped camp attire, returning home from concentration camps. Several characters in the film cannot put their camp past behind them, including the former *Kapo* (prisoner functionary) from Majdanek concentration and extermination camp, Filip (Władysław Hańcza), and his brutalized victim, the shoemaker Leon (Jacek Woszczerowicz), who is most probably Jewish, although his nationality is never clearly defined. In the film's highly dramatic final scenes, Leon kills the *Kapo*, while Leon's wife gives birth to their son. The film's dark messages, expressionistic look, and slightly stylized acting prevail over the optimistic message of "living against all odds," intended by the film's original writer, Ewa Szelburg-Zarembina (who withdrew her name from the credits). When the film was released in 1957, it was barely noticed by critics and viewers, who were at that time embracing new cinematic approaches to the war offered by the young Polish Film School filmmakers.

Given the complexities of the Polish past, it comes as no surprise that history, recent history in particular, is the traditional topic of postwar Polish films. Memories of World War II haunt Polish cinema and, like many traumatic experiences, return powerfully on the screen. Leonard Buczkowski's *Forbidden Songs*, generally regarded as the first (released) postwar Polish film, highlights this obsession. The film was made by a group of leading prewar filmmakers. It was directed by Buczkowski, who made nine feature films before the war; written by Ludwik Starski, whose name had been associated with the best-known prewar comedies; and photographed by the experienced Adolf Forbert. This film fulfilled the expectations of many Polish audiences, had 10.8 million viewers within the first three years of its release (average attendance was then high at five million viewers per film),[37] and remains one of the most popular Polish films ever.

This episodic film narrates an anthology of songs popular in Warsaw during the occupation. Although well liked by the audience, *Forbidden Songs* was criticized by communist authorities and film critics for its lack of political involvement, its alleged misrepresentation of the Germans, and a false picture of the occupation. As a result, the film was taken off the screens, remade, and then rereleased in 1948. The new version embraced stronger political accents and portrayed a darker picture of the occupation (with an emphasis on German brutality), stressed the role of the Red Army in the "liberation" of Warsaw, and provided better-developed psychological motivation for the characters' actions.

Documenting the Postwar Years

Polish filmmakers returning to Poland alongside the Red Army documented the liberation of concentration camps, postwar trials, and executions.[38] In 1944, Aleksander Ford and Jerzy Bossak produced one of the most iconic Holocaust documentaries, *Majdanek: Cmentarzysko Europy (Majdanek, the Cemetery of Europe)* that, according to Stuart Liebman, was "the first to develop visual and narrational strategies to dramatize the unprecedented story of German brutality in a camp."[39] This classic documentary features footage taken after 23 July 1944, when the Red Army captured the southeastern Polish city of Lublin, along with Majdanek, the first Nazi German death camp located in the Polish territories. The ill-equipped Czołówka camera operators—treated with suspicion by the Soviets—

were unprepared for the task and had to work with heavy and unreliable cameras and with limited supplies of film stock. Stanisław Wohl and the brothers Adolf and Władysław Forbert photographed the trial of the Majdanek SS guards and *Kapos*, along with the public execution by hanging of six Majdanek personnel. This footage was later included in the twenty-five-minute compilation documentary *Swastyka i szubienica* (*Swastika and Gallows*, 1945), produced by Kazimierz Czyński and edited by Wacław Kaźmierczak, the latter of whom was also responsible for editing some of the best-known postwar Polish documentaries. Liebman emphasizes that *Swastika and Gallows* is arguably "the first cinematic portrayal of a trial concerning what we would call today the Holocaust or Shoah,"[40]

Polish filmmakers were also among the first photographers and filmmakers at the site of another liberated camp, Auschwitz-Birkenau, on 28 January 1945. They documented trials and executions of the SS guards at other German camps, for example, in *Szubienice w Sztutthofie* (*The Gallows in the Stutthof Concentration Camp*, 1946), the special edition of the *Polish Newsreel* (*Polska Kronika Filmowa*, *PKF*) directed by Aleksander Świdwiński.

The documentarian Jerzy Bossak (Szelubski, 1910–1989) greatly shaped Polish cinema after 1945. He was a cofounder of the Czołówka Film Studio, served as a professor at the Łódź Film School, and was the first managing editor of the *Polish Newsreel* (1944–1948). The newsreel, approximately ten minutes long, was usually shown before a main feature in Polish cinemas from 1944 to 1995.[41] This "filmic newspaper," which followed the documentary tradition of early actualities, focused on local and foreign events and often attempted to comment on political, social, and cultural phenomena. *PKF* had continued the tradition of the prewar Polish Telegraphic Agency (Polska Agencja Telegraficzna, PAT) established in 1918, which had the exclusive rights to film inside state buildings since 1927. The first edition of *PKF* appeared on 1 December 1944; its first irregular editions from 1944 to 1949 were produced by Czołówka and supervised by Bossak. With some apparent propagandist bias, the newsreel mostly documented the implementation of the communist system on Polish soil: it captured images of the effects of war (material losses, devastation, and the hardship of life) and postwar reconstruction.

After 1949, *PKF* was produced by the Documentary Film Studio. It had regular weekly editions in the first half of the 1950s and two weekly editions from 1958 to 1981. The newsreel, whose musical signal was composed by Władysław Szpilman (see later discussion on Roman Polański's *The Pianist*), was appreciated by Polish audiences; many of its editions also received numerous international recognitions. For example, *Powódź* (*The Flood*, 1947, Bossak and Kaźmierczak), the celebrated documentary awarded the Grand Prix at the Cannes Film Festival, was first shown as a special edition of the *Polish Newsreel*.

Documenting Jewish Life: Kinor

Film Polski controlled the production and distribution of films, yet there was some room for other film organizations during the first postwar years. In 1947, the cooperative Kinor, an abbreviation of Kino-Organizacja (Cinema-Organization), had been reestablished by some of the surviving members of the Jewish filmmaking community who started to make films in Yiddish with the help of facilities provided by Film Polski.[42] The task of the producers Saul and Izak Goskind, the director Natan Gross, the camera operators Adolf Forbert and Władysław Forbert, and two comic actors, Israel Schumacher and Shimon Dzigan, who returned to Poland in 1948 from the Soviet Union, was to document Jewish life in Poland and to confront the immensity of the Holocaust. Working with a small budget, the Goskinds and their friends started to produce short films in Yiddish about Jewish issues, focusing on several important actual events happening in postwar Warsaw, such as the uncovering of Emmanuel Ringelblum's archives, the ceremony of handing over Torah scrolls that had survived the destruction of the Warsaw Ghetto, and numerous images of the surviving Polish Jews returning home. They also captured various cultural events on camera, including the visit of an American Yiddish cinema star, Molly Picon, known for her work in prewar classics made by Joseph Green in Poland, such as *Yiddle with His Fiddle*.

In 1947, the Goskinds produced a documentary, *Mir Lebn Geblibene* (*We Are Still Alive*) that acknowledges the horrors of the near past but focuses on the present situation. Ira Konigsberg stresses the reconciliatory tone of the film that "almost seems to be arguing that a better Poland is the result of the past horrors," and "buys into the utopianism of Poland's movement toward a Communist state. ... Jewish workers feel wanted in the new Poland, we are told, and are working together with Poles to produce civilization acceptable to both."[43]

Saul Goskind produced the first postwar narrative film in Yiddish, and the first narrative film made in Poland about the Holocaust, *Unzere Kinder* (*Our Children*, 1948), directed by Gross and with the participation of Dzigan and Szumacher.[44] In the film, Dzigan and Szumacher perform their prewar numbers for a group of Jewish orphans, who do not appreciate the references to the occupation. Later, the comedians perform once again, this time in the orphanage, and their performance brings back tragic war memories. *Our Children* was not approved for general screening by the Polish authorities and was shown in Poland only once, at a closed screening for invited guests.

After the creation of the state of Israel in 1948 and the implementation of Stalinist restrictions on cinema in 1949, there was no place for Kinor in communist Poland. In the developing political climate of the Cold War, the participation of the philanthropic Jewish organization Joint (American Joint Distribution Committee for the Aid of Jews) in the Kinor activities proved to be difficult to accept by the state authorities. In 1950, Joint's actions in Poland were terminated after the accusation of spying for foreign powers, a charge frequently employed during Stalinist times. In response, most Kinor members, including the Goskind brothers and Gross, immigrated to Israel.

Landmark Films: *The Last Stage* and *Border Street*

As stated earlier, Polish films that referenced the war and concentration camps and featured camp survivors attempting to rebuild their lives represented the main trend of postwar Polish cinema. Two major films released in the late 1940s, *Ostatni etap* (*The Last Stage*, aka *The Last Stop*, 1948, Wanda Jakubowska) and *Ulica Graniczna* (*Border Street*, 1949, Aleksander Ford), established images that influenced how subsequent filmmakers looked at Auschwitz and the Warsaw Ghetto Uprising.[45]

In *The Last Stage*, Wanda Jakubowska (1907–1988) shows the monstrosity of Auschwitz-Birkenau and draws on her own camp experiences to portray the "factory of death" (she was interned in Auschwitz-Birkenau and Ravensbrück).[46] With its dramatization of the camp experience, *The Last Stage* establishes several images that reinforced the depiction of Nazi German camps in later Holocaust narratives: the dark, "realistic" images of the camp (the film was shot on location in Auschwitz); the passionate moralistic appeal; and the clear divisions between victims and victimizers.

The film was written by Jakubowska and another Auschwitz survivor, the German communist Gerda Schneider. As stated by Jakubowska on several occasions, she was thinking about a film documenting her camp experience while still at Auschwitz; she started working on the script immediately after the war and finished the first draft in December 1945. For her, this was a personal duty as a camp survivor and as a filmmaker to bear witness to history and to register the enormity of evil.[47]

Jakubowska intended her film to be based exclusively on authentic events that either she or her fellow inmates had witnessed. To reflect the reality of the camp appropriately, she decided to produce her film on location in Auschwitz. She made her film with the participation of the local population (the inhabitants of the town of Oświęcim), Auschwitz survivors, Red Army personnel, and a small group of German prisoners of war as extras. In addition to serving as extras, the camp's former inmates played several episodic roles, which in a sense forced them to relive their Auschwitz experiences. Moreover, most of the film's crew had survived the terror of the occupation in Poland. They were knowledgeable about the history of the camps; some had even experienced incarceration in concentration camps.

This internationally acclaimed film encountered several problems during production. According to Jakubowska, only Stalin's personal approval enabled her to pursue this project. Authorities in Poland were supposedly afraid of similarities between the Soviet and German concentration camps, and preferred not to touch the sensitive topic.[48] Jakubowska also faced aesthetic problems while making this first major film about the horror of Nazi concentration camps and trying to reach large audiences. For this reason, she tried to avoid explicit imagery and instead appealed to the viewer's knowledge of the mechanisms of death camps.[49] For example, frequent shots of smoke and flames indicate rather than depict the true nature of the "factory of death"—the extermination process. In one scene, the camera tracks over the piles of belongings left after one of the Jewish transports. In another scene, Jakubowska cuts from an image of Jewish children walking toward the crematorium, unaware of their fate, to an image of burning grass and the SS men returning to their barracks.

The Last Stage opens before the credits with a brief, quasi-documentary scene of a German raid on a Warsaw street, which results in the arrest of several people, including one of the film's leading characters, Helena (Wanda Bartówna). Another scene, over the credits, moves the action to Auschwitz by portraying a train arriving at the camp. Throughout *The Last Stage*, Jakubowska depicts the nightmarish conditions in Auschwitz: recurrent roll calls, random executions and

Figure 3.2   (From the left) Maria Kaniewska (*Raportführerin*), Edward Dziewoński (SS doctor), Wanda Jakubowska, Janina Marisówna (*Aufseherin*), and Aleksandra Śląska (*Oberaufseherin*) on the set of Jakubowska's *The Last Stage* (1948). Photograph from Edward Dziewoński's archive. Courtesy of Roman Dziewoński.

selections, images of powerless people being herded to the gas chambers, and the terrifying efficiency of Auschwitz run by SS guards and camp administrators, both groups portrayed as the embodiment of evil. The filmmaker's objective, however, is not so much to portray the repelling reality of the concentration camp as it is to show the women's solidarity in their suffering, as well as in their struggle against fascism. Jakubowska focuses on carefully chosen inmates, mostly communists and supporters of the communist resistance in the camp, who represent different oppressed nationalities and groups of people.

Jakubowska's film shaped the future representation of Nazi German concentration camps. It also introduced the images of camp life that are now archetypal and notable in numerous films about the Holocaust and the "concentrationary universe." These images include, among others, morning and evening roll calls on the *Appelplatz*; the arrival of a transport train at Auschwitz-Birkenau—a steam locomotive slowly moving, in a thick fog, through the "death gate" toward the armed SS guards with dogs; the separation of families upon their arrival at the Birkenau unloading ramp; the tracking shot over the belongings left by the gassed camp victims; shots of crowded prisoners' barracks; and the juxtaposed shots of the camp orchestra playing classical music and the selection of prisoners to the gas chambers. These and other images reinforced the depiction of Nazi German concentration camps, and their influence is discernible in subsequent American films, such as *The Diary of Anne Frank* (1959, George Stevens), *Sophie's Choice* (1982, Alan Pakula), and *Schindler's List* (1993, Steven Spielberg). Scenes from *The Last Stage* are also present (without acknowledgment and, interestingly, as actual documentary footage from the camp) in films such as Alain Resnais's classic essay on memory, *Nuit et Brouillard* (*Night and Fog*, 1955).

While depicting Auschwitz-Birkenau, *The Last Stage* suffers from several weaknesses inherent in many later projects that aimed at recreating the horror of the Holocaust, including the melodramatization of situations and characters due to a dependence on mainstream narrative patterns, and the use of inspiring endings. The incorporation of some Hollywood conventions is chiefly seen in the last, much-discussed scene of the film. Portrayed with a low-angle shot, Marta Weiss (Barbara Drapińska), the heroic Jewish Polish woman working as an interpreter in the camp and involved in the communist resistance (and modeled on Mala Zimetbaum), dies a martyr's death while warning others: "You must not let Auschwitz be repeated." Marta's last words are juxtaposed with the image of (presumably Soviet) planes over Auschwitz, creating havoc among the SS guards.

Today, despite its powerful imagery, *The Last Stage* may seem in line with the official cultural policy and the dominant aesthetic modes of the late 1940s. Contemporary critics emphasize the employment of traditional cinematic conventions and the use of proper lighting and make-up not appropriate for the circumstance.[50] When *The Last Stage* was released, however, several critics praised the Russian cinematographer Boris (Bentsion) Monastyrski, who had filmed equally "unreal" images of war in Mark Donskoi's *The Rainbow*.

Despite such criticism, *The Last Stage* remains the "definitive film about Auschwitz,"[51] a seminal work about the Holocaust, and a prototype for future Holocaust cinematic narratives.[52] It deserves pioneer status with its documentary feel and searing images, and enjoys a prominent place in the history of cinema, as well as in our understanding of the past. Aside from serving as a witness of war atrocities, it is also a testimony to the postwar political climate and Jakubowska's own communist biases. Similar to several other works produced immediately after World War II, this film is not predominantly centered on presenting the wartime extermination of the European Jewry. Rather, it emphasizes the tragedy of nation-states subjected to Nazi German exterminatory policies and reflects the status of postwar debates about Auschwitz and early attempts to memorialize the former Nazi German camp.

In film criticism, *The Last Stage* is often discussed as "a model for other numerous, ideologically oriented representations of victimhood and heroism under Nazi rule."[53] This is—it must be emphasized again—a pioneering work, the first narrative film to portray the Auschwitz-Birkenau concentration/death camp. After seeing Jakubowska's film, Béla Balázs proclaimed in an unpublished essay that "a new genre was born."[54] Balázs's comments were almost of a prophetic nature, given that we are now debating the "Holocaust genre."

* * *

Another acclaimed film, the much-awaited *Border Street* by Aleksander Ford, dealt with the wartime predicament of Polish Jews and for the first time represented on the screen the Warsaw Ghetto Uprising (19 April to 16 May 1943). The film had been produced mostly at the well-equipped Czech Barrandov studio (sometimes labeled the "Slavic Hollywood") and with the Czech contingent, including the cinematographer Jaroslav Tuzar. The straightforward and realistic (although studio-made) *Border Street* shows the Germans' partitioning of Warsaw into Jewish and Aryan quarters and gives a vast panorama of Jewish and Polish characters living in a building on the street that becomes the border of the ghetto. This "cinematic monument to a trauma that was barred from any celluloid representation"[55] received many awards, including the Golden Medal at the Venice Film Festival in 1948.

Border Street had also been made by some prewar professionals. It was written by Ford, Ludwik Starski, and Jan Fethke (credited as Jean Forge) who sought the advice of a psychologist and writer, Rachela Auerbach, credited as the film's consultant. She lived in the Warsaw Ghetto during the war (where she worked together with the historian Emmanuel Ringelblum) and after her escape to the "Aryan side" was active in the Polish committee Żegota (Council to Aid Jews).

The original screenplay by Ford stressed the hostile attitude of Poles toward Jews. The final screen version, modified by Ford after severe criticism of his project, presents not so much the divisions but the solidarity between Jews and Poles across the wall (real and symbolic) dividing the city. The anti-Semitic sentiments of many Poles, however, are not suppressed in the film. In addition to images of Poles risking their lives to help the ghetto dwellers and to support the Warsaw

Ghetto Uprising, *Border Street* also shows Poles denouncing Jews to the Germans out of malice or in hopes of getting their vacated apartments. Like Jakubowska, Ford soothes the pessimistic tone of the film with a final, edifying voice-over urging the solidarity of all people as the means of destroying man-made barriers.

Border Street opens with credits over the shots of wartime Warsaw ruins. The film's action moves briefly to a period preceding the September 1939 invasion of Poland and swiftly introduces several different Polish and Jewish families living in a Warsaw apartment building on Border Street. While showing differences between the Germans' treatment of Poles and Jews, Ford constantly accentuates the need for unity and common struggle with the occupier. Children are at the center of *Border Street*. Like their families, they represent a cross-section of Warsaw and display the same qualities as their parents. As in many Italian neorealist films (that later influenced the Polish School filmmakers), children represent hope for the future. The ending of *Border Street*, with the Jewish boy Dawidek returning to fight in the ghetto, shows a group of his Polish friends standing "united as the seeds of new 'positive' Polish society."[56] This ending unmistakably shows a new, inclusive Poland where people can live together.

As stated earlier, Ford did not experience the wartime occupation of Poland firsthand. Arguably, this is why the ghetto scenes are reduced to a necessary minimum, and the film largely presents an external perspective—from the Aryan side. There are no scenes of starvation, disease, or mass deportations from the *Umschlagplatz* to the Treblinka extermination camp. Sporadically, Ford incorporates fragments of documentary newsreels to enhance the realism of the ghetto street scenes, but, apart from the portrayal of the uprising, he reduces the reality of the ghetto to several universalizing scenes.

The issue of common Polish-Jewish struggle was of utmost importance for the communist authorities—certainly more important than the homage to the victims of the Holocaust. The portrayal of Polish-Jewish unity in a country rebuilding itself from the destructions of war, from moral as well as material wounds, was encouraged and expected by the communist regime. The communists also expected to see themselves represented on the screen as leading the struggle in the ghetto. Ford's task was thus enormous, almost unattainable, although some critics praised Ford for doing the impossible. The premiere of *Border Street*, along with the unveiling of memorials and the release of documentaries and literary works paying tribute to the ghetto insurgents, coincided with the suppression of any reference pertaining to the 1944 Warsaw Uprising and the nationalist Home

Army and corresponded to the beginning of "the struggle with Zionism" within the communist bloc.

* * *

In terms of box office, the period immediately after the war certainly belonged to Leonard Buczkowski. In his next postwar film, an unpretentious comedy, *Skarb* (*Treasure*, 1949), he employed the prewar star Adolf Dymsza and two young leading actors who started their careers in *Forbidden Songs* (Danuta Szaflarska and Jerzy Duszyński). The film features the poetics of prewar comedies coupled with postwar problems (e.g., the lack of housing). Tadeusz Lubelski points out that "among all the films made after the war in Poland, *Treasure* had the most communicative features, typical of classical Hollywood cinema. The film was an example of an impersonal product, made by the crew of professionals identified with a certain style (prewar film trade), with decisions made to target the expected needs of audiences. And the public appreciated it."[57]

The audiences appreciated the lack of open didactics and the presence of actors who repeated their prewar typecasting (Adolf Dymsza and Ludwik Sempoliński). Many critics, however, considered *Treasure*'s intentional artificiality anachronistic in an age of neorealism and film noir. Yet the film's artificiality, coupled with the fact that *Treasure* was deprived of explicit political references and portrayed conventional characters in stock situations, contributed to its popular appeal in the highly politicized climate of postwar Poland.

As if in a fantasy world, the representatives of different classes and generations do not clash in Buczkowski's film but rather coexist in their futile search for a treasure hidden in their building. Instead of a treasure, the protagonists find an unexploded bomb, but the workers (who look as if taken from a socialist realist propagandist poster) save them. Films made in the next several years belong to these billboard characters.

Notes

1. The estimated figures concerning Polish and Jewish losses during World War II differ slightly in various historical accounts. See, e.g., M. B. Biskupski, *The History of Poland* (Westport, CT: Greenwood Press, 2000), 108; Lucy S. Davidowicz, *The Holocaust and the Historians* (Cambridge, MA: Harvard University Press, 1981), 6–7.

2. Eric A. Goldman, *Visions, Images, and Dreams: Yiddish Film Past and Present* (Ann Arbor, MI: UMI Research Press, 1983), 109.
3. Barbara Mruklik, "Wierność sobie: Rozmowa z Wandą Jakubowską," *Kino* 5 (1985): 6–7.
4. Compared with fifty-seven million Polish viewers in 807 cinemas before the war. Edward Zajiček, *Poza ekranem: Kinematografia polska, 1918–1991* (Warsaw: Filmoteka Narodowa and Wydawnictwa Artystyczne i Filmowe, 1992), 36; Jerzy Płażewski, "Film zagraniczny w Polsce," in *Encyklopedia kultury polskiej XX wieku: Film i kinematografia*, ed. Edward Zajiček (Warsaw: Instytut Kultury and Komitet Kinematografii, 1994), 332.
5. In the postwar period, a small group of Polish filmmakers and actors who appeared in *Heimkehr*, for example, Bogusław Samborski (who left Poland after the war), were on trial for collaborating with the Germans.
6. The name Kazimierz Junosza-Stępowski is inseparably linked with prewar Polish cinema. He started his career in 1902, acting in the first Polish films produced by Kazimierz Prószyński, and continued until the war, making several films per year (as many as ten in 1938), including some of the best-known prewar Polish works. His wife, who survived the assassination attempt, was killed nine months later. Jerzy Maśnicki and Kamil Stepan, *Pleograf: Słownik biograficzny filmu polskiego 1896–1939* (Kraków: Staromiejska Oficyna Wydawnicza, 1996), entry "Junosza-Stępowski Kazimierz," Internetowa Baza Filmu Polskiego (Polish Film Internet Database), "Kazimierz Junosza-Stępowski," http://filmpolski.pl/fp/index.php?osoba=1192110 (accessed 22 May 2018). In 1989, Jerzy Sztwiertnia made *Oszołomienie* (*Daze*), a feature film inspired by Junosza-Stępowski's life and the circumstances of his death.
7. The tragic circumstances surrounding the death of Eugeniusz Bodo are the subject of the documentary film *Za winy niepopełnione: Eugeniusz Bodo* (*Eugeniusz Bodo: For Crimes Not Committed*, Stanisław Janicki), made in 1997 for Polish State Television (Telewizja Polska SA). The title refers to Bodo's film *Za winy niepopełnione* (*For Crimes Not Committed*, 1938). The subject was first discussed by Adam Wyżyński, "Ostatnie lata Eugeniusza Bodo," *Kino* 6 (1996): 15.
8. For a book-length discussion about Polish filmmakers during World War II, see, e.g., Stanisław Ozimek, *Film polski w wojennej potrzebie* (Warsaw: Państwowy Instytut Wydawniczy, 1974); Stanisław Jewsiewicki, *Polscy filmowcy na frontach II wojny światowej* (Warsaw: Państwowy Instytut Wydawniczy, 1972). For detailed biographies of filmmakers in English, see Marek Haltof, *Historical Dictionary of Polish Cinema*, 2nd ed. (Lanham, MD: Rowman & Littlefield, 2015); Internetowa Baza Filmu Polskiego (Polish Film Internet Database), http://filmpolski.pl.
9. See Internetowa Baza Filmu Polskiego (Polish Film Internet Database), "Ina Benita," http://filmpolski.pl/fp/index.php?osoba=1180369 (accessed 20 April 2017).
10. Ryszard Ordyński had lived in France since 1937. During the war, he worked in Hollywood as an actor (often not credited) and as a technical supervisor on *To Be or Not to Be* (1942, Ernst Lubitsch). In 1947, Ordyński returned to Warsaw where he

worked for two theaters. The star of prewar cinema Jadwiga Smosarska managed to leave Poland in 1939 and settled in the United States, where she stayed until 1970. She returned to Poland one year before her death. The director Józef Lejtes remained in Israel after 1945, where he directed several films, including *My Father's House* (1947). After 1955, he directed several television films in the United States (credited as Joseph Lejtes).

11. See a very informative Polish-German documentary about Waszyński's life and career, *Książę i Dybuk* (*The Prince and the Dybbuk*, 2017, Elwira Niewiera and Piotr Rosołowski).
12. Jolanta Lemann, *Eugeniusz Cękalski* (Łódź: Muzeum Kinematografii, 1996), 104.
13. Franciszka Themerson (1907–1988) and Stefan Themerson (1910–1988) were experimental filmmakers, promoters of avant-garde cinema, writers, and publishers. The Themersons created seven experimental films from 1930 to 1945, of which only three survive: *Przygoda człowieka poczciwego* (*The Adventure of a Good Citizen*, 1937), made in Poland, *Calling Mr. Smith* (1943), and *The Eye and the Ear* (1945), the latter two produced in England. In 1937, they left for Paris and in 1940, for London. From 1948 to 1979, the Themersons ran the Gaberbocchus Press in London.
14. Norman Davies, *Heart of Europe: A Short History of Poland* (New York: Oxford University Press, 1984), 104.
15. The figures are apparent. In 1952, barely two thousand Polish citizens traveled to the West. Among them, only fifty-one were private citizens allowed to visit their families abroad. Tomasz Goban-Klas, *The Orchestration of the Media: The Politics of Mass Communications in Communist Poland and the Aftermath* (Boulder, CO: Westview Press, 1994), 84.
16. The most successful had been arguably Bronisław Kaper (1902–1983), who in 1930 moved to Germany and then to the United States. He worked as a composer, an arranger, and the conductor on nearly 150 Hollywood films, including works by well-known directors such as John Huston, King Vidor, George Cukor, and Arthur Hiller. Kaper received four Academy Award nominations and won an Oscar in 1953 for *Lili* (Charles Walters).
17. See Grzegorz Rogowski, *Skazane na zapomnienie: Polskie aktorki filmowe na emigracji* (Warsaw: Muza, 2017). Rogowski discusses the following Polish actresses who emigrated to America after World War II: Zofia Nakonieczna, Nora Ney, Renata Radojewska, Jadwiga Smosarska, Janina Wilczówna, Tamara Wiszniewska, and Lena Żelichowska.
18. Jerzy Pelz, "Zaczęło się w cukierni ojca ...," *Kino* 7 (1984): 14–20.
19. The issue of artists' collaboration with German and Soviet regimes is discussed by Tomasz Szarota, "Kolaboracja z okupantem niemieckim i sowieckim w oczach Polaków: Wówczas, wczoraj i dziś," in *Karuzela na Placu Krasińskich: Studia i szkice z lat wojny i okupacji* (Warsaw: Oficyna Wydawnicza Rytm, 2007), 71–145.

20. Jolanta Lemann-Zajiček, *Kino i polityka: Polski film dokumentalny 1945–1949* (Łódź: Łódź Film School, 2003), 16–24; Alicja Mucha-Świeżyńska, "Powikłane drogi," interview with Stanisław Wohl, *Kino* 11 (1984): 6.
21. This breaking of continuity is not a unique Polish experience. The most discussed examples include post–World War II Germany and Russia after the October Revolution.
22. Tadeusz Lubelski, *Strategie autorskie w polskim filmie fabularnym lat 1945–1961* (Kraków: Wydawnictwo Uniwersytetu Jagiellońskiego, 1992), 39.
23. Alina Madej, "100 lat kina w Polsce: 1938–1945," *Kino* 4 (1998): 50.
24. The main UFA studio was captured by the Soviets, and the Polish emissaries seized film materials from small private companies. Ibid.
25. Ewa Gębicka stresses that Polish audiences wanted to see Polish films above all. The Polish security apparatus reported that Polish audiences whistled, provided ironic comments, and laughed during the screening of several Soviet films, such as *The Vow* (*Pitsi*, 1946, Mikheil Chiaureli), a socialist realist biopic of Stalin. Gębicka enumerates Soviet films screened in Poland from 1945 to 1948: twenty-one in 1945, thirty-nine in 1946, thirty-five in 1947, and twenty-three in 1948. Ewa Gębicka, "Nie strzelać do Czapajewa! Jak po wojnie przyjmowano filmy radzieckie w Polsce," *Kwartalnik Filmowy* 2 (1993): 96–97, 99, and 107.
26. Bolesław Michałek and Frank Turaj, *The Modern Cinema of Poland* (Bloomington: Indiana University Press, 1988), 3.
27. Płażewski, "Film zagraniczny w Polsce," 333.
28. Ibid., 336.
29. Michałek and Turaj, *The Modern Cinema of Poland*, 18.
30. Małgorzata Hendrykowska, *Kronika kinematografii polskiej 1895–1997*, 2nd ed. (Poznań: Ars Nova, 2012), 170–200.
31. Alina Madej quotes an annual report from 1946 submitted by Film Polski to the Ministry of Information and Propaganda stating that they had considered 170 film projects, rejected 81, and asked for further work on 20. Alina Madej, *Kino, władza, publiczność: Kinematografia polska w latach 1944–1949* (Bielsko-Biała: Wydawnictwo "Prasa Beskidzka," 2002), 108.
32. In 1990, Andrzej Wajda directed *Korczak*. Earlier, in 1974, Aleksander Ford produced his version of Korczak's biography, the Israeli–West German coproduction *Sie sind frei, Doktor Korczak* (*Dr. Korczak, the Martyr*). For details, see Paul Coates, *The Red and the White: The Cinema of People's Poland* (London: Wallflower Press, 2005), 96–99.
33. "Protokół z posiedzenia Komisji Kwalifikującej Scenariusze z dnia 24 czerwca 1945 roku." Reprinted by Alina Madej in *Kino* 9 (1990): 16.
34. The early stages of Zarzycki's film are discussed by Barbara Mruklik, "Film fabularny," in *Historia filmu polskiego 1939–1956*, ed. Jerzy Toeplitz (Warsaw: Wydawnictwa Artystyczne i Filmowe, 1974), 223–26.

35. Piotr Zwierzchowski, *Kino nowej pamięci: Obraz II wojny światowej z kinie polskim lat 60.* (Bydgoszcz: Wydawnictwo Uniwersytetu Kazimierza Wielkiego, 2013), 27.
36. Because of political censorship, some projects either were not released or had their premieres delayed. In addition to *Two Hours*, this is the case of, for example, *Dead Track* (*Ślepy tor*, aka *Powrót*, 1947), directed by the Czech filmmaker Boživoj Zeman. In the melodramatic *Dead Track*, a concentration camp survivor, Elżbieta Gruszecka (Irena Eichlerówna), returns home and searches for her missing child. The film did not meet the expectations of the film authorities and was never theatrically released. It premiered on Polish television in 2002.
37. Ewa Gębicka, "Sieć kin i rozpowszechnianie filmów," in Zajiček, *Encyklopedia kultury polskiej XX wieku*, 433.
38. See Marek Haltof, *Polish Film and the Holocaust: Politics and Memory* (New York: Berghahn Books, 2012), 211–13.
39. Stuart Liebman, "Documenting the Liberation of the Camps: The Case of Aleksander Ford's *Vernichtungslager Majdanek—Cmentarzysko Europy* (1944)," *Lessons and Legacies VII: The Holocaust in International Perspective*, ed. Dagmar Herzog (Evanston, IL: Northwestern University Press, 2006), 334; see also the revised and enlarged Polish version, "Cmentarzysko Europy (1944): Pierwszy film o Holokauście?" *Zeszyty Majdanka* 25 (2011): 201–25.
40. Stuart Liebman, "The Majdanek Trial: The Holocaust on Trial on Film—Kazimierz Czyński's *Swastyka i szubienica* (1945)," in *The Scene of the Mass Crime: History, Film, and International Tribunals*, ed. Christian Delage and Peter Goodrich (London: Routledge, 2013), 114.
41. For information about the *Polish Newsreel*, see Marek Cieśliński, *Piękniej niż w życiu: Polska Kronika Filmowa 1944–1994* (Warsaw: Trio, 2006).
42. Eric A. Goldman, *Visions, Images, and Dreams: Yiddish Film Past and Present* (Ann Arbor, MI: UMI Research Press, 1983), 147–51.
43. Ira Konigsberg, "*Our Children* and the Limits of Cinema: Early Jewish Responses to the Holocaust," *Film Quarterly* 52, no. 1 (1998): 12.
44. For an illuminating account in English, see ibid., 7–19. According to Konigsberg, *Our Children* premiered in Tel Aviv in 1951. This was the "first film to confront the issue of whether the Holocaust is a suitable subject for art" (13).
45. See a detailed discussion on *The Last Stage* in Marek Haltof, *Screening Auschwitz: Wanda Jakubowska's* The Last Stage *and the Politics of Commemoration* (Evanston, IL: Northwestern University Press, 2018). I devote one chapter to Ford's *Border Street* in *Polish Film and the Holocaust*, 53–73.
46. Wanda Jakubowska was arrested by the Gestapo in 1942, spent six months in the infamous Pawiak prison in Warsaw, and then, from 28 April 1943 to 18 January 1945, was incarcerated in the women's concentration camp at Auschwitz-Birkenau. For the remaining months of the war, she was imprisoned at Ravensbrück.
47. See, e.g., Mruklik, "Wierność sobie," 7.

48. Tadeusz Lubelski, "Generalissumus płakał," interview with Wanda Jakubowska, *Film* 18–19 (1990): 53. In a different interview, Jakubowska stresses that the head of Film Polski, Aleksander Ford, proved to be another obstacle for her project. Alina Madej, "Jak powstawał *Ostatni etap*," interview with Wanda Jakubowska, *Kino* 5 (1998): 13–17.
49. Jakubowska commented that "the camp reality was human skeletons, piles of dead bodies, lice, rats, and various disgusting diseases. On the screen, this reality would certainly cause dread and repulsion. It was necessary to eliminate those elements which, although authentic and typical, were unbearable for the postwar viewer." Wanda Jakubowska, "Kilka wspomnień o powstaniu scenariusza (na marginesie filmu *Ostatni etap*)," *Kwartalnik Filmowy* 1 (1951): 43.
50. See, e.g., Aaron Kerner, *Film and the Holocaust: New Perspectives on Dramas, Documentaries, and Experimental Films* (London: Continuum, 2011), 20. Kerner adds that when the child is born, "a light emanates; as if the newly born baby boy signifies some 'ray of hope'" (68).
51. Annette Insdorf, *Indelible Shadows: Film and the Holocaust* (Cambridge: Cambridge University Press, 2003), 20.
52. See Hanno Loewy, "The Mother of All Holocaust Films? Wanda Jakubowska's Auschwitz Trilogy," *Historical Journal of Film, Radio and Television* 24, no. 2 (2004): 179–204.
53. Omer Bartov, *The "Jew" in Cinema: From* The Golem *to* Don't Touch My Holocaust (Bloomington: Indiana University Press, 2005), 169.
54. Béla Balázs, "The Last Stop," in "Béla Balázs on Wanda Jakubowska's *The Last Stop*: Three Texts," trans. Stuart Liebman and Zsuzsa Berger, *Slavic and East European Performance* 16, no. 3 (1996): 64. [Unpublished essay deposited in the Balázs archives in Budapest, Hungary.]
55. Bartov, *The "Jew" in Cinema*, 180.
56. Ilan Avisar, *Screening the Holocaust: Cinema's Images of the Unimaginable* (Bloomington: Indiana University Press, 1988), 40.
57. Lubelski, *Strategie autorskie*, 60.

CHAPTER 4

Screen Stalinism
Socialist Realist Films (1949–1954)

> *Both fascist and communist totalitarianisms are, in a sense, a parodic imitation of religion. ... The totalitarian system fights religion to replace it, and to become a "religion." It therefore proposes its own version of revelation, its own vision of salvation, and its own type of ties between people that resembles the mythical bond in religion.*
> — Rev. Józef Tischner, quoted from Michał Głowiński, Rytuał i demagogia

In Polish history, "Stalinism" refers to the postwar period beginning in 1949 and ending in October 1956. During that time, the one-party rule and the strict Soviet control of all aspects of Polish life[1] created a small totalitarian replica of the Soviet state. The Polish communist leader Bolesław Bierut was a faithful follower of Stalin—more accurately, he was an obedient political puppet.

The Soviet model imprinted its mark on the arts. The postwar period in Polish arts was dominated by the socialist realist doctrine, detailed in the Soviet Union by Andrei Zhdanov at the First All-Union Congress of Soviet Writers in 1934. The doctrine of socialist realism demanded the adherence to the Communist Party line, the necessary portrayal of the class struggle (the struggle between old and new), the emphasis on class-based images, the rewriting of history from a Marxist perspective, and the elimination of "reactionary bourgeois" ideology.

The Polish version of socialist realism was outlined in a speech delivered in December 1947 by Bolesław Bierut. This version was officially approved in December 1948 at the "unification congress" of the Polish Workers' Party (PPR) and the Polish Socialist Party (PPS), which saw the formation of the Polish United Workers' Party (PZPR).[2] In November 1949, the so-called congress of filmmakers met at Wisła, a small resort in the Beskid Mountains, to enforce the doctrine of socialist realism (this was preceded by similar gatherings, with similar results, of other arts organizations). The Wisła Congress condemned cosmopolitan and bourgeois tendencies supposedly present in Polish cinema, such as disregard for class struggle, nationalism, and revisionism. The speakers at the congress, including party apparatchiks, critics, writers, and filmmakers, criticized previously made films such as *Forbidden Songs*, *Treasure*, *Border Street*, and *The Last Stage* for their lack of "revolutionary spirit." Some of the two hundred participants in the congress later stressed that they had to compromise under political pressures, and blamed the atmosphere of the Stalinist period or their political blindness. Nevertheless, research shows that in many cases the initiative belonged to filmmakers who willingly went down the socialist realist path.[3] For the START members, for instance, this path was the continuation of their prewar political beliefs and the struggle for socially and politically committed cinema.

The political climate of the 1949 Wisła Congress certainly demonstrated that Stalinism was flourishing. The first Polish exhibition of portraits of work leaders took place in August, socialist realist plays dominated Polish theaters, and the new Polish literary genre, "novels about production" (*powieść produkcyjna*), came into prominence. The explicit titles of the novels tell their whole stories: *Traktory zdobędą wiosnę* (*Tractors Will Conquer the Spring*) by Witold Zalewski, or *Przy budowie* (*At the Construction Site*) by Tadeusz Konwicki.

As in the Soviet model, the reality in Polish arts was portrayed "as it should be," with clear divisions between the forces of progress, personified by a positive hero, a model to be emulated, and the dark forces of the past, embodied by a cunning opponent of the new, a model to be wary of. A leading political figure of the time, the feared minister of public security, Jakub Berman, expressed the political goal facing Polish artists: to use arts as a political weapon. In his 1951 speech, he advocated taking "aim at kulak and speculator, spy and saboteur, American warmonger and neo-Nazi."[4]

Cinema, like other arts, was treated as an instrument in the political struggle. Soviet films, rarely shown in Poland before the war for political reasons, started to dominate Polish screens after 1949. Polish cinemas were divided at that time into two categories: the "festival theaters" that showed Soviet films almost exclusively, and theaters that screened films mostly from other socialist countries.[5] It was difficult, however, to fill Polish screens with contemporary Soviet films alone; during the last years of Stalin's life, only a few films had been made, and these were mostly epic propagandist works. With the help of classic Soviet works, such as *Battleship Potemkin*, and films from the communist bloc countries, the "progressive films" constituted 78 percent of the Polish repertoire. That repertoire, however, was not numerous: from 1951 to1953, only sixty-four to sixty-six new titles were shown yearly in Polish movie theaters.[6]

Polish films did not contribute a significant percentage. Only thirty-four feature films were made in Poland from 1949 to 1955, among which thirty-one followed the socialist realist formula. They all shared thematic and stylistic affinities, provided the same didactic messages, and created similar protagonists. The exceptions, according to the Polish scholar Grażyna Stachówna, were as follows: *Pokolenie* (*A Generation*, Andrzej Wajda)—discussed in chapter 5—and two war dramas, *Godziny nadziei* (*The Hours of Hope*, Jan Rybkowski) and *Błękitny krzyż* (*The Blue Cross*, aka *The Men of the Blue Cross*, Andrzej Munk). These three films, made in 1955, were influenced by Italian neorealism and are usually discussed as the forerunners of the Polish School.[7]

With the invasion of Soviet films came the gradual elimination of Western films on Polish screens. The restrictive policy also included Italian neorealist films. Włodzimierz Sokorski, the Polish minister of culture at the time, attacked Italian neorealism as a "primitive exhibitionism of humankind's lowest instincts, the most hideous forms of cruelty, sadism, and superstition," which "has nothing whatsoever to do with a scientific analysis of life; it has to do with employing (what we have observed in fascist art) a naturalistic method to promote false, insolent arguments."[8] Because of the rejection of Western films, there was not a single American film shown in Polish movie theaters for more than seven years. For instance, only six Western films were distributed in Poland in 1951 (two French and one Dutch, Finnish, Italian, and English), and only eight in 1952 and 1953.[9]

Socialist Realist Films

The dominant theme of socialist realist films—that of the class struggle—is developed, for instance, in the classic *Dwie Brygady* (*Two Brigades*, 1950), made by the students of the Łódź Film School and supervised by Eugeniusz Cękalski. *Two Brigades* was adapted from *Parta brusiče Karhana* (Grinder Karhan's crew), a play that Mira Liehm and Antonin J. Liehm have called "one of the most primitive Czech plays of the time."[10] The film tells a story about two brigades and two forms of Stakhanovite[11] competition: workers in a factory try to increase production, and actors in a theater attempt to adapt the workers' effort for the stage. The film's message is quite straightforward: art is an imitation of life, but life as it should be, not life as it is. In the process of learning about the "true workers and the true factory life," the young actors (the old ones oppose them) gain new consciousness and, consequently, their "new style of acting" slowly emerges. Authenticity in *Two Brigades* means realistic detailed set design and crude stereotyping. Oddly enough, this film won the Best Experimental Film Award at the Karlovy Vary International Film Festival. The trite presentation of the struggle between the old and the new in two disparate fields (factory and theater) apparently was the reason for this award.

Eugeniusz Cękalski, one of the leaders of START, who spent the wartime period working on documentaries in France, England, and the United States, is also responsible for another classic socialist realist work, *Jasne Łany* (*Bright Fields*, 1947). This film, which heralded the socialist realist poetics in Polish cinema, is set in a village symbolically called Dark Fields. Its story line and its schematic propagandist message are formulated by the film's positive hero, a village teacher, whose message is that "Dark Fields must change to Bright Fields."

Bright Fields is abundant with socialist realist clichés and stereotypes, and contains explicit propagandist messages. In the artificial and chaste love story, the young and progressive protagonist, the teacher Stępkowicz (Kazimierz Dejmek), marries a local girl. She functions as a reward for his support of the communist ideology, which brings the lovers together. The film also portrays a treacherous attempt on the teacher's life, organized by a group of black marketers, and shows a cluster of negative characters populating the screen, such as the rich miller and the reactionary former teacher Leśniewski (Andrzej Łapicki), who is associated with the Polish government-in-exile in London. In the film, a politically disoriented yet talented young boy represents the generation that has a chance to thrive in the new political reality.

Bright Fields and several other films were badly received by both the public and critics. For example, *Gromada* (*The Village Mill*, 1952, Jerzy Kawalerowicz and Kazimierz Sumerski) lasted only a couple of weeks on Polish screens. Another film, *Niedaleko Warszawy* (*Not Far from Warsaw*, 1954, Maria Kaniewska), which "perfectly reconstructed on the screen the socialist realist formula," was in 1954 voted by some critics the worst Polish film ever made.[12] The poor box office performance of these films proved that in an environment tightly controlled by the guardians of the official ideology, it was almost impossible to produce a film that people would want to see yet simultaneously would advocate "the need to struggle for peace, to enhance productivity at work, to hate imperialism, and to love the communist leaders."[13]

Judging by the box office, Polish audiences wanted to see not only films referring to their wartime experiences, but also popular entertainment. One attempt to produce a politically correct yet popular film was *Przygoda na Mariensztacie (An Adventure at Marienstadt*, 1954, Leonard Buczkowski), the first Polish film in color. This film also revolves around the work competition but combines it with gender politics. Its narrative structure has all the components of a typical, socialist realist drama: work competition portrayed with a melodramatic aspect, the postwar reconstruction of Warsaw, the social advancement of the working class (the realization of a slogan "the masses will enter the city"), and "new women" who are not afraid of leaving their traditional roles to compete with men.

The film opens with a symbolic image of a small stone being crushed by a bulldozer. The camera then pulls back to show a bulldozer amid the ruins of Warsaw. With uplifting music, the scene cuts to the image of Warsaw's new construction site, Marienstadt. A montage shows the bricklayers working there; with the help of low-angle shots, they are presented as heroic figures silhouetted against the blue sky. Almost every frame in that sequence closely resembles Polish socialist realist paintings. Another dynamic montage sequence shows young people going to Warsaw. They carry red banners and slogans, and sing "To idzie młodość" (Here comes the youth), the emblematic song of the 1950s. These first images of the film establish the relationship between youth and Warsaw, between energy and the new ideology.

The film's protagonist, Hanka Ruczajówna (Lidia Korsakówna), moves to Warsaw from a small village and becomes a bricklayer in a women-only brigade. Although the film's main theme is work competition, Ruczajówna moves to Warsaw for primarily romantic/personal reasons. During her first brief visit to Warsaw, as a member of a folk ensemble, she had befriended one of the handsome socialist leaders of the work at Marienstadt, Jan Szarliński (Tadeusz Szmidt). She does not remember his name and knows only that he produces more than 300 percent of the norm. She soon finds him after seeing his huge portrait exhibited on the wall. As if to present the bricklaying job in an attractive light, the film offers yet another explanation for Hanka's move to the city. A brief glimpse of her backward village, which is shown in the manner of nineteenth-century realist paintings, completely justifies her decision.

An Adventure at Marienstadt is set in postwar Warsaw. Instead of a realistic portrayal of the city being rebuilt from ashes, it depicts "the official optimism" of the party authorities. Work is life in this world. "New women" from villages take "men's jobs" and seem to like them. The world presented on the screen resembles a hastily colored postcard, an image further enhanced the presence of the Polish folk company Mazowsze. *An Adventure at Marienstadt* features witty dialogue (written by Ludwik Starski) and popular songs (composed by the founder of Mazowsze, Tadeusz Sygietyński), which certainly have helped the film's popularity. Buczkowski's film was an effort to produce a socialist realist comedy: a difficult, if not impossible, task in a time of dreary seriousness and mandatory optimism. In the Stalinist period, there was no room for satire or for laughter at issues commonly reserved for serious treatment (the only exception was the "constructive laughter"). Despite the time period, *An Adventure at Marienstadt* proved to be one of the most popular films screened in postwar Poland, having had more viewers than, for example, *Popiół i diament* (*Ashes and Diamonds*, 1958, Andrzej Wajda) and *Star Wars* (1977, George Lucas).[14]

An Adventure at Marienstadt belongs to a small group of comedies made during a period that was not suited for entertainment films. Two other socialist realist comedies were directed by the experienced Jan Fethke: *Irena do domu!* (*Irena, Go Home!* 1955), starring Adolf Dymsza and voted the best Polish film by the readers of *Film* magazine,[15] and *Sprawa do załatwienia* (*A Matter to Be Settled*, 1953, codirected by Jan Rybkowski), featuring Dymsza in eight episodic roles. Among several attempts at action dramas, one popular film deserves attention—*Czarci żleb* (*Devil's Ravine*, 1950, Aldo Vergano and Tadeusz Kański), a suspenseful drama set in the Tatra Mountains and photographed by Adolf Forbert.

Polish films made during the Stalinist period also include biographical features, both good and bad. For instance, *Żołnierz zwycięstwa* (*The Soldier of Victory*, 1953, Wanda Jakubowska) delivers a propagandist biography of General Karol Świerczewski.[16] The two-part epic film covers forty years of Świerczewski's life beginning with the revolution of 1905; introduces many historical figures, including Lenin, Stalin, and the Cheka (Soviet secret police) founder Felix Dzerzhinsky; and portrays a multitude of then current political topics, such as spying, fascism and imperialism, and other elements of Polish internal politics. Even the presence of some of the most prominent Polish actors, including prewar stars such as Jacek Woszczerowicz and Jan Kurnakowicz, and of new, emerging talents, such as Gustaw Holoubek, Tadeusz Janczar, and Władysław Hańcza, cannot save the film.

It must be noted again that Polish filmmakers examined certain themes to please the authorities. In many cases, these themes illustrate the filmmakers' political convictions (e.g., in Jakubowska's case), sometimes political opportunism, and naïveté.[17]

Some directors, however, were able to produce biographical films of certain merit that were devoid of overtly propagandist elements. Critically acclaimed in Poland and abroad in the 1950s, *Młodość Chopina* (*The Youth of Chopin*, 1952, Aleksander Ford) traces five years of the composer's life. This epic production differs from Hollywood biographical films that usually tell stories of struggling and misunderstood geniuses; it also varies distinctly from Soviet epics, with their stress on ideological/class sources of artists' inspirations. The episodic *The Youth of Chopin* portrays Chopin (Czesław Wołłejko) as a young artist inspired by Polish history and culture—the sources of his music.[18]

Socialist Realist Characters

The representative Polish films of the Stalinist period are similar to classic Soviet examples,[19] but they tone down the extreme didacticism of the latter. They also deal with the process of gaining political consciousness. In such films, a (usually young) protagonist acquires political knowledge thanks to the guidance of the party authorities. That knowledge enables them to understand the complexities of the class struggle, to embrace the new ideology (always presented as a "natural" stage of historical development), and to improve their vigilance toward external and internal political opponents.

The "positive heroes" are usually mature party workers, security force officers, workers, or ideologically correct teachers of proper (peasant or working-class) origins. Their class background is often stressed by employing last names that indicate their peasant/working-class origins. In addition to the proper background and working-class mannerisms of speech and behavior, the schematic hero must be straightforward, open, smiling, and wise, although not necessarily well educated (the higher the level of education, the more one has doubts, and a communist hero should have none). Another feature characterizing the hero is his asexuality; he is interested only in chaste relationships that are governed by politics rather than sensual love. The protagonist has no private life and no desire to have one. Rarely shown alone, he is usually seen at work or at political gatherings.

The mature, positive protagonist commonly guides the younger one, who is typically good-natured yet politically undecided (a young female protagonist sometimes becomes the girlfriend of the mature protagonist). The Communist Party secretary or the security force officer performs the role of a good and understanding yet vigilant father who, thanks to his political instinct, is able to detect a class enemy. As proselytizing vehicles, these films are about the acquisition of consciousness; wise party workers are only too willing to convert another nonbeliever into a devoted communist.

The positive hero is portrayed as a "soldier of the new." This romantic characterization is usually reserved in Polish mythology for fighters of national freedom, not heroes of socialist work. Such a hero always remains a part of the community. For example, in *Not Far from Warsaw*, a father, himself an old, prewar communist who has "lost his revolutionary consciousness," is told that his daughter, the protagonist, was raised not by him but by the working class and the steelworks—in other words, by the community.

The communist authorities on the screen are always presented as the embodiment of the new: young, handsome, wise, and fatherly. They also have answers to all kinds of problems. They speak slowly, accentuating each word, because every single word matters—the Communist Party speaks through them. When a handsome, young security force colonel in *Not Far from Warsaw* tells the protagonist, "I trust you," and looks right into her eyes, she immediately regains her ideological confidence and is ready to face the enemies of the new.

To monumentalize the positive hero, filmmakers relied heavily on low-angle shots, usually medium shots. Afraid of being accused of "psychologization" and "formalism," they tended to avoid close-ups and used simple, nonexperimental narratives. Kazimierz Sobotka says that the growing importance of dialogue, which was easier to censor than images, caused the "theatricalization of films" and, consequently, the dominance of shots characteristic of dialogue. For example, 50 percent of all the shots in Maria Kaniewska's *Not Far from Warsaw* are medium shots.[20]

Frequently, the protagonists of Polish socialist realist films are "new women" working in fields traditionally reserved for men, such as heavy industry and construction sites. Their career choices are opposed by their families (husbands and fathers) and, sometimes, by their male superiors, who clearly lack "the revolutionary consciousness." The "new women," however, are able to win acceptance and gain new friends. For example, in *An Adventure at Marienstadt*, an older, conservative work leader, Ciepielewski (Adam Mikołajewski), claims that women should stay at home, as his wife does. In the final scene, however, he voluntarily joins the work initiated by the young female brigade (older, tired women do not appear in filmic factories).

Conflicts between generations (old versus new) are very important in these films. Films like *Trudna miłość* (*Difficult Love*, 1954, Stanisław Różewicz) or *Not Far from Warsaw* often have a primary conflict in which a young protagonist must choose between "reactionary" parents and a vision of a communist paradise on Earth. The young workers/protagonists have to convince the older workers, who are used to prewar ways of production, that the only good methods are the Soviet ones.

The positive heroes are contrasted to those who oppose the road to communism. The "enemy of the people" or "the class enemy" is usually unmasked in the film by the vigilant hero. The role of the enemy is usually reserved for a rich miller (Polish kulak), saboteur, or spy. The class enemy lacks the human qualities displayed by the positive protagonist. Foreign (Western) spies hide in the dark like cowards, waiting for the right moment to strike, while saboteurs attempt (needless to say, without success) to interrupt the Stakhanovite work competition in factories and construction sites. Their appearances betray them—they are sometimes elegant yet sinister, too well dressed, arrogant, "not ours," silent. Since they do not work (they only manipulate and exploit the masses), they are isolated from the community and surrounded by only a few other "enemies of the people" (this is always just a small number, because, the films say, the majority support the communist authorities). In *Not Far from Warsaw*, a simple woman detects the class enemy sent by "American imperialists" to destroy the prosperous (thanks to the Soviets' help) steelworks. She describes him in the following way: "He says little, as if he was afraid of every single word. Not ours, not foreign."

* * *

Gender relations are also unique in socialist realist films. Rafał Marszałek discusses "women in kerchiefs," the communist model, and "women in hats," the model desired by the masses.[21] The communist model propagates the masculinization of "new women" (women driving tractors, working in coal mines, etc.). There is no time for family, "for hats," these films seem to say, when the enemy is everywhere, when the battle for the future is the most pressing problem. There is no time for privacy, intimacy, and love. "Coquetry is killed in embryo, for it would point out the relationship with the old order," writes Marszałek.[22]

The puritan communist system promotes the emancipation of women, yet films of the Stalinist era show male heroes' rough treatment of women. Male protagonists seem to be afraid of bourgeois domesticity, and view women as an obstacle to higher production. Sobotka writes: "The male worker does not highly value his wife. More than love, he values friendship and he sings songs about it. A woman can get his friendship, and respect only when she achieves professional advancement."[23] For instance, in *An Adventure at Marienstadt*, the understanding party secretary helps the young work leaders to overcome problems in their relationship. Hanka can conquer the heart of her stubborn man only after she has proved that she can be a good bricklayer. As soon as he learns that Hanka's brigade has accomplished a record amount of work, he wants to see her.[24]

In the world of ascetic socialist realist films, in which female characters can only be with an ideologically correct man, there is no place for love, not to mention sex. Grażyna Stachówna noted that the first kiss in postwar Polish cinema occurred as late as 1954 in *Difficult Love*.[25] In socialist realist films, enhanced production equals private success; professional advancement, "class instinct," and strong belief in the new ideology can secure somebody's love. For example, in *Autobus odjeżdża 6.20* (*The Bus Leaves at 6:20*, 1954, Jan Rybkowski), Krystyna (Aleksandra Śląska) wins her husband's love only after she leaves him and moves to Silesia, where she becomes a successful industrial worker.

The Decline of the Doctrine

In the mid-1950s, some Polish filmmakers managed to retreat from the socialist realist dogma and make realistic films in the spirit of Italian neorealism. These films, however, were still set within the thematic preoccupations characteristic of socialist realism.

Though criticized by party authorities for its "bourgeois approach" to realism, the Italian neorealist movement had a great impact on Polish cinema.[26] This impact is discernible, for instance, in *Piątka z ulicy Barskiej* (*Five Boys from Barska Street*, Aleksander Ford) and Jerzy Kawalerowicz's epic diptych, *Celuloza* (*A Night of Remembrance*) and *Pod gwiazdą frygijską* (*Under the Phrygian Star*), all made in 1954. Besides neorealist inspirations, these films were also influenced by classic

Soviet biographical films, chiefly Grigori Kozintsev and Leonid Trauberg's "Maxim Trilogy" (1935-1939) and another trilogy, Mark Donskoi's biography of Maxim Gorki (1938-1940).[27] The realistic treatment of events and people was well received by both the audience and authorities. The latter were pleased to find traditional features of the socialist realist doctrine intact and a multidimensional world with well-developed characters, documentary flavor, a realistic environment, an engaging story, and professionalism in every detail.

Ford's first film in color, *Five Boys from Barska Street*, deals with juvenile delinquency, a theme previously untouched in Polish cinema. The film stresses the impact of war on the psychology of its young protagonists and shows their inability to change a lifestyle that results in crime, including murder. The five boys from a gang on Barska Street are introduced in a courtroom, where they are put under the guardianship of a bricklayer. He tries to help them with their lives, but the dangers of sinking back into crime are real. The film ends with an appeal to help the troubled youth, to offer them a chance to live normal lives. Ford won the Best Director Award for this film at the Cannes Film Festival. This film is also notable for another reason: Andrzej Wajda's debut as Ford's assistant. Soon after, Wajda would make his first feature film, *A Generation*, with several people involved in the production of *Five Boys from Barska Street*, including the assistant cinematographer Jerzy Lipman and two young actors, Tadeusz Janczar and Tadeusz Łomnicki.

Certainly, the most accomplished work of that period remains the epic diptych, *A Night of Remembrance* and *Under the Phrygian Star*, by one of the masters of Polish cinema, Jerzy Kawalerowicz. Kawalerowicz started his career as an assistant director of the first postwar Polish film, *Forbidden Songs*. After his much-criticized feature debut, *The Village Mill*, he made the acclaimed diptych, which owes a lot to its rich literary source, Igor Neverly's novel *Pamiątka z Celulozy* (*Recollection from Cellulose*, 1952). Kawalerowicz portrays in flashbacks a coming-of-age story about a peasant's son, Szczęsny (Józef Nowak), who moves to town and learns about life. The film, set in the 1930s, gives a vast panorama of prewar Poland. The second part of the diptych follows the same protagonist as he works in a cellulose factory, matures, gains "class consciousness," and becomes a communist activist. Facing arrest for his illegal activities, Szczęsny escapes to Spain to join other members of the political left in the struggles against Franco's regime.

Thematically in line with other socialist realist biographical features, the film is characterized by its novel treatment of the positive hero: it is deprived of clichés, abounds with psychological characterization, stresses the role of individual and social forces, provides a panoramic scope, and depicts realistically various social strata. One Polish critic noted: "Generally, the film got rid of the unbearably vulgar automatism controlling the lives of characters."[28] Kawalerowicz's film, however, was clearly made too late, when the principles of socialist realism were already being questioned. Had it been made earlier, it would have been an exemplary illustration of how to make a politically correct picture that succeeds artistically.

Kawalerowicz is known for his unorthodox artistic choices. His next film, *Cień* (*The Shadow*, 1956), written by Aleksander Ścibor-Rylski, was an unusual, suspenseful story set in the postwar Polish political climate. The Hitchcock-like narrative structure and composition of *The Shadow* and its sophisticated camerawork by Jerzy Lipman can be viewed almost as a mockery of the central concerns of socialist realist tenets. Thematically, however, the film was behind the times; made during the post-Stalinist thaw, it was neglected by the audience and by critics, who always favored current political content and context over style.

"Settlement of Accounts"

The socialist realist period ended in October 1956,[29] but its themes, as well as its way of presenting the world, reappeared later in several Polish films, some of them artistically accomplished works and not just blatant propaganda. During the Polish School period, several films referred to the previous thematic preoccupations, including such prominent works as *Człowiek na torze* (*Man on the Tracks*, 1957, Andrzej Munk), *Zagubione uczucia* (*Lost Feelings*, 1957, Jerzy Zarzycki),[30] and *Baza ludzi umarłych* (*Damned Roads*, 1959, Czesław Petelski). The directors of these "settlement of accounts films" (*filmy rozrachunkowe*) questioned the previous screen poetics and attempted to make the theme of work more attractive. The political motivation for work disappears in their films; what matters is money or professionalism. Problems arising at work or in everyday life are blamed not on foreign spies or class enemies, but on bureaucracy, incompetence, or crime.

Zarzycki's *Lost Feelings*, for example, presents an unflattering picture of harsh conditions and rampant hooliganism at the Nowa Huta steelworks, the pride of the communists. This film's story line also radically departs from previous, optimistic stories. A husband leaves his wife and four children to pursue his career as a union activist. The woman, a tired heroine of the socialist workforce (she is a model worker at the steelworks), cannot cope with the situation. Her teenage son, who helps her take care of his siblings, rebels, leaves home, and joins the hooligans.

Lost Feelings, neorealist in spirit, demythologizes the sugarcoated communist vision of reality. It questions the material advancement of the working class by showing nightmarish apartment buildings, tough working conditions, and a destitute landscape stripped of optimism. Zarzycki's film destroys the optimistic communist vision of the city of the future, Nowa Huta, exposing it as a claustrophobic world of concrete and mud. *Lost Feelings* is photographed as an American film noir: it shows the world deprived of sun (low-key lighting and night for night shooting), characters at the mercy of their hostile environment, present disillusionment, and pessimism.

According to Ewelina Nurczyńska-Fidelska, the author of the Polish book on Andrzej Munk, Munk's *Man on the Tracks* became the only film to overcome the shortcomings of socialist realism; it was a conscious attempt to blow up the doctrine itself from the inside.[31] Munk's film premiered on 17 January 1957, only three months after the events of the Polish October. Munk commented:

Figure 4.1 Kazimierz Opaliński in Andrzej Munk's *Man on the Tracks* (1957). Courtesy of Filmoteka Narodowa.

"By making this film, we wanted to continue a certain discussion that, at the moment of its premiere, already appeared out of date."[32] For Jerzy Płażewski, however, *Man on the Tracks* became "the first film of the Polish October."[33]

Man on the Tracks tells the story of a retired train engineer, Orzechowski (Kazimierz Opaliński), who dies under mysterious circumstances while attempting to stop a train and whose death saves the passengers of the train. The film opens in the manner of *Citizen Kane* and *Rashomon* (1950, Akira Kurosawa), films revered by young Polish filmmakers, by introducing the mystery. The rest of the film becomes a search for (unattainable) truth—for the identity of a dead man and the motivations of his actions (there are suspicions of sabotage)—and a psychological portrait of the old man. The film offers three different perspectives of the event; three different narrators complement each other and provide contradictory versions of what happened. The omniscient socialist realist narrator is replaced in *Man on the Tracks* by several narrators whose truthfulness viewers can question. The open composition of the film forces the viewer to doubt, to be active, and to engage.

The first narrator, Orzechowski's superior, accuses him of attempting to cause the accident to avenge his unwanted early retirement. The first retrospective closely resembles socialist realist narratives; Orzechowski is pictured as a classic negative character, the enemy of the new. The next retrospective belongs to Orzechowski's young apprentice, a member of the communist youth organization, and a person spying on the train engineer. However, instead of an expected simplistic portrayal of the struggle between the old and the new, the viewer learns about the psychological complexities of the dead man. The narrator himself has doubts concerning Orzechowski, and the viewer can sense his affinities with the dead man: they share the same attitude toward work. The third version of the events adds information concerning Orzechowski's life after retirement and explains the mystery of his death to the viewers (yet not to the judging committee, which must rely on the third narrator's biased account). The party representative, portrayed in the manner of classic Stalinist films, summarizes the events. The silence that follows is interrupted by one of the narrators. "It is stuffy here," he says, opening the window. That symbolic gesture and the words spoken may be seen to summarize the entire political atmosphere around the Polish October of 1956.

Man on the Tracks deals with many typical socialist realist issues (struggles between old and new, and the enhancement of work productivity) and presents some stock characters (the wise, prudently speaking party secretary; young

Orzechowski's apprentice; and Orzechowski himself as a possible villain). The focus is, however, on people and their complexities, and that makes easy generalizations impossible. The camera work supports the story. Nurczyńska-Fidelska points out that the use of deep focus photography and a panning camera in this film replaces the dynamic montage that is present in Munk's early works.[34] Munk rejects one directorial point of view and avoids imposing meaning on reality. He uses montage sequences during the committee's meeting while portraying the "judges" of Orzechowski. However, when the three narrators take the stand, the camera moves and pans, thus helping the viewer to be involved in the story and stressing the intricacy of the judged man and the different perspectives in any one man's life. "Truth, in Munk's film," writes César Ballester, "is given, returned to the individual, because there is no more collective discourse, but an individual one. The spectator is forced to come out of the collective to become an individual, having to decide for himself/herself what he or she thinks of the main character."[35]

In the spirit of neorealism, Munk paid attention to realistic details.[36] He shot on location, chose lesser-known actors/types to facilitate realism, used unpretentious dialogue (the beginning of his collaboration with Jerzy Stefan Stawiński, the Polish School's major screenwriter), used only natural noises on the soundtrack, and avoided banality and sentimentality in the portrayal of the old man.

Conclusion

The recurrent themes and stereotypes existing in Polish cinema of the Stalinist period reflect not the attitudes of Polish society but rather the perspective of the communist authorities. Rarely mentioned today, the Stalinist films ended up on a garbage heap of history—objects of ridicule for a young generation of viewers and critics, a millstone for the older generation, especially those involved in promoting the communist ideology.

A typical Polish socialist realist film resembles a poorly told fairy tale. It is predictable and didactic, uses the Orwellian "newspeak" instead of Aesopian language, and presents a simplistic vision of the world: good versus bad, new versus old, progressive forces versus reactionary forces, bright fields versus dark fields. The end of a film brings back the desired norm: the saboteurs are captured and punished, the young protagonists are (re)united, the factory production goes on undisturbed by the enemy of the people. Happiness prevails—or rather, a colorized version of the gray reality.

Films made in Poland during the Stalinist years have many elements in common, and several of them do not exhibit many individual traits. They are conventional, ritualistic, and clichéd. The socialist realist authors subdued their distinctive personalities. Wojciech Włodarczyk, in his book on Polish art from 1950 to 1954, writes that Stalinist art has no authors in the traditional sense; the author is the state.[37] Tadeusz Lubelski points out that it was a part of the game between the state, the filmmakers, and the viewers. Neither the quality of the work nor the type of contact between authors and viewers was of overriding importance. What was important was that an ideologically correct communication was produced and "dedicated" to the political authorities. For Lubelski, this was "a ritual of perverted culture."[38]

Notes

1. For example, in 1949, Konstanty Rokossowski, a Soviet general of partial Polish origin, had been appointed marshal of Poland, the Polish minister of defense, commander in chief of the Polish armed forces, and a politburo member of the Polish United Workers' Party (PZPR).
2. Włodzimierz Sokorski, "Polityka kulturalna 1944–1949," *Miesięcznik Literacki* 3 (1977): 106; Kazimierz Sobotka, "Robotnik na ekranie, czyli o tak zwanym 'filmie produkcyjnym,'" in *Szkice o filmie polskim*, ed. Bronisława Stolarska (Łódź: Łódzki Dom Kultury, 1985), 27.
3. Jolanta Lemann, "Czy istniała wymuszona estetyka? (Kilka uwag o filmie polskim wczesnych lat pięćdziesiątych)," *Film na Świecie* 320–21 (1985): 87–89.
4. Jakub Berman, "Pokażcie wielkość naszych czasów," *Nowa Kultura* 45 (1951), quoted in Tadeusz Lubelski, *Strategie autorskie w polskim filmie fabularnym lat 1945–1961* (Kraków: Wydawnictwo Uniwersytetu Jagiellońskiego, 1992), 93.
5. Alina Madej, "100 lat kina w Polsce: 1949–1954," *Kino* 6 (1998): 47.
6. Ewa Gębicka, "Sieć kin i rozpowszechnianie filmów," in *Encyklopedia kultury polskiej XX wieku*, ed. Edward Zajiček (Warsaw: Instytut Kultury and Komitet Kinematografii, 1994), 433.
7. Grażyna Stachówna, "Równanie szeregów: Bohaterowie filmów socrealistycznych (1949–1955)," in *Człowiek z ekranu: Z antropologii postaci filmowej*, ed. Mariola Jankun-Dopartowa and Mirosław Przylipiak (Kraków: Arcana, 1996), 15.
8. Włodzimierz Sokorski, *Sztuka w walce o socjalizm* (Warsaw: Państwowy Instytut Wydawniczy, 1950), 203 and 239.

9. Jerzy Płażewski, "Film zagraniczny w Polsce," in Zajiček, *Encyklopedia kultury polskiej XX wieku*, 335.
10. Mira Liehm and Antonin J. Liehm, *The Most Important Art: Soviet and Eastern European Film after 1945* (Berkeley: University of California Press, 1977), 117.
11. Alexei Stakhanov was a Soviet coal miner, a model worker who greatly surpassed his production quota. The term "Stakhanovism" was applied to all "leaders of socialist work" (Stakhanovites).
12. Stachówna, "Równanie szeregów," 16–17. The makers of *Not Far from Warsaw* (Maria Kaniewska and Adam Ważyk, the bard of socialist realist poetry) were not credited in the film. They blamed the Film Polski authorities for this film's failure. Ważyk, one of the foremost representatives of Stalinist literature at the time, is better known for his 1955 "Poemat dla dorosłych" (A poem for adults), published in *Nowa Kultura*, in which he bitterly denounced Stalinism and his former political convictions.
13. The Polish writer Leopold Tyrmand, quoted in Madej, "100 lat kina w Polsce: 1949–1954," 49.
14. Lubelski, *Strategie autorskie*, 111. It must be noted that the Polish box office differed from that of the West. The box office of certain films, including *An Adventure at Marienstadt*, was helped by the distribution of cheap (sometimes free) tickets to factories and schools. The practice continued until the late 1970s.
15. Małgorzata Hendrykowska, *Kronika kinematografii polskiej 1895–1997* (Poznań: Ars Nova, 1999), 207. *Film* readers also voted Adolf Dymsza, Aleksandra Śląska, and Danuta Szaflarska the most popular Polish actors.
16. General Świerczewski, a colorful figure, was a Polish communist living in the Soviet Union and a general in the Red Army. He fought in Spain in 1936. During World War II, he commanded the Polish troops fighting alongside the Soviets. His assassination in 1947 was blamed on the Ukrainian Insurgent Army (UPA). Michałek and Turaj justly label *The Soldier of Victory* "an aesthetic travesty" and "cinematic fiasco." Bolesław Michałek and Frank Turaj, *The Modern Cinema of Poland* (Bloomington: Indiana University Press, 1988), 13.
17. Jakubowska had always been a communist close to the official party circles. "I am a fierce and unrelenting Communist. Look at me, I am not ashamed. I am a 'Commie,'" she said in an interview with Stuart Liebman, "I Was Always in the Epicenter of Whatever Was Going On…" An Interview with Wanda Jakubowska," *Slavic and East European Performance* 17, no. 3 (1997): 29.
18. *The Youth of Chopin*, treated by Polish film critics as a masterpiece and a model film to be emulated by others, was awarded in Karlovy Vary (1952) and Ferrara (1959). The year before, Jan Rybkowski had produced *Warszawska premiera* (*Warsaw Premiere*), a film on another Polish composer, Stanisław Moniuszko.
19. Discussed, among others, by Peter Kenez, *Cinema and Soviet Society, 1917–1953* (Cambridge: Cambridge University Press, 1992); *The Birth of the Propaganda State: Soviet Methods of Mass Mobilization, 1917–1929* (Cambridge: Cambridge University

Press, 1985); also analyzed in Richard Taylor, *Film Propaganda: Soviet Russia and Nazi Germany* (London: Croom Helm, 1979).
20. Sobotka, "Robotnik na ekranie," 52.
21. Rafał Marszałek, "Kapelusz i chustka," in *Film i kontekst*, ed. Danuta Palczewska and Zbigniew Benedyktynowicz (Wrocław: Ossolineum, 1988), 35–55.
22. Ibid., 48.
23. Sobotka, "Robotnik na ekranie," 46.
24. In his psychoanalytic interpretation of *An Adventure at Marienstadt*, Wiesław Godzic writes that the film tells the story of a young woman in search of her sexual identity. Wiesław Godzic, *Film i psychoanaliza: Problem widza* (Kraków: Wydawnictwo Uniwersytetu Jagiellońskiego, 1991), 120–28.
25. Stachówna, "Równanie szeregów," 21. In Polish cinema, 1954 was "the year of kisses." Earlier, before *Difficult Love* (released in April), a kiss appeared in *An Adventure at Marienstadt* (released in January).
26. See Piotr Zwierzchowski, "*Cellulose*, Neorealism and Soviet Cinema: Inspiration and Legitimization," in *Pęknięty monolit: Konteksty polskiego kina socrealistycznego* (Bydgoszcz: Wydawnictwo Uniwersytetu Kazimierza Wielkiego, 2005), 44–63. See also Piotr Zwierzchowski, *Zapomniani bohaterowie* (Warsaw: Wydawnictwo Trio, 2000).
27. The "Maxim Trilogy" consists of *Yunost Maksima* (*The Youth of Maxim*, 1935), *Vozvrashchenie Maksima* (*The Return of Maxim*, 1937), and *Vyborgskaia storona* (*The Vyborg Country*, 1939). Donskoi adapted Gorki's autobiography as *Detstvo Gorkogo* (*The Childhood of Maxim Gorki*, 1938), *V lyudyakh* (*My Apprenticeship*, aka *On His Own*, 1939), and *Moi universitety* (*Gorky 3: My Universities*, 1940).
28. Krzysztof Teodor Toeplitz in *Nowa Kultura* 18 (1954), quoted in Michałek and Turaj, *The Modern Cinema of Poland*, 97.
29. Following Khrushchev's famous speech in which he disclosed and condemned Stalin's crimes, Poland was ready to retreat from Stalinism. In October 1956, Władysław Gomułka, recently released from prison, returned to power as first secretary of the PZPR, ending some of the Stalinist practices (e.g., the collectivization of farms), making gestures toward the Catholic Church (e.g., the releasing the Polish cardinal, Stefan Wyszyński, from prison), and making some conciliatory gestures toward the members of the noncommunist opposition against the Germans (toward the members of the Home Army).
30. Jerzy Zarzycki (1911–1971) belonged to the generation of START members. He began his career before the war, directing the much-praised *The People of the Vistula* (1938, with Aleksander Ford).
31. Ewelina Nurczyńska-Fidelska, *Andrzej Munk* (Kraków: Wydawnictwo Literackie, 1982), 38.
32. Ibid., 37.
33. Jerzy Płażewski, "Andrzej Munk, urzędnik śledczy rzeczywistości," *Życie Literackie* 5 (1975): 9.

34. Nurczyńska-Fidelska, *Andrzej Munk*, 51–52.
35. César Ballester, "Subjectivism, Uncertainty and Individuality: Munk's *Człowiek na torze / Man on the Tracks* (1956) and Its Influence on the Czechoslovak New Wave," *Studies in Eastern European Cinema* 2, no. 1 (2011): 63.
36. Munk was familiar with the world portrayed. Earlier, in 1953, he had made a documentary, *Kolejarskie słowo* (*The Railwayman's Word*), in the same milieu.
37. Wojciech Włodarczyk, *Sztuka polska w latach 1950–1954* (Paryż: Libella, 1986), 112.
38. Lubelski, *Strategie autorskie*, 95–96.

CHAPTER 5
Ashes and Diamonds
The Polish School (1955–1963)

[During World War II] death forgot about us. However, by keeping us alive, it imposed on us a duty, which is to keep memory of those who died. We were not allowed to forget; our duty to those who died was to give testimony of their death. To a certain degree, my war films narrate what is missing in my own biography, and what others had experienced. We knew that we are the voice of our dead; that our duty is to give testimony about those who were better. We saved ourselves only because we were worse; we had less courage, less bravery, less creativity, less imagination—or perhaps just too much imagination. Thus, the war became our theme, and our poignant and painful feeling was the disappointment that resulted from the wasted hope and the wasted effort; from the fact that the reality turned completely different than we had expected. The Polish Film School was born out of this very image of the war, our war, in which the struggle does not lead to victory. Hence, the irony that permeates our films and saturates Polish literature. Deceived, cheated by fate, ironically exposed to the ridicule of the world and Europe.

—Andrzej Wajda, "Moje notatki z historii"

The true birth of postwar Polish cinema had been anticipated long before the canonical films of Kazimierz Kutz, Andrzej Munk, Andrzej Wajda, and others. The term "Polish School" was coined as early as 1954 by the film critic and scholar Aleksander Jackiewicz, who expressed his desire to see a Polish School of filmmaking worthy of the great tradition of Polish art. Jackiewicz wanted to see Polish films that confronted local history and addressed social and moral problems. A filmmaker and an influential professor at the Łódź Film School, Antoni Bohdziewicz later employed the name "Polish School" when referring to Andrzej Wajda's debut film, *A Generation* (1955).[1]

Stalin's death in March 1953 created a political thaw in Poland, pushed further by Nikita Khrushchev's speech in 1956, in which he revealed some of Stalin's crimes and condemned the cult of personality. The escape of a high-ranking officer of the Ministry of Public Security, Józef Światło, from Poland in December 1953 and his broadcasts via Radio Free Europe after the fall of 1954 embarrassed the communist authorities by revealing the inner workings of the Polish security apparatus. The death (under mysterious circumstances) of Polish President Bolesław Bierut during his visit to the Soviet Union in March 1956 symbolically marked the end of the Stalinist period in Poland. It was followed by general amnesty in April 1956 and workers' strikes in Poznań in June 1956 (the "Poznań events") that were violently crushed by the security forces. The real danger of the Soviet military involvement led to a dramatic meeting in Warsaw in October 1956 between Władysław Gomułka and the high-level Soviet delegation led by Khrushchev, which resulted in the Soviet's reluctant approval of Gomułka as the new Polish communist leader.

The dramatic political events in October 1956 in Central Europe (including the uprising against the communist regime in Hungary, which was brutally crushed by the invading Soviet troops) prompted changes in Polish arts. The impatience and the desire to see the effects of the Polish October were overwhelming. Some of the writers who had produced ghastly Stalinist works emerged reborn as the champions of the new, the first to unmask the atrocities of Stalinism. The disappointment with the Stalinist period, the urge to represent reality's complex nature, and the desire to confront issues that had functioned as taboos in the Polish political as well as cultural life created a stimulating atmosphere for young filmmakers. Their works were expected to play an important role in the political changes introduced after October 1956. The new era was eagerly awaiting its debut in films.

The Polish School Phenomenon

The eruption of artistic energy and the emergence of the new wave of filmmakers in Poland after 1956 is usually described as the Polish School phenomenon. When discussing particular national schools of filmmaking or film movements, critics customarily look for works that were produced within a given period by a group of filmmakers who shared the same generational experiences and whose films embrace many thematic and stylistic similarities. Is this the case of the Polish School phenomenon?

Stanisław Ozimek, a Polish film historian, states in his seminal work that the Polish School "was the first discernible ideological and artistic formation in the history of national cinema."[2] He meticulously enumerates the characteristic tendencies within the school and proposes the following periods to describe the phenomenon: (1) the initial period (1955–1956), in which the new tendencies are only indicated, hidden under the crust of socialist realist poetics; (2) the proper period (1957–1959), during which filmmakers mostly focus on the themes of war and occupation, and situate their works within the context of the Polish romantic tradition; (3) the phase of crisis (1960–1961), characterized by the classic style and the personalization of presented themes (the importance of the plebeian protagonist); (4) the final stage (1962–1965), distinguished by superficial references to the school's poetics, as well as by the polemic concerning the school's thematic obsessions.[3] Many scholars tend to agree about the period of the origins of the school, situating it either in 1955 (the release of Wajda's *A Generation*) or in 1956 (the Polish October). There is no agreement, however, concerning the decline of the school. Most scholars locate the end of the Polish School phenomenon earlier than Ozimek does, in 1961, 1962, or 1963.[4]

Traditionally, scholars deal with a multiplicity of styles. During the Polish School period, they catalogue the major thematic and stylistic properties present during this outburst of authorial expressions. Ozimek, for instance, distinguishes the "romantic-expressive" tendency represented at its best in the films of Andrzej Wajda, *Kanał* (*Kanal*, 1957), *Popiół i diament* (*Ashes and Diamonds* (1958), and *Lotna* (*Speed*, 1959); the "rationalistic" tendency embodied in the films by Andrzej Munk, *Eroica* (1958) and *Zezowate szczęście* (*Bad Luck*, 1960); and the "psychological-existential" trend present in the films of Wojciech J. Has, Stanisław Lenartowicz, and Jerzy Kawalerowicz.[5] Another scholar, Aleksander Jackiewicz, differentiates between the romantic and plebeian traditions in Polish cinema. The first is represented by Wajda and Munk, the second by Kazimierz Kutz and other Polish filmmakers.[6]

As evidenced by the number of categories listed above, it is difficult to discuss the Polish School phenomenon in terms of thematic and stylistic similarities. Unlike the tedious era of Stalinist cinema, the Polish School period is characterized by differing themes, incompatible poetics, edginess in terms of style and ideology, and sheer entertainment value. The multiplicity of aesthetic tendencies, the various authorial expressions, and the open character of the school make defining or summarizing it an arduous task. One must take into account films set during or immediately after the war, which debate the Polish romantic mythology, and works that belong to different realms: historical epic (e.g., *Krzyżacy* [*Teutonic Knights*, 1960, Aleksander Ford]); comedy (e.g., *Ewa chce spać* [*Ewa Wants to Sleep*, 1958, Tadeusz Chmielewski]); war drama (e.g., *Wolne miasto* [*Free City*, 1958, Stanisław Różewicz]); psychological drama (e.g., *Prawdziwy koniec wielkiej wojny* [*The True End of the Great War*, 1957, Jerzy Kawalerowicz]); metaphysical drama (e.g., *Matka Joanna od Aniołów* [*Mother Joan of the Angels*, 1961, Kawalerowicz]); Holocaust drama (e.g., *Biały niedźwiedź* [*White Bear*, 1959, Jerzy Zarzycki]); the "new wave experiments" (e.g., *Ostatni dzień lata* [*The Last Day of Summer*, 1958, Tadeusz Konwicki]); black comedy (e.g., Munk's *Bad Luck*); "Eastern" (transplant of the Western genre, e.g., *Rancho Texas* [1959, Wadim Berestowski]); and others. The different, sometimes contradictory, approaches are discernible even if one analyzes films made by the same director. Films such as the neorealist *Krzyż Walecznych* (*Cross of Valor*, 1959) and the new wave (in spirit) *Nikt nie woła* (*Nobody Is Calling*, 1960), both directed by Kazimierz Kutz, or the expressionistic *Zimowy zmierzch* (*Winter Twilight*, 1957) and the war action drama *Pigułki dla Aurelii* (*Pills for Aurelia*, 1958), both directed by Stanisław Lenartowicz, belong to different realms and represent disparate film poetics.

The ambiguous criteria pertaining to the Polish School and the lack of an aesthetic program articulated by the young filmmakers allow scholars either to limit the number of films to a small group of selected examples or to consider all of the films made during the period in question. Opting for the former approach, Tadeusz Miczka writes that out of 138 feature films released from 1957 to 1963, only thirty belong to the Polish School. According to Miczka, they are distinguished by the "strategy of the psychotherapist" employed by their makers, chiefly Munk and Wajda, who "deeply influenced the social consciousness since they helped to free the national mythology from mystification and lies, permeating the socialist realist poetics."[7] Other scholars, myself included, are more cautious and choose to depart from the narrow interpretation, preferring instead to observe the complexity of the phenomenon and analyze the various means of expression that appeared during the Polish School period.

Marek Hendrykowski discusses not "the school" but "the artistic formation," and stresses that "the term Polish School has been treated ahistorically so far, that it is eliminating by definition, first, the moment of internal evolution of the formation and, second, the multiplicity of tendencies and styles of its artistic explorations."[8] Hendrykowski asserts that the artistic formation known as the Polish School was open, multifaceted, evolutionary, polyphonic, and dialogic and was created by many authors (including directors, screenwriters, cinematographers, actors, composers, and set designers).[9] Another scholar, Ewelina Nurczyńska-Fidelska, theorizes that the Polish School, as a uniform cultural marvel, did not exist; instead, we are dealing with the emergence of auteurs who initiated a serious artistic and intellectual dialogue with their viewers and reflected the spirit of the times in their works.[10]

Undoubtedly, it is more feasible to discuss the Polish School period in terms of its authors and the generational change of guard. The Polish School had been created primarily by a new generation of filmmakers—the "generation of Columbuses" (*Kolumbowie*)—born in the 1920s and embodied by the two young poets Krzysztof Kamil Baczyński and Tadeusz Gajcy, who died a soldier's death during the Warsaw Uprising of August to October 1944.[11] Maria Janion, a Polish expert on Romanticism, states that this was "the generation marked by the trauma of war and death ... born under the unhappy, perhaps cursed star."[12] The young filmmakers were united in their disenchantment with the socialist realist dogma and the simplistic aesthetics of their older colleagues. They were trying to break with their teachers—mostly prewar, left-wing filmmakers and activists whom they interestingly rarely acknowledged—and to forget their own film initiation under the auspices of socialist realism. They turned to recent history, to World War II and the postwar situation, leaving the Stalinist period virtually untouched.[13] The images of Polish history and present-day reality that they produced for the screen disturbed the communist Polish authorities.

The political changes introduced after the Polish October enabled young filmmakers to move away from socialist realism and, to a large extent, to build their films around their own experiences. Polish literature, traditionally the source for almost half of Polish films, played an even more important role in the late 1950s and in the early 1960s.[14] Unlike the prewar period, which favored adaptations of literary classics, the Polish School filmmakers preferred novels and short stories published after 1946 by their contemporaries—Jerzy Andrzejewski, Kazimierz Brandys, Bohdan Czeszko, Józef Hen, Marek Hłasko, Jerzy Stefan Stawiński, and others. For example, some of the canonical works by Andrzej Wajda and Andrzej Munk (*Man on the Tracks*, *Kanal*, *Eroica*, and *Bad Luck*) are based on scripts by Jerzy Stefan Stawiński (1920–2010). This coauthor of the Polish School's success drew on his firsthand experiences as a soldier in the September campaign of 1939 against the invading Germans. He spent time in a POW camp, from which he successfully escaped, committed himself to underground political activities, participated in the Warsaw Uprising, and, after its collapse, was interned in another POW camp. Reflecting Stawiński's personal experiences, the films made by the Polish School generation bring to light the unrepresented fate of the Home Army members—the truly national resistance against both German and Soviet occupying forces—who fought under the command of the Polish government-in-exile based in London. These films also portray the humiliating military defeat in 1939, the occupation, the Warsaw Uprising, the futility of the armed struggle, and the Polish romantic mythology.[15]

Organizational Changes

The revival of Polish cinema in the late 1950s was helped by several organizational changes that had already begun before the Polish October. Starting in May 1955, the film industry in Poland was based on a film units (*Zespoły Filmowe*) system, a new and efficient way of managing film production.[16] Each film unit was composed of film directors, screenwriters, and producers (along with their collaborators and assistants) and was supervised by an artistic director, with the help of a literary director and a production manager. Film units were considered state enterprises, yet had some rudimentary freedoms; thanks to them, many Łódź Film School graduates quickly achieved strong positions in the national film industry.

In 1957, there were eight such film companies in operation, among them the film unit Kadr, which was instrumental in developing the Polish School phenomenon. Kadr was headed by Jerzy Kawalerowicz, with Krzysztof Teodor Toeplitz (until 1957) and (later) Tadeusz Konwicki as literary directors, and Ludwik Hager as a production manager. Among its members were Andrzej Wajda, Andrzej Munk, Janusz Morgenstern, and Kazimierz Kutz. Other film units included Ludwik Starski's Iluzjon (with directors such as Wojciech Jerzy Has, Sylwester Chęciński, and Jerzy Passendorfer), Jan Rybkowski's Rytm (Stanisław Lenartowicz, Stanisław Różewicz), Aleksander Ford's Studio (Ewa and Czesław Petelski, Janusz Nasfeter), Wanda Jakubowska's Start (Jan Batory, Maria Kaniewska), Jerzy Zarzycki's Syrena, Jerzy Bossak's Kamera (formerly known as "57"), and Antoni Bohdziewicz's Droga. The literary directors included some of the most prominent writers: Anatol Stern,

Stanisław Dygat, Tadeusz Konwicki (himself a renowned filmmaker), Jerzy Stefan Stawiński, Roman Bratny, and Jerzy Andrzejewski.[17]

The year 1955 also marked the creation of the Central Film Archives (Centralne Archiwum Filmowe) in Warsaw, known today as the National Film Archives (Filmoteka Narodowa). In 1956, the Central Office of Cinema (Centralny Urząd Kinematografii, established in 1952) was replaced by the Chief Board of Cinema (Naczelny Zarząd Kinematografii), part of the Polish Ministry of Culture.

The new policy affected the distribution of films as well. Since April 1958, Polish movie theaters were obliged to screen short films (animated, documentary, or educational) before the main feature, a factor of great consequence for the future of Polish short films. In 1956, there were 2,881 cinemas in operation. From 1957 to 1961, this number increased significantly, by almost 20 percent, and by 1961 Poland had 1,490 cinemas in cities, 1,709 in rural areas, and 333 mobile cinemas. This period also marked the appearance of the first cine-clubs (as many as 170 in 1961), which played a vital role in promoting international art cinema in Poland; they often screened films that were not distributed in mainstream cinemas because of political censorship.[18]

Political events in the mid-1950s—the post-Stalinist thaw and its aftermath—also affected film distribution. Comparatively liberal politics allowed the Polish film industry to produce and import genre cinema and entertainment films from Western Europe and the Untied States. The Film Repertoire Council (Filmowa Rada Repertuarowa), an advisory body responsible for recommending foreign films, was founded in 1957 and initially headed by Jerzy Toeplitz. During the late 1950s, the number of films imported from the West increased at the expense of films from the communist countries; between 170 and 180 films from twenty-two countries were released in Poland annually, with local films making up 12 percent of the market.[19]

The new repertoire policy was characterized by its careful balance between art cinema and popular cinema. The times also required a careful geopolitical equilibrium—half of the films had to come from Soviet Bloc countries. For example, the films shown on Polish screens in 1960 consisted of forty-two Soviet, twenty-seven French, twenty-one American, twenty Polish, eighteen English, seventeen Czechoslovak, nine Italian, six East German, five Swedish, and five Yugoslavian films. The rest were from Japan, West Germany, Mexico, Hungary, Romania, Bulgaria, Austria, Argentina, Denmark, Finland, the Netherlands, China, and North Korea.[20] Despite the dominance of Soviet films (almost half of the annual Soviet production was present on Polish screens), the repertoire was rich and included the most interesting aspects of world cinema.

Immediately after World War II, the appearance of every Polish film constituted a cultural event. Local films had an average audience of about 4.7 million viewers. From 1950 to 1955, however, the average attendance at Polish films dropped to 2.6 million. In the second half of the 1950s, Polish films regained their popularity, and although attendance was never as high as immediately after the war, they drew more than three million viewers per film.[21] Total annual cinema attendance was the highest immediately after the 1956 Polish October, with 231 million viewers. Later, despite the number of successful Polish films, the diversity of imported films, and the increased number of cinemas, there was a slow decline of cinema attendance: 205 million viewers in 1958, 195.5 million in 1959, 186 million in 1960, and 179.6 million in 1961. As in other European countries, the increasing impact of television was partly to blame for the declining numbers. In 1957, for example, there were 22,000 television sets in Poland; only four years later, there were as many as 959,000.[22]

Polish films, always popular with local audiences, were starting to receive international acclaim and were winning numerous awards at various films festivals. The awards include two Silver Palms at Cannes for *Kanal* and *Mother Joan of the Angels*, the Golden Shell (the highest prize) for *Ewa Wants to Sleep* at San Sebastian, the International Federation of Film Critics (FIPRESCI) award for *Ashes and Diamonds* at Venice, the Golden Lion at Venice for *Świadectwo urodzenia* (*The Birth Certificate*, 1961, Stanisław Różewicz), the FIPRESCI award at Venice for *Nóż w wodzie* (*Knife in the Water*, 1962, Roman Polański), and the Grand Prix at San Francisco for *Jak być kochaną* (*How to Be Loved*, 1963, Wojciech J. Has). During the same period, Polish documentarians (e.g., Kazimierz Karabasz and Władysław Ślesicki) and filmmakers specializing in animation (e.g., Witold Giersz, Walerian Borowczyk, and Jan Lenica), were also being recognized abroad and winning awards at numerous film festivals.

Neorealist Influences

Starting in the mid-1950s, a split developed between young, emerging filmmakers, who were trained at the Łódź Film School and who believed in a genuine depiction of vital national themes, and older filmmakers, such as Aleksander Ford and Wanda Jakubowska, who opted for cinema imitating the Soviet epic models. The young filmmakers clearly favored the Italian neorealist approach, which offered them a chance to break with their predecessors and better reflect the spirit of the de-Stalinization period. Reproached by the communist authorities during a time of reigning socialist realism, Italian neorealism became the alternative to a portrayal of falsified reality. Though often absent on Polish screens, major works of neorealist cinema were shown during closed screenings at the Łódź Film School.[23] Neorealist influences are already discernible in some of the films made in 1954 (discussed in chapter 4): *Five Boys from Barska Street, A Night of Remembrance,* and *Under the Phrygian Star.*

Andrzej Wajda's directorial debut, *A Generation,* which premiered in January 1955, heralds the Polish School phenomenon and remains an example of a transitional work fusing the poetics of socialist realist films with neorealist observation. Essentially a coming-of-age story set during the war, this film grappled with Jewish-Polish relations from the perspective of those in the left-wing underground. The film's protagonist, Stach (Tadeusz Łomnicki), an ordinary streetwise character from a poor district of Warsaw, joins the communist resistance where he meets and falls in love with an underground communist activist, Dorota (Urszula Modrzyńska). In the film's finale, Stach leads the underground unit after Dorota is arrested by the Gestapo.

A Generation, based on Bohdan Czeszko's novel about the Gwardia Ludowa (GL; People's Guard), the communist military resistance formed in 1942, is a work tainted by political compromise. Despite its stylistic freshness, it remains, largely, a socialist realist film influenced by the neorealist style. Like Czeszko's novel, Wajda's film is heavily stereotyped, and rewrites recent Polish history from the communist perspective. It contains a distorted picture of the occupation in Poland with its black-and-white portrayal of the different factions of the underground—the nationalist Home Army members (present on the screen, although not named as such) are stereotyped as "collaborators" and "pseudopatriots," and the communist GL members are vaunted as the "true patriots."[24] The film also reverses the proportions of the Polish underground: the role of the communist underground is exaggerated at the expense of the Home Army. Like other socialist realist works, Wajda's film also has its "positive" working-class hero in the center, who acquires the correct (Marxist-Leninist) knowledge about history thanks to the guidance provided by experienced communist activists. *A Generation,* however, "successfully combines an expression of an acceptably optimistic social and political position with true lyricism, an idealization of personal experience, of remembered attitudes," Bolesław Sulik correctly observes.[25]

The action in *A Generation* often occurs near the Warsaw Ghetto walls, and part of the film takes place during the Warsaw Ghetto Uprising. In line with the political demands of the time, Wajda portrays Polish nationalistic types as treacherous and anti-Semitic, and the communists as the true helpers to the Warsaw Ghetto insurgents. "The ghetto has risen today. ... We must help our Jewish comrades," says the communist leader Sekuła. As he walks toward the ghetto, his image dissolves to several shots of burning ghetto buildings, some with waving flags on top of them (one image clearly shows a Polish flag). During this portrayal of the Warsaw Ghetto Uprising, Wajda employs images that are also present in his later films that involve the Holocaust: the carousel near the ghetto wall, the heavy smoke over the ghetto observed from the Aryan side of the wall, and smoldering pieces of burned paper flying into the Polish side. In an earlier scene, an escapee from the Ghetto, Abram, seeks the help of Jasio Krone (Tadeusz Janczar) but is rejected by his friend ("What can I do? I am just a civilian"). The scene showing the rejection by Abram's Polish friend, a "sensitive" civilian paralyzed by fear and helplessness, initiates Wajda's long-term commitment to examine Polish-Jewish wartime relations. As in his other films, Wajda is preoccupied with the Polish reactions to the uprising in the Ghetto.[26]

The straightforward story of *A Generation*, set in the working-class milieu, was shot mostly on location with young, unknown actors who were to become familiar faces of the Polish School cinema: Tadeusz Janczar (1926–1997), Zbigniew Cybulski (1927–1967), Tadeusz Łomnicki (1927–1992), and Roman Polański (1933–). The opening tracking shot of the film introduces a familiar setting from many Italian neorealist films: an impoverished Warsaw suburb with shacks and barren industrial buildings. The viewer sides with the most complex character in this film, Jasio. At first, he appears only to provide a contrast to the socialist realist hero, Stach. However, Jasio, multidimensional and ambiguous, ends up dying an unnecessary and "absurdly heroic death."[27] During the rescue mission to help the Warsaw Ghetto fighters escape via underground sewers to the "Aryan side," Jasio is a lookout on the street. He notices three approaching German patrolmen who open fire. Trying to help his comrades, Jasio runs through the bullets into a narrow street, the opposite direction of the truck with Stach and the escapees from the ghetto. His white overcoat makes him an easy target for the Germans, who pursue him toward a large apartment building. After exchanging fire with the growing number of German soldiers, Jasio finds himself trapped at the very top of the staircase. Wounded and short of ammunition, he stands on the railing and, shown in an extreme low-angle shot, tries to balance for a while before jumping to his death. Jasio is the prototype of Wajda's heroic protagonist: full of doubts, troubled, and tragic. This type of character anticipates other film personae such as Maciek Chełmicki in *Ashes and Diamonds*.

* * *

The realistic depiction of the war and postwar reality was a natural reaction against the sugarcoated poetics of socialist realism. There were both stylistic and ideological oppositions created by the Łódź Film School graduates, who wanted to manifest a personal, auteurist approach after the Stalinist period during which the author had been silenced and only the system had a voice. The dose of realism, enormous by Polish standards in the mid-1950s, was often unbearable for the censors, who reacted in several cases; they were harsher toward contemporary realistic films than toward films dealing with recent history. Jerzy Zarzycki's *Lost Feelings*, for example, was withdrawn from the screens soon after its release in 1957. The premieres of two other, lesser-known films, *Koniec nocy (The End of the Night)* and *Miasteczko (Small Town)*, both collectively directed, were delayed. The former, made in 1956, was released in December 1957; the latter, produced in 1958, premiered in March 1960.[28]

The End of the Night,[29] *Lunatycy (Moonwalkers*, 1960, Bohdan Poręba),[30] and *Lost Feelings* all deal with the themes of juvenile delinquency and hooliganism, which were "discovered" at approximately the same time by Polish documentarians. From 1956 to 1959, about twenty films of the "black series" were made, beginning with *Uwaga, chuligani! (Attention, Hooligans!* 1955, Jerzy Hoffman and Edward Skórzewski). In contrast to the socialist realist mode of representation, these documentaries portrayed the negative aspects of life as well, such as hooliganism, prostitution, and alcoholism, which were never mentioned in the previous era. Particularly known are documentaries by Kazimierz Karabasz and Władysław Ślesicki, *Gdzie diabeł mówi dobranoc (Where the Devil Says Good Night*, 1957) and *Ludzie z pustego obszaru (People from Nowhere*, 1957). The title of the latter, depicting Warsaw's rundown districts, became a description of the criminal segment of life.[31] Nurczyńska-Fidelska applies the term *czarny realizm* (literally "black realism") to a group of realistic, yet stylistically different, films including *The*

End of the Night, Small Town, Lost Feelings, Moonwalkers, Winter Twilight, Damned Roads, and *Pętla* (*The Noose*, 1958, Wojciech J. Has).[32] They formed the Polish version of Italian neorealism and, as Nurczyńska-Fidelska suggests, were characterized by a dark presentation of reality and stylistic as well as thematic borrowings from American film noir. In the context of Polish politics during the 1950s, every attempt at representing the darker side of everyday life became an explicitly political act. Hooliganism, for instance, was not portrayed exclusively as a social malady; instead, it was presented as an indirect accusation of the communist system.[33]

Damned Roads, directed by Czesław Petelski[34] and based on Marek Hłasko's novel *Następny do raju* (*Next Stop—Paradise*), frequently and deservedly appears in Polish critical works as the main example of "black realism." The film, set after the war in the sparsely populated Bieszczady Mountains (in southeastern Poland), deals with a group of brutal, rootless men working as logging truck drivers. *Damned Roads* also serves as an example of a socialist realist film about production *à rebours*—it lacks the didacticism of the previous era. The characters populating the screen (played by such popular actors as Emil Karewicz, Leon Niemczyk, Roman Kłosowski, Tadeusz Łomnicki, and others) are clearly antimodel workers—daredevils known only through their pseudonyms, shipwrecked people driving old rickety trucks.[35] Although there is one Communist Party member among them, Zabawa (Zygmunt Kęstowicz), sent there to look after the production plan, he has nothing to do with the Stalinist heroes. His wife, Wanda (Teresa Iżewska), the only woman in this male-oriented world, the equivalent of a film noir femme fatale, dreams of escaping from this god-forsaken place with any willing man from the base.

Kurt Weber's cinematography captures the gloomy scenery of the portrayed reality and stresses its fatalistic and claustrophobic aspects. Even the optimistic ending, which features new trucks coming to the base for the two remaining truck drivers, does not weaken this film's overwhelmingly pessimistic tone. Criticized in 1959 by some film reviewers for its dark portrayal of an animal-like existence and by Hłasko himself for the addition of a happy ending that is not present in his work (he withdrew his name from the credits), *Damned Roads* remains one of the darkest pictures of the "bright communist reality" and one of the best of Polish School films.

In addition to neorealism, many filmmakers adopted other cinematic styles in order to free themselves from the stiff corset of socialist realist poetics. For instance, *Winter Twilight* and *The Noose*, labeled as "black realist" films, situate themselves on the margin of mainstream Polish cinema by relying on expressionistic devices and mood. *Winter Twilight* portrays a small town somewhere in the eastern part of Poland. Its episodic narrative structure (Tadeusz Konwicki's script) focuses on an old railwayman, Rumsza (Włodzimierz Ziembiński), who is disappointed with his son Józek's choice of a wife. Józek (Bogusz Bilewski) marries a woman from outside the small community after finishing his military service. The film's plot is suggested rather than developed; the atmosphere remains more important than the action. With the help of Mieczysław Jahoda's cinematography, Stanisław Lenartowicz (1921–2010) creates a delicate mood and intimacy. The reliance on stylized flashbacks into the prewar period, the use of symbolism and expressionistic imagery, the observation of local customs and rituals produce a place that did not exist previously in the socialist realist world. The film critic Stanisław Grzelecki notes that "on the rubble of socialist realism spins what was cursed before: metaphors and symbols, moods and half-tones, dreams and fogs ... indistinct life at small railroad stations."[36] Most Polish critics, however, criticized the film's symbolism and expressionist devices. Interestingly, Lenartowicz objected to the labeling of his film as "expressionistic," considering expressionism as a distinct and closed period in film history.[37]

The Noose, another expressionistic film, deals with alcoholism and portrays a single day in the life of an alcoholic young man, Kuba (Gustaw Holoubek).[38] It is a film about the impossibility of escaping fate, about a reckless drive to destruction that ends in a suicide. The action of *The Noose* is limited to the protagonist's room and several streets that resemble a nightmarish landscape peopled by weird characters. The city serves as a reflection of Kuba's anxieties and his state of mind, which is on the verge of collapse. As in other films by Has, small objects, such as the clock and the black telephone, have important roles and virtually become characters in this film.

In *The Noose* and his other works, Wojciech J. Has (1925–2000), one of the masters of Polish cinema, ignores history and politics, that fateful fascination of Polish cinema. He does not take political stands but instead trusts his own imagination. He has always been unreceptive to artistic and political fads and the current polemics surrounding Polish film. He looks for universal themes and settings. "I reject matters, ideas, themes only significant for the present day. Art film dies in an atmosphere of fascination with the present," declares Has in a 1981 *Kino* interview.[39] Like Wajda's, Has's scripts are based on well-known works of literature, yet he always transforms them with his easily recognizable visual style.

In his films made during the Polish School period, *The Noose, Pożegnania (Farewells,* aka *Lydia Ate the Apple,* 1958), *Wspólny pokój (Shared Room,* aka *One Room Tenants,* 1960), *Rozstanie (Partings,* aka *Goodbye to the Past,* 1961), and *Złoto (Gold,* aka *Gold Dreams,* 1961), Has does not present typical Polish romantic heroes. His characters do not rebel or fight, and history seems to ignore them. The world they inhabit is built of their own dreams, fantasies, and fears. They live as if outside of history and time, trapped in a surreal reality. "The protagonists remain paralyzed by internal defeat; their world passes with cruelty, madness, and beauty, but this is a simulated movement, a simulated time," explains Piotr Wojciechowski.[40] Critics emphasize the visionary aspect of Has's cinema and how he creates his own filmic world filled with (sometimes strange) objects; they often use the Polish term *rupieciarnia* (junk room) to describe this aspect of his mise-en-scène.[41]

Reviewing Has's films for *Film Quarterly* in 1964, the critic Krzysztof-Teodor Toeplitz notes that he "gives us that part of the truth about present-day Poland, which is commonly lacking in more representative work."[42] The same applies to Has's representation of World War II. Made in 1963, his *How to Be Loved,* based on Kazimierz Brandys's story, offers a female perspective on the war. Its protagonist, Felicja (Barbara Krafftówna), finds love more important than national duty, and she pays a heavy price for it. In Has's film, Felicja narrates her story several years after the war, when she is a successful radio actor, on a plane from Warsaw to Paris. The flashbacks reveal that before the war she fell in love with a film star, Wiktor, played against type by Zbigniew Cybulski. During the occupation, Felicja offered Wiktor shelter when the Gestapo hunted him for allegedly killing a Gestapo informer. She sacrificed herself for him, including sleeping with the enemy to conceal his presence in her apartment. Cybulski's Wiktor has little in common with other characters in Polish films about the war: he is an unheroic, even a cowardly, person—a buffoon in desperate search of an audience. This is Felicja, who is an unheralded hero of the occupation.

Representations of World War II

Realistic depictions of the post-Stalinist reality did not constitute the main trend during the Polish School period. The primary concern remained history, World War II in particular. For the filmmakers, the "point of reference is not the historical reality," says Andrzej Werner, "but the notions that surround it, those mythologized forms of comprehension."[43] The Polish School filmmakers did not introduce just a single perspective on recent Polish history. Instead, they offered polemic voices and a variety of cinematic styles. The atmosphere of the post-Stalinist thaw enabled them to deal with several taboo topics, such as the Warsaw Uprising of 1944 and the fate of the Home Army fighters.

The differences in the treatment of history can be seen in numerous films polemic to the then official version of history and to each other. For example, two films dealing with the Warsaw Uprising, Wajda's *Kanal* and Munk's *Eroica*, both written by Jerzy Stefan Stawiński, portray two visions of this both cherished and criticized moment in the Polish past.[44] Most Polish scholars discuss these and other films in the context of the local romantic tradition as the works inspired by and debating this legacy. Scholars frequently juxtapose Wajda's romanticism and Munk's rationalism, comparing Wajda's dramatic characters, torn between their sense of duty to the nation and their personal happiness, to Munk's pragmatic protagonists.[45]

Wajda, a proponent of the Polish romantic tradition, deals with national history in his most important works made during the Polish School period. "Wajda's films are pervaded with the intention of interpreting the manifestations, the features and the social functions of the national mythology," writes Nurczyńska-Fidelska.[46] His protagonists are caught by the oppressive forces of history and function as its unfortunate victims. Wajda's breakthrough film, *Kanal*, produced by Kadr, concerns the final stage of the Warsaw Uprising. It narrates the story of a Home Army unit that manages to escape German troops via the only route left: the city sewers.[47] From its opening sequence, *Kanal* depicts a bleak vision of defeat. The voice-over narration introduces the leading characters, offers laconic comments on them, and tells the viewers to "watch them closely, as they live their last hours." Since the viewer is told that there is no hope for the protagonists, the film's narrative relies on "how" rather than "what." The main part of the film is set in the Warsaw city sewers, in which most of the fighters meet their deaths. The choice of this unusual environment largely explains the use of expressionistic lighting and claustrophobic camera angles, as well as the darkness of the set. The setting of the action, expressionistic in style, is also almost surrealist in spirit. The cinematographer, Jerzy Lipman (1922–1983), whose name is associated with several great achievements of the Polish School, and his cameraman, Jerzy Wójcik (1930–), depict a nightmarish underworld permeated by madness, death, and despair—full of dead bodies, German booby traps, and excrement.[48]

Kanal offers an allegory on the agony of the city and the annihilation of its inhabitants. From a contemporary perspective, however, it is easy to point out the film's historical inaccuracies, for example, that the Red Army was watching on the other bank of the Vistula River when the Germans suppressed the uprising. In a defensive comment, Wajda explains:

> The only thing that may strike one is the absence of one element, namely "force of circumstances" (let us leave it at that, in inverted commas) which precipitated the drama; but I can see no way of presenting this on the screen until the problem has first been sorted out by the historians on the basis of the evidence. Anything that I might suggest going on my own conjectures would be merely nebulous hypothesis.[49]

The Warsaw Uprising is still a controversial subject in Poland, and the release of *Kanal*, the first film to portray the legendary uprising, sparked passionate debates. In the film, Wajda neither glorifies the insurgents, as was expected by most of his compatriots in 1957, nor criticizes the official communist stand on the "liberation" of Warsaw by the Soviet troops. Instead, he stresses the patriotism of the Home Army soldiers, their sense of duty, and their heroic yet futile effort. They gain sympathy as ill-fated casualties of the war and the victims of political manipulations. Certainly, *Kanal* is not a paean to the Home Army heroes, but rather a film demythologizing Polish-style heroism. The commanding officer of the company of insurgents, Lieutenant Zadra (Wieńczysław Gliński), voices his doubts: "With small arms and hand grenades against tanks and planes. We'll never learn." His second-in-command, Lieutenant Mądry (Emil Karewicz) responds: "Orders are orders. Stop rationalizing."[50] Earlier in the film, after listening to an officer say, "We'll be hailed by posterity. They won't take us alive," Zadra bitterly responds, "That's right, the Polish way!"

One of the insurgents, Korab (Tadeusz Janczar), is severely wounded during a heroic attack on a remote-controlled German tank, "Goliath." Accompanied by his girlfriend, the fellow insurgent and messenger Daisy (Teresa Iżewska), who knows the labyrinth of underground sewers firsthand, they try to follow Zadra's group only to find themselves trapped at the barred exit into the Vistula River, where they await an imminent death. The camera slowly reveals the bank on the other side of the river, Warsaw's working-class district of Praga where (as Polish viewers were perfectly aware) the Red Army detachments were waiting for the

Germans to crush the uprising. Don Fredericksen writes: "The bars blocking his [Korab's] freedom are not self-imposed. They were, in an accurate manner of speaking, placed there by the betrayals of Poland's right to self-determination by its real and feigned allies. Thus did the hopes for a free Poland die a lonely death in the sewers of Warsaw in the autumn of 1944."[51]

Despite controversies in Poland, *Kanal* was shown at the tenth Cannes Film Festival, where it received Silver Palm—together with Ingmar Bergman's *The Seventh Seal*. This critical acclaim certainly helped its international distribution: the film was sold to twenty-four countries. *Kanal* also was successful domestically: it had 4.2 million viewers during the first year of its release.[52]

The Warsaw Uprising is also the central focus of the first part of Andrzej Munk's *Eroica: Scherzo alla Polacca*, released eight months after *Kanal*.[53] The tragic-grotesque film depicts a different, everyday face of Polish heroism stripped of romantic myths and introduces an unusual (by Polish standards) wartime antihero, Dzidziuś Górkiewicz (Edward Dziewoński). He is an opportunist, a dealer on the black market, and an accidental hero of the uprising. This protagonist is not a brave, doomed soldier as one might expect, but rather a suspicious civilian. Acting as a mediator between the Home Army command in Warsaw and the Hungarian army unit, which is stationed near his house at the outskirts of Warsaw, Munk's protagonist serves the uprising. But his motivations are not ones cultivated by the Polish romantic tradition.

Rafał Marszałek writes that Poles learned the ideals of sacrifice and martyrdom from their tragic eighteenth- and nineteenth-century history, which resulted in the standardization of the national past. This history has affected Polish "patriotic art," which is characterized by a combination of idealism and naturalism and by a reliance on pathos, national symbols, and allegories.[54] Munk's film introduces characters facing the same problems as Wajda's insurgents, yet their actions are devoid of the romantic aura. The director clearly separates himself from the dominant national mythology and offers a bitter satire on Polish-style heroism—pejoratively known in Polish as *bohaterszczyzna* (heroism for the sake of it).

Munk's next film, *Zezowate szczęście* (*Bad Luck*, aka *Cockeyed Luck*, 1960), also written by Jerzy Stefan Stawiński, belongs to the same tradition. Set from the 1930s to the 1950s, it introduces another perspective on history that is atypical for Polish cinema. The film's protagonist, Jan Piszczyk (Bogumił Kobiela), is a Polish everyman who desperately wants to play an important role in the course of events yet, with no luck on his side, becomes another victim of history.[55] Piszczyk is an antihero—a moronic opportunist and an unreliable narrator who relates the sad story of his life. In six flashbacks, he presents himself as "the eternal plaything of history whose pranks he subjectively interprets as 'bad luck.'"[56] The mixture of generic conventions (from burlesque to political satire) helps Munk to portray Piszczyk as the victim of political circumstances—totalitarian systems (communism and fascism) and the war—and an oppressive childhood. Munk's tale about the failure of political mimicry may be perceived as a very Central European story. This model had an impact on other films, for example, Péter Bacsó's *A tanú* (*The Witness*, produced in 1969, released in 1978), a Hungarian film set during the Stalinist years that introduces another hapless opportunist clashing with political circumstances beyond his understanding.

Ashes and Diamonds and *Nobody Is Calling*

The discourse on recent Polish history permeates many other films made during the Polish School period. Andrzej Wajda's *Ashes and Diamonds* and Kazimierz Kutz's *Nobody Is Calling* deal with the fate of the Home Army soldiers at a time when World War II was practically over but fighting continued between the Soviet-imposed communists and the nationalist Home Army, the two warring factions in Poland. Both films explore similar themes yet present them in a disparate manner.

Ashes and Diamonds is generally regarded as the climax of the Polish School.[57] It is considered the world cinema classic that "tamed communist Poland for the Western viewer, rendering it palatable, acceptable."[58] But when this film was made, it was attacked by the communist establishment and by Aleksander Ford, who contested its alleged "counterrevolutionary nature." The film was poorly received at the official state meeting of the film commission. It was only because of another screening organized for Communist Party intellectuals by the author of the adapted book, Jerzy Andrzejewski, that the film's release had any success.

The film takes place in a small provincial town "somewhere in Poland" with its action beginning on 8 May 1945, a date that symbolically signals the end of the war. Its action is largely confined to the Monopol Hotel, where authorities are making official preparations to celebrate the end of the war. Because of the unity of place and time (the bulk of the film is set at night) and the thespian conflict of choices, the film can be considered a classical drama. The story concerns the Home Army fighter Maciek Chełmicki (Zbigniew Cybulski), who carries out his superiors' orders and assassinates the new district secretary of the Communist Party, Szczuka (Wacław Zastrzeżyński). *Ashes and Diamonds*, however, portrays not a personal conflict but rather a conflict of opposing political forces ("The fight for Poland, the fight for what sort of country it's going to be, has only just started," explains Szczuka at the beginning of the film). The Polish communists, the security force officers, the small-town political opportunists, and the Polish and Soviet troops on the city streets represent the "new Poland." The "old Poland" is embodied by the isolated Home Army fighters and their officers, as well as by the anachronistic remnants of the prewar nobility and intelligentsia who are ridiculed in the film. Given the political circumstances, Maciek's death is inevitable: Polish soldiers shoot him, and he lies in convulsions in a fetal position as death overtakes him on the enormous city garbage heap (perhaps the Hegelian rubbish heap of history).

Maciek serves as another tragic romantic hero torn between duty to the national cause and the yearning for a normal life. The Polish romantic protagonist

Figure 5.1 Zbigniew Cybulski as Maciek (left) and Adam Pawlikowski in Andrzej Wajda's *Ashes and Diamonds* (1958). Courtesy of Filmoteka Narodowa.

always solves such a dilemma by considering national matters as having topmost priority; he knows that he must sacrifice his private happiness at the altar of national needs. Like other Polish romantic characters, Maciek is a prisoner of a fate that he is powerless to escape. By killing Szczuka, he expects to fulfill his duties to the underground Home Army and to free himself from the war. The girl he meets and falls in love with, Krystyna (Ewa Krzyżewska), offers him a chance to lead a normal life. This is, however, an illusory prospect, since the postwar Polish reality did not welcome people with Maciek's past. In Wajda's film, the Home Army Major Waga (Ignacy Machowski) elaborates on this in his comments to Andrzej (Adam Pawlikowski), Maciek's commanding officer:

> And what have you been fighting for? For a free Poland, wasn't it? But was this how you imagined it? You must be aware, Lieutenant, that in Poland as it is, the only chance for you and thousands like you is to fight on. Where can you go with your record? In this country, everything is closed to you. Except prison.

Ashes and Diamonds depicts a cross-section of Polish society. Unlike the one-dimensional archetype of socialist realist characters, Wajda's protagonists are multilayered and open to interpretation. According to his trademark formula, "lyric protagonists in dramatic situations,"[59] Wajda makes the anticommunist Maciek a seductive hero who contemplates the "to kill or not to kill" dilemma. The director contrasts the stylized acting of Cybulski (Maciek) with the restrained acting of Pawlikowski (Andrzej). Furthermore, Maciek's political enemy, Szczuka, the new party secretary and an ex-soldier of the Spanish Civil War who has just returned from the Soviet Union, is portrayed as a leader with human qualities, not a poster-like exemplar at all: he is aging, fatherly, and tired. In the opening sequence, when Szczuka meets the workers after the first failed attempt on his life, the camera portrays him in a manner typical of socialist realist films, with low-angle shots of him standing in front of the workers who are portrayed, also typically, as a group. Other diverse characters in supporting roles include the opportunist Drewnowski (Bogumił Kobiela), the alcoholic journalist Pieniążek (Stanisław Milski), the apparatchik Święcki, and Szczuka's teenage son, Marek, a Home Army soldier captured by the security forces (this aspect of the story is not present in the literary source).

Wajda comments on the tragic fate of his protagonist: "The source of his tragedy is that this boy does not accept reality, does not accept history as it is, but history as he has dreamed of it. Precisely speaking, thinking about life, about history, about the country, he uses notions he received as an inheritance from the romantic stream of Polish literature."[60] Wearing dark glasses ("During the uprising, I stayed too long in the sewers," he explains to Krystyna) and clothes that do not represent the postwar reality, Maciek serves as an exemplary hero of the late 1950s. The Polish writer and filmmaker Tadeusz Konwicki (1926–2015) writes on Cybulski's rendition of Maciek:

> *I didn't like him as Maciek in* Ashes and Diamonds *because he reminded me too much of the American actors in fashion at that time—James Dean, Montgomery Clift. ... But Home Army bumpkin that I am, it [the film] stuck in my throat. Yes, we had our fashions, fads, modes. But our fashions did not include blue jeans, sunglasses, excessive drinking, neurotic kicks, hysterical sobbing, and short-term love affairs. ... We were coarse, common; we wore knickers; we were punctual, reliable, restrained, embarrassed, hungry for death, afraid of one another, mistrustful of the elite, and timid in our feelings, gestures and words. We were simply different, we were simply genuine because we had not yet been reflected in the mirror of art.*[61]

Although Polish critics have frequently compared Cybulski to James Dean, the similarities between the two actors seem superficial. When asked about it, Cybulski said:

> *Dean had such great individuality that copying him is an unattainable dream. One can copy him in a satirical program, but not in a two-hour film. Besides, I acted in a similar manner in* A Generation, *and I did not know that he existed and I couldn't have known, because his films, as we all know, were made in 1955 and 1956. Comparisons are made because I employ the same acting method.*[62]

Ashes and Diamonds is known for its romantic celebration of doomed heroes and its flamboyant style ("baroque" is the frequently ill-used word in film criticism). Striking visual effects, references to Polish national symbolism, and its ambivalent use of religious imagery are recognizable characteristics of the film. The motif of fire in particular, here associated with death, plays an important role in Wajda's film. In the opening sequence, Maciek's victim is shot in the back and catches fire as he collapses against church doors that open, revealing the altar. In another celebrated example, Maciek and Andrzej recall (while at the hotel bar) the years of fighting, during which ideological distinctions were clear. They drink to the memory of their dead companions, lighting glasses of alcohol as blazing memorials to their fallen friends. In the final sequence, the killer and his victim embrace in a grim dance of death, with fireworks bursting suddenly behind them. The fire of Maciek's gun and the festivity's fireworks marking the end of the war provide an ironic and bitter comment on the illusory nature of peace. Wajda also employs symbols taken from Polish art iconography. Some of them border on surreal touches, for example, an upside-down crucifix in a destroyed church that separates the two lovers, Maciek and Krystyna; the presence of a white horse; and the final, drunken scene with the polonaise "Farewell to the Homeland" (composed by Michał K. Ogiński) played off-key. The accumulation of some religious symbols in *Ashes and Diamonds* and the treatment of religion in general are seen by Paul Coates as Buñuelian in spirit.[63]

Unlike Wajda, Kutz portrays surviving heroes who give up their romantic gestures; he is interested in their isolation and loneliness, which are stressed through the composition of frame and the use of landscape. Although sometimes classified with Munk as representative of the demythologizing trend in Polish cinema, Kutz focuses not on the national mythology but on the everyday, the unheroic, and the plebeian. He is interested not in symbols of national importance but in concrete situations, not in history and the fate of Poles but in detailed observations of human psychology. This treatment of common protagonists is already present in Kutz's well-received debut, *Cross of Valor*, which consists of three novellas dealing with ordinary soldiers in ordinary situations. The first one, *Krzyż* (*Cross*), narrates the story of Socha (Jerzy Turek), a soldier from a village who returns home only to find it destroyed. In this new situation, his medals and bravery make no sense. In the second part, *Pies* (*Dog*), a group of Polish soldiers cannot carry out an order to shoot a stray German shepherd although, after the dog tries to attack two concentration camp survivors (probably from Auschwitz), they realize that the SS guards in the concentration camp used it to control and kill inmates. The third novella, *Wdowa* (*Widow*), which deals with maintaining myths at all costs, tells the story of ex-soldiers who, after the war, settle in a small town. There they keep alive the myth of their dead military commander, imposing this cult onto his unhappy, young, and beautiful widow.

One of the most original, yet for a long time critically neglected, films made during the Polish School period is Kutz's *Nobody Is Calling*, written by Józef Hen and loosely based on his novel.[64] Kutz admits that his intention was to make a film polemic with *Ashes and Diamonds* since, as he puts it, Andrzejewski and Wajda's protagonist serves as an example of the very Polish form of stupidity that places the romantic gesture above one's own life.[65] Maciek's alter ego in *Nobody Is Calling*, Bożek (Henryk Boukołowski), is a Home Army fighter who is hunted by his former colleagues for an act of military disobedience: his refusal to carry out the death sentence on a communist. He hides after the war in a small town in Poland's western territories (the so-called Regained Lands). Among other displaced people, wounded by war and with complex backgrounds, he meets Lucyna (Zofia Marcinkowska) and falls in love with her.

After working together on *Cross of Valor*, Kutz and his cinematographer Jerzy Wójcik (also the cinematographer of *Ashes and Diamonds*) strove to challenge the dominant aesthetics of Polish films. The episodic, slow-paced story of *Nobody Is Calling* is maintained by means of the ascetic, frequently static black-and-white images. The youth and the physical attraction of the two lovers clash with the gloomy atmosphere of the city, as if to stress that love has been born against the environment or in spite of it. In the course of the love affair, there are fewer and fewer objects within the frame, probably to present the perspective of the lovers, who are completely obsessed with each other and shut out the world. The images of dilapidated walls, empty streets and apartments, decaying window frames, and the devastated postwar landscape register the feelings of the two protagonists and function as their psychological landscape.

Figure 5.2 Henryk Boukołowski and Zofia Marcinkowska in Kazimierz Kutz's *Nobody Is Calling* (1960). Courtesy of Filmoteka Narodowa.

The meticulous composition of frame, the scarcity and repetitiveness of dialogue that is supplemented by Bożek's voice-over narration, Wojciech Kilar's original music (his debut as a composer), and the contrasting acting personalities of Marcinkowska and Boukołowski help to create the new wave–like style of the film. Like Stanisław Lenartowicz in *Winter Twilight* and Tadeusz Konwicki in *The Last Day of Summer*, Kutz searches for a new style and new language of cinema. *Nobody Is Calling* bears similarities to the later new wave films, chiefly works by Michelangelo Antonioni. In the context of highly politicized Polish cinema, its formalist poetics, bordering on aesthetic provocation, caused consternation among film critics and the disapproval of the film authorities. As a result, voice-over narration that clarifies the action was added, but the shortened film had to wait several years to be recognized as a work of art.

Polish critics greeted Kutz's return to the realistic depiction of World War II with *Ludzie z pociągu* (*People from the Train*, 1961) with a sigh of relief. The film is set in a small provincial railway station during the war and portrays an "average day" during the occupation, with the familiar psychology of the crowd and accidental heroism. Prompted by an unusual incident (somebody throws a bouquet of flowers from a passing train), a stationmaster recalls to his assistant what happened there in 1943 when, because of a technical problem, a group of passengers were stranded at the provincial train station. Kutz presents the mosaic of intertwined incidents and the broad spectrum of Polish society, depicts gestures devoid of pathos, and relies on detailed observations that may foreshadow the "small realism" of the Czechoslovak cinema in the 1960s. Unlike Wajda, he deheroicizes the protagonists (Kutz's trademark throughout his career) and narrates their stories in a realistic manner, eschewing symbols and metaphors.

Among the many characters in the train station is a Polish war widow (Danuta Szaflarska) who is hiding a young Jewish girl, Marylka. They are endangered not only by the presence of a German SS patrol but also by a Polish *szmalcownik* (blackmailer). Later, when the Germans discover a machine gun in the station's waiting room that, unknown to them, belongs to a drunken German railway police officer, they threaten to kill every fifth passenger. Their lives are eventually spared by events that combine fortuitous acts of heroism and dark comedy. A teenage boy tries to save his fellow passengers by claiming the gun, and, before long, the stationmaster finds the drunken police officer. The SS soldiers move away after severely beating the boy—the quiet hero of "an ordinary wartime day."

***

The themes of the war and the occupation return in many films, not necessarily works entangled in the national debate about the Polish romantic legacy. Frequently, these are reconstructions of well-known military actions that do not refer to the national discussions that usually accompany the portrayal of the armed struggle. Stanisław Lenartowicz, in *Pills for Aurelia*, and Jerzy Passendorfer (1923–2003), in *Zamach* (*Answer to Violence*, 1959), focus on the sensational aspect of the occupation and portray the Home Army actions in the manner of action-suspense cinema. For example, the latter film, popular with Polish audiences, reconstructs the actual February 1944 assassination of Franz Kutschera, the commander of the SS and police forces in occupied Warsaw.

The war also features prominently in the films directed by Witold Lesiewicz (1922–2012). *Dezerter* (*The Deserter*, 1958), set during the war in Upper Silesia, concerns the fate of young Poles living in the territories that were annexed by the Reich who are forced to join the German army. The film is known for its well-used setting of a coal mine, where the main part of the action takes place, and the suspenseful chase sequence in the mine's labyrinths. Lesiewicz's next film, *Rok pierwszy* (*First Year*, 1960), narrates the story of Otryna (Stanisław Zaczyk), a communist sergeant left behind the front line who, in the fall of 1944, tries to implement communist rule in a small Polish town. At the militia station, however, the sergeant encounters members of the Home Army, led by the corporal Dunajec (Leszek Herdegen), who do not support his plans and who are his political opponents. Otryna is unable to convince them to join the new political order and is powerless to prevent six of them from joining the anticommunist partisans. The conflict in *First Year* is presented as a drama of choices; the personal conflict is related without resorting to black-and-white schemata. A similar portrayal of varied characters' psychology can be seen in Lesiewicz's subsequent film *Kwiecień* (*April*, 1961), a story concerning the soldiers of the Second Polish Army during the final stages of the war (April 1945). Although known chiefly for its epic portrayal of the war, *April* pays tribute to the common soldier, the plebeian soldier introduced by Kutz in his *Cross of Valor*.

Another common character-soldier appears in *Ogniomistrz Kaleń* (*Sergeant Major Kaleń*, 1961, Ewa and Czesław Petelski). Like the directors' earlier film, *Damned Roads*, this film is set in the Bieszczady Mountains and describes the bloody postwar conflict involving Ukrainian nationalists of the Ukrainian Insurgent

Army (UPA), remnants of the Polish underground fighting the communist government, and regular Polish troops controlled by the Soviets. The protagonist of this "cruel ballad,"[66] Kaleń (Wiesław Gołas), is portrayed almost as a folk hero. Not a typical heroic soldier, he experiences torture, betrayal, and the ferocious death of his comrades. The scene of their death at the minefield, where they are pushed by the encircling Ukrainian unit, is one of the strongest scenes in Polish cinema. The film's setting in the Polish "wild east," its lively action filled with chases and escapes, and its individualistic hero prompted some Polish critics to look for parallels with the American Western genre. The Western conventions, however, seem to be of lesser importance in *Sergeant Major Kaleń* than those of Soviet "action film classics," such as *Chapayev* (1934, Georgi Vasilyev and Sergey Vasilyev).[67]

In Polish history, September 1939 symbolizes defeat and betrayal. It also marks the end of an era harshly criticized in postwar Poland. A small group of works set at the outbreak of war include *Orzeł* (*The Submarine "Eagle,"* 1959, Leonard Buczkowski), about the escape of an interned submarine; *Free City* (Stanisław Różewicz), the story of the Polish postal workers' heroism on the first day of war in Gdańsk (Danzig); and the same director's first novella in his three-part *The Birth Certificate*. The latter portrays September 1939 through child's perspective and introduces an almost archetypal character in Polish cinema, played by Wojciech Siemion: a simple soldier entangled in the meshes of history.[68]

* * *

The release of another film, Andrzej Wajda's *Lotna* (known in English-speaking countries as *Speed*) stirred a heated national debate in Poland about the representation of the military effort in 1939. Wajda's solemn treatment of vital national concerns sometimes works against his films. The accumulation of national symbols and nostalgic images associated with prewar Poland in *Speed*—Wajda's farewell to the Polish romantic mythology—appears almost as a mockery of Polish romantic concerns. Wajda's first film in color narrates the story of a mare named Lotna, which passes from one uhlan (cavalryman) to another during the September campaign. The film also features one of the most discussed scenes in Polish cinema: the Polish cavalry's symbolic attack on the German panzer troops. Especially powerful is an image of a Polish uhlan hitting the barrel of a German tank with a sabre in an act of desperation.

Speed features uhlans, relics of the Polish romantic myth, and symbols of the Polish soldier up until World War II. Commenting on the importance of the mythology of uhlans in Poland, Marian Ursel writes: "The apotheosis of the uhlanship and its features led to the almost mythical cult of this formation. The uhlan himself became the model to be emulated. The year 1939 caused this myth to be turned into ashes by the steel caterpillar treads of German tanks."[69]

Made twenty years after the September campaign of 1939, *Speed* is saturated with images that refer to the national iconography. It resembles a "national chromolithograph" peopled not by full-blooded characters but rather by clichéd figures performing anachronistic rituals. Wajda's film refers to the patriotic paintings by Artur Grottger and Wojciech Kossak, and employs the stereotypical, almost kitschy, emblems of the "old Poland": an old country manor and an equally stereotypical image of a village; a girl from the manor paying farewell to her soldier; gallant uhlans parading to face their death; the typical Polish countryside bathed in gold and green. Alicja Helman's comment on the surreal, bordering on kitschy, symbolism of Wajda's film in her 1959 review fittingly titled "The Sarmatian on a Burning Giraffe,"[70] was in no way isolated. Summarizing the film's critical reception in Poland, Coates writes that the reviewers "repeatedly allege cheapness or vulgarity of symbolisation, indicating the relevance of the category of kitsch, which applies class judgements to forms of the aesthetic that are often mass-produced and described as simplified."[71]

Psychological War Dramas

The war also serves as a point of departure for films focusing on the psychology of their characters. This is especially evident in some of the films of Stanisław Różewicz, Jerzy Kawalerowicz, and Tadeusz Konwicki. Różewicz's *Trzy kobiety* (*Three Women*, 1957) could be considered the continuation of Jakubowska's *The Last Stage*.[72] It is a realistic story of three women of different ages who are liberated from a concentration camp and settle in a small town in the Polish Regained Lands. Różewicz is interested in friendships that survived the harsh reality of the concentration camp but are now tested by everyday life; he examines a difficult return to normality.[73]

Psychological war dramas usually narrate their stories with two planes of action. Set in the present, they stress the effects of the war, the inability to communicate and love due to the war. Memories of the war return as nightmarish flashbacks and prevent burned-out protagonists from completely returning to life. Jerzy Kawalerowicz's *The True End of the Great War* serves as a good example of this narrative strategy. It is a psychological study of a woman, Róża (Lucyna Winnicka), and the two men in her life: her emotionally disturbed husband (a concentration camp survivor) and the man she turned to when she thought that her husband was dead. Róża no longer loves her husband, yet she tries to take care of him out of pure compassion. This situation, hopeless for her and the two men involved, ends with her husband's suicide.

Kawalerowicz's intimate film, made in the spirit of the post-October thaw, breaks with the stylistic monotony of socialist realist works and relies heavily on the use of subjective camera. "The camera seems omnipresent, all knowing, taking often the point of view of one of the characters; the consistently maintained depth of focus gives it an opportunity to display its potential," writes Helman.[74] Kawalerowicz explains that he "wanted to give the film a slow, hopeless rhythm that is the rhythm of the protagonists' lives."[75] The realistic scenes, set in postwar conditions, are interrupted by flashbacks, done in an almost expressionistic manner. In the opening sequence, Róża's reminiscences of a happier past are juxtaposed by her husband's recollections of the death camp. The reality of the camp, portrayed from his point of view, is nightmarish and deformed—a reflection of his suffering of his psychological and physical disintegration.

Tadeusz Konwicki's films also move between the present and the past. He attracted the attention of critics and readers when he detached himself from the socialist realist dogma with his 1956 novel *Rojsty* (*Marshes*), which told the story of the Home Army unit that fights the Germans and then the Soviets. Konwicki's 1958 experimental film, *The Last Day of Summer,* intimate and ascetic in style, deals with his favorite themes: evocations of past times, and the impossibility of overcoming the burden of war. Although the war is not shown directly in this film, it overshadows the action of two characters who meet by chance on an empty Baltic beach. In his next film, *Zaduszki* (*All Souls Day*, 1961), Konwicki discontinues the realistic narrative by including four lengthy flashbacks that deal with the past war. The obsessive memories of Michał (Edmund Fetting) and Wala (Ewa Krzyżewska) are nearly independent filmic novellas within this film. The two protagonists, who are crippled by war experiences, are incapable of forgetting and unable to live in the present. They cannot free themselves from the war, portrayed as a destroyer of happiness, which hangs over them and meddles with their current affairs. Michał's recollections of the past feature a beautiful lieutenant Listek (Elżbieta Czyżewska). She is antiheroic, fragile (emphasized by her oversized uniform and a delicate voice when she makes patriotic speeches), and protected by the entire partisan unit, which is in love with her. When Listek dies an absurd death, she is mourned as a saint or, perhaps, the symbol of a better world.

The Holocaust Dramas

The Polish School period is also abundant with films that specifically refer to the Holocaust.[76] In the early 1960s, Wanda Jakubowska returned to the memories of Polish suffering and resistance at Auschwitz in *Spotkania w mroku (Meetings in the Twilight*, 1960) and *Koniec naszego świata (The End of Our World*, 1964). The same structure (a contemporary incident triggers the flow of past, often suppressed, memories) and the same setting (Auschwitz) are employed in Munk's psychological drama *Pasażerka (The Passenger*, 1963). The motif of Jewish hiding and Polish responses to the Holocaust are present in Wajda's *A Generation* and *Samson* (1961), Różewicz's *The Birth Certificate*, and in two lesser-known films: *White Bear* (Jerzy Zarzycki) and *Naganiacz (The Beater*, aka *Men Hunters*, 1964, Ewa and Czesław Petelski).

The Birth Certificate belongs to a small but prominent group of Polish war films focusing on the plight of children, both of Jewish and Polish origin. Różewicz is not a moralizing director. Instead of criticizing the Nazi German system, he exposes its madness. In the longest, third installment of this three-part film, *Kropla krwi (A Drop of Blood)*, a young Jewish girl, Mirka, is presented with a new birth certificate that says she is a Polish girl, and she is being moved to a provincial Polish orphanage. However, this is not the end of her ordeal. The tension mounts again with the arrival of a Gestapo officer, who is accompanied by a Nazi "racial expert," both in search of Jewish children hiding with false Polish papers. After a short examination by the "expert," Mirka is declared racially fit (having "Nordic characteristics") enough to be sent to a German orphanage. The film ends with a close-up image of Mirka's eyes, perhaps expressing wonder at the bizarre twist of fate.

Among several short films about the Holocaust made during the Polish School period, one deserves particular attention. *Ambulans (Ambulance*, 1961), directed by Janusz Morgenstern, is an outstanding black-and-white film deprived of dialogue. Presented with the Best Short Film Award in 1962 at the San Francisco

International Film Festival, *Ambulance* was made with the participation of some leading contributors to the Polish School, including the cinematographer Jerzy Lipman, the composer Krzysztof Komeda, and the actor Tadeusz Łomnicki, who is credited as the screenwriter.[77]

Morgenstern's film opens with one of Hitler's anti-Jewish speeches, followed by a German military march. The camera, positioned inside a moving truck, portrays a concrete road and the exhaust smoke. After the credits, the ambulance with a Red Cross sign enters a gate leading to a place that looks like a schoolyard surrounded by barbed wire. Watched by their old guardian, a group of children are playing on an almost empty square. Like the children at play, the viewer is also unaware that the Red Cross ambulance, a symbol of safety, help, and rescue, is a gas van—a mobile gas chamber using carbon monoxide to kill unsuspecting victims. The film portrays everyday brutality with the help of images that are suggestive rather than explicit. As the ambulance drives away from the loading zone, the viewer is spared images of the asphyxiated young victims, but strongly reminded of the mass gassings at Auschwitz and other death camps.

The End of Our World, the film Jakubowska considered her best,[78] was made in the mid-1960s, when Auschwitz became widely known in the West as the site of Jewish extermination.[79] Jakubowska's film is based on a novel of the same title published for the first time in 1958 by the writer and communist political activist Tadeusz Hołuj, who is also cast in the film.[80] The film focuses on a former (communist) political prisoner at Auschwitz, Henryk (Lech Skolimowski), whose presence at the Auschwitz-Birkenau State Museum brings back his own camp memories. Unusual for Jakubowska, the initial scenes at Auschwitz resemble the writer Tadeusz Borowski's representation of the camp. The emphasis is on the monstrous aspect of camp life, which would later be more fully developed in *Kornblumenblau* (1989, Leszek Wosiewicz). Jakubowska depicts Henryk's miraculous survival, his brush with death, the help he receives from other inmates (mostly political prisoners), and the change of his camp identity. The second half of the film is more conventional and uses elements of melodrama coupled with the ideology similar to *The Last Stage*. Like in *The Last Stage*, the most important aspect of Jakubowska's film is the protagonist's gradual involvement with the camp's resistance. Henryk becomes a reluctant *Kapo* at the request of other political prisoners. With a hidden camera, he captures images of extermination inside the camp. He even helps the Jewish *Sonderkommando* (Special Commando) to destroy the crematoria, and later he participates in the *Sonderkommando*'s uprising on 7 October 1944. The symbolic image of a communist Pole fighting and saving Jewish insurgents was a distortion of the historical reality, one that both the communist state and Wanda Jakubowska wanted to preserve and elevate.

The issue of "the common Jewish-Polish struggle" is also prominently portrayed in Wajda's second (after *A Generation*) attempt at representing the Holocaust, *Samson* (1961), an adaptation of a novel by a Polish writer of Jewish origin, Kazimierz Brandys. The film's protagonist, Jakub Gold (Serge Merlin), is introduced before the war, unaware of the "hatred that was growing intensely in those days," as the voice-over commentary explains. Attacked by a group of right-wing nationalists, Jakub accidentally kills a fellow student who, in fact, was trying to help him (the student is played by the future film director Andrzej Żuławski—not credited—who assisted Wajda on this film). While serving a prison sentence for his deed, Jakub meets a charismatic communist activist. When German bombs destroy the prison in September 1939, Jakub gets out of jail but quickly finds himself in another form of prison—locked in the Warsaw Ghetto, where he works burying the dead. After the death of his mother, Jakub escapes from the ghetto and hides on the Aryan side, counting on help from various people. The action of a large portion of the film is limited to the claustrophobic, dark cellar—another place where Jakub is "imprisoned." To tell the story about Jewish suffering, Wajda relies heavily on symbolism and Biblical associations, relegating to the margins what was earlier his forte: the historical and social background. Critics, who were previously supportive of Wajda's approach, became reluctant to embrace the abstract situation presented on the screen.

Wajda attributes the departure from Brandys's realistic depiction to his first deployment of anamorphic widescreen (Cinemascope technique).[81] The casting of the French actor Serge Merlin also greatly contributed to the film's overall shape. The way Wójcik frames him (the camera is often placed behind the protagonist) helps to emphasize the "otherness" and isolation of Jakub Gold. With no knowledge of the Polish language, Merlin rarely faces the camera, and talks as if hiding or being afraid to be noticed. Furthermore, the choice of Merlin also forced Wajda to change the original concept of *Samson*. Instead of an athletic, powerful Samson, the Hebrew hero, the viewer watches a character who is slender, intellectual, and full of doubt. Coates is arguably right when he observes that Wajda's *Samson* "represents an uneasy cocktail of communism and existentialism."[82] Wajda's reworking of the Samson myth is in line with the communist ideology with its portrayal of the prewar, bourgeois Poland as the land of anti-Semites and the communists as the only protectors of Jews. The Jewish protagonist becomes a Polish hero thanks to his (accidental in the film) association with the communist cause.

The motif of hiding, common to many Polish Holocaust narratives, for example, in *White Bear*, is presented powerfully in *The Beater*. It focuses on a reluctant Polish helper, the Warsaw Uprising insurgent (Bronisław Pawlik) who hides in the countryside after its tragic failure. Unlike several better-known protagonists of the Polish School period, he is not a heroic figure but rather a worn-out, almost resigned character who does not want to continue fighting and just tries to survive the last winter of the war. Nonetheless, pressed by circumstances beyond his control, Michał helps, albeit unwillingly, a group of Hungarian Jews who escaped from a transport to a concentration camp and are hiding in a nearby forest. The film's climax is a "hunting sequence." The SS officers organize a hunting party near the manor, and Polish villagers are forced to participate as beaters. The hunt for foxes and rabbits quickly turns into a massacre of Jews who, alarmed by the gunshots and the approaching beaters, leave the relative safety of their hidings. The prolonged carnage, without music and featuring only diegetic sounds—bullets, the moans of the dying (both people and animals—is a petrifying experience. The German officers are depicted as if enjoying the shooting regardless of the target, while the camera portrays the horror on the faces of some Polish beaters, the involuntary participants in the killing. Film officials appreciated the film's theme of making difficult moral choices under immense pressure, as revealed by the meeting minutes of the Film Approval Committee (Komisja Kolaudacyjna).[83]

The Holocaust motif is powerful in Andrzej Munk's incomplete *The Passenger*, based on Zofia Posmysz-Piasecka's novel.[84] Munk, a descendant of a Polonized Jewish family from Kraków, survived the occupation in Warsaw, where he did not reveal his Jewish ancestry and worked on the "Aryan side." During the war, he also became a member of the socialist underground (Polish Socialist Party, PPS) and later participated in the Warsaw Uprising. In 1961, Munk was killed in a car accident on the way from Warsaw to the Łódź Film Studio, where he was about to assess the set design for the next part of his *The Passenger*. The project was completed by Munk's friends, including the director Witold Lesiewicz and the writer Wiktor Woroszylski, the latter responsible for the offscreen narration.[85] They edited the existing footage and added a voice-over commentary read by Tadeusz Łomnicki. *The Passenger* premiered on the second anniversary of Munk's death, 20 September 1963. It was presented as an unfinished statement made by the tragically deceased director.

At the center of *The Passenger* is the relationship between a German overseer at Auschwitz-Birkenau, Liza (Aleksandra Śląska), and a Polish inmate, Marta (Anna Ciepielewska). Years after the war, a chance meeting between the two on a luxury liner heading from South America to Europe brings back memories of the suppressed past. The film begins with a series of private photographs introducing Munk at work and in a private setting, which is accompanied by a commentary on the making of the film and on the problems faced by Munk's friends after his premature death. The film proper opens with a frame story taking place on a transatlantic liner. Employing exclusively still photographs, it depicts the chance encounter between Liza and Marta and the threat posed by Marta's presence. The shock of seeing Marta results in a sudden, quick succession of several abrupt, nightmarish, almost hallucinatory widescreen images from Auschwitz that provided a sharp contrast to the film's prologue. The flashback from Auschwitz—the uncontrolled flow of Liza's repressed memories—includes both moving images and archival stills, among them images of naked female prisoners tormented by SS guards and *Kapos*, Alsatian shepherds sitting as if ready to attack, SS dog handlers walking along an electrified barbed wire fence, a group of prisoners pulling a road roller, and a female prisoner being tattooed.

Liza explains her strange behavior to her new husband, Walter, by admitting that she was an overseer in Auschwitz, not an inmate. Liza's attempt at explaining the past to her husband, but also to herself, introduces another flashback, this time much longer and stressing her sense of duty. In a quasi-documentary manner, Krzysztof Winiewicz's camera captures images of the camp after the gassing of one of the transports: the main gate leading to the camp, the railway, the barbed wire fence, belongings left by the victims (children's strollers, suitcases, and clothing). The panning camera stops in front of the crematorium and tilts to reveal heavy black smoke from its chimneys. Liza comments that in Auschwitz-Birkenau, she supervised a gigantic storage space, *Effektenkammer*, where goods seized from killed victims were collected and catalogued, and she tries to distance herself from crimes committed in Auschwitz, although she admits to being a witness of mass killings.

The third flashback reveals Liza's true role in the camp. From behind a fence separating the *Effektenkammer* from the crematorium, she watches the newly arrived Jewish transport walking toward the gas chamber, which is covered in black smoke. She observes two German guards on the roof of the gas chamber. One of them, wearing a gas mask, opens a canister with Zyklon B and methodically dumps it into the killing zone through ventilation openings. Liza's flashback also sheds new light on the relationship between her and Marta, how she tried to control "her prisoner," and Marta's relationship with her fiancée, Tadeusz (Marek Walczewski). The flashback ends with a cut back to the liner, and the narrator concludes in line with the politics of the day (the Berlin Wall that had just being erected), as a warning against West German politics.

The narrative aspect of *The Passenger*—the reliance on flashbacks to tell the story, may be considered Munk's favorite narrative strategy, which he employed in two earlier films. As in *Eroica* and *Bad Luck*, Munk also introduces in *The Passenger* the perspective of a character with whom the viewer cannot identify, an unreliable narrator. The scholar and Auschwitz inmate Bolesław W. Lewicki convincingly argued in his 1968 essay that *The Passenger* functions as a polemic with Jakubowska's *The Last Stage*,[86] and several elements justify such a comparison. Like Jakubowska, Munk decided to shoot his film on location at Auschwitz-Birkenau to enhance verisimilitude (he stayed in the commandant's office), which also had an enormous impact on the film's crew. Like Jakubowska, Munk was surrounded by people who experienced Auschwitz firsthand. In both films, the perpetrator is played by Aleksandra Śląska, and like Marta Weiss in Jakubowska's film, Munk's Marta is a privileged prisoner who performs a similar function in the camp's structure. Both Martas are also part of the resistance (left-wing in Jakubowska's work, unspecified in Munk's film), and they smuggle information about Auschwitz to the outside world. Both have lovers in the camp named Tadeusz (Tadek). Unlike Marta Weiss, Marta in *The Passenger* is Polish, and there is no indication that this was planned otherwise at an earlier stage. Unlike Jakubowska, Munk relies on diegetic sounds of the camp and on the almost surreal, yet historically accurate, diegetic music—for example, the march from Georges Bizet's *Carmen*, which is played by the Auschwitz orchestra near the gate leading to the camp. Like Jakubowska, in *The Passenger*, Munk de-emphasizes the issue of nationality. His film features images of the Jewish transport walking toward gas chambers and the search for a hidden Jewish newborn in Liza's *kommando*, but its focus is on political prisoners, mostly Poles. Jews are relegated to the role of passive victims. Munk, arguably, was interested in a universal dimension of his story—hence the lack of emphasis on the question of nationality of Auschwitz prisoners.

The uncompleted, fragmentary *The Passenger* "resembles antic sculptures damaged by the passing of time," writes Tadeusz Szyma.[87] The film's unfinished status helps to make this film complex, mysterious, and multilayered. Some scholars, for example, Stuart Liebman, regard the film's unfinished nature as its weakness ("merely a torso"), and the relationship between the prisoner and the overseer "seems naïve and contrived."[88] Regardless of the problematic portrayal of the relationship between the Auschwitz perpetrator and the victim, however, the strength of Munk's film lies in its powerful camp imagery, for example, a "love scene" featuring a fragment from a violin concerto by Johann Sebastian Bach performed by the camp orchestra. Separated by SS guards, Marta and Tadeusz exchange glances and move slowly toward each other with the help of other prisoners. The sudden whistles and sounds of a transport train approaching the Auschwitz ramp mark the intrusion of brutal reality. The camp concert is adjourned, and the guards anxiously rush to perform their duties.

Beyond the War

To limit the study of the Polish School only to the films that deal with World War II and the realistic works portraying Poland during the de-Stalinization period is to neglect the most important aspect of post-October cinema in Poland: its diversity. Children's films that also targeted adult audiences—such as Janusz Nasfeter's (1920–1998) *Małe dramaty* (*Small Dramas*, 1960), *Kolorowe pończochy* (*Colored Stockings*, 1960), and *Mój stary* (*My Old Man*, 1962) and Jan Batory's *Odwiedziny prezydenta* (*The Visit of the President*, 1962)—were noticed by Polish critics and received awards at international festivals. Another film by Batory, *O dwóch takich, co ukradli księżyc* (*The Two Who Stole the Moon*, 1962), an adaptation of Kornel Makuszyński's novel, is also of interest for other reasons. This entertaining film narrates the story of twin troublemakers who steal a moon in order to profit from its sale, and features two future influential Polish politicians: Lech Kaczyński, who served as the president of Poland from 2005 until his tragic death in a plane crash in 2010, and Jarosław Kaczyński, who was a Polish prime minister (2006–2007) and is now the party chairman of the ruling party, Prawo i Sprawiedliwość (Law and Justice; PiS).

This period is also marked by the international success achieved by Polish animators. The Animated Film Studio (Studio Filmów Rysunkowych) in Bielsko-Biała was established in 1956, followed by the Short Film Studio (Studio Miniatur Filmowych) in Kraków in 1966. Since 1961, the Kraków Film Festival, one of the world's oldest and most important festivals of short films, provided the venue for animated films. Relatively free from commercial restrictions, Polish filmmakers produced some truly unique works. In the 1960s, several artistic personalities, among them Walerian Borowczyk, Jan Lenica, Daniel Szczechura, Mirosław Kijowicz, and Witold Giersz, received awards at international film festivals, and critics commonly used the term "Polish School of Animation" to define this golden era of Polish animation. The animators were mostly trained at the Łódź Film School and the Academy of Fine Arts (Akademia Sztuk Pięknych) in Warsaw. The techniques employed by Polish animators and the stories they told varied significantly. Borowczyk and Lenica, for example, relied on a cutout technique to produce the absurdist spirit in animation. These two renowned animators, illustrators, and poster designers made together a series of animated short films that won international acclaim, including *Był sobie raz* (*Once Upon a Time*, 1957), *Nagrodzone uczucia* (*Love Requited*, 1957), and *Dom* (*House*, 1958). Their films were characterized by collages of geometrical forms; the absurdist *House* employed cutouts, pixilation, and object animation. Later, both animators continued their careers in France. Lenica made his first solo film, *Monsier Tete* (1959), narrated by Eugene Ionesco. He made his next films in France, Poland, the United States, and Germany. In Poland, he produced a pastiche of Henryk Sienkiewicz's novella *Nowy Janko Muzykant* (*The New Janko Musician*, 1960) and *Labirynt* (*Labyrinth*, 1963), arguably his greatest film, a political Kafkaesque animation that won the highest awards at several prestigious film festivals. Borowczyk maintained his reputation as a leading animator in France, where he made *Les Astronautes* (*Astronauts*, 1959) with Chris Marker, before switching to live narrative films.[89]

Political references permeated most films made behind the Iron Curtain, including the animated films, but were particularly visible in Kijowicz's later politically subversive films, which also offered philosophical reflection; he became the leading exponent of what Polish critics labeled the philosophical brand of Polish animation. Similar allusions to the absurdities of the communist reality, coupled with sarcastic humor, can be seen in films by Szczechura, such as *Maszyna* (*The Machine*, 1961) and *Fotel* (*The Armchair*, 1963). Other animators, for example, Giersz, relied on painterly associations in films such as *Mały western* (*Little Western*, 1960) and *Czerwone i czarne* (*Red and Black*, 1963).

Polish documentaries also had success at international film festivals, in particular films about the war and the Holocaust. Kurt Weber's *Pod jednym niebem* (*Under This Same Sky*, 1955), which features images of the hopeful postwar reality in Warsaw juxtaposed with documentary images of the Warsaw Ghetto, won awards at Karlovy Vary and Mannheim. Perhaps better known internationally is *Requiem dla 500 000* (*Requiem for 500,000* (1963), Jerzy Bossak and Wacław Kaźmierczak's compilation documentary relying on the surviving visual materials about the Warsaw Ghetto that were produced by the Germans. This chronological account of the annihilation of Polish Jewry won awards at Kraków and Florence. Another acclaimed film, *Powszedni dzień gestapowca Szmidta* (*An Ordinary Day of Szmidt, the Gestapo Man*, 1963, Jerzy Ziarnik), documents German atrocities looking at hundreds of photographs taken by the Gestapo officer and left in his apartment after his escape in 1945.

Many celebrated documentaries were, nonetheless, devoid of politics. A unique documentary by Jerzy Hoffman and Edward Skórzewski, *Pamiątka z Kalwarii* (*A Souvenir from Calvary*, 1958), winner of the International Short Film Festival Oberhausen in 1966, captures images of a pilgrimage to the sanctuary at Kalwaria Zebrzydowska. Arguably, *Muzykanci* (*Sunday Musicians*, aka *The Musicians*, 1960), one of the canonical Polish documentaries directed by Kazimierz Karabasz (1930–), remains best known outside Poland.[90] This nine-minute film captures the rehearsal of an amateur brass band established by older male tram workers in the Łódź. It starts with a series of fixed shots of the band members at work in the factory, while the soundtrack is filled with industrial noises. Later, led by an old conductor, the men are practicing in the rehearsal room. Karabasz favors simplicity paired with a meticulous observation of the subject: the camera only reveals reality, which forces it to speak for itself. Faces in close-ups tell the whole story without the need for commentary or dialogue. The film received several awards, including the Grand Prix at the International Short Film Festival Oberhausen in 1961. It also was the first winner at the inaugural Kraków Film Festival in 1961. Władysław Ślesicki (1927–2008) deservedly received similar acclaim. His documentary *Płyną tratwy* (*Rafts Are Floating*, aka *Still Floating*, 1962), a lyrical film about a youth from a village joining the local raftsmen, won the Kraków Film Festival and the festival in Venice. Ślesicki followed this success with several films that received international honors: *Wśród ludzi* (*Among People*, 1963), *Zanim opadną liście* (*Before the Leaves Fall*, 1964), and *Rodzina człowiecza* (*The Family of Man*, 1966). Critics praised Ślesicki's predilection for poetic images of people living close to nature and compared his style with Robert Flaherty.

* * *

The year 1960 marks the production of the first postwar historical epic, *Teutonic Knights* (aka *Black Cross* and *Knights of the Teutonic Order,* Aleksander Ford), an adaptation of Henryk Sienkiewicz's novel of the same title, published for the first time in 1900. This widescreen film in Eastmancolor (cinematography by Mieczysław Jahoda), the first of its kind in Poland, had fourteen million viewers in the first four years of its release and was exported to forty-six countries.[91] According to figures from 1987, *Teutonic Knights* remains the most popular film screened in Poland, with almost thirty-two million viewers, ahead of two other Sienkiewicz adaptations: the children's film *W pustyni i w puszczy* (*In Desert and Wilderness,* 1973, Władysław Ślesicki), with 30.6 million viewers, and another historical epic, *Potop* (*The Deluge,* 1974, Jerzy Hoffman), with 27.5 million viewers.[92]

The epic scope of Ford's *Teutonic Knights* had been, according to a local reviewer, "the crowning of our achievements to develop the Polish film industry, the evidence of a certain maturity in the sphere of production and organization."[93] At the center of Ford's film is the 1410 defeat of the Order of the Teutonic Knights, led by Grand Master Ulrich von Jungingen (who fell on the battlefield), by the Polish-Lithuanian forces, led by King Władysław Jagiełło. The Battle of Grunwald (aka Tanneberg), one of the biggest medieval armed encounters, marked the decline of the powerful order, which never recovered from the defeat. Ford's film combines a melodramatic love story with dynamic, often spectacular, action sequences, such as the fifteen-minute climactic battle, set against the backdrop of the military and political conflict.

The fact that the film production occurred 550 years after the battle, and almost one thousand years after the baptism of Poland (966), certainly had major political relevance. Like Sienkiewicz's novel, it reinforced images of a heroic past and functioned as "the national remedy in all colors."[94] Ford's film was also a reminder of Germany's eastward expansionism throughout history. Its black-and-white version of the past and its crude stereotyping (noble Poles fighting the corrupt and cruel Teutonic Knights) referred not only to the medieval context but also to the tense postwar relations between Poland and West Germany.

Another film, *Ewa Wants to Sleep,* directed by Tadeusz Chmielewski (1927–), became the second successful Polish postwar comedy after *Treasure.* Unlike *Treasure, Ewa Wants to Sleep* offers absurdist, grotesque, situational humor and lyricism in the spirit of René Clair, a director highly regarded in Poland. The influence

Figure 5.3 (From the left) Krzysztof Komeda, Tadeusz Łomnicki, and Roman Polański in Andrzej Wajda's *Innocent Sorcerers* (1960). Screenshot by the author.

of Clair's early sound period films (for example, *Le Million*, 1931) is visible in Chmielewski's balancing of fantasy and fact, as well as in his light and witty treatment of situations and protagonists. The simple story concerns a young woman, Ewa (Barbara Kwiatkowska), who comes to a strange town where everyone seems to be either police officers or thieves and are busy playing their games. This surreal town offers Ewa no place to sleep, and this problem of having no place to spend the night is at the center of Chmielewski's comedy. Although saturated with thinly veiled references to Polish reality, this film belongs to a group of the first postwar Polish pictures that were produced for pure entertainment. They include later comedies by Chmielewski and a series of films starring Tadeusz Fijewski as Anatol, beginning with *Kapelusz pana Anatola* (*The Hat of Mr. Anatol*, 1957, Jan Rybkowski).[95]

During this time there were also the first films about the young generation that did not refer directly to politics or social problems: *Do widzenia, do jutra* (*See You Tomorrow*, 1960, Janusz Morgenstern) and *Niewinni czarodzieje* (*Innocent Sorcerers*, 1960, Andrzej Wajda). Both featured jazz scores by Krzysztof Komeda (1931–1969) and tried to introduce new lyrical tone to contemporary films.

Jerzy Kawalerowicz

Two internationally known, stylistically refined films by Kawalerowicz, *Pociąg* (*Night Train*; aka *Baltic Express*, 1959) and *Mother Joan of the Angels* (1961), place themselves outside of mainstream Polish cinema, or at least the kind of cinema praised by local critics during the Polish School period. Both films received numerous awards, including the Georges Méliès Award, and Lucyna Winnicka's role in *Night Train* earned her the Best Actress Award at the 1959 Venice Film Festival. Kawalerowicz also won a Silver Palm at the 1961 Cannes Film Festival for *Mother Joan of the Angels*.

The protagonists of *Night Train*, Marta (Lucyna Winnicka) and Jerzy (Leon Niemczyk), are forced to share a compartment in an overnight train heading for a Baltic resort. Both characters are feeling lonely and confused: Marta wants to break up with her lover (Zbigniew Cybulski), who follows her onto the train; Jerzy is a surgeon who blames himself for the death of a patient on the operating table. The film becomes a murder mystery when an afternoon newspaper reports the case of a wife murdered by her husband; Jerzy's nervousness makes him a possible suspect. The film's action develops slowly and is mostly restricted to a train compartment, until the police board the train to search for the suspected murderer. The chase sequence, as police and passengers try to apprehend the murderer, interrupts the rhythm of the film and temporarily moves the action out of the train. The capture of the terrified murderer (which clears Jerzy from suspicion) is neither the climax nor the finale of the film. The train continues its unhurried journey and stops at its destination without any major dramatic shift. The trip ends as it began—in normality.

Kawalerowicz's film defies simple interpretations. Its narrative barely sketches the characters' psychology (similar to one's actual knowledge in comparable circumstances), yet the characters are intriguing and the story involving, almost suspenseful. *Night Train* is a film with Hitchcockian overtones. With the help of his cinematographer, Jan Laskowski, Kawalerowicz fills the story with tension and nuance with his careful composition of frame. "Through setting, rhythm, pace, lighting, physicality, in short, with his mise en scène Kawalerowicz placed himself among the great directors of Europe," write Michałek and Turaj.[96] The limited space of the action does not pose problems for the director. While the background is moving (images behind the train windows), the center of the action remains comparatively motionless. The camera captures the gestures and behaviors of the two main characters and other passengers on the crowded train. Kawalerowicz explains: "In *Night Train* I split, if I can say so, the story of one melodrama onto several characters; the yearning for feelings was granted to all the characters in the film."[97] Their expectations and unstated desires are matched by the rhythm of the moving train, the opening and closing of compartment doors, the overall monotony of the travel.

According to Helman, *Night Train* introduced the "motif of a woman who feels foreign in a world ruled by men, a woman who is not understood, and who attempts to slip away from men's hates and loves, both of which are painful."[98] This motif is also discernible in *Mother Joan of the Angels*, the film loosely based on the well-known story about possessed nuns at a seventeenth-century monastery in Loudun, France—also the subject of Ken Russell's film *The Devils* (1971). Kawalerowicz's work is an adaptation of Jarosław Iwaszkiewicz's short story set in eighteenth-century eastern Poland. This classic tale about demonic possession presents two main characters: Mother Joan (Lucyna Winnicka), the supposedly possessed mother superior, and Father Suryn (Mieczysław Voit), a young ascetic and devout exorcist. The latter is sent to the convent after one of his predecessors was burned at the stake for his involvement with Mother Joan. Others unsuccessfully try to free Mother Joan from her demons (she admits to being possessed by several demons, and she can even name them). To understand the nature of evil, Suryn visits the rabbi (also played by Voit). The exorcist is, however, unable to free Mother Joan, and the possessed nuns from demons. In the course of time, psychological tension (and perhaps a physical attraction) develops between Joan and Suryn. When Suryn exhausts the traditional methods (prescribed rituals, prayers, self-flagellation), he consciously commits a horrid crime (the killing of two stable boys) to liberate Mother Joan and the convent's sisters from demons and place them under his care.

The ascetic mise-en-scène of Kawalerowicz's film indicates the characters' psychology. Jerzy Wójcik's photography, with a clear contrast between black-and-white elements within the frame, portrays a barren, inhospitable landscape with only four buildings. The bright convent on the hill and the dark inn at its bottom play a crucial role in the film's concept. The convent is inhabited by the white figures of the nuns, whirling during the devil's activities, their robes flowing in a carefully choreographed manner. The whiteness of the nuns' robes is juxtaposed with the dark robes of the exorcists and the black or shadowy background. The carefully composed static images, with the occasional vertical and horizontal movement of the camera, capture the characters in the center of the frame.[99]

Despite its impressive formal beauty, the release of *Mother Joan of the Angels* during a decade-long *Wielka Nowenna* (religious preparations leading to the 1966 anniversary of the baptism of Poland)[100] was met by an unprecedented reaction from the hierarchy of the Catholic Church. The Polish Episcopate issued an official protest against the release of Kawalerowicz's film that was addressed to, among others, the Polish Ministry of Culture and Arts and the attorney general's office. The church strongly objected to the fact that the film includes "blasphemous scenes," is "saturated with dirty suggestions and filthy allusions," and "insults the religious beliefs" of the great majority of Polish people. Interestingly, the request to ban this film from Polish screens also included a remark about its "attractive artistic form," which "makes the matters worse."[101]

Up to the late 1950s, Polish films rarely dealt with religious issues. Film authorities, following directives from the Communist Party, generally avoided antagonizing the only real noncommunist political player in Poland: the church. During this period, there was little room for religion in the communist-run Polish film industry, although images of religious ceremonies and clergy appeared in several documentaries, including early films about the liberation of Majdanek and other Nazi German camps. Generally, religion and the clergy were portrayed as historical remnants, and religious people as trying to adapt to the new political situation. In October 1956, the new communist leader Władysław Gomułka made some positive gestures toward the Catholic Church, including the release of Cardinal Stefan Wyszyński from prison. In 1966, the celebrations of the millennium of Poland's baptism marked the height of the ideological battle between the state and the church. Reflecting this growing tension, several films released since the early 1960s dealt, often critically, with different aspects of religiosity. These include *Milczenie* (*Silence*, 1963, Kazimierz Kutz), the story of an elderly small-town priest who is weak and lonely among his parishioners, and *Drewniany różaniec* (*The Wooden Rosary*, 1965, Ewa and Czesław Petelski), a dark picture of a hypocritical prewar orphanage for girls run by nuns.[102]

Roman Polański

The first feature-length film by Roman Polański, *Knife in the Water*, which was released exactly one year after the premiere of *Mother Joan of the Angels*, offended political leaders and film authorities because of its cosmopolitan and apolitical nature. Władysław Gomułka, the First Secretary of the Polish United Workers' Party, officially condemned the film in August 1963 at the plenary assembly of the PZPR's Central Committee.[103] Like Kawalerowicz in *Night Train*, Polański employs elements of the thriller genre, avoids political or social commitment, and defies the typical communist expectations of a work of art. The film's success in the West (including the first Polish nomination for an Academy Award in 1963) was treated with suspicion in Poland and only increased the hostility toward its maker.[104]

With *Knife in the Water* Polański wanted to make a film "rigorously cerebral, precisely engineered, almost formalist." As he further explains in his autobiography: "It started out as a straightforward thriller: a couple aboard a small yacht take on a passenger who disappears in mysterious circumstances. From the first, the story concerned the interplay of antagonistic personalities within a confined space."[105] The story, limited to three characters and twenty-four hours, concerns a well-to-do Warsaw sports journalist, Andrzej (Leon Niemczyk), and his younger wife, Krystyna (Jolanta Umecka), who invite a young hitchhiker (Zygmunt Malanowicz) to a yachting weekend. The bulk of the film's action is then confined to a small boat in the Masurian Lakes, where a fierce rivalry develops between the worldly journalist and the insecure hitchhiker who challenges him. Often framed between the two men, Krystyna serves as their "prize," and is perfectly aware of her role in the conflict. The jazz score of Krzysztof Komeda, who also worked on Polański's short films, and the photography of Jerzy Lipman help to create the vibrating, jazzy tempo and mood.[106]

Many Polish critics look at Polański's film through the prism of the director's personality and biographical legend, a critical pattern in the West.[107] Polański was born in Paris to a family of Polonized Jews who returned to Poland two years before World War II. He survived the war by escaping from the Kraków Ghetto and hiding in the Polish countryside (his mother died in a concentration camp). His career started with a series of surrealistic and grotesque short films, including *Dwaj ludzie z szafą* (*Two Men and a Wardrobe*, 1958), *Gdy spadają anioły* (*When Angels Fall*, 1959), and *Ssaki* (*Mammals*, 1962). In his arguably best-known film, *Two Men and a Wardrobe*, produced by the Łódź Film School, two mysterious men carrying a large wardrobe emerge from the sea, encounter a world that is hostile to them, and eventually return with the wardrobe beneath the waves from which they came. The two good-natured, albeit somewhat grotesque, men are portrayed clearly as outcasts in a town that is reluctant to accept them. Given its open, multifaceted structure and ambiguity associated with the two characters, Polański's film is sometimes discussed as featuring two Holocaust survivors who are carrying their burden in the form of a wardrobe and return to their hometown to face a crowd of hostile inhabitants, their former neighbors.[108]

The End of the Formation

Numerous voices in recent Polish scholarship favor the assertion that the decline of the Polish School was not "natural"—that it was not related to the exhaustion of its themes and the manner in which they were presented—but rather that it had to do with the pressure of politics and the increasing conflict between the filmmakers and the communist regime.[109] The demands for greater independence and softer censorship for the film units were incompatible with the Communist Party's attempts to regain total control over the filmmaking process, which had been characteristic of the pre-October period.

Toward the end of the 1950s, communist authorities had been sending many signals that the relative freedom of expression would no longer be tolerated. The party was disappointed with the messages and themes permeating Polish films and with the "westernization" of Polish filmmakers. As a result, the autonomy of film units was gradually limited, and stricter control of films was administratively implemented. Although the Main Office for Control of the Press, Publications, and Public Performances (Główny Urząd Kontroli Prasy Publikacji i Widowisk) was responsible for media censorship in general, censorship was frequently much harsher at the film units level. The Committee for Evaluation of Scripts (Komisja Ocen Scenariuszy) was the first major obstacle for a film project to be approved.

The restrictive policy of the Communist Party can be observed toward some of the representative films of the Polish School. The most frequent way to punish the makers of "unwanted films" was the limited distribution of their works (as in the case of *Nobody Is Calling*, *Winter Twilight*, and *The End of the Night*). Another form of punishment was delaying the premiere of some films, and in extreme instances even banning them, as was the case with *Ósmy dzień tygodnia* (*The Eighth Day of the Week*, Aleksander Ford). This Polish–West German production, based on Marek Hłasko's story and starring Zbigniew Cybulski and the German Sonja Ziemann, was made in 1958 and distributed in Germany (as *Der Achte Wochentag*); it did not premiere in Poland until as late as 1983.[110] The third practice, which reflects the suspicion, as well as the aversion, of the communist leaders toward some of the films, was the reluctance to send some of them to international film festivals.[111]

The Resolution of the Central Committee Secretariat of the Polish United Workers' Party, issued in June 1960, marked the actual end of the Polish School.[112] In this document, the communist authorities criticized the pessimism of many

Polish films, their lack of compliance with the party line, and the strong role played by Western cinema in Poland. As a remedy, the resolution imposed stricter limits and more rigorous criteria on films imported from the West. It also postulated that films purchased from other socialist countries, chiefly from the Soviet Union, should be privileged. As a result, from 1961 to 1969, the number of films from the Soviet Bloc countries increased to 57 percent (for 35mm films) and 75 percent (for 16mm films).[113] This same party document also postulated making political and educational films needed in the process of "building socialism," films that reflected current problems from the socialist perspective, and works inspired by the "progressive tendencies" in Polish history. The document also referred to the role of "socialist film criticism." It recommended increasing the number of pro-party writers and party functionaries in the processes of screenwriting and script approval, and proposed to develop "socialist entertainment films." The intentions behind the latter directive, which were fully implemented in the 1960s, were twofold: to neutralize the popularity of foreign "bourgeois" films and to turn Polish society's attention away from the pressing economic problems experienced under Władysław Gomułka's regime.

The Polish School began to lose its impetus in the early 1960s. Although political developments once again defined the Polish cinema, nonpolitical reasons also contributed to this decline. In September 1961, Andrzej Munk died tragically while making his film, *The Passenger*. Andrzej Wajda began making films abroad: in 1962, *Sibirska Ledi Makbet (Siberian Lady Macbeth*, aka *Fury Is a Woman)*, produced in Yugoslavia; an episode in France for *Love at Twenty*; then, in 1967, *Gates to Paradise* in England, the latter never released in cinemas. Additionally, a group of young filmmakers emerged for whom the point of reference was no longer local history or other concerns associated with the Polish School. For example, the first films by Roman Polański and Jerzy Skolimowski were similar to current international cinema and influenced by their own personal experiences. Polański migrated to France after making *Knife in the Water*, his only full-length film made in Poland.[114]

Several films made in the mid-1960s, however, returned to Polish history and the moral dilemmas of World War II. These films, including *Salto* (*Somersault*, 1965, Tadeusz Konwicki), debunk the Polish war mythology and focus on the impossibility of freeing oneself from the shadow of the war, as in *Szyfry* (*Cyphers*, aka *Codes*, 1966. Wojciech J. Has) and *Powrót na ziemię* (*Return to Earth*, 1967, Stanisław Jędryka). Another prominent group of films refers directly to the war: moral dilemmas of the underground fighters in *Stajnia na Salwatorze* (*Stall on Salvador*, 1967, Paweł

Komorowski) and the tragedy of September 1939 in *Westerplatte* (1967, Stanisław Różewicz). The main preoccupations of the Polish School also return in some films made in the 1970s, for instance, in *Hubal* (1973, Bohdan Poręba). The real end of the Polish School, and the farewell to its poetics, is probably marked by *Pierścionek z orłem w koronie* (*The Ring with a Crowned Eagle*, 1992, Andrzej Wajda), the film that examines issues first explored in *Ashes and Diamonds*.[115]

Notes

1. Aleksander Jackiewicz, "Prawo do eksperymentu," *Przegląd Kulturalny* 51–52 (1954), quoted in Stanisław Ozimek, "Konfrontacje z Wielką Wojną," in *Historia filmu polskiego 1957–1961*, vol. 4, ed. Jerzy Toeplitz (Warsaw: Wydawnictwa Artystyczne i Filmowe), 14.
2. Stanisław Ozimek, "Spojrzenie na szkołę polską," in Toeplitz, *Historia filmu polskiego 1957–1961*, 201.
3. Ibid., 206–7.
4. Tadeusz Lubelski, *Strategie autorskie w polskim filmie fabularnym lat 1945–1961* (Kraków: Wydawnictwo Uniwersytetu Jagiellońskiego, 1992), 113–93; Bolesław Michałek and Frank Turaj, *The Modern Cinema of Poland* (Bloomington: Indiana University Press, 1988), 19–34; David A. Cook, *A History of Narrative Film* (New York: Norton, 1996), 684.
5. Ozimek, "Spojrzenie na szkołę polską," 205–6.
6. Aleksander Jackiewicz, "Kordianowskie i plebejskie tradycje w filmie polskim," *Kino* 11 (1969): 2–11; Aleksander Jackiewicz, "Powrót Kordiana: Tradycja romantyczna w filmie polskim," *Kwartalnik Filmowy* 4 (1961): 23–37.
7. Tadeusz Miczka, "Cinema under Political Pressure: A Brief Outline of Authorial Roles in Polish Post-war Feature Film 1945–1995," *Kinema* 4 (1995): 37. The term "psychotherapy" had been also used consciously by some filmmakers, for instance, by Wajda, who stated that Polish filmmakers "approach their work seriously, as a kind of psychotherapy." Stanisław Janicki, *Polscy twórcy filmowi o sobie* (Warsaw: Wydawnictwa Artystyczne i Filmowe, 1962), 84.
8. Marek Hendrykowski, "Polska szkoła filmowa jako formacja artystyczna," in *"Szkoła polska": Powroty*, ed. Ewelina Nurczyńska-Fidelska and Bronisława Stolarska (Łódź: Wydawnictwo Uniwersytetu Łódzkiego, 1998), 9.
9. Ibid., 10–11.
10. Ewelina Nurczyńska-Fidelska, "'Szkoła' czy autorzy? Uwagi na marginesie doświadczeń polskiej historii filmu," in Nurczyńska-Fidelska and Stolarska, *"Szkoła polska,"* 30–31.
11. Andrzej Munk and the screenwriter Jerzy Stefan Stawiński were born in 1921, Jerzy Kawalerowicz in 1922, Stanisław Różewicz in 1924, Wojciech J. Has in 1925,

Tadeusz Konwicki and Andrzej Wajda in 1926, and Kazimierz Kutz in 1929. The term *Kolumbowie* (Columbuses) comes from the celebrated novel by Roman Bratny, *Kolumbowie rocznik 20* (*Columbuses Born in 1920*), published for the first time in Warsaw in 1957. The novel was adapted in 1970 as a popular television series, *Kolumbowie* (five episodes), directed by Janusz Morgenstern.

12. Maria Janion, "Jeruzalem Słoneczna i Zaklęty Krąg," *Kwartalnik Filmowy* 17 (1997): 5.
13. Stalinism was unavailable to filmmakers because of censorship. One may speculate that perhaps another reason was the involvement of some of the filmmakers with the socialist realist dogma—they would have to deal with their own fascination with Stalinism. For instance, Andrzej Munk, who later made seminal Polish School films, started his career at the beginning of the 1950s with several documentaries made in the spirit of socialist realism. They include, among others, *Zaczęło się w Hiszpanii* (*It Started in Spain*, 1950), *Kierunek Nowa Huta* (*Direction: Nowa Huta*, 1951), and *Pamiętniki chłopów* (*Peasant Diaries*, 1953).
14. The importance of Polish literature as a source for Polish films is discussed in the context of postwar cinema by, among others, Marek Hendrykowski, "Zagadnienie kontekstu literackiego filmu na przykładzie polskiej szkoły filmowej," in *Film polski wobec innych sztuk*, ed. Alicja Helman and Alina Madej (Katowice: Wydawnictwo Uniwersytetu Śląskiego, 1979), 44–60; Wojciech Soliński, "Podłoże literackie filmów szkoły polskiej," in *Polska Szkoła Filmowa: Poetyka i tradycja*, ed. Jan Trzynadlowski (Wrocław: Ossolineum, 1976), 31–39; Maryla Hopfinger, "Adaptacje utworów literackich w polskim filmie okresu powojennego," in *Problemy socjologii literatury*, ed. Janusz Sławiński (Wrocław: Ossolineum, 1971), 467–89.
15. Reflecting on Jerzy Stefan Stawiński's personal experiences, described in his novels and short stories published since 1952, Wajda's *Kanal* (1957) and Munk's *Eroica* (1958) and *Bad Luck* (1960) brought to light the unrepresented fate of the Home Army (AK) members. Stawiński also wrote several other notable films produced during this period, such as *Man on the Tracks* (1957, Munk) and *The Teutonic Knights* (1960, Aleksander Ford). In 1964, Stawiński made his directorial debut, *Rozwodów nie będzie* (*No More Divorces*, 1964), followed by a series of popular psychological comedies, including *Pingwin* (*Penguin*, 1965) and *Urodziny Matyldy* (*Matilda's Birthday*, 1975). In addition, during his multifaceted career Stawiński acted as a literary director of several film units: Kamera (1957–1965), Panorama (1972–1974), and Iluzjon (1977–1981). See Barbara Giza, *Do filmu trafiłem przypadkiem* (Warsaw: Trio, 2007), a book-length interview with Jerzy Stefan Stawiński; Barbara Giza, *Stawiński i wojna: Reprezentacje doświadczenia jako podróż autobiograficzna* (Warsaw: Wyższa Szkoła Psychologii Społecznej / Trio, 2012).
16. The concept of film units goes back to the ideas propagated before the war by the Society for the Promotion of Film Art (START). Before 1955, there were unsuccessful attempts to create film units. For example, three such units were founded in 1948 in order to stimulate film production: Blok, managed by Aleksander Ford; Zespół

Autorów Filmowych (ZAF), by Wanda Jakubowska; and Warszawa, by Ludwik Starski. They were disbanded in 1949.
17. I refer to data in Edward Zajiček, *Poza ekranem: Kinematografia polska 1918-1991* (Warsaw: Filmoteka Narodowa and Wydawnictwa Artystyczne i Filmowe, 1992), 142 and 202.
18. Jerzy Toeplitz, "Drogi rozwoju kinematografii," in Toeplitz, *Historia filmu polskiego 1957-1961*, 381-83, and 388.
19. Ewa Gębicka, "Sieć kin i rozpowszechnianie filmów," in *Encyklopedia kultury polskiej XX wieku: Film i kinematografia*, ed. Edward Zajiček (Warsaw: Instytut Kultury and Komitet Kinematografii, 1994), 436.
20. Jerzy Płażewski, "Film zagraniczny w Polsce," in Zajiček, *Encyklopedia kultury polskiej XX wieku*, 341.
21. Edward Zajiček, "Szkoła polska: Uwarunkowania organizacyjne i gospodarcze," in Nurczyńska-Fidelska and Stolarska, *"Szkoła polska,"* 177 and 180. For example, *Ewa Wants to Sleep* had 3.6 million viewers; *Answer to Violence*, 3.8 million; and *Ashes and Diamonds*, 3.4 million.
22. Toeplitz, "Drogi rozwoju kinematografii," 388 and 417.
23. Bolesław Michałek, "Polska przygoda neorealizmu," *Kino* 1 (1975): 30.
24. In an interview accompanying the 2005 Criterion edition of *A Generation*, titled *Andrzej Wajda: On Becoming a Filmmaker*, Wajda stresses that it was not his intention to caricature the Home Army and blames his lack of knowledge and limited experience for such a portrayal.
25. Bolesław Sulik, "Introduction," in *Ashes and Diamonds, Kanal, A Generation: Three Films*, by Andrzej Wajda (London: Lorrimer, 1973), 12.
26. For more detailed discussion of *A Generation* in the context of Polish cinematic responses to the Holocaust, see Marek Haltof, *Polish Film and the Holocaust: Politics and Memory* (New York: Berghahn Books, 2012), 78–84.
27. Ibid., 13.
28. Aleksander Jackiewicz, in a review of *The End of the Night* titled "Neorealizm Polski" (Polish neorealism), stated that this modest film fully implemented the neorealist tenets for the first time in Polish cinema. Another critic, Juliusz Kydryński, compared this film with *Blackboard Jungle* (1955, Richard Brooks), then not shown in Poland. Lubelski, *Strategie autorskie*, 123.
29. *The End of the Night* is truly a cooperative effort. In addition to the three directors (Julian Dziedzina, Paweł Komorowski, and Walentyna Uszycka), it has six screenwriters (including Professor Antoni Bohdziewicz of the Łódź Film School and the writer Marek Hłasko—the symbol of the post–Polish October literature), and three cinematographers (including Jerzy Wójcik, the cinematographer of *Ashes and Diamonds*, *Nobody Is Calling*, and *Mother Joan of the Angels*).
30. Bohdan Poręba (1934-2014), the director chiefly known for his 1973 film *Hubal*, discussed in the next chapter, also made two other noteworthy films during the Polish School period: *Droga na zachód* (*The Road West*, 1961), about the last days

of World War II, and *Daleka jest droga (Far Is the Road*, 1963), about a Polish officer returning after the war from Scotland to Poland.
31. See Andrzej Szpulak, "Czas przeobrażeń 1956–1960," in *Historia polskiego filmu dokumentalnego (1945–2014)*, ed. Małgorzata Hendrykowska (Poznań: Wydawnictwo Naukowe Uniwersytetu im. Adama Mickiewicza, 2015), 87–148.
32. Ewelina Nurczyńska-Fidelska, "Czarny realizm: O stylu i jego funkcji w filmach nurtu współczesnego," in Nurczyńska-Fidelska and Stolarska, "*Szkoła polska*," 33–47.
33. Ibid., 38.
34. Czesław Petelski (1922–1996) and Ewa Petelska (Poleska, 1920–2013), a married couple working together on most of their films, also worked together on *Damned Roads*. Although only Czesław Petelski is credited as the director, Ewa Petelska, who gave birth at that time, was involved in directing interior scenes. Łukasz Figielski and Bartosz Michalak, *Prywatna historia kina polskiego* (Gdańsk: słowo/obraz terytoria, 2006), 140.
35. Critics often compare this film to *Le salaire de la peur (The Wages of Fear*, 1953, Henri-Georges Clouzot), popular on Polish screens since its 1955 premiere.
36. Quoted in Stanisław Ozimek, "Od wojny w dzień powszedni," in Toeplitz, *Historia filmu polskiego 1957–1961*, 139.
37. Janicki, *Polscy twórcy filmowi o sobie*, 50.
38. Gustaw Holoubek (1923–2008) excelled in several films directed by Wojciech J. Has. In addition to *The Noose*, during the Polish School phenomenon he also appeared in *Farewells* and *Shared Room*, and starred in Jerzy Zarzycki's Holocaust drama *White Bear*.
39. Piotr Wojciechowski, "Prorok naszych snów," *Kino* 4 (1995): 20.
40. Ibid.
41. Several Polish-language books published on Wojciech J. Has's films in recent years discuss eloquently the complexities of his cinematic style. They include Marcin Maron, *Dramat czasu i wyobraźni: Filmy Wojciecha J. Hasa* (Kraków: Universitas, 2010); Iwona Grodź, *Zaszyfrowane w obrazie: O filmach Wojciecha Jerzego Hasa* (Gdańsk: słowo/obraz terytoria, 2009); Małgorzata Jakubowska, *Kryształy czasu: Kino Wojciecha Jerzego Hasa* (Łódź: Wydawnictwo Uniwersytetu Łódzkiego, 2013). See also the first English-language study by Annette Insdorf, *Intimations: The Cinema of Wojciech Has* (Evanston, IL: Northwestern University Press, 2017).
42. Krzysztof-Teodor Toeplitz, "The Films of Wojciech Has," *Film Quarterly* 18, no. 2 (1964): 6.
43. Andrzej Werner, "Film fabularny," in *Historia filmu polskiego 1962–1967*, vol. 5, ed. Rafał Marszałek (Warsaw: Wydawnictwa Artystyczne i Filmowe, 1985), 21.
44. Another film set during the Warsaw Uprising, *Kamienne niebo (A Sky of Stone*, 1959, Ewa Petelska and Czesław Petelski), deals with the fate of a group of Warsaw dwellers buried in a cellar of a collapsed building.

45. For example, the difference is already stressed in the table of contents of Michałek and Turaj, *The Modern Cinema of Poland*: "Andrzej Munk: The Perspective of a Sceptic" and "Andrzej Wajda: The Essential Pole."
46. Ewelina Nurczyńska-Fidelska, "Romanticism and History: A Sketch of the Creative Output of Andrzej Wajda," in *Polish Cinema in Ten Takes*, ed. Ewelina Nurczyńska-Fidelska and Zbigniew Batko (Łódź: Łódzkie Towarzystwo Naukowe, 1995), 9.
47. The Polish title of the film, *Kanał*, literally means "sewer." This was also the route taken by the film's screenwriter Stawiński, who during the uprising was a commanding officer in the Home Army (pseudonym Łącki). He led seventy of his men through the sewers. After thirteen hours, he emerged from the sewers with only five insurgents. See Jerzy Stefan Stawiński, *Notatki scenarzysty* (Warsaw: Czytelnik, 1988), 63.
48. Jerzy Lipman and Jerzy Wójcik are responsible for several classic Polish films. Lipman started his career in 1953 working on Aleksander Ford's *Five Boys from Barska Street*. He worked as a cinematographer on Wajda's *A Generation*, *Kanal*, and *Speed*, Jerzy Kawalerowicz's *The True End of the Great War*, and Roman Polański's *Knife in the Water*, among others. Wójcik was a cinematographer on several films, including Wajda's *Ashes and Diamonds*, Andrzej Munk's *Eroica*, Kazimierz Kutz's *Nobody Is Calling*, and Jerzy Kawalerowicz's *Mother Joan of the Angels* and *Pharaoh*.
49. Bolesław Michałek, *The Cinema of Andrzej Wajda* (London: Tantivy Press, 1973), 32.
50. All of the Home Army fighters' names are war pseudonyms, for example, "Zadra" means "splinter," "Mądry" means "wise."
51. Don Fredericksen and Marek Hendrykowski, *Wajda's Kanal* (Poznań: Wydawnictwo Naukowe Uniwersytetu im. Adama Mickiewicza, 2007), 102.
52. Ibid., 33, Marek Hendrykowski's chapter.
53. The second part, *Ostinato Lugubre*, which narrates the story of Polish prisoners of war in a German camp, is a satire on heroism and the anachronistically understood "soldier's honor." The third segment, *Con bravura*, different in spirit since it uses the Polish romantic legend, deals with the experiences of the wartime couriers crossing the Tatra Mountains. Munk decided to drop *Con bravura* from the final version of his film; it premiered in 1972 on Polish television. The "musical titles" are obviously of parodic nature, but they also testify to Munk's interest in music. See, for example, his 1958 short film *Spacerek staromiejski* (*A Walk in the Old Town*).
54. Rafał Marszałek, *Filmowa pop-historia* (Kraków: Wydawnictwo Literackie, 1984), 344.
55. In the *Scherzo alla Polacca* part of *Eroica*, as well as in *Bad Luck* and later in *The Passenger*, Munk introduces the perspective of characters with whom the viewer cannot identify—that of the sly dog, the opportunist, and the German officer from the concentration camp, respectively. Munk's merciless satire on opportunism and bureaucracy, *Bad Luck*, is continued by Andrzej Kotkowski in *Obywatel Piszczyk* (*Citizen P.*, 1989) and by Kazimierz Kutz in *Straszny sen Dzidziusia Górkiewicza* (*The Terrible Dream of Dzidziuś Górkiewicza*, 1993), both written by Jerzy Stefan Stawiński.
56. Alicja Helman, "Andrzej Munk: *Cockeyed Luck*," *MovEast* 2 (1992): 101.

57. See the meticulously researched monograph on *Ashes and Diamonds* by Krzysztof Kornacki, *"Popiół i diament" Andrzeja Wajdy* (Gdańsk: słowo/obraz terytoria, 2011).
58. Tadeusz Konwicki, *Moonrise, Moonset*, trans. Richard Lourie (New York: Farrar, Straus & Giroux, 1987), 56.
59. Wajda's comment originally published in *Przegląd Kulturalny* 15 (1959), quoted in Marian Ursel, "Legenda romantyczna w polskiej szkole filmowej," in Trzynadlowski, *Polska Szkoła Filmowa*, 83.
60. Bolesław Michałek, "Mówi Andrzej Wajda," *Kino* 1 (1968), 42 (an interview with Wajda).
61. Konwicki, *Moonrise, Moonset*, 56–57.
62. Konrad Eberhardt, *Zbigniew Cybulski* (Warsaw: Wydawnictwa Artystyczne i Filmowe, 1976), 59.
63. Paul Coates, "Forms of the Polish Intellectual's Self-Criticism: Revisiting *Ashes and Diamonds* with Andrzejewski and Wajda," *Canadian Slavonic Papers* 38, nos. 3–4 (1996): 294–96. The scene with the inverted crucifix that separates the two lovers may be understood as a symbol of the overthrown values; it "mordantly fuses the Wellesian and the Buñuelian" (294).
64. Józef Hen's novel dealt with a taboo topic: the fate of the Polish citizens in the Soviet Union after the outbreak of World War II and the annexation of the Polish Eastern Provinces by the Soviets. The book was banned for almost thirty-three years; it was not published until 1990.
65. Elżbieta Baniewicz, *Kazimierz Kutz: Z dołu widać inaczej* (Warsaw: Wydawnictwa Artystyczne i Filmowe, 1994), 152.
66. Ozimek, "Konfrontacje z Wielką Wojną," 121.
67. Ibid., 120–21. Ozimek quotes the 1974 interview with the Petelskis in which they stress that their Łódź Film School generation was educated on *Chapayev* and that the ending of *Sergeant Major Kaleń* (the death of the protagonist) testifies to this inspiration.
68. The actor Wojciech Siemion (1928–2010) almost repeated his role from *The Birth Certificate* in Jerzy Passendorfer's films, chiefly in *Kierunek Berlin* (*Heading for Berlin*, 1969) and its sequel, *Ostatnie dni* (*The Last Days*, 1969).
69. Ursel, "Legenda romantyczna w polskiej szkole filmowej," 74.
70. Alicja Helman, "Sarmata na płonącej żyrafie," *Ekran* 42 (1959): 3. *Sarmata* is sometimes used as an ironic synonym for the Polish character.
71. Paul Coates, *The Red and the White: The Cinema of People's Poland* (London: Wallflower Press, 2005), 123.
72. Aleksander Jackiewicz stresses this aspect in his review of Różewicz's film, "*Ostatniego etapu* ciąg dalszy" [*The Last Stage* continues] reprinted in his *Moja filmoteka: Kino polskie* (Warsaw: Wydawnictwa Artystyczne i Filmowe, 1983), 196.
73. A highly respected Polish filmmaker, Stanisław Różewicz wrote several films with his brother, the accomplished Polish poet and writer Tadeusz Różewicz (1921–2014). Among the films they wrote together are restrained psychological dramas such

as *Miejsce na ziemi* (*A Place on Earth*, 1960), *Głos z tamtego świata* (*The Voice from Beyond*, 1962), *Samotność we dwoje*, (*Lonely Together*, 1969), and *Echo* (1964).

74. Alicja Helman, "Jerzy Kawalerowicz: A Virtuoso of the Camera," in Nurczyńska-Fidelska and Batko, *Polish Cinema in Ten Takes*, 53–54.
75. Ozimek, "Konfrontacje z Wielką Wojną," 82.
76. See the chapter on "Images of the Holocaust during the Polish School Period (1955–1965)" in Haltof, *Polish Film and the Holocaust*, 74–114. This fragment is based on that chapter.
77. Interestingly, despite Janusz Morgenstern's Jewish background and the fact that he survived the war in occupied Poland in the ghetto and then hiding in the countryside, *Ambulance* serves as his only film openly dealing with the Holocaust. Morgenstern commented that he never wanted to make films that would be too close to his own story of survival. After the war, he "didn't want to remember the Holocaust at all. I told myself—that's it! I am beginning a new life." Katarzyna Bielas and Jacek Szczerba, "Życie raz jeszcze," *Gazeta Wyborcza* 29 (21 November 2002): 18.
78. Kornatowska, "Kto ratuje jedno życie," 37; Barbara Hollender, "Nie można nikogo nauczyć żyć," *Rzeczpospolita* 11 (1997): 25.
79. The film was made after the capture of Adolf Eichmann by Israeli Mossad agents in Argentina, his historic trial in 1961, and his conviction and execution in Jerusalem. The film also coincided with the much-publicized Frankfurt Auschwitz trial of twenty-two SS guards from Auschwitz (1963–1965).
80. This was one of Hołuj's several returns to his own experiences in Auschwitz, where he was imprisoned in 1942 (camp no. 62937). Jakubowska and Hołuj, however, were not the only Auschwitz survivors who worked on this film. Wiesław Kielar, assistant to the camera operator, and Marian Kołodziej, costume designer, were sent to Auschwitz in May 1940 with the first transport of 728 Polish men, mostly political prisoners, from the Tarnów prison (camp nos. 290 and 432, respectively).
81. Janina Falkowska, *Andrzej Wajda: History, Politics, and Nostalgia in Polish Cinema* (New York: Berghahn Books, 2007), 85, originally published in Jerzy Płażewski, Grzegorz Balski, and Jan Słodowski, *Wajda Films*, vol. 1 (Warsaw: WAiF, 1996), 110.
82. Coates, *The Red and the White*, 163.
83. "Protokół z kolaudacji filmu *Naganiacz* w dniu 29 VI 1963," National Film Archive in Warsaw, A-216/4.
84. Zofia Posmysz-Piasecka (1923–) was incarcerated in Auschwitz from 1942 to 1945. Her radio broadcast, *Passenger from Cabin Number 45* (*Pasażerka z kabiny 45*), aired on Polish radio in August 1959. Munk, who listened to the broadcast, asked Posmysz-Piasecka to write a television play, which he later directed. The psychological drama was set entirely on the ocean liner; it dealt with the issue of guilt and forgetting on the part of the Germans, and offered only four comments by Liza on her Auschwitz past. In 1962, after Munk's death, Posmysz-Piasecka published her novel *The Passenger*, one of her many attempts to deal with the legacy

of Auschwitz. Details about the early stages of *The Passenger* come from Ewelina Nurczyńska-Fidelska, *Andrzej Munk* (Kraków: Wydawnictwo Literackie, 1982), 131–44.
85. According to Wajda, Munk's assistant directors were deeply affected by his tragic death and unable to continue with the project. Wajda was approached by Jerzy Bossak, head of the film unit Kamera and the film's producer, and asked to finish the film. He declined the offer after evaluating the materials left by Munk. "I'm afraid," commented Wajda, "that Andrzej [Munk] believed too much in improvisation, which was meant to get from the script more than it was written there, and that he started to doubt the result." See Wajda's introduction to Marek Hendrykowski, *Andrzej Munk* (Warsaw: Więź, 2007), 10.
86. Bolesław W. Lewicki, "Temat: Oświęcim," *Kino* 6 (1968): 16–18.
87. Tadeusz Szyma, "Szkic do portretu Andrzeja Munka," *Kino* 9 (2001): 9.
88. Stuart Liebman, "Man on the Tracks, Passenger, Bad Luck, Eroica," *Cineaste* 32, no. 2 (2007): 64.
89. Walerian Borowczyk (1923–2006) received critical acclaim for his first two feature films, *Goto, l'île d'amour* (*Goto, Island of Love*, 1969) and *Blanche* (1972), often described as surrealist and erotic, but after making *Contes immoraux* (*Immoral Tales*, 1974), a compilation of four explicitly sexual stories, critics started accusing him of producing exploitative art porn. For more information on Borowczyk, see Aga Skrodzka, "Woman's Body and Her Pleasure in the Celluloid Erotica of Walerian Borowczyk," *Studies in European Cinema* 8, no. 1 (2011): 67–79; Kamila Kuc, Kuba Mikurda, and Michał Oleszczyk, eds., *Boro, l'Île d'Amour: The Films of Walerian Borowczyk* (New York: Berghahn Books, 2015). For more information on Jan Lenica (1928–2001), see Steve Weiner, "Jan Lenica and Landscape," *Film Quarterly* 45, no. 4 (1992): 2–16.
90. For information about Karabasz's cinema, see Mikołaj Jazdon, *Kino dokumentalne Kazimierza Karabasza* (Poznań: Wydawnictwo Naukowe Uniwersytetu im. Adama Mickiewicza, 2009).
91. Stanisław Janicki, *Aleksander Ford* (Warsaw: Wydawnictwa Artystyczne i Filmowe, 1967), 81.
92. Małgorzata Hendrykowska, *Kronika kinematografii polskiej 1895–1997*, 2nd ed. (Poznań: Ars Nova, 2012), 427. The figures clearly show the preference for local films, mostly adaptations of national literary canon; out of twenty films listed, as many as thirteen are Polish productions.
93. Jerzy Pelc, "Krzyżacy," *Film* 36 (1960): 5.
94. The title of Zygmunt Kałużyński's review, "Lekarstwo narodowe we wszystkich kolorach" [National remedy in all colors], quoted in Ozimek, "Od wojny w dzień powszedni," 187.
95. Its continuations were made in 1959: *Pan Anatol szuka miliona* (*Mr. Anatol Seeks a Million*), and *Inspekcja pana Anatola* (*The Inspection of Mr. Anatol*), both also directed by Jan Rybkowski.

96. Michałek and Turaj, *The Modern Cinema of Poland*, 101.
97. Janicki, *Polscy twórcy filmowi o sobie*, 35.
98. Helman, "Jerzy Kawalerowicz," 55. The emergence of the new protagonists during the Polish School period, both men and women, deserves a separate publication. Unlike the socialist realist characters, who were immune to sex and unwilling to give up production for love, the new protagonists are multidimensional, torn between duty to the nation and private aspirations, and frequently interested only in personal issues. For example, Urszula Modrzyńska, the socialist realist star in *Not Far from Warsaw* and *A Generation*, displays different qualities in *Deszczowy lipiec (Rainy July*, 1958, Leonard Buczkowski). Lucyna Winnicka in *Night Train*, the insurgent Daisy (Teresa Iżewska) in *Kanal*, and other female characters are experienced, strong, sexual, and in charge of men. The issue of the representation of female characters by the Polish School filmmakers is discussed by Joanna Pyszny, "Kobieta w filmach szkoły polskiej," in Trzynadlowski, *Polska Szkoła Filmowa*, 91–101. See also Elżbieta Ostrowska, "Caught between Activity and Passivity: Women in the Polish School," in Ewa Mazierska and Elżbieta Ostrowska, *Women in Polish Cinema* (New York: Berghahn Books, 2006), 75–91.
99. Michałek and Turaj, *The Modern Cinema of Poland*, 104.
100. The Polish ruler Mieszko I of the Piast dynasty was baptized in the year 966. Celebrations of the millennium of Poland's baptism were held in 1966.
101. Krzysztof Kornacki, *Kino polskie wobec katolicyzmu (1945–1970)* (Gdańsk: słowo/obraz terytoria, 2005), 213–14.
102. Also in the 1960s, Mieczysław Waśkowski presented in *Zacne grzechy (Respectable Sins*, 1963) images of monks and priests in the manner of a folk ballad. Later, images of the Vatican bureaucracy were at the center of Janusz Majewski's television film *Urząd (The Office*, 1969). Krzysztof Kornacki discusses this issue extensively in *Kino polskie wobec katolicyzmu*, 256–98.
103. Grażyna Stachówna, *Roman Polański i jego filmy* (Warsaw, Łódź: Wydawnictwo Naukowe PWN, 1994), 42.
104. I am writing here about the "official hostility" toward Polański's film in Poland. *Knife in the Water* won the "Złota Kaczka" (Golden Duck) award for the best Polish film of 1962 in the popular plebiscite organized by *Film* magazine.
105. Roman Polański, *Roman* (New York: William Morrow, 1984), 156–57.
106. Marek Hendrykowski compares the composition of Polański's film to modern jazz compositions. Marek Hendrykowski, "*Nóż w wodzie*: Modern Jazz," *Kwartalnik Filmowy* 17 (1997): 86–96.
107. Polański's life often overshadows his films. His films are (pop)psychoanalyzed to excess. The number of books on Polański does not match their quality. These are mostly biographies, sometimes scandalizing ones, which cannibalize Polański's much publicized "private" life.

108. See, e.g., Herbert J. Eagle, "Power and the Visual Semantics of Polanski's Films," in *The Cinema of Roman Polanski: Dark Spaces of the World*, ed. John Orr and Elżbieta Ostrowska (London: Wallflower Press, 2006), 40–41.
109. E.g., Ewa Gębicka, "Partia i państwo a kino: Przypadek 'szkoły polskiej'—O ideologicznym stylu odbioru filmów i jego konsekwencjach," in Nurczyńska-Fidelska and Stolarska, *"Szkoła polska,"* 129–44; Alina Madej, "Bohaterowie byli zmęczeni?" in *Syndrom konformizmu? Kino polskie lat sześćdziesiątych*, ed. Tadeusz Miczka and Alina Madej (Katowice: Wydawnictwo Uniwersytetu Śląskiego, 1994), 10–26.
110. The dark picture of Polish reality portrayed in *The Eighth Day of the Week* was unacceptable for the Communist Party authorities. The banning of Ford's film served as a clear signal that nobody was exempted from communist censorship. Ford "was the Film Polski" for many years, and still an influential and well-connected person in the late 1950s. Problems experienced with *Eighth Day of the Week*, however, did not prevent Ford from making the epic superproduction *Teutonic Knights* just two years later.
111. This is the case of *Ashes and Diamonds*. Wajda's film had not been sent to Cannes because, in Aleksander Ford's words, it had "ambiguous political meaning." Madej, "Bohaterowie byli zmęczeni," 15.
112. "Uchwała Sekretariatu KC w sprawie kinematografii," National Film Archives in Warsaw (no. 130). Reprinted in Miczka and Madej, *Syndrom konformizmu?* 27–34.
113. Ewa Gębicka, "Obcinanie kantów, czyli polityka PZPR i państwa wobec kinematografii lat sześćdziesiątych," in Miczka and Madej, *Syndrom konformizmu?* 42.
114. Polański made films outside of Poland, in England, France, and the United States. They include *Repulsion* (1965), *Cul-de-sac* (1966), *The Fearless Vampire Killers* (1967), *Rosemary's Baby* (1968), *Macbeth* (1971), *Chinatown* (1974), *Le Locataire (The Tenant,* 1976), *Tess* (1979), *Frantic* (1988), *Bitter Moon* (1992), and *The Ninth Gate* (2000). Polański's artistic output, because of its diversity, manipulation of the genre's rules, and cosmopolitan nature, is not easily defined. There is, presumably, nothing Polish about his films, unless we tend toward the bizarre and the grotesque as a typical Polish feature. Despite their diversity and genre-oriented nature, Polański's films break conventional formulae and are characterized by the strong presence of the authorial self. The films exhibit the director's highly visual style, his personal thematic obsessions, prevailing images of the violent and the grotesque, and an adept mastery of manipulating the viewer's emotions.
115. As described by Andrzej Wajda. See Bożena Janicka, "Żegnaj, szkoło polska" [Farewell, the Polish School] *Film* 4 (1993): 2–3. Paul Coates writes: "It is tempting to describe *The Ring with a Crowned Eagle* as frustrated dreamwork upon *Ashes and Diamonds*." Coates, "Forms of the Polish Intellectual's Self-Criticism," 300.

CHAPTER 6
Adaptations, Personal Style, and Popular Cinema (1964–1975)

The spirit of the 1956 Polish October was short-lived and gave way to a period commonly known in Poland as the "small stabilization" of the 1960s. The term was adopted from the title of the play *Świadkowie albo nasza mała stabilizacja* (*Witnesses or Our Small Stabilization*, 1962), written by a distinguished Polish playwright, Tadeusz Różewicz. This expression serves as an ironic comment on the period of Władysław Gomułka—the Communist Party leader from 1956 to 1970. The term does not refer to socialist prosperity, as one might expect, but calls for tougher measures in politics and empty rituals.

Generally, Polish films of the 1960s do not reveal disenchantment with the state of affairs, that is, the fiasco of the limited democratization introduced for a brief period during the events of October 1956. Because of harsh communist censorship, Polish filmmakers were unable to voice their real concerns about recent national history, politics, and social issues. Rather, they retreated to safer adaptations of the national literary canon and popular cinema. "The cinema of small stabilization created an image of the nonexistent country," writes Krzysztof Kornacki, who adds that this cinema reflected the personal stabilization of Polish filmmakers rather than the economic and political stabilization of the country.[1]

Political developments once again contributed to the state of the Polish film industry. Filmmaking was affected by the events of 1968: brutally crushed student demonstrations in Warsaw (the March Events), and the anti-Semitic campaign orchestrated by a nationalistic faction of the Communist Party in order to remove some seasoned party and security force members, many of whom were Jewish, from their privileged positions. The Polish film industry was heavily affected by the emigration of numerous filmmakers of Jewish origin, among them director Aleksander Ford,[2] cinematographers Jerzy Lipman and Kurt Weber,[3] and a large group of experienced production managers, including Ludwik Hager.

After 1968, the communist authorities tightened censorship, criticized "commercialism," and called for films reflecting the true spirit of socialism. They also reorganized the existing film units to introduce a more centralized organization of the film industry. In 1969, the following six film units were in operation: Iluzjon, Kraj, Nike, Plan, Tor, and Wektor. Founded in 1967, Tor, managed by Stanisław Różewicz, drew such prominent directors as Andrzej Wajda, Krzysztof Zanussi, and Janusz Majewski. Kazimierz Kutz, Jerzy Hoffman, Jerzy Skolimowski, and Andrzej Żuławski worked for another unit, Wektor, headed by Jerzy Jesionowski. The third important unit, Ryszard Kosiński and Stanisław Zieliński's Plan, employed, among others, Tadeusz Chmielewski, Wojciech J. Has, Jerzy Kawalerowicz, and Jan Rybkowski.

The December 1970 workers' strikes in the Baltic ports, which were violently suppressed by the communist authorities, led to the downfall of Gomułka. The more pragmatic Edward Gierek became the new party leader and introduced some minor economic reforms. With the help of foreign loans, he focused on economic investments and consumer goods. The first half of the 1970s also brought changes to film practice in Poland. Another reorganization of the film units granted them more artistic freedom. As Bolesław Michałek and Frank Turaj write, "Top management was composed of—miracle of miracles in any country or field—people of genuine professional accomplishment, who enjoyed the confidence of the cinema community. This was indeed why the seventies became such a thoroughly successful time for Polish film."[4] In 1972, there were seven film units: Tor, Czesław Petelski's Iluzjon, Jerzy Kawalerowicz's Kadr, Jerzy Passendorfer's Panorama, Aleksander Ścibor-Rylski's Pryzmat, Andrzej Wajda's X, and the only unit established outside of Warsaw—Kazimierz Kutz's Silesia in Katowice.

This period of relative prosperity, heightened by the "propaganda of success" in Poland, ended in the late 1970s. Workers' protests in 1976 (caused by food price increases) spotlighted the growing problems of the Gierek administration: mismanagement of foreign credits, corruption, and the deepening economic crisis barely masked by the triumphant propaganda.

Although European art films and selected American films (usually the best) dominated the repertoire of Polish cinemas in the second half of the 1960s, the most popular fare among Polish audiences remained commercially oriented productions, for example, *Winnetou* (aka *Apache Gold*, 1965, Harald Reinl), released in 1968 (4.7 million viewers), and *Cleopatra* (1963, Joseph L. Mankiewicz), released in 1970 (5.7 million viewers).[5] Polish films, mostly adaptations of the Polish literary canon, successfully competed with foreign products. For example, Jerzy Hoffman's version of Henryk Sienkiewicz's classic, *Pan Wołodyjowski* (*Pan Michael*, aka *Colonel Wolodyjowski*, 1969), had nearly ten million viewers. Another film, *Faraon* (*Pharaoh*, 1966, Jerzy Kawalerowicz), based on Bolesław Prus's novel, had 8.5 million viewers.[6]

In 1965, Poland had the most cinemas in its history: 3,935, including 381 mobile cinemas, with 732,000 seats. Later, until the mid-1970s, this number was drastically reduced to 1,296 cinemas and almost 180,000 seats. During the 1970s, Albania was the only European country with fewer cinema seats per number of inhabitants than Poland.[7] Cheap admissions, the deterioration of the remaining cinemas, the disregard for genre cinema, fewer imports from the West, and the continuous preference for films from other Eastern Bloc countries contributed to the growing financial deficit and the decreasing number of cinemas. In the course of time, only art house theaters and cine-clubs were offering a variety of films from the West, and their number was increasing. For example, the number of cine-clubs reached 241 in 1968, with as many as 351 in 1972.[8]

Television Films and Documentaries

As elsewhere in Europe, the decline in cinema attendance can be attributed to the popularity of television. The number of television sets grew from 3,389,000 in 1968 to 5,200,000 in 1972.[9] The most popular films were television productions, such as *Czterej pancerni i pies* (*Four Tankmen and a Dog*, twenty-one episodes, 1966–1970), directed by Konrad Nałęcki, and *Stawka większa niż życie* (*More than Life at Stake*, eighteen episodes, 1965–1967), directed by Janusz Morgenstern and Andrzej Konic. Despite being loaded with pro-Soviet propaganda, both have achieved cult series status not only in Poland but also in other countries of the Eastern Bloc. The former series, based on Janusz Przymanowski's novel (also the co-screenwriter of the film), is an adventure war film featuring the tank "Rudy" (Ginger, literally "red haired") and its crew on their road to Poland from the Soviet Union. The latter, also set during the war, offers an equally cartoonish, simplified, and stereotypical version of history. The film narrates the story of Hans Kloss (Stanisław Mikulski), a Polish superspy dressed in a German uniform (codename J-23). Thanks to this role of a double agent in the *Abwehr* (German military intelligence), Mikulski became one of the most popular Polish actors of the day.[10] The popularity of these two television series prompted their makers to release theatrical versions in 1968 and 1969.[11] Subsequent television series, for example, *Chłopi (Peasants*, 1973, Jan Rybkowski), an adaptation of the Polish Nobel laureate Władysław Stanisław Reymont's epic novel, were frequently made with the theatrical release in mind. Jerzy Antczak, the director of the historical film *Hrabina Cosel (Countess Cosel*, 1968), first began this practice.

In 1965, Polish viewers watched the first locally made television series, *Barbara i Jan (Barbara and Jan)*, directed by Hieronim Przybył and Jerzy Ziarnik, followed by Stanisław Bareja's crime series *Kapitan Sowa na tropie (Captain Sowa Investigates)* and the most popular early series: Jerzy Gruza's satirical comedy *Wojna domowa (War at Home)*. In the second half of the 1960s, Polish television films were produced by established filmmakers and recent graduates from the Łódź Film School. The latter often started their careers by producing medium-length television films. For example, Krzysztof Zanussi attracted international attention with his diploma film *Śmierć Prowincjała (The Death of a Provincial*, 1965), which won awards at the Venice and Mannheim film festivals, and two other television films, *Twarzą w twarz (Face to Face*, 1967) and *Zaliczenie (Pass Mark*, 1968).

Beginning in the late 1960s, television also became a training ground for many young documentarians, as well as a venue for documentaries, sometimes of great importance for Polish cinema. For example, in 1967, Kazimierz Karabasz produced his classic full-length documentary, *Rok Franka W. (A Year of Franek W.*, 1967), a coming-of-age film about an undistinguished young man from a rural area. Another production studio, Wytwórnia Filmów Oświatowych (Educational Film Studio), founded in 1950 in Warsaw, also sponsored some notable documentaries, including two classics by Wojciech Wiszniewski (1946–1981): *Wanda Gościmińska: Włókniarka (Wanda Gościmińska, the Textile Worker*, 1975, released in 1981), which examines Stalinist work competition, and *Elementarz (The First Textbook*, 1976), a philosophical essay on the nature of patriotism. It must be emphasized that several award-winning documentaries were made by female filmmakers, such as Krystyna Gryczełowska (1931–2009) and Danuta Halladin (1930–1987). For example, Gryczełowska's classic film *Nazywa się Błażej Rejdak (His Name Is Błażej Rejdak*, 1968) and Halladin's *Moja ulica (My Street*, 1965) were winners of the Kraków Film Festival.

Kazimierz Karabasz's student, Krzysztof Kieślowski, graduated from the Łódź Film School in 1968 and made several important documentaries, including *Urząd (The Office*, 1966),[12] *Zdjęcie (The Photograph*, 1968), *Z miasta Łodzi (From the City of Łódź*, 1969) and *Pierwsza miłość (First Love*, 1974). In his early films, Kieślowski dealt with several individual cases representing a universal meaning; they were, pars pro toto, studies of the communist system. Unable to criticize the system openly, he focused on its several micro aspects in the hope of presenting its unveiled, true nature.

Kieślowski and some of the members of his class at the Łódź Film School, among them Andrzej Titkow (1946–), Krzysztof Wojciechowski (1939–), and Tomasz Zygadło (1947–2011), were chiefly interested in documenting reality. They appeared as a group at the Documentary Filmmakers' Forum during the 1971 Kraków Film Festival. Together with Grzegorz Królikiewicz (1939–2017), Marcel Łoziński (1940–), and Marek Piwowski (1935–), to name just a few, they developed and shaped documentary film in Poland in the years to come. According to Mirosław Przylipiak, their concept of documentaries stressed the following: the need to describe reality and to present its truthful picture; the call to contest the political system (although their films were produced within this system); the necessity to "activate reality" in order to "expose the hidden truth"; and the urge to speak metaphorically (because of political censorship) about reality.[13] The year 1971 saw the production of such classic Polish documentaries as Zygadło's *Szkoła podstawowa* (*Elementary School*, 1971) and *Ziemia* (*The Land*, 1971), Wojciechowski's *Wyszedł w jasny, pogodny dzień* (*He Left on a Bright, Sunny Day*, 1971), Titkow's *W takim niedużym mieście* (*In Such a Small Town*, 1971), and Piwowski's *Korkociąg* (*Corkscrew*, 1971) and *Hair* (1971).

Unlike documentarians who were interested in recording reality, filmmakers such as Grzegorz Królikiewicz and Wojciech Wiszniewski started to incorporate techniques of fictional cinema into their documentaries. They contributed to a unique brand of Polish documentary cinema that Polish critics labeled "creative documentary" (*dokument kreacyjny*).[14] For example, Wiszniewski made, among others, a stylized documentary about the Stalinist period, *Opowieść o człowieku, który wykonał 552% normy* (*The Story of a Man Who Produced 552 Percent of the Norm*, 1973), which portrays the life of a coal miner–Stakhanovite, Bernard Bugdoł, "the Polish People's Republic Citizen Kane."[15]

Adaptations

Film adaptations of the national literary canon had the most successful ticket sales in Polish cinema during the mid-1960s. They were also well received by Polish critics. Most adaptations stirred heated national debates, usually dealing with historical and political issues surrounding the films rather than with the films themselves. Some were also received as historically distant parables on contemporary Poland. This way of reading films was an established tradition in Poland; it became even more prominent in the late 1970s and after the introduction of martial law in December 1981. The acclaimed Polish writer Ryszard Kapuściński aptly described the peculiar situation under communist rule:

> *In Poland every text is read as allusive, every written situation—even the most distant in space and time—is immediately, without hesitation, applied to the situation in Poland. In this way, every text is a double text, and between the printed lines we search for sympathetic messages written in invisible ink, and the hidden message we find is treated as the most valid, the only real one. The result stems not only from the difficulty of open speech, the language of truth. It is also because this country of ours has suffered every possible experience in the world, and is still exposed to dozens of different trials, so that now in the normal course of things every Pole sees in histories that are not ours, connections with his own life.*[16]

Popioły (*Ashes*, 1965, Andrzej Wajda), an adaptation of Stefan Żeromski's novel, serves as a good example here. This almost four-hour-long black-and-white film generated one of the most intense debates in Poland; its filmic aspects were of secondary importance in this discussion.[17] Set in the Napoleonic era and portraying the fate of the young Polish legionnaires, *Ashes* is "not a straightforward historical novel in the Dumas genre, but a giant historical and historico-philosophical fresco which resembles, if anything, Stendhal and Tolstoy."[18] The film covers the public disillusionment with Napoleon and the loss of hope that he will restore the Polish state. Discussions about Wajda's film, as always, touch on the issue of faithfulness to the literary source and emphasize parallels between Wajda's generation of Columbuses and the young generation of Polish legionnaires, both outsmarted by "the forces of history." Tadeusz Sobolewski expresses the issue as follows: "*Ashes* opposed the propaganda, which stated that the Polish People's Republic was crowning the dreams of independence, by portraying history as a cemetery of Polish hopes."[19] Despite its ambitious theme, epic scope, and painterly black-and-white photography (Jerzy Lipman), *Ashes* does not belong to Wajda's successful works. Its incoherent narrative, superfluous plots, and multitude of characters, with whom a viewer cannot identify, weaken the impact of this film.

One of the best Polish historical films, Jerzy Kawalerowicz's epic production *Pharaoh*, was given the same political reading as its contemporaries. The script by Kawalerowicz and Tadeusz Konwicki follows Bolesław Prus's celebrated novel about a young, fictitious pharaoh, Ramses XIII, who tries to modernize Egypt but is defeated by his antagonists: the priests led by the archpriest Herhor. Faithful to the literary source, Kawalerowicz's film narrates the story of a young, impatient, and impulsive heir to the throne in ancient Egypt (Jerzy Zelnik), who is eager to limit the priests' impact on politics. When Ramses XIII becomes pharaoh, after the death of his father, he attempts to reform the country with the aid of treasures held by the priests. Since he cannot count on popular support, he decides to use force to take the labyrinth where the treasures are kept. The knowledgeable

Figure 6.1 (a) A scene from Jerzy Kawalerowicz's *Pharaoh* (1966); (b) Jerzy Zelnik as the young pharaoh (left) and Leszek Herdegen as a priest. Screenshots by the author.

priests use the eclipse of the sun, which coincides with the attack, to threaten the soldiers, who consequently flee in panic. Ramses XIII later dies at the hand of his double, Lykon (also played by Jerzy Zelnik), who has been prepared by the priests to replace the young pharaoh.

Pharaoh was released at the height of the ideological battle between the Polish Roman Catholic Church and the communist regime, and was used in this conflict. The story of a young heir unable to reform the country, the struggle for power between the church and secular rulers, the role of "progressive" priests supporting the ruler, and the impact of religion happened to be very close to the complexities of Polish politics in the 1960s. Later, the same political readings of the film were applied to *Bolesław Śmiały* (*Bolesław the Bold*, 1972, Witold Lesiewicz), the story of the Polish king Bolesław II the Generous (aka the Bold, 1041–1081) and his conflict with Bishop Stanislaus, who was found guilty of treason and executed by the king.

Today, however, Kawalerowicz's historical epic, enormous by Polish standards, is absorbing not only for its theme but chiefly for its grand formal beauty. Eisensteinian compositions of frame (cinematography by Jerzy Wójcik), stylized gestures and movements of actors, creative design by Jerzy Skrzepiński, and original, subjective shots (for example, the battle between Egypt and Assyria is seen from a common soldier's point of view) make *Pharaoh* intriguing to audiences. Despite its anti-Hollywood treatment of history, Kawalerowicz's *Pharaoh* received an Oscar nomination for Best Foreign Film in 1967.

In the mid-1960s, Wojciech J. Has changed the intimate style that were characteristic of his films made during the Polish School period and moved to the realm of historical spectaculars based on great literary works. His 1965 black-and-white *Rękopis znaleziony w Saragossie* (*The Saragossa Manuscript*) was adapted from the 1813 French novel published by a writer of the European Enlightenment, Count Jan Potocki (1761–1815). Like the novel, Has's film offers a complex, labyrinthine narrative structure that is open to interpretation. The viewer follows Captain Alfons van Worden (Zbigniew Cybulski) and his improbable voyages across eighteenth-century Spain, the land populated by evil spirits, bandits, mysterious characters, and attractive women. The logic of dreams governs van Worden's surreal journey.[20]

The dreamlike dimension of this travel, the motif of a journey into one's past, and the appearances of characters who emerge from the realm of dreams or memories also characterize some of Has's later films, including *Sanatorium pod klepsydrą* (*The Hourglass Sanatorium*, aka *The Sandglass*, 1973), an adaptation of

Bruno Schulz's (1892–1941) prose. Schulz's prose, which deals with the theme of childhood recollections, seems to be almost unadaptable for the screen; it would be like making a film based on paintings by Marc Chagall. Following Konrad Eberhardt's 1973 essay published in the monthly *Kino*, Polish critics frequently analyzed adaptations of Schulz's works, which depict Jewish communities in small-town, southwest Poland before the war, as narratives foreshadowing the Holocaust.[21] Has's *The Hourglass Sanatorium*, inspired by Schulz's short stories published in 1937,[22] succeeds in representing Schulz's moody evocation of the lost Jewish world. Like Schulz, Has creates a poetic, almost surreal landscape peopled by characters who move as if in a dream.[23] The film's protagonist, Józef (Jan Nowicki), travels in time; painterly dreamlike and surrealist images accompany his voyage. Time is Has's obsession. The film blends the past and the present, the living and the dead. The richness of the images, the panorama of characters, and the lyricism of this vision, permeated by nostalgia, contributed to this film's artistic success. Although *The Hourglass Sanatorium* is not, strictly speaking, about the Holocaust, the viewer is compelled to look at this film through the prism of Schulz's tragic death (killed by a Gestapo officer) in 1942, and cannot ignore what happened to the Jews of Drohobycz and other towns in former eastern Poland.

In 1968, Has adapted Bolesław Prus's novel *Lalka* (*The Doll*) in a more conventional manner. Set in the late nineteenth century, *The Doll* (Has's first film in color) tells a love story between an impoverished aristocratic young woman, the countess Izabella Łęcka (Beata Tyszkiewicz), and a rich merchant, Stanisław Wokulski (Mariusz Dmochowski). *The Doll* centers around two worlds of conflict: emerging Polish capitalism, represented by Wokulski and his class, and the old Polish romantic tradition, represented by Łęcka, her family, and Wokulski's shop assistant Rzecki (Tadeusz Fijewski). "With painterly compositions," Annette Insdorf writes about Wokulski, "*The Doll* traces his economic rise and romantic fall."[24] This film's art direction and a vast panorama of Polish society, conscious of the failed January Uprising of 1863–1864 against Russia, greatly contributed to its critical and box office success.[25]

Vast panoramas, epic scopes, historical adventure stories using Polish history, and, above all, Henryk Sienkiewicz's name proved to be enough to attract millions to *Pan Michael* and *The Deluge*, both directed by Jerzy Hoffman (1932–).[26] Like the earlier popular success, Aleksander Ford's *Teutonic Knights*, adaptations of Sienkiewicz were eagerly awaited by Polish audiences for whom this writer and the characters populating his historical novels were and still are household names.

Sienkiewicz, the "peddler of pleasant dreams," as writer Witold Gombrowicz referred to him, promoted "national self-assertion and pride, which compensated for the collective low esteem and feeling, stemming from continuous defeats on the battlefield."[27]

Pan Michael deals with the seventeenth-century defense of Christianity against the Islamic Turks. It is a generic adventure film, almost a "cloak and dagger" with elements of romance, set in an environment that is a stereotype of Polish history. This film's likeable protagonists, Michał Wołodyjowski (Tadeusz Łomnicki) and his beloved Basia (Magdalena Zawadzka), and the straightforward, colorful version of the not-so-colorful past generated success with local as well as foreign audiences; from 1969 to 1986, the film was sold to twenty-eight countries.[28]

The two-part, five-hour-long epic *The Deluge* is also set in the turbulent mid-seventeenth century, during the Swedish invasion of Poland known as the "Swedish Deluge." Hoffman's film narrates a melodramatic love story between the color sergeant Andrzej Kmicic (Daniel Olbrychski) and Oleńka Billewiczówna (Małgorzata Braunek). Kmicic swears an allegiance to the Lithuanian prince Janusz Radziwiłł, who later betrays the Polish king to the Swedish invaders. Torn between his loyalty to Radziwiłł and a sense of patriotism, Kmicic changes sides. He defends the holy monastery at Częstochowa under a different name. Thanks to his heroic deeds, he is pardoned by the Polish king for his treason and later reconciled with Oleńka. The transformation of a fun-loving, irresponsible young man into a national hero is at the structural center of this film. Another adaptation of Sienkiewicz, Władysław Ślesicki's *W pustyni i w puszczy* (*In Desert and Wilderness*, 1973), proved to be the most popular film for children and one of the most popular films in Polish history.

Noce i dnie (*Nights and Days*, 1975), Jerzy Antczak's (1929–) faithful adaptation of Maria Dąbrowska's revered epic novel, also belongs to a group of Polish critical and box office successes.[29] This epic melodramatic account of love between the emotional and ambitious Barbara (Jadwiga Barańska) and the down-to-earth Bogumił (Jerzy Bińczycki) begins and ends with the outbreak of World War I, which destroys the tranquility experienced in the past, and covers almost forty years. The film deals with Barbara's reminiscences of her life, and the theme of long-lasting love against all odds. Like Dąbrowska's family saga, Antczak's film offers a nostalgic venture into the past and an evocation of life and models of behavior for the impoverished Polish gentry (*szlachta*). *Nights and Days* won the 1975 Festival of Polish Films in Gdynia, was nominated for the Best Foreign Language Film Academy Award in 1977, and Barańska and Bińczycki received several acting awards.

Another popular adaptation was made by Walerian Borowczyk, a Polish graphic artist and filmmaker living in France, who returned to Poland in 1975 to produce *Dzieje grzechu* (*The Story of Sin*, 1975), an adaptation of Stefan Żeromski's "scandalous novel" published in 1908. This undervalued, stylish, and erotic drama—a style that could be expected from the maker of *Goto, l'Île d'amour* (*Goto, Island of Love*, 1969), *Blanche* (1972), and *Contes immoraux* (*Immoral Stories*, 1974)—tells the story of the unhappy life of a young woman, Ewa (Grażyna Długołęcka), and her descent into prostitution and crime.

Andrzej Wajda's Films: 1969–1975

In 1969, Andrzej Wajda released his most personal film, *Wszystko na sprzedaż* (*Everything for Sale*), following the tragic death of his *Ashes and Diamonds* star, Zbigniew Cybulski (1927–1967). Although Cybulski's name is not mentioned, the film deals with Cybulski's legend—and what is left of it after the hero's death. By 1969, Wajda's films had become identifiable by certain themes and by his well-developed and personal visual style. As Bolesław Michałek suggests, the director may have become "a prisoner of his themes and his obsessions with national cross-purposes."[30] If an artist wants to develop his art, the title of the film suggests, he must put everything up for sale.

Everything for Sale, though, is not so much a film about Cybulski as it is about Wajda, his actors, his other films, and the uncertainty of the future of his artistic career. The protagonist, the film director Andrzej (Andrzej Łapicki), clearly serves as Wajda's alter ego. "How could he do this to me?" he asks of the deceased actor. The enactment of Cybulski's life and death constitutes the narrative axis of the film. The film is cast with real-life characters, friends of Cybulski and Wajda who appear under their own names: Beata Tyszkiewicz as Beata, Elżbieta Czyżewska as Ela, Bogumił Kobiela as Bobek, and Daniel Olbrychski as the rising new star Daniel, who replaces the dead actor. Wajda's film tries to discover Cybulski through memories of those who knew him and ultimately remarks on the impossibility of recreating a true picture. Konrad Eberhardt comments: "Wajda made a ballet of forms and ostentatiously bright colors. His film is nervous, breathless, and has a rhythm of a chase. In it there is a search for the film's idea, and also for the shadow of a person who has passed away."[31]

Every aspect of life, including death or an artistic crisis, can be turned into art. Like *Otto e mezzo* (*8½*, 1963, Federico Fellini) and *La nuit américaine* (*Day for Night*, 1973, François Truffaut), *Everything for Sale* is a self-reflexive, exhibitionist film about a creative process—a film within a film. During the last scene of Wajda's film, the camera focuses on Olbrychski. He is "Wajda's new-found symbol of the Polish consciousness," remarks Paul Coates, who goes on to say, "The camera turns away from the railway tracks that recall the death of Cybulski. One may almost feel it licking its lips at the prospect of filming Olbrychski in later works."[32]

Daniel Olbrychski (1945–), who in the film rejects the identification with Cybulski, became the most popular Polish actor in the early 1970s. He debuted in 1964 in *Ranny w lesie* (*Wounded in the Forest*, Janusz Nasfeter) and then starred in Wajda's *Ashes* and several other films in the late 1960s, including *Bokser* (*The Boxer*, 1966, Julian Dziedzina) and *Jowita* (1967, Janusz Morgenstern). Olbrychski's lead roles established him as a charismatic generational actor, known for his screen characters who were sometimes hot tempered, emotional yet intellectual, athletic, and energetic. In the early 1970s, he became the most popular Polish actor, once again being identified with Wajda's films that displayed the range of his talent and earned him critical acclaim as well. He sealed his popularity in Jerzy Hoffman's adaptations of Sienkiewicz. The role of Kmicic in *The Deluge* was perhaps the pinnacle of his career.[33]

Most of Wajda's films, all starring Olbrychski, constitute adaptations of the Polish national literary canon. In the early 1970s, Wajda produced several important adaptations revolving around the characters' psychology rather than the historical and political contexts. They include *Krajobraz po bitwie* (*Landscape after Battle*, 1970), based on Tadeusz Borowski's short stories; *Brzezina* (*Birchwood*, 1970), an adaptation of Jarosław Iwaszkiewicz's short story; *Wesele* (*The Wedding*, 1973), an adaptation of the canonical Polish drama by Stanisław Wyspiański; and *Ziemia obiecana* (*The Promised Land*, 1975),[34] based on Władysław Stanisław Reymont's novel about the birth of Polish capitalism in Łódź.[35]

Landscape after Battle opens with a memorable sequence that sets the tone for the whole film: the liberation of a German concentration camp by American troops. Lacking dialogue and accompanied by Antonio Vivaldi's *Four Seasons*, the sequence portrays the first minutes of freedom. The prisoners in their striped camp clothing run through a snow-covered field, finally encountering a barbed wire fence. They wait, confused and tired, before one of them (Mieczysław Stoor) touches it and discovers that it is not electrified. A sharp contrast follows when the prisoners avenge their misery by killing a *Kapo*. They literally stamp him into the dirt after an American officer-liberator's lofty speech. The camera then introduces the film's protagonist, the writer Tadeusz (Daniel Olbrychski), who has the low number "105" tattooed on his arm, indicating a long stay in the camp. He appears to be an almost stereotypical young intellectual: he wears wire-rimmed glasses, is absent minded, and rescues books from a fire while others search for food and clothing.

The film's action then moves to a displaced persons camp, organized in a former SS barracks. The concentration camp prisoners, POWs, Jewish refugees from Poland, and survivors from other camps live in this place under the watch of American soldiers. Although Wajda portrays political differences among the Poles, he is primarily concerned with the love that surfaces between two survivors: Tadeusz and Nina (Stanisława Celińska), a Jewish refugee from Poland. As often happens in Wajda's films, the sudden manifestation of love serves only as a romantic interlude before death. Ironically, an American guard accidentally kills Nina while she returning with Tadeusz to the camp. As in Wajda's later film *Birchwood*, the death of a loved one enables the protagonist to awaken psychologically and regain some human emotions. In the film's finale, Tadeusz boards a train to Poland with numerous other refugees.

The situation represented in the film includes some unambiguous references to the late 1960s in Poland. Wajda seems to mock the nationalist communists in a bombastic scene featuring a recreation of the national past (the Battle of Grunwald). Moreover, Nina's character must be seen in the context of the political atmosphere preceding the release of Wajda's film. She is clearly an escapee from post–March 1968 Poland who wants to study and live a quiet life somewhere in the West.[36]

In 1970, Wajda paired once again with his cinematographer Zygmunt Samosiuk to produce *Birchwood*, a modest television film (first distributed theatrically), that was of great importance for Wajda. The story, set in the 1930s, concerns the relationship between two brothers. The older, Bolesław (Daniel Olbrychski), is a widower who works as a forest warden and lives with his daughter, Ola. The younger brother, Stanisław (Olgierd Łukaszewicz), who is dying of tuberculosis, has just returned from a sanatorium in Switzerland to spend the last moments of his life with Bolesław. A local woman, Malina (Emilia Krakowska), serves as the very embodiment of life force and the symbol of sexuality. The brothers become rivals when they realize that they both want this woman. When Stanisław dies, he is buried next to Bolesław's wife in the birchwood. Revitalized, Bolesław leaves both the forest and Malina, who is about to marry her village suitor.

The themes of love and death permeate the film. The Polish art nouveau painter Jacek Malczewski serves as the source of painterly inspirations.[37] Bolesław Michałek says

> The colour is certainly eerie, ugly in its way, "cadaverous" as it was called—a mélange of putrid yellows, greens and violets. These tones dominate the photography of human bodies with their faces splodged by sickly, sinister stains. The use of the same spectrum as Malczewski lent the film's images a disquieting, misty, but ever-present air of disease, decomposition and death.[38]

The presentation of the struggle between Eros and Thanatos (love and death) in this life-affirming film is new for Wajda. As Ewelina Nurczyńska-Fidelska points out, Wajda has dealt with the themes of love and death and with protagonists who experience love for only a short time before their deaths. This is a common theme in his films *A Generation, Kanal, Ashes and Diamonds, Speed, Ashes,* and *Landscape after Battle*.[39] The deaths in *Landscape after Battle* and in *Birchwood*, however, are deprived of the political dimension; they are not at the altar of national needs.

Wajda's next film is abundant with national symbolism and alludes to Polish mythology, history, and national complexes. An adaptation of *The Wedding*, the play written by the multitalented fin de siècle artist Stanisław Wyspiański, was staged for the first time in Kraków in 1901. It deals with the actual wedding of a Kraków poet, Lucjan Rydel, and a peasant girl, Jadwiga Mikołajczyk, in the village of Bronowice, just outside of Kraków. Set in 1900, the play portrays the illusory unity of the intelligentsia and the peasants, explores the different political goals of these two groups, and stresses the impossibility of overcoming the burden of the past. Wajda's film faithfully follows the play, preserving its rhymed dialogues and stressing its dreamlike qualities. The director reinforces symbolism that refers to the Polish past, adds the aura of uncanniness to Wyspiański's phantoms from the nation's history, and injects a vibrating rhythm to this national psychotherapeutic drama. Similar to *Ashes and Diamonds*, the psychedelic rhythm of *The Wedding* culminates in another symbolic dance in the film's finale. Wajda's "masterpiece of cinepainting"[40] relies on familiar Polish iconography more than his other films do, and draws inspirations from the local painting tradition.[41]

The painterly aspect is also important in Wajda's next film, *The Promised Land*.⁴² Its action, set in the fast-growing industrial city of Łódź, introduces three protagonists/friends: a Pole, Karol Borowiecki (Daniel Olbrychski); a Jew, Moryc Welt (Wojciech Pszoniak); and a German, Max Baum (Andrzej Seweryn), all of whom attempt to build a textile factory. The film, also written by Wajda, tells how the three young entrepreneurs try to establish themselves in Łódź, yet it is essentially the story of the city: multicultural, dynamic, vulgar, and tempting. Wajda paints an almost Marxist image of the city devouring its children. He follows Reymont's portrayal of the end of the romantic era on the Polish territories, the loss of traditional values, and the triumphant march of uncouth and dynamic nineteenth-century capitalism. Like Reymont, Wajda portrays Łódź as having energy, potential, wealth, and national and class diversity. He also deals (and sympathizes) with the plight of the remnants of the pauperized nobility, who were forced to move from their country manors—the bastions of traditionally understood Polishness—to newly developed industrial cities. Łódź, the land of promise for many, means destruction for others in this film.

The Promised Land received an Oscar nomination for Best Foreign Film and won the Festival of Polish Films in Gdańsk and film festivals in Moscow, Valladolid, and Chicago. In 1996, *The Promised Land* was chosen the best film in the history of Polish cinema in a popular plebiscite of the local monthly *Film* and to this day is often voted in Poland the best Polish film ever made. Despite this critical acclaim, however, the film's unfavorable portrayal of other ethnicities, in particular the Jewish bourgeoisie, resulted in accusations of anti-Semitism, particularly in the United States, where the film was rarely shown and was rejected by several

Figure 6.2 (From the left) Andrzej Seweryn as Max Baum, Daniel Olbrychski as Karol Borowiecki, and Wojciech Pszoniak as Moryc Welt in Andrzej Wajda's *The Promised Land* (1975). Photograph by Renata Pajchel. Courtesy of Film Studio Zebra.

distributors.⁴³ One distributor wrote the following in his letter to Wajda after the film's pilot screening for a Jewish audience in New York: "For me, it is a masterpiece of filmmaking, so rich and wonderfully made, a feast for the eyes. Unhappily, however, the feeling among several people in the audience is that the film is open to anti-Semitic interpretation. ... This said, it will be impossible for me to open the film in New York."⁴⁴ Commenting on his film's negative reception in the United States, Wajda stated bitterly that he "understood that American Jews do not want to come from the aggressive Łódź capitalists. They prefer to think of themselves as descendants of the romantic *Fiddler on the Roof*."⁴⁵ In Poland, interestingly, Wajda's representation of the national complexities of nineteenth-century Łódź was largely discussed as historically accurate and relatively unbiased, especially when compared with Reymont's literary source.

The War Experiences

The war still features prominently in Polish films made in the second half of the 1960s and the early 1970s. The best-known works return to the main preoccupations and poetics of the Polish School. The events of September 1939 are depicted in *Westerplatte* (1967), Stanisław Różewicz's film about the defense of the Polish garrison at the Westerplatte peninsula near Gdańsk. Różewicz reconstructs the one-week battle in a realistic manner, even incorporating newsreels, and avoids romanticizing this habitually mythologized aspect of the year 1939. The garrison's commander, Major Henryk Sucharski (Zygmunt Hübner), is portrayed as a brave, well-disciplined, and pragmatic officer. He cares about his people, not history.⁴⁶

In *Hubal*, Bohdan Poręba deals with another legend, that of Major Henryk Dobrzański, known as Hubal (portrayed by Ryszard Filipski in a memorable performance), who kept fighting the Germans after the Polish armies were defeated in September 1939 until he died in action in the spring of 1940. The film alludes to the romantic tradition in Polish arts and immortalizes Hubal, but it also stresses the practical aspect of the protagonist's actions. At first glance, the setting of Poręba's film resembles Wajda's earlier *Speed* (in which cavalrymen struggle with the Germans during the September campaign), but the issue of heroism is treated differently. Heroism is mixed here with everyday struggle. The cavalrymen turned partisans are heroic but also tired men making a futile effort to reverse history.

A distinct group of films, epic in scope and aspirations, affirms, rather than questions, Polish history. These films, told from the perspective of a common soldier advancing westward with the First Polish Army, lack the dilemmas that permeate Wajda's films; their interest lies not in tragedy but in glory. *Kierunek Berlin* (*Heading for Berlin*, aka *Destination Berlin*, 1969, Jerzy Passendorfer) and *Jarzębina czerwona* (*The Rowan Tree*, 1970, Ewa and Czesław Petelski), although made in the spirit of the Soviet epic war films, stress the everyday aspect of war and the ordinary heroism of common soldiers. Both films portray the last days of war: the Battle of Berlin and the Battle of Kołobrzeg (Kolberg, an important Baltic seaport), which was one of the bloodiest combat battles fought by Polish soldiers during the war. Piotr Zwierzchowski coined the term "cinema of new memory" to describe their representation of World War II as the foundational myth of the Polish People's Republic. He stresses that in the 1960s, approximately three hundred feature and documentaries dealt with the war. Their main political task, regardless of the filmmakers' political and aesthetic preferences, was to create and propagate the official version of history, images approved by the communist regime that supported the construction of new national identity.[47]

In 1967, two modest, realistic films were made, portraying an average day under the occupation: *Stajnia na Salwatorze* (*Stall on Salvador*), directed by Paweł Komorowski (1930–2011), and *Kontrybucja* (*Contribution*), directed by Jan Łomnicki (1929–2002). Both examine the moral dilemmas of the underground fighters whose psychology and dramatic choices are of utmost importance. These dramas of choices have much in common with Kazimierz Kutz's and Stanisław Różewicz's depictions of the war. The protagonists do not serve as personifications of different ideological stands; they are psychologically complex characters with family lives, fears, and responsibilities.

In *Stall on Salvador*, an underground soldier, Michał (Janusz Gajos), gets an order to kill a friend who, because of tortures inflicted by the Gestapo, has betrayed the organization and endangered the lives of others. *Contribution* deals with an underground fighter's attempts to free his brother-in-law, who has been captured by the Germans. He does not obey his superiors' orders and pays the highest price for it. Both films are presented in an almost documentary tone and offer psychological landscapes rather than epic scope and action. They refrain from breakthrough moments in Polish history and concentrate on everyday experiences in order to understand history. As Aleksander Jackiewicz writes, they "reflected the time, which cannot be compared to ordinary time, although it was ordinary at the time."[48]

Two films from that period aptly address the plight of children during the occupation. *Twarz anioła* (*The Face of an Angel*, 1971, Zbigniew Chmielewski) is set in a concentration camp for Polish children in Łódź and focuses on an eleven-year-old boy who survives the war and a German guard's attempt to Germanize him. In another film, the Polish–Soviet Union coproduction *Zapamiętaj imię swoje* (*Remember Your Name*, 1974, Sergei Kolosov), a Russian mother who survived Auschwitz tries to find her son from whom she was separated in the camp. Twenty years later, she learns that he is alive and was adopted by a Polish family after the war. The story of *Remember Your Name* most probably owes its inspiration to a ten-minute documentary, *Dzieci rampy* (*Children of the Ramp*, 1963, Andrzej Piekutowski), which consists of interviews with those who survived Auschwitz as children, among them a young woman who, several years after the war, found her real parents in the Soviet Union. A fragment of this documentary is used as a citation in an earlier psychological film, *Julia, Anna, Genowefa* (1968, Anna Sokołowska). It deals with a young woman (Wanda Neumann) who learns that she was adopted and tries to find her biological parents.

Given the political climate after 1965, very few films attempted to deal with the Holocaust directly. *Długa noc* (*The Long Night*, Janusz Nasfeter) was produced in 1967, immediately shelved by the authorities, and not released until 1989. Set one week before Christmas of 1943 in a small Polish town, the film's story revolves around a young Pole, Zygmunt Korsak (Józef Duriasz), who hides in his small flat a Jewish escapee from the ghetto. Like Zbigniew Cybulski's Maciek in Wajda's *Ashes and Diamonds*, Korsak represents more his contemporaries rather than the wartime generation. The tall, blond, well-informed protagonist does not look like a typical villager; he resembles a Polish artist from the 1960s in a desperate clash with the merciless political system. The attempts at modernizing and thus universalizing the protagonist were, however, criticized at the meeting of the Film Approval Committee, particularly by Wanda Jakubowska, who largely praised the film's realistic and truthful portrayal of wartime.[49]

The Long Night contained several images that the censor did not want to release, chiefly the representation of some segments of Polish society as anti-Semites. The film also openly questioned the myth of generous Polish wartime help for the Jews, thus making Poles morally responsible for what happened. In addition, the Six-Day War between Israel and the Arab states in June 1967 and the tense situation within the Soviet Bloc contributed to the shelving of the film.[50]

Another film about the Holocaust, Jan Rybkowski's intimate psychological drama *Wniebowstąpienie* (*Ascension Day*, 1969), was also affected by the political situation in the late 1960s. Like Nasfeter in *Unloved*, Rybkowski tells a story about damaging love that can only bring unhappiness and death. The film opens on 22 June 1941 with a precredit long shot image of a group of SS men on motorcycles in a rural landscape and then a cut to a medium close-up of goggled riders over the credits. The commentary reminds the viewer that on this particular day Hitler's Germany attacked the Soviet Union, and portrays the situation in Lwów (modern Lviv) without mentioning that the town had been occupied by the Soviets since September 1939.

Rybkowski's drama revolves around two Jewish protagonists: a beautiful music student, Raisa Wolkowa (Małgorzata Braunek), and a promising scientist with psychological problems, Sebastian Goldstein (Andrzej Antkowiak). Against all odds, they decide to get married in a traditional ceremony and to stay in the occupied town. After the murder of Sebastian's parents, the couple leaves Lwów and stays at the outskirts of Warsaw assuming a Polish identity. Raisa's "Aryan looks" allow her to work and to take care of her ailing husband. Sebastian's recklessness, however, and his growing isolation—a result of his mental illness— endanger not only him but also Raisa and those who offer them shelter and help.

Ascension Day is deprived of a larger social and political context. The recurrent images of the SS men on motorcycles—"the emissaries of hell," as one Polish film reviewer called them[51]—serve as constant reminders about the impending danger. Because of the political atmosphere of the late 1960s, the authorities decided to shelve the film and to screen it later, when there would be another film released about the occupation that would offer a different perspective.[52] One must add that Jan Rybkowski (1912–1987) also experienced problems with his earlier film, *Kiedy miłość była zbrodnią* (*Rassenschande; When Love Was a Crime*, 1968), a Polish–West German coproduction about forbidden love during World War II. As a result, his later films were safer adaptations and films devoid of explicit political issues.[53]

Other films depict the war in a different manner. For example, Andrzej Żuławski's first feature film, *Trzecia część nocy* (*The Third Part of the Night*, 1972), based on the novel written by the director's father, Mirosław Żuławski (and partly based on his war experiences), is governed by the logic of a nightmare. It introduces a young man, Michał (Leszek Teleszyński), who after witnessing the killing of his son and wife (Małgorzata Braunek), manages to escape from a country manor to a city and tries to survive in a cruel world reminding him of his loss. He falls in love with another woman (also played by Braunek) who just lost her husband. He takes care of her family by becoming a "lice feeder" at Prof. Rudolf Weigl's laboratory in Lwów (Lviv), where successful experiments to find a cure for typhoid were conducted in the 1920s and where the production of typhus vaccine continued during the war, under the Soviet and then under the Nazi German occupation.[54]

The Third Part of the Night is a film that is difficult to classify, replete with shocking images, doppelgängers, symbolism, stylized dialogues, expressionistic, almost "hysteric" acting, prolonged tracking shots, profile shots, and perplexing dynamic editing. Andrzej Korzyński's psychedelic rock music enhances the film's pulsating rhythm and emotional power. Analyzing the camerawork (by Witold Sobociński), Monika Maszewska-Łupiniak writes:

> *Blinking, unsteady, incomplete, fragmentary—the pictures are to trigger particular associations rather than presenting the course of events. Individual scenes have their own rhythm, emotional intensity, and even style. What is common for the majority of images is a kind of detachment from reality, a phantasmagorical character; after all, we enter into the realm of memory, and, moreover, we touch on matters which contradict the commonsensical, habitual way of perceiving reality. The arrangement of elements which constitute the presented world resembles an almost fractal structure, whose deformed, misshapen matter contains a logic measured by the adopted viewing perspective.*[55]

The mannerism, violent imagery, exhilarating camera movement, and nonconformity of Żuławski's (1940–2016) early films surprised and shocked both audiences and film authorities. Because of its accumulation of shocking imagery, Żuławski's next film, *Diabeł* (*Devil*, 1972), frequently labeled a horror film, was not released until 1988. Authorities stopped the two-year-long production of Żuławski's lavish science fiction film, *Na srebrnym globie* (*On the Silver Globe*), in 1977 for allegedly going over budget (a reconstructed version of this film was premiered by the director in 1989). Consequently, Żuławski decided to move permanently to France, where he directed several controversial and violent art house films, including *Possession* (1981), *La femme publique* (*The Public Woman*, 1984), *L'amour braque* (*Mad Love*, 1985), *Boris Godunov* (1990), *La note bleue* (*Blue Note*, 1991), and *La fidélité* (*Faithfulness*, 2000). In 1996, Żuławski returned briefly to Poland to direct *Szamanka* (*She-Shaman*), fittingly nicknamed by Polish critics as "Last Tango in Warsaw."

* * *

Several films reflect the divisions among the Polish underground toward the end of the war and the plight of the Home Army and other underground units after 1945. They include, among others, *Barwy walki* (*Scenes of Battle*, 1965, Jerzy Passendorfer), *Potem nastąpi cisza* (*Then There Will Be Silence*, 1966, Janusz Morgenstern), *Ciemna rzeka* (*Dark River*, 1974, Sylwester Szyszko), and *Znikąd donikąd* (*From Nowhere to Nowhere*, 1975, Kazimierz Kutz). With the exception of the action-oriented, propagandist *Scenes of Battle*, based on the book written by Minister of the Interior Mieczysław Moczar, which celebrates the communist partisans, other films deal with the political divisions after the war, the moral aspect of the war, and the struggles between the remaining Home Army units and the regular Polish troops.

The postwar situation is also present in the embryonic Polish genre cinema. The influences of the Western genre are transparent in films such as *Prawo i pięść* (*The Law and the Fist*, 1964, Jerzy Hoffman and Edward Skórzewski) and *Wilcze echa* (*Wolves' Echoes*, 1968, Aleksander Ścibor-Rylski). The action's scenery becomes the postwar reality in the Regained Lands and the Bieszczady Mountains in southeast Poland. Both films employ the motif of a lone official who defends the law and clashes with gangster types. These superficial transplants of the Western genre became popular partly because of the absence of American popular cinema on Polish screens. In *The Law and the Fist*, Gustaw Holoubek plays Andrzej Kenig, a concentration camp survivor who moves to a small deserted town in western Poland, where a criminal gang confronts him. Unlike the East German *Indianerfilm* or the Hungarian "Goulash Westerns," Polish Westerns do not feature stock Western characters but instead focus primarily on American Western narrative conventions, employ Western-like music (for example, by Krzysztof Komeda in *The Law and the Fist*), and feature the new Polish frontiers. The protagonists in this new Polish cinematic "Wild West," often loners with a wartime past, are fighting not just with some criminal elements but the enemies of the new system.

Third Polish Cinema

The tendency to disregard the prewar period in Polish cinema and discuss only its postwar achievements is reflected in the term *Trzecie kino polskie* (Third Polish

Cinema), coined by some Polish critics in the mid-1960s.⁵⁶ They wanted to stress another generational change occurring in Polish cinema. For them, the "third generation" consisted of filmmakers raised, sometimes even born, in postwar Poland, whose political baptism by fire was not the war and its aftermath, but rather the events of the Polish October and the Gomułka years of "small stabilization." After the "first generation"—the postwar generation represented by, among others, Wanda Jakubowska and Aleksander Ford—and the "Polish School (second) generation," the late 1960s marked the emergence of filmmakers for whom national history and politics are less important. Reality and philosophical reflections on culture are of prime significance. These filmmakers are characterized by their different interests and cinematic styles; they are preoccupied with reality, skeptical about the world, suspicious of the national romantic tradition, and interested in personal cinema. Jackiewicz observes:

> *Polański, Skolimowski, Majewski, and now Kluba. Maybe this is another generation of Polish cinema? After Munk, Wajda, Kawalerowicz, Has, after the Polish School, new generation? The earlier filmmakers were serious, excessive, baroque, expressionistic, and naive. The latter with a distance, a smile, with tendencies to mystification and caricature. The earlier came from romanticism, surrealism, Wyspiański, Buñuel, Olivier's "theater," and Kurosawa. The latter from Beckett, Mrożek, Godard, and the "new cinema."*⁵⁷

Rafał Marszałek states that the third generation not only introduced the new language of cinema but also complicated the one-dimensional worldview that had dominated Polish cinema: "We know that univocality was for many years the aesthetic ideal of Polish cinema. Before the war, it relied on the mass audience and after the war was subordinated mainly to educational and propagandist norms." According to Marszałek, the newcomers "proposed a different aesthetic hierarchy based on the multilayered status of the work of art and its equivocal reading."⁵⁸

The term "Third Polish Cinema," which also appears in books published in North America,⁵⁹ has little explanatory power. It covers disparate film poetics and distinct directorial personalities. Among the new filmmakers emerging after the Polish School period, two stand out from the rest: Jerzy Skolimowski (1936–) in the mid-1960s and Krzysztof Zanussi (1939–) in the late 1960s and early 1970s. Both created personal films that are unique in the context of Polish cinema, and introduced characters with personal rather than political problems, moral dilemmas rather than disputes about history, and new generational experiences reflected in a refreshing style.

Jerzy Skolimowski

In his trilogy about the new generation—*Rysopis* (*Identification Marks: None*, 1965), *Walkower* (*Walkover*, 1965), and *Bariera* (*The Barrier*, 1966)—Skolimowski introduces an outsider who searches for his own way of life, a nonconformist who refuses to accept reality. The protagonist, played in the first two films by Skolimowski, does everything to destroy any possibility of entering the mainstream of life. Although frequently analyzed in the context of European new wave cinema,[60] the protagonist is much in line with the traditional Polish romantic hero, with his rebellious, self-destructive nature.[61] Skolimowski's stylized language, full of references to Polish culture and politics and to his own biographical legend (as a poet, a screenwriter for *Innocent Sorcerers* and *Knife in the Water*, and a boxer), attacks the post-Stalinist conformity. The protagonist's search for the new, his journey (both physical and psychological), defies the world of "small stabilization." Skolimowski's presence on the screen and many autobiographical features certainly help to make the film a personal statement and to reflect on the texture of the epoch.

As stated earlier, Skolimowski's films have a style similar to the new wave trends in European cinema of the 1960s. His films are open, documentary-like constructs, shot on location without artificial lighting, frequently improvised on the set,[62] and characterized by their reliance on long takes (for example, there are only thirty-five cuts in *Walkover*).[63] This style was already evidenced in Skolimowski's diploma film made at the Łódź Film School, *Identification Marks: None*, which was produced from numerous student exercises, filmic etudes made since the second year of Skolimowski's studies.[64] The episodic film centers on Andrzej Leszczyc (Skolimowski), who is expelled from the university because of his own mistake, not because he supported some political causes. The protagonist does not want to live like the older generation did and attempts to prolong his youth by avoiding personal or professional commitments. Skolimowski produces the "spiritual generational biography"[65] and offers the essence of authorial cinema: he is the director-screenwriter-actor of the film, which features his then wife, Elżbieta Czyżewska, and his Łódź Film School friends. Skolimowski's next film,

Walkover, continues to follow the story of Andrzej Leszczyc, now a thirty-year-old boxer, living on his modest boxing prizes. When he tries to win another boxing tournament and faces a stronger opponent, he decides not to give up. This decision signals that he wants to embrace a mature life, which requires fight and commitment.

Certainly, the most elaborate is the third part of the generational trilogy, *The Barrier*. Jan Nowicki replaces Skolimowski as a nameless outsider about to begin a new life. In the first sequence, the protagonist leaves a university campus with a suitcase containing a piggy bank won at the student hall. Convinced that ideals are meant to be lost eventually, he decides to speed up the process, marry a rich woman, and quickly establish himself within the society of "small stabilization." A chance meeting with a young female tram driver (Joanna Szczerbic) leads to an internal confrontation with his ideas about life.

The Barrier works against mainstream Polish cinema, which is obsessed with the romantic, martyrological aspect of the past—World War II in particular. By introducing some characters against a white background, with their hands held tightly behind their backs, the opening scene of *The Barrier* looks like another Polish war/partisan film. The viewer learns later that this is a part of the absurd student game. The very title of the film introduces the theme of a generational conflict: the barrier has been built between the generation of fathers, locked in their past, not in touch with the new reality, and the new generation, which was too young to be active during the war. The protagonist's alienation from the older generation as well as the grotesque aspect of the war veterans' behavior are ridiculed in a scene in which numerous male war veterans sing a patriotic song. Not understood by the protagonist (or by the viewers), they sing asynchronously, sometimes not even remembering the lyrics, while the camera pans over a group of women sitting at the tables, waiting patiently. Skolimowski also mocks the exaggerated and fake wartime stories of the older generation, for example, in the encounter with a man faking his blindness and inventing his tragic war story. The protagonist compares those who helped to develop the "small stabilization" to geese: "You get fat and lose bird's ambition to fly. I understand you."

Because the film is set around Easter time, the theme of resurrection, both personal and generational, comes to the foreground. The music, composed by Krzysztof Komeda, with the Hallelujah sung by a vocal group, provides an ironic, sometimes almost tragic comment on the action. To make *The Barrier* even more personal, a cleaner in a restaurant visited by the protagonist unexpectedly begins a song to the poetry of Skolimowski (she is played by Maria Malicka, but the song is performed by Ewa Demarczyk). Michael Walker comments: "Sequences of 'pure fantasy' are blended with stylised visualisations of reality, creating a richly poetic (*and* homogeneous) texture."[66] The film's poetic stylization and ornate symbolism refer to Polish history and culture. Carrying his father's saber, the protagonist wanders through an artificial space that is frequently only a white, dreamlike, and surrealist landscape.

The Barrier proved to be the last film Skolimowski was able to produce and release in the 1960s in Poland. His next project, *Ręce do góry (Hands Up)*, about the postwar generation that quickly gave up its ideals and turned to a middle-class existence and middle-class aspirations, was completed in 1967 but released as late as 1985. This film, one of the first to deal with the Stalinist years, was too difficult for communist authorities to take. One scene from *Hands Up* is usually singled out for emphasis. A group of once-ambitious students in the 1950s (now conformists addressing each other by the names of their cars) recall an incident from their youth involving Stalin's image. While preparing parts of an enormous portrait of Stalin for the state event, they paint an extra pair of eyes by mistake. When the portrait is assembled and raised publicly, Stalin appears with four eyes. He is sinister (no one can escape his scrutiny) yet grotesque.

Unable to continue his career in Poland, Skolimowski left the country. He went on to make several films in the West, including *The Shout* (1978, UK), *Moonlighting* (1982, UK), *Success Is the Best Revenge* (1984, UK), *The Lightship* (1985, US), and *Torrents of Spring* (1989, France/Italy).

Krzysztof Zanussi

Krzysztof Zanussi's unusual road to filmmaking is clearly reflected in his films. After years of studying physics and philosophy and making amateur films, he enrolled at the Łódź Film School. Zanussi attracted international attention with his medium-length diploma film, *The Death of a Provincial,* and two television films made in 1968, *Face to Face* and *Pass Mark*. These films contain many thematic features characteristic of his later films: the mystery of death, the conflict between the individual and society, existential problems, and moral choices. For example, in an intimate, well-received film, *The Death of a Provincial,* Zanussi focuses on a young art historian working in a monastery who witnesses the agony of an old monk.

Zanussi's Bergmanesque themes and his austere, noncommittal style became his trademarks. Usually, Zanussi avoids films that make a social commitment, that refer to the romantic roots of Polish culture. He prefers multidimensional and detailed realistic observation. Coates aptly writes: "Not until the arrival of Zanussi was a new style created that other directors could assimilate: that of the low-key television drama. Zanussi replaced the pathos-laden style of the Polish school with scrupulous attention to the everyday.... The bad faith of faithful reconstruction of irrelevant pasts gave way to a careful examination of the present."[67] Zanussi's realism refers less to the social and more to the psychological and philosophical reality; therefore, the terms "intellectual cinema" and "artist-intellectual" are frequently applied to his works.[68]

Zanussi's full-length films, beginning with *Struktura kryształu* (*The Structure of Crystals*, 1969), created his reputation as an auteur interested in specific characters, known as "Zanussoids"—young intellectuals questioning the corrupt world.[69] Several young members of the Polish intelligentsia identified with the protagonist of *Iluminacja* (*Illumination*, 1973) and later praised the parable on politics presented in *Barwy ochronne* (*Camouflage*, 1977). Zanussi started to function as the representative of "intellectual cinema," a cosmopolitan Pole at home everywhere, a cultural ambassador of the Catholic Poland.

Jackiewicz commented: "With *The Structure of Crystals*, a long-awaited personality in Polish cinema has been born."[70] Zanussi's film was also the start of his permanent collaboration with the renowned composer Wojciech Kilar. This modest black-and-white film, made during the era of big-budget historical adaptations, was shot entirely on location. It is very authentic, resembling a documentary, and is addressed to sophisticated viewers. "For the first time, we get into a filmic reality that is not simulated," states Rafał Marszałek.[71] Written by Zanussi, who writes or cowrites all his films, *The Structure of Crystals* depicts young intellectuals and their moral choices and ethical problems. The story concerns the meeting of two physicists, former university friends: Marek (Andrzej Żarnecki), who lives in Warsaw and has just returned from a fellowship in the West, and Jan (Jan Mysłowicz), who works at a provincial meteorological station and lives with his wife, Anna (Barbara Wrzesińska), in a remote village. The worldly Marek tries to convince Jan to return to the university and gradually learns the reasons behind his friend's decision to live a quiet life. The film introduces two personalities and two ways to succeed in life: dynamic expansion and professional success versus calmness and independence—the narrow approach (Marek specializes in the structure of crystals) versus the broad, humanistic outlook. Zanussi grants virtues evenly to both protagonists and does not offer easy solutions in the choice between *vita activa* and *vita contemplativa*.

In the psychological drama *Życie rodzinne* (*Family Life*, 1971), Zanussi introduces another conflict between differing philosophies of life and moral issues. The director queries whether one has the right to get rid of one's roots if they prove to be an obstacle to living a desired life. He narrates the conflict between the father (Jan Kreczmar), the prewar factory owner out of touch with the new reality, and the son, Wit (Daniel Olbrychski), who loosens his ties to family. Zanussi's favorite actress, Maja Komorowska (1937–), made her film debut in *Family Life* as Wit's sister, Bella. She had begun her long collaboration with Zanussi the year before, appearing in the television film *Góry o zmierzchu* (*Mountains at Dusk*). Her next television film for Zanussi, *Za ścianą* (*Next Door*, 1971), fully demonstrated her ability to convey the uneasiness and psychological torment of her characters. Both she and another prototypical "Zanussian actor," Zbigniew Zapasiewicz (1934–2009) as a reserved docent, greatly contributed to the success of this classic Polish television production.

Bilans kwartalny (*A Woman's Decision*, aka *Balance Sheet*, 1975), one of Zanussi's finest films, also stars Komorowska as Marta, an altruistic accountant who is always thinking of others yet is bored with her own life. She has a short-lived extramarital affair with Jacek (played by a director, Marek Piwowski), a free-spirited man not preoccupied with the material aspects of life. In this story of a marital triangle, Marta's husband, Janek (Piotr Fronczewski), is portrayed as a person obsessed with work and unable to show his true emotions. The whole affair is depicted in an observational manner, with much attention paid to everyday details, to the Polish reality of the 1970s. The linear, slow-paced narrative of this well-received, internationally known film is devoid of the structural complexities of Zanussi's previous film, *Illumination*.

Illumination is a philosophical essay unusual in Polish cinema. The film links an episodic, fictional narrative with documentary fragments (newsreels, interviews with noted Polish scientists, and fragments of their lectures). It begins with an explanation of the film's title delivered by a prominent Polish philosopher, Władysław Tatarkiewicz. *Illuminatio* (illumination), a medieval philosophical term introduced by St. Augustine, stands for an intellectual and spiritual enlightenment gained through intellectual hardship and purity of heart.[72] The film's narrative concerns ten years in the life of a young physicist, Franciszek Retman (Stanisław

Latałło). The camera follows him from his matriculation in a small-town school, through his studies in physics, his first sexual experience with an older woman, his marriage to Małgosia (Małgorzata Pritulak), the birth of their child, work, the death of a friend, personal crisis, the search for answers at the Cameldolite monastery, the return to his family, and the acceptance of his fate. Zanussi admits that he uses the term "illumination" in a bitter sense.[73] Although convinced that truth can be fathomed rationally, the film's protagonist gains illumination through his life experience. Zanussi employs real scientists, nonprofessional actors (such as Latałło, a camera operator), and the form of a filmic essay to tell the story of a typical individual almost in the manner of a clinical case. "Zanussi's film belongs to those rare moments in film history," writes Jackiewicz, "when a film seems to be granted the grace of illumination."[74]

Films by Edward Żebrowski (1935–2014) thematically and stylistically resemble the cinema of Zanussi. A collaborator with Zanussi (the co-screenwriter of several of Zanussi's films), Żebrowski started his career with *Ocalenie* (*Deliverance*, 1972). The film deals with a scientist (Zbigniew Zapasiewicz) whose busy routine is interrupted when he contracts a fatal illness, forcing him to reflect on his life. In his next film, *Szpital Przemienienia* (*The Hospital of Transfiguration*, 1979), based on Stanisław Lem's novel, Żebrowski continues his examination of a character facing dramatic choices. Set in September 1939, the film tells a story about the Germans' killing of patients in a mental asylum. Żebrowski portrays the microcosm of Polish prewar society through the divisions among the hospital staff who experience the extreme situation.

Searching for a New Style

Żywot Mateusza (*The Life of Matthew*, 1968), directed by Witold Leszczyński (1933–2007), is certainly a unique film of the late 1960s in Poland. The slow-paced story, an adaptation of Tarjei Vesaas's novel, is divided into seven chapters and concerns the forty-year-old Matthew (Franciszek Pieczka), an oversensitive person whom his neighbors consider mentally handicapped. Living with his sister, Olga (Anna Milewska), in virtual isolation on the lake, Matthew develops an unusual closeness to nature. When the outside world turns on Matthew (his sister falls in love with an outsider, a woodcutter), he paddles to the middle of the lake and punches a hole in the bottom of his boat. The director introduces the

Figure 6.3 Franciszek Pieczka as Matthew, Małgorzata Braunek (left), and Maria Janiec (right) in Witold Leszczyński's *The Life of Matthew* (1968). Photograph by Jacek Mierosławski. Courtesy of Film Studio Zebra.

psychological study of loneliness and of the relationship between man and nature. Exquisite cinematography by Andrzej Kostenko and the skillful use of classical music by Arcangelo Corelli enhance the poetic atmosphere of the film.

The co-screenwriter of *The Life of Matthew*, Wojciech Solarz, one year later directed his debut film, *Molo* (*Jetty*), an ingeniously—in the French New Wave spirit—narrated story dealing with the middle-age crisis of a ship designer from the Gdańsk Shipyard (Ryszard Filipski) for whom his fortieth birthday serves as a reminder of things he missed in life.

It must be noted that innovative films were often produced by some older filmmakers, for example, Władysław Ślesicki and Jerzy Ziarnik (1931–1999), both better known for their classic documentaries. In 1969, Ślesicki directed *Ruchome piaski* (*Shifting Sands*), starring Małgorzata Braunek and Marek Walczewski. Jerzy Ziarnik's psychological drama *Wycieczka w nieznane* (*A Journey into the Unknown*, aka *Across the Unknown*, 1968) focuses on a young and carefree writer, Andrzej Miller (Ryszard Filipski), for whom a chance trip to Auschwitz, to watch the production of a film based on his friend's script, forever changes his perspective on life. Ziarnik's film, among others, deals with the issue of memorializing Auschwitz. The young writer observes the inept film crew at work on location in Auschwitz and the touristy aspect of the Auschwitz museum. A film-within-a-film segment of *A Journey into the Unknown*, the fictionalization of the camp experience, includes several pointed observations and appears to be the strongest part of the film, although Polish critics did not take it as such. Like István Szabó in *Father* (*Apa*, 1966), Ziarnik interweaves the past (photographs and names of the murdered) with the present; he also comments on role playing/reversal by showing the film crew in action: extras playing SS guards flirt with "female prisoners" during the break in shooting.

One of the most independent Polish filmmakers, Grzegorz Królikiewicz, made another rare film. After a series of short films, he made an ambitious and provocative documentary-like film, *Na wylot* (*Through and Through*, aka *Clear Through*, 1973), a work based on a well-publicized murder case in prewar Poland. The Malisz couple—unemployed, alienated from society, and desperate to change their miserable conditions—murder a mail carrier and the elderly couple who witnessed their deed. Królikiewicz shows the ugliness and despair of the characters, played by Franciszek Trzeciak and Anna Nieborowska, and the revolting reality that surrounds them; he is not afraid to portray the repulsive physicality of the murder, an animal-like attack that shocks an unprepared viewer. Atypical camera movement, bizarre angles, merciless close-ups that disfigure the protagonists, images difficult to decipher, and bizarre sound effects help to intensify the emotional aspect of the film.

Królikiewicz is not only a screenwriter-director but also a film theorist who has taught at the Łódź Film School since 1977. His theoretical works, especially his examination of the offscreen space,[75] are reflected in techniques used in *Through and Through*: rudimentary dialogues, unusual camera angles, and the uncommon composition of frame. For example, in the murder scene, the viewer sees one of the images upside down, with the victim's blood dropping from bottom to top of the screen. Królikiewicz also experiments with sound; he relies on sound and unusual sound effects to tell the story when the action is outside of the camera's gaze or when the camera pans away. The search for a new cinematic language and the avoidance of psychologization resulted in the mixed reception of some of Królikiewicz's later films, such as *Fort 13* (1983) and *Zabicie ciotki* (*The Killing of Aunt*, 1984). His formal experiments were often unintelligible, even to critics.

Slightly older than Skolimowski and Zanussi, Janusz Majewski (1931–) began his career in the 1960s with films in a variety of genres. Trained as an architect and later at the Łódź Film School, Majewski started out as an art director and a documentarian. His *Album Fleischera* (*Private Fleischer's Photo Album*, 1963), which portrays the war through the eyes of an ordinary German soldier, became a classic example of Polish documentary cinema. Majewski also made several successful television films, mostly mysteries, such as *Awatar, czyli zamiana dusz* (*Awatar, or the Exchange of Souls*, 1964) and *Ja gorę!* (*I Am Burning!* 1967). His range is demonstrated by another well-received television drama, the psychological study *Czarna suknia* (*The Black Dress*, 1967), starring Ida Kamińska and Aleksandra Śląska.

Majewski is chiefly known for his well-crafted, stylish literary adaptations made in the late 1960s and the 1970s. He began with a black comedy, *Sublokator* (*The Lodger*, 1967), which was followed by a crime film, *Zbrodniarz, który ukradł zbrodnię* (*The Criminal Who Stole a Crime*, 1969), frequently cited as one of the best Polish crime films. In *Lokis* (*The Bear*, 1970), based on Prosper Mérimée's short story, Majewski continued his fascination with the horror genre. Critical acclaim, however, allowed him to make subtle adaptations of the prewar Polish literary canon: *Zazdrość i medycyna* (*Jealousy and Medicine*, 1973), based on Michał Choromański's novel, and *Zaklęte rewiry* (*Hotel Pacific*, 1975), an adaptation of Henryk Worcell's fiction.

In *Jealousy and Medicine*, Ewa Krzyżewska (known for her role in Wajda's *Ashes and Diamonds*) appears in the role of Rebeka Widmar, an object of desire of two men: her husband (Mariusz Dmochowski) and lover (Andrzej Łapicki). Krzyżewska's portrayal of Rebeka shares many similarities with other female Jewish characters in Polish cinema, often portrayed as attractive, sexual, and competing for a Polish man with a plain, down-to-earth Polish woman (sometimes represented by an iconic figure of a Polish Mother).[76]

Hotel Pacific, Majewski's Polish-Czechoslovak coproduction, narrates the experiences of a young waiter (Marek Kondrat) working in an exclusive Kraków hotel in the 1930s. The film's detailed reconstruction of the past (with cinematography by Miloš Forman's collaborator Miroslav Ondříček) is combined with a psychological observation of the power struggle and mechanisms of power in the small, hierarchic world of the restaurant.

Unlike Majewski, numerous young, emerging filmmakers in the early 1970s dealt with different aspects of contemporary life. Their equally young protagonists learn about life, experience first love, get first jobs, and follow their dreams in a conformist world. For example, in *Kardiogram* (*Cardiogram*, 1971) Roman Załuski (1936–) portrays the Polish province as seen through the eyes of a young physician (Tadeusz Borowski), who chooses to settle and start his career in a small town. Another physician, also played by Borowski, appears in Załuski's next film, *Zaraza* (*The Outbreak*, 1972), a psychological drama about the outbreak of black smallpox in Wrocław. In 1972, Załuski also made *Anatomia miłości* (*Anatomy of Love*, 1972), starring Jan Nowicki and Barbara Brylska, which offered a popular, contemporary love story.

Janusz Zaorski's debut at the age of twenty-four, *Uciec jak najbliżej* (*Escape as Near as Possible*, 1972), paints a realistic picture of the younger generation. It introduces a young man who travels across Poland on business, representing a small company that produces road signs. Zaorski portrays a typical generational character. Symbolically, the protagonist carries only road warning signs and signs that must be obeyed—no directional signs. He also comes from a town that is the geographical center of Poland. In the final scene, he enters a sports stadium in which the young women are practicing gymnastics for the state holiday and searches for the girl he has just met and spent the night with. Suddenly, the women form the map of Poland, and he finds himself in its middle: undecided, confused, and without direction.

Chudy i inni (*Skinny and Others*, 1967) and *Słońce wschodzi raz na dzień* (*The Sun Rises Once a Day*, 1967, not released until 1972),[77] directed by Henryk Kluba (1931–2005) and written by Wiesław Dymny, offer different film poetics. *Skinny and Others*, a socialist realist production film *à rebours*, introduces antiheroic workers. *The Sun Rises Once a Day* focuses on the postwar reality in the Beskid Mountains and the clash between the new communist reality and the self-governing aspirations of the mountaineers. It is a highly stylized folk ballad—with a choir of village elders commenting on the action—that portrays public distrust of the new political order.

Another film, *Palec Boży* (*God's Finger*, 1973), directed by Antoni Krauze (1940–),[78] is about a man who is so focused on his future profession as an actor that it becomes the source of his psychological problems. Marian Opania stars as the oversensitive, small-town protagonist. Several films also deal with juvenile crime in a realistic manner, for example, *Trąd* (*Leprosy*, 1971) and *Zapis zbrodni* (*Record of Crime*, 1974), both directed by Andrzej Trzos-Rastawiecki (1933–). *Record of Crime* in particular refers to an actual murder case and offers a paradocumentary examination of the sociological and psychological circumstances leading to crime.

Probably the finest film concerning the younger generation was made by the Polish School generation filmmaker Janusz Morgenstern. His *Trzeba zabić tę miłość* (*Kill That Love*, 1972), written by Janusz Głowacki, depicts love between two young people who did not get enough points to enter university. They start their first jobs to support themselves and to prepare for future studies. Jadwiga Jankowska-

Figure 6.4 Jadwiga Jankowska-Cieślak as Magda and Władysław Kowalski in Janusz Morgenstern's *Kill That Love* (1972). Photograph by Renata Pajchel. Courtesy of Film Studio Zebra.

Cieślak as Magda, a girl dreaming about becoming a doctor, created one of the most interesting characters in Polish cinema of the 1970s. The film presents the Polish reality—a degraded world in which everybody cheats—as an obstacle to happiness. The protagonists' love is not strong enough to survive the grotesquely portrayed socialist reality. This aspect of the film owes greatly to the screenwriter, Głowacki, who was then known for his short stories and a column published in the weekly *Kultura*. Głowacki's feel for the propagandist's newspeak, as well as his ironic and grotesque comments, enrich Morgenstern's film. *Kill That Love* also has a subplot without dialogue that comments on the action. It concerns the warehouseman (Jan Himilsbach) who sells cement on the black market while he is supposed to be on guard. In the film's final scene, he wants to kill his faithful dog, who barked at his "clients," by attaching a stick of dynamite to him. The dog, however, hides in a warehouse (the place where the lovers first met), and the explosion that follows serves as an ironic reference to *Zabriskie Point* (1969), a film about youth rebellion.

Kazimierz Kutz's Silesia

In the 1960s, Kazimierz Kutz made a series of realistic films set in provincial Poland that received mixed reviews from Polish critics: *Tarpany* (*Wild Horses*, 1962), the film that marks the beginning of Kutz's collaboration with the cinematographer

Wiesław Zdort; *Milczenie* (*Silence*, 1963); *Ktokolwiek wie* (*Whoever Knows*, 1966); and *Skok* (*Robbery*, 1969). As always, Kutz worked against mainstream Polish cinema. In the decade of epic adaptations, his films were realistic pictures, new wave narrative experiments, and examinations of provincial places, simple people, and everyday rituals. The failed attempt to steal money in *Robbery* is only a pretext to portray a realistic picture of young people. *Silence* describes the small-town indifference faced by a young boy who was blinded by an accident. In *Whoever Knows*, a young investigative reporter (Edward Linde-Lubaszenko) searches for a missing girl. He discovers her background and family history, the pressure of her social circle, and her alienation. Made in the spirit of Michelangelo Antonioni's early works, Kutz's film offers no solutions; the reporter simply gives up his search.

Kutz's return to his roots, his native Upper Silesia,[79] proved to be one of the most important moments in Polish postwar cinema. He produced a trilogy of personal films that form the contemporary Polish canon: *Sól ziemi czarnej* (*Salt of the Black Earth*, 1970), *Perła w koronie* (*The Pearl in the Crown*, 1972), and *Paciorki jednego różańca* (*Beads of One Rosary*, 1980). Traditionally regarded by the Warsaw-based Polish film industry as an unglamorous, unphotogenic province of hard work, coal mines, and unfamiliar history, Silesia burst into the Polish consciousness thanks to Kutz' powerful vision. Unlike the realistic *Beads of One Rosary*, set in the late 1970s, the first two parts of the trilogy deal with modern history and the culture of Silesia. Written by Kutz, and with music by Wojciech Kilar, all these films introduce authentic places and real people with local dialects, modes of thinking, and dreams. Kutz continues his interest in "simple people" with the plebeian character that he developed during the Polish School period. He does not want to follow the filmic fashions that Polish cinema often slavishly emulates. As he explains, "Instead of narrating about a human being, it [Polish film] relates the cause, mostly the patriotic one, which has to elevate that person, give him some worth, and show it in the context of Polish suffering."[80]

Salt of the Black Earth deals with the second Polish uprising in a series of three armed uprisings against the German rule of Silesia during August 1920.[81] The story concerns the Basista family: the patriarchal father, the silent mother and sisters, and the seven miner brothers. The Basista family house serves as the bastion of Polishness and traditional rituals concerning family life, work, and the love for the region. The youngest son, Gabryel (Olgierd Łukaszewicz), and his coming-of-age story remain at the center of the film. The film depicts his political and sexual initiation, his infatuation with a German nurse, and his irresponsible behavior as an insurgent in the uprising when, in a stolen German uniform, he moves into enemy territory to see the nurse. In the final days of the uprising, the wounded Gabryel is carried to the Polish border by four young women angels.

Although the film is set during the actual political event, it surprisingly neglects politics at the cost of creating a poetic image of the province. In folk ballad form, Kutz shows grayish images of industrial Silesia—coal mines, piles of waste coal, steelworks, and railway tracks—contrasted with the reddish color of miners' brick houses.[82] The regional costumes, folk art, chants, everyday rituals, and customs enhance the authenticity. Several images resemble medieval, perhaps naive paintings. Rafał Marszałek justly compares Kutz's symbolism in *Salt of the Black Earth* with that of Sergei Parajanov in *Sayat-nova* (*The Color of Pomegranates*, 1969, released in 1972). In both films, everyday rituals are full of symbolic meaning.[83]

While agreeing with Marszałek's comment, I would also like to point out similarities with Miklós Jancsó's 1960s Hungarian films. Both filmmakers use similar rhythms, symbolism, and choreographed movements of actors. For example, in the final sequence of Kutz's film, the defeated and encircled insurgents try to break through German positions to reach the nearby Polish border. They rip their jackets off in the futile hope of running faster. The bullets strike them in the back, and their white shirts get soaked with red blood—the colors of the Polish flag. The scene, shown partly in slow motion, was filmed with a handheld camera for point-of-view shots. Finally, the street is white and red, covered by fallen insurgents. Gabryel's nurse moves among the dead and the wounded, beginning her work. In the next scene, while some insurgents lie dead in the street, their bodies arranged in an orderly manner like animals killed after the hunt, the execution of others begins.

There are, obviously, numerous differences between the styles of Kutz and Jancso. Wiesław Zdort's camera in *Salt of the Black Earth* is not circling; there is no elaborate panning, lengthy take, or tracking. Unlike Jancsó's solemn metaphorical imagery, Kutz's film introduces comic interludes during fights, and folk festivities between them. Kutz portrays death as an everyday phenomenon and uses pointed, sometimes crude, dialogue in the Silesian dialect. The composition of frame relies primarily on long shots with distant figures of insurgents moving through the industrial landscape. The characters, however, are not alienated from this landscape; the mise-en-scène stresses that the characters belong there.

Kutz juxtaposes the images of industrial Silesia with the pastoral vision of Poland. For example, when Gabryel conquers a German tower, he looks through

Figure 6.5 (From the right) Jerzy Bińczycki, Olgierd Łukaszewicz, Jan Englert, and Jerzy Cnota in Kazimierz Kutz's *Salt of the Black Earth* (1970). Courtesy of Filmoteka Narodowa.

a military telescope at the idyllic landscapes of nearby Poland: the tranquil splendor of green valleys and the dangerous beauty of the mountains. Kutz also pictures the pragmatism of the Silesians and clashes it with the traditional Polish romanticism. The uprising is portrayed almost like a job that must be done, and patriotism is understood as love for the region. The Basista brothers go to the uprising without any romantic notions; when overpowered by the Germans, the commander of the insurgent unit, Erwin (Jan Englert), simply announces the end of the uprising. This pragmatic approach is sharply contrasted with the idealism of a young Polish artillery officer (Daniel Olbrychski), as handsome as a figure in a romantic chromolithograph, who helps the miners against his superiors' orders and dies a clichéd, romantic death. His appearance, short participation in the uprising, death, and burial epitomize the essence of traditional Polish romantic ideals. Commenting on the differences between Silesia and Poland, Kutz observes:

> Poland appears to us as a land of gentry, the nobility living in whitewashed manors, with obedient and backward peasantry dependent on them. The peasants are educated by virtuous maidens who do so because of a shortage of more useful occupations. In a sentence, this is a country where work is not the basis of existence. In my memory, there was nothing like that in Silesia. I grew up in a world of concrete work, in a harrowing landscape, and my surrounding was always the family group, generations living in the same place, and inheriting professions and the customs.[84]

The second part of the trilogy, *The Pearl in the Crown*, concerns the coal miners' strike in the 1930s, which was brought on by the closure of their mine, Zygmunt.

Although this part of Silesia now belongs to Poland, the mines are administered by German owners and protected by Polish police. The miners try to prevent the mine's flooding by occupying it. When negotiations fail, they continue with a hunger strike. The film's protagonist, Jaś (Olgierd Łukaszewicz), remains with the strikers out of solidarity, although he would rather have stayed at home with his wife, Wichta (Łucja Kowolik), and their two small sons. The strikers, led by their leader, Hubert Siersza (Franciszek Pieczka), are supported by the Silesians on the ground and organized by Erwin (Jan Englert), the former insurgent in *Salt of the Black Earth*, now unemployed. The first sequences of the film portray the harsh reality of the economic crisis, the closure of the mines, and the small coal pits run by the unemployed miners.

The Pearl in the Crown provides discourses on class solidarity, family ties, tradition, love for the family, and love for the land. The film also serves as a powerful love story: the intensity of its lyricism and eroticism is probably unparalleled in Polish cinema. As in *Salt of the Black Earth*, Kutz portrays Silesia—a region traditionally seen as colorless and almost inhuman—in a poetic, folk ballad manner. Similarly, he glorifies the traditions and celebrates the patriarchal order with highly stylized images. Simple, everyday rituals attain a symbolic meaning. For example, the protagonist's sons always wait for him after work and escort him home, where his wife washes his feet and assists with his bath. Further links with the first part of the trilogy are established by using the same actors, such as Olgierd Łukaszewicz, Jan Englert, and the "Silesian actors," such as Jerzy Cnota and Bernard Krawczyk.

In *The Pearl in the Crown*, Kutz moves further with stylization, symbolism, and mythologization of everyday rituals. He introduces authentic people playing themselves, speaking their own dialect, and celebrating their own customs. Kutz claims without exaggeration that his films could be called scientific ethnographic works.[85] With the help of his cinematographer, Stanisław Loth, the director also relies on contrast, this time between the harsh reality inside the mine (blackness, hunger strike) and the colorful reality on the ground (the picturesque crowd waiting for the strikers). Kutz also shows the differences between the happiness of the protagonist's home and the brutal reality outside. In the course of the film, the juxtaposition of the gloomy underworld of the mine and the vibrant world outside gains more and more importance: "The more the miners melt into a black, amorphous mass, the more replete with the bright colours of regional costume becomes the world of the surface."[86] In the final scene, the triumphant strikers—

exhausted, deprived of food and oxygen, and holding each other—emerge from the shaft of the coal mine to face an almost medieval carnival in front of the mine: the colorful crowd in folk costumes, exotic animals, and a brass orchestra.

The realistic picture of Silesia portrayed in *Beads of One Rosary* is the story of a retired miner, Karol Habryka (Augustyn Halotta), who does not want to leave his old house, scheduled for demolition, and move to a new apartment building. In his house, Habryka recalls that he "has survived the two world wars, the emperor, unemployment, strikes, different debasements, Hitler, and other humiliations." The protagonist belongs to the insurgents' generation (he also took part in the Silesian Uprising), yet to the authorities, his refusal to leave his home constitutes an example of antisocial behavior. Finally, recognizing his glorious past (he was also an exemplary miner), the authorities give him a modern house in which he feels completely out of place. A few months after moving, Habryka dies. His burial, and the burial of old culture, is Kutz's farewell to the old Silesia.

As in his two previous "Silesian films," Kutz elevates ordinary activities, such as having breakfast and smoking a pipe, and grants them symbolic status. He also relies on nonprofessional actors from Silesia, this time casting them in the leading roles (Halotta, and Marta Straszna as Habryka's wife). Their personalities, feeling for the local dialect, peculiar humor, and behavior create the intimate atmosphere of this film.[87]

Popular Cinema: Crime and Militia Films

In the aftermath of World War II, cinema in Poland was generally regarded as more than just entertainment. There was little room for commercial cinema within the framework of socialist art. Film's task was to communicate, educate, and perform other social duties.

Although it had the support of an audience, genre cinema in Poland never constituted a distinct part of national film production. This type of cinema was also rarely supported or treated seriously by Polish film critics, who looked for great authors dealing with great themes of national importance. Similarly, this cinema was ignored in the West, which was chiefly interested in films that gave insight into Central European politics. For many critics, certain popular genres, such as the crime film, were impossible to make in the highly politicized climate of communist Poland. Adam Zagajewski comments on the absence of certain popular genres in totalitarian states: "Murder mystery novels are impossible here: everyone always knows who the guilty party is—the state."[88] Zagajewski observes that in totalitarianism, the state monopolizes every aspect of life—including its evil dimensions—and, consequently, becomes "by necessity" the only wrongdoer.

Despite the political obstacles, there were several attempts to make genre cinema—American in form but with "socialist" overtones and messages. For example, the adaptations of "militia novels"[89] resulted in a peculiar version of the detective genre: "militia films," frequently known as "democratic thrillers." These were popular films during the communist period that told stories about the heroes in blue uniforms—representatives of Milicja Obywatelska (MO), a civic militia created in 1945 in the Soviet Bloc to replace the prewar police.

Several filmmakers attempted to make crime films that both imitated American models and echoed ideological messages. *Dotknięcie nocy* (*The Touch of the Night*, 1961, Stanisław Bareja) is usually considered the first Polish postwar crime film. Bareja also produced the first television series about militia work, *Captain Sowa Investigates* (1965), starring Wiesław Gołas as the likeable militia officer. Militia officers, repeatedly portrayed as being highly professional and attractive, were almost always played by likeable and handsome actors, such as Wieńczysław Gliński, who stars as a militia lieutenant in *Ostatni kurs* (*The Last Ride*, 1963, Jan Batory). The film was based on a script by Joe Alex (artistic pseudonym of Maciej Słomczyński) the author of numerous popular detective novels and television plays. Batory later employed dark humor in *Lekarstwo na miłość* (*A Cure for Love*, 1966), starring Andrzej Łapicki as a militia captain. Next year, Łapicki repeated the role of a militia officer in *Gdzie jest trzeci król?* (*Where Is the Third King?* 1967, Ryszard Ber). His character speaks fluent French and has an expert knowledge of art history. In addition to Łapicki and Gliński, other stars of Polish cinema also appeared in these films. Zbigniew Cybulski, for example, played Captain Ziętek in *Zbrodniarz i panna* (*The Criminal and the Maiden*, 1963, Janusz Nasfeter) in which he was again paired with Ewa Krzyżewska, his love interest from *Ashes and Diamonds*.

The Criminal Who Stole a Crime (1969, Janusz Majewski) serves as probably the best example of that genre. Zygmunt Hübner portrays Captain Siwy, an MO officer who successfully continues his search for justice after his retirement. Unlike the protagonists in other Polish crime films, Siwy's character is more than a stereotypical militia officer; he is a multifaceted individual with strengths and weaknesses, a tired hero of socialist work. The villain is played by Ryszard Filipski, who delivered strong performances in several other crime films as both villain and militia officer. For example, also in 1969, he starred as a militia captain in *Tylko umarły odpowie* (*Only the Dead Will Answer*, Sylwester Chęciński).

The militia films also proved to be popular in the 1970s. They included television series such as Krzysztof Szmagier's *Przygody psa Cywila* (*The Adventures of the Police Dog Cywil*, 1970) and, in particular, the series *07 zgłoś się* (*07 Report*, 1976–1987), starring Bronisław Cieślak as Lieutenant Borewicz (unusually, in the Polish context, Cieślak was not a professional actor but a journalist). The genre, however, was changing. In several other films, including *Brylanty pani Zuzy* (*The Diamonds of Mrs. Zuza*, 1972, Paweł Komorowski) and *Strach* (*Fear*, 1975, Antoni Krauze), the focus was no longer on the militia officers but on the more exciting world of crime.

Unlike their Western counterparts, Polish popular genres had to perform several political duties outlined in the state's propagandist cultural policy. In her examination of Polish crime films of the 1960s, Agnieszka Ćwikiel lists the various social roles these films had to perform. First, they had to be ambitious, artistic works that scrupulously reflected life in Poland and contained the truth about its inhabitants. Another task was to show the achievements of the militia and thereby serve as a form of crime prevention. Finally, they had to entertain.[90] Thus, the "popular genres" belonged to the domain of "ambitious cinema." They had to be didactic, touching on political and social issues to justify their existence. For local filmmakers, it was almost impossible to meet the demand of making an entertaining film that would also be apologetic toward the state and its representatives in blue uniforms.

The political correctness of the time required the modification of imported formulae by establishing the militia as the protagonist. The educational tasks of the "militia genre" were achieved by including several stereotyped elements: the emphasis on the futility of crime ("crime does not pay"), the emphasis on the infallibility of the system, and the presentation of militia officers as dignified yet sympathetic characters with proper (usually working-class) backgrounds and beliefs. These attributes were seldom questioned. An example of this type of film would be *Przepraszam, czy tu biją?* (*Foul Play*, 1976, Marek Piwowski), a crime picture starring two boxing champions (Jerzy Kulej and Jan Szczepański) as unconventional police inspectors who are not afraid to employ brutal yet apparently successful methods in their investigative work.

Politics aside, the malfunctioning Polish economy proved to be another obstacle for the production of local popular genres. The colorless reality produced equally unglamorous, paltry crimes. The boring, politically correct militia officers represented an equally boring political system. High-speed chases, car crashes, and luxurious clothes and interiors belonged to a different world. Local audiences could only dream foreign dreams.

Comedies

Alicja Helman wrote in 1971, "We have cultivated an art film whose makers cannot produce popular culture."[91] After 1961, however, comedies began to play a more important role in Polish cinema. Of the 119 films produced from 1961 to 1965, twenty-four are listed as comedies.[92] This genre gained immediate prominence on television as well. *Kabaret Starszych Panów* (*Cabaret of Elderly Gentlemen*), created by the writer Jeremi Przybora and the composer Jerzy Wasowski (the two "elderly gentlemen" of the title), featured some of the best Polish actors: Wiesław Michnikowski, Mieczysław Czechowicz, Wiesław Gołas, and Irena Kwiatkowska, among others. The absurdist, sophisticated, and elegant humor of Przybora and Wasowski, and their delicate mockery of the communist reality, can also be seen in the full-length comedy *Upał* (*Heat*, 1964, Kazimierz Kutz), which continues with the same formula as the cabaret.

Comedies were very popular among the Polish audiences yet rarely appreciated by critics, who awaited the next *Eva Wants to Sleep or Treasure*. The names of Tadeusz Chmielewski (1927–2016), Stanisław Bareja (1929–1987), and Sylwester Chęciński (1930–) became synonymous with comedy, although these filmmakers were also working in other genres. Chmielewski's *Gdzie jest generał?* (*Where Is the General?* 1964), *Jak rozpętałem II wojnę światową* (*How I Unleashed World War II*, three parts, 1970), and *Nie lubię poniedziałku* (*I Hate Mondays*, 1971), despite their popularity, never achieved the critical success of his earlier *Eva Wants to Sleep*. Chęciński became very successful with his trilogy written by Andrzej Mularczyk— *Sami swoi* (*All among Ourselves*, aka *Our Folks*, 1967), *Nie ma mocnych* (*Big Deal*, 1974), and *Kochaj albo rzuć* (*Love It or Leave It*, 1977)—now considered classic Polish comedies. They are structured around a feud between two families who, because of postwar politics and changing borders, were transplanted from their eastern village to the Polish western Recovered Lands. Kazimierz Pawlak (Wacław Kowalski) and Władysław Kargul (Władysław Hańcza), the two heads of the quarrelling families, seem inseparable: they fight yet cannot live without each other. The situational humor of these comedies, their tempo, and the protagonists' accent, which plays a prominent role in their witty dialogues, all contributed to the box office success of these films.[93]

Most Polish comedies in the late 1960s and the early 1970s were highly didactic. Unable to laugh openly at political and social issues, they portrayed a "wishful thinking" reality. The film protagonists frequently travel to the West (a prospect unattainable for the majority of Poles), only to stress the authorities' desired message that "there is nothing like home" and that "there is no place for sincere Poles in the West." When Polish comedies feature love across the borders, for example, in Żona dla Australijczyka (A Wife for an Australian, 1964, Stanisław Bareja), the love "never jeopardizes our political alliances."[94] Comedies of the 1960s and 1970s range from situational comedies, such as Rzeczpospolita babska (Women's Republic, 1969, Hieronim Przybył), set during the postwar period and focusing on the gender relations between male and female veterans who have settled on two neighboring farms, to satires such as Polowanie na muchy (Hunting Flies, 1969, Andrzej Wajda).

Among the many attempts at comedy, one stands out from the rest: Rejs (The Cruise, 1970), directed by Marek Piwowski, who also wrote the film with Janusz Głowacki. The film took Polish critics by surprise, and their opinions were initially polarized. Today, this is one of a few cult films in Poland. At first glance, Piwowski's film looks like an amateurish production without an underlying structure because of its improvised dialogues, its quasi-documentary look, and the presence of nonprofessional actors/types. The Cruise portrays a group of people on board the Dzerzhinsky during a leisurely tour on the river. The film clearly serves as a Polish parable; its situational humor and dialogues refer to the current political reality and laugh at the schizophrenic absurdities of communist Poland. Piwowski's film speaks with an idiom distinctly Polish, virtually inaccessible to a Westerner. It is a satire on communism with its references to newspeak, the Gomułka epoch, and the private and official truth. It also serves as a satire on any totalitarian system, a "bitter comedy about a collective escape from freedom."[95]

Influenced by the poetics of Les Vacances de Monsieur Hulot (1953, Jacques Tati) and Miloš Forman's early films, The Cruise features many standup comedians as well professional character actors, including Jan Himilsbach, Stanisław Tym, and Zdzisław Maklakiewicz. In a memorable scene, Maklakiewicz as the engineer Mamoń delivers a frequently cited talk about the misery of Polish cinema: "In Polish film it is as follows: boredom ... nothing happens ... poor dialogues, very poor dialogues. ... In general, there is no action, nothing happens. One wonders why do they not copy foreign films." Maklakiewicz, paired with another character actor from Piwowski's film, Himilsbach, also appears in Andrzej Kondratiuk's two television films, *Wniebowzięci* (*The Ascended*, 1973) and *Jak to się robi* (*How It Is Done*, 1973), which enjoy cult status in Poland.

***

Polish cinema of the 1960s and 1970s was also shaped by other filmmakers determined to continue their personal style. For example, Tadeusz Konwicki's *Jak daleko stąd, jak blisko* (*How Far from Here, How Near*, 1972) is, like his novels, a filmic essay replete with autobiographical features, an "illogical" film narrative that is "governed by laws of dream."[96] The film's protagonist, Andrzej (Andrzej Łapicki), searches for an explanation regarding the death of his friend Maks (Gustaw Holoubek). The oneiric narrative of Konwicki mixes past and present, different genres, and styles. Basically a poetic evocation of times past, it contains thinly veiled political observations, references to history, and the new wave narrative devices.

In the 1970s, Janusz Nasfeter (1920–1998) continued to make important films, primarily addressed to children but with a universal meaning, such as *Abel, twój brat* (*Abel, Your Brother*, 1970) and *Motyle* (*Butterflies*, 1973). A versatile filmmaker, he also succeeded in making a psychological war drama, *Weekend z dziewczyną* (*Weekend with a Girl*, 1968), as well as a crime film, *The Criminal and the Maiden*. One of his most interesting works, however, remains *Niekochana* (*Unloved*, 1966), based on Adolf Rudnicki's short story. It deals with the unhappy, obsessive, and damaging love of a young Jewish woman, Noemi (Elżbieta Czyżewska), for a Polish fine arts student. Set before the war, the film portrays the story of their separations and reunions and her mental breakdown, set against the background of claustrophobic corridors, streets, and unappealing rooms. Noemi's love destroys her life; in the final scene, she faces the outbreak of the war alone and depressed. The Holocaust seems to loom over this unhappy love story, making it even more impossible.

In the mid-1970s, a growing number of filmmakers became interested in recording reality and favored the style of documentary cinema. Television films such as *Personel* (*Personnel*, 1975, Krzysztof Kieślowski) and *Historia pewnej miłości* (*The Story of a Certain Love*, 1974, not released until 1982, Wojciech Wiszniewski) heralded the tone and the thematic preoccupations of a group of films that critics called the "Cinema of Moral Concern."

Notes

1. Krzysztof Kornacki, "Bohater w przydeptanych kapciach," in *Człowiek z ekranu: Z antropologii postaci filmowej*, ed. Mariola Jankun-Dopartowa and Mirosław Przylipiak (Kraków: Arcana, 1996), 77.
2. The events of 1968 isolated Ford as both a person of Jewish origin (born Mosze Lifszyc) and an activist linked with the group removed from power. As a result, Ford emigrated from Poland in 1969 and tried to continue his career in West Germany, Denmark, and the United States. In Germany, he directed *Den Foerste Kreds* (*The First Circle*, 1971) and *Dr. Korczak, the Martyr*. In 1980, at the age of seventy-two, Ford committed suicide in Naples, Florida. Details of his eventful life are discussed in Stanisław Janicki's documentary *Kochany i znienawidzony: Dramat życia i śmierci twórcy Krzyżaków* (*Loved and Hated: The Tragedy of Life and Death of the Maker of The Teutonic Knights*, 2002).
3. Lipman was born in an upper-middle-class, assimilated Jewish family. During the war, he hid in Warsaw with false papers, and later, masquerading as a German officer and maintaining contacts with the Polish underground, he traveled extensively throughout occupied Europe smuggling goods and weaponry. In 1968, he left for West Germany, where he worked until 1982, mostly for television. See Tadeusz Lubelski, ed., *Zdjęcia: Jerzy Lipman* (Warsaw: Wydawnictwa Artystyczne i Filmowe, 2005). Weber, born in a Jewish family in Cieszyn (border town in southern Poland), immigrated in 1969 to West Germany, where he worked as a camera operator and a lecturer at several universities.
4. Bolesław Michałek and Frank Turaj, *The Modern Cinema of Poland* (Bloomington: Indiana University Press, 1988), 50.
5. Ryszard Koniczek, "Kultura filmowa, polityka repertuarowa i produkcyjna," in *Historia filmu polskiego 1968-1972*, vol. 6, ed. Rafał Marszałek (Warsaw: Wydawnictwa Artystyczne i Filmowe, 1994), 486.
6. Edward Zajiček, *Poza ekranem: Kinematografia polska, 1918-1991* (Warsaw: Filmoteka Narodowa and Wydawnictwa Artystyczne i Filmowe, 1992), 190.
7. In the 1970s, Poland had only 21.1 cinema seats per one thousand inhabitants. Ewa Gębicka, "Sieć kin i rozpowszechnianie filmów," in *Encyklopedia kultury polskiej XX wieku: Film i kinematografia*, ed. Edward Zajiček (Warsaw: Instytut Kultury and Komitet Kinematografii, 1994), 440–41.
8. Koniczek, "Kultura filmowa," 489.
9. Ibid., 478.

10. According to the *Express Wieczorny*'s poll, Stanisław Mikulski (1929–2014) was the most popular Polish actor in 1965, 1966, and 1968 and second most popular in 1967 and 1969. Mikulski was known for playing mostly military men, partisans, and insurgents (he plays the Home Army fighter Smukły/Slim in Wajda's *Kanal*).
11. In 2012, Patryk Vega made *Hans Kloss: Stawka większa niż śmierć* (*Hans Kloss: More than Death at Stake*), the big-screen reworking of Captain Kloss's exploits starring two popular stars from the original television series: Stanisław Mikulski (Kloss) and Emil Karewicz as Sturmbannführer Hermann Brunner.
12. See *Short Film Studies* 5, no. 1 (2015), a special issue devoted to Kieślowski's *The Office*. For a discussion in English on Kieślowski's documentaries, see the chapter on "Documenting the Unrepresented World" in Marek Haltof, *The Cinema of Krzysztof Kieślowski: Variations on Destiny and Chance* (London: Wallflower Press, 2004), 1–23. For a discussion in Polish, see Mikołaj Jazdon, *Dokumenty Kieślowskiego* (Poznań: Wydawnictwo Poznańskie, 2002).
13. Mirosław Przylipiak, "Polish Documentary Film after 1989," in *The New Polish Cinema*, ed. Janina Falkowska and Marek Haltof (London: Flicks Books, 2003), 144–46.
14. Discussed in detail by Mirosław Przylipiak, *Poetyka kina dokumentalnego* (Gdańsk: Wydawnictwo Uniwersytetu Gdańskiego, 2000), 185–93.
15. Tadeusz Sobolewski, "100 lat kina w Polsce: 1974–1976," *Kino* 5 (1999): 52. Andrzej Mellin's documentary *Szajbus: Film o Wojtku Wiszniewskim* (*Lunatic: The Film about Wojciech Wiszniewski*, 1985) provides an insight into the life and work of Wojciech Wiszniewski, one of the most innovative of Polish documentarians.
16. Ryszard Kapuściński, *Lapidarium* (Warsaw: Czytelnik, 1990), 39, quoted in Carl Tighe, "Ryszard Kapuściński and *The Emperor*," *Modern Language Review* 91, no. 4 (1996): 933–34.
17. The political and cultural context of Wajda's *Ashes* is discussed by Tadeusz Miczka, "Tekst jako 'ofiara' kontekstu," in *Syndrom konformizmu? Kino polskie lat sześćdziesiątych*, ed. Tadeusz Miczka and Alina Madej (Katowice: Wydawnictwo Uniwersytetu Śląskiego, 1994), 147–66. The Polish reception of *Ashes* is discussed by Andrzej Werner, "Film fabularny," in *Historia filmu polskiego 1962–1967*, vol. 5, ed. Rafał Marszałek (Warsaw: Wydawnictwa Artystyczne i Filmowe, 1985), 28–33.
18. Bolesław Michałek, *The Cinema of Andrzej Wajda* (London: Tantivy Press, 1973), 82.
19. Tadeusz Sobolewski, "100 lat kina w Polsce: 1965–1966," *Kino* 1 (1999): 52.
20. See Izabela Kalinowska, "From Orientalism to Surrealism: Wojciech Jerzy Has Interprets Jan Potocki," *Studies in Eastern European Cinema* 4, no. 1 (2013): 47–62.
21. Konrad Eberhardt, "Sny sprzed potopu," *Kino* 12 (1973): 12–19.
22. Published in English as Bruno Schulz, *Sanatorium under the Sign of the Hourglass*, trans. Celina Wieniewska (New York: Walker & Company, 1979).
23. For a detailed analysis, see Małgorzata Jakubowska, *Laboratorium czasu: Sanatorium pod klepsydrą Wojciecha Jerzego Hasa* (Łódź: Łódź Film School, 2010).

24. Annette Insdorf, *Intimations: The Cinema of Wojciech Has* (Evanston, IL: Northwestern University Press, 2017), 65.
25. *The Doll* was adapted once again in 1977, this time by Ryszard Ber for television (nine episodes). See Elżbieta Ostrowska, "Dreaming, Drifting, Dying: The Narrative Inertia in Wojciech Has's *Lalka / The Doll* (1968)," *Studies in Eastern European Cinema* 4, no. 1 (2013): 63–78; Paul Coates, "'Choose the Impossible': Wojciech Has Reframes Prus's *Lalka*," *Studies in Eastern European Cinema* 4, no. 1 (2013): 79–94.
26. Jerzy Hoffman, who is of Jewish origin, survived the war in Siberia where the Soviets deported his family in 1940. He returned to Poland in 1945 (his father served in the Tadeusz Kościuszko division) but studied at (and in 1955 graduated from) the Moscow Film School (WGiK).
27. Ewa Hauser, "Reconstruction of National Identity: Poles and Ukrainians among Others in Jerzy Hoffman's Film *With Fire and Sword*," *The Polish Review* 14, no. 3 (2000): 306.
28. Rafał Marszałek, "Film fabularny," in Marszałek, *Historia filmu polskiego 1968–1972*, 71.
29. In 1987, a list was created of the twenty films, both local and foreign, that had the most viewers in Poland. *Nights and Days* is ranked fifth with 22.3 million viewers. Małgorzata Hendrykowska, *Kronika kinematografii polskiej 1895–1997*, 2nd ed. (Poznań: Arcana, 2012), 427. Jerzy Antczak also produced a television series of *Nights and Days* (thirteen episodes), which premiered on Polish television after the film's theatrical release.
30. Michałek, *The Cinema of Andrzej Wajda*, 99.
31. Konrad Eberhardt, "Wajda—epoka błękitna," *Ekran* 6 (1969), quoted in Marszałek, *Historia filmu polskiego 1968–1972*, 361.
32. Paul Coates, *The Story of the Lost Reflection: The Alienation of the Image in Western and Polish Cinema* (London: Verso, 1985), 37.
33. Olbrychski's widespread popularity perhaps caused him later, during the Cinema of Distrust period, to remain outside its main realistic trend with the exception of *Kung-fu* (1980, Janusz Kijowski). His most important films at that time include Wajda's nostalgic evocation of the past, *The Maids of Wilko* (1979), and Volker Schlöndorff's adaptation of Günter Grass, *Die Blechtrommel* (*The Tin Drum*, 1979, Germany). In the 1980s, Olbrychski acted in several films made outside of Poland, including *Bolero* (aka *Within Memory*, 1981, Claude Lelouch) and *Rosa Luxemburg* (1986, Margarethe von Trotta). He appeared infrequently on Polish screens in films such as *Dekalog 3* (1988, Krzysztof Kieślowski). In the 1990s, Olbrychski also acted in films made in Hungary, Russia, France, and Italy. He regained popularity in Poland starring in several big-budget adaptations of the national literary canon that were very well received by local audiences. For example, he appeared in leading roles in Wajda's *Pan Tadeusz* (1999) and *Revenge* (2002), Hoffman's *With Fire and Sword* (1999) and *The Old Tale* (2004), and Bajon's *Early Spring* (2001). Olbrychski continues to appear in foreign films playing, for example, a Russian spy in Phillip Noyce's *Salt* (2011).

34. In 2000, Wajda prepared a different, significantly shorter, reedited version of the film with improved sound. He also produced a television series of *The Promised Land*, eight one-hour-long episodes that premiered on Polish television in 1975 and 1976.
35. Wajda's adaptations are discussed extensively in Ewelina Nurczyńska-Fidelska, *Polska klasyka literacka według Andrzeja Wajdy* (Katowice: Śląsk, 1998) [expanded edition published 2010 by Wydawnictwo Uniwersytetu Łódzkiego (Łódź)]. She focuses on *Ashes, The Promised Land, Birchwood, The Wedding*, and *Danton*. Wajda also produced *Smuga cienia* (*The Shadow Line*, 1976), a lesser-known adaptation of Joseph Conrad.
36. For more information about Wajda's film, see Tomasz Łysak, "Reconstruction or Creation? The Liberation of a Concentration Camp in Andrzej Wajda's *Landscape after Battle*," *Slovo* 25, no. 2 (2013): 31–47.
37. Discussed extensively in Dariusz Chyb, "Malarstwo w filmach Andrzeja Wajdy: *Brzezina*," *Kino* 11 (1988): 20–25.
38. Michałek, *The Cinema of Andrzej Wajda*, 138.
39. Nurczyńska-Fidelska, *Polska klasyka literacka według Andrzeja Wajdy*, 162.
40. Tadeusz Miczka's term in "Polskie czary," *Kwartalnik Filmowy* 18 (1997): 72. One must stress the role of the cinematographer, Witold Sobociński, and the set designer, Tadeusz Wybult.
41. The painterly aspect of Wajda's film is discussed by, among others, Tadeusz Miczka, "Inspiracje malarskie w *Weselu* Andrzeja Wajdy: Krążenie komunikatów plastycznych w artystycznych medytacjach o historii," in *Analizy i interpretacje: Film polski*, ed. Alicja Helman and Tadeusz Miczka (Katowice: Wydawnictwo Uniwersytetu Śląskiego, 1984), 131–58; Dariusz Chyb, "Malarstwo w filmach Andrzeja Wajdy: *Wesele*," *Kino* 12 (1988): 24–28.
42. The visual side owes much to three cinematographers, Witold Sobociński, Edward Kłosiński, and Wacław Dybowski, set design by Tadeusz Kosarewicz, and costumes by Barbara Ptak.
43. For comments about the reception of *The Promised Land* in the United States, see Janina Falkowska, *Andrzej Wajda: History, Politics, and Nostalgia in Polish Cinema* (New York: Berghahn Books, 2007), 150–52.
44. Daniel Talbot (New Yorker Films) in a letter to Andrzej Wajda dated 14 October 1977, Andrzej Wajda Archives in Kraków, quoted in Falkowska, *Andrzej Wajda*, 151.
45. Maria Malatyńska, "Siedmioramiennie," an interview with Andrzej Wajda, *Tygodnik Powszechny* 9 (1996): 7.
46. In 2013, Paweł Chochlew returned to this much-discussed fragment of Polish history in *Tajemnica Westerplatte* (*The Secret of Westerplatte*, Poland-Lithuania) with Michał Żebrowski starring as Major Sucharski.
47. Piotr Zwierzchowski, *Kino nowej pamięci: Obraz II wojny światowej w kinie polskim lat 60*. (Bydgoszcz: Wydawnictwo Uniwersytetu Kazimierza Wielkiego, 2013), 9–10.
48. Aleksander Jackiewicz, *Moja filmoteka: Kino polskie* (Warsaw: Wydawnictwa Artystyczne i Filmowe, 1983), 357.

49. "Stenogram z posiedzenia Komisji Kolaudacyjnej w dniu15 VI 1967: *Noc*," Filmoteka Narodowa, Warsaw, A-216/132, quoted in the minutes published in *Iluzjon* 1 (1993): 80–81.
50. For details concerning the politics surrounding Nasfeter's film, see Marek Haltof, *Polish Film and the Holocaust: Politics and Memory* (New York: Berghahn Books, 2012), 126–31.
51. Danuta Karcz, "Requiem dla obłąkanego," *Kino* 12 (1969): 22.
52. "*Wniebowstąpienie*: Stenogram z posiedzenia Komisji Kolaudacyjnej w dniu 2 VII 1968," National Film Archive in Warsaw, A-344/442.
53. Jolanta Lemann-Zajiček, "Jan Rybkowski: Baron polskiej kinematografii," in *Autorzy kina polskiego*, ed. Grażyna Stachówna and Bogusław Żmudziński (Kraków: Wydawnictwo Uniwersytetu Jagiellońskiego, 2007), 24–27.
54. The fascinating story concerning the Polish scientist Dr. Rudolf Weigl is the subject of Arthur Allen's book *The Fantastic Laboratory of Dr. Weigl* (New York: Norton, 2015). Allen writes that Weigl's laboratory offered shelter to numerous members of Polish intelligentsia and members of the underground (Home Army) by employing them as "lice feeders" in order to produce a vaccine.
55. Monika Maszewska-Łupiniak, "War Beading Up into a Red Dot: Autobiographical Discourse in Andrzej Żuławski's *The Third Part of the Night*," special issue in English on "Polish Film Scholars on Polish Cinema," *Kwartalnik Filmowy* (2013): 99.
56. The term was coined by Jerzy Płażewski and propagated by Janusz Gazda and Konrad Eberhardt. Marszałek, "Film fabularny," 12.
57. Jackiewicz, *Moja filmoteka*, 389.
58. Marszałek, "Film fabularny," 120–21.
59. See, e.g., David A. Cook, *A History of Narrative Film*, 5th ed. (New York: Norton, 2016), 486.
60. E.g., Michael Walker, "Jerzy Skolimowski," in *Second Wave* (London: Studio Vista, 1970), 34–62.
61. See Mariola Jankun-Dopartowa, "*Rysopis* jako duchowa biografia pokolenia," *Kwartalnik Filmowy* 17 (1997): 101.
62. Skolimowski discusses his method of making films in a detailed conversation with Jerzy Uszyński, "Jerzy Skolimowski o sobie: Całe życie jak na dłoni," *Film na Świecie* 373 (1990): 3–47.
63. Walker, "Jerzy Skolimowski," 40.
64. Uszyński, "Jerzy Skolimowski o sobie," 8.
65. This aspect is indicated in the very title of Jankun-Dopartowa, "*Rysopis* jako duchowa biografia pokolenia" [*Identification Marks: None* as a spiritual generational biography], 98.
66. Walker, "Jerzy Skolimowski," 48.
67. Coates, *The Story of the Lost Reflection*, 140.

68. Michałek and Turaj stress this aspect of Zanussi by titling a chapter on him: "Krzysztof Zanussi: The Cinema of Intellectual Inquiry," in *The Modern Cinema of Poland*, 173–95.
69. Tadeusz Sobolewski's term ("Zanussoid") used in his review of *The Touch*: "Zanussi: Posłaniec," *Kino* 10 (1992): 10–11.
70. Jackiewicz, *Moja filmoteka*, 421.
71. Marszałek, "Film fabularny," 118.
72. According to St. Augustine, our cognition depends not on our intellectual activities or senses but on illumination granted by God. The philosophical aspect of the film is discussed by Łukasz Plesnar, "W poszukiwaniu absolutu (*Iluminacja* Krzysztofa Zanussiego)," in Helman and Miczka, *Analizy i interpretacje*, 179–91.
73. Krzysztof Zanussi, "Iluminacja: Nowela filmowa," *Kino* 5 (1973): 25.
74. Jackiewicz, *Moja filmoteka*, 427.
75. Grzegorz Królikiewicz is the author of a theoretical study on the offscreen space, originally written in 1968, "Przestrzeń filmowa poza kadrem," *Kino* 11 (1972): 25–28. He also published a series of books—detailed examinations of film masterpieces.
76. The otherness of Jewish women is discussed by Elżbieta Ostrowska, "Otherness Doubled: Representations of Jewish Women in Polish Cinema," in *Gender and Film and the Media: East-West Dialogues*, ed. Elżbieta Oleksy, Elżbieta Ostrowska, and Michael Stevenson (Frankfurt: Peter Lang, 2000), 120–30.
77. Kluba's presentation of the conflict between the villagers and communist authorities was the main reason behind the shelving of this film. The director had to change the ending three times before the film was released after five years. Marszałek, "Film fabularny," 91–92.
78. Antoni Krauze previously made television films such as *Monidło* (1970) and *Meta* (*Shelter*, 1971, not released until 1981), both adaptations of Jan Himilsbach's and Marek Nowakowski's fiction, respectively.
79. Kazimierz Kutz was born in 1929 in Szopienice (today part of Katowice). He was the founder and head of the film studio Silesia from 1972 to 1978, and later the cofounder and head of the Silesian Film Society (1981–1988), as well as a lecturer at the Katowice Film School (1979–1982).
80. Elżbieta Baniewicz, *Kazimierz Kutz: Z dołu widać inaczej* (Warsaw: Wydawnictwa Artystyczne i Filmowe, 1994), 177.
81. The first Polish uprising in Upper Silesia took place in August 1919; the third, which followed the March Plebiscite in Upper Silesia, broke out in May 1921.
82. Bolesław Kamykowski created the set design for the first two parts of the trilogy.
83. Marszałek, "Film fabularny," 66.
84. Baniewicz, *Kazimierz Kutz*, 166.
85. Ibid., 193.
86. Elżbieta Ostrowska, "Silesian Landscapes of Kazimierz Kutz," in *Polish Cinema in Ten Takes*, ed. Ewelina Nurczyńska-Fidelska and Zbigniew Batko (Łódź: Łódzkie Towarzystwo Naukowe, 1995), 90.

87. The Silesian themes return in Kutz's later films: *Na straży swej stać będę* (*I Will Stand on my Guard*, 1983), *Śmierć jak kromka chleba* (*Death as a Slice of Bread*, 1994), and *Zawrócony* (*The Turned Back*, 1994). To be discussed later in this book.
88. Adam Zagajewski, *Solidarity, Solitude*, trans. Lillian Vallee (New York: Ecco Press, 1990), 140.
89. Stanisław Barańczak's term from *Czytelnik ubezwłasnowolniony* (Paris: Libella, 1983), 96–132.
90. Agnieszka Ćwikiel, "U nas na komendzie," in Miczka and Madej, *Syndrom konformizmu?* 84.
91. Alicja Helman, "Start i po starcie," *Kino* 4 (1971), quoted in Iwona Rammel, "Dobranoc ojczyzno kochana, już pora na sen... Komedia filmowa lat sześćdziesiątych," in Miczka and Madej, *Syndrom konformizmu?* 63.
92. Rammel, "Dobranoc ojczyzno kochana," 59. Citing figures from the 1976 *Kino* article by Edward Zajiček, "Film jako towar," Rammel remarks that several films labeled as "comedies" did not meet generic expectations—they were not funny.
93. Sylwester Chęciński's *Big Deal* and *Love It or Leave It* belong to the most popular films ever screened in Poland. According to 1987 figures, the former is ranked twentieth and the latter seventeenth. Hendrykowska, *Kronika kinematografii polskiej 1895–1997*, 427.
94. Rammel, "Dobranoc ojczyzno kochana," 66–67.
95. Małgorzata Hendrykowska, "100 lat kina w Polsce: 1969–1970," *Kino* 3 (1999): 49.
96. Alicja Helman, "*Jak daleko stąd, jak blisko*: Analiza kilku wybranych motywów," *Kino* 4 (1972): 18.

CHAPTER 7

Camouflage and Rough Treatment
The "Cinema of Distrust" (1976–1981)

> *Living in an undescribed world is hard. ... It is like having no identity.*
> —*Krzysztof Kieślowski*, I'm So-So

The era of relative prosperity under Edward Gierek was gradually ending in the late 1970s. The strikes in June 1976, triggered by the introduction of price increases, signaled the decline of the Gierek regime. In October 1978, the archbishop of Kraków, Karol Wojtyła, was elected pope as Pope John Paul II, and in June 1979, he triumphantly visited Poland. The workers' protest that erupted in August 1980 culminated in the emergence of a mass-supported movement, Solidarność (Solidarity), headed by the future Polish president Lech Wałęsa. In September 1980, Stanisław Kania replaced Edward Gierek as the new party first secretary. The period of Solidarity ended on 13 December 1981, with General Wojciech Jaruzelski's imposition of martial law.

In the late 1970s, Polish cinema underwent another generational change of guard: the advent of filmmakers born after the war, whose first major political initiation was the March Events of 1968. The collection of essays written by two Polish poets, Julian Kornhauser and Adam Zagajewski, *Świat nie przedstawiony* (*The Unrepresented World*, 1974),[1] became both the manifesto and the theoretical formula for this generation sometimes known as the "Young Culture" (*Młoda Kultura*) formation.[2] In an essay on postwar Polish literature, Zagajewski writes that the most basic disparity in Polish culture is between "what is and what should be; the disparity between the dreamed picture of the society, between the idealized picture of human personality and the actual state of things, full of conflicts and animosity in relations between people. ... Due to the fact that what exists remains unrecognized, the very existence of reality is incomplete and lame, because to exist means to be described in culture."[3] The presence of the official and the unofficial culture characterized Polish artistic life in the late 1970s. The former was approved and censored by the state, and the latter existed in opposition to the communist regime. The lines between these two spheres of culture were often blurred.

The absence of life "as it is" on Polish screens prompted audiences to practice allegorical Aesopian readings.[4] The audiences often looked for references, frequently nonexistent ones, to Polish reality. Many filmmakers had advocated the need to describe the unrepresented world, the world not present in official arts. In publications and interviews, they strongly manifested their generational bonds. Agnieszka Holland explains:

> *I know that this was the formation created thanks to a certain generational experience—the meeting of people sharing a similar sensibility and a strong need to receive feedback from the audience. This was not the film criticism that invented "moral concern." ... This phenomenon was not artificial; it truly existed based on "social request." It was created by the viewers.*[5]

A group of films called the Cinema of Moral Concern (aka Cinema of Moral Anxiety; *Kino moralnego niepokoju*) explored the corrupted side of communism in the late 1970s.[6] The filmmaker Janusz Kijowski (1948–) coined the term, and Andrzej Wajda first used it in a public speech delivered at the 1979 Festival of Polish Films.[7] The term refers to realistic films that examine contemporary issues and were made primarily from 1976 to 1981 by, among others, established masters like Krzysztof Zanussi and Andrzej Wajda, and young filmmakers such as Krzysztof Kieślowski (1941–1996), Feliks Falk (1941–), Piotr Andrejew (1947–2017), Agnieszka Holland (1948–), Janusz Kijowski, and Janusz Zaorski (1947–).

Several Polish critics and filmmakers have objected to the term "Cinema of Moral Concern."[8] The Polish scholar Mariola Jankun-Dopartowa proposed a new label, the Cinema of Distrust (*Kino nieufności*), to describe films characterized by contemporary themes, realism, and the social initiation of a young protagonist.[9] Jankun-Dopartowa explains that the term refers only to a group of selected films made during this period: Zanussi's *Barwy ochronne* (*Camouflage*, 1977); Falk's *Wodzirej* (*Top Dog*, 1978) and *Szansa* (*The Chance*, 1980); Kijowski's *Indeks* (*Index*, 1977, released in 1981) and *Kung-fu* (1980); Holland's *Aktorzy prowincjonalni* (*Provincial Actors*, 1979); and Kieślowski's *Amator* (*Camera Buff*, 1979). Jankun-Dopartowa also includes Wajda's *Bez znieczulenia* (*Rough Treatment*, 1978) and

Dyrygent (*The Conductor*, 1980); Marcel Łoziński's *Jak żyć?* (*How Are We to Live?* aka *Recipe for Life*, 1977, 1981); Andrejew's *Klincz* (*Clinch*, 1979); and the later continuations of the Cinema of Distrust: Barbara Sass's *Bez miłości* (*Without Love*, 1980), and Zaorski's *Dziecinne pytania* (*Child's Questions*, aka *Childish Questions*, 1981).[10]

This series of contemporary realistic films centers on the conflict between the state and the individual, and examines the massive gap between the official "progressive" postulates and their implementation. Because of state censorship, the system is not attacked directly; the films target its institutions and functionaries, and focus on corruption and social maladies. The mechanisms of manipulation and indoctrination are examined on a metaphorical level. The summer camp in *Camouflage* and *How Are We to Live?*, school in *The Chance*, the world of show business in *Top Dog*, sport in *Clinch*, and the media in *Rough Treatment* and *Without Love* serve as microcosms of Polish society. These films also portray the emergence of the arrogant communist elites, hypocrisy, conformity, and other social and political effects of the communist system. Often set in provincial Poland (perhaps to indicate that these problems are far from the center), they provide thinly veiled allusions to the political and social present.

Uncovering the Unrepresented Reality: Krzysztof Kieślowski's First Films

In the second half of the 1970s, several documentary and narrative films attempted to uncover the unrepresented reality and to examine social issues. Interestingly, some of them were produced by Polish television, the institution usually associated with manipulation and indoctrination. Kieślowski's semiautobiographical *Personel* (*Personnel*, 1975),[11] for example, introduces the coming-of-age story about a young trainee theater dresser working in the wardrobe department of the Wrocław Opera, and focuses on his professional initiation, as well as his initiation into the world of art and politics. Romek Januchta, played by the future film director Juliusz Machulski, is an idealistic young man, an observer rather than a participant in the internal games and quarrels of the opera house. Later, however, he must take sides in a power struggle at the opera. The opera management and the head of the communist youth organization test his friendship with an older theater worker (Michał Tarkowski), who is critical about the artistic program of the theater and who is in a conflict with one of the narcissistic and confrontational opera singers. The opera director pressures Romek to write a report denouncing his colleague in order to succeed in his profession. The open, ambiguous ending of *Personnel* shows Romek sitting in front of a blank page in the opera director's cabinet, with the pen ready in his hand. He seems to know perfectly that, regardless of his comments, his written statement will be used against Sowa.

Personnel deals with the confrontation between crude reality and the idealistic concept of theater envisioned by Romek, between dreams about artistry and the prose of life. Kieślowski examines the issue of being loyal to one's convictions in the manner of documentary cinema. Several Polish film critics rightly point out the Formanesque observations in *Personnel*, especially the influence of *Černy Petr* (*Black Peter*, 1963). Both films share a simplicity of narrative (disregard for a well-developed narrative), an unobtrusive, documentary-like observation of the portrayed group of people, an improvisation on the set, an episodic plot, a reliance on many nonprofessional actors, a handheld camera, the focus on people's faces and everyday behavior, and finally, a thinly veiled political and social criticism.

Reality, however, was far better represented in documentary cinema. Several films dealing with everyday hardships, social pathologies, and the world of cynicism and incompetence were shelved by authorities, not to be released until the Solidarity period. Some of the finest examples include Marcel Łoziński's *Próba mikrofonu* (*The Microphone Test*, 1980), Irena Kamieńska's *Robotnice* (*Female Workers*, aka *Workwomen*, 1980), Piotr Szulkin's *Kobiety pracujące* (*Working Women*, 1978), Krzysztof Kieślowski's *Z punktu widzenia nocnego portiera* (*From the Point of View of the Night Porter*, 1977), and Tomasz Zygadło's *Mikrofon dla wszystkich* (*Microphone for Everybody*, 1976). Later, Zygadło made realistic narrative films, including *Rebus* (1977) and the more complex *Ćma* (*The Moth*, 1980). In the latter, Roman Wilhelmi stars as the broadcaster of an all-night radio talk show, whose own personal problems reflect those of his listeners. The concern for real life and authentic characters is also present in Krzysztof Wojciechowski's narrative films. In *Kochajmy się* (*Let Us Love*, 1974) and later in *Róg Brzeskiej i Capri* (*The Corner of Brzeska and Capri*, 1980), he employs a cast of nonprofessional actors and offers an almost "ethnographic experience" concerned with, respectively, the developing village and the impoverished working-class Warsaw suburb.[12]

In 1976, Kieślowski made two feature films that reflect the 1970s reality in Poland: *Blizna* (*The Scar*, 1976) and *Spokój* (*Calm*, 1976, released in 1980). Although critical about the former film (he calls it a socialist realist film *à rebours*),[13] in *The Scar* Kieślowski portrays a multifaceted, well-meaning manager of a huge chemical industrial complex, Stefan Bednarz (Franciszek Pieczka). After almost twenty years,

Bednarz returns to his small hometown, where he builds a chemical plant despite the vocal opposition of the local residents. The construction of the plant, which is administered by the over ambitious and simple-minded town authorities, completely changes the local community. People must be resettled, houses bulldozed, and the forest clear. Although Bednarz succeeds with the construction site, he ends his career and returns to his family in Silesia. The film's ending, showing the embittered manager helping his baby grandson learn to walk, may be described as typical of later Kieślowski: it offers a retreat from politics, an escape from the political to the private, a move portrayed in his later films.

Although the film is set in the late 1960s, its spirit, its images referring to sped-up yet badly planned industrialization, and the idea of political leaders being isolated from the masses by the Communist Party apparatchiks clearly refer to the mid-1970s in Poland. The realistic, sometimes even paradocumentary, portrayal of the Polish managerial class in *The Scar* and the atmosphere surrounding typical "communist industrial sites" are well balanced and devoid of clichés. The camera records the pomposity, rituals, and communist decorum of the 1970s: official visits by party authorities (all driving the emblematic communist cars: the black Volgas), the masses organized by party activists to cheer and show support for their plans and then silently leave after they are no longer needed, May Day parades, the ritualistic opening of the plant, social functions, and professional meetings.

The Scar largely reveals the documentary style that originated in Kieślowski's early films. Apart from being a political drama, it also offers a psychological portrait of the managerial class in Poland. As always in Kieślowski's early films, dialogue aptly captures the official language of the 1970s: newspeak. *The Scar*, however, is not the only Polish film in the mid-1970s that deals with communist managers and their dilemmas. The realm of the managerial class and communist politics is also examined in several popular television series, ranging from the reflective picture of factory managers presented in the very well-received television series *Dyrektorzy* (*Directors*, six episodes, 1975, Zbigniew Chmielewski) to the humorous depiction of life during the Gierek period in *Czterdziestolatek* (*The Forty-Year-Old*, twenty-one episodes, 1974–1976, Jerzy Gruza) and its big-screen version, *Motylem jestem, czyli romans czterdziestolatka* (*I Am a Butterfly, or the Love Affair of the Forty-Year-Old*, Jerzy Gruza, 1976). Other television films, for example, *Znaki szczególne* (*Identification Marks*, 1976, six episodes, Roman Załuski) and *Ślad na ziemi* (*The Sign on Earth*, 1978, seven episodes, Zbigniew Chmielewski), also deal with similar issues. Directors of mainstream films in the 1970s, however, abstained from these subjects, never popular among Polish audiences, tainted by the socialist realist dogma and clichés, and dangerously close to the domain of schematic propagandist works. Some notable exceptions include, for example, Kazimierz Kutz's ambitious but failed *Linia* (*Line*, 1974), a film about a provincial party secretary, described by several Polish critics as a work about "the dilemmas of the authorities" (similarly to *The Scar*), and Roman Załuski's *Rdza* (*Rust*), made during the Solidarity period but not released until 1982, after the introduction of martial law.

Jerzy Stuhr (1947–), who plays a supporting role in *The Scar* as an opportunistic assistant to the director Bednarz, appears in the leading role in Kieślowski's next film, *The Calm*. He stars as Antoni Gralak, a simple man recently released from prison who wants to lead a calm life and stay out of trouble. He explains his dreams to his new colleagues: "A woman, children, a place of one's own." Drab reality, however, offers him no such chance to fulfill his modest dreams. He is caught in the middle of the growing conflict between the director of the small plant, where he was employed despite his prison record, and his fellow workers. The protagonist is rejected by both sides—manipulated by the management and beaten by his colleagues in the final scene. The painful realism of Kieślowski's film and the inclusion of some images forbidden by the state, such as workers' strike (though the word strike is not uttered there, but the simple phrase "we don't work" is) and prisoners working outside of a prison, resulted in the belated premiere of *The Calm*. Made during the period of unrest in 1976, the film premiered in 1980, weeks after signing the "August Agreements" between the striking Solidarity members led by Lech Wałęsa and representatives of the Communist Party.[14]

The Calm strikes the viewer with its paradocumentary flavor: down-to earth story and characters, everyday situations, and colloquial dialogue. Stuhr's pragmatic Gralak is deprived of any romantic gestures and grand romantic aspirations; he just yearns for basic privacy. In the context of Polish cinema, favoring the portrayal of individuals at the mercy of cruel history (history as a destroyer of happiness and a meddler into private affairs), Kieślowski's character seems apolitical, to the point of being narrow-minded, in his focus on private life.[15]

Camera Buff, Kieślowski's first internationally acclaimed film, remains the most intricate work of that period. The deceptively simple story of *Camera Buff* introduces Filip Mosz (Jerzy Stuhr), an ordinary thirty-year-old man working in a small-town factory as a purchasing agent. When his wife Irena (Małgorzata Ząbkowska) becomes pregnant, he buys an 8mm movie camera to record the growth of their child. Raised in an orphanage, Filip has everything the protagonist of *The Calm* truly

Figure 7.1   Jerzy Stuhr in Krzysztof Kieślowski's *Camera Buff* (1979). Courtesy of Filmoteka Narodowa.

wanted: a family, a place to live, a job, and a group of friends. His friend and supervisor Stanisław Osuch (Jerzy Nowak) comments when he observes the joyous Filip after the birth of his child: "Now I can see what happiness is all about." Yet, as Filip later tells his wife, filmmaking means more for him than his home and family.

Filip begins his career by making a home movie that documents the birth and first months of his baby daughter. Later, however, he becomes increasingly preoccupied with the world around him. Invited by the factory manager, he becomes the visual chronicler of official factory functions and an observer of simple everyday events in his small town. The camera enables him to see more, to go beyond the facade of things, and to grow as a person and as a political being. While making a film about his hometown, he documents his small discoveries: the divergence between the main streets and the back streets, the shabbiness behind a pretty facade. In a memorable and symbolic scene, in a long handheld take, Filip moves from the front of a well-kept street through the gate leading to a dilapidated rear side. He portrays the two sides of reality in one take: the official truth and the unrepresented reality.

The themes of Filip's first films are not necessarily expected by the director of the factory, who would like to see a straightforward documentation of factory life rather than films peppered with small, sometimes critical, social observations. Filip wins the prize at an amateur film festival and gets an invitation to work for a manipulative television producer. Gradually, Filip learns the responsibilities of being a filmmaker. One of his films destroys the career of some other people, including Osuch. As a result, the shaken Filip destroys his new film about brickworks, produced for television. He overexposes the film when he suspects that his new work, which uncovers the mismanagement of the brickworks, can be used against the people he portrayed there. His problems as a filmmaker are paralleled by his personal problems; the more he focuses on filmmaking, the more estranged he becomes from his wife, who finally leaves him, taking their daughter with her. In the frequently cited final scene, the disappointed protagonist takes his new 16mm camera and turns it on himself. After exposing the lives of others, he is now exposing himself, retreating from socially committed observations to the exploration of his own life and mind.

As observed by several critics, Kieślowski produces a self-reflexive film—a meditation on filmmaking, its pleasures and dangers, an essay about being faithful to oneself and personal sacrifice, as well as about the responsibilities of being an artist. *Camera Buff* examines the impact of film on one's life, the process of self-discovery through the arts, and the pressures of censorship. *Camera Buff* can be also discussed as an essay on censorship and self-censorship; on making compromises and learning that the world is gray rather than black and white. Filip, the passionate neophyte who gets a camera, a tripod, and an editing table, intends to "make simple films about people and their feelings," as he explains to his colleagues. Soon, however, he learns that the plant director demands the editing out of some scenes, simple observations of reality that do not comply with the official truth.

The problems that the filmmaker-amateur encounters in his small town certainly parallel the problems of the Polish professional filmmaking community. Paul Coates comments that *Camera Buff* "hovers between the Fellinian mode of autobiography and straight narrative."[16] Krzysztof Teodor Toeplitz writes in a similar manner that, thematically, *Camera Buff* can be approached as the 8½ of contemporary Polish cinema. The unique character of Kieślowski's film, writes Toeplitz, has to do with its protagonist and his moral dilemmas. He is neither a filmmaker, as was the protagonist in Federico Fellini's film or in Wajda's *Everything for Sale*, nor a refined intellectual as in Zanussi's films, but rather a simple character with sophisticated dilemmas. The film tells us that "problems concerning the creativity and morality of art—often ascribed to the neurosis or hypersensitiveness of overly-sensitive artistic people—are in fact universal problems, accessible to anybody who, even by a small degree, crosses the border of everyday 'peaceful calm.'"[17] Here, Kieślowski works against the pervasive stereotype (prevalent not only in Polish cinema) that certain topics are reserved for specific social groups. For example, when Filip discovers the camera's ability to immortalize, thanks to casual footage of his friend's mother taken shortly before her death, he expresses some ontological questions about the nature of cinema asked by several filmmakers and film theorists. As if to stress Zanussi's importance for the Polish film community, and for Kieślowski himself (he made *Camera Buff* for the Tor studio headed by Zanussi since 1979), Zanussi participates in a meeting after a screening of his *Camouflage*, and comments on the filmmakers' moral obligations.

Man of Marble

Krzysztof Zanussi's *Camouflage* and Andrzej Wajda's *Człowiek z marmuru* (*Man of Marble*)—two internationally known films that were made in 1976 and released at the beginning of 1977—had the biggest impact on the Cinema of Distrust filmmakers. Wajda's search for a sincere picture of the Stalinist era, based on the script written by Aleksander Ścibor-Rylski, suffered from the restrictions imposed

Figure 7.2   Jerzy Radziwiłowicz in Andrzej Wajda's *Man of Marble* (1977). Photograph by Renata Pajchel. Courtesy of Film Studio Zebra.

by the communist state. Although it was not banned, the film was shown in a limited number of copies and was not considered for awards by the jury at the Festival of Polish Films in Gdańsk.

Man of Marble is a pioneer narrative film that denounces Stalinism and retells the 1950s.[18] The film deals with cynical manipulation and repression, and successfully captures the atmosphere of the 1950s with its totalitarian mentality. The film's protagonist, Mateusz Birkut (Jerzy Radziwiłowicz), is an honest bricklayer at the Nowa Huta steelworks near Kraków; he is an exemplary worker, courted and exploited by communist authorities as a national hero. The structure of Man of Marble, as pointed out by many scholars, resembles that of Orson Welles's Citizen Kane (1941). The film student Agnieszka (Krystyna Janda) performs the role of Thompson, the reporter in search of Rosebud. While making her student documentary about a model worker, Birkut, she discovers secrets of the real Birkut and learns the true history of the Stalinist period. A marble statue of Birkut that she finds in the basement of the museum initiates her search for the "man behind the mask." Like Thompson, Agnieszka starts with the "official truth" (a newsreel featuring her protagonist), but as she gradually learns the story behind the facade, a more complete picture of the period emerges. Agnieszka approaches people who used to know Birkut—those who loved him, surrounded him, and spied on him. Extensive flashbacks portray the rise of the simple-minded worker to communist stardom and expose the hypocrisy and dirty politics of Stalinism. Unlike Thompson, Agnieszka encounters political obstacles while attempting to unveil the truth about her protagonist. Her opportunistic producer tells her that she should instead choose another topic because "nobody has touched the 1950s."[19]

As the first powerful political, as well as artistic, work dealing with Stalinism, Man of Marble established a certain method of approaching that period in Polish history. To venture into the forbidden past, Wajda employs authentic black-and-white newsreels, several flashbacks in color, and skillfully made black-and-white pseudo-documentaries and fabricated newsreels, which are virtually undistinguishable from the real ones. The fabricated footage is presented as recently unearthed documents, and Wajda's imitations of the official communist propaganda style are as effective as the actual propagandist work.[20] Wajda reproduces past modes of representation not to make his film look more "real" but rather to examine the past—to search for the roots of Polish Stalinism and to capture the mood of that period. As Janina Falkowska explains, "the Stalinist totalitarian spirit is referred to in every discursive layer of the film, and it monologically conditions and manipulates the spectator's reaction toward the film. The Polish spectator, living most of his or her life under the influence of the Stalinist aura, felt especially overwhelmed by the hopelessness and oppressiveness of some scenes."[21]

Many scenes in *Man of Marble* stress the paranoia, cynicism, and oppressive nature of Stalinism. This is a Kafkaesque world ruled by manipulation and fear, the world of accusations fabricated by the Urząd Bezpieczeństwa (Office of Security), show trials and sinister cabinets of security officers—the places where people disappear without a trace. Wajda recreates the 1950s not only by referring to that period's propaganda newsreels, but also by alluding to classic socialist realist paintings and the most popular Polish socialist realist film, *An Adventure at Marienstadt*.[22] Manipulative diegetic and nondiegetic music and a stern voice-over in a pseudo-documentary expose "traitors" and refer to the socialist realist discourse. In many cases, the ironic use of music, especially the sarcastic use of well-known musical pieces from the 1950s,[23] and visual references to 1950s arts border on mockery of the socialist realist concerns. According to Stephen Schiff, Wajda's style in *Man of Marble* is "a perfect distillation of the tricky game that is survival in Poland. Wajda's camera feints, winks, jabs, and then drops back, as if to avoid reprisal, and beneath every shot one can feel the turbulent energy of an artist reining in his rage."[24]

Man of Marble also serves as a statement on filmmakers' responsibility for the distorted images of the Stalinist era. In the propagandist mock documentary *Architects of Our Happiness*, a film within a film credited to the young and determined director Burski (perhaps Wajda's alter ego), Wajda lists himself as an assistant director. The film portrays a sharp contrast between Agnieszka's youthful, committed, and, as a result, perhaps naive approach and Burski's conformist, communist, celebrity-like lifestyle. But the inclusion of mock documentary footage and genuine archival material, as Bjørn Sørensen writes, "lends a sense of authenticity to the fictional account, functioning as a guarantee for the validity of the portrait of the historical period in question."[25]

Camouflage, Politics, and Aesopian Reading

Zanussi's *Camouflage* portrays the conformity of the Polish intelligentsia, and it is a continuation of his cerebral, documentary-like style. Unlike Zanussi's previous philosophical examinations of moral issues, *Camouflage* is more political and social satire. For most Polish viewers in 1977, the film served as a clear metaphor for Polish society and an allegory of the corruptive nature of the system. Zanussi stresses, nonetheless, that this film has a universal meaning: "My film deals with a broader phenomenon, which I attempted to show in an individual case. This phenomenon refers not only to a university, and not only to our country."[26]

Set at a linguistics summer camp, the film is built around a psychological struggle between two academics: the pragmatic and cynical middle-aged professor Jakub Szelestowski (Zbigniew Zapasiewicz) and the younger and idealistic teaching assistant Jarosław Kruszyński (Piotr Garlicki). Like other films by Zanussi, *Camouflage* examines the confrontation of two moral stands, perhaps just the two stages of the development of the same character. The Mephistophelian professor tests the young assistant and tries to deprive him of illusions about life. Their conversations, often taking place in the tranquil milieu of the summer retreat, form the main part of the film.

In *Camouflage*, both the students and their teachers are portrayed as pitiful characters who deserve their fate—conformists subjected to manipulation who change their colors rather than fight, and hide rather than attack. The theme of social and political mimicry is introduced by the very title of the film and by referencing creatures who resort to camouflage to hide; later, it is reinforced by the professor's frequent comments on the natural world.

Marcel Łoziński depicts a similar milieu and theme of manipulation (set in a summer camp for young couples) in his para-documentary *How Are We to Live?* The themes of manipulation and corruption appear in numerous films, for example, in Piotr Andrejew's *Clinch*, a film about the corrupt world of boxing, starring Tomasz Lengren.[27] The world of show business also serves as a metaphor for the Polish reality in Feliks Falk's *Top Dog*, which narrates the story of Lutek Danielak (Jerzy Stuhr), the ruthless dance leader in a provincial town, and his climb to power in the world of Polish small town entertainment. Danielak's ambition is to lead an anniversary ball in his town, which will be broadcast on television. In order to get this job, he eliminates his rivals by employing blackmail, payoff, anonymous letters, and the betrayal of his friend, and by offering his sexual services. The emblematic Polish actor of the late 1970s, Jerzy Stuhr, must be largely credited as the coauthor of this film. His monstrous yet sympathetic character never rests, running from place to place to entertain people, to give them "what they want."

In a tightly controlled political system, almost every situation portrayed, no matter how far removed from politics, prompted Polish viewers to practice Aesopian reading. In Polish cinema of the 1970s, the world of theater frequently served as a coded image of the country and as a microcosm of Polish society. Referring to his film *Personnel*, Krzysztof Kieślowski stressed this theme in the following way: "Theatre and opera are always a metaphor for life. It's obvious that the film was about how we can't really find a place for ourselves in Poland. That our dreams and ideas about some ideal reality always clash somewhere along the line with something that's incomparably shallower and more wretched."[28]

Zdjęcia próbne (*Screen Tests*, 1977), directed by Agnieszka Holland, Paweł Kędzierski, and Jerzy Domaradzki,[29] depicts the initiation of a group of young and aspiring film actors. In another film, *Provincial Actors*, Holland portrays a group of dissatisfied young actors unable to fulfill their artistic dreams. The relationship between Anna (Halina Łabonarska), a puppet theater actress, and Krzysztof (Tadeusz Huk), the most talented actor in a provincial theater, is permeated with an aura of hopelessness; their lives are full of professional and personal frustrations. The staging of Stanisław Wyspiański's classic drama *Wyzwolenie* (*Liberation*), despite the initial outburst of creative freedom, brings Krzysztof only disappointment; his and other actors' hopes for personal liberation turn sour. The spectacle becomes yet another safe "avant-garde event" devoid of references to contemporary life.

The world of journalism, a traditional Polish villain during the late 1970s and afterward, is portrayed in *Without Love*, the first feature film directed by Barbara Sass. The journalist Ewa Bracka (Dorota Stalińska) yearns for a career at all costs. Like Danielak in *Top Dog*, she hurts other people and herself to achieve her goals. She loses her faith in love and other values to be "tougher than men." Stalińska, the star of Sass's early works, creates the portrait of a woman who is "extremely dynamic, rarely reflects, instead works too much," and "tries not to show her weaknesses, even to herself."[30] Her next performances—as a sturdy young woman who is without family and real friends in *Debiutantka* (*Debutante*, 1982) and in *Krzyk* (*The Shout*, 1983)—were equally successful. The former film describes the professional initiation of a young architect who is manipulated by her boss. The latter narrates the story of a young ex-convict who tries to get rid of her circle of friends and family and to lead a normal life. Both films are set in 1981 and depict an unattractive, hopeless reality. Although deprived of direct references to politics, they reflect the atmosphere of the Solidarity period.[31]

Andrzej Wajda's *Rough Treatment* (aka *Without Anesthesia*) introduces another representative of the media, Jerzy Michałowski (Zbigniew Zapasiewicz), a middle-aged journalist who specializes in foreign affairs. A politically incorrect comment broadcast on television causes his fall from grace. The film centers on Michałowski's professional and personal downfall: he can no longer lecture at the university, he loses some small personal privileges (for example, his supply of foreign newspapers), and his wife, Ewa (Ewa Dałkowska), leaves him for her younger lover (Andrzej Seweryn), who is a career-oriented, hard-line party activist. Political and personal pressures prove too much for Michałowski, who falls into alcoholism and is consoled by a young student (Krystyna Janda). Ambiguity surrounds his loss of a career as well as his later death, supposedly accidental (an explosion of a gas stove). Cowritten by Wajda and Holland, *Rough Treatment* deals with a Polish-style "conspiracy theory." When the protagonist's privileges are stripped away and his wife deserts him, he discovers the oppressive side of the system, which formerly favored him. "How are you going to prove what isn't true?" Ewa asks her manipulative divorce lawyer (Jerzy Stuhr). His response, "Proof is never a problem," aptly describes the presented reality. That oppressive reality is aptly captured by Edward Kłosiński's camera, as described perceptively by Marcin Maron:

> *We watch the mental and physical demise of the main protagonist in a whole range of close-ups. ... Throughout the film, the camera work is chiefly focused on observing the gradual process whereby energy for life drains from the hero. The spaces in which he moves—the anonymous lobby of the publishing house, the crowded law office, the court (where the divorce case takes place) and other offices—which are shown as we follow the disastrous trials and tribulations of the hero, are contrasted with the space of his home, which until now was a refuge for him and yet turns out to be a death trap in this new situation (the final explosion of gas). Despite the limited space of action and a certain "transparency" of operational methods used by Kłosiński (open compositions, hand-held camera motion, natural light, and sparse use of artificial light indoors),* Rough Treatment *convincingly depicts the drama of a hunted man, mainly thanks to Zapasiewicz's own performance and the precise organization of the screen space in Kłosiński's shots.*[32]

The films of the Cinema of Distrust portray stories of the generation who experienced the 1968 March Events as students. For example, Janusz Zaorski's *Child's Questions* tells the story of six university friends, their political initiation in

1968, and their adult battleground—the Gierek era. Another film, Janusz Kijowski's *Index*, introduces a student, Józef Moneta (Krzysztof Zaleski), who is expelled from the university for defending a fellow student who participated in the March Events and was ousted from the university. Unwilling to compromise, Moneta works as a laborer and writes a novel. Later, as a high school teacher, the disillusioned protagonist punishes an equally rebellious student. Both *Index* and *Child's Questions* portray their protagonists as struggling to maintain their moral views during the period of communist conformity.

* * *

Several films made during the period in question share many thematic similarities with the Cinema of Distrust. For example, in his two films released in 1980, Zanussi deals with the issues of corruption, moral compromise, and moral choices. His *Kontrakt* (*Contract*) caricatures both the communist nouveaux riches and the corrupt Polish intelligentsia. Zanussi's satire tells the story of a wedding that does not happen (the bride escapes from the altar), but this development does not prevent the guests from celebrating. Described as "*The Wedding* of the Solidarity period,"[33] *Contract* mocks the morally bankrupt elites of the Polish People's Republic.

Another "unattractively" titled film, *Constans* (*The Constant Factor*),[34] is more in line with the tone of Zanussi's earlier films. The young idealist Witold (Tadeusz Bradecki) wants to live honestly, which proves difficult in a depraved reality: the people around him are involved in petty corruption. Unwilling to compromise his high standards, Witold rejects the temptation of being involved in the world of communist conformity. Zanussi, however, reveals a sense of irony in the film's finale, when the protagonist accidentally causes the death of a young boy. At the Cannes Film Festival, the film won the Jury Prize and the Prize of the Ecumenical Jury.

The representatives of the Cinema of Distrust frequently emphasized the utilitarian role of their films. "We took part in something important. I had the impression then that I was making something more than a film, something more than art. This was a kind of work for the society," says Feliks Falk.[35] In many cases, however, this functional attitude resulted in films that lack psychological or sociological depth. For instance, the world vision presented in Kijowski's *Kung-fu* or Falk's *The Chance* is uncomplicated and sketchy. Both films deal with the 1968 generation and show how the student riots impact on the student's lives.

Psychological motivation in characterization is particularly bland in *Kung-fu*. Furthermore, social phenomena in the film are inadequately described: the group of young protagonists defend their nonconformist friend against the small-town coterie by using the methods of their opponents. The pro-communist representations are often reversed, proving that when fighting an established political system, one frequently falls into its way of thinking. *The Chance* narrates the conflict between two high school teachers who represent different moral values. The struggle for the "students' souls"—between a good history teacher and a simplistic and authoritarian physical education teacher—is heavy-handed, almost socialist realist in spirit.

Andrzej Wajda's *The Conductor*, a film about an old and famous orchestra conductor (John Gielgud) who is visiting Poland, his country of origin, offers a similar scenario. The conflict between the old master and an opportunistic provincial orchestra conductor (Andrzej Seweryn) is presented as the struggle between the old and the new, between the sensitive music lover and the unscrupulous careerist. As Maron writes about Sławomir Idziak's cinematography in Wajda's film:

> *The limitations of the space of action and the lack of a strong dramatic storyline meant that the film lacked convincing detail; furthermore, the methods of shooting and directing, focusing on a "behavioural" description, were not able to penetrate the psyche of the characters, recording only their grimaces (Andrzej Seweryn) or their statuesqueness (John Gielgud). They failed even in the case of the main protagonist, played by Krystyna Janda.*[36]

In an interview conducted in 1993, Agnieszka Holland comments: "We were delighted that we could code the message in a film that 'evil is linked with communism.' It seems that this is the basic weakness of these films."[37] Several films suffered from this schematic approach. The clear divisions between the positive and the negative characters, inherited from socialist realism, frequently produce types rather than real-life characters. Maria Kornatowska distinguishes the following types present in Polish cinema in the late 1970s: "the old, 'sincere' party activist, cynical youth movement activist, career-oriented opportunist, pragmatic technocrat, vile representative of the mass media (primarily television), nouveau riche cosmopolitan and neurotic member of the intelligentsia suffering from a complex of defeat and inability."[38] As in the world of socialist realist films, there is no love, and no time for love, in the reality presented in the Cinema of Distrust. In this world of predominantly male characters, who are slowly entering middle age and are usually portrayed without sympathy, the supporting female characters are unwilling to understand the psychological torment of the protagonist; they betray and leave him.

The films of the Cinema of Distrust tell stories that were familiar to most viewers. Kornatowska comments about these films:

> *Employing the positivist, socialist realist viewpoint, they simplified the image of the world by cleverly avoiding issues and situations that were complicated. By and large, these films did not attempt to examine ambivalent, unclear complications of reality. ... They were repeating some obvious truths, the pertinence of which nobody could question: neither the authorities tirelessly trying to "restore the country," nor the society that was, in its majority, passively waiting for that restoration.*[39]

As if to stress generational and other links, the Cinema of Distrust filmmakers appear in each other's films. For example, Agnieszka Holland has a cameo as a secretary in *The Scar* and as a prisoner in Ryszard Bugajski's *Przesłuchanie* (*Interrogation*, 1982, released in 1989); Tomasz Lengren and Tomasz Zygadło act in *Personnel*; Lengren also stars in Piotr Andrejew's *Clinch*, and Zygadło in *Provincial Actors*; Krzysztof Zanussi and Andrzej Jurga appear as themselves (filmmakers-mentors) in *Camera Buff*.

Two fine actors imprinted their mark on the Cinema of Distrust: Jerzy Stuhr and Zbigniew Zapasiewicz. The versatile Stuhr, known for his feel for everyday language (he is often credited as a writer),[40] created a panorama of characters ranging from uprooted careerists (*The Scar, Top Dog, Rough Treatment*) and people struggling with the pressure of politics and everyday hardship (*Calm*), to passionate and sincere ordinary characters (*Camera Buff*). Zapasiewicz continued his characterization of a pragmatic intellectual that he started in Zanussi's *Next Door*. Zapasiewicz's portrayal of a journalist disenchanted with his professional and private life (*Rough Treatment*) and, in particular, that of a cunning, almost diabolical, professor (*Camouflage*), for which he received the Best Actor Award at the Festival of Polish Films in Gdańsk, became the classic characterizations of the period.

The Solidarity Period

Although the spirit of Solidarity from 1980 to 1981 stimulated both the quality and quantity of locally made films, the film infrastructure in Poland was deteriorating. Comments such as "never before had Polish films attracted so much popular attention,"[41] although true regarding Western critics' interest, seem wishful thinking in the local context. For example, 144 million viewers visited Polish cinemas in 1976, including 45 million who saw Polish films. The gradual elimination of films from the West (fifty-five in 1975, and only fourteen in 1981) and the disintegration of the existing infrastructure contributed to the rapid decline in attendance. In 1981, only eighty-eight million viewers went to cinemas, and only thirty-one million to watch Polish films. From 1976 to 1982, 554 permanent cinemas and 150 mobile theaters closed.[42]

With their revolutionary atmosphere and uncertainty, the years 1980 and 1981 better suited documentary cinema. The documentary directed by Andrzej Chodakowski and Andrzej Zajączkowski, *Robotnicy '80* (*Workers 1980*, 1981),[43] was one of the most popular works produced and released in Poland during the Solidarity period. Probably the most sincere Polish narrative film about the working class is Kazimierz Kutz's *The Beads of One Rosary* (discussed in chapter 6), which was produced in 1979 and premiered in March 1980—months before the birth of the Solidarity movement. This modest film about the struggle for human dignity, depicting the clash between individualism and the power of the state, won the 1980 Festival of Polish Films in Gdańsk.

The biggest critical success of the Solidarity period, *Człowiek z żelaza* (*Man of Iron*, 1981), Andrzej Wajda's sequel to *Man of Marble*, won the Palme d'Or (grand prize) at the Cannes Film Festival. *Man of Iron* preserves the narrative structure of its famous predecessor and relies on flashbacks to tell the story of Birkut's son, Maciek Tomczyk (again, Jerzy Radziwiłowicz), a Gdańsk Shipyard worker and a Solidarity activist married to Agnieszka (Krystyna Janda). Another media man, the alcoholic journalist Winkiel (Marian Opania), who is blackmailed by the state authorities, searches for Birkut's son in order to discredit him. The viewer learns about Tomczyk through the converted sinner Winkiel, who changes his views after meeting the Solidarity activists and learning about their goals.

Wajda incorporates documents, newsreels, fragments of *Man of Marble*, television programs, and real-life political figures (among them the Solidarity leader Lech Wałęsa) to produce an explicitly political work. The flashbacks in the film refer to the recent political events in Poland: the students' strikes of 1968 and the workers' protests in 1970; the father-son conflict, which is of both political and generational nature; and the death of Birkut in 1970.

The flashbacks provide a sense of the Solidarity movement's roots. As a work of art, however, the hastily made and edited *Man of Iron* does not belong to Wajda's foremost films. Time constraints and the demand for "the correct film" resulted in shallow, melodramatic aspect and one-dimensional characterization typical of socialist realist cinema. Only in flashbacks is Agnieszka dynamic and herself; when she marries the spotless hero Tomczyk, her dramatic role is finished—there is no place for her in this men-only world of Polish politics of the early 1980s. Coates aptly comments: "The tigress Krystyna Janda is miscast as a plaster saint of the overnight revolution, whilst the hero, played by Jerzy Radziwiłowicz, has all the callowness of a socialist realist icon and none of the vibrancy he possessed in *Man of Marble*."[44] With some exceptions, Wajda portrays the clear divisions between "us" and "them." The party functionaries and security force members are depicted as caricatures—ruthless apparatchiks who are losing their ground.

The ending of *Man of Iron* unmistakably anticipates martial law. The party apparatchik, played by Franciszek Trzeciak, tells Tomczyk that the recent agreement between the shipyard workers and the authorities is invalid because it was signed under pressure. Wajda's film may fail as a work of art, but it fittingly captures the spirit of the time, which was both majestic and kitschy—full of passion, tragedy, and anxiety.

Gorączka (*Fever*, 1981, Agnieszka Holland) and *W biały dzień* (*In Broad Daylight*, 1981, Edward Żebrowski) return to the 1905 revolutionary movement in the Russian-controlled part of Poland. In these films, Holland and Żebrowski are interested in psychological issues and the moral dilemmas of the revolutionaries, rather than historical reconstructions of past events. Holland adapts Andrzej Strug's now forgotten novel concerning the young Polish revolutionaries fighting the tsarist regime. Żebrowski examines the issues of political terrorism and fanaticism, telling the story of an assassin in an underground organization who is torn between obedience and conscientiousness and who searches for truth concerning the guilt of his victim. Both films offer many references to the political situation in Poland during the Solidarity period.

Also in 1981, Holland produced for Polish television one of the darkest and most brutally honest films ever made in Poland: *Kobieta samotna* (*A Woman Alone*, released in 1988). Unfolding in a series of episodes, the film concerns a single mother, the postal worker Irena (Maria Chwalibóg), who struggles in a joyless Polish reality. Her new relationship with the equally unhappy, young, but handicapped ex-miner Jacek (Bogusław Linda) offers her a chance to change her life. Out of desperation, Irena steals money from her workplace, buys an old car, and decides to move abroad with Jacek. After giving her son to an orphanage, they travel toward the border, but the voyage ends in an accident. When Irena confesses to Jacek that she has stolen the money, he strangles her out of mercy. Jacek Petrycki's cinematography portrays the hopeless existence of the protagonists—victims of social and political circumstances. It stresses unfriendly landscapes, gloomy reality, and everyday hardship.

While Kieślowski's earlier narratives demonstrate his fascination with capturing life as it is, they go beyond the ramifications of narrowly understood realism. The script of *Przypadek* (*Blind Chance*) was written before the Solidarity period and was later published in 1981 in a prestigious journal on drama, *Dialog*.[45] Produced in 1981, the film was immediately shelved by authorities until 1987. A still from *Blind Chance* appeared on the front cover of the last issue of the monthly *Kino*, published before the introduction of martial law in Poland.

Blind Chance, which attained dissident cult status after the introduction of martial law, portrays an undergraduate medical student, Witek (Bogusław Linda), whose future is determined by whether he is able to jump onto a moving train. The three separate stories originate with a simple incident at the Łódź train station. This is the beginning of Witek's three different life paths: he is a young party apparatchik manipulated by old party functionaries, a dissident activist involved in underground publishing, and a person isolated from others by his desire for privacy. In each "what if" scenario, an accidental element determines the protagonist's life—a fact stressed by the film's title.[46]

Blind Chance might be considered a pessimistic philosophical parable on human destiny shaped by occurrences beyond individual control. On the one hand, Kieślowski's treatment of the matter stems in large part from his documentary beginnings; in this light, the film could be considered a political essay. On the other hand, by introducing the element of chance (perhaps destiny) into his protagonist's actions, the director is able to deal with questions present in his later, internationally acclaimed films, starting with *Decalogue*. Kieślowski commented that his films "are always observations of a person who must choose in order to define one's place. This is always an attempt to consider what proper, objective reality is, or to understand the motives of a person who acts against this reality."[47] The almost clinical study of the three life variants, presented by Kieślowski, has more in common with Krzysztof Zanussi's philosophical parables such as *The Structure of Crystals* and *Illumination* than with the Cinema of Distrust from the late 1970s.

In *Blind Chance*, Kieślowski questions the "us" and "them" division that defined Polish political as well as cultural life under communist rule. He expresses disillusionment with life in Poland and favors the model of life revolving around the personal rather than the public. In all three parts of *Blind Chance*, regardless of his political stand, Witek is the same: sincere, honest, decent, passionate, eager to act, and trying to do his best in given circumstances. In every story, Witek also finds for himself a different surrogate father and falls in love with a different (with regard to her appearance, psychology, and aspirations) woman. Although fate meddles in Witek's affairs and alters (or ends) his life, he remains good by nature. Perhaps Kieślowski argues that decency can be found on both sides on the political division in Poland—certainly an unpopular view in the bitter atmosphere of the early 1980s in Poland.

Another film by Kieślowski, *Krótki dzień pracy* (*Short Working Day*), made in 1981 for Polish television but with a possible theatrical release in mind, was immediately shelved by authorities and never released. *Short Working Day* retells the 1976 workers' strike in the city of Radom in an unusual manner—through the eyes of a local Communist Party secretary. Kieślowski often stressed the weaknesses of this film and, in time, was against its release. The film premiered on Polish television after Kieślowski's death, to little critical response.

Like *The Scar* and many of Kieślowski's documentaries, *Short Working Day* deals with the mechanisms of power portrayed from within the system. The film's photography emulates the roughness of documentaries, which is enhanced by the incorporation of documentary footage. The film offers the point of view of the local Communist Party secretary (Wacław Ulewicz), whose office building is besieged by striking workers. Despite the secretary's voice-over narration, his apparently endangered life, and his position as a loner facing the hostile and unpredictable crowd, it is difficult, if not impossible, to sympathize with him. Narrating the film through the eyes of the communist apparatchik certainly alienated Polish viewers and most Polish critics uncertain of Kieślowski's intentions.

Representation of Stalinist Years: The Impact of *Man of Marble*

Wajda's *Man of Marble* influenced many films dealing with the Stalinist past, made by a group of young filmmakers during the brief Solidarity period. These included *Dreszcze* (Shivers, Wojciech Marczewski), *Niech cię odleci mara* (The Haunted, 1983, Andrzej Barański), *Był jazz* (There Was Jazz, 1984, Feliks Falk), *Wielki bieg* (The Big Run, 1987, Jerzy Domaradzki), and the television film *Wahadełko* (Shilly Shally, 1984, Filip Bajon). In 1982, after the introduction of martial law, two prominent films were finished and promptly shelved by authorities: *Matka Królów* (The Mother of Kings, 1987, Janusz Zaorski) and *Interrogation* (1989, Ryszard Bugajski). The same happened to a medium-length film, *Niedzielne igraszki* (Sunday Pranks, finished in 1983, released in 1988, Robert Gliński). Had these temporally dislodged films been released earlier, all may well have played an important role in Polish cultural and political life.

Commenting in 1989 on the Cinema of Moral Concern, Frank Turaj sees the emergence of films examining the Stalinist epoch in the following way:

There continued to be a fascination with the Stalinist years, partly because that period is intrinsically interesting but also because Stalinism is a good target. It is a way of criticizing the system without being blamed for criticizing the system. It is permissible to denigrate Stalinism, as long as it is Polish Stalinism (any criticism involving the Soviets is the ultimate taboo), since it was officially acknowledged as an erroneous phenomenon.[48]

Several films made during the brief Solidarity period denounce the Stalinist system and follow the poetics of *Man of Marble*. As Turaj accurately observes, they focus exclusively on the Polish aspect of Stalinism. Because of 1980s censorship practices in Poland, nobody openly criticized the Soviet involvement in Polish politics.

Wojciech Marczewski's *Shivers*, a coming-of-age story set in the 1950s, deals with institutionalized indoctrination and manipulation. Tomasz Hudziec stars as a young teenage boy, Tomasz, who is sent to a scouts' camp after Stalin's death. In the camp, designed to train future party activists, Tomasz falls under the spell of the communist ideology even though his father is a political prisoner. His enchantment with the new ideology parallels Tomasz's erotic fascination with a young woman (Teresa Marczewska), an idealistic counselor from the communist youth organization (ZMP).

In the beginning of the film, Marczewski (1944–) paints a picture of Tomasz's family and friends, creating a world deprived of emotions and populated by young adolescents framed by a cold landscape. Heavy, sometimes too obvious, symbolism permeates *Shivers*: a photograph of Karl Marx is shown with tears in his eyes, and in the final scenes, the same picture is seen in the mud. The oppressive atmosphere of *Shivers* distinctly resembles that of Marczewski's earlier film *Zmory* (*Nightmares*, 1979); both films are set in an oppressive environment (Austro-Hungarian Galicia at the turn of the century in *Nightmares*), deal with a combination of erotic and political fascinations, and introduce demonic teachers/manipulators (a Catholic priest in *Nightmares*).

Marczewski's tale about indoctrination was followed by Bugajski's *Interrogation*, a shocking portrayal of ruthlessness and dehumanization set in early 1950s Poland. Photographed by Jacek Petrycki and produced by Wajda's X film unit, *Interrogation* is arguably the strongest work on the Stalinist past ever made in Central Europe. This film was a battering ram, revealing hidden taboos; like a bulldozer, it demolished existing images about the Stalinist period. *Interrogation* is the preeminent Polish film of the early 1980s. It describes the imprisonment and torture of an innocent young woman, Antonina "Tonia" Dziwisz (Krystyna Janda) wrongly charged by the Stalinist secret police. In an interview, Janda said:

> *The story was really based on the lives of two real women who lived through the Stalinist hell: Tonia Lechmann and Wanda Podgórska, the secretary to Władysław Gomułka [former Communist Party Secretary—M.S.]. Mrs. Podgórska, who spent six years in prison, including two in an isolation cell, served as my consultant on the film. ... We had to make sure that we documented the film very well because we had to defend everything we did in front of a review board. That is why the French reaction at the Cannes festival showing, that the film was unreal, made me angry. It was remarkably factual.*[49]

Interrogation, set predominantly in a prison, graphically shows the horror and brutality of the times. Bugajski's film is built around the sharp opposition between the oppressive Stalinist system (represented by the interrogators played by Janusz Gajos, Adam Ferency, and others) and its innocent victims (exemplified by Tonia and her prison mates, among them a character played by Agnieszka Holland). The protagonist of *Interrogation* suffers enormously, even attempts suicide, but refuses to help fabricate evidence against her friend (who is killed despite her silence).

Tonia's confrontation with the Stalinist system brings her a Pyrrhic victory—after years behind bars, she is released and can be reunited with her young daughter who had been born in the prison hospital and taken away from her. The girl's father is one of the interrogators, who, influenced by Tonia, begins to doubt the communist dogma and eventually shoots himself. Bugajski avoids the black-and-white characterization found in many postwar Polish productions. He abstains from merely reversing the stereotypical images of brave functionaries of the communist system who clash with the "reactionary elements," and creates an intricate nightmarish film about the rituals of Stalinist questioning.

Finished after the introduction of martial law in Poland, *Interrogation* was immediately shelved by the communist regime. Bugajski, unable to produce films in his own country, was forced to emigrate.[50] His film, perhaps the most famous Polish work of the 1980s, was seen by viewers in Poland on illegal video copies until its release in 1989. In 1990, *Interrogation* received several awards at the Festival of Polish Films in Gdynia, including the Special Jury Prize for Bugajski and the Best Actress Award for Janda, who also received the Best Actress Award at the 1990 Cannes Film Festival.

Another film about Stalinism, Andrzej Barański's *The Haunted*, portrays a provincial town somewhere in central Poland in 1951. The film's personal, almost

Figure 7.3 Krystyna Janda as Antonina Dziwisz (right) and Adam Ferency as one of the interrogating officers in Ryszard Bugajski's *Interrogation* (1982/1989). Photograph by Renata Pajchel. Courtesy of Film Studio Zebra.

nostalgic tone stands in sharp contrast to the explicitly political works of that period. As in his other works, Barański is preoccupied with small people in small places and their personal versions of history. The film depicts the struggles of a shopkeeper to keep his family business alive under communist rule. After several years of futile struggle, he loses the store and ends up working for the state.

The film introduces a different perspective on Stalinism. The shopkeeper's son, Witek (Marek Probosz), tells the story about his father, an opportunist defeated by the system. Black-and-white flashbacks and dream sequences peer into periods before, during, and immediately after the war. These recollections from the past provide information about the town itself (for example, that half of the prewar population was Jewish), and about the intrusion of postwar politics into the town's sleepy atmosphere. The last scenes of *The Haunted* clearly indicate that the communist takeover in this Polish provincial town in the early 1950s changed life forever. When the shopkeeper gives up his struggles to maintain his business, his store is transformed into a warehouse for the local branch of the Communist Party. The final camera pan over communist paraphernalia (red flags, portraits of communist leaders, socialist realist portraits) reveals the "landscape after the battle."

Neglected Cinema?

Critical works on Polish cinema after 1976 tend to examine political films or films of social concern at the expense of other genres. For example, Gustaw Moszcz (Gary Mead) speaks of the makers of "the mass of dull literary adaptations and trivial costume dramas" as opposed to those who "are working towards a revitalization of the industry under the impetus of Solidarity."[51] Literary adaptations, however, constitute the most popular Polish films. For example, two such successful films were released in 1979: Wojciech Marczewski's *Nightmares*, based on Emil Zegadłowicz's anticlerical novel, and Andrzej Wajda's *Panny z Wilka* (*The Maids of Wilko*), his other (after *Birchwood*) adaptation of Jarosław Iwaszkiewicz's prose. *Nightmares* tells the coming-of-age story of a sensitive boy in a small Galician town (then part of the Austro-Hungarian monarchy). Set at the beginning of the twentieth century in a brutal junior high school environment, the film is about the boy's confrontation with some sadistic teachers, his brief fascination with socialist ideology, and his first erotic fascinations. This first film by

Marczewski, although set in the past, offers several relevant discourses on topics including educational methods, maintaining one's individuality at all costs, and the dangers of totalitarianism.

Wajda's Oscar-nominated (Best Foreign Film) *The Maids of Wilko* introduces the forty-year-old protagonist, Wiktor Ruben (Daniel Olbrychski), who is depressed after the death of a friend and moves to the village of Wilko to revive happy memories from his first visit there before World War I. The erotic and moody photography (by Edward Kłosiński) evokes a Chekhovian atmosphere. The feeling of nostalgia and the theme of the impossibility of reversing time permeate this story of the "five unhappy women from Venus and a tired man from Mars."[52]

Another prominent group of films consists of works that refer to recent Polish history, such as *Śmierć Prezydenta* (*Death of a President*, 1977, Jerzy Kawalerowicz) and *Gdziekolwiek jesteś, Panie Prezydencie* (*Wherever You Are, Mr. President*, 1978, Andrzej Trzos-Rastawiecki). Kawalerowicz's film depicts the 1922 assassination of the first Polish president, Gabriel Narutowicz (Zdzisław Mrożewski), by a nationalist fanatic (Marek Walczewski). The film portrays the turbulent political climate in Poland, the political right's dirty campaign directed against Narutowicz, and the outburst of hatred that resulted in the assassination. Another successful historical reconstruction, *Wherever You Are, Mr. President* describes the life of the legendary prewar Warsaw president Stefan Starzyński (Tadeusz Łomnicki). In September 1939, Starzyński was arrested in his office by the invading Germans and later perished during the war. Trzos-Rastawiecki incorporates archival footage into black-and-white photography to produce a documentary-like experience (cinematography by Zygmunt Samosiuk). Unlike the historical reconstructions by Kawalerowicz and Trzos-Rastawiecki, Ryszard Filipski's *Zamach stanu* (*Coup d'état*, 1980) and Bohdan Poręba's *Polonia Restituta* (1981, also a television series in 1982), both massive (by Polish standards) historical epics, offer unsophisticated chronicles of the events that led to Marshal Józef Piłsudski's coup d'état in 1926 and Poland's independence (*Polonia Restituta*).[53]

A small group of films dealt with World War II and the occupation. *Akcja pod Arsenałem* (*Operation Arsenal*, 1978, Jan Łomnicki) focuses on the actions of the Polish underground in occupied Warsaw. Janusz Morgenstern's popular television series *Polskie drogi* (*Polish Ways*, 1976–1977, eleven episodes) portrays a vast panorama of Polish characters living under German occupation. Revolving around the wartime accounts of two characters, Władysław Niwiński (Karol Strassburger) and Leon Kuraś (Kazimierz Kaczor), the films deal with the Polish fate and refers to the communist resistance (GL) and the Home Army, to Auschwitz, and to the plight of Polish Jews.

Janusz Majewski's films made in the late 1970s were also set in the past. *Sprawa Gorgonowej* (*The Gorgon Affair*, 1977) and *Lekcja martwego języka* (*The Lesson of a Dead Language*, 1979) established him as a filmmaker sensitive to the nuances of the past and able to capture its tone. The former, set in the 1930s, relates the actual trial of Rita Gorgon (Ewa Dałkowska), who was accused of murdering her employer and lover's teenage daughter. Although Gorgon maintained her innocence, she received the death sentence, which was later changed to eight years in prison. Majewski deals with the atmosphere of hysteria surrounding the trial and the xenophobic attitudes toward Gorgon (she was a foreigner). *The Lesson of a Dead Language,* based on Andrzej Kuśniewicz's novel, concerns the demise of the Austro-Hungarian Empire, the end of a historical epoch. Set in 1918, the film narrates the story of the uhlan lieutenant Alfred Kiekeritz (Olgierd Łukaszewicz) who is dying of tuberculosis and has been sent to a sanatorium in a small Carpathian town situated on the periphery of the monarchy. The lieutenant, a known art collector and connoisseur, awaits his death there. The motif of death, both personal (Kiekeritz) and political (the empire), permeates the film.

Often absent in critical works on Polish cinema of that period, published outside of Poland, are popular comedies directed by Stanisław Bareja (1929–1987). Bareja's films, generally undervalued both then and now, appropriately reflected the absurdity of Polish life under communist rule. Konrad Klejsa fittingly labels Bareja's approach to Polish reality as "socialist hyperrealism."[54] Beginning with *Poszukiwany, poszukiwana* (*Wanted*, 1972), Bareja started to infuse his films with harsh observations of everyday political reality. His bitter political satires, such as *Co mi zrobisz jak mnie złapiesz* (*What Will You Do With Me When You Catch Me*, 1978) and, in particular, *Miś* (*Teddy Bear*, 1981), reveal more about that period than does the whole roster of politically oriented Polish cinema. Both films portray situations that are surrealist in spirit, people whose stupidity is of epic proportions, and an everyday existence that is kitschy, ridiculous, and painful.[55]

In the late 1970s, Polish critics coined the term "creative cinema" (*kino kreacyjne*) to distinguish between those filmmakers who focused on everyday problems and politics and those who were more interested in cultural issues and formal concerns. The Polish critic Czesław Dondziłło coined a more appropriate term in 1979—"the cinema reflecting on culture" (*kino kulturowej refleksji*)—to contrast the "journalistic cinema" of the politically minded filmmakers and a group of films that were "oneiric, sophisticated, and aesthetically refined."[56] As the best examples, he briefly discusses Marczewski's *Nightmares*, Filip Bajon's *Aria dla atlety* (*Aria for an Athlete*, 1979), Piotr Szulkin's *Golem* (1980), and Tadeusz Junak's *Pałac* (*The Palace*, 1980).

Aria for an Athlete by Bajon (1947–) and his later films—*Wizja lokalna 1901* (*Inspection at the Scene of the Crime, 1901*, 1981) and *Magnat* (*The Magnate*, 1987)—deserve attention. The Polish critic Waldemar Chołodowski writes: "Bajon does not employ a social background; he manages without it. His cinematographically well-defined protagonists are located in a culture of street songs and kitchen romances (*Aria*), and in the law-abiding culture (*Inspection*). These films are closer to a circus tradition or theatrical conventions; closer to decorativeness than an authentic story about life."[57] *Aria for an Athlete* introduces a nostalgic look at the turn of the twentieth century. The story, written by Bajon, revolves around a freestyle-wrestling champion, Władysław Góralewicz (Krzysztof Majchrzak), his rise to fame from a humble beginning in a provincial circus, and his love for the opera. The painterly quality and the mood of this film, which is based on the life of the famous Polish athlete Zbyszko Cyganiewicz, owe much to the stylish cinematography by Jerzy Zieliński, who also worked on Bajon's next two films.[58]

Inspection at the Scene of the Crime, 1901 reconstructs a school strike that happened in 1901 in the small town of Września, then part of Germany. Bajon portrays the fight to use the Polish language at school without resorting to national stereotyping and without imitating Polish sentimental patriotic films. The very title of the film indicates an attempt at an objective representation of past events. The symbolic nature of several scenes, their painterly quality, and the meticulous composition of the frame distinguish Bajon's film from the dominant "journalistic" tone and style of several Polish films made at that time. Stylish ventures into the past became Bajon's trademark. *The Magnate*, which deals with Polish-German relations, provides references to actual events and places. The demise of the German aristocratic family von Teuss in Upper Silesia is the central story of *The Magnate*, an epic film covering the first half of the century. Jan Nowicki, who plays the family patriarch, leads a cast of several known Polish actors in the film in which the family saga merges with a careful re-creation of actual historical events.[59]

Known for a series of excruciatingly contemporary science fiction films, Piotr Szulkin (1950–2018) began his career with *Golem* (1980), inspired by Gustav Meyrink's writings and the Golem legend. This dystopian fiction describes the problem of dehumanization and portrays animal-like existence in a futuristic, postnuclear world. *Golem*'s cold beauty of painterly images (cinematography by Zygmunt Samosiuk) is repeated in Szulkin's next film, *Wojna światów: Następne stulecie* (*War of the Worlds: Next Century*, 1981, released in 1983). Dedicated to H. G. Wells and Orson Welles, the film depicts another futuristic society as revealed during the landing of the Martians. It is not surprising that Szulkin made a film about a totalitarian system that uses television as its main tool of control. The young, emerging Polish filmmakers, including Szulkin, often cast the world of media in the role of the traditional Polish villain. "Reality—we create it," reads the slogan in the film. Roman Wilhelmi stars as a television anchor manipulated by "the system," thus allowing for numerous allusions to the 1981 political situation in Poland. Because of obvious parallels between the film's images and its political context, it was banned after the introduction of martial law.[60]

Polish cinema in the late 1970s and during the Solidarity period also paid attention to sociological observations and moral issues, often without linking them to current politics. For example, *Tańczący jastrząb* (*Dancing Hawk*, 1978, Grzegorz Królikiewicz), based on Julian Kawalec's novel, is about social advancement and its consequences: social uprooting. The film tells the story about the rise of an ambitious villager (Franciszek Trzeciak) who graduates from a university, breaks links with his roots (divorcing his first wife and marrying a socialite), and sacrifices everything for his career, with tragic repercussions.[61] Sociological observations also dominate films made by Ryszard Czekała: *Zofia* (1976) and *Płomienie* (*Flames*, 1979). Both deal with generational conflicts, the disintegration of traditional values, and the confrontation between different (city/village) values.[62]

In the highly political atmosphere in Poland, critics often overlooked films devoid of politics. Among them was *Grzeszny żywot Franciszka Buły* (*The Sinful Life of Franciszek Buła*, 1980, Janusz Kidawa), a down-to-earth comedy that uses the prewar folklore of Silesia; *Wśród nocnej ciszy* (*Silent Night*, aka *In the Still of the Night*, 1978), a moody thriller set in the 1920s and directed by Tadeusz Chmielewski, a filmmaker better known for his classic film comedies; and *Con Amore* (1976, Jan Batory), a melodrama that was popular in Poland and abroad.

Spirala (*Spiral*, 1978, Krzysztof Zanussi), a continuation of the director's earlier meditations on death, is also unique in the context of the Cinema of Distrust. Instead of social or political issues, in this film Zanussi tackles moral and philosophical dilemmas. The film's protagonist, Tomasz (Jan Nowicki), a middle-aged, professional man, faces a terminal disease. The grief-stricken Tomasz rebels against death and society. He escapes from the hospital to die on his own terms:

climbing in the Tatra Mountains. The film poses many questions concerning the process of dying and the intimacy of death.

* * *

The introduction of martial law by General Jaruzelski in December 1981 was followed by eighteen months of curfew and militarized administration and then by the "period of normalization" (1983–1986). Despite the name, this was an era of political struggle to change the system, an era of hopelessness, economic stagnation, and harsh living conditions.

Notes

1. Julian Kornhauser and Adam Zagajewski, *Świat nie przedstawiony* (Kraków: Wydawnictwo Literackie, 1974).
2. The term refers to the title of a Kraków periodical.
3. Adam Zagajewski, "Rzeczywistość nie przedstawiona w powojennej literaturze polskiej," in Kornhauser and Zagajewski, *Świat nie przedstawiony*, 32.
4. Michał Głowiński describes the weak foundations of the communist system in his seminal works and analyzes the use of language—the Orwellian "newspeak." See, e.g., Michał Głowiński, *Nowomowa po polsku* (Warsaw: Open, 1990); *Rytuał i demagogia: Trzynaście szkiców o sztuce zdegradowanej* (Warsaw: Open, 1992); *Peereliada: Komentarze do słów 1976–1981* (Warsaw: Państwowy Instytut Wydawniczy, 1993).
5. Tadeusz Sobolewski, "Wyzwoliłam się: mówi Agnieszka Holland," *Kino* 12 (1992): 8.
6. Various authors translate "Kino moralnego niepokoju" differently—as the Cinema of Moral Anxiety or the Cinema of Moral Unrest. Daniel Bickley prefers another term: the Cinema of Moral Dissent. Daniel Bickley, "The Cinema of Moral Dissent: A Report from the Gdańsk Film Festival," *Cineaste* 11, no. 1 (1980–1981): 10–15.
7. Many sources cite Kijowski as the one who coined "Cinema of Moral Concern." His fellow filmmakers, for instance, Feliks Falks, also acknowledged the term. See, e.g., Tadeusz Sobolewski, "Braliśmy udział w czymś poważnym: Mówi Feliks Falk," *Kino* 12 (1992): 11.
8. In her detailed monograph on the Cinema of Moral Concern, Dobrochna Dabert summarizes Polish debates surrounding this very term, which she translates in the "Summary" as the Cinema of Moral Anxiety. Dobrochna Dabert, *Kino moralnego niepokoju: Wokół wybranych problemów poetyki i etyki* (Poznań: Wydawnictwo Naukowe Uniwersytetu im. Adama Mickiewicza, 2003), 30–33.

9. Mariola Jankun-Dopartowa, "Fałszywa inicjacja bohatera: Młode kino lat siedemdziesiątych wobec założeń programowych Młodej Kultury," in *Człowiek z ekranu: Z antropologii postaci filmowej*, ed. Mariola Jankun-Dopartowa and Mirosław Przylipiak (Kraków: Arcana, 1996), 108.
10. Ibid., 109.
11. *Personnel* belongs to Kieślowski's more autobiographical films. Like the film's protagonist, Kieślowski graduated from the Warsaw College for Theater Technicians (Państwowe Liceum Techniki Teatralnej) in 1962 and spent one year working as a dresser at the prestigious Teatr Współczesny in Warsaw.
12. Krzysztof Wojciechowski (1939–) is the author of educational films, television films and programs, and documentaries. He became known for his documentary classic *Wyszedł w jasny, pogodny dzień* (*He Left on a Bright, Sunny Day*, 1971). In 1997, he made *Historia o proroku Eliaszu z Wierszalina* (*The Story of Prophet Elijah of Wierszalin*)—another "ethnographic film" set before the war in the Polish eastern provinces.
13. Danusia Stok, ed., *Kieślowski on Kieślowski* (London: Faber & Faber, 1993), 99.
14. When screened at the 1981 Festival of Polish Films in Gdańsk, *The Calm* won the Special Prize shared with another "unshelved" film, *Meta* (*Shelter*, 1971, Antoni Krauze), also made for Polish television.
15. For more information about *The Scar* and *The Calm*, particularly their Polish context, see Marek Haltof, *The Cinema of Krzysztof Kieślowski: Variations on Destiny and Chance* (London: Wallflower Press, 2004): 34–42.
16. Paul Coates, *The Story of the Lost Reflection: The Alienation of the Image in Western and Polish Cinema* (London: Verso, 1985), 45.
17. Krzysztof T. Toeplitz, "*Amator* czyli moralność sztuki," *Miesięcznik Literacki* 12 (1979): 83.
18. In the early 1970s, several Polish documentaries tried to uncover the Stalinist past, including Wojciech Wiszniewski's stylized films about Stalinist work competition, *The Story of a Man Who Produced 552 Percent of the Norm* (1973) and *Wanda Gościmińska, the Textile Worker*, 1975); Krzysztof Kieślowski's *Murarz* (*Bricklayer*, 1973); and Ryszard Bugajski's *Słowo o Wincentym Pstrowskim* (*A Word on Wincenty Pstrowski*, 1973). They were released in 1981 and banned after the introduction of martial law in December 1981.
19. For insightful comparative comments on *Citizen Kane* and *Man of Marble*, see Maureen Turim, "Remembering and Deconstructing: The Historical Flashback in *Man of Marble* and *Man of Iron*," in *The Cinema of Andrzej Wajda: The Art of Irony and Defiance*, ed. John Orr and Elżbieta Ostrowska (London: Wallflower Press, 2003), 95–98.
20. This aspect of *Man of Marble* is discussed by Wiesław Godzic, "Metafora polityczna: *Człowiek z marmuru* Andrzeja Wajdy," in *Analizy i interpretacje: Film polski*, ed. Alicja Helman and Tadeusz Miczka (Katowice: Wydawnictwo Uniwersytetu Śląskiego, 1984), 106–21.

21. Janina Falkowska, *The Political Films of Andrzej Wajda: Dialogism in* Man of Marble, Man of Iron, *and* Danton (New York: Berghahn Books, 1996), 74.
22. The influence of socialist realist paintings and *An Adventure at Marienstadt* is apparent mostly in scenes with the young Birkut at the construction site (low-angle shots against the sky).
23. For instance, "Murarski walczyk" (The little waltz of bricklayers), played by the Gypsy band, when drunken Birkut throws a brick at the state (perhaps security service) building. The use of music in *Man of Marble* is extensively discussed by Iwona Sowińska-Rammel, "Emocjonalna i ideologiczna funkcja muzyki w *Człowieku z marmuru* Andrzeja Wajdy," in Helman and Miczka, *Analizy i interpretacje*, 122–29.
24. Stephen Schiff's review of *Man of Marble* in *Foreign Affairs: The National Society of Film Critics' Video Guide to Foreign Films*, ed. Kathy Schulz Huffhines (San Francisco: Mercury House, 1991), 254.
25. Bjørn Sørensen, "'Visual Eloquence' and Documentary Form: Meeting *Man of Marble* in Nowa Huta," in Orr and Ostrowska, *The Cinema of Andrzej Wajda*, 112.
26. Marek Radziwon, "Barwy ochronne nie wyblakły," *Kwartalnik Filmowy* 18 (1997): 134.
27. Tomasz Lengren (1945–2008) was also a film director, the author of the medium-length *Choinka strachu* (*The Christmas Tree of Fear*, 1982, released in 1989), and the full-length *Tanie pieniądze* (*Cheap Money*, 1986).
28. Stok, *Kieślowski on Kieślowski*, 96.
29. After making several films in Poland, including *Bestia* (*The Beast*, 1979), *Planeta krawiec* (*The Planet Tailor*, 1984), and *Łuk Erosa* (*Cupid's Bow*, 1988), Jerzy Domaradzki (1943–) continued his career in Australia, where he directed two critically acclaimed films: *Struck by Lightning* (1990) and *Lilian's Story* (1996). He was the head of the Polish Filmmakers Association from 1994 to 1996.
30. Joanna Korska, "Barbara Sass-Zdort: Kobiety pod presją w Polsce lat osiemdziesiątych," in *Kobieta z kamerą*, ed. Grażyna Stachówna (Kraków: Wydawnictwo Uniwersytetu Jagiellońskiego, 1998), 82–83.
31. For more information, see Monika Talarczyk-Gubała, *Wszystko o Ewie: Filmy Barbary Sass a kino kobiet w drugiej połowie XX wieku* (Szczecin: Wydawnictwo Uniwersytetu Szczecińskiego, 2013).
32. Marcin Maron, "Head of Medusa, or Realism in Films of the Cinema of Moral Anxiety," special issue in English on "Polish Film Scholars on Polish Cinema," *Kwartalnik Filmowy*: 241–42.
33. Aleksander Jackiewicz, *Moja filmoteka: Kino polskie* (Warsaw: Wydawnictwa Artystyczne i Filmowe, 1983), 517.
34. I am referring here to films such as *Illumination* or Zanussi's films made abroad: *Imperative* (1982) and *Paradigm* (1985).
35. Sobolewski, "Braliśmy udział," 10.
36. Maron, "Head of Medusa," 237.
37. Sobolewski, "Wyzwoliłam się," 8.

38. Maria Kornatowska, *Wodzireje i amatorzy* (Warsaw: Wydawnictwa Artystyczne i Filmowe, 1990), 184.
39. Ibid., 173.
40. See Piotr Litka, "Najważniejszy jest dialog," an interview with Jerzy Stuhr, *Kino* 12 (1999): 22–24.
41. Tomasz Warchol, "The End of the Beginning," *Sight and Sound* 55, no. 3 (1986): 190.
42. Ewa Gębicka, "Sieć i rozpowszechnianie filmów," in *Encyklopedia kultury polskiej XX wieku: Film i kinematografia*, ed. Edward Zajiček (Warsaw: Instytut Kultury and Komitet Kinematografii, 1994), 442–44. The number of films from Western countries was even lower in 1982—nine out of the eighty-seven imported films. Jerzy Płażewski, "Film zagraniczny w Polsce," in Zajiček, *Encyklopedia kultury polskiej*, 348.
43. The title refers to an earlier documentary, *Robotnicy '71: Nic o nas bez nas* (*Workers 1971: Nothing about Us without Us*, 1972), directed by Krzysztof Kieślowski, Tomasz Zygadło, Wojciech Wiszniewski, Paweł Kędzierski, and Tadeusz Walendowski.
44. Coates, *The Story of the Lost Reflection*, 152.
45. Krzysztof Kieślowski, "Przypadek," *Dialog* 5 (1981): 7–25.
46. The Polish title *Przypadek* is usually translated as *Blind Chance*, but it could as easily be translated as "the coincidence" or "the case" (i.e., the case of Witek).
47. Konrad J. Zarębski, ed., "*Przypadek*," *Filmowy Serwis Prasowy* 5 (1987): 17.
48. Frank Turaj, "Poland: The Cinema of Moral Concern," in *Post New Wave Cinema in the Soviet Union and Eastern Europe*, ed. Daniel J. Goulding (Bloomington: Indiana University Press, 1989), 160.
49. Michael Szporer, "Woman of Marble: An Interview with Krystyna Janda," *Cineaste* 18, no. 3 (1991): 14.
50. Ryszard Bugajski settled in Canada where he directed *Clearcut* (1991). He returned to Poland in the mid-1990s, making *Gracze* (*Players*, 1996), a political drama set during the first presidential elections after the fall of communism.
51. Gustaw Moszcz (Gary Mead), "Frozen Assets: Interviews on Polish Cinema," *Sight and Sound* 50, no. 2 (1981): 87
52. "*The Maids of Wilko*: Five Unhappy Women from Venus and a Tired Man from Mars" is a translation of the title of Teresa Rutkowska's Polish text, "*Panny z Wilka*: Pięć nieszczęśliwych kobiet z Wenus i zmęczony mężczyzna z Marsa," *Kwartalnik Filmowy* 18 (1997): 141–52.
53. Bohdan Poręba, a controversial communist activist and head of film studio Profil, also made a film about an idealistic party functionary in *Gdzie woda czysta i trawa zielona* (*Where the Water Is Clear and the Grass Is Green*, 1977).
54. Konrad Klejsa, "Stanisław Bareja: Nadrealizm socjalistyczny," in *Autorzy kina polskiego, tom 2*, ed. Grażyna Stachówna and Bogusław Żmudziński (Kraków: Wydawnictwo Uniwersytetu Jagiellońskiego, 2007), 79–128.
55. A documentary film by Agnieszka Arnold, *Bareizm* (*Bareism*, 1997), deals with Bareja's career and his exceptional popularity among young viewers in particular. Bareja's earlier television film, *Niespotykanie spokojny człowiek* (*An Unusually Quiet*

Man, 1975), has been voted the best television film in a plebiscite organized by the weekly *Polityka*. Zdzisław Pietrasik, "Złota dziesiątka," *Polityka* 31 (3 August 2002): 48. For more information about Bareja, see Maciej Łuczak, *Miś, czyli rzecz o Stanisławie Barei* (Warsaw: Wydawnictwo Prószyński i S-ka, 2002); Maciej Replewicz, *Stanisław Bareja: Król krzywego zwierciadła* (Poznań: Zysk i S-ka, 2009).

56. Czesław Dondziłło, *Młode kino polskie lat siedemdziesiątych* (Warsaw: Młodzieżowa Agencja Wydawnicza, 1985), 92.
57. Waldemar Chołodowski, *Kraina niedojrzałości* (Warsaw: Czytelnik, 1983), 121.
58. Zieliński (1950–) received praise in the late 1970s for his work on several critically acclaimed short films, including Zbigniew Rybczyński's *New Book* (1975) and Wojciech Wiszniewski's *The First Textbook* (1976) and *Foreman on the Farm* (1978). Critics in Poland commended his stylish photography of Bajon's first films. He began working abroad in the 1980s, photographing, among other films, Agnieszka Holland's *Washington Square* (1997) and *The Third Miracle* (1999), and John Kent Harrison's *The Courageous Heart of Irena Sendler* (2009).
59. See Ewelina Nurczyńska-Fidelska, *Czas i przesłona: O Filipie Bajonie i jego twórczości* (Kraków: Wydawnictwo Rabid, 2003).
60. The representation of Winkiel, a television reporter in *Man of Iron*, serves here as a good example. The issues of manipulation by "the system" also appear in *Czułe miejsca (Sensitive Spots*, 1981, Piotr Andrejew) and in Szulkin's next films: *O-bi, o-ba: Koniec cywilizacji (O-bi, o-ba: End of Civilization*, 1985), and *Ga, Ga: Chwała bohaterom (Ga, Ga: Glory to the Heroes*, 1986).
61. *Dancing Hawk*'s cinematographer was Zbigniew Rybczyński, later known for a series of experimental films that he directed, including *Tango* (1980), for which he received an Academy Award for Best Short Film in 1983.
62. Ryszard Czekała (1941–2010) started his career in the late 1960s with a series of animated films that were well received by Polish critics. His arguably best-known animated short is *Apel* (*The Roll Call*, 1970), a black-and-white film about the reality of a concentration camp. In the 1970s, animated films flourished in Poland. In addition to Czekała and Rybczyński, one must mention, among others, the ascetic and philosophical films by Jerzy Kucia (sometimes labeled in Poland "the Bresson of Polish animation") and the noncamera films by Julian Józef Antonisz. The early 1980s mark the appearance of the first animated films by Piotr Dumała and Aleksander Sroczyński, among others.

CHAPTER 8
The Cinema of Martial Law and Afterward (1982–1988)

> *If we were to judge only by their films, the Poles would seem the most depressed people on earth.*
>
> —Gerald Pratley, "Gdańsk: Metaphors for Poland"

Leaving its political implications aside, the implementation of martial law on 13 December 1981 by General Wojciech Jaruzelski seriously affected Polish cinema. The film landscape was changed by the communist ban on "unwanted" films, by the emigration of young filmmakers such as Ryszard Bugajski and Agnieszka Holland,[1] and by the silence ("internal exile") of others such as Wojciech Marczewski. Accused of oppositional activities, Andrzej Wajda was removed as the head of the film studio X in April 1983, together with his close collaborators—the producer Barbara Pec-Ślesicka and the literary director Bolesław Michałek. Wajda also resigned as the head of the Polish Filmmakers Association, which was suspended, like most other Polish associations, after December 1981.[2]

The political situation after 1981 deepened the divisions between the filmmakers who supported the introduction of martial law (the minority) and those who opposed it. Comments such as "Poland's quality cinema is now either silent or working in exile"[3] certainly simplified the problem yet aptly reflected the heated atmosphere, with its intensified divisions between "us" and "them." Once again, the political aspects became more important than the films themselves. The unofficial boycott of certain pro-communist filmmakers and the attempt to boycott filmmaking in general—and filmmaking for state television in particular—were unsuccessful. The boycott did not affect established filmmakers (some of whom were making films or teaching abroad) and negatively influenced the careers of young, emerging filmmakers and actors. The latter either were unable to produce films or had to comply with the dominant aesthetics in order to be considered true artists. The film director Waldemar Krzystek (1953–) commented sarcastically: "Immediately after martial law, it was not the best time to break with the artistic preferences of 'moral concern.' The country was again in need, the nation suffered, and the mothers shed tears."[4] Because of the absence of locally made films that expressed dissenting views, distorted pro-communist interpretations of recent events were propagated in films such as *Godność* (*Dignity*, 1984, Roman Wionczek), which tells the story of an old worker, a party member, who is humiliated by Solidarity activists.

Authorities immediately banned several films made and released during the brief Solidarity period, among them Andrzej Wajda's *Man of Iron* and Wojciech Marczewski's *Shivers*, which premiered on 12 December 1981—one day before the declaration of martial law. The same thing happened to a group of films finished at the beginning of 1982, including Ryszard Bugajski's *Interrogation* and Janusz Zaorski's *The Mother of Kings*. The latter, based on Kazimierz Brandys's novel, is a saga about a working-class family led by a widowed mother, Łucja Król (Magda Teresa Wójcik). Unlike Brandys's story about a communist activist who is disenchanted after the end of the Stalinist period, Zaorski's film covers more than twenty years of Polish history by focusing on the mother.

In 1987, *The Mother of Kings* was quietly released with a group of other distinguished banned films including Krzysztof Kieślowski's *Blind Chance* and Jerzy Domaradzki's *The Big Run*. At the 1987 Polish Film Festival in Gdańsk, Kieślowski received the Best Screenplay Award for *Blind Chance*, and its star, Bogusław Linda, received the Best Actor Award. In 1988, Agnieszka Holland's *A Woman Alone* was "unshelved," as was the preeminent Polish film of the early 1980s, Ryszard Bugajski's *Interrogation*, one year later.

The banning of several Polish films, the significant reduction of Western films in Poland (only nine such films in distribution in 1982),[5] and the impact of the (mostly pirated) video market alienated many sophisticated Polish viewers. In 1982, the biggest box office hit on Polish screens was the belated release of Bruce Lee's 1973 *Enter the Dragon*. Polish films released in 1982, such as Tadeusz Konwicki's adaptation of Czesław Miłosz's *Dolina Issy* (*The Valley of Issa*) and Janusz Kidawa's para-documentary *Anna i wampir* (*Anna and the Vampire*, 1982), telling the story of a serial killer who terrorized the inhabitants of Silesia in the late 1960s (an actual crime case), were no match for imported works.

In 1978, a second film school was established in Poland, originally for the television industry exclusively, the Katowice Film and Television School.[6] In the early 1980s, it emerged as a competitor for the well-known Łódź Film School and was essential in invigorating the Polish film industry. By the end of the 1980s, the Katowice School was dominating its famous rival by graduating such talented directors as Maciej Dejczer, Waldemar Krzystek, and Piotr and Magdalena Łazarkiewicz, to name just a few. The strength of the Katowice School also lay with its distinguished teachers, some of who were "unwanted" at the Łódź Film School for political reasons. They included Krzysztof Kieślowski, Kazimierz Kutz, Andrzej Wajda, and Krzysztof Zanussi. Critics in Poland often juxtaposed the documentary-oriented style of Katowice with the formal concerns of Łódź. The competition between the two film centers had produced some engaging artistic results. The young filmmakers, sometimes labeled in Poland the "Martial Law Generation,"[7] had a difficult start in the mid-1980s. Caught in political divisions among the filmmakers, they produced their crucial films in the late 1980s and after the 1989 return of democracy.

In 1981, a new experimental production collective, the Karol Irzykowski Film Studio, produced several significant films made by younger filmmakers, such as *Kartka z podróży* (*A Postcard from the Journey*, 1984), directed by Waldemar Dziki (1956–2016), and *Nadzór* (*Custody*, 1985), directed by Wiesław Saniewski (1948–). *Custody* is one of the most important Polish films made in the mid-1980s. This prison film, set in a women's penitentiary, traces the life of Klara (Ewa Błaszczyk), who is arrested on the day of her wedding in 1967, accused of misappropriating money, and sentenced to life in prison, which is then changed to twenty-five years. Klara's struggles for dignity and internal freedom and her attempts to see her born-in-prison child are at the center of the film. *Custody* also deals with the issue of manipulation and the psychology of female prisoners. The film's dark portrayal of the prison reality (a topic untouched by Polish films, with the exception of *Interrogation*) contributed to the limited release of this powerful film.

The director of *Custody*, Wiesław Saniewski, a former film critic (the author of three books of film criticism) and a reporter, also made *Wolny strzelec* (*The Freelancer*, 1981, released in 1988) and *Sezon na bażanty* (*The Season of Dead Birds*, aka *The Stalking Season*, 1986) during this period. Though Saniewski has not won many critical fans in Poland, his films have been consistently well received and awarded abroad, especially in the United States. With the exception of the psychological drama *Dotknięci* (*The Touched*, 1988), labeled by some critics as the Polish version of *One Flew over the Cuckoo's Nest* (1975, Miloš Forman), films by Saniewski were not successful locally. This is also true of his later films from the

1990s, such as *Obcy musi fruwać* (*The Stranger Must Fly*, 1993) and *Deszczowy żołnierz* (*The Rainy Soldier*, 1996), which received awards at film festivals in Phoenix, Charleston, and Houston, among others, yet were ignored by local film audiences and critics.

***

A penetrating observer of the new Polish cinema, the critic Tadeusz Sobolewski, commented: "The experiences of martial law developed ritual reactions within the Polish culture: poetry was composed to commemorate particular occasions, along with paintings depicting the martyrdom of victims of the regime, Romantic Messianism came back to life, or rather the parody of it."[8] During that dark period, however, there were some success stories. Zbigniew Rybczyński's experimental film *Tango* (1980) received several festival awards, including the Academy Award for Best Animated Short Film in 1983, the first for a Polish production. Rybczyński (1949–), chiefly known as a director of experimental animated films and music videos, earlier also worked as a cinematographer on documentaries with directors such as Andrzej Barański and Wojciech Wiszniewski (e.g., *Wanda Gościmińska, the Textile Worker*, 1975) and on one feature film, the classic *Dancing Hawk* (1978) by Grzegorz Królikiewicz. After immigrating to the United States in 1983, Rybczyński made many acclaimed music videos (including for John Lennon's "Imagine" in 1986) and several distinguished films, among them *Steps* (1987), *The Fourth Dimension* (1988), *The Orchestra* (1990, Emmy Award for special effects), and *Kafka* (1992).

In 1984, *Rok spokojnego słońca* (*Year of the Quiet Sun*, 1985), Krzysztof Zanussi's tale of unfulfilled love, won the Venice Film Festival (Golden Lion), which only raised suspicions in Poland that the award was politically motivated (as in the case of *Man of Iron*). Zanussi's excellent film portrays an impossible love between two lonely, middle-aged people—the American soldier Norman (Scott Wilson) and the Polish war widow Emilia (Maja Komorowska). Both are scarred by the war. Norman, who is a former prisoner of a German POW camp, works for the Allied War Crimes Commission investigating the death of captured American pilots. Emilia takes care of her ailing mother (Hanna Skarżanka). Their chance meeting in a small town deserted by the Germans, now part of the Polish Regained Lands, offers them an opportunity to overcome the burden of the past. The language barrier (they must communicate through interpreters) is not an obstacle to their

Figure 8.1 Scott Wilson and Maja Komorowska in Krzysztof Zanussi's *Year of the Quiet Sun* (1985). Courtesy of Filmoteka Narodowa.

love. Emilia, however, does not follow her heart and decides to stay in Poland, even though her mother dies early on and everything is ready for her escape abroad. Suffering unnecessarily, Emilia gives up her love and her chance to be free. The lovers are united only after death in a powerful, symbolic, and emotional last scene showing them dancing at Monument Valley.

Zanussi's reconstruction of the postwar period is devoid of the optimism present in numerous Polish films. The director is interested in not political but personal dilemmas; he focuses on divisions not between Poles and Germans, but rather between honest and devious people. Poland's small town in the Regained Lands is a drab, sinister place populated by crooks, gangsters, prostitutes, and the people lost in this new reality like Emilia and her mother. Sławomir Idziak's camera captures inhospitable, chilly landscapes, brownish images of an unfriendly town, as if providing a bitter comment on the "year of the sun." Despite its careful balance between melodrama and psychological drama, as well as its formal beauty, Zanussi's film was not very well received in Poland because of its mood of despair, its uncommitted portrayal of the postwar reality, and the presentation of the postwar situation as the end of the world instead of the beginning of a new one.

The Catamount Killing (1974, US) began a series of films that Zanussi made abroad periodically, and he made several of them in the 1980s. Two of them, *Imperative* (1982, France–West Germany) and *Paradigm* (1985, France-Italy), stand out from the rest and are on the level of Zanussi's most accomplished Polish productions.[9]

Popular Cinema

The elimination of politically minded cinema in distribution and the growing importance of locally made popular genre films prompted several Polish critics, who supported the thematic preoccupations of the Cinema of Distrust, to speak of the danger of imminent commercialization. These comments, however, overstated the danger of the specter of commercialism in the early 1980s.

The first films by Juliusz Machulski (1955–), very popular among audiences, must be mentioned in this context: *Vabank* (*Va Banque*, 1982), its sequel *Va Banque II* (1985), and *Seksmisja* (*Sex Mission*, 1984). A former leading actor in Kieślowski's *Personnel*, a film heralding the Cinema of Distrust, Machulski was nevertheless openly critical about his colleagues' films. He accused Polish filmmakers, with the exception of Holland and Kieślowski, of superficiality and the lack of professionalism.[10]

Machulski's films refer to Western cinema rather than a national context, to cinema conventions rather than life "as it is." His *Va Banque*, a retro gangster comedy set in the 1930s in Warsaw, was clearly influenced by American films such as *The Sting* (1973, George Roy Hill). It tells the story of a professional safecracker Kwinto (Jan Machulski, the director's father), who, with the help of his new friend "Duńczyk" (Witold Pyrkosz), avenges the betrayal by his former partner, a respected banker, who convinced Kwinto to rob his bank to cover misappropriations, but then called the police.

Another film by Machulski, *Sex Mission*, is a science fiction farce about a futuristic society formed after a nuclear disaster by (as it appears later) an impotent older man disguised as a woman. In this women-only world, men are excluded because they are blamed for the disaster. When two hibernated male protagonists (Jerzy Stuhr and Olgierd Łukaszewicz) awaken, a series of comic situations develop that provide some clear references to gender politics in Poland and the Polish political reality.

The style of another popular director, Radosław Piwowarski (1948–), had already emerged in the 1970s in two successful television films: *Ciuciubabka* (*Blind Man's Bluff*, 1977) and *Córka albo syn* (*A Daughter or a Son*, 1979). These introduced characters who were down to earth, likeable, and sometimes mildly grotesque and who told stories that were lyrical, nostalgic, and bordering on the sentimental. Piwowarski often dealt with coming-of-age problems and told stories set in small provincial towns against the backdrop of politics. After directing one of the most unusual Polish television series, *Jan Serce* (*John Heart*, 1982), about a sensitive Warsaw sewer maintenance worker (Kazimierz Kaczor), Piwowarski released his first theatrical film, *Yesterday* (1985), about the Beatles phenomenon in Poland. Equally popular became his *Pociąg do Hollywood* (*Train to Hollywood*, 1987), about a small-town bartender (Katarzyna Figura) and her dream of becoming Marilyn Monroe.

Another screenwriter-director, Wojciech Wójcik (1943–2018), specialized in crime films, although at the beginning of his career he also made a psychological drama, *Okno* (*Window*, (1981/1983) and a postwar drama, *Sam pośród swoich* (*Alone among His Own*, 1985). His action film *Karate po polsku* (*Karate Polish Style*, 1983) set the pattern for his later works. They were mostly action-oriented crime films that incorporated the style of American cinema to describe unglamorous Polish reality. In *Prywatne śledztwo* (*Private Investigation*, 1987), for example, Roman Wilhelmi plays a character seeking revenge after a drunken truck driver killed his family.

Genuinely popular among Polish viewers, but underestimated by critics, were *Łuk Erosa* (*Cupid's Bow*, 1988, Jerzy Domaradzki), and some Janusz Zaorski films such as *Baryton* (*The Baritone*, 1985), starring Zbigniew Zapasiewicz; *Jezioro Bodeńskie* (*Sons and Comrades*, aka *Bodensee*, 1986), the winner of the Locarno Film Festival; and *Piłkarski poker* (*Soccer Poker*, 1989). Despite the popularity of films by Machulski, Piwowarski, and Zaorski, and films like *Znachor* (*Quack*, 1982, Jerzy Hoffman) and *Wielki Szu* (*The Big Rook*, 1983, Sylwester Chęciński), Polish cinemas recorded a steady decline in attendance. In 1985, only nine million viewers visited cinemas to watch Polish films, compared with thirty-one million in 1981, and forty-five million in 1976.[11] The exceptional situation occurred in 1984, when a record number of viewers visited Polish cinemas (127.6 million); Polish films were seen by as many as 56.6 million. The popularity of *Sex Mission* (thirteen million viewers) and a children's film, *Akademia pana Kleksa* (*Mr. Blot's Academy*, 1984,

Krzysztof Gradowski), with ten million viewers, helped to achieve such remarkable results.[12]

Polish critics, largely favoring politically committed cinema, wanted to protect this type of cinema against the growing importance of commercially minded films. Some critics saw the appearance of popular cinema as a cynical move on the part of state authorities to divert the attention of Polish viewers to matters of secondary importance. They did not object to Machulski's films or the unpretentious *Yesterday*. Their prime target remained films such as the erotic *Thais* (1984, Ryszard Ber) and *Widziadło* (*Phantom*, 1984, Marek Nowicki); a barrack comedy set in 1918, *C.K. Dezerterzy* (*Deserters*, 1986, Janusz Majewski); and an erotic comedy, *Och, Karol* (*Oh, Charles*, 1985, Roman Załuski). The problem, however, was not a group of genuinely popular films, but rather the mass of mediocre products—neither popular nor artistically or politically minded—that were swiftly rejected by new audiences that, by means of pirated videos, had been educated by American popular cinema.

Personal Cinema and Adaptations

Intimate psychological dramas and safe literary adaptations formed the canon of Polish cinema in the mid-1980s. The highly politicized atmosphere of these years better suited films such as the winner of the 1985 Festival of Polish Films, *Kobieta w kapeluszu* (*A Woman with a Hat*, 1985), written and directed by one of the quiet masters of Polish cinema, Stanisław Różewicz. It is a subtle morality play, devoid of direct references to Polish political reality, and tells the story of a young actress, Ewa (Hanna Mikuć), who lives her unfulfilled dream of becoming a successful actress. Another film released in 1985, Andrzej Barański's *Kobieta z prowincji* (*Woman from the Provinces*, aka *Life's Little Comforts*, 1985), introduces a sixty-year-old woman named Andzia (Ewa Dałkowska) living in a small town. Her difficult, yet not unhappy, life is portrayed in a series of lengthy flashbacks. The film registers her modest everyday life devoid of politics and stresses the simplicity of her existence—its hardships and life's little comforts—as well as the old-fashioned charm of ordinary, banal situations. An interest in "simple people," sympathy (without sentimentality) for the underprivileged, and a warmth emanating from characters like Andzia became Barański's trademarks.

Another film, the "seniors' road movie," *Prognoza pogody* (*Weather Forecast*, 1983, Antoni Krauze), provides commentary on the turbulent year 1981. Set in the fall, it tells the story of the boarders of a seniors' home who escape and regain some freedom and dignity while wandering through Poland. They escape because they fear for their lives. After watching a television news program that forecasts extremely harsh winter conditions, they secretly observe their director (Witold Pyrkosz) helping to transport some coffins to their home during the night. The seniors' panic is stronger than their fear of leaving the safety of their house. After a few days of enjoying their freedom and encountering different people, including young drug addicts, the seniors are found by militia using helicopters and sent back to their home. Clear references to the atmosphere preceding martial law, the themes of distrust toward the authorities, and the idea of regaining one's freedom at all costs make this film a political metaphor of the year 1981.

In the oppressive 1980s, adaptations of national literature belonged to the most successful films. For example, among the thirty-five Polish films released in 1986, the most significant and the most popular were adaptations: *Cudzoziemka* (*Foreigner*, Ryszard Ber), based on Maria Kuncewiczowa's novel; *Kronika wypadków miłosnych* (*Chronicle of Amorous Accidents*, Andrzej Wajda), based on Tadeusz Konwicki's novel; *Sons and Comrades* (Janusz Zaorski), based on Stanisław Dygat's novel; *Siekierezada* (*Axiliad*, Witold Leszczyński), based on Edward Stachura's novel; and Barbara Sass's *Dziewczęta z Nowolipek* (*The Girls of Nowolipki*) and its continuation *Rajska jabłoń* (*Crabapple Tree*), both adaptations of Pola Gojawiczyńska's novel. The popular novel by Gojawiczyńska, first published in 1935, was already successfully adapted by Józef Lejtes in 1937. Faithful to the literary source, Sass tells the story about four Warsaw girls before World War I (the 1920s in *Crabapple Tree*). The films reflect Sass's interest in feminist issues and gender relations. Although melodramatic, these films provide a sociological examination of the girls' social background and confront their youthful aspirations with somber reality, while they search for love with the disappointments that it brings.

The most popular film screened in 1987 in Poland, with six million viewers, was another adaptation, *Nad Niemnem* (*On the Niemen River*, Zbigniew Kuźmiński), based on Eliza Orzeszkowa's novel.[13] Considering the popularity of film adaptations, it is surprising that the last films made by one of the old masters of Polish cinema, Wojciech J. Has, received lukewarm reviews from critics and were virtually ignored by audiences. They include *Nieciekawa historia* (*An Uneventful Story*, 1983), an adaptation of Anton Chekhov's short story; *Pismak* (*The Scribbler*, aka *Write and Fight*, 1985), based on Władysław Terlecki's novel; *Osobisty pamiętnik grzesznika przez niego samego spisany* (*Memoirs of a Sinner*, 1986), adapted from James Hogg's 1824 novel *The Private Memoirs and Confessions of a Justified Sinner*; and *Niezwykła podróż Baltazara Kobera* (*The Fabulous Journey of Balthazar Kober*, aka *The Tribulations of Balthazar Kober*, 1988), based on Frédéric Tristan's novel. New Polish audiences did not appreciate Has's dreamlike narratives, his films' stylistic extravagance, and their disregard for linear development. Stressing Has's desire to continue the type of cinema that brought him critical and popular recognition in the 1960s and the early 1970s, and—as expected—his unwillingness to compromise and incorporate new models of cinema, Alicja Helman writes in her essay fittingly titled "The Masters Are Tired":

> *Has does not seem interested in narrating a story; the linear progression of events in his films is always broken, violated or purposely blurred because he is concerned with an integral vision, a certain unusual atmosphere and an emotional intensity, all of which function to convey the message. His most recent films, to a degree far greater than the films of the Polish School period, require interaction on the part of the viewer and familiarity with the literary sources. For Has does not adapt literature, but rather creates a dialogue with it by making choices and selections from it without restraint, by abbreviating and transforming literature, and by not bothering to inform the audience at all about the basic determinants of the story.*[14]

In the early 1980s, many established filmmakers released their major film adaptations, including Witold Leszczyński's *Konopielka* (1982), and Andrzej Wajda's *Danton* (1983, Poland-France).

The black-and-white *Konopielka*, based on a popular novel by Edward Redliński, portrays a grotesquely backward rural community. The appearance of a beautiful, young teacher (Joanna Sienkiewicz) brings energy and a breath of fresh air into the village. Under her influence, the film's central character, Kaziuk (Krzysztof Majchrzak), begins to question old customs, taboos, and superstitious practices. Majchrzak's fine performance, the film's multilayered structure and its bizarre humor, mocking observations, and sensuality result in a work that equals Leszczyński's classic debut, *The Life of Matthew*. Leszczyński's next film, *Axiliad*, based on the writer Edward Stachura's writings and life (which he ended prematurely in 1979 by committing suicide), won the 1986 Polish Film Festival.

Stanisława Przybyszewska's play *Sprawa Dantona* (*The Danton Affair*), which premiered in 1931, provided a literary source for Wajda's *Danton,* one of the best films of his career. It is a complex historical drama about the French Revolution of 1789, set during its crisis in the spring of 1794. Unlike Przybyszewska, who portrayed Maximilien Robespierre as a hero, Wajda shifts his sympathy toward Georges-Jacques Danton. He juxtaposes the likeable and mass-supported Danton (Gérard Depardieu) and the ascetic doctrinaire Robespierre (Wojciech Pszoniak), who is obsessed with his ideas about the revolution and is unwilling to compromise. Like many other Polish films in the past, *Danton* was read by viewers in Poland as an allegorical reference to the country's political situation.[15] The political and physical similarities between the two leaders (Jaruzelski as Robespierre and Wałęsa as Danton), their confrontation, and the situation of revolutionary chaos and food shortages in 1981 prompted such a double reading. *Danton* depicts people who set the revolution in motion but are crushed when it spins out of control. For many critics in Poland, this is a film, born out of the experience of the Solidarity movement, about the "birth of modern totalitarianism."[16]

Films about Polish-Jewish History

Remarkably, several films about Polish-Jewish relations and the Holocaust were made during one of the darkest years in postwar Polish history, following the introduction of martial law.[17] Some of those projects originated during the Solidarity period and were largely unaffected by the communist ban on "unwanted" films after the declaration of the martial law. *Ryś* (*Lynx*), directed by Stanisław Różewicz in 1981 and released in March 1982, three months after the introduction of martial law, is set in a small town after the deportation of the local Jewish community to a concentration camp. The story revolves around a Polish artisan, Alojz (Franciszek Pieczka), who receives a death sentence from the Polish underground for allegedly collaborating with the occupier. A young local parish priest, Konrad (Jerzy Radziwiłowicz), learns that Alojz is hiding a Jewish family who evaded the transport, and tries to postpone the execution.[18]

As many as four films dealing with the Holocaust were presented at the 1984 Festival of Polish Films in Gdańsk (the first festival since 1981), including *Austeria* (Jerzy Kawalerowicz), *A Postcard from the Journey* (Waldemar Dziki), and *Wedle wyroków Twoich* (*According to the Decrees of Providence,* 1983, Jerzy Hoffman).[19]

One of the most impressive debuts, *A Postcard from the Journey*, is set in 1941 in a Jewish ghetto and portrays a middle-aged office worker, Jakub Rosenberg (Władysław Kowalski), now degraded to a street cleaner, who tries to cope with the growing fear with dignity. While awaiting inevitable deportation, he methodically, almost obsessively, pays attention to small practical details in order to battle his fear and to prepare for death. Unlike his friends and neighbors, Rosenberg attempts to separate himself from the external world. He exercises, psychologically as well as physically, so he is prepared for deportation, transport, and stay in a camp. Preoccupations with detail, slow pace, limited dialogue, and emotional distance make Dziki's film an uneasy experience. Wit Dąbal's camera does not emphasize elements that viewers habitually associate with Holocaust cinema; instead, it mostly captures images of claustrophobic and dilapidated interiors. Although a communist official pointed this out as the film's weakness during the meeting of the Film Approval Committee, the film received the overwhelming praise from, among others, Wanda Jakubowska and Janusz Morgenstern.[20]

Possibly the most accomplished film made in the early 1980s is Kawalerowicz's *Austeria*, based on Julian Stryjkowski's novel of the same title published in 1966 that offers a nostalgic account of a lost Jewish world.[21] *Austeria*, which won the Grand Prix at the 1984 Festival of Polish Films in Gdańsk, portrays an idealized Jewish world of a small eastern Galician town at the outbreak of World War I. Its protagonist, Tag (Franciszek Pieczka), the innkeeper at "Austeria," witnesses diverse communities who gather in his inn on the eve of the war. The last scene of this stylized film shows the destruction of Jews, in a sense heralding events that would happen thirty years later. Several critics justly argued that the characters and the world represented in *Austeria* were shaped by the Holocaust with its "metaphoric visualization of dying."[22] However, after the meeting of the Commission for Film Approval (Komisja Kolaudacyjna) in May 1982, the Soviet embassy objected to the film's alleged anti-Russian bias. The embassy demanded that *Austeria* be released in a limited number of copies and that the final scene be changed. In the original scene, the Tsarist Cossacks approach the river where the Hasidim are bathing and spray them with bullets until the water is red.[23] Following the instructions, Kawalerowicz changed the last fragment to a scene of a distant artillery fire hitting the water and killing the bathing Hasidim.

Austeria premiered on Polish screens in March 1983 and was shown outside of Poland. Iwona Irwin-Zarecka suggests that General Jaruzelski's government used the film outside of Poland as "both an 'ambassador' and an important component of the regime's celebration of Jewish culture."[24] Gabriella Safran comments in a similar manner: "In the capacity of a quasi-official expression of Polish regret at the passing of Jews, and perhaps as a demonstration of liberalism aimed at the western critics of the new regime, *Austeria* was widely promoted and exported to film festivals abroad."[25]

Three other films were released in the mid-1980s that dealt with the Holocaust and Polish-Jewish wartime relations: *Nie było słońca tej wiosny* (*There Was No Sun That Spring*, 1984, Juliusz Janicki); *Zaproszenie* (*The Invitation*, 1985), the last installment of Wanda Jakubowska's sequence of films about Auschwitz; and *W cieniu nienawiści* (*In the Shadow of Hatred*, 1986, Wojciech Żółtowski).

There Was No Sun That Spring, a wartime melodrama set in the winter of 1943, revolves around a difficult love between a sophisticated Jewish woman from a city and a simple, uneducated farmer. Chaja (Ernestyna Winnicka), a physician, escapes from a transport that is headed to a concentration camp, and gets safely to a house on the outskirts of a nearby village. Her quick action saves the lives of a young farmer, Piotr (Maciej Kozłowski), and his family, who suffered carbon monoxide poisoning. Piotr's distressed wife, who is able to convince the partisans to take Chaja as their doctor, interrupts the doomed romance with the Holocaust in its background.

The narrative of Janicki's film brings to mind Agnieszka Holland's 1985 well-received film (Academy Award nomination for Best Foreign Film) made in West Germany, *Bittere Ernte* (*Angry Harvest*), which examines the psychological and social mechanisms within a relationship between a Polish farmer and a Jewish fugitive. Holland's portrayal prompted Karen Jaehne to write that the film "explores the peasant/Jew relationship with more insight and less self-righteousness than all nine and a half hour of *Shoah*."[26]

The issue of Polish help for the Jews—a recurring motif in several Polish films—features prominently in Wojciech Żółtowski's cinematic debut, *In the Shadow of Hatred*. The film is based on true events involving a group of workers at the Warsaw Health and Social Welfare Department, including Irena Sendler (1910–2008), who rescued some 2,500 Jewish children from the Warsaw Ghetto and placed them in foster homes and Catholic orphanages.[27] The first scenes introduce the reluctant hero, Zofia (Bożena Adamek), a middle-class mother of a young son who is just trying to survive the occupation and hopes to see her husband-officer released from a POW camp. Despite her initial unwillingness,

Zofia risks her life to save a Jewish child. The film presents a panorama of Polish characters and their attitudes toward Jews and strives for a balanced image of the occupation. The character of Zofia may serve as a modernized version of the mythical figure of the Polish Mother (*Matka Polka*). Her strength and dignity are intact despite the hardships she must face in order to keep up the household on her own.

Krzysztof Kieślowski's *No End* and *Decalogue*

The first film that Kieślowski made after the imposition of martial law in December 1981, *Bez końca* (*No End*, 1985) avoids easy, generic classification. It contains elements of psychological drama, political film, ghost story, romance, and metaphysical film. Kieślowski tells the story of mourning after the death of a lawyer Antoni Zyro (played by the symbol of Solidarity cinema, Jerzy Radziwiłowicz), who defended political prisoners. He dies in 1982, leaving his confused and grieving wife, Urszula (Grażyna Szapołowska), and a young son. The metaphysical element, present earlier in Kieślowski's *Blind Chance*, dominates the story in *No End*. The ghost of the lawyer, who introduces himself in the opening scene, intervenes with daily matters; his widow feels his presence. The reality of 1982 is indicated in the film only because the psychological reality is more important here; it is not politics but a personal loss that matters to Urszula.

Cowritten by Kieślowski and Krzysztof Piesiewicz, *No End* reflects the disheartening reality of martial law—eighteen months of curfew and militarized administration in Poland. The metaphysical element, earlier present in Kieślowski's *Calm* (the intriguing, symbolic horses appearing on the television screen) and, more importantly, in *Blind Chance* (the discourse on chance and destiny), governs the story of *No End* from its precredit scene—a bird's eye view of a cemetery with flickering burning candles during the All Souls' Day on 1 November. Zbigniew Preisner's intense, repetitive, and somber musical score supports this image. The scene sets the dreary and melancholy tone of the film and introduces its major themes of death, memory, and love.

When *No End*, released in a limited number of prints several months after its production, finally reached divided and highly politicized Polish society, critics, regardless of their political stance, attacked the film. Consequently, it received no prize at the 1985 Festival of Polish Films. This can be attributed to the film's complex poetics, its mood of despair and defeat, its prominent metaphysical component, and its retreat from the paradocumentary realism that had been much praised by Polish critics in Kieślowski's earlier productions. The Polish Roman Catholic Church despised the film's aura of hopelessness, the graphic portrayal of casual sex, the protagonist's suicide, and the depiction of love for a dead husband being stronger than maternal love. The film, obviously, did not meet expectations of communist authorities either and was criticized by pro-communist party critics because it portrayed martial law as the defeat of the communist regime. Solidarity activists and critics associated with this political formation also found it impossible to embrace *No End*. Instead of an atmosphere of death and despair, they expected a film more in the spirit of Wajda's propagandist *Man of Iron* that encourages the suppressed union members to maintain their struggle. The harsh criticism of *No End*, and the sense of being ostracized, would later contribute to Kieślowski's reluctant and bitter attitude toward Polish critics, his aversion to politics, and his move to international coproductions.

Kieślowski's next project, *Dekalog* (*Decalogue*, 1988), a ten-part series of contemporary television films loosely based on the Bible's Ten Commandments, was hailed as a great achievement and incontestably placed its director in the realm of renowned filmic authors. *Krótki film o zabijaniu* (*A Short Film about Killing*) and *Krótki film o miłości* (*A Short Film about Love*), the extended feature versions of two parts of *Decalogue*, were exceptionally well received in Europe. *Decalogue* was produced with the involvement of nine leading Polish cinematographers (Piotr Sobociński worked on two parts) and Kieślowski's regular collaborators since *No End*—the composer Zbigniew Preisner and the screenwriter Krzysztof Piesiewicz. Among several Kieślowskian actors, there is also Artur Barciś, who appears in episodic yet important roles in almost all parts of the series. He is the enigmatic angel-like character who appears in some decisive scenes, the silent witness to events in other people's lives.

Despite its religious connotations, *Decalogue* is not an exploration of supernatural phenomena but an acute analysis of the mental condition of Polish society before 1989. The film, written by Kieślowski with Piesiewicz, portrays a pessimistic picture of a harsh world in which moral choices must be made against the pressure of politics and economics. The bulk of the action takes place in the same drab Warsaw apartment building complex. The ugliness and grayness of the dehumanized urban landscape dominate the screen, together with close-ups of people who endure these harsh conditions. The *Decalogue* series introduces undistinguished characters, mostly intelligent professionals dwarfed by the oppressive political system. The viewer watches them in situations that require immediate and vital decisions and is introduced to their moral dilemmas. Arguably the products of specific East-Central European historical and cultural circumstances, these characters also face universal, truly Bergmanesque dilemmas. Such situations depicted in *Decalogue* are not surprising, given Kieślowski's admiration of some of Bergman's films, *Tystnaden* (*The Silence*, 1963) in particular.[28]

Kieślowski's "entomological observations" of desperate and unhappy characters inhabiting the unfriendly space give *Decalogue* the feeling of a documentary. The semidocumentary aspect of *Decalogue* is particularly evident in *A Short Film about Killing*, which alludes to the Fifth Commandment. The film tells the story of a young drifter, Jacek (Mirosław Baka), who brutally murders a taxi driver (Jan Tesarz), is sentenced to death for his crime, and is hanged. Kieślowski's film presents three distinct viewpoints and crosscuts between the sociopathic murderer, the taxi driver who later becomes his victim, and the idealistic

Figure 8.2 Mirosław Baka (Jacek) and Jan Tesarz (taxi driver) in Krzysztof Kieślowski's *A Short Film about Killing* (1988). Courtesy of Filmoteka Narodowa.

lawyer (Krzysztof Globisz) whose first case is defending the killer. Kieślowski brings into focus small, gritty, realistic details. He stresses the graphic, dreadful aspect of both the murder of the taxi driver and the killing authorized by the state. The long sequence during which the taxi driver is killed leaves nothing to the imagination. By also depicting Jacek's execution with all the terrifying details, Kieślowski almost equates the two killings. The capital city of Warsaw, where the film is set, is depicted as a repellent, depressing place: gray, brutal, and peopled by alienated characters. The greenish filters used by the cinematographer Sławomir Idziak not only dehumanize and distort the images of Warsaw but also leave some diffused colors in the center of the frame. *A Short Film about Killing* received the FIPRESCI Award and the Jury Prize at the 1988 Cannes Film Festival, earned the Best European Film Award ("Felix"), and received the Grand Prix at the Festival of Polish Films in Gdańsk with *A Short Film about Love* (1988), the theatrical version of *Decalogue 6*.

A Short Film about Love is a story of voyeurism, stalking, lust, and sexual humiliation. It introduces Tomek (Olaf Lubaszenko), a nineteen-year old postal clerk attracted to an older woman who lives in the apartment building opposite his, an artist named Magda (Grażyna Szapołowska). Tomek steals a telescope from a school and spies on her every evening from his bedroom. Gradually, he begins to meddle in her life. His infatuation with Magda leads him to admit his activities and to reveal his love to her, which results in his humiliation and attempted suicide. The film ends by reversing the watcher/watched roles.

Unlike the shorter television version, *A Short Film about Love* includes a framing story that places the bulk of the film in a flashback. The film opens and ends with an image of Magda in Tomek's room. While he is asleep after his return from the hospital, she looks through his telescope at her apartment, imagines herself and Tomek talking to each other, and reflects on their relationship. The action of the film is essentially confined to two apartments, the square that separates them, and the nearby housing estate post office. Witold Adamek's camera carefully replicates the perspective of a person watching. Both the theme of voyeurism and the dependence on point-of-view long shots from the perspective of a peeping Tom bring to mind several classic films such as *Rear Window* (1954, Alfred Hitchcock) and *Monsieur Hire* (1988, Patrice Leconte). Preisner's haunting music elicits feelings of unrequited love that contribute to the critical reception of the film as a study of the obsessive and destructive love.[29]

***

The oppressive political system started to crumble toward the end of the 1980s. In 1987, new legislation abolished the state monopoly on film production, distribution, and purchase of foreign films. Two years later, the impossible happened: the communist system ended, initiating peaceful—albeit difficult—transition to democracy.

Notes

1. After the declaration of martial law, Agnieszka Holland decided to remain in France. She directed several internationally acclaimed films in Germany, France, and the United States. In Germany she made *Angry Harvest* (1985) and *Europa, Europa* (1991), and in France *To Kill a Priest* (1988), *Olivier, Olivier* (1992), and *Total Eclipse* (1995, French-English coproduction). Her later Hollywood films include *Secret Garden* (1993), *Washington Square* (1997), and *The Third Miracle* (1999).
2. Wajda's next films were made abroad. For example, he made the historical drama *Danton* in France and the war melodrama *Eine Liebe in Deutschland (A Love in Germany)* in West Germany, both in 1983.
3. Gary Mead, "Volksfilm for the 1980s: Prospects for Polish Cinema after Martial Law," *Sight and Sound* 52, no. 4 (1983): 231.
4. Waldemar Krzystek, "Było sobie kino," *Kino* 12 (1995): 8.
5. Jerzy Płażewski, "Film zagraniczny w Polsce," in *Encyklopedia kultury polskiej XX wieku: Film i kinematografia*, ed. Edward Zajiček (Warsaw: Instytut Kultury and Komitet Kinematografii, 1994), 348. Płażewski points out that between 1982 and 1989, Poland imported only six films from Italy (349).
6. Wydział Radia i Telewizji im. Krzysztofa Kieślowskiego, Uniwersytet Śląski w Katowicach. In 2000, the Katowice Film and Television School was named after Kieślowski, who taught there for several years.
7. Piotr Wasilewski, *Świadectwa metryk* (Kraków: Powiększenie, 1990), 8.
8. Tadeusz Sobolewski, "Peace and Rebellion," in *Polish Cinema in Ten Takes*, ed. Ewelina Nurczyńska-Fidelska and Zbigniew Batko (Łódź: Łódzkie Towarzystwo Naukowe, 1995), 133.
9. Other films made by Krzysztof Zanussi outside of Poland include *Wege in der Nacht* (*Ways in the Night*, TV, 1979, Germany), *From a Far Country: Pope John Paul II* (1981, Italy, UK, Poland), *Versuchung* (*The Temptation*, TV, 1982, Germany), *Die Unerreichbare* (*The Unapproachable*, TV, 1982, Germany), and *Blaubart* (*Bluebeard*, TV, 1984, Germany).

10. E.g., Zdzisław Pietrasik, "Klasa i kasa: Rozmowa z Juliuszem Machulskim, reżyserem filmu *Girl Guide*," *Polityka* 8 (1996): 46.
11. Ewa Gębicka, "Sieć i rozpowszechnianie filmów," in Zajiček, *Encyklopedia kultury polskiej XX wieku*, 445.
12. Edward Zajiček, "Kinematografia," in Zajiček, *Encyklopedia kultury polskiej XX wieku*, 91.
13. Małgorzata Hendrykowska, *Kronika kinematografii polskiej 1895–1997* (Poznań: Ars Nova, 1999), 427.
14. Alicja Helman, "The Masters Are Tired," in *The New Polish Cinema*, ed. Janina Falkowska and Marek Haltof (London: Flicks Books, 2003), 39.
15. I refer extensively to my own recollections concerning this period. I have experienced the Solidarity period and martial law firsthand, having lived at that time in Poland.
16. Jan F. Lewandowski, *100 filmów polskich* (Katowice: Videograf II, 1997), 158.
17. For a more detailed discussion, see Marek Haltof, *Polish Film and the Holocaust: Politics and Memory* (New York: Berghahn Books, 2012): 139–53.
18. The Holocaust references are also present in Różewicz's later film *Anioł w szafie* (*An Angel in the Wardrobe*, 1988) in which the protagonist meets an old Jew at a Jewish cemetery who tells him about his escape from a transport to a death camp.
19. *According to the Decrees of Providence* is Hoffman's only film dealing with the Holocaust. This director, better known for his adaptations of Sienkiewicz's epic novels, was born in 1932 into a secular, assimilated Jewish family.
20. "Stenogram z posiedzenia Kolisji Kolaudacyjnej Filmów Fabularnych w dniu 2 marca 1983," National Film Archive in Warsaw, A-344/322.
21. Published in English as Julian Stryjkowski, *The Inn*, trans. Celina Wieniewska (New York: Harcourt Brace Jovanovich, 1972).
22. Daria Mazur, "Paradoks i topika judajska: *Austeria* Jerzego Kawalerowicza," in *Gefilte film: Wątki żydowskie w kinie*, ed. Joanna Preizner (Kraków: Azolem Alejchem, 2008), 147.
23. The report issued after the meeting by a communist apparatchik Stanisław Stefański, while generally defending the film, suggested some revisions: "The last scene may be treated as a metaphor anticipated the future tragedy of European Jews during the fascist period. ... However, given the possibility of imposing an anti-Soviet interpretation on the film by antisocialist elements, it is necessary to eliminate accents that enable such an interpretation of the work." Documents related to *Austeria*, held at the archive of the Central Committee (KC) of PZPR, were reprinted by Przemysław Kaniecki, "Z archiwum KC PZPR: Sprawa *Austerii* Jerzego Kawalerowicza," *Studia Filmoznawcze 30*, ed. Sławomir Bobowski (Wrocław: Wydawnictwo Uniwersytetu Wrocławskiego, 2009), 207.
24. Iwona Irwin-Zarecka, *Neutralizing Memory: The Jew in Contemporary Poland* (New Brunswick, NJ: Transaction, 1989), 119.

25. Gabriella Safran, "Dancing with Death and Salvaging Jewish Culture in *Austeria* and *The Dybbuk*," *Slavic Review* 59, no. 4 (2000): 761.
26. Karen Jaehne, "Angry Harvest," *Cineaste* 15, no. 1 (1986): 39.
27. In 2009, John Kent Harrison directed a film about Sendler, *The Courageous Heart of Irena Sendler*, with Anna Paquin in a Golden Globe–nominated performance.
28. Interestingly, in his 1995 interview, announced as "the last one," Bergman listed *Decalogue* as one of the five contemporary films that he "most benefited from." Kieślowski's fascination with Bergman is discussed extensively in Tadeusz Szczepański, "Kieślowski wobec Bergmana, czyli Tam, gdzie spotykają się równoległe," in *Kino Krzysztofa Kieślowskiego*, ed. Tadeusz Lubelski (Kraków: Universitas, 1997), 163–71. Szczepański quotes Jannike Åhlund's interview with Bergman, "Sista intervjun med Bergman," *Expressen* (23 November 1995).
29. Apart being a cowinner of the Gdynia Film Festival, *A Short Film about Love* received several other awards, including Best Script for Kieślowski and Piesiewicz and Best Actress for Szapołowska. Readers of the popular Polish weekly *Film* voted Szapołowska and her screen partner Lubaszenko the best Polish actors in 1988.

CHAPTER 9
A Fistful of Dollars
Polish Cinema after the Wall Came Down (1989–1998)

The communist system in Poland started to show signs of decline toward the end of the 1980s. At the beginning of 1989, roundtable discussions were arranged between the communists and the representatives of the opposition to find solutions to Poland's political problems and poor economy. The negotiations led to a compromise that, consequently, enabled the change of the political formation. The summer of 1989 is usually cited as a turning point in Polish history, marking the peaceful transition from the totalitarian system to democracy. Tadeusz Mazowiecki formed the first noncommunist government in postwar Polish history after the stunning election victory of Solidarity's Civic Committee in June 1989. Although General Wojciech Jaruzelski remained the president, the communists' monopoly had been brought to a decisive end. Lech Wałęsa's presidential victory in December 1990 definitively ended one-party rule and started a new era in Polish history.

Cinema Industry: From the State Monopoly to Free Market

The year 1989 was also a turning point for the Polish film industry. Once again, it was not a cinematic movement but rather a political transformation—this time, a bloodless one—that defined the new period. The nationalized and centralized film industry, entirely dependent on government funding, was transformed into a free market economy subsidized by the state. In post-totalitarian Poland, filmmakers and other artists were relieved from their traditional duties to the nation, liberated from political pressures and commitments. The political role commonly reserved for artists returned to politicians, political commentators, and historians. Filmmaking once again became a strictly professional endeavor and started to exist somewhere on the margin of mainstream Polish life.

Earlier, the year 1987 brought new legislation that abolished the state monopoly in the sphere of film production, distribution, and the purchase of foreign films. This act, more fully introduced after 1989, transformed the state-owned and -controlled film industry, based on film units—the core of the local film business since 1955—into independent studios. The new legislation and the abolition of censorship in 1990 made film producers and directors responsible for both the content and the financial success, or failure, of their products. On the one hand, this decision gave considerable freedom to the companies mainly in the sphere of coproductions and distribution in the West. On the other hand, despite limited government subsidies via the Cinema Committee of the Ministry of Culture and Arts (also established in 1987), this independence forced the companies to concentrate on the commercial aspect of their productions. At the beginning of 1992, the following film studios were in operation: Filip Bajon's Dom, Jerzy Kawalerowicz's Kadr, Tadeusz Chmielewski's Oko, Janusz Morgenstern's Perspektywa, Bohdan Poręba's Profil, Krzysztof Zanussi's Tor, Juliusz Machulski's Zebra, Jerzy Hoffman's Zodiak, and the Karol Irzykowski Film Studio managed by Jacek Skalski and Ryszard Bugajski.[1]

The process of democratization began with releasing several films shelved by the previous regime, including, among others, Ryszard Bugajski's *Interrogation*, Jerzy Domaradzki's *The Big Run*, Agnieszka Holland's *A Woman Alone*, Krzysztof Kieślowski's *Blind Chance*, and Janusz Zaorski's *The Mother of Kings*. These films deal with Stalinism—the period euphemistically called by the communist regime in Poland "the age of mistakes and blunders." In addition, films concerned with Polish-Russian history, like Tadeusz Chmielewski's adaptation of *Wierna rzeka* (*Faithful River*, 1983), the classic novel by Stefan Żeromski about an anti-Russian uprising in 1863, had also been suppressed.

The move toward a market economy in Poland coincided with the universalization of coproductions in Europe and the incorporation of popular American cinema into that market. The end of a fully subsidized and centralized Polish film industry controlled through state censorship and the emergence of a new audience, for whom communism and Solidarity were historical subjects, have brought some inevitable changes to film production and distribution, as well as to film themes and styles. Coproductions, multinational enterprises, competition with Hollywood, a plurality of styles and genres were all changing the film landscape in Poland.

The transition to a market economy in Poland had not been an easy process. In the early 1990s, there were symptoms of a deep economic crisis in the film industry. Figures show that the number of cinemas decreased rapidly, from 1,830 toward the end of the 1980s to 1,195 in 1991 and 755 in 1993 (compared with 1,200 in the Czech Republic, 3,709 in Germany, and 4,397 in France in 1993). Another alarming figure was the extremely low average number of cinema visits per inhabitant: 0.35 in 1993 compared with 1.26 in Hungary, 2.06 in the Czech Republic, and 2.15 in Germany.[2]

Some Polish critics and filmmakers believed that free market reforms had created a situation in which Polish films could not compete with American products. With the gradual Americanization of the local market, it was also difficult to see Western European films, and almost impossible to see Central European and Russian works. For instance, from 1991 to 1995, only six Italian, nineteen German, forty-one English, and forty-five French films were released in Poland. Interestingly, there was not a single Russian film among 122 new titles exhibited in Poland in 1992.[3]

In accordance with expectations, American films clearly dominated the market: more than 60 percent of the Polish repertoire consisted of American films (as much as 73 percent in 1992). They were heavily promoted and well distributed. The average number of prints used for the release of an American film ranged from twenty to fifty. Only five to fifteen copies of films from Poland and other parts of Europe were distributed at release. Polish films accounted for only 18 percent in 1991, 14 percent in 1992, 20 percent in 1993, 12 percent in 1994, and 10 percent in 1995 of the total number of films released in Poland. The number of local films distributed in Poland, however, did not match their market share. Because of lower inflation rates and increasing cinema ticket prices ($2 to $3 in 1995), the total box office had been steadily growing and reached $40 million in 1995. The percentage earned by Polish films had been low, ranging from 9.4 in 1991 to 5.2 in 1995.[4]

In the early 1980s, the film industry in Poland was a workplace for almost ten thousand people, half of whom were employed by state institutions. Throughout the 1990s, this number decreased rapidly. For example, the Film Production Company in Łódź, whose personnel numbered 1,100 in the 1980s, employed only 350 in 1992.[5] While the transfer of Poland's economy from the public to the private sector had been conducted in quite an efficient manner, the privatization of the film industry had proved difficult.

To stimulate and protect the indigenous film industry, the following three government-funded bodies were created in 1991: the script, production, and distribution agencies.[6] The goal of the Script Agency (Agencja Scenariuszowa) was to create a market for film scripts in Poland by supporting script development and preproduction work—more than 50 percent of Polish scripts originated with the agency's financial support.

The Film Production Agency (Agencja Produkcji Filmowej) was involved financially in the production of feature, documentary, animated, and educational films. Its main goal was to cofinance projects that were "of cultural value." The selection process was carried out by a panel of experts appointed by the chair of the Cinema Committee. Each feature project was evaluated by a commission of nine experts picked randomly from a group of fifty-seven. The commission was always composed of two critics or screenwriters, two production managers, two distributors, and three cinema managers. The agency coproduced seventeen features in 1992, eighteen in 1993, and fifteen in 1994.

The main task of the Film Distribution Agency (Agencja Dystrybucji Filmowej) was to stimulate the distribution of films that are considered important from the point of view of the state's cultural policy. This was done through the agency's financial participation in the distribution mostly of Polish films but also of artistically significant foreign films. With the help of this agency, Polish cinemas had screened films by directors such as Jim Jarmusch, Derek Jarman, and Peter Greenaway, as well as most Polish features.

Given the difficulties of the transitional period, it is worth noting that the Polish film industry had consistently been able to annually produce more than twenty feature films. Every year during the 1990s, at least two or three films were made independently, without the state's involvement. Independent film producers, such as Dariusz Jabłoński (Apple Film Production) and Lew Rywin (Heritage Films), became major players in the local film industry. Since 1993, an unconventional film festival, International Film Festival of the Art of Cinematography Camerimage, has been organized by its founder-director, Marek Żydowicz. This prestigious film festival celebrates cinematographers and awards films for their visual and photographic values. The festival's Lifetime Achievement Award in the 1990s went to some of the finest cinematographers, including Sven Nykvist (1993), Vittorio Storaro and Witold Sobociński (1994), Conrad Hall (1995), Haskell Wexler (1996), Vilmos Zsigmond (1997), László Kovács (1998), and Giuseppe Rotunno (1999).

Since the crisis in the early 1990s, the number of cinemas has been increasing slowly but steadily. In 1992, Poland joined the Eurimages Foundation (established in 1989), which sponsors European films. Krzysztof Kieślowski's last films were made with its help. Polish cinema, however, was increasingly dependent on television. In 1995, state-run television participated in the production of almost all feature films in Poland and acted as a sole producer of four. The private television network Canal+ coproduced three films. Certain acclaimed filmmakers, for example, Andrzej Barański and Jan Jakub Kolski, made all their films with the help of state television.

These changes created a new system in which state patronage coexisted with private initiatives. The main task was to defend the national film industry; in a country with a population of approximately thirty-eight million, it is understandable that virtually no local film can recoup its cost without foreign sales. Statistics show that one hundred thousand viewers in cinema theaters are considered high by Polish standards of the 1990s. For example, if we look at Polish films released in 1996, only five of them achieved these modest results: *Słodko-gorzki* (*Bittersweet*, Władysław Pasikowski) leads with 344,635 viewers, followed by *Girl Guide* (Juliusz Machulski), *Szamanka* (*She-Shaman*, Andrzej Żuławski), *Pestka* (*Pip*, Krystyna Janda), and *Nic śmiesznego* (*Nothing Funny*, Marek Koterski). Many films, often made by internationally renowned directors, had only a limited audience. For instance, *Wielki Tydzień* (*Holy Week*, 1996, Andrzej Wajda) had 9,740 viewers, *Cwał* (*In Full Gallop*, Krzysztof Zanussi) 23,176, and *Za co?* (*For What?* Jerzy Kawalerowicz) 2,840.[7] During the mid-1990s in Poland, it was still easier to produce a film than to exhibit it in movie theaters.

Filmmakers after the Wall Came Down

In Robert Gliński's 1989 film, *Łabędzi śpiew* (*Swan Song*), a successful Polish screenwriter returns from abroad only to learn that his ideas for future films have nothing to do with the changed reality around him. He tries to survive this difficult time by producing some desperate "postmodern" versions of Polish history and by cannibalizing American models. The effect is unintentionally comic, absurd, and out of place.

For many filmmakers in Poland, as was the case for Gliński's protagonist, the new reality came as somewhat of a shock; the relationships between the state and the artist, as well as between the artist and its audience, had changed dramatically. The traditional antagonist (the totalitarian state) had disappeared and, with it, a polarized world in which the only meaningful distinction was between the pro-communist side ("them") and the "right side" ("us"). One must remember that the artistic criteria in Poland were repeatedly subordinated to political criteria. To be a dissident meant to be a true artist; some artists were canonized simply because their work was incompatible with the communist system. For some, being on the right (dissident) side was enough reason to be hailed as a great artist. In a sense, it was an anachronistic, romantic Polish extension of the artist-as-torch-bearer myth. In this context, the quality of artistic output was often of minor importance. In Wajda's classic *Ashes and Diamonds*, the two Home Army survivors engage in a conversation that could easily be a commentary on the situation of a filmmaker in post-1989 Poland. "Those were the days!" says Maciek recalling his dead friends. "We knew what we wanted, and what was expected of us," responds Andrzej.[8]

Given the complexity of Polish history, cinema—and, for that matter, all Polish art—had generally been regarded as more than just entertainment. The artist's "mission" was that of a prophet and teacher bringing a message to society. Film and other art forms acted as safety valves in the controlled, corrupt political system. Filmmaking was a platform on which political debates were sometimes argued openly, and sometimes in an Aesopian language. Politically active filmmakers were always at the foreground of Polish life. The artists felt an immense responsibility. Conversely, they were also accustomed to a situation in which their voices were heard and analyzed by the people and by the authorities.

In the early 1990s, economics superseded politics. New audiences demanded new films. The marginalization of traditional filmic themes like Polish martyrology and history (only two of the films at the 1996 Festival of Polish Films in Gdynia dealt with such themes) proved that the time had come for Polish cinema to be free from political and social obligations. But what does this freedom mean—queried Andrzej Wajda in his 1991 diagnosis of the state of Polish cinema—in these changed political, economic, and social situations? He ironically suggested that such freedom is a freedom from the audience, criticism, authority, ideology, and artistic criteria.[9]

Polish filmmakers had to defend themselves exclusively with their films. They had to fight for audiences that they depended on to exist. State-run political censorship had been replaced by the economic censorship of the producer, which, in many aspects, was even harsher. The Polish film critic Tadeusz Sobolewski stated that many filmmakers and critics started out believing in the victory of freedom but immediately felt disappointed with it.[10] One of the leading Polish Catholic intellectuals, Józef Tischner, expressed this concern bluntly in the title of his book *The Unhappy Gift of Freedom*.[11]

A new market came into being. Nevertheless, Kazimierz Kutz maintained in the early 1990s that the quality of Polish cinema had reached rock bottom. For him, Poland was allowing itself to be flooded with anonymous international coproductions rather than supporting national films.[12] In his view, the production of films was becoming exclusively an opportunity for grabbing money; the producers were behaving in the manner of the capitalists from early Soviet cinema.[13] Others, like the influential *Kino* critic Jerzy Płażewski, claimed that coproductions would guarantee survival for the local film industry.[14] The figures, which show the increasing number of coproductions, support the critic's claim: between 30 and 40 percent of Polish films from that period are international coproductions.

After the 1989 freedom shock, there were claims—supported by leading Polish filmmakers such as Wajda and Zanussi—that Polish cinema was in danger of becoming commercialized, especially after Western distributors entered the Polish market. Some believed that free market reforms would create a situation in which Polish films cannot compete with Western "B" products, such as "the collected works of Chuck Norris." Another concern was the feigned reorientation of Polish filmmakers toward commercialism. For many critics and filmmakers, the specter of commercialism haunted Polish cinema. Disappointed with the first flood of commercially minded products, some filmmakers went so far as to emphasize the positive role of state censorship in the totalitarian period.[15] For instance, Kutz asserted that political censorship was a main factor behind the origins of artistic cinema in Poland. He maintained that there were some positive aspects to political censorship, which motivated the best artists to work harder and to speak in purely visual terms. For him, this laid the foundation of the Polish School in the late 1950s and early 1960s. According to Wajda, the figurativeness of Polish cinema was a crucial element in its fight against political censorship. In contrast to dialogue, symbolic pictures are very difficult to censor, claims Wajda, giving examples from his *Ashes and Diamonds*.[16] Commenting on censorship, Kieślowski once remarked that filmmakers in Poland "were in a luxurious and unique situation. We were truly important ... precisely because of censorship. We're allowed to say everything now but people have stopped caring what we're allowed to say."[17]

The whole discussion about the future of the Polish film industry vacillated between voices emphasizing the importance of the national character of Polish films and those advocating the universal, cosmopolitan nature of art. Taking the first perspective, the Polish film critic and writer Anita Skwara stated, "Polish cinema stands a chance of survival and development only when it is national in character, when it arises directly from the traditions, culture and myths forming Polish awareness."[18] Some directors, however, moved beyond the limits of narrowly understood "national themes" or the "Polish perspective" and focused on what can be called "a European consciousness."[19] The then popular slogan in Poland, "catching up with Europe," expressed a desire to create new post-totalitarian art that, while addressing some universal issues, will reflect national uniqueness. The problem facing new cinema, not only in Poland but also in all of Central Europe at the time, was to find a new voice to adequately express the "national" while incorporating other cinematic discourses.

Some established filmmakers, however, were unable to find quickly a new voice in this altered situation. For instance, Feliks Falk's *Koniec gry (The End of the Game*, 1991) and *Daleko od siebie (Far from the Other*, 1996) are full of clichés from the poetics of the Cinema of Distrust. *The End of the Game* portrays a sensitive young mathematician (who resembles the early protagonists of Zanussi) and tells the story of his uneasy love affair with the leader of a political party. The world vision presented in the film is journalistic and sketchy, in line with the bland psychological characterization of the protagonists. An old master, Jerzy Kawalerowicz, experienced similar problems with two films released after the Berlin Wall came down. *Jeniec Europy (The Prisoner of Europe*, 1989) and *For What?* (1996) were poorly received by critics and ignored by audiences. Some of Wajda's films met the same indifference: *Pierścionek z orłem w koronie (The Ring with a Crowned Eagle*, 1992), *Holy Week*, and *Panna Nikt (Miss Nobody*, 1996).

Krzysztof Zanussi: Moral Dilemmas

The early 1990s had been very productive for the self-declared cosmopolitan filmmaker Krzysztof Zanussi. He made a series of popular television films, *Opowieści weekendowe (Weekend Stories*, 1996–2000), aptly labeled by Larson Powell as the "moral microhistory of post-communism."[2] Zanussi also directed several documentaries and many feature films, including *Gdzieśkolwiek jest, jeśliś jest... (Wherever You Are*, 1989, Poland–West Germany–UK), *Stan posiadania (Inventory*, 1989), *Życie za życie: Maksymilian Kolbe (Life for Life: Maximilian Kolbe*, 1991, Poland–Germany), *Dotknięcie ręki (The Silent Touch*, 1992, Poland–UK–Denmark), *In Full Gallop*, and *Brat naszego Boga (The Brother of Our God*, 1997).

Films made by Zanussi in the late 1980s and the 1990s, however, did not provoke the same disputes and controversies as his earlier works did. For example, in *Inventory* Zanussi centers on three characters: two women—the former communist censor (Krystyna Janda) and a devout Catholic (Maja Komorowska), who represent two different worldviews and two different groups of the Polish society ("us" versus "them")—and a sensitive young man acting as a mediator (Artur Żmijewski). Improvised elements play a major role in this ascetic film characterized by the minimal use of cinematic techniques and an emphasis on moralizing dialogues. In *Inventory*, Zanussi pushes his style to the extreme and thus several Polish reviewers considered it too verbal at the expense of imagery and too artificial in its construction of the conflict.

Zanussi's international coproduction *Wherever You Are* narrates the story of an honorary consul of Uruguay in Poland who moves to Poland before the outbreak of World War II with his wife. The consul's wife suffers from mental illness after an accident and begins to perceive the world as slowly revealing its hidden, terrifying dimension—a premonition about the future genocide. When her husband must leave Poland on business, the war begins, and she is doomed—killed by the Germans while hospitalized in a psychiatric hospital.

Another multinational production by Zanussi, this time in English, is *The Silent Touch*, which tells the story of a young musicologist from Kraków (Lothaire Bluteau) who has a dream about an unknown musical masterpiece. He writes down its basic tones and travels abroad to an old eccentric composer (Max von Sydow), once famous and worldly, now living in seclusion, to convince him to write the piece. The composer has been silent for almost forty years, withdrawn from the musical life. The young messenger from Poland must awaken him from artistic inertia, awaken his sexuality, and enable him to compose the work of his life. (The film includes Wojciech Kilar's magnificent score.)

Earlier, Zanussi produced the filmic biography of the "Polish Pope": *Z dalekiego kraju* (*From a Far Country: Pope John Paul II* (1981, Poland-Italy-UK). In 1997, he also adapted for the screen *The Brother of Our God*, an early play by Karol Wojtyła. Starring Scott Wilson as Adam Chmielowski, the film relies heavily on theological/philosophical dialogue. Zanussi, who knew the pope personally, frequently joked while introducing the film that making it may be considered his penance.

Zanussi's earlier work, *Life for Life*, is a biographical film about the Franciscan saint Maksymilian Kolbe (Edward Żentara), who was beatified in 1971 and canonized in 1982 by John Paul II, which some scholars saw as an attempt to

"Catholicize Auschwitz."[21] Written by Zanussi and the writer Jan Józef Szczepański, the film opens in Auschwitz in 1941 with the scene of a prisoner's escape. The escapee, Jan Tytz (Christoph Waltz), later hides in a monastery and learns that, as a reprisal for his action, the Auschwitz guards randomly selected ten prisoners and sentenced them to death by starvation. He also learns that a volunteer, Father Kolbe (Edward Żentara), replaced one of the selected prisoners. Employing a flashback structure, the film tells the story of Kolbe's life—his arrest, imprisonment, and death by starvation in the Auschwitz's "hunger bunker"—through testimonies of those who knew him. It ends with a scene of Kolbe's beatification that is witnessed by Jan, now living in the United States.

Biopics of prominent religious figures, like Zanussi's *Life for Life*, form an important trend in contemporary Polish cinema. For example, *Faustyna (Faustina*, 1995, Jerzy Łukaszewicz) depicts the life of Sister Faustyna Kowalska (1905–1938), known as Saint Faustina (Dorota Segda), who was canonized by Pope John Paul II in 2000. The release of this popular film, the recipient of several awards at the Festival of Polish Films in Gdańsk, coincided with the beatification of Sister Faustina, a mystic who had visions of Jesus during her lifetime.

Return of the Repressed: Reclaiming the Past

Focusing on the past seems almost natural in Polish cinema. Like Central European cinema in general, it has familiarized viewers with its political contexts and messages by presenting Central Europeans as victims of a dark history. In the novel political situation in Central Europe after 1989, one could expect "the return of the repressed" in cinema and other art forms, the return of history, and a certain boldness in a critical reappraisal of the not-so-distant past. In a time of considerable political openness, however, in which (almost) everything could be said candidly, the double talk and subversive messages provided by the old Polish cinema were no longer needed.

Several films released during the transition to democracy were unable to break with the previous mode of thinking. *Bal na dworcu w Koluszkach (The Ball at the Koluszki Railway Station*, 1990, Filip Bajon), *The End of the Game, Stan strachu (The State of Fear*, 1990, Janusz Kijowski), Waldemar Krzystek's *Ostatni prom (The Last Ferry*, 1989) and *Zwolnieni z życia (Dismissed from Life*, 1991), and particularly *Po *upadku* (*After the Fall*, 1990, Andrzej Trzos-Rastawiecki) were made too late. Viewed after 1989, they had lost their relevance and, as a result, their audience.

The success of *Ucieczka z kina "Wolność"* (*Escape from the "Liberty" Cinema*, 1990, Wojciech Marczewski) was merely an exception to the rule that political films were difficult to market in post-1989 Poland.[22] On the surface, Marczewski's film looks like a tribute to *The Purple Rose of Cairo* (1985, Woody Allen). The story is set in a movie theater called Liberty in which a fictitious Polish film titled *Jutrzenka* (*Morning Star*) is shown. The characters in the film within a film rebel against the roles they must perform; they do not follow the script, and, in an act of defiance, utter their own words. They cannot be subjected to any external pressures. The mutiny on the screen spreads rapidly; real people from the street, regardless of their political standing, sing Mozart's Requiem as a way of showing their resistance. A government censor (Janusz Gajos, in an impressive performance) is unable to do anything and eventually falls under the spell of the film. Finally, afraid that the copy of the film will be burned, the screen characters escape to the roof of the cinema building.

On the simplest level, *Escape from the "Liberty" Cinema* offers a story about a disillusioned censor, rejected by his family, who comes to fathom the misery of his present life. On another level, however, this multilayered film clearly serves as an allegory of the situation in the 1980s, a reminder of the supremacy of politics over people's lives, or, perhaps, as an allegorical story about rebellion. Marczewski's film is not as visually refined as his earlier *Nightmares* or *Shivers*. The emphasis is on direct political references and on an examination of the near past from the perspective of a newly regained freedom. With its clear divisions between what is right and wrong, between the rulers and the ruled, *Escape from the "Liberty" Cinema* accurately reflects the spirit of the former period. Nevertheless, intellectually, for these same reasons, it also belongs to that era.

One might well have expected a flood of artistic works reclaiming the past after the political events of 1989. Indeed, in the early 1990s, the distribution of major awards at Polish film festivals demonstrated a consistent preference for honoring films that deal with various aspects of Polish history. Awards were presented to *Wszystko, co najważniejsze* (*All That Really Matters*, 1992, Robert Gliński), an examination of the fate of Polish citizens deported by Stalin to Kazakhstan after the outbreak of World War II, and to Grzegorz Królikiewicz for his study of Polish history as seen through the eyes of a handicapped person in an unsuccessful search for his unknown mother in *Przypadek Pekosińskiego* (*The Case of Pekosiński*,

1993). Other well-received films dealing with recent history included, among others, *300 mil do nieba* (*300 Miles to Heaven*, 1989, Maciej Dejczer), *Kornblumenblau* (1989, Leszek Wosiewicz), *Pokuszenie* (*Temptation*, 1995, Barbara Sass), *Pułkownik Kwiatkowski* (*Colonel Kwiatkowski*, 1996, Kazimierz Kutz), and *Gry uliczne* (*Street Games*, 1996, Krzysztof Krauze).

300 Miles to Heaven won the European Film Award (the "Felix") in 1989 as the Young European Film of the Year. This well-made and moving film, written by Dejczer and Cezary Harasimowicz and based on real events, tells the story of two young brothers (Rafał Zimowski and Wojciech Klata, the latter also starring in *Decalogue 1*) who, during martial law, escape to Sweden hidden on the underside of a huge truck. Despite the tendencies inherent in such topics, Dejczer avoids sentimentality and never resorts to stereotypes or filmic clichés. The first part of the film portrays a hopeless picture of Polish "socialist" reality—the ugliness of the environment, the corruption, the futile struggles with authorities—and serves as justification for the boys' desperate departure from the country. The second part shows the two alienated teenage protagonists in prosperous, though cold, "capitalist landscapes." The final scene, a telephone conversation between the two boys and their parents in Poland, is among the most powerful sequences in Polish cinema. "Don't ever return here," their father states. This cruel sentence might serve as one of the strongest criticism of the communist regime.

In *Kornblumenblau*, Leszek Wosiewicz offers a completely different treatment of Polish martyrology—a different look at World War II and wartime sufferings. One of the most accomplished films of that period, *Kornblumenblau* (the title of a German song) also works against the romantic tradition that permeates Polish literature and film. Moreover, since the film is set in Auschwitz and its protagonist's name is Tadeusz, it is inviting to treat it as another reading of the laconic postwar prose of Tadeusz Borowski. In Borowski's world, all characters are infected by the devastating degeneration of human values. Everyday existence is marked by compromises and resignation, and viewed through a personal philosophy adopted in order to survive. Like Borowski, Wosiewicz focuses not on the psychology but on the physiology of the dehumanized hero. Tadeusz (Adam Kamień) survives by instinct: he tries to be loyal to the guards and to stay on good terms with the other inmates. For them, he remains an enigma. "Is he a sly dog or an imbecile?" wonders one of his fellow prisoners. "The saintly cretin," says another.

The film starts with a skillfully edited precredit, slapstick-like sequence that summarizes the early stages of Tadeusz's life. Wosiewicz employs old documentary footage and fragments of a Polish prewar film, intercut with original footage (also in sepia tones) showing the protagonist's parents, his birth, and the beginnings of his career as a musician. This silent part of the film (only a few captions are employed) ends with the outbreak of the war and Tadeusz being sent to a concentration camp for his supposed political activities.

It is tempting to read *Kornblumenblau* in broader terms, as a parable on the situation of an artist in a totalitarian state, but the film's protagonist is quite pragmatic, a chameleonlike person able to fit into different situations, an amiable conformist. Tadeusz fulfills his parents' dream by becoming an artist, but to secure his future, he also becomes an engineer. As if to emphasize this aspect of his personality, in the last, symbolic scene, after the liberation of the camp, he voluntarily joins a group of Soviet soldiers and starts entertaining them.

The protagonist of *Kornblumenblau* tries to survive at all costs, as if detached from the grim reality surrounding him. He acts like a voyeur. He is watching a group of newly arrived young Hungarian Jewish women, and each morning he witnesses their gradual deterioration. The Jewish tragedy, although not in the center of this film, is addressed in several brief, laconic, but powerful scenes. Like Borowski, Wosiewicz depicts the camp without attempting to elevate the history of suffering. He mixes horror and banality, tragedy and farce. In one scene deprived of tragicomic dimensions, he also breaks the taboo by depicting the industrialized killing inside the gas chamber, a scene that had never been portrayed in Polish cinema and is generally avoided in Holocaust narratives.[23]

Street Games, directed by Krzysztof Krauze (1953–2015), centers on an event in recent Polish history: the death of Stanisław Pyjas, a student and a member of the opposition, who was murdered in 1977. According to the film, the mystery surrounding Pyjas's death does not belong to a faded past. In *Street Games*, the past affects the present. The ghosts from the past emerge as important players in contemporary political life. These include not only members of the disgraced Security Force (SB) but also a former dissident with an obscure past as a collaborator and informer, who is possibly involved in the murder. The young television reporter Janek (Redbad Klijnstra) investigates the past, although the subject initially seems to be too removed for him. Gradually, he develops a spiritual bond with the murdered student, becomes almost obsessed with the case, and, finally, must die.

The look of Krauze's film is American, but its content is unmistakably Polish; it is a classic political thriller set in contemporary Poland. Łukasz Kośmicki's stylish cinematography creates a cinematic trip into the complexities of the past. *Street Games* is clearly a modern political film, successful in its attempts to capture the change of political systems and the spirit of the communist past. Similar to Agnieszka in Wajda's *Man of Marble*, Janek from *Street Games* also goes back almost twenty years and investigates the 1970s. In both cases, the past emerges in its dangerous intricacy and overshadows the present. The mosaic stylistics of Krauze's film (e.g., the insertion of animated clips into the realistic story), references to American cinema, and the use of modern Polish rock music clearly target young viewers.

Another filmmaker, a prominent member of the Polish School generation, Kazimierz Kutz, continued to be one of the key figures in Polish cinema of the 1990s. Despite his harsh criticism of the new reality, he seemed to have no problems in adjusting to it. Active in the theater and television, and a regular contributor to a much-discussed column in the journal *Kino* in the mid-1990s, Kutz directed, among others, *Zawrócony* (*The Turned Back*), the winner of the 1994 Festival of Polish Films; *Śmierć jak kromka chleba* (*Death as a Slice of Bread*), Special Award of the Jury at the same festival; and *Colonel Kwiatkowski*, one of the best of Polish films released in 1996.

The Turned Back and *Death as a Slice of Bread*, films also written by Kutz, are set in Silesia, shortly before and after the introduction of martial law. The director, independent as usual and unconcerned with current political and aesthetic fashions, deals with the myth of Solidarity and the political atmosphere of 1981. Both films differ distinctly in their treatment of the subject. The tragedy and pathos of *Death as a Slice of Bread* is replaced by the almost farcical events of *The Turned Back*. For Kutz, these two films also mark a return to his favorite Silesian themes, which are present in his earlier best-known works.

The sit-in strike at the coal mine Wujek is the subject of *Death as a Slice of Bread*. The film is a faithful reconstruction of those events: it starts with the introduction of martial law and the arrest of the mine's Solidarity leader, and ends with the brutal pacification of the mine, during which nine people were killed. Working on the project for almost ten years, Kutz was faced with the challenge of making a film that would neither trivialize the events nor fall into the now obsolete category of "patriotic pictures." The result is an almost documentary record of those events, a tragedy without individual heroes. The film lacks a typical narrative yet is laden with pathos in its celebration of everyday situations. Its characters are simple yet dignified, as if taken from a Solidarity poster. Kutz's film alienates the viewer with its refusal to introduce distinguishable characters. In the period characterized by the depreciation of the myth of Solidarity, Kutz's film went against the trend and attempted to animate a myth that was already dead. *Death as a Slice of Bread* is, arguably, a powerful farewell to the epoch of Solidarity.

The Turned Back tells a tragicomic story about an ordinary man, the simple worker and party member Tomasz Siwek (Zbigniew Zamachowski), who, sent as a communist informer to a Solidarity demonstration, returns as a changed man (the title of the film is a play on words: in Polish *zawrócony* = turned back is close to *nawrócony* = converted). At the gathering, Tomasz is overwhelmed by the exhilarating atmosphere and starts to sing religious and patriotic songs. Barely escaping the pursuit of militia special forces, he is later mistakenly identified as an active agitator and brutally interrogated by the secret police. Finally, the disillusioned Tomasz finds his own direction and protection in the Catholic Church.

The above account may be understood in symbolic terms as a story about political initiation. The protagonist is not an opportunist but a simple man lost in the complex reality of 1981. He is an ordinary man who comes from a village and feels alienated in a new industrial environment. Manipulated by representatives of the communist system and, accidentally, involved in Solidarity's actions, he starts the rapid process of self-education. Tomasz is not a converted sinner, but a person who is "turned back" from being an object of manipulation. Kutz stresses the grotesque, tragicomic aspect of his protagonist's adventures, particularly in the famous slapstick-like sequence in which Tomasz is chased by a group of riot militia.

Representation of Stalinism in Polish Cinema

As stated earlier, several openly political films, made in the early 1990s, referred to recent Polish history but reflected immorality and corruption in 1980s terms: they were both commercial and artistic failures. Some attempts to reconstruct events experienced under martial law never received the critical or public acclaim they deserve. Kazimierz Kutz's passionate film about the tragedy at the Wujek coal mine, *Death as a Slice of Bread*, is just one example of a political work that has gone largely unnoticed. Even though Polish audiences and critics alike grew tired of history, politics, and national martyrology, films featuring recent Polish history that attempted to recover long-suppressed levels of "national memory" did exist in post-1989 Polish cinema. Among them are films portraying the Stalinist past and dealing with complex Polish-Jewish relations.

Because of strict political censorship, the question of the legacy of Polish Stalinism remained virtually untouched until the mid-1970s.[24] The process of unveiling the Stalinist years started in Polish as well as in Hungarian cinema in the late 1970s and was followed by the "perestroika films" in the 1980s in the former Soviet Union. Earlier, a group of distinguished films made in the former Czechoslovakia—*Žert* (*The Joke*, 1968, Jaromil Jireš), *Skřivánci na niti* (*Larks on a String*, 1969, Jiří Menzel), and *Všichni dobří rodáci* (*All My Good Countrymen*, 1969, Vojtěch Jasny)—had dealt with this problem.

Hungarian filmmakers, in particular, contributed extensively to this "genre." In the late 1970s, they were quite politically blunt and moved out of the safe territory of Aesopian language. The denunciation of Stalinism was reflected in such critically acclaimed films as Péter Bacsó's *The Witness* (released in 1978 after being shelved for almost nine years), András Kovács's *Ménezgazda* (*The Stud Farm*, 1978), Pál Gábor's *Angi Vera* (1978), and Márta Mészáros's *Napló gyermekeimnek* (*Diary for My Children*, 1982) and *Napló szerelmeimnek* (*Diary for My Loves*, 1987). *Egymásra nézve* (*Another Way*, 1982, Károly Makk) and *Megáll az idő* (*Time Stands Still*, 1981, Péter Gothár) put the issues of sexual nonconformity and political nonconformity into the foreground.[25] David Paul aptly observed that the relative openness of the Hungarian regime allowed the filmmakers to explore the Stalinist period in Hungarian history. The number of these films and their reception in Hungary prompted Paul to say: "Ironically, just when the Soviet cinema began at last to peel back the layers of restriction that had so long buried the past, Hungarian moviegoers considered Stalinism old hat."[26]

Stalinism also appeared as a filmic genre on its own in the former Soviet Union, starting with *Pokayanie* (*Repentance*, 1987, Tengiz Abuladze), the film that, as Anna Lawton puts it, "brought the vampire out of its bunker for all to see."[27] In Russian cinema, Stalinism and Stalin himself became almost "fashionable." According to Svetlana Boym, Stalin became "a mythical fetish of the new Soviet cinema," and his "cinematic repertoire includes the tragic and the farcical, the sublime and the ridiculous, the terrifying and the banal, fiction and documentary."[28]

Given the similarities between the Stalinist period and the situation after the introduction of equally oppressive martial law and before the transitional year of 1989, it was inevitable that films about Stalinism would be almost impossible to make. In *W zawieszeniu* (*Suspended*, 1987), Waldemar Krzystek tells the story of a former Home Army member who is sentenced to death but escapes from prison, moves to a provincial town, and hides several years in the cellar of the house belonging to his wife, whom he had secretly married during the war. Like his predecessors, Krzystek directly condemns Stalinism while indirectly criticizing the communist system. To stress the link between his film and works by Andrzej Wajda, he casts in the main roles two of Wajda's actor-symbols, Krystyna Janda and Jerzy Radziwiłowicz. Krzystek, however, is not interested in the epic scope and the "poetics of red banners" of *Man of Marble*. Instead, he focuses on the everyday ugliness of Stalinism and its impact on ordinary yet heroic people. He is interested not in disillusioned or mesmerized communists but in people whose lives were destroyed by communism.

Interestingly, in comments made about *Suspended* in 1990, Krzystek indicates that he views this work not as a "historical film" but rather as a film relevant to the present. He states that the Stalinist system permeates many spheres of Polish life: "We now barely fight its foundations. By reaching the roots of degeneration, I wished to show that the reconstruction will not be helped by repainting the buildings, but that thorough changes are needed."[29]

Documentaries, which were earlier shown as supplements to the main program in cinemas, became the domain of television after the transition to democracy in 1989. This fact hugely increased the number of films produced but ended one quality that Polish documentaries were known for: metaphorical, poetic depictions of reality. The most prominent trend in films made in the 1990s had to do with coming to terms with the communist past and uncovering historical moments buried or distorted by the communists. A great number of documentaries made in Poland examined the Stalinist mentality, hypocrisy, and indoctrination. Marcel Łoziński's *45–89 (Polish People's Republic 1945–1989* (1990) and *Las katyński (The Katyń Forest* (1991), Józef Gębski's *Film znaleziony w Katyniu (The Film Found in Katyń*, 1992), and Iwona Bartólewska's *Bezpieka 1944–1956 (Secret Service 1944–1956*, 1997) serve as good examples here.[30]

Some critics and filmmakers had seen many of the films dealing with earlier "forbidden topics" in Polish history as "cheap shots at the past." A film director and a sharp polemicist, Konrad Szołajski stated in a 1995 article: "Historical films continuously dominate the screens. Their makers demonstrate the courage that they did not show ten or fifteen years ago. The new filmmakers, cherished by television bosses, mainly denounce the Stalinists' crimes and other sins of the Polish People's Republic or fill the screens with terribly boring pictures of pilgrimages and sanctuaries."[31]

This is not the case with *Defilada* (*The Parade*, 1989, Andrzej Fidyk), a documentary depicting the nature of totalitarianism in North Korea. Fidyk portrays preparations for the celebration of the fortieth anniversary of Kim Il-sung's Korea. Every person appearing before the camera seems to be under the spell of the communist dictator; everybody seems to be happy in this totalitarian system. The tone of *The Parade* resembles an entomological documentary. Fidyk's camera dispassionately portrays the complete subordination of any individuality within the personality cult of Kim Il-sung—"the Great Leader," as Fidyk's interlocutors call him. Equally interesting was this film's reception, which deserves a separate chapter. *The Parade* was applauded in North Korea as a great propagandist film. For Polish audiences, or any Western audiences for that matter, Fidyk's film clearly uncovers the true nature of the Stalinist regime.

Reviewing Krzysztof Zanussi's 1996 film *In Full Gallop*, Jerzy Płażewski asserts: "After *Shivers* or (in another dimension) *Interrogation*, it is more and more difficult to reveal something about the Stalinist system that captivated minds. That system has always been the same. More interesting, however, are the reactions of people who survived the system."[32] The shift from political to personal, suggested by Płażewski, may be observed in several Polish films that attempted to describe the reactions of ordinary people surviving or even outsmarting the system. The martyrological tone of former films had been replaced by cathartic humor, epic scope by personal qualities. These films include intimate psychological dramas set in the 1950s such as Barbara Sass's *Temptation*, and films giving a panorama of Polish history, including Stalinism, such as Grzegorz Królikiewicz's *The Case of Pekosiński*. Some are comedies taming the past or films with grotesque or comic touches, such as *In Full Gallop*, *Colonel Kwiatkowski*, and Leszek Wosiewicz's *Cynga* (*Scurvy*, 1993) and *Kroniki domowe* (*Family Events*, 1997). *Poznań 56* (*Street Boys*, 1996, Filip Bajon) and *The Ring with a Crowned Eagle* (Andrzej Wajda) are examples of historical reconstructions devoid of irony and humor.

As if to illustrate the burden of history, the protagonist of *The Case of Pekosiński* is a hunchback—an older, ill, and alcoholic man who appears in the film playing himself. He has no knowledge of who he is. Everything about him is symbolic: his date of birth is at the outbreak of World War II, his place of birth is the Nazi German concentration camp in which he miraculously survived by being pushed through a barbed wire fence by his (most probably Jewish) mother, and his surname is an acronym of a Polish charitable institution (PKOS). Taking all this into account, the protagonist serves as another Central European victim of history.

Known for his bold experiments, Królikiewicz is not afraid to employ the authentic person to reconstruct episodes and scenes from his life and, consequently, to block the viewer's identification with the protagonist. Pekosiński does not act in the film (apart from some basic tasks); he is only the object of actions and manipulations of several people who surround him. From that perspective, however, as Mirosław Przylipiak writes, the director's name could be added to a long list of persons who simply exploited Pekosiński.[33] Interestingly, Jan Kidawa-Błoński's *Pamiętnik znaleziony w garbie* (*Diary in Marble*, aka *Memoirs Found in a Hunched Back*, 1994) shows another handicapped, hunchbacked protagonist reflecting on his past. The film is set in Polish Silesia and looks at the complex history of this region via the personalized story of two brothers (Olaf Lubaszenko and Bogusław Linda) and their uneasy relationship.[34]

The Stalinist past also returns in intimate and intense psychological dramas set in the harsh political climate of the 1950s. Barbara Sass directed what was arguably one of the finest Polish film produced in 1995, *Temptation*. Set in 1953, the film tells the story of a young nun, Anna (Magdalena Cielecka's award-winning debut performance), who is transferred from a prison to a remote location where a high-ranked Catholic priest is being held. They had known each other; he had convinced her to become a nun, and her decision to enter a convent was partly motivated by her love for him. The secret police try to take advantage of their relationship and pressure the nun to inform on the man she loves. To a certain extent, Sass's film is inspired by the factual experience of the Polish Roman Catholic primate Stefan Wyszyński. The director, however, is more preoccupied with the personal than with the political, more interested in the situation between a man and a woman than in the political circumstances.

Temptation differs distinctly from other Polish films about the Stalinist period, especially those made before 1989. Its story is told without ridiculing the system. Wiesław Zdort's camera portrays a gloomy picture deprived of the sun and dominated by the darkness of the priests' and nuns' frocks, the dirty green colors of the soldiers' uniforms, and the faded color of the old brick buildings. In the last scene, the protagonist—oppressed by two systems—is left at the train station and given an opportunity to make a choice concerning her life.

As mentioned earlier, Polish films made after 1989 no longer employed the accusatory tone of many earlier films dealing with the Stalinist past. Sporadic returns to earlier Solidarity poetics were met by indifferent audiences and mixed critical reviews. This happened, for instance, to Bajon's semiautobiographical

Street Boys,[35] which, through the perspective of two boys, narrates the story of the violent workers' protest in Poznań in June 1956. During the strike, which concerned the reduction of work norms and salary increase, riots started, and the army and the security force opened fire.

Another film, Wajda's *The Ring with a Crowned Eagle*, which discusses issues the director first addressed in *Ashes and Diamonds*, was both a critical and box office failure.[36] The opening sequence of Wajda's film introduces the Warsaw Uprising of 1944; the action then cuts abruptly to the last days of the uprising and moves quickly to the postwar period. After the war, a young officer from the uprising, Marcin, attempts to take care of his surviving soldiers and secure their future in Soviet-occupied Poland. "To collaborate with the communists or not" is the issue posed by the film. To stress the link between *The Ring with a Crowned Eagle* and *Ashes and Diamonds*, Wajda even reconstructs the famous symbolic scene in a bar with the flaming glasses of alcohol, each symbolizing a fallen member of the protagonist's Home Army unit. In the last scene, the politically naive protagonist, now bitter and disillusioned, leaves the Security Office (UB) building and hides on the street, realizing that he is no longer in his own country.

More popular among critics and moderately popular among audiences were comedies that tamed the past. In the center of Zanussi's semiautobiographical *In Full Gallop* is an aging protagonist, Idalia Dobrowolska (Maja Komorowska). She is proud, yet willing to compromise—a Catholic at heart and a communist on the surface.[37] The doubleness of the protagonist has a symbolic dimension: it represents the double talk and double behavior of most of her compatriots. If we consider this, we realize that it could be a film about surviving in the Stalinist period, about political mimicry. Jerzy Płażewski writes that, despite its apparent autobiographical nature, often emphasized by Zanussi, this film is about a "philosophy of survival" in an era unfriendly to humans.[38]

Kutz's *Colonel Kwiatkowski* shares similar features. Its protagonist, a picaresque hero, is Kwiatkowski (Marek Kondrat), an army physician who assumes the false identity of a high-ranking officer in the secret police. Accompanied by a small group of friends, he travels throughout Poland and releases political prisoners, causing consternation among provincial functionaries. His actions, however, are not motivated by patriotic or political impulses. He takes this new identity to save himself after an argument with a Soviet officer and maintains it to impress his girlfriend.

The film works against Polish national stereotypes and romantic myths, which demand that the protagonist sacrifice his life for a noble national cause. As in most of his films, starting with *Cross of Valor*, Kutz prefers to focus on ordinary people absorbed by history rather than on history epitomized by individual cases. Kutz's film laughs at issues usually reserved in Poland for martyrological works. His supposedly real story (as indicated by the credits) introduces a character unusual by Polish standards. This character is not another victim of history but almost a folk hero who beats the system with wisdom and wit.

Leszek Wosiewicz emphasizes the grotesqueness of history in his *Scurvy*, a film about the fate of Poles who, after the September 1939 German and Soviet aggression, found themselves in Soviet-occupied territories and were deported by Stalin to Siberia. Wosiewicz uses a montage of documentary footage to reveal the historical context and, in broader terms, to show his protagonist surfing on the wave of history. In the final sequence, the protagonist returns from a Soviet concentration camp to Poland and is promptly arrested by the Polish military as a spy (a fact indicated in documents fabricated by the Soviet security service). He is kept in a former German concentration camp, now a place for POWs and alleged collaborators, including Polish freedom fighters. Trying to escape, he finds himself in a crematorium and hides in a furnace where two soldiers, a Russian and a Pole, spot him. With its stress on the grotesque, absurdist aspect of history, *Scurvy*, like Wosiewicz's earlier *Kornblumenblau*, shares many characteristics with Agnieszka Holland's acclaimed *Europa, Europa* (1991, France-Germany). Wosiewicz's later film, *Family Events*, differs distinctly from his previous works. It is a semiautobiographical story set in a small town during the Stalinist years. Wosiewicz divides the film into five chronological chapters and offers an almost idealistic evocation of childhood, despite the troubled political time.

The Stalinist period attracted filmmakers not only for political but also for purely artistic reasons. Robert Gliński, writer-director who started his career with the medium-length *Niedzielne igraszki* (*Sunday Pranks*, 1983, released in 1988), a film exposing the brutal, grotesque banality of Stalinism, said that "this was the period extremely abundant with human dramas; there were clashes of different attitudes, a different model of life prevailed. Conflicts between new and old were distinct. Furthermore, the iconography of that period was extremely filmic."[39]

The cinematic images of Stalinism were created in the 1990s predominantly by younger filmmakers such as Gliński who, unlike Wajda and Kutz, did not know Stalinism firsthand, having been being born in the late 1940s and the 1950s. They relied heavily on socialist realist aesthetics. The kitsch iconography of that period, as represented in Polish cinema, is very filmic indeed: communist slogans; red banners; portraits of Lenin, Stalin, and Bierut; May Day parades; sports parades; monumental construction sites; red stars; the masses of people enthusiastically greeting the leaders; black limousines of the infamous security service; and members of the communist youth organization in uniform. Socialist realist songs, associated with May Day parades, and the phraseology of the period fill the soundtrack.

Flashbacks to the Stalinist past are usually constructed of stylized images employing a similar color palette: typically gray or blue, with elements of red (for banners, posters, etc.). Several Polish films use sequences resembling images associated with that period; frequently, to heighten their verisimilitude, they incorporate actual newsreels and other documentary materials into their narrative (in *The Mother of Kings*, a black-and-white film, Zaorski extensively employs prewar and postwar newsreels). To stress the oppressive nature of Stalinism further, these films are frequently set in places of confinement such as prisons (*Interrogation*; many sequences of *The Mother of Kings*), labor camps (*Scurvy*), internment sites (*Temptation*), hiding places (*Suspended*), and schools and scouts' camps (*Shivers*).

There is nothing fascinating about the Polish version of Stalinism, nothing seductive; the only discernible nostalgia is for lost innocence. Stalinist kitsch is an object of ridicule. Polish cinema shows Stalin's image in white uniform as he appears in documentary clips, billboards, and portraits. A mixture of fear and an almost surrealist quality is also inseparably linked with contemporary images of Stalin and other communist leaders. Deprived of their threatening aura, they appear almost like Grand Guignol characters: farcical, devilish, grotesque. For example, in the ironic *Femina* (1991), a film abundant with symbols, Piotr Szulkin mocks the emptiness of Polish political and religious rituals. He debunks the ritual aspect of Polish culture and its martyrological character. The protagonist (Hanna Dunowska) is torn between Catholicism and the communist ideology: oneiric flashbacks full of bizarre images reveal the oppressiveness of her childhood. The reappearing image in the film is that of Stalin hanging from a chandelier. This treatment of totalitarianism is new to Szulkin's works. His earlier antitotalitarian science fiction films employed barely hidden political messages, easily deciphered by his audiences.

To conclude, after years of the mythologization of history, Polish postwar history finally belonged to Polish screens. Although primarily the domain of documentary cinema, the Stalinist past also appeared in mainstream narrative films. Coming to terms with the past had produced some interesting films. The Stalinist period was safely distant enough to enable some "filmic fascination" with these years, yet close enough to provide many strong parallels with the present. For years, Polish postwar history has attracted several leading filmmakers whose struggles with state censorship and other political obstacles were frequently as absorbing as their completed works. In the early 1990s, they could freely deal with various formerly taboo themes. The irony is that during the transitional period, the new audiences seemed to be tired of politics and did not care what the filmmakers had to say.

"The Poor Poles Look at the Ghetto": Representations of the Holocaust

Since the return of democracy in Central Europe, a great number of narrative and documentaries, as well as literary and academic works, dealing with Jewish themes have surfaced. The quantity of works focusing on Polish-Jewish relations was unprecedented and usually interpreted as an indication of a will and commitment to come to terms with the complex and frequently suppressed past. In postcommunist Poland, the reassessment of history had resulted in, among other things, the emergence of a significant number of films that deal with Polish-Jewish relations at a level of intensity unparalleled by earlier works.

The Polish approach to the common Polish-Jewish history changed earlier, toward the end of the 1980s. The television screening of Claude Lanzmann's *Shoah* (1985) stimulated a heated debate in the Polish media. Although generally praised for his forceful account of the Holocaust, Lanzmann had been accused by many Polish commentators of being biased in his selection of material and thus of presenting an incomplete picture of the occupation in Poland. As some authors observed, Lanzmann's partial emphasis on anti-Semitic traits in Polish society prevented him from telling a more balanced version of what really happened.[40] Another important event was the publication of an essay by Jan Błoński, "The Poor Poles Look at the Ghetto," which appeared in 1987 in the Catholic weekly *Tygodnik Powszechny*.[41] Błoński explores the Poles' repression of the Jewish tragedy and the degree to which the Polish people are morally responsible, as "silent witnesses," for what happened on their soil. In this now classic text, the title of which directly refers to Czesław Miłosz's poem "A Poor Christian Looks at the

Ghetto," Błoński focuses on the question of repressed national memories and the necessity of mourning the dead. He also poses a crucial question: can the Poles be blamed for their indifference? Błoński pronounces that the Polish soil was tainted and desecrated, and needs to be exculpated from guilt. What remains now, he says, is to see the Polish past truthfully.

In his intense essay, Błoński also refers to another well-known poem by Miłosz, "Campo dei Fiori," written in Warsaw in 1943. It shows the indifference of Poles to what happened in the Warsaw ghetto at the time of the Jewish uprising. In this poem, Miłosz compares the fate of Giordano Bruno—burned to death as a heretic in the presence of an unconcerned mob at Rome's Campo dei Fiori—and the fate of Polish Jewry. Miłosz's image of a carousel close to the ghetto wall is very emblematic, almost the essence of the problem. The carousel, as Błoński explains, is a historical fact. It was installed at Krasiński Square in Warsaw just before the uprising in the ghetto and was in operation for its duration.[42] It is no wonder that this very image is employed in two films discussed later in this chapter. Janusz Kijowski uses the image of the carousel extensively in *Tragarz puchu* (*Warszawa. Année 5703*, 1992, Poland-France-Germany), and it is present in Andrzej Wajda's *Holy Week* (1996).

Like its Central European neighbors, let us emphasize again, Poland is a history-conscious nation; films dealing with the past were and are the core of serious mainstream cinema. After the 1989 "freedom shock," a prominent group of feature films about Polish-Jewish history had been released: Wajda's *Korczak* (1990) and *Holy Week*, Kijowski's *Warszawa. Année 5703*, Filip Zylber's *Pożegnanie z Marią* (*Farewell to Maria*, 1993), Jan Łomnicki's *Jeszcze tylko ten las* (*Just Beyond this Forest*, 1991), and Ryszard Brylski's *Deborah* (1995). The Holocaust theme is not limited to these films. It also appears in *Kornblumenblau* (Leszek Wosiewicz), *All That Really Matters* (Robert Gliński), and *Pogrzeb kartofla* (*The Burial of a Potato*, 1991, Jan Jakub Kolski).

To make the list of films dealing with Polish-Jewish relations complete, one must also take into account films dealing with the 1968 anti-Semitic campaign in Poland: *Marcowe migdały* (*March Almonds*, 1990, Radosław Piwowarski) and *1968: Szczęśliwego Nowego Roku* (*1968: Happy New Year*, 1993, Jacek Bromski) and films made abroad by Polish filmmakers, for instance, Agnieszka Holland's German-made *Bittere Ernte* (*Angry Harvest*, 1985) and *Europa, Europa*.[43] It is also essential to mention foreign films shot in Poland and with a strong Polish involvement, most notably Steven Spielberg's *Schindler's List* (1993). Three Poles who contributed to this film, Allan Starski (set design), Ewa Braun (costumes), and Janusz Kaminski (who lives in the United States, cinematography), received Academy Awards.

The Holocaust does not appear explicitly in Kolski's fine debut film, *The Burial of a Potato*. In this film that combines poetic metaphors with grotesque images of Polish postwar reality, a former concentration camp prisoner, Mateusz Szewczyk (Franciszek Pieczka), faces a hostile village after his unexpected and unwanted return several years after his incarceration. The village has already taken possession of his belongings and is after his land. Mateusz's fellow neighbors reject him as an alien and as a Jew, although he is neither. In one poignant scene, he puts on a striped concentration camp uniform with the number 23423 and a "P" inside a triangle (indicating that he is Polish) and stands half naked, with his pants down, in front of his neighbors to prove that he is not a Jew.[44]

The essence of the film is Mateusz's struggle for acceptance, not the political reality of postwar Poland (portrayed powerfully, albeit in an uncanny manner). Kolski is not afraid to demythologize Polish peasants. While they function as the defenders of traditional nationalistic values in several Polish literary and filmic works, they are portrayed in *The Burial of a Potato* as brutal, superficially religious, xenophobic, and anti-Semitic caricatures, almost in the manner of Jerzy Kosiński's representation in his controversial novel *The Painted Bird*.[45]

Andrzej Wajda devoted more time to Polish-Jewish relations than any other major Polish director did.[46] His *Korczak*, the "casualty of Jewish Polish polemics," as Lawrence Baron rightly describes it,[47] portrays a figure of great importance for both Polish and Jewish cultures—Dr. Janusz Korczak (in reality, Henryk Goldszmit). Korczak, a famous writer, a well-known pediatrician, and a devoted pedagogue, in his writings and in practice always stressed the dignity of childhood. On 6 August 1942, he marched in the Warsaw Ghetto to the *Umschlagplatz* with two hundred of "his orphans" from a Jewish orphanage. They all died in the gas chamber of Treblinka.

In the film written by Agnieszka Holland, Korczak (played memorably by Wojciech Pszoniak) is described by one of his senior pupils as "the world's greatest Pole ... and the greatest Jew, too." Wajda has always been interested in Korczak's martyrdom and legend, so he swiftly moves to the final stages of his life. The film starts immediately before the war and briefly indicates the intricacies of Polish-Jewish relations and anti-Jewish sentiments in prewar Poland. The war is announced by a few street scenes intercut with the much-cited Polish documentary footage showing the burning King's Castle in Warsaw in September 1939. A cut to an image of marching Polish prisoners of war announces the stage of resignation and despair. Another scene introduces the terror of the occupation: the creation of the Warsaw ghetto on 13 September 1940.

From the beginning, Wajda insists on an almost documentary quality for his film, chiefly by choosing black-and-white photography and by inserting newsreels and documentary footage, both Polish and German. The film introduces familiar images of ghetto life: hunger, brutality, overcrowding, death in the streets. Wajda, however, is not afraid to show the less familiar side of the ghetto: Jewish police and Jewish martyrs, rich and poor Jews, Polish anti-Semites, and those who risked their lives to help the Jews. He also portrays the tragedy of Adam Czerniakow, the chairman of the Jewish Council (Judenrat) in the Warsaw ghetto. Polish characters appear only as supporting figures in *Korczak*; their attitudes toward the Jews and the separation between the Poles and the Jews range from passive sympathy and active help (punished by death) to silent approval.

The last sequence of Wajda's film shows the deportation of the Jewish orphans and their instructors to Treblinka. Led by Korczak, who refuses to abandon his children, the orphans carry a flag with the Star of David on one side and a four-leaf clover (the orphanage emblem) on the other as they march to meet their doom. In a poetic, symbolic, and emotional final scene, shown in slow motion, the children disembark from the mysteriously disconnected railway wagon and fade into a peaceful rural landscape. When the image whitens, a sentence appears leaving no doubt about their actual fate: "Korczak died with his children in the gas chambers of Treblinka in August 1942." *Korczak*, although well received in Germany and Israel (among other countries), stirred many controversies in France.[48] Some French critics and filmmakers (like Lanzmann) accused Wajda and his screenwriter, Holland (herself half-Jewish), of being anti-Semites and of misrepresenting the Holocaust, and castigated them for choosing a Polonized Jew as a hero.[49]

Unharmed by some negative responses to *Korczak*, Wajda returned to an examination of Polish-Jewish wartime relations in *Holy Week*, which is based on Jerzy Andrzejewski's short story written soon after the Warsaw Ghetto Uprising.[50] Like the short story, the film is set during Easter Week of 1943, during the first seven days of the uprising. The film's Jewish protagonist, Irena Lilien (Beata Fudalej), seeks sanctuary on the Aryan side of the ghetto with her Polish friend, Jan Małecki (Wojciech Malajkat), and his pregnant wife. During the film, Irena spends several days in her hiding place, feeling constantly threatened by the outside world. The last montage sequence depicts Irena moving toward the ghetto, Jan killed by the Gestapo while attempting to recover Irena's belongings from her former hiding place, and his wife praying in a church. The powerful final scene portrays Irena returning to the ghetto, now in flames and almost destroyed, passing some weary German soldiers returning from their deadly shift in the ghetto and not even reacting to her presence. The parallel between the Jewish tragedy and the meaning of Easter Week, which is present in the literary source, provides an artistic framework carefully devised and developed by Wajda.

As in his first films from the Polish School period, Wajda emphasizes the tragic aspects of life. *Holy Week* is dominated by symbolism, a feature surely expected in Wajda's cinema but sometimes disparaged by critics.[51] The film examines Polish morality—with the ghetto insurgents offscreen, it deals with the Polish experience of the Holocaust. Irena Lilien is sent among Poles to "test the nation."[52] She acts like a litmus paper to check the attitudes of her Polish hosts. Wajda portrays Irena in an unconventional way: she is not a sympathetic character, not a typical Holocaust victim. Unlike most figures in Holocaust narratives, she refuses to remain silent and obedient, out of German sight, and she "ungratefully" questions the attitude of her Polish hosts.

The symbolic image of the carousel in front of the ghetto wall also appears in the film to stress the Polish indifference. A group of young Polish fighters, probably members of the Gray Ranks (Szare Szeregi), the underground Polish scouting organization during World War II, employs the carousel to look behind the wall before entering the ghetto to help the Jewish insurgents.[53] The image of the carousel on the Polish side of the ghetto wall also appears several times throughout Janusz Kijowski's *Warszawa. Année 5703*. Unlike Wajda, Kijowski employs it exclusively as a symbol of the outside world's indifference and of the indifference of Poles living on the Aryan side of the wall. He tells the story of a young couple escaping through sewers from the Warsaw ghetto and finding refuge on the Polish side of the wall in an apartment owned by Stefania (Hanna Schygulla), a half-German, middle-aged woman whose Polish husband is in a POW camp. Alek (Lambert Wilson), who first gets to the hiding place, becomes Stefania's lover. To prolong his and his wife Fryda's (Julie Delpy) stay at Stefania's place, and because he is afraid to tell the truth, he pretends to be Fryda's brother, despite her violent objections.

Warszawa. Année 5703 opens with several negative images showing mysterious faces and characters. It then cuts to an image of a photographer surreptitiously taking pictures of the horrors transpiring in the ghetto. He gives the negatives to

Alek, hoping that he will deliver them to a Polish photographer on the Aryan side. The photographer, however, was arrested (and probably killed) for hiding a Jew, and this situation forces Alek to accept Stefania's help. After these brief, promising initial scenes, the action moves to Stefania's apartment. From this point on, the film relies heavily on the three leading stars, and increasingly resembles a theatrical play. The camera rarely ventures outside of Stefania's apartment, and if it does, the results are sketchy and unconvincing, for example, the two scenes set in the sewers, which invite comparisons with Wajda's *Kanal* or Ford's *Border Street*. The nightmarish external circumstances only serve to bring the three characters more intimately, claustrophobically together.[54]

Like Kijowski, Ryszard Brylski also attempted to incorporate the Holocaust into mainstream melodramatic formulae in his debut film, *Deborah*. The action of the film is set before the outbreak of World War II in a small Polish provincial town with a significant Jewish population. The film's protagonist, the painter Marek Wawrowski (Olgierd Łukaszewicz), is preoccupied with restoring the newly uncovered frescoes in a local Catholic church. Rumors about war enhance the feeling of fear in the sleepy town. The Jewish population is afraid of what looms ahead. At the outbreak of the war, the married painter begins an affair with a young, beautiful Jewish woman, Deborah Grossman (Renata Dancewicz). After the war begins, he hides Deborah in an empty apartment, then in a cellar, while the Germans are exterminating the Jewish population of the town, including Deborah's father and friends.

Brylski aims creating an atmosphere of despair. The imminent war and then its reality overshadow the characters' actions. In Brylski's film, the Holocaust functions as the background for a tale about a passionate love, doomed from its very inception. Poles are generally shown to be sympathetic to the plight of the Jews; most are depicted helping the Jews, with many being killed by the Germans as a result. The theme of deeply rooted anti-Semitism, however, is introduced by an anti-Jewish tale portrayed in the church's frescoes ("We work on the same theme," the Nazi officer says to the Polish painter). In Brylski's film, however, the Holocaust functions as the background for a tale about a passionate love, doomed from its very inception. Like Kijowski's *Warszawa. Année 5703*, *Deborah* attempts to exploit the Holocaust, to incorporate it into mainstream cinema formulae.

Filip Zylber's *Farewell to Maria*, loosely based on Tadeusz Borowski's powerful short story,[55] differs from other films dealing with the occupation, the war, and Polish-Jewish relations. Modern jazz compositions by Tomasz Stańko and stylized photography by Dariusz Kuc stress the morbid melancholy initially introduced by edifying dialogues about love, war, and poetry. Slow-motion photography, used consistently throughout the film, functions here not as a clichéd cinematic device but as a means of building atmosphere. This is not to say that Zylber builds an atmosphere at the cost of aestheticizing the Holocaust. The film offers a new reading of a classic text and of history. Zylber does not follow the partly autobiographical, laconic, and verging-on-cynical vision of Borowski. The film revolves around the story of two Jewish women who manage to escape from the ghetto. The older of the two (Danuta Szaflarska), escapes from the ghetto thanks to her prewar connections on the "Aryan side," but later, choosing inevitable death, she returns to be with friends and relatives. The young and beautiful Sara (Katarzyna Jamróz) performs a different role. According to Zylber, she "propels the action, circles like a moth, perturbs people. In a sense, she provokes her own death."[56] Like Irena in Wajda's *Holy Week*, Sara serves as a reminder of what is going on behind the ghetto wall. She upsets people by her very presence.

In Borowski's short story, the emphasis is on the old Jewish woman; the nameless young one performs only a marginal role. Jerzy Antczak repeated this characterization in his memorable 1965 television adaptation of the story with Ida Kamińska (the star of *The Shop on Main Street*) in the leading role. Tadeusz Lubelski calls Zylber's film "a drama of helplessness" and Borowski's short story "a drama of mutual responsibility."[57] According to Lubelski, the filmic *Farewell to Maria* creates two distinct realms: the realm of private rituals and the realm of death. Young Polish intellectuals attending the wedding of their friends know that the nightmarish world behind the ghetto wall exists, but they feel unable to do anything about it. Insulated from the realm of death by their artificial rituals, they can only powerlessly watch the death of Sara, killed by a Polish *granatowy* (navy blue) police officer.

Jan Łomnicki's *Just Beyond this Forest*, a Polish anti–*Schindler's List*, low-budget, antispectacular film, introduces an ordinary hero performing ordinary deeds in exceptional circumstances. The film's opening scenes, set in the Warsaw Ghetto in June 1942, show an elderly woman wandering fearfully through impoverished streets. The impassioned camera portrays an overcrowded ghetto in an almost semidocumentary manner. A washerwoman, Kulgawcowa (the outstanding Ryszarda Hanin), is introduced clearly as an outsider, an observer of a world that is far removed from her own. This simple woman, previously employed by a rich Jewish doctor and his family, is now about to help them. She is asked to take their only child, the young girl, Rutka, out of the ghetto. Reluctantly, she agrees because she knows the danger involved—also because she is prejudiced against the Jews.

The film follows Kulgawcowa and Rutka's dangerous journey beyond the ghetto wall and their short stay at Kulgawcowa's home. Facing an open hostility of Kulgawcowa's grown-up daughter, they are forced to continue their journey to a village where Kulgawcowa hopes to hide Rutka. Conversations with fellow passengers on a train reveal Polish attitudes toward the Jews. Kulgawcowa and Rutka are blackmailed by one of the passengers and rescued by another. When they continue walking toward the village that is "just beyond the forest," they encounter a German gendarme. During a routine control, Rutka drops a photograph of her parents that she smuggled out of the ghetto, and her identity is revealed. In the last scene, Kulgawcowa accompanies Rutka to the police station where death most likely awaits them.

Just Beyond this Forest does not portray a favorable picture of Polish reality. The Poles in the film are presented as poorly educated people, as a collection of low Polish types, blackmailers, and often anti-Semites. Łomnicki's aim is not to present a well-known figure (like Korczak in Wajda's film). Rather, he is interested in small, insignificant people overwhelmed by history. These people are the center of this modest film. Whereas Wajda gives a lesson on history and Polish-Jewish relations, Łomnicki creates characters and situations entrenched in realism with seemingly contemporary dilemmas.

The political atmosphere in 1968 (the year of the anti-Semitic campaign in Poland)[58] is addressed in two films: Radosław Piwowarski's *March Almonds* and Jacek Bromski's *1968: Happy New Year*. Both make no direct references to the Holocaust, but they recreate the 1968 events through the eyes of young protagonists, high school and university students, respectively, who experience their political initiation and are forced to make their first adult choices. In *March Almonds*, Piwowarski tells the story in his usual, lyrical style that resembles some Czech and Slovak films from the 1960s; the characters are likeable, warm, mildly grotesque, but not villainous. He deals with coming-of-age problems in a small provincial town against the backdrop of the political atmosphere of the late 1960s. The peaceful atmosphere of the small town ends abruptly with the intrusion of politics that starts to overshadow the characters' lives. One of the protagonists, Marcyś (Piotr Siwkiewicz), learns that he is of Jewish origin and is eventually forced to leave the country with his father. At the beginning of the film, supposedly unaware of his Jewishness, Marcyś carries an anti-Semitic slogan at the smalltown gathering in support of the official party line.

March Almonds is nostalgic for the 1960s, Piwowarski's generation. To enhance this mood, the film features 1960s music groups from the West as well as their Polish counterparts, such as Breakout and Czerwone Gitary (Red Guitars). At the film's end, the song "Ta nasza młodość" (That youth of ours) is heard, and a brief postscript describing the fates of the nonfictional characters who inspired their screen counterparts passes before the viewer. Despite the director's hazardous tendency to sentimentalize, the film may serve as a good example of the new political cinema emerging in Poland at that time. Contrary to pre-1989 works, *March Almonds* avoids martyrological gestures and clear divisions between good and bad. It also offers a satirical look at political opportunism, primitive indoctrination, and doublespeak.

The theme of the Holocaust is not limited to feature film: a large number of documentaries made after 1989 also deal with Poland's Jewish history. Many films show the surviving Polish Jews returning to places where they lived before the war, revisiting the sites of concentration and death camps where their relatives perished, and talking to Polish eyewitnesses, often people who helped them. The survivors' testimonies are sometimes supported by a combination of archival photographs and footage, usually produced by the Germans in the ghettos. Among several documentaries, there are three classic examples of Holocaust cinema: *Miejsce urodzenia* (*Birthplace*, 1992, Paweł Łoziński), *Kronika powstania w getcie warszawskim według Marka Edelmana* (*Chronicle of the Warsaw Ghetto Uprising According to Marek Edelman*, 1993, Jolanta Dylewska), and *Fotoamator* (*Photographer*, 1998, Dariusz Jabłoński).

Birthplace revolves around Henryk Grynberg's return to Poland in order to learn more about the circumstances surrounding the death of his father and brother during the war.[59] In 1992, accompanied by Łoziński's camera, Grynberg revisits places where his family hid during the occupation and meets with many old villagers who remember him and his family. After talking to several people, some of whom helped the Grynbergs to survive, the grim truth about his father's fate is revealed: he was killed by two brothers, village dwellers, who were hoping to prosper from the crime. In the film's finale, Grynberg discovers the place where some villagers buried his father after his body had been lying in the field for days. Łoziński's film follows Claude Lanzmann's strategy of revisiting the places of the Holocaust and letting the eyewitnesses provide their own testimonies. Praising his work, Mirosław Przylipiak writes: "The creation of a time-bridge between two points over fifty years apart is the exceptional achievement of this film. It seems that Łoziński managed to 'reverse time' without using any archival materials."[60]

Two internationally known Polish films continued the long tradition of local documentaries based on archival photographs. Dylewska in *Chronicle of the Warsaw Ghetto Uprising according to Marek Edelman* creatively employs footage shot by the Germans in the Warsaw Ghetto in 1943. Jerzy Bossak brought the materials to Poland after the war and used them in his classic documentary *Requiem for 500,000*. Later, this footage appeared in many other films, but Dylewska treats it differently. She creates new images from old ones, editing within a frame; by magnifying and slowing frames, she accentuates details missed by previous filmmakers. Through this process, she transforms anonymous and deprived-of-humanity victims into suffering and dignified characters. A member of the Jewish underground leadership in the Warsaw Ghetto, Marek Edelman, candidly narrates the powerful documentary that won several international film festival awards, including the Grand Prix in Munich.[61] Edelman's face, shown in close-ups and hidden in darkness, is juxtaposed with archival materials. The film ends with images of those who fought in the ghetto alongside Edelman, among them Mordecai Anielewicz.

Another film, Jabłoński's *Photographer*, the recipient of several awards including the Grand Prix in Amsterdam, uses a collection of four hundred color slides that were uncovered in 1987 in Vienna. The film juxtaposes Walter Genewein's pictures taken in the ghetto after 1940, as well as his offscreen comments (read by an actor) based on his letters and other documents, with the narration by the physician and writer Arnold Mostowicz who survived the Łódź Ghetto. The contrast between the past captured by Genewein in color and the present introduced in black and white structures the film and, perhaps, adds a commentary that to see the Holocaust in color may be "inappropriate" and "causes spontaneous resistance."[62] Genewein's images do not capture the extermination of the Jewish population of Łódź. In his words, they portray the ghetto not as a *Konzentrationslager* but as a small Jewish town (*kleine jüdische Stadt*). Jabłoński's film demonstrates the extent to which Genewein's photographs removed the grim reality of the ghetto by including the eyewitness testimony. Without Mostowicz's account, the viewer would be helpless "facing the lie of the colored images."[63]

Polish Films with an American Accent

Anita Skwara's essay published in 1992, "Film Stars Do Not Shine in the Sky Over Poland: The Absence of Popular Cinema in Poland," emphasizes the lack of popular cinema traditions. In this work, written before the wave of Polish action films, Skwara states that "the poetics of American genre cinema transplanted to Poland turned out to be dysfunctional, alien, astonishingly naive or vulgar, and simplistic."[64] Harsh in her criticism of the "Polish-made American films" (a term used in Poland to describe the local versions of Hollywood), Skwara stresses that these "clumsy imitations" were not made for the more sophisticated viewer and, deprived of a Polish national context, had no chance of survival.

The number and popularity of genre films released in Poland after 1989 suggested the opposite. The poetics of Hollywood transferred to Polish reality was seen at its best in such action films as *Zabić na końcu* (*To Kill at the End*, 1990, Wojciech Wójcik), *Miasto prywatne* (*The Private Town*, 1993, Jacek Skalski), *Młode wilki* (*Fast Lane*, 1995, Jarosław Żamojda), *Nocne graffiti* (*Night Graffiti*, 1997, Maciej Dutkiewicz), and, in particular, Władysław Pasikowski's *Kroll* (1991), *Psy* (*The Pigs*, 1992), and its sequel, *Psy 2: Ostatnia krew* (*The Pigs 2: The Last Blood*, 1994). In addition, several action films made in the late 1990s incorporated the poetics of American action films. This was evident in films like Pasikowski's *Demony wojny według Goyi* (*The War Demons According to Goya*, 1998) and *Operacja Samum* (*Operation Samum*, 1999).

The adoption of the genre cinema formulae was, of course, not restricted to genuine action films. For example, the return of melodrama could be observed in *Tato* (*Daddy*, 1995), a debut film by Maciej Ślesicki (1964–). His *Sara* (1997) went even further with its incorporation of Hollywood formulae; it cannibalized many genres and cleverly played with cinematic clichés. Another film, the Polish-Czech production *Zabić Sekala* (*To Kill Sekal*, 1998, Vladimir Michálek), successfully transplanted the poetics of the Western to the war reality of the Protectorate of Bohemia and Moravia.

Films by Juliusz Machulski were also inspired by American genre cinema, from his very well-received *Va Banque* (1982) to box office successes in the 1990s: *Kiler* (1997) and its sequel, *Kiler-ów 2-óch* (*Kiler 2*, 1999), both starring one of the most popular Polish actors of the 1990s, Cezary Pazura. The commercial and critical success of these films in Poland relied on yet another important ingredient: formulaic structures were saturated with numerous references to Polish politics and everyday life. This was also evident in Machulski's *Girl Guide* (the title refers to a stolen nuclear warhead guidance system named GIRL), winner of the 1995 Festival of Polish Films and advertised as "an amusing story combining rock and roll, spies, and highland folk, with a thriller element."[65] As this brief description suggests, the film employs elements of Hollywood genre cinema but fuses them with a distinctly Polish idiom. It targets young Polish viewers with its postmodern references to world cinema, its depiction of the local rock scene, and its mockery of Polish political life, as well as with its humor. As if to prove that he was capable of moving to the realm of "art cinema," Machulski also made the stylish, although neglected by Polish critics, historical drama *Szwadron* (*Squadron*, 1993).

One of Machulski's best films from this period, however, is *Déjà Vu* (1989, Poland-Soviet Union), which employs pastiche as a dominant form of expression. Set in 1925 and narrated in English and Russian, *Déjà Vu* tells the story of Johnny Pollack (Jerzy Stuhr), an American gangster of Polish origin sent by mobsters from Chicago to Odessa. What follows are Pollack's adventures in a land governed by its own principles, principles incomprehensible to Westerners. Pollack's pragmatic professionalism is out of place in the land of the Bolsheviks.

The title *Déjà Vu* implies events already seen, and, indeed, Machulski builds his film from clichés, fills it with references to world cinema, and thus creates a film for cinema buffs. In this multilayered pastiche, he employs familiar images from numerous films and quotes both early Soviet and American cinemas extensively. He borrows from Lev Kuleshov and Sergei Eisenstein, as well as from Boris Barnet's comedies about everyday life under the New Economic Policy (NEP) program. He also borrows heavily from burlesque and American gangster films set during the prohibition era. *Déjà Vu* is peopled with American gangsters bearing familiar names (Cimino, Pacino, Scorsese, Coppola, etc.) and icons of an early Soviet culture: Vladimir Mayakovsky, Lili and Osip Brik, and Sergei Eisenstein. In the most famous sequence, frequently cited by scholars, Johnny Pollack, who is pursuing another gangster, finds himself on the steps of Odessa during Eisenstein's shooting of *Battleship Potemkin* (1925). Because Pollack is wearing a stolen officer's jacket, the film crew mistakes him for an actor who is supposed to be playing a commanding officer on the steps. Eventually, Chicago gangsters watch Pollack as he leads the Cossacks in the released version of *Battleship Potemkin*. With the exception of Zbigniew Rybczyński's short film *Steps* (1987), this is probably the most intelligent use of Eisenstein's famous sequence.

Figure 9.1 Jerzy Stuhr as an American gangster on the Odessa Steps in 1925 in Juliusz Machulski's *Déjà Vu* (1989). Courtesy of Film Studio Zebra.

In box office terms, action films were the most successful Polish films of the early 1990s and were the only works effectively competing with American products. For instance, of the Polish films released from 1990 to 1996, the top three are action films: *The Pigs 2: The Last Blood* (684,946 viewers), *Fast Lane* (542,955), and *Night Graffiti* (606,046).[66] Their popularity on video matches that of American action films. The title of Zdzisław Pietrasik's article in the influential weekly *Polityka* emphasized the preferences of Polish audiences clearly: "Defend Yourself: Most of All We Enjoy Watching Polish-Made American Films."[67] If we take into account films released in the 1990s, action films account for as many as seven titles among the most popular ten.[68]

Awards at the Festival of Polish Films in Gdynia indicated a change of direction favoring genre cinema: the 1993 award went to a romantic comedy, *Kolejność uczuć* (*The Sequence of Feelings*, 1993, Radosław Piwowarski); the 1994 festival winner, *The Turned Back*, was a political comedy by Kazimierz Kutz; and the 1995 award went to Juliusz Machulski's *Girl Guide*. In addition, a growing number of young Polish directors were increasingly interested in telling stories and in making well-narrated commercial films. As they often insisted, their goal was not to perform any national or social mission, discuss "important issues," or focus on traditional filmic themes like Polish history. They wanted cinema to be free from political and social obligations. Their films were no longer made for the young Polish intelligentsia. The word "art" seemed to be forbidden in these young filmmaking circles. Sporadic voices stressing the importance of art cinema seemed to be taken from a previous political reality.[69]

The transfer of Hollywood poetics to Polish reality was primarily visible in popular Polish television series, such as *Ekstradycja* (*The Extradition*, 1995–1998, twenty five episodes, Wojciech Wójcik). In this production, Marek Kondrat stars as Olgierd Halski, a Warsaw police inspector fighting international drug gangs that smuggle heroin and amphetamines from Russia via Poland to the West. Kondrat plays an aging, almost stereotypically hard-bitten cop who uses brutal methods in his work. In the series, the Polish viewer encounters clear references to contemporary political and criminal affairs, like the well-publicized racketeering in Warsaw's Old Town. *The Extradition* demonizes the Russians, the Russian mafia, and former KGB officers, now involved in large-scale criminal activities. It also stresses the helplessness of the Polish police and the corruption of its high-ranking officers. Another successful television series, *Akwarium* (*The Aquarium*, 1995, four episodes, Poland-Germany-Ukraine), directed by Antoni Krauze, goes even further with its morbid fascination with the Soviet secret services. Based on Victor Suvorov's famous account, *The Aquarium* is a psychological, rather than an action, film about espionage.

There is no doubt that certain action films were popular partly because of their exploration of realms that earlier could not be depicted in a negative fashion. For instance, Pasikowski's *Kroll* and Feliks Falk's *Samowolka* (*AWOL*, 1993) create a dark picture of a formerly taboo topic: the military. The screen protagonists' vulgar language reflects an unrefined actual Polish reality of that time based on corruption, depravity, and primitive indoctrination. *AWOL* is less action oriented and more a journalistic film made in the Cinema of Distrust tradition. Falk's film revolves around the conflict between new soldiers and the old guard about to retire from active duty. The older soldiers, led by a criminal nicknamed Tiger, rule the garrison and drill the newcomers in order to avenge their own earlier humiliation. Everything happens with the silent approval of the officers. Despite its popularity in the Polish video market, this type of cinema—a substitute for independent media before 1989—is rife with clichés and does not go beyond common knowledge of the subject.

The opening scenes of *Kroll* suggest a typical Polish "war film": in a dark, rainy atmosphere soldiers load heavy tanks onto a train. Vulgar language and scenes showing the humiliation of a young soldier introduce a reality never before seen in Polish cinema. What follows is the suicide of the victimized soldier, which is falsely reported as an accident to avoid controversy. His distraught friend and protector, Kroll (Olaf Lubaszenko), leaves the barracks illegally and goes to see his own family. Lieutenant Arek (Bogusław Linda) and one of his soldiers, Wiaderny (Cezary Pazura), try to bring Kroll back so that he will not be prosecuted. The worlds in and out of the barracks contain the same ugly features: corruption, violence, alcoholism, and betrayal.

Kroll sets the tone for subsequent films by Pasikowski. It introduces a harsh, violent world reserved for equally violent and tough men with clearly misogynist attitudes. The film also stresses the message that is present in almost all Polish action films: the friendship between men matters most. Kroll's friend, Kuba, who has a romance with Kroll's wife, finally saves Kroll and their friendship by taking on the identity of the AWOL soldier. In the final scene, Kuba asks the lieutenant, who knows of the switch and accepts the deception, "How is it here?" The lieutenant's spasmatic laughter is the only answer—and an excruciating comment on the situation in the Polish armed forces.

Pasikowski's Neo-noir, Neo-militia Film, *The Pigs*

The incorporation of American models is seen at its best in *The Pigs*, directed by Władysław Pasikowski (1959–). Pasikowski draws heavily on the formula of American police/gangster films and quotes extensively from several makers of quality action films. The mise-en-scène is distinctly American; the viewer encounters "American locations" (luxurious interiors, rainy streets, underground parking lots, a deserted factory), excessive violence shown in extreme slow motion, vulgar language, and tough talk in the world of rough men. The film relies on action instead of dialogue, an unusual feature compared to most Polish productions. The cinematographer, Paweł Edelman, captures images with a tracking camera, frequently in slow motion and sometimes portrayed as tableaux-like compositions.

Despite the aforementioned features, *The Pigs* is "very Polish." Set in 1989, the film incorporates many factual events into its narrative and shows Poland in a process of transition from one political system to another, in which all principles are shaken and everything is possible. In Poland, 1989 was marked by verifications of the former members of the secret police (SB), by burned secret police files, and by open corruption. The film also portrays a world in which colleagues from the former Soviet KGB, East German STASI, and Polish SB join forces to fight for control of the illegal, but lucrative, drug market.

The protagonist of *The Pigs*, Franciszek "Franz" Maurer (played memorably by Bogusław Linda), a lieutenant in the secret police, tries to survive in an "age of verifications," lost privileges, and his own personal problems. Franz, dressed formally but without a tie, sits nonchalantly before the verification commission, smoking a cigarette and listening to his work record. The camera portrays him frontally, from the commission's point of view. The viewer learns that Franz is thirty-seven, is married to a daughter of the former vice minister of internal affairs, and has one child. In his professional career, he was honored but also disciplined several times and almost discharged from the police force. The most serious crime he has been accused of is killing Captain Nowakowski, who tried to establish free trade unions in the police force in 1980, the year of Solidarity. Franz defends himself by saying that Nowakowski was a mentally unstable person who killed his wife and dragged his daughter onto the roof of a building demanding the registration of the trade unions and an increase in his salary. Franz proudly admits that he shot him from 220 meters with a Mauser 7.8 mm. After bragging about his marksmanship ("I shot his head off"), he adds in a poignant voice, "He was my colleague."

With Michał Lorenc's music evoking spaghetti Westerns and gangster classics, the camera cuts to the building that houses the Ministry of Internal Affairs. Franz and his colleagues from the security force pack confidential documents and police files onto a truck and later burn them at an abandoned dumping ground. In one of the scenes, Franz approaches some barking police dogs in their cages. The dogs bark viciously, but are contained, alluding to the situation of the secret police members—once above the law but now controlled by the former dissidents.[70] The film shows the end of a certain political formation; its now unwanted pretorians fight for survival. At the dumping ground, Franz's friend Olo (Marek Kondrat) tells a police newcomer (Cezary Pazura), who spies on them: "When you grow up, you'll understand that politics is not the evening news. We are the politics, here on this dumping ground. Either we manage to get out of this or we stay here forever."

Immediately after its release, *The Pigs* became a cult film for many young viewers in Poland, which confused some established film critics and filmmakers. Pasikowski's viewers side with a member of the disgraced former secret police, an individual whose world collapses, who was and is surrounded by corrupt politicians, and who exists in a world without moral values. The viewer sides with a classic loser: a lonely tough guy, betrayed by "his system," his wife, his best friend, and his girlfriend. The protagonist, formerly in a position of power and money, finds himself deprived of his privileged status. He loses his loved ones and his material

Figure 9.2 Bogusław Linda as Franz Maurer (left) and Cezary Pazura in Władysław Pasikowski's *The Pigs* (1992). Courtesy of Film Studio Zebra.

possessions, and his career comes under investigation. After destroying the police documents that relate to his professional past, Franz burns family documents and photographs in the backyard of his empty villa (his private past).

Pasikowski's film was probably the first artistic work to capture the death of the Solidarity movement's ethos. In a scene that aggravated some Polish film critics, the drunken members of the infamous security force carry one of their completely drunk colleagues on their shoulders toward the camera while singing "Janek Wiśniewski padł" (Janek Wiśniewski has fallen). Andrzej Wajda previously employed the song in his *Man of Iron* to refer to the Solidarity movement because of its associations with the 1970 strike in Gdańsk. The young audience of *The Pigs*, never exposed to political thinking prevalent in the communist era, appreciated the debunking of the oppositional myths.[71]

According to some critics and filmmakers, *The Pigs* did not exploit the post-1989 situation but merely unveiled the state of mind in postcommunist Poland. For instance, Bogusław Linda stated: "People have had enough of martyrology, veterans, selling out. They're angry about what is happening in the country. My role in *The Pigs* was born out of this anger and hatred toward the new reality."[72] Other voices defended *The Pigs*, stressing its moral dimensions. The film director Piotr Szulkin noted the similarities between *The Pigs* and Wajda's *Ashes and Diamonds*: "*The Pigs* does not have the literary dimension of Andrzejewski's novel [the literary source of Wajda's film], but ... communicates similar astonishments that, for Andrzejewski, could have been a discovery but, for Pasikowski, are only a statement."[73]

The parallels between Maciek, the protagonist of Wajda's classic *Ashes and Diamonds*, and Franz, of *The Pigs*, seem unlikely at first but eventually appear legitimate. For different reasons, both bear the burden of the past and try to survive in a new political reality. Both suffer defeat. In one of the final scenes of *The Pigs 2: The Last Blood*,[74] the wounded Franz runs into a field away from a train filled with ammunition. The way he moves and the way he is followed by the camera, as well as his groaning and exaggerated gestures, emulate Wajda's dying hero.

The Pigs 2, commercially one of the most successful Polish films of the 1990s,[75] reinforces images from the first part, images also present in other Polish action films. The film opens with newsreel-like scenes from the Balkan War. A man whom the viewer later recognizes as Wolf (Artur Żmijewski), an arms dealer, poses in front of the camera with two severed heads. Another man briskly approaches, points a gun to the camera (and the viewer), and shoots. After a short period of blackness, the camera cuts to a prison cell that Franz shares with a convicted murderer who hastily reveals his crimes. In a scene likely referring to Krzysztof Kieślowski's *A Short Film about Killing*, the murderer is taken out of the cell by force to be executed.

Upon his release from prison, after serving several years, Franz is greeted by his former colleague from the police force, nicknamed Nowy (Cezary Pazura). Fired for not joining the strike in the factory and unable to find a permanent job, Franz pairs up with Wolf, and together they become involved in an illegal international arms deal. For unclear reasons (perhaps conscience), Franz single-handedly prevents the sale of arms to the Balkans. In the film's finale, he blows up a train filled with firearms.

The Pigs and its sequel created a new charismatic Polish star, Bogusław Linda (1952–). He is another generational actor who follows two acting personalities known for their roles in Wajda's films: Zbigniew Cybulski and Daniel Olbrychski. Like his predecessors, and unlike most Polish actors, he is known exclusively for his filmic roles, although he is also a film and theater director (in 1989, he made his first feature film, *Seszele* [*Seychelles*], which was well received by young audiences). He started his acting career in the early 1980s in a series of acclaimed political films, including Agnieszka Holland's *Fever* and *A Woman Alone*, Andrzej Wajda's *Man of Iron* and *Danton*, Krzysztof Kieślowski's *Blind Chance*, and Janusz Zaorski's *The Mother of Kings*. He became an idol of the Solidarity generation, although the censor shelved most of the films he appeared in. In the 1990s, he became an icon for another generation, the post-Solidarity generation, and represented its nihilism and disillusionment with the new reality. The "tough guy" aura and the cynical attitude of the protagonists he portrayed reflected the reality of the first period of unfettered Polish capitalism.

Linda's character in *The Pigs* introduced a completely new hero, different from any former Polish screen star. The protagonist representing the young intelligentsia had been replaced by a tough guy, passivity by action. Male solidarity and money are what really matter for the new hero; male bonding and a foreign car are more important than political ideals and lasting male-female relationships. Like some of his American predecessors (beginning with Clint Eastwood's Dirty Harry), the new Polish action hero does not want to wait for justice; he does not even believe that it exists. Rather, he takes the initiative and the law into his own hands. Franz Maurer is not a vigilante, however. In a manner resembling Dirty Harry, in *The Pigs 2* he claims: "I am nobody. I only remove weeds." Also in the sequel, parodying Dostoevsky (perhaps a Dostoevsky for the masses), Franz remarks, while standing next to the body of the Russian mafia boss whom he has just killed, "If there is no god, what kind of a Satan are you?"

Both parts of *The Pigs* and most Polish action films of the 1990s were male-oriented films—masculine spectacles celebrating machismo Polish style. These male melodramas, notable for their sense of melancholy, depicted the breakdown of law and order that prompted the characters, usually bearing foreign names, such as Kroll, Maurer, Wolf, or Kossot, to resort to violent methods. With the exception of *Fast Lane*, which portrayed inexperienced teenagers tempted by the big money that can be made almost overnight by smuggling, the protagonists were middle-aged men, usually former security agents, military men, or sometimes petty criminals (*The Private Town*). Customarily dressed in black suits and dark ties, they resembled FBI agents or stereotypical businessmen. According to Polish folk wisdom from the 1990s, gangsters and businessmen had a lot in common in the post-1989 period; their moralities fused.

In *The Pigs*, Pasikowski shows a degraded world with clichéd female characters. His clichés, however, have more to do with the stereotype found in American action cinema than with stereotypes of women in Polish films. Piotr Szulkin, who contributes to this discussion with his film *Femina*, points out that women in Polish films never had time for love because they were busy making national banners.[76] Pasikowski is not interested in this aspect of Polishness; like some of their American counterparts from the 1980s, both *Pigs* films represent female characters as voiceless figures who inhabit male-dominated landscapes. Their task is no longer to "stand by their men," as in classical Hollywood cinema, but to find a place for themselves in a ruthless world where only their sexuality matters.

Similar treatment of female characters spreads across other genres. The melodramatic *Daddy*, for example, a film employing stars from *The Pigs* (Bogusław Linda and Cezary Pazura), tells the story of a bitter divorce case between a successful filmmaker and his wife, who shows signs of mental illness. This well-narrated film, full of references to contemporary American cinema, portrays however a one-dimensional world with black-and-white divisions between genders. Ślesicki, who skillfully retains precise control of the mood and atmosphere of the film, portrays a clearly misogynist landscape where almost all female characters border on caricatures.

* * *

In the early 1990s, Polish action filmmakers employed hybrid, transgeneric constructs to tell stories similar to those of numerous American films. These filmmakers, mostly first-time directors, created films predominantly for viewers of the younger generation who were untainted by the politically draining 1980s in Poland—people who grew up in the transitional period of the early 1990s—and were no longer interested in the political complexity of the past and the problems experienced in the post-totalitarian period.

The ambition of action filmmakers in Poland (and anywhere else, for that matter) was to beat Hollywood on its own terms, yet, paradoxically, their films relied on the Polish social context for success. These films referred to contemporary political, financial, and criminal affairs, and reflected the unstable political and economic life, as well as moral chaos. Many critics perceived action films made in Poland in the early 1990s as a threat to a national cinema that needed to speak with a discrete Polish idiom. Others, myself included, looked at their "positive unoriginality" as a chance to rejuvenate Polish film: to make it well narrated and absorbing for the viewer.[77]

Laughter after Battle: Comedies

In the early 1990s, a few attempts to make deliberately commercial films resulted in some miserable releases. Intended as commercial endeavors, some films by formerly respected, artistically inclined directors proved to be both artistic and commercial failures, for example, *Panny i wdowy* (*Maidens and Widows*, 1991,

Janusz Zaorski) and *Pajęczarki* (*Spider Women*, 1992, Barbara Sass). Fortunately, there were some exceptions. In addition to Radosław Piwowarski and Juliusz Machulski, who succeeded in making intelligent and popular films, other directors made single films that enjoyed moderate success. These include *Wielka wsypa* (*The Big Giveaway*, 1993, Jan Łomnicki), *Lepiej być piękną i bogatą* (*It's Better to Be Beautiful and Rich*, 1993, Filip Bajon), and *Szczęśliwego Nowego Jorku* (*Happy New York*, 1997, Janusz Zaorski), the latter about six miserable Polish migrants in New York and an adaptation of a satirical novel by Edward Redliński.

Since his first feature film, *Aria for an Athlete,* Filip Bajon has made many highly original, artistically sound films, like his stylish historical *The Magnate*, which covered the first half of the twentieth century and told the story of the demise of the aristocratic German family von Teuss in Upper Silesia. His comedy, *It's Better to Be Beautiful and Rich*, a modern version of the Cinderella story with a distinct Polish flavor, is his successful first venture into mainstream commercial cinema. His young protagonist, a weaver played by Adrianna Biedrzyńska, works in a declining factory that is permanently on strike. One day, she learns that she has inherited the factory. The implausible becomes possible in the film, which meanders toward an unavoidable happy conclusion that implicitly mocks popular films on success stories. The film has two layers: a melodramatic success story and an ironic commentary on the new Polish dream of becoming rich overnight. Bajon also plays with stereotypical Polish images of the West and of the "Wild East" (Ukraine). The film features many excellent Polish actors—among others, Daniel Olbrychski, Anna Prucnal, Bronisław Pawlik, and Marek Kondrat—who act (perhaps overact) in the manner of American prime-time television productions. The music and flamboyant photography emphasize the fairy-tale aspect of the film.

Another film, Radosław Piwowarski's award-winning *The Sequence of Feelings*, tells the story of a famous aging actor (Daniel Olbrychski) who goes to a provincial theater in Silesia to direct *Romeo and Juliet* and subsequently has a romance with a teenager, Julia (Juliet, played by Maria Seweryn). The love story is set, atypically, against the background of industrial Silesia. This lyrical but unsentimental film, at times reminiscent of American romantic screwball comedies of the 1940s and 1950s, plays with Olbrychski's own star persona, which he earned in the late 1960s and the 1970s. His performance (a near mockery of "Olbrychski," a figure he created during his long career) also comes as a refreshing turn in his career.

It is often stated, accurately, that Polish cinema is not internationally known for its comedies. The atmosphere of Polish films is usually serious, in keeping with the topics presented in these films: politics, social issues, and local history. Sylwester Chęciński's film about the introduction of martial law, *Rozmowy kontrolowane* (*Controlled Conversations*, aka *Calls Controlled*, 1992) offered some hope that in Poland it could be possible to laugh at matters normally reserved for serious treatment. Chęciński's film, written by a former contributor to Stanisław Bareja's comedies, Stanisław Tym (who also plays the main role), is set shortly before and after the implementation of martial law in Poland. Significantly, its innovation lies in its mockery of both sides. The protagonist (Tym), entangled in events that overwhelm him, unwillingly becomes a hero of the underground Solidarity. His undeserved fame spreads. Chęciński's mockery of Polish-style heroism and worn-out romantic gestures belongs to the tradition started by Andrzej Munk's antiheroic *Eroica*. The likeable hero of *Controlled Conversations* is involved in farcical adventures in the gloomy reality of the early 1980s in Poland. There is no ambiguity about him; he is a simple-minded, career-seeking individual, a product and a victim of the system.

Two later films, though lacking the strength of Chęciński's work, deal with similar issues told in a similar fashion. Marek Piwowski, the maker of the Polish cult film *The Cruise*, directed *Uprowadzenie Agaty* (*The Kidnapping of Agata*, 1993), based on a true story, about a politician who abuses his power to get rid of his daughter's lover. The new political situation, with its hastily created political elites, and the Catholic Church are the object of laughter and mockery. Piwowski's film, despite its satirical and comic potential, loses its initial impetus and turns out to be a collection of humorous yet disconnected and visually dry cabaret sketches. *Człowiek z...* (*Man of...*, 1993, Konrad Szołajski) goes so far as to mock Wajda's *Man of Marble* and *Man of Iron* and ridicule the "men of Styrofoam," the descendants of brave dissidents turned new-style apparatchiks. In addition to direct references to Wajda's films, this sadly ineffective film tries to laugh at the current state of affairs, which is portrayed as corrupt, manipulated, and hopeless. In this world, there are no ideas, and there is no protagonist to identify with.

Although most comedies in the 1990s dealt with the current political situation, some films focused more on characters than on politics. The exhibitionist film *Nothing Funny*, directed by Marek Koterski (1942–), is such an example. The film starts with an image of the deceased filmmaker, who tells the sad story of his life. One misfortune follows another from the time he is in diapers. Cezary Pazura plays the unfortunate loser, who goes through a midlife crisis and suffers from permanent artist's block. *Nothing Funny* can also be taken as a parody of the filmmaking community in Poland: several (frequently crude) gags ridicule its alleged lack of professionalism and stupidity. Koterski blends fine humor and well-observed situations with lavatory jokes and unsophisticated imagery. Laughing at the state of the film industry, yet exhibiting a lack of filmic refinement himself, the director falls victim to his own mockery.

Jacek Bromski's *Dzieci i ryby* (*Seen but Not Heard*, 1996) and *U pana Boga za piecem* (*Snug as a Bug in a Rug*, 1998; its sequels made in 2007 and 2009) belong to the most interesting comedies made in the 1990s. *Seen but Not Heard* is the story of a forty-something generation trying to find itself in the new Polish reality. It narrates the story of a romance between a well-to-do woman (Anna Romantowska), running her own advertising business and raising a daughter, and her old romantic interest (Krzysztof Stroiński), once an aspiring scientist, now a provincial teacher.

Personal Cinema

In the 1990s, several Polish filmmakers made low-budget, personal, easily recognizable films, for example, *Rozmowa z człowiekiem z szafy* (*Conversation with a Person in a Wardrobe*, 1993, Mariusz Grzegorzek), a film about an unusual case of motherly love, isolation, and rejection. In the opening scene in a mortuary that sets the tone of the whole film, the protagonist (Bożena Adamek) goes into labor while identifying her husband's body. She isolates herself and her son, Karol, from the outside world. Karol grows up alienated, paranoid, and wild. Finally, she leaves her totally dependent seventeen-year-old son to take up with a lover. Karol is passed on to a special institution in which he learns basic life skills and painfully enters adult life. Slow camera work, voice-over narration, and attention to detail set the mood for this unusual film.

Two leading "personal directors," Andrzej Barański and Jan Jakub Kolski, deal with provincial Poland and the small, "insignificant" characters populating this landscape. From 1989 to 1995, Kolski and Barański were the most prolific of Polish filmmakers, with six feature films, produced mostly by state television. Exceptional in the context of Polish cinema is the case of Andrzej Kondratiuk's *Wrzeciono czasu* (*The Spinning Wheel of Time*, 1995) and *Słoneczny zegar* (*The Sundial*, 1997), both low-budget, personal films produced by the director's family and friends.

Andrzej Kondratiuk (1936–2016) started his career in 1965 with the television film *Monolog trębacza* (*The Trumpeter's Monologue*) and made several films in the 1970s, including *Dziura w ziemi* (*The Hole in the Ground*, 1970), *The Ascended*, and *Pełnia* (*Full Moon*, 1979). With his wife, actor Iga Cembrzyńska (1939–), he made *The Spinning Wheel of Time* and *The Sundial*, both semiautobiographical stories about an aging filmmaker obsessed with the passage of time, cinema, and a young woman. These films are a continuation of Kondratiuk's earlier *Cztery pory roku* (*Four Seasons*, 1984), a work resembling a family album that portrays the Kondratiuks vacationing in their secluded family cabin. These films, however, are not family movies, nor are they narcissistic pictures of the Polish intelligentsia. The discourse on aging, temporality, family bonds, and art is enhanced by the films' exhibitionist style, the creation of characters who border on being pretentious, and the inclusion of clever dialogues about existential problems. *The Spinning Wheel of Time*, in particular, succeeds in capturing the grotesque aspect of life as well as its poetry.[78] Critics in Poland labeled this type of cinema "private/separate cinema."[79] The film's slow-paced scenes, unmistakable self-mockery, sarcastic humor, visual beauty, and Kondratiuk's perseverance in pursuing his vision were honored with the Special Award of the Jury at the 1995 Festival of Polish Films.

Since his impressive 1985 film, *Woman from the Provinces*, Andrzej Barański (1941–) had made several notable films in the early 1990s, including *Kramarz* (*The Peddler*, 1990), *Kawalerskie życie na obczyźnie* (*A Bachelor's Life Abroad*, 1992), and *Dwa księżyce* (*Two Moons*, 1993). He is not a storyteller but rather a philosopher interested in the banality of everyday life. His films, although frequently set in the 1950s and the 1960s, ignore politics and are devoid of Polish romantic clichés. They resemble intimate miniatures, naive pictures that put everyday banality on the pedestal of art. Barański shows his protagonists' lives as heroic—tough but charming. His pragmatic protagonists are preoccupied with work and life; they do not shape history, ask "important questions," or fight/build the communist system. Instead, they approach life as a task to accomplish. They retain their composure when confronting everyday reality and survive day by day.

Barański's subtle version of realism has no predecessors in Polish cinema; it also differs from a version of realism developed in the early films of Jiří Menzel and Miloš Forman. The uniqueness of Barański's poetics is seen at its best in *The Peddler*. The protagonist, Chruścik (Roman Kłosowski), is another deromanticized, hardworking individual who is preoccupied not with politics or history but with the everyday struggle for survival. Barański tells the story of his life in an extended flashback. Before the court, Chruścik narrates the futility of his past exertions, his failed attempts to fulfill the dream of his life (to own a small house), and his struggles with provincial authorities and unfair competition. The protagonist endures all the hardships of life, yet, surprisingly, his account of Polish postwar history is deprived of politics. Politics plays a role in his life not unlike that of the elements and is treated accordingly. A perpetual optimist with no luck on his side, Chruścik never complains.

The Peddler is permeated with images of provincial Poland and the slow-paced lives of the province dwellers. Because of the nature of his work (as an itinerant salesman), Chruścik moves from one small place to another. The camera follows him in these colorful places avoided by mainstream Polish cinema: country fairs and sleepy provincial towns. The importance of Barański's work lies in his painstaking recreation of the material aspect of the Polish communist past. In this film, the paraphernalia of the Catholic Church and the communist system blend into an idiosyncratic mélange characteristic of postwar Polish reality. Answering a question about the alleged banality of his films, Barański remarks: "It is not that I love banal aspects of life. I am, however, charmed by a certain order. Such an order with which one can live and die."[80]

Jan Jakub Kolski (1956–) is arguably one of the most original filmmakers who emerged during the postcommunist period. Trained as a cinematographer at the Łódź Film School, he began his career directing short films. He has made many highly original films since his well-received 1991 debut, *The Burial of a Potato*. They include *Pograbek* (1992), *Jańcio Wodnik* (*Johnnie the Aquarius*, 1993), *Cudowne miejsce* (*Miraculous Place*, 1994), *Szabla od komendanta* (*The Sabre from the Commander*, 1995), and *Grający z talerza* (*The Plate Player*, 1995), and the winner of the 1998 Festival of Polish Films, *Historia kina w Popielawach* (*The History of Cinema Theater in Popielawy*). His slow-paced films are characterized by their fine cinematography (by Piotr Lenar) and stylized acting, particularly from Franciszek Pieczka, Mariusz Saniternik, and Grażyna Błęcka-Kolska (the director's wife). Kolski's films resemble in atmosphere Witold Leszczyński's classic *The Life of Matthew*, also starring Pieczka, and his later film *Konopielka*. Kolski's films share with *The Life of Matthew* the same obsession with mythologized rural communities and down-to-earth yet multidimensional protagonists who feel a sense of mystery when close to nature. In some of his films, however, the protagonists have more in common with characters depicted in *Konopielka*—characters who are backward, ignorant, and xenophobic. Kolski creates a private world, a mythical village, and protagonists who are outside of history. However, he makes not "rural films," as he frequently declares, but rather films that are set in a rural milieu; the problems they touch upon have universal appeal.

Kolski's prolific nature and his obsession with the private world lead inevitably to a certain mannerism, apparent in *The Sabre from the Commander* and *The Plate Player*. To be sure, from a "personal director" we expect an "authorial style," and this frequently involves the repetition of themes, structures, and cinematic devices. Writer-director Kolski (all scripts are his own) is haunted by the same picturesque landscapes and characters and by the presence of the religious/supernatural element in the lives of his down-to-earth yet unique characters.

The direct political references present in Kolski's first film, *The Burial of a Potato*, gradually disappear from his later works, replaced by metaphysical meditation and folk wisdom combined with a unique version of lyricism and humor. Kolski is interested in oversensitive, weird, and marginalized characters whose worlds are limited to their village and end with the horizon. His protagonists live as if outside of history; they are not political animals but simple people whose often banal and uneventful lives are limited to their village or small town and a marginal profession. Their aspirations follow suit. In Kolski's world, supernatural events are everyday phenomena, and Christianity coexists with remnants of Slavic pagan beliefs.

Johnnie the Aquarius is the essence of Kolski's stylized poetic, perhaps magic, realism.[81] The film portrays a village thinker, Jańcio (Johnnie, played by Franciszek Pieczka), who discovers his unusual ability to "control" water, which, under his power, is no longer constrained by the laws of gravity. Blessed with miraculous abilities and driven by a sense of mission, Jańcio leaves his secluded village and his pregnant, faithful wife, Weronka, for the outside world. Prosperity and fame change his life forever, endangering his marriage and, finally, bringing unhappiness to him and to those whom he loves. His son, born in a barn, has a devilish tail, the result of a spell thrown by a beggar for somebody else's wrongdoing. Desperate, Jańcio tries to reverse time and to repair the damage he has done to Weronka. He loses the battle with time, but, by accepting things as they are, he finds peace of mind while surrounded by his family.

With its multilayered construction and many references to religion, politics, and literature, *Johnnie the Aquarius* could be taken as a philosophical, political, or poetical parable, depending on a critic's predilection. Kolski's unusual story has no equivalent in Polish cinema; it has the appeal of a chromolithograph, of "primitive poetry," and of a philosophical folktale. Stylized dialogues and songs commenting on the action are combined with tableaux-like compositions of a world ruled by mysticism. The frequent use of slow motion stresses the importance of the moment and of the characters inscribed in a rural landscape.

Kolski's poetics and his portrayal of the farmers' class, as well as Barański's vision of provincial life, were not challenged in Poland in the 1990s. An important stream of "Polish rural literature" has no filmic counterparts. For instance, Ryszard Ber's adaptation of Wiesław Myśliwski's prose, *Kamień na kamieniu* (*Not One Stone Upon Another*, 1995), resulted in a disconnected picture devoid of the epic scope of the novel (interestingly, Myśliwski is credited as a screenwriter of the film). Practically, the only picture that must be mentioned here is *Śmierć dziecioroba* (*Death of a Childmaker*, 1991, Wojciech Nowak). This film belongs to a different kind of realism. Like Kolski's *The Burial of a Potato*, it is a cruel, merciless picture of the province. The reality Nowak presents is loathsome, peopled by grotesque, vulgar characters. The film's protagonist, a provincial Don Juan (Marek Kasprzyk), refuses to marry a pregnant security officer's daughter. His refusal is not a nonconformist act, a Don Juan's revolt, or a political gesture. Instead, he is at pains to emphasize his separation from a world he despises but of which he is paradoxically a part. The film's mise-en-scène stresses the ugliness and trashy characteristics of a degraded world. This black vision of reality prompted one reviewer to claim that *Death of a Childmaker* is a new Polish film about love.[82]

Female Filmmakers

In the early 1990s, several films made by female Polish filmmakers enjoyed critical and/or commercial success, including works by Dorota Kędzierzawska, Teresa Kotlarczyk, Magdalena Łazarkiewicz (Agnieszka Holland's younger sister), and, in particular, Barbara Sass.

Dorota Kędzierzawska (1957–) started her career with *Koniec świata* (*The End of the World*, 1988, television film) and *Diabły, diabły* (*Devils, Devils*, 1991). Her subsequent films, *Wrony* (*Crows*, 1994), *Nic* (*Nothing*, 1998), and *Jestem* (*I Am*, 2005) have been popular on the international film festival circuit. *Crows* tells the story of a lonely twelve-year-old girl who kidnaps a two-year-old toddler, plays at being her mother, and then returns her many hours later. The slow narration centers entirely on the two girls and their journey; other characters appear and then quickly fade away in this episodic film about the need for love. Artur Reinhart beautifully visualizes the film's simple, poetic narrative; his splendid cinematography captures sophisticated images of an old town, of beaches, and of the sea—the scenery of the journey. In these beautiful yet cold landscapes, the older girl's desperate search for love becomes almost a cry in the dark.

Another female director who started her career in the 1990s is Teresa Kotlarczyk (1955–). She is the author of *Zakład* (*The Reformatory*, 1990), an intriguing film dealing with the problem of manipulation and, on a different level, with moral questions involved in filmmaking. Kotlarczyk's *Odwiedź mnie we śnie* (*Visit Me in My Dream*, 1996) is the Polish equivalent of *Ghost* (1990, Jerry Zucker). Ala (Danuta Stenka), a beautiful and successful writer, dies in a car accident, leaving her three children and husband (Zbigniew Zamachowski) unable to cope with their loss. The parallel action portrays Ala in a kind of heavenly waiting room reconsidering her past life and watching her family on Earth learning to live anew. In an emotional finale, she returns to Earth disguised as a different woman and is recognized by her family.

Magdalena Łazarkiewicz (1954–) became known for the youth-oriented *Ostatni dzwonek* (*The Last Bell*, 1989), the politically oriented *Odjazd* (*Departure*, 1992, directed with her husband, Piotr Łazarkiewicz), and *Białe małżeństwo* (*White Marriage*, 1993). The latter deals openly with young female sexuality as well as female psychology. Set against the backdrop of the idyllic scenery of prewar Poland—a picturesque country landscape with a pleasant manor, marching cavalrymen, and burgeoning girls in virginal white dresses—the film mixes subjective and objective reality, dreams and waking reality, and various genres. The young protagonist rebels against her own gender and the traditional role prescribed for her. She despises and is afraid of matrimonial sex without love, with all its biological connotations, and does not want to follow the example of other women in her family. *White Marriage* is a clever discussion of female sexuality with strong Freudian overtones, something of a rarity in Polish cinema.

In the shadow of Poland's internationally known filmmakers, Barbara Sass (1936–2015) developed her own personal style. After working as an assistant director on films by Wajda, Has, and Skolimowski, she started her independent career in 1980 with *Without Love*. Following the film's success, she developed a body of work characterized by thematic unity (she was also a screenwriter) and by a simple documentary-like visual style (her husband, Wiesław Zdort, always participated as a cinematographer). Like Márta Mészáros of Hungary, Sass presented a feminist perspective and confronted issues largely ignored in overtly political Central Europe: gender relations and the plight of women. Like Mészáros and most Central European female filmmakers, Sass also objected to narrow feminist interpretations of her films. Nevertheless, given Sass's manifest interest in feminist issues, her works almost force critics to take a feminist perspective. For instance, her early works—starting with *Without Love* through *Debutante*, *The Shout*, and *The Girls of Nowolipki* and its sequel, *Crabapple Tree*—portray young women struggling to achieve their goals despite political and other pressures. These films center more on characters than on action; Sass appropriately calls her early films "psychological portraits narrated in a rhythm corresponding to that of the contemporary world: dynamic, sharp, and fast."[83]

In the 1990s, Sass completed four films: *Historia niemoralna* (*An Immoral Story*, 1990), *Tylko strach* (*Only Fear*, 1993), *Temptation*, and *Jak narkotyk* (*Like a Drug*, 1999). *An Immoral Story* comments on the creative process of filmmaking. Featuring the star of Sass's early films, Dorota Stalińska, the film tells a fictional story about an actress and reflects on being an artist (actor/filmmaker) at the same time. Throughout the film, a director comments offscreen to her editor on several scenes from her film in the making. *An Immoral Story* is full of intertextual references to Sass's early films, to Polish cinema, and to Stalińska's acting career. Despite its significance, this intricate and brutally honest work did not receive the critical acclaim it deserves in Poland. After *Only Fear*, the story of a successful television journalist, Katarzyna (Anna Dymna's winning performance), struggling to overcome alcoholism, Sass directed one of the finest Polish films produced in 1995, *Temptation* (discussed earlier in this chapter).

Krzysztof Kieślowski's Phenomenon

Arguably the best-known contemporary Polish filmmaker, Krzysztof Kieślowski died in March 1996 following heart bypass surgery. His last films, *Podwójne życie Weroniki* (*The Double Life of Véronique*, 1991) and the *Three Colours* trilogy—*Three Colours: Blue* (*Trois couleurs: Bleu*, 1993), *Three Colours: White* (*Trois couleurs: Blanc*, 1994), and *Three Colours: Red* (*Trois couleurs: Rouge*, 1994)—premiered at major film festivals, won numerous awards, and consolidated his position as a household name in European art cinema.[84]

A closer look at Kieślowski's oeuvre and his artistic persona reveals that he does not fit the traditional image of a "great Central European auteur" obsessed with politics and history. For many critics who are used to Polish film functioning, for the most part, as an expression of Polish history and political tensions, Kieślowski's films (especially his 1990s international coproductions) can be puzzling. Kieślowski's last films embrace many stylistic and thematic obsessions characteristic of European art cinema and therefore should be examined in a larger-than-national context.

As opposed to other internationally known Polish filmmakers, like Wajda or Zanussi, Kieślowski was never directly involved in politics, nor was he ever explicitly political in his films or in public appearances. Although persistently subjected to an Aesopian reading by Polish critics and filmgoers alike, his early (at that time, underappreciated) films, such as *Camera Buff* or *Blind Chance*, do not demonize the communist system. Rather, they show the system as an obstacle to achieving happiness and—to use the title of his 1976 film—calm. Discussing Kieślowski's career, Tadeusz Sobolewski points out the problem that Kieślowski's "apolitical" stand generated in Poland: "None of the critics in Poland had the foresight to perceive the uniqueness and specificity of Kieślowski's films, except in terms of their being a function of social, political or religious aspirations. The Polish critic persistently forces the artist to answer the questions concerning social issues."[85]

Perpetually independent, Kieślowski operated outside of mainstream Central European aesthetics. Within this highly politicized culture, in which political choices were of greater importance than aesthetic priorities were, Kieślowski was clearly an outsider, not afraid of expressing unpopular views concerning, for example, religion and political commitment. Kieślowski frequently stressed his disillusionment with politics. In 1994, explaining his surprising decision to retire from filmmaking at the age of fifty-three, he claimed, "One of the reasons of my departure from the cinema is my dislike for fulfilling public roles, and a longing for privacy."[86]

Some Polish critics thought Kieślowski's move to international coproductions and his subsequent critical recognition was suspicious.[87] Unlike other Polish artists, Kieślowski achieved his international auteur status without relying on the Polish romantic tradition. Western critics often allegorically read Kieślowski's Polish-French coproductions, starting with *The Double Life of Véronique*, as commentaries on the relationship between Poland and Western Europe. *The Double Life of Véronique* is a rare "art film" dealing with the subject of doubleness. This is presented in the story of two young women, Weronika in Poland and Véronique in France, both memorably played by Irène Jacob (winner of the Best Actress Award at Cannes), who do not know each other but whose lives have

Figure 9.3 Irène Jacob in Krzysztof Kieślowski's *The Double Life of Veronique* (1991). Screenshot by the author.

several mysterious parallels. Polish Weronika lives for the art of singing. During a brilliant performance featuring Van den Budenmayer's music (a fictional composer—Zbigniew Preisner's creation), she collapses on stage and is pronounced dead. The story of Weronika then dissolves into the story of Véronique, who works as a primary school teacher. She is unaware of Weronika's existence, yet thanks to the mysterious link between the two women, she learns from Weronika's mistakes.

The element of chance is a driving force in the film. The protagonists' "double life" is intensified by Sławomir Idziak's remarkable cinematography and its reliance on yellowish filters, which help to create warmth and a sense of otherworldliness, and by fuzzy images and landscapes, which generate a dreamlike atmosphere. This slow-paced enigma, beautifully crafted and governed by a sense of mystery, appears to be almost the essence of "European art cinema," because of its personal character, sensuality, and self-referentiality and because it is saturated with art film clichés. Kieślowski's episodic film, full of unexplained occurrences, relies heavily on magnification, enigmatic doubling, and symbolism. Its elliptical narrative construction, which is mysterious to the point of teasing the spectator, resists any explicit interpretation. The story about duality is told with the help of point-of-view shots, upside-down and mirror images, distorted images through windows and from behind massive doors with tiny glass ornaments, and blurred images seen through a transparent toy ball. They not only multiply space but also make the whole film a spectacle of ambiguity. The film's energy and breadth does not allow it, however, to be another "fairly conventional box of ontological tricks, recycling traditional metafictional paradoxes."[88]

Kieślowski's formalist exercise probably did to art films in the 1990s what Sergio Leone's spaghetti Westerns did to the Western in the 1960s—the accumulation and intensification of features characteristic of the "genre." The accumulation of symbolic associations and other art cinema qualities in *The Double Life of Véronique* prompted Gaylyn Studlar to remark that it looks almost like "a virtual parody of all the established stereotypes of Continental filmmaking associated with an earlier generation of filmmakers, such as Ingmar Bergman and Alain Resnais."[89]

For Kieślowski, this film also marks a radical departure from his early film essays to polished international and "unpolitical" coproductions. This is a turn toward privacy and "calmness," a retreat from the pressure of politics, which is openly manifested in the Polish part of the film. For instance, Weronika does not notice a huge statue of Lenin being towed away on a truck, signaling, perhaps, the fall of communism. In another scene, when Weronika stares at her double among the tourists, she seems unaware of the political demonstration and the riot police surrounding her at Kraków's Main Square. Weronika is as free from politics as is the film, to the astonishment of many critics.

Kieślowski's *Three Colours*, a major cinematic achievement of the 1990s, is a trilogy inspired by the French tricolor flag, in which blue stands for liberty, white for equality, and red for fraternity. Despite these connotations, Kieślowski does not seem to be particularly interested in politics or social issues; instead, once again, he deals with protagonists facing moral dilemmas, with their individual quests for the three values embodied in the French flag. Although carefully designed as a trilogy and released as such within a short span of time, the three French-Polish-Swiss productions can be viewed separately, as Kieślowski indicated on several occasions.

The first part of the trilogy, *Blue*, tells the story of Julie (Juliette Binoche), who endures the death of her husband and child in a car accident. The camera captures Julie's grief, her attempts to detach herself from her friends, to free herself from the past ("I don't want any belongings, any memories. No friends, no love. Those are all traps"). When Julie accidentally learns about her husband's infidelity and discovers that his mistress is pregnant with her husband's child, she gradually embraces the life she has attempted to suppress. As in *The Double Life of Véronique*, the striking musical score by Zbigniew Preisner dominates the trilogy, especially the *Blue* part. It replaces dialogue and strengthens the narrative. *Blue*, in fact, is also about music. Julie's late husband was a famous composer who left an unfinished piece devoted to the idea of Europe's unification. At the end of the film, Preisner's music explodes with the "European Concerto," which employs St. Paul's letter to the Corinthians.

The first part of *Blue*, almost purely visual and prominently featuring the color blue and blue objects, sets the tone for the whole film. The cinematographer Sławomir Idziak employs blue filters extensively and neutralizes the cold color blue by the warm color amber. Like the flashes of memory, the color blue bursts onto the screen unexpectedly, strengthened by bits of pieces of the unfinished concerto. These flashes of blue and the bursts of the "European Concerto" that occasionally overtake the screen emphasize the importance of memory.

In *Blue*, Kieślowski attempts to represent mental states that remain the domain of literature, a superior art according to several of his comments. In order to do so, he tries to invent a new cinematic language. To stress the importance of memories that haunt Julie, Kieślowski uses four blackouts—fades to black lasting several seconds before the action resumes from the moment before the blackout. The director employs the obsessions, intensity, and strategies characteristic of art cinema. He also portrays a protagonist typical of art cinema: alienated, sensitive, with psychological problems, and observed during an existential crisis. Like other great art cinema auteurs, Kieślowski is preoccupied with the exploration of his protagonist's mind. The stillness of the screen during blackouts, episodic and random incidents that are both frustrating and puzzling, action that is difficult to predict, and mysterious characters and objects that populate the screen all reflect Julie's "mindscreen," to use Bruce F. Kawin's term,[90] her mental landscape filled with painful emotions. Kieślowski resorts to breaking the visual flow of the action by the blackness of the screen that marks the "return of the repressed"—painful memories associated with the past that Julie attempts to suppress in the name of liberty.

White, the "Polish" part of *Three Colours*, portrays Karol (Zbigniew Zamachowski), a Polish hairdresser living in Paris and going through a bitter divorce with his French wife, Dominique (Julie Delpy). After Karol is (improbably) smuggled into Poland in a suitcase, he quickly amasses a fortune by speculating on land. In order to get even with his wife, he fakes his own death. When Julie appears in Poland to claim his legacy, she is arrested and accused of murdering Karol. In the final scene, a "typical Kieślowskian happy ending," Karol stands outside Dominique's prison, tears in his eyes, exchanging secretive sings.

Most critics discuss *White* as, to use Geoff Andrew's description, "a droll black comedy, complete with such generic staples as missing corpses, cunning schemes and sexual humiliation."[91] Western critics in particular also see the second part of the trilogy, like the earlier *The Double Life of Véronique*, as commenting on the ties between Poland and the West. Paul Coates, for instance, states that *White* "dramatizes Polish fears of exclusion from Europe," and "Karol's impotence may be that of the Pole confronting locked European doors."[92] Such political interpretations of the film seem to be valid—the film includes some penetrating, humorous references to Polish "capitalist reality"—yet this is not the tone of most reviews published in Poland. *White* was discussed there as merely a "comic interlude" within the trilogy, a film devoid of serious examination of Polish reality and filled with suspicious art house clichés.[93]

White paints a bleak vision of the post-1989 Polish state of affairs: a country populated by crooks, nouveaux riches, bandits pretending to be businessmen, foreign currency dealers, thieves at the airport, and backward farmers. "This is Europe now," says Karol's brother (Jerzy Stuhr), explaining the flashy neon sign "Karol" that advertises his "hairdressing salon" located in a dilapidated building near impersonal apartment complexes. Kieślowski's sharp satire on the new capitalist Poland includes several scenes pointing to Karol's "capitalist behavior," for example when he captures the satisfaction on Karol's face as he orders construction workers to knock down the wall surrounding his manor house and build a new one, only four centimeters thicker. He also refers to the powerful role played by the Catholic Church in Poland in the scene of the confrontation between Karol and his boss, who intimidates him at home.

Kieślowski's *Red*, probably the most sophisticated part of the triptych, tells the story of a young fashion model, Valentine (Irène Jacob), and her chance encounter with a retired judge (Jean-Louis Trintignant) who is obsessed with illegal electronic surveillance. The complex relationship that develops between them is at the center of the film. Another character is also introduced, Valentine's neighbor, Auguste (Jean-Pierre Lorit), a young law student whose life mirrors that of the old judge. Kieślowski once commented: "The theme of *Red* is the conditional mood—what would have happened if the judge had been born forty years later."[94] The "what if" structure of several of his earlier films is cleverly retold in *Red*, which offers a game of associations, a story of chance encounters, double chances, mystifying coincidences, and destiny.

At the end of the film, Valentine and Auguste are shown among the mere seven survivors out of the 1,435 ferry passengers, but despite their mysterious connection, emphasized throughout the film, the final freeze frame with the red background suggests that they do not yet know each other: they appear together within one frame but look into different directions. In an attempt to sum up the trilogy, the film also lists additional survivors whose names include the earlier protagonists: Julie and Olivier from *Blue*, as well as Karol and Dominique from *White*. Although Kieślowski is known for his particular understanding of "happy endings," it is not easy to bring together such an idea with the immensity of the tragedy. Several hundred passengers are dead, but the chosen ones, "our protagonists," are saved. As depicted in *Red*, the ending serves almost as a mockery of happy endings and seems to be closer to the realm of disaster genre rather than art cinema.

Kieślowski's *Three Colours* trilogy is ostensibly self-reflective and self-referential. As in *Decalogue*, characters appear and reappear and Van den Budenmayer's music is quoted extensively. Kieślowski remarked that these interconnections are "for the pleasure of some cinephiles who like to find points of reference from one film to another."[95] The director employs chance scenes with no apparent link to the story, rejects causal narrative, and peoples his films with familiar supporting characters. The same tendency toward mannerism is evident in the cinematography and mise-en-scène, including the extensive use of the films' key colors to stress the films' themes, and the reliance on mirror images, filters, and views through windows and doors. Kieślowski made films for cinema buffs; there are more questions than answers in his cinema, and everything here is geared toward mystery.

Tadeusz Szczepański comments:

Kieślowski ingeniously multiplies subtle refrains, parallelism, counterpoints, correspondences, symmetries, echoes, and mirror effects not only on the level of narrative threads, situations, characters or props in the roles of res dramatica, *but also in mise-en-scène, use of color, sound, and, of course, music.*[96]

Another Polish scholar, Grażyna Stachówna, lists recurrent motifs in the trilogy that also refer to Kieślowski's earlier films: "colors, slogans of the French Revolution, blind chance, Van den Budenmayer, voyeurism and eavesdropping, an old woman with a bottle, the final cry of the protagonists, windows, beads made of glass, two frank coin, loneliness, jealousy, humiliation, contempt, sex, suicide."[97]

For many Polish critics, Kieślowski seems to be the true hero in his films. Tadeusz Sobolewski writes that despite Kieślowski's often-declared agnosticism, his films are imbued with strong religious overtones. For instance, the judge in *Red* "becomes simultaneously the figure of Kieślowski and the Lord God as imagined by common folk." Kieślowski abandoned "tales of fictitious characters, much in the same way he had once abandoned the documentary for fiction, for something in a way of an 'inner documentary' attempting to render inexpressible, agnostic states."[98]

* * *

Although Kieślowski's films are unique in the Polish context, one may see a continuation of his cinema in films made by Jerzy Stuhr, such as *Spis cudzołożnic* (*The List of Adulteresses*, 1994) and *Historie miłosne* (*Love Stories*, 1997). *The List of Adulteresses*, with Stuhr in the leading role, tells the story of a middle-aged academic who thinks back on his old girlfriends and women from his past during the official visit of a Swedish academic. Stuhr's film offers not only a nostalgic journey into one man's past but also a loving introduction to the unique character of Kraków.

One of Kieślowski's favorite actors, Stuhr also wrote and directed the 1997 winner of the Festival of Polish Films, *Love Stories*. Kieślowski helped with the script, and the film is dedicated to him. Stuhr presents four parallel stories with four different protagonists: a university teacher, a priest, an army officer, and a convicted thief (all played by Stuhr). They must choose between love and career, between the complications that love might introduce into their lives and the boredom of illusory stability. Stuhr employs an "art film atmosphere," down-to-earth characters facing moral choices, and mysterious, otherworldly figures like the "Master Pollster" (played by Jerzy Nowak) who questions the four protagonists about the true nature of their choices. *Love Stories* resembles a morality play permeated with the very metaphysical ingredients that are so characteristic of Kieślowski's final films.

Stuhr is not alone. Many films made in Poland in the mid-1990s seem to owe their inspiration to Kieślowski's cinema. They include, for example, a series of television films produced by Kieślowski's mentor and friend Krzysztof Zanussi, *Weekend Stories*, which are similar in spirit to *Decalogue*. Another filmmaker often discussed in the context of Kieślowski's legacy is the documentarian Paweł Łoziński, son of the acclaimed Polish documentarist Marcel Łoziński. Paweł Łoziński worked as an assistant to Kieślowski on his *Three Colours* trilogy. His debut, the medium-length television film *Kratka* (*The Manhole*, 1996), was based on Kieślowski's idea and made under his artistic supervision. The story revolves around a fierce competition between a ten-year-old boy and a retired man for a 500 franc banknote found near a central Warsaw hotel. Both characters notice the banknote at the bottom of a manhole and try to retrieve it by either competing or collaborating with each other. The film, however, is not so much about their struggle for the banknote, which because of strange circumstances takes almost the whole day, but about their developing understanding and friendship.

In the late 1990s, Kieślowski's screenwriter Piesiewicz started collaborating with a younger film director, Michał Rosa (1963–), a 1992 graduate of the Katowice Film School. At the time of their meeting, Rosa was known chiefly for his early realistic films, such as the medium-length *Gorący czwartek* (*Hot Thursday*, 1993) and the feature *Farba* (*Paint*, 1997). Rosa's name became associated with painstaking observations of everyday reality, adeptly captured on camera by his cinematographer Mieczysław Anweiler. *Hot Thursday*, written and directed by Rosa, offers a realistic depiction of young delinquent boys from the impoverished parts of Silesia. It portrays mundane reality marked by unemployment, poor living conditions, and lack of perspective. His work received the Best First Film Award at the Festival of Polish Films in Gdynia. He followed this success with another well-received film, the road movie *Paint*, about young people searching for the meaning in life, looking for their own identity. The girl nicknamed Paint (Agnieszka Krukówna) tries to find her grandmother, accompanied by an accidental fellow traveler.

Given Kieślowski's international status and the fact that he occupies a unique position within Polish cinema, it is perhaps expected that several Polish films would contain references to Kieślowski's cinema. Although direct references to Kieślowski films (pastiches, parodies, continuations of his films) had not been frequent in Polish cinema of the 1990s, several films either thematically or stylistically evoked Kieślowskian cinema, or cannibalized it to the point of parodying its characteristic features. For example, as early as in 1993, Rafał Wieczyński wrote, directed, and produced a film whose very title bluntly refers to Kieślowski's preoccupations: *Naprawdę krótki film o miłości, zabijaniu i jeszcze jednym przykazaniu* (*A Truly Short Film about Love, Killing and One More Commandment*, Poland-France). Wieczyński's film, an unconvincing parable loosely referring to Kieślowski's *Decalogue* and two related "short" films is set in a small town in 1989; its thematic and stylistic concerns border on unsophisticated parody of Kieślowski's cinema.

***

Political and economic transformations profoundly affected the Polish film industry in the 1990s. The transition to a market economy changed the relationship between the filmmakers and the state, and between the filmmakers and their audiences. After a period of noticeable crises in the early 1990s, later years brought some moderate optimism: Polish films started to compete successfully with Hollywood on Polish screens. In addition, several established filmmakers regained their popularity and emerging innovative auteurs like Kolski and Krauze found loyal audiences and critical recognition.

Notes

1. See Edward Zajiček, "Kinematografia," in *Encyklopedia kultury polskiej XX wieku: Film, kinematografia*, ed. Edward Zajiček (Warsaw: Instytut Kultury and Komitet Kinematografii, 1994), 93.
2. Monique van Dusseldorp and Raphaël Loucheux, eds., *Towards the Digital Revolution: European Television and Film between Market and Revolution* (Liege: European Institute for the Media, 1994), 50 and 53.
3. *Polish Film Guide 1996/97* (Warsaw: Film Polski, 1997), 9; Barbara Hollender, "Kronika: Bilans roku 1992 w kinach," *Kino* 1 (1993): 2.
4. Ibid.
5. Zajiček, "Kinematografia," 92 and 97.
6. *The Catalogue of the XX Festival of Polish Feature Films in Gdynia* (Gdynia, 1995), 111–15; "Jak powstaje film," *Kino* 11 (1994): 14–16.
7. Krzysztof Kucharski, *Kino plus: Film i dystrybucja kinowa w Polsce w latach 1990–2000* (Toruń: Oficyna Wydawnicza Kucharski, 2002), 385; Krzysztof Kucharski, "Popularność filmów polskich 29.12.95–29.08.96," *Film Pro* 10, no. 18 (1996): 11.
8. Wajda also mentioned this fragment of *Ashes and Diamonds* in his address at the Congress of Polish Film. Andrzej Wajda, "Co się stało z polskim kinem?" *Kino* 2 (1997): 5.
9. Andrzej Wajda, "Wolni od czego?" *Kino* 1 (1992): 3–5.
10. Tadeusz Sobolewski, "Filmy polskie mówią: W tym kraju nic się nie zmieni," a statement of the Polish critic at the Forum of the Polish Filmmakers Association in Gdynia, 1991, *Kino* 1 (1992): 2.
11. Józef Tischner, *Nieszczęsny dar wolności* (Kraków: Znak, 1996).
12. Kazimierz Kutz, "Przestaliśmy istnieć," a fragment of a discussion: "Co z polskim kinem?" *Kino* 11 (1992): 21.
13. Kazimierz Kutz, "Z mojego młyna," *Kino* 7–8 (1995): 70.

14. Wanda Wertenstein and Jerzy Płażewski, "Współprodukcje: Hydra czy szansa," *Kino* 6 (1993): 6–9.
15. For instance, opinions expressed in "Tren na śmierć cenzora," special issue, *Reżyser* 11 (1992): 1–8, published with *Kino* 11 (1992). Also, an interview with writer and filmmaker Tadeusz Konwicki: "Wróżby z dnia dzisiejszego," *Kino* 1 (1991): 5–6.
16. "Tren na śmierć cenzora," 2.
17. Danusia Stok, ed., *Kieślowski on Kieślowski* (London: Faber & Faber, 1993), 151–52.
18. Anita Skwara, "Film Stars Do Not Shine in the Sky over Poland: The Absence of Popular Cinema in Poland," in *Popular European Cinema*, ed. Richard Dyer and Ginnette Vincendeau (London: Routledge, 1992), 230.
19. See Krzysztof Zanussi, "Obrona kosmopolityzmu," *Kino* 2 (1992): 16–18.
20. Larson Powell, "The Moral Microhistory of Post-Communism: Zanussi's *Weekend Stories*," in *European Visions: Small Cinemas in Transition*, ed. Janelle Blankenship and Tobias Nagl (Bielefeld: Transcript, 2015): 285–98.
21. See Andrew Charlesworth, "Contesting Places of Memory: The Case of Auschwitz," *Environment and Planning D: Society and Space* 12, no. 5 (1994): 585.
22. Marczewski's film was the winner of the 1990 Festival of Polish Films in Gdynia. After the introduction of martial law in Poland, as a sign of protest, the director had remained silent for almost ten years ("internal exile" was the Polish term to describe such acts).
23. For more, see Marek Haltof, *Polish Film and the Holocaust: Politics and Memory* (New York: Berghahn Books), 162–64; Libby Saxton, *Haunted Images: Film, Ethics, Testimony and the Holocaust* (London: Wallflower Press, 2008).
24. One of the first attempts to examine the Stalinist period was Janusz Morgenstern's *Życie raz jeszcze* (*Life Once Again*, 1965), based on Roman Bratny's novel.
25. Discussed, among others, in Marek Haltof and Donald Smith, "An Aborted Revolution, a Stillborn Generation: Generational Politics and Gender Relations in Péter Gothár's *Time Stands Still*," *Canadian Journal of Film Studies* 6, no. 2 (1997): 51–64.
26. David Paul, "Hungary: The Magyar on the Bridge," in *Post New Wave Cinema in the Soviet Union and Eastern Europe*, ed. Daniel J. Goulding (Bloomington: Indiana University Press), 207.
27. Anna Lawton, "The Ghost That Does Return: Exorcising Stalin," in *Stalinism and Soviet Cinema*, ed. Richard Taylor and Derek Spring (London: Routledge, 1993), 188.
28. Svetlana Boym, "Stalin Is with Us: Soviet Documentary Mythologies of the 1980s," in Taylor and Spring, *Stalinism and Soviet Cinema*, 201.
29. Piotr Wasilewski, *Świadectwa metryk: Polskie kino młodych w latach osiemdziesiątych* (Kraków: Oficyna Obecnych, 1990), 224.
30. Any list of important Polish documentaries made after the transition to democracy should also include *Nienormalni* (*Developmentally Challenged*, 1990, Jacek Bławut)—the only documentary made in the 1990s with a regular distribution in Poland—and *Usłyszcie mój krzyk* (*Listen to My Cry*, 1991, Maciej Drygas).

31. Konrad Szołajski, "Świat nie przedstawiony," *Kino* 7–8 (1995): 13.
32. Jerzy Płażewski, "Przetrwać cwałem," *Kino* 4 (1996): 18.
33. Mirosław Przylipiak, "Pekosiński jako znak," *Kino* 1 (1994): 44–45.
34. Jan Kidawa-Błoński (born in 1953 in Chorzów, Upper Silesia) often deals with Silesian themes. He started his career with a well-received *Trzy stopy nad ziemią* (*Three Feet above the Ground*, 1983), a film about an engineering student who tries to avoid military service by working in a Silesian coal mine.
35. Bajon discusses the autobiographical aspect of *Street Boys* in a book-length interview: Włodzimierz Braniecki, *Szczun* (Poznań: W drodze, 1998), 132–48.
36. I am referring here to critics' indifference and, consequently, to the fact that Wajda's film did not have a successful theatrical distribution in Poland. This is not the whole picture, however. Polish films were present and very popular on Polish television. Sometimes, as statistics show, they had ten million or more viewers. When *The Ring with a Crowned Eagle* was shown on Channel 1 (Polish State Television), it had 17.6 million viewers. Despite that record number, Wajda's film did not stir any major debates. Jolanta Rodziewicz-Rayzacher, "Raport z Agencji," *Reżyser* 1 (1997): 2–3 and 4, published with *Kino*.
37. At the 1996 Festival of Polish Films in Gdynia, *In Full Gallop* received several awards, including the Best Actress Award for Maja Komorowska and the Special Award with Bajon's *Street Boys* and Krauze's *Street Games* (there was no Grand Prize in 1996).
38. Płażewski, "Przetrwać cwałem," 18.
39. Wasilewski, *Świadectwa metryk*, 101.
40. See, e.g., André Pierre Colombat, *The Holocaust in French Film* (Metuchen: Scarecrow Press, 1993), 299–344; Stefan Korboński, *The Jews and the Poles on World War II* (New York: Hippocrene Books, 1989), 107–25; Jean-Charles Szurek, "Shoah: From the Jewish Question to the Polish Question," in *Claude Lanzmann's Shoah: Key Essays*, ed. Stuart Liebman (Oxford: Oxford University Press, 2007), 149–69.
41. Jan Błoński, "Biedni Polacy patrzą na getto," *Tygodnik Powszechny* (11 January 1987), 1 and 4. For the translation of Błoński's essay and the discussion it initiated in Poland, see Anthony Polonsky, ed., *My Brother's Keeper? Recent Polish Debates on the Holocaust* (London: Routledge, 1990).
42. Błoński, "Biedni Polacy," 1. See also Tomasz Szarota, *Karuzela przy Placu Krasińskich: Studia i szkice z lat wojny i okupacji* (Warsaw: Oficyna Wydawnicza Rytm, 2007).
43. Holland's *Angry Harvest* received an Academy Award nomination for Best Foreign Film. *Europa, Europa* received a Golden Globe Award for Best Foreign Film. The subject matter of this factual story of the survival of Solomon Perel, with its blending of humor and horror and its almost absurdist yet true story, perhaps prompted the Germans to decline to nominate *Europa, Europa* for an Academy Award.
44. Jan Jakub Kolski stressed in an interview that the story presented in *The Burial of a Potato* is authentic and happened to his grandfather, Jakub Szewczyk, a Home Army (AK) officer who survived Auschwitz and was marginalized by the village

after his late return in 1946. The film's protagonist wears the camp uniform with Jakub's actual number from the camp. The subplot regarding Mateusz's son, an officer in the AK who was killed after the war, is also authentic, along with the names of several villagers. The film was shot in the village of Popielawy, the actual place of the postwar drama and a mythologized space in several later films made by Kolski. Marek Hendrykowski, ed., *Debiuty polskiego kina* (Konin: Wydawnictwo Przegląd Koniński, 1998), 312.

45. Jerzy Kosiński, *The Painted Bird* (New York: Harcourt Brace Jovanovich, 1970).
46. See, e.g., Michael Stevenson, "Wajda's Representation of Polish-Jewish Relations," in *The Cinema of Andrzej Wajda: The Art of Irony and Defiance*, ed. John Orr and Elżbieta Ostrowska (London: Wallflower Press, 2003): 76–92. For a more extensive discussion of Wajda's *Korczak* and *Holy Week*, see Marek Haltof, "Andrzej Wajda Responds: *Korczak* (1990) and *Holy Week* (1996)," in Haltof, *Polish Film and the Holocaust*, 187–210.
47. Lawrence Baron, *Projecting the Holocaust into the Present: The Changing Focus of Contemporary Holocaust Cinema* (Lanham, MD: Rowman & Littlefield, 2005), 48.
48. Colombat, *The Holocaust in French Film*, 113–16; Tzvetan Todorov, "Umrzeć w Warszawie," *Kultura Niezależna* 49 (1989), reprinted in *Kino* 7 (1991): 41–42 (trans. Jagoda Engelbrecht).
49. For more comments on *Korczak* and "the French controversy," see Haltof, *Polish Film and the Holocaust*, 191–200; Terri Ginsberg, "St. Korczak of Warsaw," in *Imaginary Neighbors: Mediating Polish-Jewish Relations after the Holocaust*, ed. Dorota Glowacka and Joanna Zylinska (Lincoln: University of Nebraska Press, 2007): 110–34; Omer Bartov, *The "Jew" in Cinema: From* The Golem *to* Don't Touch My Holocaust (Bloomington: Indiana University Press, 2005): 153–58.
50. Jerzy Andrzejewski, *Wielki Tydzień* (Warszawa: Czytelnik, 1993), published in English as *Holy Week: A Novel of the Warsaw Uprising*, trans. Daniel M. Pennell, Anna M. Poukish, and Matthew J. Russian (Athens: Ohio University Press, 2007).
51. For example, Piotr Wojciechowski referring to Wajda's characters employs the term "a symbolic theme park." Piotr Wojciechowski, "Rekolekcje w skansenie," *Tygodnik Powszechny* 12 (1996): 9.
52. Maria Malatyńska, "Między winą a rozgrzeszeniem," *Tygodnik Powszechny* 10 (1996): 13.
53. In Wajda's earlier *A Generation*, the young underground fighters gathering on Krasiński Square near the carousel are members of the communist People's Guard (GL).
54. The subtle Polish title of Kijowski's film, *Tragarz puchu*, means, in direct translation, "a person who carries downy feathers." This title would be more appropriate for this intimate psychological drama than the adopted English title *Warszawa. Année 5703*, which suggests a film of almost epic proportions. A television film with the same Polish title, directed by Stefan Szlachtycz, had been made in 1983 and presented the next year at the Festival of Polish Films in Gdańsk. Kijowski's multinational

production, though far superior in almost every aspect, shares the same weaknesses as its predecessor.
55. Tadeusz Borowski, "Pożegnanie z Marią," the title piece of a collection of short stories, *Pożegnanie z Marią*, first published in Warsaw in 1947.
56. Bożena Janicka, "Coś zostało w powietrzu: Mówi Filip Zylber," *Kino* 3 (1994): 13.
57. Tadeusz Lubelski, "Borowski na dziś," *Kino* 3 (1994): 15.
58. The year 1968 in Poland, as elsewhere in Europe, was marked by student demonstrations. The ban on Adam Mickiewicz's classic romantic drama *Dziady* (*Forefathers*) and the brutality of the police provoked student demonstrations. Some Communist Party members used these events to get rid of old guard communists, many of whom were of Jewish origin. They blamed "Zionist elements" for the eruption of political protests directed against the party. The "anti-Zionist" campaign resulted in not only in purges within the party but also attacks on people of Jewish origin in other spheres of life. The canonized drama by Mickiewicz was adapted for the screen in 1989 by Tadeusz Konwicki as *Lawa: Opowieść o Dziadach* (*Lava: The Story of Forefathers*).
59. Henryk Grynberg (1936–) is a Jewish Polish writer well known for his books about the Holocaust and the fate of Polish Jewry. Several members of his family perished during the war; he and his mother survived, hiding with "Aryan papers." In 1967, Grynberg defected to the United States when his theatrical company, the State Jewish Theater in Warsaw, was on tour.
60. Mirosław Przylipiak, "Polish Documentary Film after 1989," in *The New Polish Cinema*, ed. Janina Falkowska and Marek Haltof (London: Flicks Books, 2003), 155.
61. Marek Edelman is also the narrator of one of the most powerful accounts of the Warsaw Ghetto Uprising, a book by Hanna Krall, *Shielding the Flame: An Intimate Conversation with Dr. Marek Edelman, the Last Surviving Leader of the Warsaw Ghetto Uprising*, trans. Joanna Stasińska and Lawrence Weschler (New York: Henry Holt, 1986).
62. Tomasz Łysak, "O niemożliwej wierze w dokument: *Fotoamator* Dariusza Jabłońskiego," *Kwartalnik Filmowy* 43 (2003): 72; *Od kroniki do filmu posttraumatycznego: Filmy dokumentalne o Zagładzie* (Warsaw: Instytut Badań Literackich PAN, 2016).
63. Tomasz Majewski, "Getto w kolorach Agfa: Uwagi o *Fotoamatorze* Dariusza Jabłońskiego," in *Między słowem a obrazem*, ed. Małgorzata Jakubowska, Tomasz Kłys, and Bronisława Stolarska (Kraków: Rabid, 2005), 334. For a detailed analysis in English, see Frances Guerin, "Reframing the Photographer and His Photographs: *Photographer* (1995)," *Film and History* 32, no. 1 (2002): 43–54.
64. Skwara, "Film Stars Do Not Shine in the Sky over Poland," 230.
65. *The Catalogue of the XX Festival of Polish Feature Films*, 46.
66. Kucharski, *Kino plus: Film i dystrybucja kinowa w Polsce w latach 1990–2000* (Toruń: Oficyna Wydawnicza Kucharski, 2002), 387. Pasikowski's *The Pigs* had 400,505 viewers.

67. Zdzisław Pietrasik, "Broń się: Najbardziej lubimy oglądać amerykańskie filmy polskie," *Polityka* 15 (1997): 72–73.
68. Looking at the box office in the 1990s, Machulski's *Kiler* is third with 2,200,943 viewers, after two historical epics, *With Fire and Sword* and *Pan Tadeusz*. See Appendix B.
69. E.g., a defense of art cinema, Mariusz Grzegorzek, "Żal tak młodo umierać," *Kino* 11 (1994): 12–13.
70. The Polish title of the film, *Psy*, literally means "the dogs." The connotation of "dog" in Polish is pejorative; the word, which implies servility and subhuman qualities, is frequently used to denigrate another person.
71. In a 1996 interview with Zdzisław Pietrasik, Wajda made the following observation on the scene from *The Pigs*: "I understood that something important had happened in Poland, something that may have unforeseeable consequences. That is why I was not surprised with the later election results [the defeat of the pro-Solidarity parties and the victory of the former communists], not to mention the latest presidential elections [the defeat of Lech Wałęsa by Aleksander Kwaśniewski, the former Communist Party member]." Zdzisław Pietrasik, "Andrzej Wajda: Na moich warunkach," *Polityka* 10 (1996): 45–48.
72. *The Catalogue of the XIX Festival of Polish Feature Films in Gdynia* (Gdynia, 1994): 78, reprint from Stanisław Zawiśliński, *Powiedzmy Linda* (Warsaw: Taurus, 1994).
73. Piotr Szulkin, "Psy wieszane non stop," *Kino* 5 (1993): 13.
74. The title of the film, *The Pigs 2: The Last Blood*, clearly refers to the Rambo films of the 1980s: *First Blood* (1982, Ted Kotcheff) and *Rambo: First Blood Part II* (1985, George P. Cosmatos).
75. *The Pigs 2* was the sixth most popular film in the 1990s with more than 684,000 viewers.
76. Manana Chyb, "Otoczony przez niemych Maurów: Rozmowa z Piotrem Szulkinem," *Kino* 4 (1992): 3.
77. I discuss *The Pigs* referring to Meaghan Morris's concept of "positive unoriginality" in "'Amerykańskie kino polskie': *Psy* (1992), pozytywna wtórność i polityczny przekaz," in *Polskie kino popularne*, ed. Piotr Zwierzchowski and Daria Mazur (Bydgoszcz: University of Bydgoszcz Press, 2011), 177–86.
78. *The Spinning Wheel of Time* was virtually a family enterprise. Andrzej Kondratiuk was the writer-director-star and co-cinematographer of this film. His wife, Iga Cembrzyńska, a well-known actor-singer, acted as producer-star. Among the few actors in this intimate film is Janusz Kondratiuk (1943–), Andrzej's brother, a director known mostly for his distinguished television films made in the spirit of an early Miloš Forman, for example, his cult film in Poland, *Dziewczyny do wzięcia* (*Marriageable Girls*, 1972). He also made full-length films in the 1990s, including *Głos* (*The Voice*, 1992) and *Złote runo* (*The Golden Fleece*, 1997).

79. See Iwona Guść, "Polish Film Culture in Transition: On the 'Private Films' of Andrzej Kondratiuk (1985–1996)," in *European Visions: Small Cinemas in Transition*, ed. Janelle Blankenship and Tobias Nagl (Bielefeld: Transcript, 2015), 299–316.
80. Tadeusz Sobolewski, "Realizm Andrzeja Barańskiego," an interview with Barański, *Kino* 11 (1992): 12.
81. See Aga Skrodzka, *Magic Realist Cinema in East Central Europe* (Edinburgh: Edinburgh University Press, 2012).
82. Jerzy Krysiak, "Bunt Don Juana," *Konkurs* 4–5 (1991): 6.
83. Maciej Maniewski, "Między miłością a dojrzałością," an interview with Barbara Sass, *Kino* 6 (1996): 6.
84. The awards for *Three Colours* include the Golden Lion for *Blue*, the Best Actress Award for Juliette Binoche, and the Best Photography Award for Sławomir Idziak at the Venice Film Festival. *White* received the Silver Bear at the Berlin International Film Festival (Best Director). Although *Red* received no award at Cannes (the grand prize, the Palme d'Or, was given to Quentin Tarantino for *Pulp Fiction*), it received numerous other awards, including three Academy Award nominations in 1995 (direction, screenplay, and cinematography), four BAFTA nominations (direction, screenplay, actress, and non-English language film), and several other festival awards.
85. Tadeusz Sobolewski, "Peace and Rebellion: Some Remarks on the Creative Output of Krzysztof Kieślowski," *Polish Cinema in Ten Takes*, ed. Ewelina Nurczyńska-Fidelska and Zbigniew Batko (Łódź: Łódzkie Towarzystwo Naukowe, 1995), 124.
86. Ibid., 125.
87. Mirosław Przylipiak writes about the reception of Kieślowski's films in Poland, "Filmy fabularne Krzysztofa Kieślowskiego w zwierciadle polskiej krytyki filmowej," *Kino Krzysztofa Kieślowskiego*, ed. Tadeusz Lubelski (Kraków: Universitas, 1997), 213–47; "Monter i studentka," *Kino* 3 (1997): 6–9 and 50.
88. Jonathan Romney, "The Double Life of Véronique," *Sight and Sound* 1, no. 11 (1992): 43.
89. Gaylyn Studlar, "The Double Life of Véronique," *Magill's Cinema Annual 1992: A Survey of the Films of 1991*, ed. Frank N. Magill (Pasadena, CA: Salem Press, 1992), 120.
90. Bruce F. Kawin, *Mindscreen, Godard, and First-Person Film* (Princeton, NJ: Princeton University Press, 1978).
91. Geoff Andrew, *The "Three Colours" Trilogy* (London: BFI, 1998), 38.
92. Paul Coates, "The Sense of Ending: Reflections on Kieślowski's Trilogy," *Film Quarterly* 50, no. 2 (1996–1997): 23–24.
93. The titles of several reviews published in Polish major journals are self-explanatory: Tadeusz Sobolewski, "Równanie w dół. *Trzy kolory. Biały*" [Downward: Three Colours: White], *Kino* 2 (1994): 10–11; Piotr Lis, "Chłód" [Cold], *Kino* 6 (1994): 16; Piotr Mucharski, "Bez koloru" [Without color], *Tygodnik Powszechny* (27 March 1994): 11.
94. Stok, *Kieślowski on Kieślowski*, 218.

95. Serge Mensonge, "Three Colours: *Blue, White* and *Red*—Krzysztof Kieślowski and Friends," interview, *Cinema Papers* 99 (1994): 30.
96. Tadeusz Szczepański, "Kieślowski wobec Bergmana, czyli Tam, gdzie spotykają się równoległe," in *Kino Krzysztofa Kieślowskiego*, ed. Tadeusz Lubelski (Kraków: Universitas, 1997), 165.
97. Grażyna Stachówna, "*Trzy kolory*: Wariacje na jeden temat," in Lubelski, *Kino Krzysztofa Kieślowskiego*, 102.
98. Sobolewski, "Peace and Rebellion," 136 and 123.

CHAPTER 10
Adapting the National Literary Canon and Reclaiming the Past (1999–2004)

Toward the end of the 1990s, the film industry in Poland was less than perfect: it combined elements of the pre-1989 cinema with the free market economy. The five state-owned and Warsaw-based film studios remained active: Filip Bajon's Dom, Tadeusz Chmielewski's Oko, Janusz Morgenstern's Perspektywa, Krzysztof Zanussi's Tor, and Juliusz Machulski's Zebra. They produced films and supported themselves by having legal rights to films made before 1989. Among numerous, but mostly small, private production companies, some began to play an important role in the Polish cinema industry, for example, Dariusz Jabłoński's Apple Film Production, Lew Rywin's Heritage Films, and Waldemar Dziki's Pleograf. Television, both state-owned—Polish State Television (Telewizja Polska SA)—and private channels (such as Canal Plus and HBO) continued to play essential roles in invigorating the industry.

In addition to the well-established state schools, the Łódź Film School and the Katowice Film School, two new private professional film schools launched their operations in Warsaw. Andrzej Wajda's Master School of Film Directing (Mistrzowska Szkoła Reżyserii Filmowej Andrzeja Wajdy) was founded in November 2001 by Wajda, Wojciech Marczewski, and the Documentary and Feature Film Studio in Warsaw, under the honorary patronage of the European Film Academy. Unlike existing film schools, its instruction has been based on project development and practical issues. The school has produced numerous short films and documentaries that won awards at major film festivals.

The actor Bogusław Linda and the director Maciej Ślesicki founded another training ground, the Warsaw Film School (Warszawska Szkoła Filmowa), in 2004. Later, in 2011, the school became a vocational film college under the patronage of the Ministry of Culture and National Heritage. Aside from its founders, the school has been home to numerous distinguished teachers and film professionals, including the film directors Krzysztof Zanussi, Filip Bajon, Wojciech Wójcik, Andrzej Titkow, and Jan Kidawa-Błoński; the cinematographers Andrzej Jaroszewicz and Andrzej Ramlau; and the actors Sonia Bohosiewicz and Beata Fudalej. The school's intensive courses emphasize the practical aspect of filmmaking, and cover nine areas ranging from directing and screenwriting to cinematography and editing.

In 1999, members of the Polish Film Academy (Polska Akademia Filmowa) granted the first Polish Film Awards "Eagles" (Polskie Nagrody Filmowe "Orły"). Similar to the Academy Awards, Polish films are awarded in eighteen categories. The first winners in the Best Film category include *The History of Cinema Theater in Popielawy* (Jan Jakub Kolski, 1998), *Dług* (*Debt*, Krzysztof Krauze,1999), *Życie jako śmiertelna choroba przenoszona drogą płciową* (*Life as a Fatal Sexually Transmitted Disease*, Krzysztof Zanussi, 2000), *Cześć Tereska* (*Hi, Tereska*, Robert Gliński, 2001), *The Pianist* (Roman Polański, 2002), *Zmruż oczy* (*Squint Your Eyes*, Andrzej Jakimowski, 2003), and *Wesele* (*The Wedding*, Wojciech Smarzowski, 2004). In addition, the Polish Film Academy members annually select the Best European Film shown on Polish screens, and present the Lifetime Achievement Award. The latter was awarded to some of the most accomplished Polish filmmakers, including Wojciech J. Has, Andrzej Wajda, Roman Polański, Kazimierz Kutz, and Jerzy Kawalerowicz.

From 1999 to 2004, a period dominated by big-budget adaptations of the national literary canon, Polish cinema also received prestigious international awards. For example, in 2000, Andrzej Wajda received the Academy Honorary Award. In 2002, Roman Polański's Holocaust epic *Pianista* (*The Pianist*, France-Poland-Germany-UK) received international acclaim and three Academy Awards, including Best Director. Another film, Krzysztof Krauze's biopic *Mój Nikifor* (*My Nikifor*, 2004) received critical acclaim in Poland and won top prizes at the international film festivals in Chicago and Karlovy Vary. Earlier, in 2000, Krzysztof Zanussi's *Life as a Fatal Sexually Transmitted Disease*, a continuation of his earlier meditations on death, was announced the winner of the Moscow International Film Festival.[1]

Nostalgic Heritage Cinema: Adaptations

After overcoming the rough transitional period in the early 1990s, a group of well-established Polish filmmakers, whose names are often synonymous with Polish national cinema, succeeded in winning back their audiences toward the end of the decade. Their commercial success came with films that were always popular in Poland—lavish adaptations of the Polish national literary canon.[2] Thanks to Jerzy Hoffman's *Ogniem i mieczem* (*With Fire and Sword*) and Andrzej Wajda's *Pan Tadeusz*, which together had more than thirteen million viewers in 1999, Polish cinema shared an unprecedented 60 percent of the local market. The success of Polish films prompted the influential *Rzeczpospolita* film critic, Barbara Hollender, to title her review article "Hoffman and Wajda won over Hollywood."[3] Another prominent critic, Zbigniew Pietrasik of the weekly *Polityka*, proclaimed in his 1999 article the long-awaited "true victory" of Polish cinema.[4]

Poor financial results in 2000, despite a small group of remarkable films, were blamed on the lack of big-budget literary adaptations. This situation prompted some filmmakers to choose the much-traveled path and rely on well-known literary sources. Thus, the beginning of this century brought new adaptations of Henryk Sienkiewicz: *Quo Vadis* (2001, Jerzy Kawalerowicz), clearly the most expensive Polish film ever made with its budget of almost $18 million, and *W pustyni i w puszczy* (*In Desert and Wilderness* (2001, Gavin Hood).[5] Other adaptations, labeled in Poland as belonging to the "cinema of school canon," followed quickly: Stefan Żeromski's novel *Przedwiośnie* (*Early Spring*, 2001, Filip Bajon),[6] Aleksander Fredro's classic play *Zemsta* (*Revenge*, 2002, Andrzej Wajda), and Józef Ignacy Kraszewski's popular pseudohistorical novel *Stara baśń* (*The Old Tale*, 2003, Jerzy Hoffman). Like earlier adaptations, these films also successfully competed with Hollywood products and dominated the box office: *Quo Vadis* (4.3 million viewers), *In Desert and Wilderness* (2.2 million viewers), *Revenge* (1.9 million viewers), and *Early Spring* (1.7 million viewers). They left behind a prominent group of (mostly) American films such as *Shrek, Bridget Jones's Diary, Cast Away,* and *Pearl Harbor*.[7]

The popularity of local historical adaptations is reflected by the statistical data; the ten most popular films released in Poland after 1989 include three Polish adaptations topping the list: *With Fire and Sword, Pan Tadeusz,* and *Quo Vadis*. In addition, there are six adaptations of canonical literary works among the fifteen most financially successful Polish films from 1990 to 2015.[8] Perhaps these impressive figures prompted Dina Iordanova to comment, "If one looks at the wider European context, Poland's record in producing heritage cinema may yield only to France and Britain."[9] However, contrary to frequently voiced opinions about the dominant role of contemporary adaptations of the Polish literary canon after 1989, these films form merely 25 percent of the total local film production.

Their enormous popular appeal also does not match their critical acclaim. For example, among fourteen Grand Prix awards at the annual Festival of Polish Films from 1989 to 2005, only three went to film adaptations (the main prize was not awarded in 1989, 1991, and 1996).

Although adaptations do not constitute most films produced in Poland, do not receive important festival awards, and are relatively unknown outside Poland, they are the most prominent part of the Polish film industry in terms of their popularity and prestige. How shall we then look at the successes of Polish adaptations in 1999 and after? How do we explain the nostalgia for Sienkiewicz in postcommunist Poland? How can we explain the popularity of works written in a different epoch in order to promote "national self-assertion and pride, which compensated for the collective low esteem and feeling, stemming from continuous defeats on the battlefield"?[10]

In an article on Polish adaptations, symptomatically titled "In the Land of Noble Knights and Mute Princesses: Polish Heritage Cinema," Ewa Mazierska applies the term "heritage cinema" (although this is not the term used by Polish film critics and scholars) to a group of historical films based on masterpieces of Polish literature, and focuses her attention on *With Fire and Sword* and *Pan Tadeusz*. Mazierska examines these films almost as commentaries on problems permeating contemporary Poland, as a reflection of the dominant Polish ideology and of the state of Polish cinema. She also analyzes these films as part of a "nostalgia business" that attempts to achieve the impossible—to create an imaginary "land of noble knights and mute princesses." Mazierska stresses that the popularity of heritage films in Poland "can be largely explained by the anxieties and uncertainties Poland experienced after the collapse of communism and introduction of the market economy."[11] Furthermore, she notices that heritage films, which are partly subsidized and fiercely promoted by the state as "national events," support the dominant "conservative ideology" and help to affirm Polish national identity experiencing profound crisis. Mazierska concludes her highly critical analysis of Polish adaptations by saying that local "heritage films typically create an image of Poland in days gone by as a feudal and patriarchal country, where loyalty to one's motherland and the Catholic faith was regarded as of the highest value. This Poland is idealized by the films' authors and thus (albeit indirectly) they elevate the political forces that facilitate and strengthen nationalism, Catholicism, patriarchy, sexism and elitism." She concludes by stressing that Polish heritage cinema "promotes a conservative, reactionary ideology."[12]

It is difficult to argue with Mazierska's comments. To a certain degree, the popularity of Polish heritage films reveals frequently voiced fears of exclusion from Europe, the difficulty of Poles finding themselves in a new political situation, and skepticism concerning contemporary politics and politicians. Furthermore, if we look at Merchant/Ivory historical films and follow Andrew Higson's much-quoted description of British heritage cinema of the 1980s, the similarities between the two are striking.[13] Heritage films are, largely, lavish "quality" productions relying on reputable literary works, offering slow-paced pastoral images, revealing the same fascination with the romanticized past, and dealing with the upper-class milieu. Like their British counterparts, Polish adapters of the national literary canon favor safe literary works set in an equally safe history. Their films do not deconstruct the past or stir up vitriol. Instead, they offer romantic, nostalgic images of the past and rely on the popularity of their literary sources for success.

Aspiring to make big-budget "quality pictures," Polish filmmakers, however, produce film adaptations inferior to Hollywood products, despite their growing budgets, epic scopes, local stars, and thousands of extras. These films' spectacular sets, colorful costumes, and household literary names in the credits provide only "signs of art." Audiences are reassured rather than challenged. Despite the cinema industry's large-scale publicity machine that stresses the contemporary relevance of a given literary work (see numerous interviews with Wajda concerning his adaptation of *Pan Tadeusz* and *Revenge*), audiences are taken to places that bear little significance to the present but that for many Poles represent the stereotypical, nostalgic images of "Polishness." According to a *Polityka* film critic, the mass audience watching *With Fire and Sword* proves that contemporary Poles are "modern but without a modern ideology."[14]

In the past, Polish intellectuals frequently objected to Sienkiewicz's vision of history and tried to eradicate the national image he promoted. Although such reservations were frequently voiced, they had been marginalized in the state of almost "national euphoria" that surrounded the release of Polish heritage films. Their box office success also had to do with aggressive media campaigns, unprecedented by Polish standards. Several scholars analyzed this aspect, the sociological and cultural phenomena of mass pilgrimages to see *Pan Tadeusz* and *With Fire and Sword*. These films' promotional campaigns constituted a marketing achievement in themselves, with the involvement of the Polish press, critics, and cultural organizations inside and outside of Poland, emphasizing that it would be almost "unpatriotic" not to see films such as *Pan Tadeusz* and *With Fire and*

Sword.[15] Interestingly, the promotional campaign had not only been reserved, traditionally, to film journals and tabloid press. For example, *Gazeta Wyborcza*—a leading Polish daily newspaper—published more than five hundred articles about *With Fire and Sword*.[16]

* * *

According to the makers of Polish heritage films, their films performed a very important nation-building task. For example, in 2002 Jerzy Hoffman commented: "In a year, 20 films are produced and five per cent of them are historical films. And we are happy that this five per cent of these films are based on Polish history. In two or three years we will join the European Union [Poland joined the EU in 2004]. There are huge opportunities for unification and communication. But what will differ us will be our culture, our history and our traditions."[17] Hoffman also revealed in an interview after the premiere of *With Fire and Sword* that he intended to produce a "Polish-Ukrainian version of *Gone with the Wind* ... a story of great passions, of human fates thrown into the tragic whirlpool of civil war."[18] Unlike Sienkiewicz's novel, however, Hoffman's film promotes reconciliation between Poland and Ukraine via, among other things, the elimination of several scenes, which would be offensive to contemporary Ukrainians. Ewa Hauser argues persuasively that "this film's popularity reflects the desire on the part of the Polish audience to revise the eastern mission myth, and redefine the borders of Polishness."[19] Likewise, Andrzej Wajda commented on the vital role that heritage cinema plays in contemporary Poland. Elżbieta Ostrowska fittingly summarizes Wajda's attempts in *Pan Tadeusz* by saying that his "effort aims to save the landscapes of collective memory from oblivion and to create in the contemporary collective consciousness of Poles a little space for the shadows of ancestors not to be forgotten."[20]

A *Central Europe Review* critic noticed that Hoffman's film, "with its depiction of a territorially powerful Polish state, use of well-loved Polish novel as a source and its sheer epic scale and box-office prowess, might make it a candidate for a 'nationalist' film."[21] In several interviews, however, the director strongly rejected this notion, and, interestingly, liberally minded film critics in Polish debates surrounding the release of Hoffman's film carefully avoided the word "national" (*narodowy*) because it had been appropriated by the Polish political right. Wajda, however, did not seem to be afraid of the term when he emphasized that his film celebrates Polishness and is the result of a nostalgic yearning for a lost home.[22] The image of a stork that appears in the last shots of *Pan Tadeusz*, that clichéd emblem of tranquil rural Poland, serves as a visual exclamation mark (perhaps redundant?) for this very Polish film.

The commercial success of Polish adaptations of the national literary canon is usually guaranteed. These films serve many generations of Poles as handy, albeit sometimes naive, illustrations of the national literature and the national past. Schools (schoolchildren on cinema trips in particular) make extensive use of them. Their artistic merit as films, however, is questionable. *Pan Tadeusz, With Fire and Sword*, and several other adaptations fare poorly among those who lack familiarity with their literary sources and the elaborate knowledge that surrounds their literary and political contexts. Unlike most English heritage films, popular on the international art house circuit and shown in mainstream theaters, the films by Wajda and Hoffman are specifically Polish products, incomprehensible to outsiders. The bigger budgets, and the competition between Polish blockbusters have proved difficult for some Polish film producers to recoup their films' growing production costs through domestic sales alone.

Reclaiming the Past

Several films made at the beginning of the new millennium dealt with the blessing and the curse of the local national cinema: its preoccupation with history. Like Barbara Sass's *Temptation* (1995), Teresa Kotlarczyk's *Prymas: Trzy lata z tysiąclecia (The Primate: Three Years Out of the Millennium*, 2000) stirred debates about the communist past by telling the story of communist authorities' internment of the Polish Catholic primate Stefan Wyszyński (Andrzej Seweryn). The communist past also returns in *Tam i z powrotem (There and Back*, 2002, Wojciech Wójcik), an absorbing political drama set in the 1960s. This film, which won Wójcik a Best Director Award at the Festival of Polish Films in Gdynia, tells the story of a Polish physician (Janusz Gajos) who uses desperate measures to be reunited with his English wife and daughter. Another film, *Weiser* (2001, Wojciech Marczewski), an adaptation of a critically acclaimed novel by Paweł Huelle, also deals with the 1960s. It introduces several middle-aged characters who try to fathom what happened to their childhood Jewish friend, David. His mysterious disappearance brings back conflicting memories about the past. This is not, however, a film about politics, Jewish-Polish relations, or Jewish history but, as stated by several Polish critics, a "film about mystery."

Jewish-Polish relations and the Holocaust are represented in four films from that period. In 2000, attempting to broaden his oeuvre, Jan Jakub Kolski directed the Holocaust drama *Daleko od okna* (*Keep Away from the Window*). Three years later, he also adapted Witold Gombrowicz's novel *Pornografia* (*Pornography*), saturating the film with references to the Holocaust.[23] *Keep Away from the Window*, based on Hanna Krall's short story published in 1994 and based on real events, revolves around a young woman, Helusia, born in 1943. Several years later, she learns that her biological mother was a Jewish woman, Regina, who hid in her parents' apartment during the war. The childless couple, Jan and Barbara, sheltered Regina, and when she became pregnant with Jan, Barbara pretended to be an expecting mother for the outside world and, after the birth of a baby girl, took the child as her own. In July 1944, before the Soviets entered the city, Regina disappeared, and the Polish couple raised the child and refused to give it to the mother who settled in Hamburg after the war. The mature Helusia tries to establish a relationship with her birth mother, but Regina rejects her because she wants to forget that nightmarish part of her life.

The bulk of *Keep Away from the Window* is set in the claustrophobic interiors of a house belonging to the Polish couple. The first scenes, taking place before the war, introduce the couple whose lack of a child appears to be the main concern. The film moves quickly to the war period, which is announced by a brief scene with jerky images of an empty baby carriage and fleeing people, among them Hassidic Jews. During the occupation, despite his wife's objections, Jan shelters Regina in his studio and in a huge wardrobe, which occupies the center of their living room. Regina is told to keep away from the window and to hide in the wardrobe when guests are coming, in particular during the often-unexpected visits by a blue police officer, Jodła. Several point-of-view shots employed throughout the film (Arkadiusz Tomiak's cinematography) reflect Regina's perspective from inside the wardrobe.

Kolski interrupts the realistic narrative of his film to insert three highly stylized, dreamlike images of a shtetl. When Regina hides in a wardrobe and starts calmly singing, two flashbacks take her to images of a dwarfed shtetl community—a girl is standing among miniature houses, half her size. The scenery may resemble Chagall's paintings. It may also symbolize Regina's mental landscape: her yearning for a happier place, a nostalgic return to her roots (although she is an assimilated

Jewess). Although Kolski's film was often hailed as the best film released locally in 2000, it nevertheless was distributed in five copies and had only 6,700 viewers.[24] The film also never received much deserved exposure at the international film festival circuit partly because of its unfortunate timing. It was released soon after the Polish premiere of an Oscar-nominated Czech film, *Musimé si pomahát* (*Divided We Fall*, 2000, Jan Hřebejk), a domestic drama about a young childless couple hiding a Jewish man, their former neighbor David.

Kolski followed *Keep Away from the Window* with an adaptation of Witold Gombrowicz's novel *Pornography*, published in 1966. The film's action takes place during German occupation and revolves around two middle-aged Warsaw *literati*, the film's narrator, Witold, and his companion Fryderyk (Krzysztof Majchrzak), who are visiting their friend, involved in underground activities. Kolski infuses Gombrowicz's narrative with references to the Holocaust and moves Fryderyk's character to the center of the film. As the viewer learns toward the end of the film, Fryderyk failed to save his half-Jewish daughter, Hela, who died in a concentration camp. After the Germans arrested her, Fryderyk somehow managed to follow her to the camp on the same transport train. When she recognized him at the entrance to the camp, however, he hid from his own child because he was paralyzed by fear and brutalized by the whole ordeal. After a successful escape from the camp, all his encounters were marked by the burden of the past. Unable to carry on, and trying to redeem himself, he commits suicide.

Two prestigious coproductions dealing with the Holocaust, *Boże skrawki* (*Edges of the Lord*, 2001) and *The Pianist*, were made by Polish émigré directors, Yurek Bogayevicz and Roman Polański, respectively, on location in Poland, and with substantial Polish involvement. Actor turned director Yurek Bogayevicz (1948–) left Poland in 1976 for the United States, where he made, among others, two well-received films—*Anna* (1987) and *Three of Hearts* (1992). His first film made in Poland, the American-Polish coproduction *Edges of the Lord*, shares many similarities with earlier Polish Holocaust narratives about hiding, in particular with films featuring a child's point of view of the war, for example, *Birth Certificate*. Set in 1942, the story of *Edges of the Lord* follows an eleven-year-old Jewish boy, Romek (Haley Joel Osment), whose parents send him away from the Kraków Ghetto to the countryside.[25] Pretending to be a farmer's nephew from the city, Romek stays in the village, passing for a Catholic. A local priest (Willem Dafoe) knows the child's secret but allows Romek to participate in preparations for the first communion. Portrayed unconventionally in the context of Polish cinema, the priest teaches Romek the Catholic catechism but respects his Jewish background. The priest also encourages children to replay some scenes from the life of Jesus to learn their catechism. To their surprise, the children discover that Jesus was Jewish but are unaware of Romek's Jewishness.

Polish critics praised Bogayevicz's ability to work with child actors but voiced their reservations concerning the film's clichéd story line, superficiality of the characters, and some artificiality regarding the representation of the rural community. At the 2011 Festival of Polish Films in Gdynia, the film was perceived as an American product. It is in English (with the exception of a Polish prayer in the church) with (often) fake Polish accents, has recognizable American stars, and offers an "external look" at the Polish countryside that is captured by Paweł Edelman's camera in a picturesque manner, as if evoking distant childhood memories.[26]

The Pianist (2002)

Roman Polański's celebrated Holocaust drama, *The Pianist*, is based on the memoirs written by the Jewish Polish composer and pianist Władysław Szpilman (1911–2000) and published for the first time in an abbreviated, censored version in 1946.[27] Polański's Polish, French, and British coproduction in English premiered at the Cannes Film Festival, where it won the Golden Palm. Among numerous awards that *The Pianist* later received are three Academy Awards: Best Director (Polański), Best Adapted Screenplay (Ronald Harwood), and Best Actor (Adrien Brody).[28]

The Pianist, Polański's second film made in Poland since his 1962 debut, *Knife in the Water*, also marks his first cinematic return to his own wartime childhood experiences. Polański was born in 1933 in Paris to a family of Polonized Jews who returned to Poland two years before World War II. He survived the war by escaping from the Kraków Ghetto and hiding in the Polish countryside (his mother died in a concentration camp). Polański often stated that he became attracted to Szpilman's account of survival because the book described events that he remembered from his own childhood in the Kraków Ghetto, the experiences he extensively discussed in his memoir, *Roman by Polanski*.[29] Earlier, Polański never cinematically returned to the places associated with his childhood trauma, although critics analyzed several of his films through the prism of his biography. Critics often attributed certain elements of his cinema, namely the prevailing

Figure 10.1 Adrien Brody as Szpilman (center) and his family in Roman Polański's *The Pianist* (2002). Screenshot by the author.

images of the violent and the grotesque, to darker sides of Polański's life (such as surviving the Holocaust and the murder of his wife, Sharon Tate). Like *The Pianist*, in which Szpilman and his family lose control over their fate and experience entrapment in the ghetto, some of Polański's earlier films, most notably *Repulsion* (1965) and *Le Locataire* (*The Tenant*, 1976), deal with the loss of personal space and its impact on the protagonist.

The Pianist opens with a brief documentary prologue featuring black-and-white shots of prewar Warsaw and then introduces the twenty-eight-year-old Szpilman (in Adrien Brody's memorable performance) playing Chopin in the final broadcast of the Polish Radio on 23 September 1939. The concert continues despite the bombardment of the city and is abruptly terminated only when a bomb hits the station. Polański's film continues to narrate the linear story of Szpilman's survival in the Warsaw Ghetto, the separation from his family at the *Umschlagplatz*, his escape from the ghetto and hiding on the Aryan side, and his ordeal after the Warsaw Rising in the city that became destroyed and desolate. *The Pianist* ends with postwar scenes portraying Szpilman resuming his work for the Polish Radio and trying to learn about the fate of Captain Hosenfeld (Thomas Kretschmann), one of many people who helped him to survive.[30]

Following most Polish Holocaust films, Polański portrays in *The Pianist* an assimilated middle-class Jew who, like Korczak, is both Polish and Jewish, proudly bearing the emblems of the two nationalities and being respected by both. The beginning of the occupation separates him from the Poles, brutally reminds him of his Jewishness, castigates him as the "other," and imperils his life. His friends, "the poor Poles" from the Aryan side, watch his misery and try to help him. In the film, Szpilman is portrayed not as a heroic man but as a character overwhelmed by the reality that surrounds him. He survives because of a combination of blind chances and sheer luck. He is portrayed as a helpless eyewitness to the horrors that are difficult for him to comprehend. Brody's understated performance brings to mind Tadeusz Borowski–like detachment and irony. The camera is on Brody when he wanders the streets of Warsaw; it registers his transformation from a successful middle-class musician to a hunted fugitive in desperate search for shelter and food. With luck on his side, he survives random executions and is able to meet some honest people—Poles, Jews, and a German officer—who make his survival possible.

Polański resorts to long shots to portray Szpilman's loneliness. For example, after he is separated from his family at the *Umschlagplatz*, where he witnessed them and other Jewish people being herded onto the train, he walks in despair on a desolated street, surrounded by belongings left behind by those who were sent to death camps. Another memorable shot, an extreme long shot, depicts Szpilman crawling over the ghetto wall and entering the almost completely destroyed part of Warsaw. The camera portrays him as a twentieth-century, urban Robinson Crusoe amid the ruins of Warsaw.

In *The Pianist*, Szpilman seems almost detached "as if he himself was watching a film."[31] He "meanders through the confined space of the ghetto and of Warsaw and he looks obliquely through windows, small gaps and around corners at the catastrophe, he never sees the totality of the action, the complete picture, and neither do we."[32] The viewer follows Szpilman during his odyssey through Warsaw and witnesses the horror of destruction. Szpilman is a passive observer of atrocities in the ghetto, and later, from his shelter on the Aryan side, he watches the Warsaw Ghetto Uprising. The passivity of Szpilman's character, so vehemently criticized by communist authorities immediately after the war, still seems to trouble some critics who would like to see a "man of action" rather than a passive spectator. Comments stressing that Szpilman's character "learns nothing from his horrific experiences" follow this line of criticism, which prevented Szpilman's story from being adequately portrayed in 1950.[33]

After Kieślowski

Despite Krzysztof Kieślowski's frequent remarks on early filmmaking retirement due to fatigue and health problems, his premature death in 1996 came as a profound shock to the Polish filmmaking community.[34] He died at the age of fifty-four, at the peak of his artistic powers and, despite his much-heralded retirement from filmmaking, embarking on a new project with his long-time collaborator, screenwriter Krzysztof Piesiewicz. They started working on another trilogy of films titled *Raj* (*Heaven*), *Piekło* (*Hell*), and *Czyściec* (*Purgatory*). It is likely that Kieślowski never intended to direct the new trilogy, but he wanted to supervise the project. He wrote the first part, *Heaven*, together with Piesiewicz, and Piesiewicz wrote the next two parts after the director's death. Tom Tykwer's *Heaven*, first shown at the 2002 Berlin International Film Festival, also polarized Polish film critics who largely discussed the degree of fidelity to the spirit of Kieślowski's cinema, and considered Tykwer almost a director working on behalf of Kieślowski. Although Tykwer's film had several recognizable elements of Kieślowski's last works (slow pace, art film atmosphere, ambiguous ending, lyricism, hypnotic photography, and a story about deadly choices, among others), most of these critics said it did not duplicate the earlier experience. In 2005, Danis Tanović directed the second installment of the trilogy in France, *L'enfer* (*Hell*), which also received mixed reviews.

In 1998, Piesiewicz authored another trilogy in the spirit of Kieślowski: *Wiara-Nadzieja-Miłość* (*Faith-Hope-Love*), originally written for Italy's national public broadcasting company, RAI. Stanisław Mucha, a Polish actor and director who has resided in Germany since 1995, directed the trilogy's first part, *Nadzieja* (*Hope*), which received lukewarm reviews after its premiere at the 2007 Festival of Polish Films in Gdynia. For a careful reader of Polish film journals and websites, it was noticeable that Piesiewicz's continuation of his screenwriting career after Kieślowski's death came as a surprise to some Polish critics who, perhaps, expected to close that chapter of Polish cinema.

The collaboration between Piesiewicz and Michał Rosa resulted in the production of *Cisza* (*Silence*, 2001), based on Piesiewicz's script, a film that was well received by the judges at the 2001 Festival of Polish Films in Gdynia but that failed at the box office.[35] *Silence* opens with brief scenes set in 1978 in Łódź that introduce a young boy who, while playing pranks with his friends, unintentionally causes a deadly car accident. The action then moves to 2000 and focuses on Szymon (Bartosz Opania), the boy responsible for the accident twenty-two years ago, who befriends Mimi (Kinga Preis), the girl who survived the car crash, in which both her parents were killed. Szymon, whose guilty conscience prevents him from living a "normal life," is unable to get over the past. For many years, he acts like a "silent angel," watching Mimi and trying to help her. The film juxtaposes two different characters living worlds apart. Mimi has several attributes of the new Polish managerial class: nice apartment, car, and clothes and a lifestyle for which she sacrifices her personal life. To live a "successful modern life," she has no time for love or for her young daughter, who is staying with her grandmother. Mimi is portrayed as cold on the surface, showing no emotions, relaxing in dance halls playing techno music, and preferring casual sex over long-term relationships. Thanks to the encounter with Szymon, her repressed memories from childhood come back, and she embarks on a journey of self-discovery and embraces her motherhood. Unlike Mimi, Szymon lives a modest existence as a railroad engineer of cargo trains. As depicted in the film, he most probably missed the speedy Polish transformation after 1989. Is Szymon's character really a patient and understanding angel, a sinner trying to save his and his "victim's" soul, or is he perhaps a stalker infatuated with Mimi? Unimpressed by the film, Andrew James Horton writes that it "depicts a victim of stalking who uncovers the obsessive relationship after a chance friendship turns out to have more intense and premeditated origins" and that "its portrayal of a woman falling in love with her stalker will be morally sickening and insensitive and outweigh Piesiewicz's otherwise worthy aims."[36] *Silence* aspires to possess the metaphysics of *The Double Life of Veronique*, yet is preoccupied with realistic depiction. The film is also abundant with metaphorical images that stress the role of mystery and fate.

Although Kieślowski's films are unique in the Polish context, several critics see the legacy of his cinema in films directed by Jerzy Stuhr: *Tydzień z życia mężczyzny* (*A Week in the Life of a Man*, 1999), *Duże zwierzę* (*The Big Animal*, 2000), and *Pogoda na jutro* (*Tomorrow's Weather*, 2003). In *A Week in the Life of a Man*, Stuhr casts himself as the public prosecutor Adam Borowski, who is eager to prosecute others yet in his private life is equally guilty. He has an extramarital affair, attempts to avoid paying taxes, and does not understand his wife's (Gosia Dobrowolska) urge to adopt a child. The contrast between the public and private sphere of life and the subtle criticism of the emerging postcommunist middle class in Poland are stressed by the ironic use of a line from *Hamlet,* sung in a song composed by Wojciech Kilar. The choir, to which the prosecutor belongs, rehearses several times "What a piece of work is a man," an ironic comment on the duality of the main protagonist.

Stuhr's later film, *The Big Animal*, is based on a script written by Kieślowski in 1973. This black-and-white film (Paweł Edelman's cinematography) tells the story of a simple office worker, Mr. Sawicki (Stuhr), who, despite problems with his neighbors and the authorities, takes care of a camel that was abandoned by a wandering circus. The camel clearly serves as a poetic metaphor of tolerance and personal freedom in Stuhr's realistic observations of small-town mentality. What Kieślowski (and the writer Kazimierz Orłoś, the author of the short story) originally envisioned as a surreal story about the absurdities of the communist bureaucracy and about intolerance Stuhr adapted into a poetic tale that lacks historical context and extensively refers to Kieślowski's realistic and metaphysical films.[37]

Polish critics often stressed that Iwona Siekierzyńska's first major film, *Moje pieczone kurczaki* (*My Roast Chicken*, 2002), the sixty-three-minute television production, is a feminist version of Kieślowski's classic *Camera Buff*. Although at first glance this assumption may seem exaggerated, several characteristics justify such a comparison. In the center of Siekierzyńska's film is a young protagonist with a camera, Magda (Agata Kulesza), trying to impose her cinematic perspective on the world that surrounds her, attempting, in a distinct style, to tell the story of the psychological condition of her own (as well as Siekierzyńska's) generation of thirty-somethings. Although narrated differently from Kieślowski's classic, Siekierzyńska's film revolves around similar issues, among them the finding of self-fulfillment through filmmaking. The film deals with the marital crisis of a couple who have just returned to Poland (Łódź) from an unsuccessful (as hinted in the film) attempt to settle permanently in Canada and who struggle with everyday problems, such as the inability to find employment, lack of money, and, consequently, housing problems (they stay with Magda's mother). The modern, dynamic narration of Siekierzyńska's film, with its set of problems pertinent to postcommunist Poland, helped this film to become a prime example of what Polish critics describe (or perhaps overstate) as the new Polish cinema made by the "Pokolenie 2000" (Generation 2000). The term refers to a successful series of medium-length films directed by talented young directors and produced by Polish State Television and the Irzykowski Film Studio. They include debuts such as *Moje miasto* (*My Town*, 2002, Marek Lechki), *Bellissima* (2001, Artur Urbański), and *Inferno* (2001, Maciej Pieprzyca).

In several young filmmakers' first films, the viewer may find reminiscences of Kieślowski's early attempts to uncover the gray yet somehow photogenic aspect of communist Poland. For example, Leszek David's short film produced by the Łódź Film School, *Moje miejsce* (*My Place*, 2004), may be discussed in the context of Kieślowski's *Personnel*. The spirit of the "late Kieślowski," full of metaphysical associations, can be found in films such as *Trzeci* (*The Third*, 2004), directed by Jan Hryniak (1969– , married to Kieślowski's daughter, Marta), which at first glance deliberately refers to Polański's *Knife in the Water*. The reworking of Polański's classic, however, replaces the young hitchhiker with an angel-like character played by Marek Kondrat ("the third" of the title). He accompanies a young, financially successful couple on their yachting vacation. He helps Paweł (Jacek Poniedziałek) and Ewa (Magdalena Cielecka), sometimes against their will, to overcome their marital crisis, and meddles in their private affairs. This intriguing film by Hryniak, while remaking Polański's canonical work, moves it to the realm of Kieślowski's Polish-French-Swiss coproductions.

References to Kieślowski, bordering on parody of his aesthetic choices, may be found, interestingly, in films directed by his former actors. For example, in *Chłopaki nie płaczą* (*Boys Don't Cry*, 2000, Olaf Lubaszenko), the director, known outside of Poland mostly for his breakthrough role of Tomek in Kieślowski's *A Short Film about Love*, quotes the ending of *Three Colours: White* in one of the final scenes: the bandit behind prison bars is exchanging mysterious signs with his girlfriend, who is standing outside of the prison. Earlier she had given him a hand-knitted red sweater. *Superprodukcja* (*Super Production*, 2003, Juliusz Machulski) features another clear reference to Kieślowski. In this bitter comedy, which targets the Polish film industry, an uncompromising young film critic, Yanek Drzazga (Rafał Królikowski), is forced to direct a film, an epic super production, for mafia bosses. Artur Barciś, the actor known for his role as the enigmatic angel-like character who appears in some decisive scenes of *Decalogue*, comes into view several times, when the main protagonist is about to make an "important decision," such as calling or not calling an escort agency. In another scene, when the film critic sends a negative review as an email attachment, the camera frantically follows the electronic impulse in the way Kieślowski opened *Red*: a psychedelic sped-up sequence filmed with an extensive use of Steadicam.

Despite the infrequent dissenting voices questioning Kieślowski's legacy, he is still not only remembered but also highly respected in his own country. Although it is difficult to talk about the "Kieślowski school of cinema" in Poland, the international stardom that he achieved in the art house world functions as an inspiration for younger Polish filmmakers. He also serves as an inspiration for those who believe in the concept of auteurism in cinema.

Independent Cinema: Rebellion and Images of Poverty

Although the most prominent in terms of popularity, film adaptations did not constitute most films produced in Poland. Among thirty-one films competing for awards at the 2001 Festival of Polish Films in Gdynia were works inspired by Quentin Tarantino, such as *Sezon na leszcza* (*Sucker Season*, Bogusław Linda); action films bordering on self-parodies, such as *Reich* (Władysław Pasikowski), starring Bogusław Linda; and highly personal, poetic cinema by Lech Majewski (*Angelus*) and Witold Leszczyński (*Requiem*).

The most visible, however, were twelve films by first-time directors, including six films made independently outside of the existing funding system, often with tiny budgets, filmed on location and with the use of digital cameras. Anna Jadowska and Ewa Stankiewicz, both recent graduates of the Łódź Film School, directed *Dotknij mnie* (*Touch Me*, 2003), a low-budget, realistic film revolving around young people searching for love and acceptance in the grim scenery of the realistically portrayed Łódź. A new group of directors, however, whose names are not among the graduates of the established film schools, entered the film industry. First works by Jacek Borcuch, Bodo Kox, Piotr Matwiejczyk, and Przemysław Wojcieszek, among others, not only received awards at different "off-cinema" festivals but were also praised by mainstream film critics for their realistic, albeit habitually harsh, portrayal of the new capitalist Polish reality. The scenery from Kieślowski's *Decalogue*—ugly, postcommunist apartment buildings—returns powerfully in a group of films of uneven quality, often featuring nonprofessional actors, MTV style editing, vulgar language, an abundance of social problems, and contempt for "quality cinema." *Blok.pl* by actor-director Marek Bukowski, ... *Że życie ma sens* ... (*... That Life Makes Sense* ....) by Grzegorz Lipiec, and others deal with the plight of people who inhabit impersonal building complexes (*blokowiska*), once considered the pride of the former communist system.

Of particular importance are independently made films by writer-director (also a playwright and a theater director) Przemysław Wojcieszek (1974–) and photographed by the experienced and accomplished cinematographer-director of documentary films Jolanta Dylewska. Wojcieszek's *Zabij ich wszystkich* (*Kill Them All*, 1999) and *Głośniej od bomb* (*Louder than Bombs*, 2002) introduce nonconformist young Poles who oppose "the system" and struggle in the new reality, yet desperately try to find a place for themselves in their own country instead of considering emigration. Polish critics commended Wojcieszek for his fresh portrayal of Poland as the place to be for young people, for his sincerity, and, interestingly, for (an unusual in Polish cinema) a dose of optimism that his characters demonstrate despite facing some overwhelming odds. In *Louder than Bombs*, for example, a twenty-one-year old Marcin (Rafał Maćkowiak) tries to envision his future on the day of his father's funeral. A university dropout who lives in a small provincial town, Marcin is a fan of James Dean and the Smiths, and is in love with Kasia (Sylwia Łuszczak), who is about leave Poland to study in Chicago. Marcin must bury his father (his mother is long dead) and convince his girlfriend to stay with him in their small, gloomy town and to live "louder than bombs." A *Gazeta Wyborcza* reviewer aptly commented:

> *This is a strong voice of the younger generation. Instead of whimpering about the hopeless life that young people lead among housing blocks or confusing himself with unsuccessful formal experimentation, Wojcieszek finally gives us a film with guts, an interesting story line and a slightly anarchic and somewhat grim sense of humor. ... He treats his characters seriously, but a note of irony is easily perceptible throughout this work. There is no masochism here, no excessive Hamletizing, just drama mixed with comedy. ... It has been long since we have seen a Polish film that would be so formally fresh, yet so mature in the manner in which it examines the world. Though the director treats his protagonists seriously, his retelling of their adventures is anarchic and somewhat grimly humorous.*[38]

Wojcieszek continued such portrayal later in *W dół kolorowym wzgórzem* (*Down the Colorful Hill*, 2005), for which he received the Best Director Award in Gdynia, and in *Doskonałe popołudnie* (*A Perfect Afternoon*, 2005, released in 2007).

The same degraded reality—devoid, however, of optimism—is also present in a powerful film made by an established director, Robert Gliński (1952–). His realistic black-and-white film *Hi, Tereska*, the winner of the 2001 Festival of Polish Films in Gdynia and a winner at the Karlovy Vary International Film Festival, is among the best Polish films made at the beginning of the new millennium. Featuring nonprofessional actors in the leading roles, this tragic coming-of-age story deals with fifteen-year-old Tereska (Aleksandra Gietner). Humiliated and unable to adjust to a brutal world, the girl becomes a murderer of a person in a wheelchair, whom she earlier befriended.

Action Cinema and Comedy

Some Polish action films, such as *Night Graffiti* (1997, Maciej Dutkiewicz) and *Prawo ojca* (*Father's Law*, 1999, Marek Kondrat), continued a long tradition of films dealing with the necessity of taking the law into one's own hands. In *Night Graffiti*, an inconsistent yet popular film, the captain of an elite army troop and his friends from the military fight a war against drug dealers. Captain Kossot, played by Marek Kondrat, in what is almost a continuation of his earlier role from the television series *Extradition*, is an avenger in the inner-city asphalt jungle. *Night Graffiti* also shows the corruption of a high-ranking police officer who, in the film's finale, is killed in a cover-up to preserve the good name of the police force. The first screen appearance of Kasia Kowalska, a young Polish rock star, as a troubled drug addict contributed to this film's commercial success. However, according to a *Kino* critic, *Night Graffiti* is still "devoid of a scrap of probability, an ersatz youth action film."[39]

One may certainly find a better example of an "ersatz youth action film" in Jarosław Żamojda's 1995 directorial debut, *Fast Lane*, and its 1998 sequel, *Fast Lane 1/2*. The plot describes the dilemmas of the new generation, teenagers who face their first adult choices. "An intelligent person has money" is the advice given to Robert, the best student in a high school class, prompting the young wolf[40] to join a gang of smugglers operating between Poland and Germany. *Fast Lane* and *Night Graffiti* are works without secrets, clumsy imitations of American genres made purely for entertainment. When compared with them, the much-criticized classic film *The Pigs* appears not only professionally made but also multidimensional and very Polish, despite its borrowings from American cinema.

Marek Kondrat's directorial debut, *Father's Law* (in which he plays the role of a single father avenging his teenage daughter), develops the theme of police corruption and ineffectuality, the topic present later in films such as *Pitbull* (2005, Patryk Vega) and its continuations, and *Drogówka* (*Traffic Department*, 2013, Wojciech Smarzowski). In the final scenes of Kondrat's film, the victorious yet wounded protagonist addresses the prosecutor and the police officer: "Where are you when they kill people? Law is for ordinary people, not for bandits." The thematic similarities between *Father's Law* and *Dirty Harry* (1971, Don Siegel) have been stressed by Polish critics, for example, by Zdzisław Pietrasik in his *Polityka* article entitled "Brudny Marek" (Dirty Marek).[41] The very title of Kondrat's film, with its biblical connotations, suggests that the father has the right to avenge his daughter's sufferings and to protect her. His methods, though not approved by law, help to restore "good, old values" endangered by the liberal policy makers. *Father's Law* received the Audience Award at the 1999 Festival of Polish Films in Gdynia, a sure testimony that this film, in addition to its well-executed American accent, also articulated some of the pressing problems of the postcommunist reality.

Well-written, "serious" action and suspense films, such as *Ostatnia misja* (*The Last Mission*, 2000, Wojciech Wójcik) and *Stacja* (*Station*, 2001, Piotr Wereśniak), usually feature major stars of Polish cinema, for example, Bogusław Linda, Katarzyna Figura, and Zbigniew Zamachowski in the latter. Crime comedies continued to be popular as well, including works by actor-director Olaf Lubaszenko (1968–). In addition to appearing in numerous films such as the successful Polish-Czech production *To Kill Sekal* (1997), Lubaszenko began his career as a film director with a crime comedy, *Sztos* (*The Sting*, aka *Polish Roulette*, 1997). *The Sting* was followed by several popular films, mostly unsophisticated crime comedies, such as *Boys Don't Cry, Poranek kojota* (*The Morning of Coyote*, 2001), and *E=mc²* (2002). They all tell entertaining but unrefined stories, introduce likeable although clichéd and petty characters, and feature popular Polish actors, including Cezary Pazura, Maciej Stuhr, and Edward Linde-Lubaszenko (Olaf's father).

In addition to Lubaszenko's films, other films popular with audiences proved to be absurdist crime comedies, such as the postmodernist comedy *Ciało* (*Body*, 2003, Tomasz Konecki and Andrzej Saramonowicz) and *Show* (2003, by Maciej Ślesicki). The latter is set in the world of television reality shows and stars Cezary Pazura. Established director and screenwriter of all his films, Juliusz Machulski maintained popularity with a stylish heist film set in Kraków, *Vinci* (2004), which became also a breakthrough film for one of the best contemporary Polish actors, and the face of the new Polish cinema, Robert Więckiewicz.

Dzień świra (*The Day of the Wacko*, 2002), an outrageously funny comedy by writer-director Marek Koterski, won much deserved acclaim in Poland. Koterski is chiefly known for a series of exhibitionist, largely autobiographical, bitter satires featuring Adam (or Michał) Miauczyński (the name may indicate whining). Miauczyński is an unfortunate loser with intellectual pretensions who suffers from never-ending midlife crises and permanent writer's block. Cezary Pazura, the lead actor in Koterski's 1996 film, *Nothing Funny*, also starred in his next comedy, *Ajlawju* (*I Love You*, 1999). *The Day of the Wacko*, however, relies heavily on the performance of Marek Kondrat, an actor who had also appeared in Koterski's 1984 satire, *Dom wariatów* (*The House of Fools*). In *The Day of the Wacko*, Kondrat plays another incarnation of Miauczyński—a middle-aged teacher of Polish language

Figure 10.2 Marek Kondrat as Adam Miauczyński (near the window) in Marek Koterski's *The Day of the Wacko* (2002). Screenshot by the author.

who is struggling with himself, his environment, unruly neighbors, the stupidity of his compatriots, and life in Poland in general.[42] Miauczyński—in a way a product and a victim of the previous political system—comments constantly on his neurotic behavior and his allergy to the outside world. The language is in the center of this film—its leitmotif and the main character.[43]

The obsessive-compulsive character played by Kondrat is described by a *Variety* reviewer as a "a histrionic misanthrope that makes Jack Nicholson's turn in *As Good as It Gets* look positively serene. Though many of the barbs seem aimed at particular Polish sacred cows and more than a few sequences fall flat, sheer chutzpah alone should propel this unique item to brave fests and perhaps a bit of business."[44] Despite its roughness, *The Day of the Wacko* was very successful at the 2002 Festival of Polish Films in Gdynia, where it received the main prize. Polish critics also complimented the director for his apt portrayal of the unrefined Polish reality.

Unfriendly Capitalist Landscapes

Awarded the Grand Prix at the 1999 Festival of Polish Films in Gdynia, Krzysztof Krauze's celebrated psychological thriller about the weakness of law, *Debt*, refers to a well-publicized event. A group of young entrepreneurs, unable to secure a loan from a bank, borrow money from mobsters in order to import scooters to Poland. At a certain point, the gangster they deal with tries to collect a nonexistent debt and turns violent. Out of desperation, the protagonists take the law into their own hands, kill the thug debt collector and his bodyguard, and dispose of their bodies. For their deed, they receive long-term sentences. Although the psychological relations between the young businessmen and the gangster are at the center of Krauze's film, it took part in a national discussion concerning the weakness of the law, the helplessness of ordinary citizens facing a corrupt underworld, and the links between organized crime and the political elite.

The dark aspects of the emergent Polish capitalism—the world full of dirty money, greed, drugs, and a rat race mentality—are featured in several films released during this period. Some are satires on politics, such as *Bajland* (2000), directed by the documentary filmmaker Henryk Dederko, with Wojciech Pszoniak as a cynical Polish presidential candidate, and *Kariera Nikosia Dyzmy* (*The Career of Nikoś Dyzma*, 2002), Jacek Bromski's mockery of politics and political elites. The latter film, focusing on a simpleton (Cezary Pazura) who forges an astonishing political career, is inspired by Tadeusz Dołęga-Mostowicz's 1932 novel and a popular television series from 1980 (under the same title and starring Roman Wilhelmi) directed by Jan Rybkowski and Marek Nowicki.

Several films revolve around young characters who work for major international cooperations and rapidly adapt to the new Polish-style capitalist reality but pay a heavy price for their success. Films such as *Billboard* (1998, Łukasz Zadrzyński), *Egzekutor* (*Executor*, 1999, Filip Zylber), *Amok* (*Stupor*, 1999, Natalia Koryncka-Gruz), *Pierwszy million* (*First Million*, 2000, Waldemar Dziki), and *Nie ma zmiłuj* (*No Mercy*, 2000, Waldemar Krzystek) portray an unflattering, cruel world ruled by fast money and moral relativism. *O dwóch takich, co nic nie ukradli* (*The Two Who Did Not Steal Anything*, 1999, Łukasz Wylężałek) depicts an equally unattractive Polish province by focusing on characters who display all the negative features that are usually associated with the past communist system. Piotr Trzaskalski's debut, *Edi* (2002), the recipient of several awards at the Festival of Polish Films in Gdynia, introduces a middle-aged homeless person, Edi, played by Henryk Gołębiewski, a former child actor known for his roles in the 1970s in the films directed by Janusz Nasfeter and Stanisław Jędryka. Edi survives by collecting scrap metal with another outsider, his friend Jureczek (Jacek Braciak). Trzaskalski places them in a hostile and dangerous landscape, and he idealizes the saintly protagonist by portraying him as gentle, selfless, and bookish.

Auteur Cinema

Several filmmakers/auteurs continued to pursue their own vision of cinema. One of them is Lech Majewski (born in 1953 in Katowice), who is truly a renaissance man: film, theater, and opera director; screenwriter, cinematographer, and producer; writer, poet, and painter. The multitalented Majewski graduated from the Łódź Film School in 1977, established himself as a theater director, and became known for his intensely personal, poetic, and highly stylized cinema, as evidenced by *Rycerz* (*The Knight*, 1980). In 1981, he moved to England and then to the United States, where he made *Flight of the Spruce Goose* (1985) and *The Gospel According to Harry* (1992, with Polish involvement). He also made another international coproduction, *The Prisoner of Rio* (1988, UK, Brazil, Switzerland, and Poland), and several video installations.⁴⁵

Arguably, Majewski's best-known work in Poland is *Wojaczek* (1999), an atypical, unsentimental biopic of the Silesian poet Rafał Wojaczek (1945–1971), for which he received the best director award at the Festival of Polish Films in Gdynia. This black-and-white episodic film covers select events from the turbulent and self-destructive life of Wojaczek (played by another Silesian poet, Krzysztof Siwczyk) that was ended prematurely in suicide. The film is not only about Wojaczek's downfall and his struggles with the grim reality of the late 1960s in Poland, but above all about rebellion.

Majewski's next film, *Angelus* (2001), deals with a Silesian occult group that became known thanks to some of its members, such as Teofil Ociepka, now a celebrated painter. It was photographed by Adam Sikora (also the cinematographer of *Wojaczek* and frequent collaborator of Majewski) who won the Silver Frog for this film at the Camerimage festival. Majewski's later projects include *The Garden of Earthly Delights* (2003, Poland-Italy-UK) and *Szklane usta* (*Glass Lips*, 2007). His 2010 art film in English, *Młyn i krzyż* (*The Mill and the Cross*, 2011, Poland-Sweden), proved to be his biggest critical success at several film festivals. Majewski's hypnotic and lavish film essay recreates "The Way to Calvary," Pieter Bruegel the Elder's 1564 masterpiece, and examines the painter's (Rutger Hauer) creative work and the times in which he lived in Flanders. In line with several other American critics, Daniel M. Gold praised the film in his *New York Times* review as "an inspiring, alluring meditation about imagery and storytelling, the common coin of history, religion and art." He added:

Figure 10.3 Rutger Hauer in Lech Majewski's *The Mill and the Cross* (2011). © Lech Majewski, 2010. Published with permission.

> *It isn't the artist, it's the art that's the star here, and Mr. Majewski lavishes sophisticated, enchanting detail on its re-creation. He's painting cinematically, shooting in Europe and New Zealand for the right locations and applying several layers of technology: blue screen, backdrops, digital footage.*[46]

In 2000, Krzysztof Zanussi returned to the theme of death—present in his earlier films, beginning with his student work, *The Death of a Provincial*—in his multi-award winning *Life as a Fatal Sexually Transmitted Disease*. The story revolves around a terminally ill physician, Tomasz Berg, played memorably by one of Zanussi's favorite actors, Zbigniew Zapasiewicz. Andrew James Horton reported after seeing Zanussi's film at the Karlovy Vary International Film Festival:

> *Zanussi's early work from the late 1960s and 1970s explored the soul-searching of young men, usually scientists, as they tried to grapple with themselves and the world around them and find a place for themselves in life. Życie jako śmiertelna choroba continues these metaphysical journeys, although with a protagonist whose age is closer to that of the 62-year-old director. … Zanussi is a devout Catholic (he has filmed the Pope's official biography and acts as his special cultural advisor), and while you can watch his early films and not know the way Zanussi has answered his own existential quests, Życie jako śmiertelna choroba is distinctly a piece of Catholic proselytizing. However, if you can accept that the film chooses a limited philosophical framework, it is an absorbing and thought-provoking film. My fellow viewers at the screening I*

attended seemed to be clearly affected by the film's reflective nature, and the film's eschewal of the formal devices and vertiginous photography that gives, say, Constans *bite means that the film is stripped back to its screenplay, written by Zanussi himself. In an age that worships directing talent as the most supreme in the film world, it is refreshing to see a director who chooses to express himself primarily through a strongly written, well-constructed script.*[47]

Zapasiewicz also stars in Zanussi's next film, the bitter political satire *Persona non grata* (2005), as a Polish ambassador in Uruguay grieving over the sudden death of his wife. Also featuring Jerzy Stuhr, Nikita Mikhalkov, and Andrzej Chyra, this film garnered four Festival of Polish Films awards. Despite modest critical attention paid to Zanussi's recent films,[48] he still plays a very important role in Polish cultural life. He is not only a film director and screenwriter but also a stage and opera director, film professor at the Katowice Film and Television School, teacher at several universities in Poland and abroad, columnist, head of Tor since 1979, and a member of several international professional organizations.

One of the biggest critical successes of 2004 was Krzysztof Krauze's *My Nikifor* (*Mój Nikifor*), a biography of the well-known "naive painter" Nikifor Krynicki (1895–1968), played by actress Krystyna Feldman. The story of Nikifor is told from the perspective of a professional painter, Marian Włosiński (Roman Gancarczyk), who gives up his own career and sacrifices his personal life in order to become Nikifor's caretaker and promoter. Feldman, mostly known for dozens of strong supporting roles, delivers a striking performance as a "primitive" painter. As Renata Murawska writes: "Small-framed, with hair sticking out of his/her ears, broken glasses and mumbling to him/herself incomprehensibly, Feldman's Nikifor is a masterpiece of transgender acting."[49]

The years 2003 and 2004 marked the emergence of several new, talented directors. With his debut film, *Warszawa* (*Warsaw*, 2003), Dariusz Gajewski won several awards, including Golden Lions and the Best Director Award, at the Festival of Polish Films in Gdynia. His well-narrated, multilayered film deals with five different characters whose paths cross while visiting Warsaw. In 2004, the year Poland joined the European Union, the winner of the Gdynia festival was Magdalena Piekorz's first film, *Pręgi* (*The Welts*), a tense psychological drama about a father-son relationship. The screenwriter-director of documentary and feature films Małgorzata Szumowska debuted with *Szczęśliwy człowiek* (*Happy Man*, 2000), but she received critical attention with her next film, *Ono* (*Stranger*,

2004), which tells the story of a pregnant woman trying to prepare her baby for the outside world. Together with Wojciech Smarzowski, who started his career with The Wedding (2004), Andrzej Jakimowski, whose debut was Squint Your Eyes (2003), and several other auteurs, she will define the next decade.

Notes

1. The annual Gdynia Film Festival, which presents Polish feature films, was organized for the first time in Gdańsk in 1974 as the Festival of Polish Films in Gdańsk. In 1996, the festival moved to the neighboring town of Gdynia. In 2011, the festival changed its name to Gdynia Film Festival (Gdynia—Festiwal Filmowy). The festival grants its main prize, the Golden Lion (Złote Lwy), as well as other awards in several different categories (ranging from best direction to costumes).
2. For more on this issue, see Marek Haltof, "Adapting the National Literary Canon: Polish Heritage Cinema," *Canadian Revue of Comparative Literature / Revue Canadienne de Littérature Comparée* 34, no. 3 (2007): 298–306; Marek Haltof, "Narodowe nostalgie: Uwagi o współczesnych adaptacjach klasyki literackiej," in *Najnowsze kino polskie*, ed. Piotr Zwierzchowski and Daria Mazur (Bydgoszcz: University of Bydgoszcz Press, 2007), 79–87.
3. Barbara Hollender, "Hoffman i Wajda wygrali z Hollywood: Podsumowanie roku 1999 w polskich kinach," *Rzeczpospolita* 21 (26 January 2000): 8.
4. Zdzisław Pietrasik, "Opakowanie zastępcze: Czy *Ogniem i mieczem* nadal krzepi?" *Polityka* 16 (1999): 52.
5. The budget of *Quo Vadis* amounted to 68 million zlotys (approximately $18 million). In terms of budget, Kawalerowicz's film was followed by *With Fire and Sword* and *Early Spring*. Tadeusz Kowalski, ed. "Raport o stanie kultury: Kinematografia—W kierunku rynku i Europy" (Warsaw: Ministerstwo Kultury i Dziedzictwa Narodowego, 2009), 9, http://www.kongreskultury.pl/library/File/RoSK%20 kinematografia/kinematografia_kowalski.pdf.
6. In 2010, Bajon made a modern adaptation of the 1832 play by Aleksander Fredro, *Śluby panieńskie (Maiden Vows)*, which had more than one million viewers.
7. Barbara Hollender, "Amerykanie kontratakują: Rok 2002 w polskich kinach," *Rzeczpospolita* 302 (30 December 2002): 8; Barbara Hollender, "Więcej widzów, więcej niepokoju," *Rzeczpospolita* 302 (27 December 2001): 8.
8. "Top 20: Filmy polskie 1990–2015," in *Polskie filmy 2016* (Warsaw: PISF, 2016), 181. See Appendix B.
9. Dina Iordanova, *Cinema of the Other Europe: The Industry and Artistry of East Central European Film* (London: Wallflower Press, 2003), 49.

10. Ewa Hauser, "Reconstruction of National Identity: Poles and Ukrainians among Others in Jerzy Hoffman's Film *With Fire and Sword*," *The Polish Review* 14, no. 3 (2000): 306.
11. Ewa Mazierska, "In the Land of Noble Knights and Mute Princesses: Polish Heritage Cinema," *Historical Journal of Film, Radio and Television* 21, no. 2 (2001): 168.
12. Ibid., 180.
13. For example, the following works by Andrew Higson: "Re-presenting the National Past: Nostalgia and Pastiche in the Heritage Film," in *Fires Were Started: British Cinema and Thatcherism*, ed. Lester Friedman (Minneapolis: University of Minnesota Press, 1993); *Waving the Flag: Constructing a National Cinema in Britain* (Oxford: Oxford University Press, 1995); *English Heritage, English Cinema* (Oxford: Oxford University Press, 2003).
14. Pietrasik, "Opakowanie zastępcze," 53.
15. Zygmunt Kałużyński and Tomasz Raczek, "Aria na ściśniętym gardle," *Wprost* (10 February 2000): 18.
16. Hauser, "Reconstruction of National Identity," 309.
17. Andrew James Horton, "Tales of Hoffman," *Central Europe Review* 3, no. 14 (23 April 2001). http://www.ce-review.org/01/14/kinoeye14_horton.html.
18. Hauser, "Reconstruction of National Identity," 310.
19. Ibid., 306.
20. Elżbieta Ostrowska, "Landscape and Lost Time: Ethnoscape in the Work of Andrzej Wajda," *Kinoeye* 4, no. 5 (2004), www.kinoeye.org/04/05/ostrowska05.php.
21. Horton, "Tales of Hoffman."
22. Tadeusz Lubelski, "Radość i melancholia *Pana Tadeusza*," *Kino* 11 (1999): 28.
23. For a more detailed discussion of Jan Jakub Kolski's Holocaust films, Yurek Bogayevicz's *Edges of the Lord*, and Roman Polański's *The Pianist*, see Marek Haltof, *Polish Film and the Holocaust: Politics and Memory* (New York: Berghahn Books), 166–71 and 173–80.
24. Krzysztof Kucharski, *Kino plus: Film i dystrybucja kinowa w Polsce w latach 1990–2000* (Toruń: Oficyna Wydawnicza Kucharski, 2002), 387.
25. Several Polish reviewers noticed that the choice of the main character's name, Romek, is not accidental in the film and bears strong resemblance to Roman (Romek) Polański's story of survival.
26. Interestingly, Bogayevicz received the Best Screenplay Award at the Gdynia Film Festival, and the film received nominations in several categories for the Polish Film Awards "Eagles." *Edges of the Lord* was theatrically released in Poland and several other Western European countries. In the United States, however, the film was released only on DVD, and as late as 2005, which is surprising given the presence of two American stars, Osment and Dafoe.
27. Władysław Szpilman, *Śmierć miasta: Pamiętniki Władysława Szpilmana*, ed. Jerzy Waldorff (Warsaw: Wiedza, 1946). Fragments of Szpilman's memoirs appeared earlier, in 1946, in the Polish journal *Przekrój*. The censor changed the nationality

of Captain Hosenfeld from German to Austrian. Born in Sosnowiec, Władysław Szpilman established himself as a composer and pianist. Before World War II, he worked in Polish radio. During the war, he performed in a duet with Artur Goldfeder in the Warsaw Ghetto cafés. Since 13 February 1943, he was hiding on the Aryan side, where he survived the Warsaw Uprising and its aftermath until January 1945, when the Soviets entered the city. After the war, he returned to the radio, founded the Warsaw Quintet, and performed in Poland and abroad. He is also the author of dozens of popular Polish songs. In 2004, Marek Drążewski made a biographical, medium-length documentary about Szpilman's life, *Władysław Szpilman 1911–2000: In His Own Words* (*Władysław Szpilman 1911–2000, własnymi słowami*).

28. In addition, *The Pianist* won eight Polish Film Awards "Eagles," including best film, director, cinematographer (Paweł Edelman), set designer (Allan Starski), music (Wojciech Kilar), costume designer (Anna Sheppard), and editor (Jean-Marie Blondel). The film also won three BAFTA awards, seven French César Awards, and Edelman won the European Film Award for Best Cinematography.
29. Roman Polański, *Roman by Polanski* (New York: William Morrow, 1984), 21–35.
30. Marek Drążewski in his documentary film *Dzięki niemu żyjemy* (*We Owe Him Our Lives*, 2008) covered the sad irony of Hosenfeld's life, the officer who died in 1952 in a Soviet camp, as *The Pianist*'s postscript informs the viewer.
31. Wojtek Kość, "Weirdness through Simplicity: Roman Polanski's *The Pianist*," *Kinoeye* 2, no. 20 (2002). http://www.kinoeye.org/02/20/kosc20.php.
32. Michael Stevenson, "*The Pianist* and Its Contexts: Polanski's Narration of Holocaust Evasion and Survival," in *The Cinema of Roman Polanski: Dark Spaces of the World*, ed. John Orr and Elżbieta Ostrowska (London: Wallflower Press, 2006), 149.
33. Michael B. Oren, "Schindler's Liszt: Roman Polanski's Mistake about the Holocaust," *The New Republic* 228, no. 10 (2003): 25.
34. For a more detailed discussion of this issue, see Marek Haltof, "Still Alive: Krzysztof Kieślowski's Influence on Post-Communist Polish Cinema," in *After Kieślowski: The Legacy of Krzysztof Kieślowski*, ed. Steven Woodward (Detroit: Wayne State University Press, 2009): 19–33.
35. *Silence* received the Best Director Award and the Best Actress Award for Kinga Preis. The film also received the Best Actress Award for Kinga Preis and the Ecumenical Jury Award at the 2002 Karlovy Vary International Film Festival.
36. Horton, "Tales of Hoffman." Perhaps the same can be said, however, about some earlier characters of Kieślowski and Piesiewicz, for example, the voyeur Tomek in *A Short Film about Love* and the manipulative puppet master Alexandre in *The Double Life of Véronique*.
37. See Renata Murawska, "Turning Director: Jerzy Stuhr Does Jerzy Stuhr," in Woodward, *After Kieślowski*, 58–61.
38. Tomasz Tiuryn's review of *Głośniej od bomb* in *Gazeta Wyborcza* (13 December 2002), http://culture.pl/en/work/louder-than-bombs-przemyslaw-wojcieszek.
39. Konrad J. Zarębski, "Zwyczajny cynizm," *Kino* 3 (1997): 34.

40. The original Polish title, *Młode wilki*, literally means "young wolves."
41. Zdzisław Pietrasik, "Brudny Marek: Samotny mściciel w polskich realiach," *Polityka* 6 (2000): 44–45.
42. Marek Kondrat also appeared as fifty-five-year old Adam Miauczyński in Koterski's later project, *Wszyscy jesteśmy Chrystusami* (*We Are All Christs*, 2006), a film about alcoholism.
43. Małgorzata Miławska published a book on the linguistic aspect of *The Day of the Wacko*, in which she emphasizes that "language is this film's protagonist." Małgorzata Miławska, *Język bohaterem filmu: Analiza lingwistyczna "Dnia świra" Marka Koterskiego* (Lublin: Wydawnictwo Katolickiego Uniwersytetu Lubelskiego, 2015).
44. Eddie Cocrell, "Review: *Day of the Wacko*," *Variety* (18 February 2003), http://variety.com/2003/film/reviews/day-of-the-wacko-1200543373.
45. The MoMA (Museum of Modern Art) in New York organized a retrospective of Lech Majewski's works in 2006 titled "Lech Majewski: Conjuring the Moving Image." See Piotr Zawojski, "Nomada ze stałym adresem: Lech Majewski," *Postscriptum* 1–2 (2003): 88–97; Piotr Zawojski, "Poezja kamerą (za)pisana: Od *Wojaczka* do *Krwi poety* i *Szklanych ust* Lecha Majewskiego," in *Sztuka obrazu i obrazowania w epoce nowych mediów* (Warsaw: Oficyna Naukowa, 2012), 118–42.
46. Daniel M. Gold, "Creating a Cinematic Picture of a Flemish Masterpiece," *New York Times* (13 September 2011).
47. Andrew James Horton, "Concern for the Devil: Polish Film at the 36th Karlovy Vary Film Festival," *Kinoeye* 1, no. 3 (2001), http://www.kinoeye.org/01/03/horton03.php.
48. Krzysztof Zanussi has released a group of films including *Serce na dłoni* (*And a Warm Heart*, 2008), *Rewizyta* (*Revisited*, 2009), and *Obce ciało* (*The Foreign Body*, 2014).
49. Renata Murawska, "New Polish Cinema: The 29th Polish Feature Film Festival in Gdynia," *Senses of Cinema* 34 (2005), http://sensesofcinema.com/2005/festival-reports/polish_film_festival_2004.

CHAPTER 11

The Transforming Years (2005–)

At the beginning of the new millennium, there was an urgent need for substantial structural changes in the Polish film industry. Not only did the production of films decrease to approximately twenty features per year, but most films released from 2000 to 2004 were low-budget productions, either independently created or television films.[1] On 30 June 2005, the Polish parliament (Sejm) passed the Act on Cinematography, setting the new film law in Poland. The breakthrough moment was the founding of the Polish Film Institute (Polski Instytut Sztuki Filmowej, PISF), within the Ministry of Culture (Ministerstwo Kultury i Dziedzictwa Narodowego), which replaced the Cinema Committee established in 1987 and the Script, Production, and Distribution Agencies created in 1991. The main goal of the PISF, headed from 2005 to 2015 by Agnieszka Odorowicz, is to create conditions for the development of local film production and to promote Polish cinema in Poland and abroad. The institute's mission is to support local cinema at all stages of film production by subsidizing the development of film projects (in most cases, up to 50 percent of the total production budget) and by assisting during the production, promotion, and distribution of films.

As specified in the Act on Cinematography, the PISF's task in particular is to support young filmmakers and art cinema, to increase the presence of Polish films at international film festivals, and to support the current film institutions, such as the National Film Archive (Filmoteka Narodowa) in Warsaw.[2] The annual budget of PISF has been roughly $42 million during recent years, in part funded by a 1.5 percent tax imposed on television, cinema, and cable television operators.[3] (For comparison, the entire budget of the former Cinema Committee amounted only to $3.5 million to 4.2 million from 1996 to 2000.)[4] The PISF finances four major programs: film production (including script scholarships, project development, and production of feature, documentary, and animated films); education and dissemination of film culture; development of cinema infrastructure; and promotion of Polish films abroad.

The introduction of the new film law, the establishment of the Polish Film Institute, and the launching of several regional film bodies funding local film production successfully stimulated the film industry. Among several regional film funding institutions is, for example, Silesia Film (Instytucja Filmowa Silesia-Film) in Katowice, which continues the tradition of the Silesia Film Unit (Zespół Filmowy Śląsk) founded by Kazimierz Kutz in 1972 in Katowice. Silesia Film supports film production through its Silesian Film Fund (Śląski Fundusz Filmowy) and organizes or co-organizes several regional film festivals, such as the Cinema on the Border (Kino na Granicy) and Summer Frames (Wakacyjne Kadry), both in Cieszyn, a border town in southern Poland. Silesia Film also runs several art house theaters and the Silesian Film Archive. Among recent films produced or coproduced by Silesia Film are noteworthy works such as *Senność* (*Drowsiness*, 2008, Magdalena Piekorz), *The Mill and the Cross* and *Onirica* (*Field of Dogs*, 2014, Lech Majewski), and *Jesteś bogiem* (*You Are God*, 2012, Leszek Dawid).

Because of the stimulating organizational changes, the annual production of feature films increased quickly from twenty-three in 2003 and as few as twelve in 2004, to thirty-nine in 2014 and forty-one in 2015. As elsewhere in Europe, Hollywood films clearly dominated and continue to dominate the Polish box office. Their market share is always above 50 percent (67 percent in 2015); their biggest market share was in 2004 (80 percent) and 2003 (79 percent).

Polish films are generally very popular among local audiences. For example, Polish films shared 28.4 percent of total box office sales in 2011 and 25.6 percent in 2014, compared with 8.8 and 3.5 percent in 2004 and 2005, respectively. The number of premieres on Polish screens has also increased significantly from roughly 200 annually from 2000 to 2005, to more than 340 in 2014 and 2015.[5] In addition, the number of cinemas in Poland continues to grow slowly but steadily and reached eight hundred in 2010, including seventy-seven multiplexes and nine IMAX cinemas.[6] For comparison, there were 1,435 cinemas in 1990, but their numbers decreased rapidly to only 705 in 1993 and 555 in 2004.[7]

The state-owned Documentary and Feature Film Studio (WFDiF), which incorporated the Czołówka studio in 2010, is the biggest film studio in Poland, financing and producing approximately five films per year. Private companies produce more and more films; a significant number of them are international coproductions, several of them cofinanced by the PISF. Numerous foreign films are also made with the Polish financial involvement, including films by directors such as Peter Greenaway (*Nightwatching*, 2007) and Volker Schlöndorff (*Strike*, 2006).[8]

Historical Cinema

The Polish Film Institute has been generously funding films that refer to Polish history, which have been always popular among Polish audiences. One of the PISF's stated priorities is to provide "funding to feature, documentary, and animated films that deal with an important historical subject, are made with artistic merit, touch upon issues of key importance for Polish national heritage and culture, and have educational qualities."[9] From 2005 to 2015, as many as sixty-nine full-length historical films were made, and cofinanced by the PISF, with total support of roughly $100 million. From 2006 to 2014, the PISF also provided support for 176 documentaries that focused on Polish history, and, interestingly, for sixteen animated films, which promoted various aspects of local history. Historical films, according to the PISF's policy, may be granted maximum financial support of 6 million zlotys (approximately $1.7 million).[10]

Both parties ruling in post-2005 Poland, the centrist Civic Platform (Platforma Obywatelska, PO) and the Christian, right-wing Law and Justice (Prawo i Sprawiedliwość, PiS), have supported several historical projects that deal with significant, albeit often fiercely contested and controversial, moments in the Polish past. The Polish Film Institute financially supported several film projects that were designed to remind the younger generations of Poles about historical figures and events that the communist regime deleted from Polish official memory. Many major films, such as Andrzej Wajda's *Katyń* (2007), were not only cofinanced by the PISF but also heavily promoted by the Polish Ministry of Culture and its institutions such as the National Center for Culture (Narodowe Centrum Kultury, NCK) and the Adam Mickiewicz Institute (Instytut Adama Mickiewicza).

It is important to emphasize that through its funding, the PISF and other government institutions have created and disseminated images that had often been either suppressed or falsified during the communist period. Interestingly, the peaceful transition to democracy in Poland has not been an important subject in Polish documentary or feature cinema (Władysław Pasikowski's 1992 film, *The Pigs*, should be mentioned here). Commenting on postcommunist East-Central European politics, James Mark writes in his book *Unfinished Revolution* that the "task for producers of new public memories was the construction of a believable popular narrative of a revolutionary rupture between dictatorship and liberal democracy, despite the absence of an actual revolution to mythologize." Mark discusses two types of institutions that emerged in postcommunist East-Central

Europe: history commissions and institutes of national memory. In Poland, the latter role has been chiefly performed by the Institute of National Remembrance (Instytut Pamięci Narodowej, IPN), created by the Polish parliament in 1998. This vital national institution was established, like other comparable institutions in the former communist bloc, to "preserve and regulate access to the voluminous records of the former secret police, but also out of a sense of confidence that these sources could be employed to create a nationally unifying account of Communism, based on rigorous and scholarly archival research, which could overcome the divided nature of post-Communist memory."[11] The IPN, by definition an apolitical institution established to gather and disseminate historical information pertaining to Nazi German occupation and the communist period, has nonetheless been regularly blamed for its alleged attempts to rewrite history and to offer its politicized version, particularly during the PiS rule.[12]

Katyń, Andrzej Wajda's representation of the Katyń massacre, the Soviet NKVD's mass execution of Polish officers in 1940, is among the best-known historical works in Poland. Wajda's Oscar-nominated war drama was anxiously awaited by Polish audiences and largely met their high (almost impossible to fulfill) expectations; the film received several Polish Film Awards, including best film, best cinematography (Paweł Edelman), and best music (Krzysztof Penderecki). It is also one of the most popular films at the box office with more than 2.7 million viewers, number 7 on the list of the most popular Polish films released after 1990 (see Appendix B). The 2007 screening of *Katyń*, the first narrative film dealing with a traumatic tragedy that was suppressed for decades, was a national event. Nonetheless, a series of documentaries about Katyń, which

Figure 11.1 Artur Żmijewski (left) and Andrzej Chyra as Polish officers in Andrzej Wajda's *Katyń* (2007). Screenshot by the author.

were released after the return to democracy in 1989, had prepared the ground for Wajda's film. These documentaries include *Las Katyński* (*The Katyń Woods*, 1990, Marcel Łoziński), *Zbrodnia katyńska* (*The Katyń Massacre*, 1991, Maciej Sieński), *Film znaleziony w Katyniu* (*The Film Found in Katyń*, 1992, Józef Gębski), *Katyń: Prawda i kłamstwo o zbrodni* (*Katyń: The Truth and the Lie about the Crime*, 2005, Grzegorz Szuplewski), and *Katyń* (2007, Józef Gębski), among others.

In *Katyń*, Wajda powerfully recreates the slaughter of approximately twenty-two thousand Polish officers who were captured by the Red Army after its attack on Poland on 17 September 1939 and murdered on Stalin's order in a series of executions in the Katyń Forest near Smolensk and at other locations. Among the officers killed in April and May of 1940 was Wajda's father, Captain Jakub Wajda, who was executed in the NKVD prison in Kharkiv. The Germans first discovered the mass graves at Katyń in 1943. The Soviets initially denied their responsibility and blamed the Nazi Germans. They officially admitted their culpability as late as 1990.[13]

The script of *Katyń* is based on Andrzej Mularczyk's filmic novella and cowritten by Wajda, Władysław Pasikowski, and Przemysław Nowakowski.[14] It revolves around the actual uncovered documents from the Katyń graves and preserved by the victims' families. Made with the participation of some of Poland's finest actors, including Jan Englert, Andrzej Chyra, Artur Żmijewski, Maja Komorowska, and Magdalena Cielecka, Wajda's solemn film tells the story not only of the massacre but also of the postwar years when the Katyń crime became a taboo topic in Soviet-controlled Poland. The film opens with footage of the invasion of Poland in September 1939 by Nazi Germany from the west and by Soviet Russia from the east and briefly summarizes events leading up to the massacre. The story unfolds through the perspective of several women. These daughters, mothers, sisters, and wives—guardians of national virtues—search in vain for their loved ones and later, after the war, struggle to keep the knowledge of Katyń alive.

Stylistically, *Katyń* is a mainstream film, even an example of good, old-fashioned filmmaking, the work heavy with symbolism and cultural and religious references. It attempts to tell "the whole story" of Katyń; this ambitious endeavor arguably contributes to its almost educational dimensions. Explaining numerous difficulties encountered during the preproduction stage of the film, Wajda noticed:

> For the first film, I had to show the crime and its consequences. The next film could show just the crime or just the lie. Future directors could do a fine

psychological drama, showing the victims' internal plights. Or one could do a purely political film. ... But the first film had to show the crime—and the lie. The crime: that was indeed my father who was murdered there. The lie: my mother was one of the ladies who was constantly trying to find information, she was writing to the Red Cross in London and Switzerland, she clung on to the hope that her husband would return from the war. She was lied to that he didn't die in Katyń, and only gradually did we discover the truth. We learnt that there were other camps, and those camps were also liquidated. In short, we learnt about the machinery of death.[15]

Katyń might be discussed as a "patriotic picture" with its easily decipherable Christian and national iconography, somber and elevated tone, and characters who represent various traits of national history. Some palpable dangers inherent in such "national projects" are that they tend to show a panorama of vital historical events and a multitude of characters representing different strata of society. Wajda's film, however, defies these dangers by its chilling and emotional final sequence. As Geoffrey Macnab writes:

The massacre itself is shot in brutal but haunting fashion. Officer after officer is bundled out of Soviet trucks, shot in the back of the head and left to topple forward into a pit. Wajda doesn't shrink at showing the sheer scale of the slaughter. What makes the sequences all the more chilling is the lack of emotion of the Soviet assassins.[16]

While pointing out some inevitable weaknesses of the film, most foreign reviewers emphasized the film's "stately, deliberate quality that insulates it against sentimentality and makes it all the more devastating."[17] In addition to reconstructing the Katyń crime on screen, Wajda's film (like some of his earlier films, such as *Ashes and Diamonds*) also serves as a powerful farewell to the prewar political and social order. Two of the film's characters embody it well: the proud wife of the general murdered at Katyń, Róża (Danuta Stenka), and her prewar servant, Stasia (Stanisława Celińska). The latter, married to a left-wing partisan during the war and now a regional administrator in postwar Poland, represents things (and the social class) to come.

Another significant film that deals with suppressed earlier events, *Czarny czwartek: Janek Wiśniewski padł* (*Black Thursday*, 2011, Antoni Krauze), is an intense reenactment of the general strike in the shipyards of Gdynia and Gdańsk in December 1970, which was brutally crushed by the regime (eighteen people were killed). Krauze's docudrama commemorates the events in the manner of the critically acclaimed *Bloody Sunday* (2002, Paul Greengrass, UK, Ireland), the documentary-like recreation of the 1972 events in Northern Ireland. Jacek Petrycki, the cinematographer known for his work on Krzysztof Kieślowski's early realistic films, captures images of the striking shipyard workers, bloody clashes with the riot police and regular army troops, stunned and angry top communist politicians reacting to the strikes, and wounded and dead workers and their grieving families. The photography is dark and grayish and blends easily with documentary archival footage, which adds an extra layer of faithfulness. To make this docudrama more appealing on a human level, *Black Thursday* focuses on the family of a young shipyard worker who is accidentally killed at the beginning of the strike. As in other Polish films that refer to tragic events in Polish history and often focus on surviving women, the bulk of Krauze's film deals with the fate of the grieving widow and her children, who are unable to mourn their dead husband and father properly and are forced by the system to remain silent.

Historical films coproduced by the Polish Film Institute also include some genre-defying films, such as Marcin Krzyształowicz's wartime thriller *Obława* (*Manhunt*, 2012); Adrian Panek's costume drama set in the eighteenth century, *Daas* (2011); and Maciej Sobieszczański's dark love triangle set in 1945 on the grounds of the former Auschwitz-Birkenau complex, *Zgoda* (*The Reconciliation*, 2017). The PISF's support for historical pictures that focus on important moments in Polish history has not always resulted in films that received critical recognition or met audiences' expectations. Among them are some of the most expensive Polish films made in recent years, such as Jerzy Hoffman's historical epic *1920 Bitwa Warszawska* (*Battle of Warsaw 1920*, 2011) about the decisive Polish victory during the Polish–Soviet War in 1920. This expensive production by Polish standards (its budget was $9 million, including $3 million provided by the PISF) was the first Polish 3-D feature film (photographed by Sławomir Idziak) and offers a clichéd, almost patriotic textbook-like story about an event of national importance, known as the Miracle on the Vistula.[18] For similar reasons, another highly anticipated yet failed film was *Syberiada polska* (*Siberian Exile*, 2013, Janusz Zaorski), about the fate of Poles sent to Siberia after the Soviet occupation of eastern Poland in 1939. Perhaps the most spectacular was the failure of Łukasz Barczyk's epic costume drama *Hiszpanka* (*Influence*, 2015, with a budget of $7 million), which was advertised as a spiritual thriller.[19] *Influence* attempts to depict events leading to the Greater Poland Uprising (Powstanie Wielkopolskie, 1918–1919), but its treatment of Polish history, and the abundance of real and fictional characters (such as a group of patriotically minded clairvoyants) in search of a story, resulted in an epic fiasco despite some remarkable special effects, camerawork, and set design.

Commemorating the Warsaw Uprising

The Warsaw Uprising Museum (Muzeum Powstania Warszawskiego), which opened in 2004 on the sixtieth anniversary of the uprising, is now among the most popular museums in Poland, visited by more than half a million people annually. Its founding not only renewed interest in this topic, especially among the younger generation of Poles, but also prepared the ground for recent films such as *Miasto 44* (*Warsaw '44*, 2014, Jan Komasa), produced to commemorate the seventieth anniversary of the uprising. Screenwriter-director Komasa (1981–) unmistakably targets young Polish viewers.[20] His popular film introduces the language of violent video clips, computer game tactics, the latest technology, blood, slow motion, nondiegetic pop music, and national sacrifice.

Warsaw '44 tells the story of the legendary uprising, which is also present in several canonical Polish films such as Andrzej Wajda's *Kanal*, Andrzej Munk's *Eroica*, and Janusz Morgenstern's television series *Columbuses*, among others. Before 1989, approximately twenty films were made about the 1944 Warsaw Uprising or referred to this event. These works often generated national debates and controversies. As if paying tribute to those earlier films, particularly to works by Morgenstern and Wajda, Komasa's dramatic narrative of the uprising also tells the story of initiation and love amid brutal scenery, but this time in a big-budget and commercialized version. After the film's premiere, Tadeusz Sobolewski proclaimed Komasa's film to be a "perfect imitation of great cinema." He said that the "uprising has become today a mine of easy emotions and melodramatic effects. ... [In] *Kanal* it was about underscoring the monstrosity of the war, the absurdity of the uprising—this is about the intensity of survival. This is the shift in memory of the uprising toward pop culture."[21]

Despite being safely located in history and now debated mostly by historians, the subject of the uprising still unleashes heated disputes in Poland. In his film, however, Komasa is not asking questions, taking sides, or offering new perspectives.

His objective is to memorialize the traumatic event by resorting to the language of the cinema of excess and carnage. The idealistic young insurgents in *Warsaw '44*, convincingly played by a group of talented, emerging Polish actors, are portrayed as tragic figures in a ghastly, hyperreal world; their sacrifice serves the nation.

Komasa also dealt with the Warsaw Uprising in his fictionalized documentary *Powstanie Warszawskie* (*Warsaw Uprising*, 2014) and its slightly modified (and shorter) export version in English, *Warsaw Uprising* (2014). The latter is advertised as an "87-minute film, made of completely restored, colorized archive footage, which shows the Warsaw Uprising in an extremely touching way and with unparalleled realism."[22] The film uses exclusively authentic newsreels from August 1944 with an added voice-over dialogue and diegetic sound. The opening credits pay tribute to several camera operators, members of the Home Army, who captured the struggle with their cameras. This riveting documentary footage from the uprising also proved very popular among audiences (almost six hundred thousand viewers) despite the addition of a fictitious story, which probably weakened its overall impact.

Other cinematic tributes to young people who fought in the uprising also include low-budget films such as *Był sobie dzieciak* (aka *Taniec śmierci: Sceny z Powstania Warszawskiego*; *Once upon a Time in Warsaw*, 2013, Leszek Wosiewicz) and *Sierpniowe niebo: 63 dni chwały* (*August's Sky: 63 Days of Glory*, 2013, Ireneusz Dobrowolski). Clearly overshadowed by Komasa's *Warsaw '44*, both narratives use archival footage to authenticate their stories. Another popular film, *Kamienie na szaniec* (*Stones for the Rampart*, 2014, Robert Gliński), which also targets younger viewers with its story of wartime bravery and sacrifice, is an adaptation of Aleksander Kamiński's 1943 book about the Gray Ranks—the Polish underground scout movement during World War II.[23] Like an earlier film by Jan Łomnicki, *Operation Arsenal* (1978), *Stones for the Rampart* focuses on the action of the underground scout unit led by "Zośka" (nom de guerre of Tadeusz Zawadzki) to free one of its leaders, "Rudy" (in reality, Jan Bytnar), imprisoned and tortured by the Gestapo. The operation near the Warsaw armory (arsenal) building in the city center succeeded in liberating Rudy (whose injuries inflicted by the Gestapo, however, proved fatal, and he died several days later) and other prisoners who were transported from the Pawiak prison to the Gestapo headquarters on Szucha Street.

After Gross: Representations of the Holocaust

The renewed interest in the Polish-Jewish past and the Holocaust has been demonstrated, among other things, by the release of several films dealing with this ideologically charged subject. They include significant, internationally known films such as *Joanna* (2010, Feliks Falk), *W ciemności* (*In Darkness*, 2012, Agnieszka Holland), *Pokłosie* (*Aftermath*, 2012, Władysław Pasikowski), and *Ida* (2013, Paweł Pawlikowski). The list of recent Polish films on this topic is extensive and includes works directly facing the Holocaust, such as *W ukryciu* (*In Hiding*, 2013, Jan Kidawa-Błoński), advertised as an "erotic thriller," and *Klezmer* (2015, Piotr Chrzan). Another cluster of films places the Holocaust in the background: *Z daleka widok jest piękny* (*It Looks Pretty from a Distance*, 2012, Wilhelm and Anna Sasnal), *Sekret* (*Secret*, 2012, Przemysław Wojcieszek), *Noc Walpurgi* (*Walpurgis Night*, 2015, Marcin Bortkiewicz), *Demon* (2015, Poland-Israel, Marcin Wrona), and *Letnie przesilenie* (*Summer Solstice*, 2016, Poland-Germany, Michał Rogalski).

A group of recently released films takes part in a discussion initiated in 2001 by the publication of Jan Gross's *Neighbors: The Destruction of the Jewish Community in Jedwabne, Poland*. The book depicted the massacre of a Jewish population by their Polish neighbors that took place on in July 1941 in the small Polish town of Jedwabne, at that time occupied by Nazi Germany.[24] The Polish edition of Gross's book, which appeared one year earlier, sparked a heated discussion about Polish complicity in this crime and revived the debate on Polish-Jewish wartime relations.[25] This debate revealed once again the double (Polish and Jewish) memory of the war and the occupation, and it showed the continuous presence of two different narratives regarding this period.[26]

Despite the frequent critical voices questioning Gross's methodology and his merciless destruction of a generally accepted and rarely questioned version of recent Polish history, the impact of his *Neighbors* has been lasting and is seen as part of a significant group of recent Polish narrative films. Like Gross's book, they attempt to reexamine the Polish wartime experience and behavior toward Jews. A prominent number of documentaries and a relatively small group of narrative films, known mostly locally, attempt to counterbalance a largely critical portrayal of the Polish wartime actions that, according to many Poles, prevails in Western films about the Nazi German occupation. They attempt to correct the accusatory tone of Gross's monograph by emphasizing the Polish wartime help for the Jews. Thus, the Polish Righteous among the Nations feature prominently in television series, such as *Sprawiedliwi* (*The Righteous*, 2010, seven episodes, Waldemar Krzystek), which moves between the present and the past to tell the story of the members of the Polish Council to Aid Jews (Żegota). Other films, such as television series *Czas honoru* (*Time of Honor*, 2008–2013) and television docudrama *Historia Kowalskich* (*The Story of the Kowalskis*, 2009), emphasize the complexity of the occupation and focus on the courageous responses of Poles who witness the Jewish tragedy and risk their lives to offer help.

The award-winning feature *Joanna*, by the veteran director Feliks Falk, belongs to the same category. It tells the story of a young Polish woman in Kraków (played persuasively by Urszula Grabowska) who takes care of a young Jewish girl, Róża. Her mother, who was betrayed by a Polish *szmalcownik* (blackmailer), tries to save her daughter and sends her to a nearby Polish church where Joanna prays. Although the film's story may sound familiar in the context of Polish cinema, Falk intelligently narrates the complexity of the situation during the war and avoids clichéd aspects of some previously made films. In order to protect the Jewish girl, whose presence was discovered by a German officer (played by German actor Joachim Paul Assböck, who appeared in supporting roles in several Holocaust films), the saintly Joanna becomes his lover. She pays for his silence with her body. Fellow Poles, who are not aware that she is sheltering a Jewish child, accuse her of collaborating with the occupier (her husband has been in a POW camp since the September 1939 campaign). The film portrays the loneliness of a Polish helper, ostracized by her family and fellow nationals.

Commenting on another much-debated book in Poland by Jan Gross, *Golden Harvest: Events at the Periphery of the Holocaust*,[27] the writer Andrzej Stasiuk expresses eloquently the complexity of the Polish memory of the Holocaust:

> There have been no Jews in Poland for a long time now, yet in some unfathomable way we are condemned to each other. ... The Germans got rid of the ashes, thereby ridding themselves of the guilt and cleansing themselves. We had lived with the Jews for centuries and now we live with their ashes, with their spirits, and this is how it will be until the end of the world. It is quite possible that we will never come to terms with it.[28]

One of Poland's leading contemporary dramatists, Tadeusz Słobodzianek, the author of a celebrated and much-debated play about the Jedwabne massacre, *Our Class* (*Nasza klasa*, 2009), proposes that "the Germans should make films about Auschwitz, the Russians about Katyń, and the Poles about Jedwabne."[29] Indeed, such films are being made in Poland—films that question the noble and heroic images of the war and the Polish behavior (which Poles would like to nurture) and blend the present and the past to uncover the darker aspects of the past (including Jedwabne). They are also better known internationally.

In 2012, after several years of silence, Władysław Pasikowski wrote and directed *Aftermath*, which indirectly addresses the Jedwabne massacre. Its script, designed as a continuation of Gross's book and originally titled *Kaddish*, was ready in 2005 but received no funding.[30] This historical drama, presented as a thriller with elements of the Western, sparked a heated controversy in Poland concerning Polish-Jewish relations during World War II. *Aftermath* was sometimes labeled a tool in the "pedagogy of shame" (*pedagogika wstydu*)—deliberate attempts to deprive Poles of their national pride.[31]

Set in the 1990s, *Aftermath* centers on two brothers overwhelmed by the burden of the past. The older, Franciszek Kalina (Ireneusz Czop), a Polish émigré in Chicago, returns unannounced, after twenty years, to his village located somewhere in central Poland. He is alarmed by the actions of his brother, Józef (Maciej Stuhr), who runs the family farm: the villagers ostracize him, and his wife and children left him for the United States. Franciszek learns that his younger brother is an outcast in the village because of his unwelcome interest in its Jewish past. Józef uncovers dozens of Jewish gravestones dispersed throughout the village, which the locals have used in and around their farmhouses. Józef (literally) unearths his village's Jewish past (he even learns enough Hebrew to read the epitaphs). He makes the Jewish past public, unlike other villagers who want to keep it silent. Later, joined by his "American brother," he fathoms what happened to the murdered Jews and how the village, including his own family, benefited from their disappearance by taking possession of their belongings.

The Polish debates concerning *Aftermath* dealt almost exclusively with its political and historical context (with predictable political divisions among reviewers), not the film itself. Following Gross, Pasikowski demystifies the Polish past. Subtlety, however, is not this film's forte. The passionate (almost obsessive) main character, the modern Polish Righteous, faces a hostile and backward crowd who has the support of a young anti-Semitic priest (the older, soon-to-retire priest, played by the actor and Solidarity symbol Jerzy Radziwiłowicz, is more understanding). Several scenes, including the villagers' final "crucifixion" of Józef, seem heavy-handed and bordering on the grotesque. As a *Variety* reviewer fittingly noticed: "The action mounts to a near-hysterical pitch with occult occurrences (the brothers' gruesome unearthing of old bones intercut with the kindly priest's sudden illness) and a denouement straight out of the Middle Ages. But the more the action hews to a Hammer horror template, the less congruent it feels with historical revelation."[32] Polish audiences expected a more nuanced film, given that it was made several years after the publication of Gross's book and after numerous public debates.

A similar portrayal of Polish farmers as backward, superficially religious, and anti-Semitic creatures, which is also present in several earlier Polish films, can also be encountered in *It Looks Pretty from a Distance*, an allegorical film abundant with clear references to the Holocaust without uttering the word "Jew," and in the celebrated *Ida*. Unlike the screen images of members of Polish intelligentsia—usually shown as helpless witnesses to the genocide committed on their soil by the Nazi German invaders—the villagers in these films represent everything the townspeople would like to forget. According to the much-quoted, fitting

Figure 11.2 Itay Tiran (center) in Marcin Wrona's *Demon* (2015). Photograph by Marta Gostkiewicz for Magnet Man Film. Courtesy of Kino Świat.

description by the Polish writer Sylwia Chutnik, in Poland "a village is Jedwabne; a town is Żegota [Council to Aid Jews]."[33]

Several other films are also set in the present and provide references to the past, among them the Polish-Israeli coproduction *Demon*, directed by the recently deceased Marcin Wrona.[34] Often described as a horror film,[35] although it also displays elements of an absurdist comedy and a love story, *Demon* introduces another disastrous wedding. Piotr from England (played expressively by an Israeli actor, Itay Tiran) and his Polish bride, Żaneta (Agnieszka Żulewska), marry at her family house in the Polish countryside—a gift for the newlyweds from the bride's father. Before the wedding, however, the groom falls on a pile of human remains in a muddy terrain and later is possessed by a Jewish dybbuk, a character from Yiddish mythology usually defined as "a wandering soul believed in Jewish folklore to enter and control a living body until exorcised by a religious rite."[36] Wrona's *Demon* tells the story of a land filled with the unexcavated skeletons of the past. His return-of-the-repressed narrative deals with specters that haunt the Polish landscape.

Another film that blends the present and the past is Paweł Pawlikowski's *Ida*, the recipient of many prestigious international awards, including the 2015 Academy Award for Best Foreign Language Film. Pawlikowski was born in 1957 in Poland, but at the age of fourteen moved to England, where he later established himself with a series of documentaries and well-received features such as *Last Resort* (2000) and, in particular, the BAFTA-winning *My Summer of Love* (2004). *Ida* marks his return to the Poland he remembers from childhood; it is, in his own words, "an attempt to recover the Poland of my childhood," "a film about identity, family, faith, guilt, socialism, and music."[37]

Set in 1961, during the post-Stalinist years, *Ida* opens with images of an eighteen-year-old Catholic novice, Anna (played by the newcomer Agata Trzebuchowska), about to take her final vows. Her Mother Superior, however, wants Anna to see her only living relative in Łódź, her mother's sister, Wanda Gruz (Agata Kulesza). Wanda is the former top communist prosecutor ("Red Wanda") who played a prominent role in the political show trials of "enemies of the people" but now is disillusioned and marginalized by the same system after the political thaw. From her aunt, the young novice learns that she is Jewish, that her real name is Ida Lebenstein, and that her parents and brother were killed during the war. Together they travel across the Polish countryside in search of their family's resting place. They learn that during the war the Lebensteins were sheltered by a

Figure 11.3 Agata Trzebuchowska as Ida (left) and Agata Kulesza in Paweł Pawlikowski's *Ida* (2013). Screenshot by the author.

Polish peasant family and later murdered and buried in a nearby forest by the same people who hid them. After her aunt's suicide (most probably the result of grief or, as several reviewers have suggested, survivor's guilt), Ida briefly tests the limits of her relative freedom (including casual sex with a young saxophone player whom she met earlier). In the final scene, she returns to the convent—the only place she has known since childhood.

Pawlikowski's representation of "Red Wanda" refers to a historical figure, Helena Wolińska-Brus, a prominent Stalinist prosecutor involved in show trials of many legendary members of the Polish underground, including General August Emil Fieldorf, the deputy commander-in-chief of the Home Army after the Warsaw Uprising, who was executed in 1953 (see later discussion on *General Nil*). The Polish Institute of National Remembrance accused Wolińska of Stalinist crimes and unsuccessfully tried to extradite her from England (where she died in 2008). Pawlikowski knew her personally and at one point attempted to produce a documentary about her.[38] Thematically, Pawlikowski also pays tribute and models its story on Henryk Grynberg's return to a wartime crime scene shown in Paweł Łoziński's classic documentary *Birthplace* (see chapter 9). Like Grynberg, Ida Lebenstein and her aunt talk to local peasants and learn what happened to their family; they also discover the place in the forest where the victims are buried. Unlike *Birthplace*, however, in which the motif for murder is money, the murderer of Ida's family—the farmer's son Feliks, who confesses to the crime ("what happened, happened")—was afraid that his family would be denounced and experience serious consequences (the death penalty in the occupied Polish territories) for hiding the Jews.

Reviewing the film, Megan Ratner writes, "Ida Lebenstein stands for the Jewish wartime victims as well as the psychologically displaced persons of Communist Poland, hectored by the state into conformity."[39] *Ida*'s narrative of discovery (of the crime, but also of her identity) is similar to numerous recent Polish literary and filmic accounts. For example, a comparable unusual story of survival is portrayed in the documentary *Wpisany w gwiazdę Dawida-Krzyż* (*The Cross Inscribed in the Star of David*, 1997, Grzegorz Linkowski), about the Catholic priest Romuald Jakub Weksler-Waszkinel (he bears the names of his Jewish and Polish families), who learned about his Jewish origin at the age of thirty-two.

Pawlikowski produces a powerful multilayered art film in which blocks of silence and stillness of inhospitable cold landscapes have the power of a cathartic thunderstorm. *Ida*'s black-and-white photography by Łukasz Żal and Ryszard Lenczewski (both nominated for Oscars), use of the Academy ratio (1.37:1), empty spaces, stillness of the camera with characters regularly framed off-center, and unhurried pace contribute to comparisons of films made by world cinema giants—Carl Theodor Dreyer and Robert Bresson.[40] But it is also a film about the Holocaust with Jews and Poles only, as if suggesting that Poles were responsible for what happened. Such a representation of the Polish experience of the Holocaust contributed to a polarized reception of *Ida* in Poland, where, as Dorota Glowacka and Joanna Zylinska write, "narratives of heroism, oppression, and liberation have yielded stories of sacrifice for the fatherland, including tales of the selfless rescue of the Jews. They stand in stark contrast to the Jewish narratives of suffering, senseless death, and betrayal."[41] Distributed in Poland in the relatively small number of seventy-five copies (the smallest among the top twenty Polish films released in 2003), *Ida* had only 243,466 viewers (number 10 on the list of Polish films released in 2013).[42]

Another internationally known film that faces the Holocaust is *In Darkness* (Agnieszka Holland, 2012, Poland-Germany-Canada), an Oscar-nominated drama adapted from Robert Marshall's book documenting the actual story of survival, *In the Sewers of Lvov*.[43] Photographed by the documentarian Jolanta Dylewska,[44] the film tells the true story of a Catholic Pole, Leopold Socha, a simple sewer worker and a petty thief, who for fourteen months hid a group of Jews in the sewers of Lvov (today Lviv in Ukraine), occupied by the Germans. Dedicated to Marek Edelman (the last surviving leader of the Warsaw Ghetto Uprising who passed away in 2009), this is Holland's third film dealing with the Holocaust (after *Angry Harvest* and *Europa, Europa*) and her third Oscar nomination.

In Darkness opens in 1941, after Germany's attack on the Soviet Union, without, however, referring to an earlier period when the Soviets occupied Lvov after their 1939 invasion and annexation of the Polish Eastern Provinces and deportations of Polish intelligentsia and Ukrainian nationalists. As Timothy Snyder comments on the wartime situation in Lvov and Western Ukraine:

> *This is the rich and complex world that the Germans destroyed, with some help from the Soviets. The mass murder of the Jews was an unprecedented assault on a group defined zoologically; it was the extinction of life of millions of individuals, but it was also a successful attack on an old world that, although full of the hostility and prejudice that Holland fearlessly presents, nevertheless defied a homology of race, nation, and culture.*[45]

Robert Więckiewicz, a leading actor of his generation,[46] plays an unsentimental and reluctant hero, who is transformed from an anti-Semite to a rescuer of Jews. In the first scenes, Socha witnesses an execution of Jews in the forest; later he encounters another group of them hiding in the sewers after their escape from the Lvov Ghetto in June 1943. He initially helps the Jews solely for money, but then, establishing an emotional bond with them ("these are my Jews," he says in the final scene) and not afraid to risk everything, he hides them in the elaborate labyrinth of sewers beneath the town.

Though coproduced Holocaust films (such as *The Pianist*) are often narrated in English, Holland's actors reflect the multinational and multilingual Lvov by speaking the actual languages of the real-life characters: Polish, German, Hebrew, Yiddish, Russian, and Ukrainian. In addition, unlike too-often idealized Jewish characters in filmic representations of the Holocaust, Holland's Jews have all-too human flaws. According to the director, they

> *aren't one-dimensional angelic, they are full-bodied human beings with anger, sex, weakness and selfishness, and generosity and love as well. That was another thing that irritates me in English-language Holocaust movies: that in most of them the Jews are turned into some kind of non-living, positive stereotypes. I think that in doing so, in some way you are killing them again. They become unreal.*[47]

From its opening scene, *In Darkness* relies heavily on scenes doubling the Polish and Jewish experience as if commenting on the double memory of the wartime period.⁴⁸ Holland cuts between images of the Jewish escapees from the ghetto, led by Mundek Margulies (Benno Fürmann), and the "Polish Schindler" Socha and his family. Although the true story of *In Darkness* can possibly be labeled a "standard conversion melodrama,"⁴⁹ this Holocaust film is, however, absorbing, multifaceted, and harrowing. Holland, as Snyder aptly concludes, "overdoes nothing. She does just enough, and the consequence is an extraordinary work of art that brings us closer to the reality of the Holocaust than we will be comfortable going."⁵⁰

The Return of History as the Biopic

General interest in historical cinema in Poland, as evidenced by the box office and the stated goals of the PISF, stimulated the production of films that refer to various aspects of post-1945 Polish history. In recent years, however, the screen has become a battleground of memory: different political factions try to enforce their cinematic vision of the past through funding (or the lack of it) and by exerting political pressure. Political divisions deepened after the tragic plane crash near Smolensk North Airport (western Russia) on 10 April 2010, which killed ninety-six people, including Polish President Lech Kaczyński and several senior government and military officials. They were traveling to attend the official ceremony marking the seventieth anniversary of the Katyń massacre.⁵¹

Like other films, the biopic (biographical film) is a site of competing memories; it also offers commentaries on the intricate rapport between memory and historical events. Through its funding, the PISF has been involved in bringing back memories of those who were earlier wiped out from the official history textbooks, including the nationalist underground fighters during the postwar period. Labeled "bandits" by the communist regime, but now hailed heroes of the anticommunist resistance, these "cursed soldiers" (*żołnierze wyklęci*) continued their struggle against the Polish security forces and the Soviet NKVD after 1945, well into the 1950s. *Wyklęty* (*Cursed*, aka *The Damned*, 2017, Konrad Łęcki), a film based on historical facts, tells the story of Franciszek "Lolo" Józefczyk, who continues his doomed struggle against the communist regime after the war (Wojciech Niemczyk plays the fictitious character, who is modeled on several "cursed soldiers").⁵²

In another film, *Generał Nil* (*General Nil*, 2009), Ryszard Bugajski introduces a hero of the Polish wartime resistance, General Emil Fieldorf (1895–1953, nom the guerre "Nil"), who, among other exploits, in February 1944 oversaw the assassination of SS-Brigadeführer Franz Kutschera, the commander of the Warsaw SS and police. Fieldorf surrendered himself during the 1948 amnesty but later was accused of treason, and after a show trial based on fabricated evidence, the communists executed him in 1953. Bugajski focuses on Fieldorf's last years, but flashbacks reveal his years during the occupation and arrest by the Soviet secret service (NKVD) after the war when, unrecognized (under the assumed name of Walenty Gdanicki), he was sent to a labor camp in the Ural Mountains and then returned to Poland in 1947. Olgierd Łukaszewicz plays General Fieldorf as a dignified yet pragmatic leader in this film, which was rightly summarized in the title of Sobolewski's review: "An honorary salvo commemorating General Fieldorf."[53]

Ryszard Bugajski, of *Interrogation* fame, earlier directed a television play about the heroics of another eminent Polish wartime figure, Witold Pilecki (1901–1948), titled *Śmierć rotmistrza Pileckiego* (*The Death of Cavalry Captain Pilecki*, 2006). Pilecki, a prewar cavalry officer and member of the Home Army during the war, was incarcerated in 1940 at Auschwitz in order to provide the Western Allies with information about the camp. On 27 April 1943, he escaped from Auschwitz and later took part in the Warsaw Uprising. Imprisoned by the communists after the war and accused of espionage, after a show trial he was executed in May 1948.[54] Interestingly, Bugajski's most recent film, *Zaćma* (*Blindness*, 2016), is inspired by the life of a person from the other side of the political spectrum—the prominent member of the communist security apparatus Julia Brystiger (Brystygier, played by Maria Mamona). Nicknamed Bloody Luna (Krwawa Luna) by former prisoners for her sadistic interrogations and use of torture, Brystiger also headed the Fifth Department of the Ministry of Public Security (MBP), which was responsible for the persecution of Polish religious leaders, among others.

Like biopics made elsewhere, this subgenre in Poland dramatizes biographies of important historical personages, crosses the boundaries of many genres, and covers religion, war, music, and art. The biopic is usually perceived as a domain of "quality cinema" and a "vehicle for prestige projects." But, as Belén Vidal writes, it is also "often perceived as a throwback to old-fashioned models of storytelling—a sort of heavy armor that constrains filmmakers' creative movements."[55] Andrzej Wajda's two most recent films, *Wałęsa: Człowiek z nadziei* (*Walesa: Man of Hope*, 2013) and *Powidoki* (*Afterimage*, 2016), may serve here as good examples. *Afterimage* focuses on the last years of Władysław Strzemiński (1893–1952), a Polish avant-garde painter and theoretician, the author of *Teoria widzenia* (*The Theory of Vision*, published for the first time after his death, in 1958). Strzemiński was a professor at the Academy of Fine Arts (Państwowa Wyższa Szkoła Sztuk Plastycznych) in Łódź, but was later dismissed by communist authorities for noncompliance with the tenets of socialist realist art.

Several critics look at *Afterimage*, Wajda's last film (he died two weeks after its premiere at the Gdynia Film Festival, at the age of ninety), and its main character (Bogusław Linda) as a personal and self-reflexive film about Wajda's own struggles with censorship and the communist dogma in arts. They also emphasize that the film's classical structure[56] is somehow incompatible with the image of Strzemiński—a left-leaning avant-garde artist, unwilling to compromise, handicapped (Strzemiński lost an arm and a leg serving in the Russian army during World War I), and struggling with the oppressive system that first tries to lure him but then shuns him. However, as the Polish film critic and scholar Michał Oleszczyk observes:

> *The irony of* Afterimage ... *is that Wajda himself actually did master the game that Strzemiński, who died of tuberculosis and starvation after having been repeatedly denied the right to ply his trade, proved incapable of grasping: that of making one's art under the watchful eye of the Communist authorities—and then turning it against them. Wajda's last film, then, is a very particular sort of tribute: a salute to a fiercely avant-garde artist, as well as a record of unqualified resistance from a filmmaker who knew exactly how much subterfuge was needed to remain active in a state-approved system of production.*[57]

The subtitle of Wajda's earlier film, *Walesa: Man of Hope*, suggests that it is a companion piece to his widely known films *Man of Marble* and *Man of Iron*. Based on the novelist and playwright Janusz Głowacki's script, this traditional biopic recreates the turbulent period in Polish history and the life of a man who became one of the most internationally recognizable Poles. Lech Wałęsa (outstanding Robert Więckiewicz) is shown as a political figure and a family man whose wife, Danuta (Agnieszka Grochowska), plays an important role in his life. In fact, the scenes featuring Danuta Wałęsa's acceptance of the Nobel Peace Prize on behalf of her husband, and her degrading strip search conducted by Polish authorities at the Warsaw airport after she returns from Stockholm belong to the film's strongest parts.

The film centers on the 1981 interview that Wałęsa gave to a prominent Italian journalist, Oriana Fallaci. The plot then takes the viewer back to the 1970 strike in the Baltic ports and covers the birth of the Solidarity movement. Today a polarizing figure in Poland, Wałęsa is shown during his prime trade union years when he leads the workers' mass movement, experiences blackmail by the communist secret service, and tries to outsmart them and the system. The film ends with Wałęsa's speech before the US Congress on 15 November 1989. Więckiewicz expertly captures Wałęsa's characteristic way of speaking, charisma, firm beliefs, arrogance, and self-assurance. Black-and-white archival footage from the past, including newsreels and television reports, as well as fragments from *Man of Iron*, are used to authenticate the story and to blend with the contemporary setting in color (cinematography by Paweł Edelman).[58]

The period of the Polish People's Republic also returns in a film dressed as a historical spy thriller, *Jack Strong* (2014, Władysław Pasikowski), a biopic about Ryszard Kukliński (Marcin Dorociński), a gifted Polish colonel with access to classified materials, who worked for the CIA from 1971 to 1981 (codenamed Jack Strong). Disenchanted with the growing Sovietization of Poland and afraid that his country may become a nuclear wasteland in a future war between the superpowers, Kukliński passed several Soviet secrets to the CIA, including vital military plans (Patrick Wilson plays his CIA handler). Regrettably, Colonel Kukliński remains a controversial figure in Poland (he was sentenced to death in absentia by the communist regime, and even today some Poles consider him a traitor).

Jack Strong, a suspenseful Cold War thriller, shows the world of spies and political intrigues in the manner of John le Carré's novels. The film received several awards at the Gdynia Film Festival and as many as fourteen nominations at the Polish Film Awards (but won only one Eagle, for Best Actress, which went to Maja Ostaszewska starring as Hanna Kuklińska, the colonel's wife).[59] The writer-director Pasikowski skillfully maintains suspense, balances tension with moments of dark comedy, and introduces several historical figures, including the Soviet leader Leonid Brezhnev and the general Viktor Kulikov, commander-in-chief of the Warsaw Pact (both characters played with gusto by Russian actors, Siergiej Kriuczkov and Oleg Maslennikov, respectively). In addition, he introduces a climactic car chase on the snowy streets of Warsaw and a suspenseful standoff at Checkpoint Charlie in Berlin—the crossing point between East and West Berlin. Narrated in three languages, *Jack Strong* also has as its executive villain (the chief villain is always the communist state) the KGB officer Ivanov (Dimitri Bilov).

Another important moment in Polish history, the communist secret service's 1984 political murder of Father Popiełuszko, is portrayed in *Popiełuszko, wolność*

Jest w nas (*Freedom Is within Us: Popiełuszko*, 2009, Rafał Wieczyński), starring Adam Woronowicz as Jerzy Popiełuszko. The murder of Popiełuszko, a priest and a Solidarity supporter who was beatified in 2010, is also the subject of Agnieszka Holland's English-language *To Kill a Priest* (1988, French-US production, Polish premiere in 1991), starring Ed Harris as an obsessed security service officer and Christopher Lambert as Popiełuszko.

A prominent group of films deal with the life and the papacy of John Paul II, including two multinational films, which were produced with significant Polish involvement: *Karol: A Man Who Became Pope* (*Karol: Człowiek, który został papieżem*, 2005) and its continuation *Karol: The Pope, the Man* (*Karol: Papież, który pozostał człowiekiem*, 2006), both made by the Italian director Giacomo Battiato and starring the Polish actor Piotr Adamczyk as Karol Wojtyła.[60] Another popular film about the pope, the 2008 paradocumentary *Świadectwo* (*John Paul II: The Testimony*, Paweł Pitera), which had more than one million viewers in Polish cinemas, is narrated by Stanisław Dziwisz, a long-time personal secretary to John Paul II and a cardinal since 2006. Another film, the equally popular full-length documentary *Jan Paweł II: Szukałem was ...* (*John Paul II: I Looked for You*, 2011, Jarosław Szmidt), addressed, among others, the issue of the pope's legacy.

Several other biopics also reflect on the communist past, but focus on prominent figures outside of politics and religion, among them *Sztuka kochania Michaliny Wisłockiej* (*The Art of Loving: The Story of Michalina Wisłocka*, 2017, Maria Sadowska),[61] and *Bogowie* (*Gods*, 2014, Łukasz Palkowski). Well received by Polish critics and audiences, both films successfully competed with foreign and local products by offering stories of medical celebrities, characters who succeeded despite overwhelming odds. *The Art of Loving* tells the story of the Polish gynecologist and sex educator Michalina Wisłocka (1921–2005), the author of the first book on sex education published in the communist bloc. Her book *The Art of Loving* (translated into English in 1978 as *A Practical Guide to Marital Bliss*) was published for the first time in 1976 and quickly became a bestseller (seven million copies sold).[62] The cardiac surgeon Zbigniew Religa (1938–2009), who performed the first successful heart transplant in Poland in 1987, is the protagonist of *Gods*, which received the main prize (the Golden Lion) at the Gdynia Film Festival and several Polish Film Awards.

Both films are written by Krzysztof Rak, employ witty dialogue, and offer fast-paced success stories that are reminiscent of American productions about rebellious and determined characters. The Polish underdogs challenge the political structure and moral as well as religious taboos obstructing change and innovation, especially when it comes from the West. Religa (Tomasz Kot) and Wisłocka (Magdalena Boczarska) are shown as highly motivated albeit slightly eccentric characters who are larger than the gray and fossilized political (and medical) reality that surrounds them. Their actions seem to induce psychological, generational, and political change. The reality of the 1980s in Poland, despite its ugly political context, is not demonized but only somewhat ridiculed in *Gods*. *The Art of Loving* also features politically turbulent times in the background (the postwar years, Stalinism, the 1970s "era of Gierek"), but the focus is on the woman who, as often stated, "opened the doors of Polish bedrooms." Two young cinematographers, Michał Sobociński in *The Art of Loving* and his older brother, Piotr Sobociński Jr., in *Gods*,[63] aptly capture the period's atmosphere and trigger almost nostalgic evocations of the past, tinted with irony. This past, like memories of one's youth, emerges no longer as a dark stage in Polish history but as its colorized and slightly sugarcoated variety.

The director of *Gods*, Palkowski, started his career (and Sonia Bohosiewicz's acting career) with *Rezerwat* (*The Reserve*, 2007), a film about a unique old district of Warsaw, Praga, and some of its unconventional inhabitants. *Najlepszy* (*The Fastest*, 2017), his latest film, however, continues taming the 1980s and offers after *Gods* another mass therapy for a nation that yearns for its own superheroes. *The Fastest*, inspired by Jerzy Górski's story, is a biopic about a former drug addict who became a triathlon champion in 1990 (played by one of Poland's rising stars, Jakub Gierszał). Although not a subtle story of fighting inner demons (shown in this film almost literally), its "from drug addict to Ironman" inspirational story guaranteed box office success in Poland.

Among several biopic films made recently in Poland, two stand out: *Papusza* (2013) and *Ostatnia rodzina* (*The Last Family*, 2016). Krzysztof Krauze and his wife, Joanna Kos-Krauze, made *Papusza*, about the Gypsy poet Bronisława Wajs (1908–1987), better known as Papusza, played by Jowita Budnik. This award-winning film is not only a biopic of the first female poet from the Roma community in Poland, but also a work that offers insights into Roma life. The film unfolds unhurriedly in a series of nonchronological vignettes introducing different episodes from Papusza's life, often featuring images of visually striking landscapes. Superbly photographed in black-and-white by Krzysztof Ptak and Wojciech Staroń, the film offers a story of Papusza's life from her childhood, being on the road with her extended family, her forced marriage to an older controlling man (her uncle), and a friendship with a Polish poet, Jerzy Ficowski, who joined the traveling Gypsies and encouraged her to write poetry.

The 2016 winner of the Gdynia Film Festival, *The Last Family*, the debut film of Jan P. Matuszyński (1984–), focuses on the renowned painter Zdzisław Beksiński (1929–2005), played by Andrzej Seweryn, and his family: son Tomasz (Dawid Ogrodnik) and wife Zofia (Aleksandra Konieczna). Tomasz (Tomek) is a known music journalist with emotional problems who committed suicide in 1999. His mother, Zofia, is shown as a sympathetic character who is the unheralded hero of this family. Written by Robert Bolesto, the script focuses on complicated family dynamics and is largely based on Beksiński's own video footage.[64]

Zdzisław Beksiński's obsessive videotaping of his everyday life influences and shapes the film. His apocalyptic and surreal paintings, which are familiar in Poland, do not influence the look of this unsettling film. Its action is mostly confined to two flats in an unglamorous high-rise apartment complex in Warsaw. The outside reality is on the margins of this film and intrudes sporadically. Although *The Last Family* covers twenty-seven years in Polish history, the period filled with important political events, the film centers almost exclusively on a self-obsessed family. The compositions are static, observational, and almost detached. A *Variety* critic film rightly describes the film as

> *a remarkable, frequently unsettling exercise in staged voyeurism. ... Visually, the mixture of fixed master shots with recreated early home videos makes it feel at times like we're watching the Beksińskis as viewed through a diorama. The apartments themselves lend a sense of intimacy, practically become characters in their own right, thanks to [Kacper] Fertacz's camerawork as well as Jagna Janicka's production design, flawless in capturing the period.*[65]

The Return of History as Genre Film

History, neither triumphant nor demythologized, also returns in genre cinema: crime films, melodramas, and road movies. Discussing what he labels "new Polish historical cinema," Thomas Anessi writes that it addresses

> *the way in which the collective consciousness about history is structured, about how the past is understood. Genre and cinematic techniques are used not to*

Figure 11.4 (From the left) Dawid Ogrodnik (Tomasz Beksiński), Aleksandra Konieczna (Zofia Beksińska), and Andrzej Seweryn (Zdzisław Beksiński) in Jan P. Matuszyński's *The Last Family* (2016). Photograph by Hubert Komerski for Aurum Film. Courtesy of Kino Świat.

achieve a reality effect, but to provide innovative formulae by which to explore a world that can only be accessed through stories, and the understanding of which is a direct result of the modes of depictions employed.[66]

Films set during the communist period are often interpreted dubiously as displaying nostalgic features for the communist times. Commenting on the proliferation of academic studies concerning the issue of nostalgia about the communist past, Maria Todorova states ironically, "A spectre is haunting the world of academia: the *study* of post-Communist nostalgia."[67] There are, however, people in Poland who were left behind during the transformation period, who are dissatisfied with the new reality and nostalgically look back at the communist past (at least at its more prosperous years, such as the 1970s).[68] Despite vast support for the European Union in Poland (at 75 percent in 2017), 40 percent of Poles in a representative survey conducted in 2011 described their lives as better before the transition to democracy.[69]

Many recent films look at the communist past, which serves more than just an exotic (for younger viewers) or personal nostalgic background. The episodic road movie with elements of comedy, *Bilet na księżyc* (*One Way Ticket to the Moon*, 2013), written and directed by Jacek Bromski, may serve as a good example. Set in the summer of 1969, it tells the story of a shy young man, Adam (Filip Pławiak), who is passionate about aviation but, disappointingly, is drafted into the navy. Accompanied by his worldly older brother, Antoni (Mateusz Kościukiewicz), who wants to prepare him well for a harsh, three-year life in the military, Adam travels through Poland to his naval base unit on the Baltic seaside. During the journey that lasts several days, the brothers visit old friends, befriend new people, and have some romantic adventures. Bromski narrates a personal nostalgic tale with a romantic subplot, set against harsh reality, with the ultimate culprit lurking in the background: the communist state.

The interest in the past also resulted in a proliferation of quality crime films, such as *Fotograf* (*The Photographer*, 2014, Waldemar Krzystek), *Czerwony pająk* (*Red Spider*, 2015, Marcin Koszałka), *Jestem mordercą* (*I'm a Killer*, 2016, Maciej Pieprzyca), and *Ach śpij kochanie* (*Lullaby Killer*, 2017, Krzysztof Lang). All of them are about a hunt for a serial killer, are inspired by actual historical events, and skillfully recreate different periods in Polish history. In *The Photographer*, the Russian investigative team moves from contemporary Moscow to Legnica (southwestern Poland) to learn more about a serial killer. The flashback reveals images of the former Soviet garrison town in the 1970s and its intricate Polish-Soviet relations. The retro thriller *Red Spider* is set in the decaying, foggy Kraków of the 1960s, and *Lullaby Killer* is set in Stalinist Warsaw.

I'm a Killer, Maciej Pieprzyca's psychological crime film, belongs to the best works recently released in Poland. Inspired by true events, it tells the story of a serial killer known as the "Vampire of Zagłębie" (the region bordering Upper

Figure 11.5 Mirosław Haniszewski (standing) as a militia lieutenant in Maciej Pieprzyca's *I'm a Killer* (2016). Courtesy of Renata Czarnkowska-Listoś and RE Studio.

Silesia), who was accused of killing fourteen women and attempting to kill more, and sentenced to death in 1975. Mirosław Haniszewski plays a young, energetic, and determined militia investigator, Lieutenant Janusz Jasiński, heading a unit formed to find a killer who terrorizes the whole region. Pressured by his superiors, he arrests a man fitting the killer's profile (Arkadiusz Jakubik), almost a trapped character who is not comprehending the whole situation and who signs a confession. Pieprzyca, a native of Silesia, makes more than a crime film; he recreates the world of smoke-filled cabinets, a communist bureaucracy that overwhelms the young investigator, and the pathologies of the system.[70]

Occasionally, like in *The Photographer,* a crime film's action may be set in the present in order to reveal some darker aspects of the past. For example, *Ziarno prawdy (A Grain of Truth,* 2015, Borys Lankosz), a crime thriller based on Zygmunt Miłoszewski's novel, is set in the contemporary picturesque town of Sandomierz (southeastern Poland), but the search for truth takes the viewer back to the postwar years. Robert Więckiewicz stars as the prosecutor Teodor Szacki who tries to solve the mystery of a brutal murder that forces him to look at the postwar history of the town with its complicated Polish-Jewish relations.

Preoccupation with the past, this time shown as an intruder and destroyer of families, is also seen in domestic dramas. Michał Rosa's multi-award-winning film about the burden of the past, *Rysa (Scratch,* 2008), a political film disguised as a domestic drama, tells the story of a woman (Jadwiga Jankowska-Cieślak) who learns that her husband (Krzysztof Stroiński) was a former communist security service informer. Another suspenseful film, *Kret (The Mole,* 2011, Rafael Lewandowski, Polish-French), tells the story of a former Solidarity activist (Marian Dzięaziel), now the owner of a secondhand clothing business, who is accused by the tabloid press of collaborating with the communist secret police. His son (Borys Szyc) is shocked to learn that his father, a respected and widely known member of Solidarity, was an informer ("the mole"), and tries to uncover the truth. In these and other films, the intrusion of the murky past, usually in the form of some devilish characters associated with the former communist regime, destroys families who are trying to rebuild their lives in the new reality.

Another film, Borys Lankosz's black-and-white *Rewers (The Reverse,* 2009), is set in the early 1950s and offers a pastiche of noir cinema. The judges at the Gdynia Film Festival, who gave this film eleven awards, including for Best Film, appreciated its unconventional take on the past. *The Reverse* focuses on three generations of women living in Warsaw during the Stalinist period (played by

Agata Buzek, Krystyna Janda, and Anna Polony) and the intrusion of politics (Marcin Dorociński as a security agent). Another successful film, *Różyczka* (*Rosebud*, 2010, Jan Kidawa-Błoński), the winner of the Gdynia Film Festival, focuses on the true life story of the Polish dissident writer and historian Paweł Jasienica (Andrzej Seweryn) and his marriage to a communist agent codenamed Rosebud. (The agent is played compellingly by Magdalena Boczarska, who received the Best Actress Award at the Gdynia Film Festival and the Polish Film Award.) The past also returns in *Mała Moskwa* (*Little Moscow*, 2008), Waldemar Krzystek's melodrama about forbidden love between a Polish officer and a married Russian woman in Legnica, the Soviet garrison town in Poland (also the setting of *The Photographer*).

Romantic Comedy and Musical

In recent years, comedies, particularly romantic comedies, defined broadly as "a genre in which the development of romance leads to comic situations," proved to be the most successful Polish films at the box office.[71] Nine out of the twenty most profitable Polish films released from 1990 to 2015 were comedies, including five romantic comedies.[72] The list includes films directed by Tomasz Konecki—such as *Lejdis* (*Ladies*, 2008) and *Testosteron* (*Testosterone*, 2007, with Andrzej Saramonowicz)—and many romantic comedies that possess universal messages but nonetheless carry a distinct Polish idiom. They include Mitja Okorn's box office successes *Listy do M.* (*Letters to Santa*, 2011) and *Planeta singli* (*Planet Single*, 2016), Piotr Wereśniak's *Nie kłam kochanie* (*Don't Lie, Honey*, 2008), and Ryszard Zatorski's *Nigdy w życiu!* (*Never Ever!* 2004) and *Tylko mnie kochaj* (*Just Love Me*, 2006).

Polish romantic comedies, although not particularly visible internationally, have always been popular in Poland. Their presence was particularly notable after the advent of sound with films such as *Forgotten Melody*, *Is Lucyna a Girl?*, *Jadzia* (1936, Mieczysław Krawicz), and *Piętro wyżej* (*Upstairs*, 1937, Leon Trystan). They were popular after the war and during the Stalinist period. The "proletarian romantic comedy" *An Adventure and Marienstadt* may serve as the most accomplished example. Romantic comedies survived the tenets of the imposed ideology and became popular in the 1960s, for example, *A Wife for an Australian*, and later reemerged in the early 1990s with films such as *Papierowe małżeństwo*

(*Paper Marriage*, 1992, Poland-UK, Krzysztof Lang) and, one year later, *The Sequence of Feelings*.

Most Polish romantic comedies, although profitable domestically, are easy to discredit. Like some of their foreign counterparts, they lack refinement and artistic merit, and offer unsophisticated urban love stories, typically set in well-known, big cities, with predictable characters and situations. Known for their unashamed product placement, these films largely feature prosperous young Poles working in fashionable corporate offices and living in designers' apartments—the polar opposite of the characters in Kieślowski's *Decalogue*. The protagonists' lifestyles imitate glossy sensational papers; the witty, often crude, dialogue refers to political and cultural life. Images of prosperity, certainly a refreshing sign in Polish cinema after decades of depressing landscapes, and characters driven by love seem to suggest that some Poles have no other problems. Like American or British romantic comedies, Polish films often rely on class/cultural differences and employ similar clichéd supporting characters that verge on stereotypes. Unlike their foreign counterparts, however, Polish comedies rarely deal with ethnic/national differences, although, occasionally, love knows no boundaries – even in Poland. In the unremarkable *Mała wielka miłość* (*Expecting Love*, 2008, Łukasz Karwowski), for example, a young American lawyer follows his pregnant Polish girlfriend who left America for Poland.

Contemporary Polish romantic comedies aspire to match the level of British films, chiefly *Four Weddings and a Funeral* (1994, Mike Newell). The heartwarming and well-written films directed by the Slovenian-born Mitja Okorn (1981–), *Letters to Santa* and *Planet Single*, are modeled on another box office success, *Love Actually* (2003, Richard Curtis), which is referenced in *Letters to Santa*. Set on Christmas Day, this film centers on five men and five women living in Warsaw who experience love or try to rediscover it. They are played by an ensemble of popular Polish actors, among them Maciej Stuhr and Roma Gąsiorowska. Everything in Okorn's film is picturesque and romantic, including Warsaw, the city not particularly known for its beauty or romantic appeal.[73]

After decades of comedies that subtly poked fun at the absurdities of the communist system, some popular new Polish comedies, such as *Ladies* and *Testosterone*, may seem unsophisticated for a foreign viewer; too often they rely on sexist jokes and lavatory humor. Subtle comedies are infrequent, for example, *Statyści* (*Movie Extras*, 2006, Michał Kwieciński), which revolves around a group of supporting Polish actors who appear in a Chinese film being shot on location in

Poland. (The Chinese producers, who need extras with sad faces, are able to find them only in Poland.) Juliusz Machulski, a director who specializes in comedy, should be mentioned in this context. He has maintained popularity with releasing films such as *Ile waży koń trojański? (How Much Does the Trojan Horse Weigh?* 2008), an intelligent comedy set in communist times, *Kołysanka (Lullaby,* 2010), a successful Polish version of *The Addams Family* (1991, Barry Sonnenfeld), and *Volta* (2017), a crime comedy.

In recent years, a group of filmmakers tried to revive a much-neglected genre in Polish cinema: the musical. Advertised as the "angry musical," the forcefully titled *Polskie gówno (Polish Shit,* 2015, Grzegorz Jankowski), shows an indie rock group touring around Poland. *Disco Polo* (2015, Maciej Bochniak), set in the 1990s, deals with a uniquely Polish phenomenon of unsophisticated yet popular dance music known as disco polo, usually associated with provincial Poland. In *#WszystkoGra (Game On,* 2016), which tells the story of three women trying to save their family house in Warsaw, Agnieszka Glińska offers classic Polish songs in modern arrangements. *Ekscentrycy, czyli po słonecznej stronie ulicy (Eccentrics, the Sunny Side of the Street,* 2016, Janusz Majewski), set in the late 1950s, deals with a topic that was present earlier on Polish screens: the postwar popularity of jazz coupled with politics lurking in the background.

Three films in particular should be mentioned in this context: two mostly known locally, *Skazany na bluesa (Destined for Blues,* 2005, Jan Kidawa-Błoński) and *Jesteś bogiem (You Are God,* 2012, Leszek Dawid), and the internationally known *Córki dancingu (The Lure,* Agnieszka Smoczyńska). *Destined for Blues* is set in Silesia and focuses on the life of Ryszard Riedel (the director's cousin, played convincingly by Tomasz Kot), the leader of a popular rock blues band Dżem, who died from drug overdose in 1994 at the age of thirty-seven. Similar images of the unglamorous Silesian reality are also featured in *You Are God,* a box office success (1.4 million viewers; see Appendix B) about the Polish hip-hop group Paktofonika (the film's title refers to a song by the band).

The Lure is a genre-defying and daring debut by Agnieszka Smoczyńska that combines elements of musical, vampire/mermaid horror, feminist fantasy, and grotesque love story. Written by Robert Bolesto, *The Lure* refers to Hans Christian Andersen's "The Little Mermaid" and other literary and mythological sirens (perhaps even to the sword-wielding symbol of the Polish capital: the Warsaw Mermaid). Unusual in the context of Polish cinema, this film introduces two man-eating mermaid sisters, Silver (Marta Mazurek) and Golden (Michalina Olszańska), who emerge from the Vistula River ashore lured by a tender song, which they reciprocate with their angelic voices. Since the out-of-the-water mermaids have humanlike legs, they join a lead singer (Kinga Preis) and a group of other performers at a Warsaw sleazy nightclub in the 1980s. Only when sprinkled with water or when bathing do the sister mermaids display their huge fish tails. The photography by Jakub Kijowski (who earlier worked as a camera operator on the Academy Award–nominated *In Darkness*) expertly captures the glitter of the dance halls with their showy musical numbers and the perilous-looking exteriors often shot with greenish and bluish filters.

The Lure received several awards at international festivals of independent cinema, including the Special Jury Prize at the 2016 Sundance Film Festival. The film took audiences by surprise as "a coming-of-age fairy tale with a catchy synth-fueled soundtrack, outrageous song-and-dance numbers, and lavishly grimy sets," and with its exploration "of themes of emerging female sexuality, exploitation, and the compromises of adulthood with savage energy and originality."[74] Angela Lovel praises the film in an essay for the Criterion Collection, which released the film, as a "meditation on innocence, violence, family dynamics, sexual exploitation, and feminine nature." She adds: "The resulting film, with its wildly original soundtrack that glides from wistful ballads to disco to show tunes to Europop to punk, is a colorful, exuberant, and absurdist genre experiment that introduces a distinctive new directorial sensibility in Smoczyńska. You can practically taste the salt water—and the blood."[75]

Figure 11.6 (From the left) Marta Mazurek (Silver), Kinga Preis (Krysia), and Michalina Olszańska (Golden) in Agnieszka Smoczyńska's *The Lure* (2015). Screenshot by the author.

Auteur Cinema

Several Polish filmmakers have continued to make personal films, often repeating their earlier style and, in some cases, broadening their oeuvre. For example, Jan Jakub Kolski, after reprising his earlier poetics in films such as *Jasminum* (2006) and *Afonia i pszczoły* (*Happy Aphonia*, 2009), found more success with films such as *Zabić bobra* (*To Kill a Beaver*, 2014), a story of a soldier returning from the war. Another established filmmaker with a distinct visual style, Andrzej Barański, made many films, including *Parę osób, mały czas* (*A Few People, a Little Time*, 2007) and *Księstwo* (*Heritage*, 2012), the latter on the level of his classic *Woman from the Provinces* (1985).

Bodo Kox (1977–), who earlier had become an icon of Polish independent cinema, graduated from the Łódź Film School in 2012. His two recent films, *Dziewczyna z szafy* (*The Girl from the Wardrobe*, 2012) and *Człowiek z magicznym pudełkiem* (*The Man with the Magic Box*, 2017), mark his transition into mainstream cinema. However, his films' freshness and energy, unpretentious stories, eccentric yet likeable characters, and original soundtrack belong to the world of indie cinema. Kox's playfulness with genres (e.g., melodramatic plot, dystopian futuristic world, and time travel to the 1950s in *The Man with the Magic Box*), distinct sense of humor, and warmth are combined with a dose of anticipated weirdness and visual innovation (cinematography by Arkadiusz Tomiak).

Distinctive personalities have also emerged in popular cinema. For example, Patryk Vega (1977–) produced a sequence of popular action films, which feature several top Polish actors. His action-packed films tell realistic and brutal stories about police work and the Warsaw underworld. Vega's films, such as *Pitbull* (2005—and its continuations, *Pitbull: Nowe porządki* (*Pitbull: New Order*) and *Pitbull: Niebezpieczne kobiety* (*Pitbull: Tough Women*), both released in 2016—transfer the world of gritty television reality programs and documentaries into mainstream action cinema. Vega, in fact, started his career by working on several documentary television shows and series, such as *Taśmy grozy* (*Tapes of Horror*, 2002), which captured the everyday aspect of police work and the shady world of crime that officers try to eradicate. In his fictional films, Vega uses this same documentary-like style to portray the unglamorous characters on both sides of the division (the world of the police and the criminals is blurred) and enhances it by using the vulgar vernacular. Vega's violent action films, also written by him, resemble, however, unfinished products—big-budget extensions of sensational reality shows, which are saved by the presence of quality actors and sensational topics that usually make headlines. Michał Oleszczyk rightly stresses that Vega has created his own genre: "Vega's signature mix of fast action, highly profane, slang-ridden dialogue and a slew of distinctive characters is box office magic. Whether he's the poor man's Scorsese or a Guy Ritchie for the pierogi-loving crowd, there's no denying Vega's supreme reign with Polish wide audiences right now."[76] The box office figures confirm Oleszczyk's comment about Vega's "local magic." For example, his most recent film, *Botoks* (*Botox*, 2017), about the corrupt health care system and its representatives, has secured more than 2.3 million viewers. Three of his films (*Pitbull: New Order* and *Pitbull: Tough Women*) are among the top twenty-five Polish box office hits released after 1990.

***

After making several films abroad and acting in films made by other directors, Jerzy Skolimowski returned to Poland and made two films: *Cztery noce z Anną* (*Four Nights with Anna*, 2008) and *Essential Killing* (2010), both expertly photographed by Adam Sikora. The former is a suspenseful drama about voyeurism, stalking, and unhealthy, obsessive infatuation made in the spirit of Alfred Hitchcock and Krzysztof Kieślowski (sometimes compared to *A Short Film about Love*). The film introduces the working-class character Leon (Artur Steranko) who lives with his mother and works as a stoker in the hospital crematorium. This shy loner spies on a hospital nurse, Anna (Kinga Preis), who lives across the courtyard, "visits" her at night, and, after adding sleeping pills to her night tea, watches her longingly. The film's flashbacks reveal a backstory: Leon served time for raping Anna (a charge he denies).

Skolimowski followed the unsettling and creepy atmosphere of *Four Nights with Anna* with a political action thriller, *Essential Killing*, starring Vincent Gallo. The film deals with an Afghan Taliban POW (captured after killing three American soldiers) who escapes from a secret American interrogation center in northeastern Poland. This chase film, almost without dialogue and often narrated from the fugitive's perspective, refrains from making political statements and tells the story of survival in the harsh, wintry landscape of the Masurian region in Poland (where Skolimowski resides). The film won four Polish Film Awards, including for Best Film, and received a Special Jury Prize at the Venice Film Festival.

Skolimowski's most recent film, *11 Minut* (*11 Minutes*, 2015, Poland-Ireland), offers many overlapping narratives, often repeating from different angles the eleven minutes between 5:00 and 5:11 p.m. in the lives of several characters. The intersecting narratives introduce several Warsaw inhabitants and predictably lead to a cinematically effective yet narratively frustrating climax. Often comparing Skolimowski's narrative strategy to films such as *21 Grams* (2003, Alejandro G. Iñárritu) and *Crash* (2004, Paul Haggis), many critics praise his film's visceral energy and employment of different camera techniques. Some, however, are less enthusiastic. For example, A. O. Scott in the *New York Times* notices that Skolimowski's film

> *seems more than anything else like a belated entry in the speedy, teasingly philosophical Euro-pop cinema of the late 1990s, as if the director had finally caught up with* Run Lola Run. *But the compressed, elliptical plot lines also suggest an anthology of lost or unmade Jerzy Skolimowski films, a mini-retrospective of sad comedies, absurd tragedies and deadly serious Polish jokes.*[77]

Skolimowski's film may remind viewers of several recent Polish productions that offer similarly interwoven and puzzlingly narrated stories, beginning with Dariusz Gajewski's *Warsaw* (2003), the unexpected but worthy winner of the Gdynia Film Festival. The film follows five different characters whose paths intertwine when they move to Warsaw. Paweł Borowski's *Zero* (2009) and Maciej Ślesicki's *Trzy minuty: 21:37* (*Three Minutes: 9:37 p.m.*, 2010) revolve around several interwoven stories and many characters whose actions affect each other. In another film, *Matka Teresa od kotów* (*Mother Teresa of Cats*, 2010), perhaps inspired by the classic *Memento* (2000, Christopher Nolan), Paweł Sala tells backward the story of a matricide. Employing flashbacks, the director attempts to uncover the motivations leading to this brutal crime.

Among several filmmakers who have developed their personal styles in recent years is the writer-director Andrzej Jakimowski (1963–), a graduate in philosophy from the University of Warsaw and in film directing from the Katowice Film and Television School. In true authorial fashion, Jakimowski writes, directs, and produces his cleverly constructed films that are unhurriedly narrated, poetic and tender, imaginative, and devoid of politics. Jakimowski often works with the same collaborators, including the cinematographer Adam Bajerski, the set designer Ewa Jakimowska (his wife), and the composer Tomasz Gąssowski. Since his debut at the age of forty, Jakimowski has made four theatrical films—distinct, popular, and critically recognized at film festivals in Poland and abroad.

Jakimowski's modestly budgeted debut, *Zmruż oczy* (*Squint Your Eyes*, 2003), tells the story of an outsider, a former teacher working as a night guard living on a postcommunist farm (Zbigniew Zamachowski). He is confronted with a preteen girl who has escaped from the city and her affluent, yet emotionally distant parents. Jakimowski's next film, *Sztuczki* (*Tricks*, 2007), introduces a young boy, Stefek, who, with the help of his older sister, Elka, tries to get closer to his absent father by playing games with fate—small tricks that may change the course of events. Jakimowski's *Imagine* (2013, Poland-France-Portugal), set in Lisbon, Portugal, and narrated in English, deals with the themes of blindness and nonconformity. It follows an unconventional, blind teacher who walks without a cane into his new school for blind children and teaches imagining the world—echolocation—in order to navigate the world. Jakimowski's latest production, *Pewnego razu w listopadzie* (*Once Upon a Time in November*, 2017), tells the story of a mother (Agata Kulesza), a former teacher living with her student-son, evicted from their Warsaw apartment and searching for a place to stay. Unfortunately, images of poverty, indifference toward the homeless, and inefficiency of the social system are too close to journalistic headlines (wild reprivatization, police brutality, and nationalist fervor). Jakimowski—the keen and tender observer of everyday reality—with his new film moves into the realm of Ken Loach's cinema but employs the poetics found in the earlier cinema of distrust.

Another emerging filmmaker, Małgorzata Szumowska (1973–), who debuted in 2000 with *Szczęśliwy człowiek* (*Happy Man*), received critical attention with her next film, *Ono* (*Stranger*, 2004), which tells the story of a pregnant woman trying to prepare her baby for the outside world. Szumowska's breakthrough film, however, came in 2008 with *33 sceny z życia* (*33 Scenes from Life*, Poland-Germany), starring the German Julia Jentsch as a talented photographer and Maciej Stuhr as her composer-husband, a film with recognizable references to her own life. Written by Szumowska, this film, which focuses on a crisis experienced by a well-established artistic family in Kraków, received the Silver Leopard at the Locarno Festival. Her next film, *Sponsoring* (*Elles*, 2012, France-Poland), tells an unpersuasive story of a Parisian journalist (Juliette Binoche) who is writing an investigative piece about prostitution among students. Szumowska's recent *W imię…* (*In the Name of …*, 2013) introduces a Catholic priest (Andrzej Chyra) who is in a homosexual relationship with a younger man.

Szumowska's latest film, *Body* (*Body/Ciało*, 2015), is arguably her most accomplished work. It narrates the story of an older, successful criminal prosecutor (Janusz Gajos) who lost his wife recently; his suicidal, anorexic daughter, Olga (Justyna Suwała), who loathes him; and an unconventional therapist, Anna (Maja Ostaszewska), whose specializes in eating disorders. The latter also can communicate with the dead by transmitting their messages via automatic writing. Szumowska's transgeneric film—a family drama about loss coupled with a supernatural element, but also a film about a father-daughter relationship—may look like a take on Krzysztof Kieślowski's cinema. Like Kieślowski, Szumowska focuses on individuals and relegates politics to the background (she only alludes to front-page scandals and debates). What separates her film from the world of Kieślowski's characters, however, is delicate irony, an absurd deadpan sense of humor, and self-mockery.

Szumowska belongs to Poland's new internationally visible auteurs. Her films are screened in the main competition section at the Berlin International Film Festival, where *Body* won her the Silver Bear for Best Director. Despite Szumowska's reluctance to face political or historical issues head-on, many critics see her films as commentaries on present-day Poland. For example, Peter Debruge reporting for *Variety* from the Berlin festival, writes that *Body* "depicts a country with a conflicted sense of self, torn between modern conveniences and a certain Old World mentality (neither the bureaucracy nor the plumbing seems to work correctly) ... [where] religion has failed the country."[78]

The National Auteur: Wojciech Smarzowski

Wojciech (Wojtek) Smarzowski (1963–) is arguably the most important contemporary Polish filmmaker, though he is still relatively unknown at the festival circuit outside Poland. He studied cinema at the Jagiellonian University in Kraków and later graduated in cinematography from the Łódź Film School. His career started with a self-reflexive television film, *Małżowina* (*Earlobe*, 1998). His first theatrical film, the low-budget *Wesele* (*The Wedding*, 2004), which can be seen as a grim and modernized version of Stanisław Wyspiański's classic play (as well as Andrzej Wajda's 1973 adaptation), shows the world of corrupt, drunken, and vicious provincial Poland. The film follows the father of the bride (Marian Dziędziel in his breakthrough role),[79] who offers the groom a new car in exchange for

Figure 11.7   Marian Dziędziel (center) as the father of the bride, Tamara Arciuch (bride), and Bartłomiej Topa (groom) in Wojciech Smarzowski's *The Wedding* (2004). Courtesy of Film It/Krzysztof Wiktor.

marrying his pregnant daughter, and the former lover of the bride (Maciej Stuhr) as he documents the calamitous wedding with his video camera (creating a film within a film). Vodka, sex, diarrhea, exploding toilets, and death are featured in this commanding film.

Smarzowski's film about a disastrous wedding received many honors in Poland, including several Polish Film Awards "Eagles" (for Best Film, Best Direction, Best Script, and Best Actor for Marian Dziędziel). It also sets the tone for future films written and directed by Smarzowski. He is one of the harshest commentators on Polish reality, focusing on its dark aspects and social plagues. He pictures a depraved, rotten world filled with brutal crime and plenty of greed, alcohol, and corruption. He creates images that often border on caricature and break generic conventions.

Unlike Małgorzata Szumowska, who established herself internationally, Smarzowski is a "national director," a national auteur. In his next film, the multi-award-winning *Dom zły* (*The Dark House*, 2009), set in southeastern provincial Poland, Smarzowski tells another story of crime, alcoholism, and corruption at a regional level and offers one of the darkest portrayals of the communist past. The film opens after the introduction of martial law, in 1982, during the inspection of a scene of a brutal crime committed a couple of years earlier. The flashbacks take us back four years. We follow an ordinary character, Edward Środoń (Arkadiusz Jakubik), who after the sudden death of his wife and a period of heavy alcohol abuse, moves to a different part of Poland to start his life anew. On the way to a new place, he stops at a remote farmhouse that belongs to the Dziabas family (Marian Dziędziel and Kinga Preis), but his short overnight stay ends in tragedy. The crime scene is revisited four years later with Środoń, accused of murder, in an attempt not only to uncover what happened on that fateful night but also to cover up the police abuse, corruption, and crime that were sanctioned by the state officials. One of the investigating officers, Mróz (Robert Więckiewicz), learns about the involvement of his superior officers, who sacrifice him. With the accused Środoń and investigator Mróz dead, the films ends with an image of a childbirth amid the ruins of the old farm—the pregnant police officer gives birth to Mróz's child.

The wintry landscape and some characters (including the pregnant police officer) may remind viewers of *Fargo* (1996, Joel and Ethan Coen). Comparing Smarzowski's film to *Fargo*, Sobolewski writes:

> The Dark House *is not a classic tragedy, which is supposed to awaken "pity and terror," bring purification. Here, there is no mercy, there is no purification. This is the cinema, which breaks conventions, mixes styles and genres. ... We watch the world immersed in mud and slurry—literally and figuratively. All the heroes of this bloody story—zootechnics, peasants, and militia—are mired in the same mud.*[80]

One of Smarzowski's most accomplished work to date is *Róża* (*Rose*, 2012), which received several Polish Film Awards but was ignored by the international jury at the Gdynia Film Festival.[81] The film's action occurs in the postwar period in the northeastern region of Poland, Masuria, part of East Prussia, which was incorporated into Poland in 1945 (also the scenery of Roman Polański's classic *Knife in the Water*). This gritty postwar drama shows the encounter between a former Polish Home Army officer, Tadeusz (Marcin Dorociński), who tries to rebuild his life, and a widowed Masurian woman, Rose (Agata Kulesza), who is repeatedly raped by the marauding Soviet soldiers. In the opening scenes, Tadeusz witnesses the rape and death of his wife, committed by the Germans during the Warsaw Uprising. He heads for the Masurian farm to inform Rose about the death of her husband (the

German Wehrmacht soldier), which he had witnessed, and to return her husband's photograph and a wedding ring. Both Tadeusz and Rose are portrayed as victims of the war, scarred characters in the new postwar order. He must hide in his own country, which is now occupied by the Soviets and ruled by its communist puppets. Rose, the indigenous woman of Masuria, is no longer welcomed there; classified as a German and facing expulsion, she is violated and treated like an enemy. Overwhelming violence, widespread national migrations and expulsions, and brutal rapes by the Soviet soldiers test their mutual understanding (perhaps secret love) that somehow appeared amid continuing conflict and hopelessness.

Rose offers arguably one of the bleakest stories of the postwar years; it is deprived of any glimpse of optimism that is present in many films about this period in Polish history. Its brutal depiction of the war aftermath has no equivalent in Polish cinema, perhaps with the exception of Krzysztof Zanussi's *A Year of the Quiet Sun* (1985; interestingly, Zanussi and his studio, Tor, coproduced the film). In an article titled "*Rose*: The minefield of history," Sobolewski writes: "this is a film filled with violence, which is over the norm of Polish cinema. Evil has no uniform or nationality here; it lurks on all sides. The story of the Masurians has more general dimension: this is the drama of raped, disregarded identity."[82] The Soviet soldiers, portrayed in the spirit of *A Woman in Berlin* (2008, Max Färberböck), are the embodiment of evil, shown not as liberators but as looters and rapists. The presence of a "good Russian" officer/doctor—a recurrent feature in Polish film and literature—does not soften the devastating images of lawlessness and the colorless landscape peopled by almost demonic invaders from the east.

Izabela Kalinowska praises Smarzowski for the way in which he "has chosen to follow in the footsteps of his predecessors, in his perennial concern with individuals caught up in history, and yet not fearing to reveal the abyss of life's meaninglessness."[83] For foreign audiences, however, the complexity of the political situation in *Rose* and the significance of certain places and names might be difficult to fathom. A *Variety* critic, while calling the film "unbearably brutal yet hauntingly romantic," addresses this problem by suggesting additional "contextual info about the period's historical and geographical complexities [that] could ease pic beyond the fest and Polish-lingo circuit offshore." She favorably compares Smarzowski's film with František Vláčil's *Adelheid* (1969) and Elem Klimov's *Come and See* (1985), which "should assure Smarzowski's status as an internationally recognized auteur."[84]

Smarzowski followed *Rose* with two films that were popular at the box office but do not match the artistry of his earlier works: *Drogówka* (*Traffic Department*,

2013) and *Pod Mocnym Aniołem* (*The Mighty Angel*, 2014). *Traffic Department*, his next attempt at a crime and police drama after *The Dark House*, narrates the story of seven Warsaw police officers and the mysterious death of one of them. With contemporary Warsaw in the background, the film tells the story about drugs, corruption, alcoholism, prostitution, and murder. *The Mighty Angel*, starring Robert Więckiewicz as the alcoholic writer Jerzy, is an adaptation of Jerzy Pilch's novel about addiction and redemption.

In his most recent film, the epic *Wołyń* (*Volhynia*, aka *Hatred*, 2016), perhaps the most important work in his career so far, Smarzowski deals another national trauma, another taboo topic inherited from the communist period: the 1943/1944 massacre of Poles in Volhynia and Eastern Galicia occupied by Nazi Germany. According to Ewa Siemaszko, from 1943 to 1945, Ukrainian nationalists murdered 130,000 Poles (and other nationalities who had Polish papers), now known in Poland as the Volhynia Slaughter (Rzeź Wołyńska).[85] Another expert on this subject, the Polish historian Grzegorz Motyka, estimates that ten thousand to fifteen thousand Ukrainians were killed in retaliatory Polish actions. Additionally, thousands more Ukrainians were killed by their own nationals (members of the Ukrainian Insurgent Army, UPA) for aiding the Poles.[86] To honor the Volhynian Poles, in July 2016 the Polish parliament almost unanimously (with only ten votes abstaining) adopted a resolution declaring 11 July the National Day of Remembrance of Victims of the Genocide Committed by Ukrainian Nationalists on Citizens of the Second Polish Republic.[87]

Referring to a prolonged silence over this painful moment in Polish history, *Volhynia* opens with an epigraph stating that *Kresowianie*, the people living in the former Polish Eastern Provinces known as Kresy (the eastern borderlands/frontiers), "were killed twice—once with an axe, the second time by silence. And the second death was much worse than the first." The film's first sequence, set in the summer of 1939, introduces a village wedding between a Polish woman and a Ukrainian man, which some Polish reviewers compared to the opening scenes of *The Deer Hunter* (1979, Michael Cimino). Although the atmosphere is festive, the first scenes of *Volhynia* reveal deep distrust and conflict along the ethnic divisions among the Polish, Ukrainian, and Jewish inhabitants of this region, later called the "bloodlands" of Europe by Snyder to define these lands "between Hitler and Stalin."[88]

The film is largely told from the perspective of the bride's groom, Zosia Głowacka (Michalina Łabacz's impressive debut), who is in love with a Ukrainian man, Petro (Vasili Vasylyk), but forced by her parents into marrying an older Polish

Figure 11.8 Michalina Łabacz (center) as Zosia Głowacka in Wojciech Smarzowski's *Volhynia* (aka *Hatred*, 2016). Courtesy of Film It/Krzysztof Wiktor.

neighbor, Maciej Skiba (Arkadiusz Jakubik), a rich farmer-widower with two children. The tension displayed during the wedding scenes foreshadows the gruesome events that follow. The region becomes the backdrop for an ethnic cleansing that often involves neighbors killing neighbors, and Smarzowski realistically depicts the outburst of nationalism on screen. As Snyder writes about those historical events: "According to numerous and mutually confirming reports Ukrainian partisans and their allies burned homes, shot or forced back inside those who tried to flee, and used sickles and pitchforks to kill those they captured outside. Churches full of worshippers were burned to the ground. Partisans displayed beheaded, crucified, dismembered, or disemboweled bodies, to encourage remaining Poles to flee."[89] Arguably, the same people who took part in the wedding later behead Zosia's sister, whose braids were earlier cut off with an axe during the opening wedding festivities. Showing the ethnic cleansing in its brutality, Smarzowski tries to keep balance and be historically objective by referring to the Poles' earlier harsh treatment of the Ukrainians, the prewar Polish expansionism and colonization, and by introducing Ukrainian characters who object to the killing, offer assistance, and are sometimes killed with the Poles.

In *Volhynia*, the camera by Piotr Sobociński Jr. is not shy of showing mass atrocities. The graphic images and the timing of the film's release stirred controversy: its premiere occurred during the ongoing war in eastern Ukraine between the Russian-backed separatists and government troops and the reemergence of the far right forces in this region. The film's release also prompted many critics to claim that its depiction does not help the Polish-Ukrainian reconciliation, as if the film should be used as a political tool. Smarzowski's film was banned in Ukraine, after being accused of political and historical bias, but its popularity in Poland has been an indication of a continued interest in historical issues.

Realistic Observations

The most financially successful Polish films deal with historical subjects or feature characters who benefited from the post-1989 market transformation. However, many films also focus on those who missed the recent speedy recovery of the Polish economy: the poor, the unemployed, the homeless, and those who were forced to seek jobs and better standards of living abroad. These films do not tell success stories of young professionals but deal with everyday life situations of Poles left behind. Several such films were made from 2002 to 2007, when the unemployment rate in Poland was particularly high. From only 0.3 percent in January 1990, the unemployment rate increased to 15.2 percent in 1995, reached 19.5 percent in 2002, and continued at this high level until 2007. In recent years, it has been gradually decreasing and is currently at 6.8 percent.[90]

Many films mentioned in chapter 10, such as *Hi, Tereska* (2001) and *Edi* (2002), addressed social problems. In 2005, *Komornik* (*The Debt Collector*, Feliks Falk) won the Gdynia Film Festival. It is a satirical social drama about forty-eight hours from the life of a ruthless debt collector, convincingly played by Andrzej Chyra. Another winner of the Gdynia Film Festival, *Plac Zbawiciela* (*Savior Square*, 2006, Krzysztof Krauze and Joanna Kos-Krauze), portrays a married couple in their mid-thirties who lose their money (and dreams about owning their own apartment) after investing everything they had with a developer who has gone bankrupt. Heavily in debt, Beata (Jowita Budnik) and Bartek (Arkadiusz Janiczek) accept his mother's offer and stay with their two small sons in her apartment, which overlooks one of Warsaw's central places, Savior Square. Their marriage collapses because of the lack of privacy, animosity between the overbearing mother (Ewa Wencel) and her depressed daughter-in-law, and Bartek's infidelity. The Krauzes produce a gritty social drama, which is loosely based on several reports published in the Polish press. They tell the story of the disintegration of a hard-working family—luckless people with limited options.

The postindustrial landscape of Silesia, a region greatly affected by a crisis in the coal mining industry, also attracted several filmmakers and serves as a backdrop for stories about lawbreaking, poverty, and lack of perspectives. They include films made by Michał Rosa, *Co słonko widziało* (*What the Sun Has Seen*, 2006); Robert Gliński, *Benek* (2007/2010); and Adam Sikora and Ingmar Villquist, *Ewa* (2010).[91] Another film set in Silesia, *Z odzysku* (*Retrieval*, 2006) directed by Sławomir Fabicki (1970–), introduces a nineteen-year-old amateur boxer (Antoni Pawlicki) who is in love with an older Ukrainian woman staying illegally in Poland with her child. In order to help her, the young man begins working for a local criminal. The film's characters and subject, its emotional dimension, and its frequent use of handheld cameras situate it close to the cinematic world of Mike Leigh.

Fabicki became known for his honest portrayals of an unglamorous reality. In his first work, *Męska sprawa* (*A Man Thing*, 2001), a black-and-white short film set in a rundown part of Łódź, he focuses on a thirteen-year-old boy who is abused by his father. The portrayal of a cruel adult world and the boy's loneliness secured Fabicki many prestigious awards, including an Oscar nomination. His more recent film, *Miłość* (*Loving*, 2013), loosely based on real events (a known case of sexual harassment involving a prominent city official), offers another portrayal of the Polish reality. Fabicki tells the story of a married couple, Maria (the outstanding Julia Kijowska) and her husband, Tomek (Marcin Dorociński), during their marital crisis.

Images of hopelessness and violence are also present in Leszek Wosiewicz's *Rozdroże Cafe* (*The Crossroads Café*, 2005), which intriguingly narrates the story of a group of young people committing a senseless, brutal murder during a bank robbery. The inefficiency of the legal system that leaves people at the mercy of corrupt officials is shown in two thrillers, both inspired by true events: *Układ zamknięty* (*The Closed Circuit*, 2013, Ryszard Bugajski) and *Lincz* (*Lynching*, 2010, Krzysztof Łukaszewicz). Bugajski's political thriller presents the world of shady regional state officials who attempt to take over a new, successful high-tech company by falsely accusing young executives of money laundering. The film is based on the much-publicized case of a group of entrepreneurs who were imprisoned after fabricated accusations by a local prosecutor and a tax office. Several years later, the businesspeople received only a symbolic compensation when the case against them was dismissed because of lack of evidence. Another film about the ineptitude of law, *Lynching*, takes place in a small village terrorized by a sixty-year-old man recently released from prison, who assaults the villagers and demands money. Unable to receive help from the authorities, local vigilantes take the law into their own hands and beat the man, causing his death.

Realistic films about difficult, everyday problems may comprise humor and lighthearted depictions of issues usually reserved for serious treatment. For example, *Boisko bezdomnych* (*The Offsiders*, 2008, Kasia Adamik) tells the story of a group of homeless people coached by a former soccer player who take part in the Homeless World Cup in Germany. Another film, *Chce się żyć* (*Life Feels Good*, 2013, Maciej Pieprzyca), a rare example of disability drama in Polish cinema, tells the uplifting story of Mateusz with cerebral palsy who was misdiagnosed in childhood as mentally disabled ("he is a vegetable"). Based on a true case, this (arguably first) Polish film focusing on a handicapped person received several prestigious awards, including Grand Prix and other prizes at the Montreal World Film Festival.

In *Life Feels Good*, the humorous voice-over of its protagonist, Mateusz (Kamil Tkacz as a boy and Dawid Ogrodnik as a grown-up character), comments on the action and offers an intimate look into his mind. The viewer knows from the beginning that he is an intelligent man who is just unable to communicate. The film begins in the 1980s and covers twenty-six years of Mateusz's solitude. His caring mother (Dorota Kolak) believes that her son responds to her questions ("he understands me"), and she seeks help. After the death of Mateusz's good-natured father (Arkadiusz Jakubik), he is placed in a home for the mentally disabled until the true nature of his disability is discovered.

The director Maciej Pieprzyca produces a touching, highly manipulative film (the mood switches constantly) about a difficult subject. *Life Feels Good* is an impressive story of disability, dignity, and human spirit. Unlike some internationally known films, for example, *The Diving Bell and the Butterfly* (2007, Julian Schnabel), Pieprzyca does not rely on the subjective camera. His style is observational and emotional, alternating between drama and comedy, with Oscar-deserving performances. The film's universal story about a person who is a prisoner of his body has been well received by audiences worldwide.

Another film that displays similar features, *Wszystko będzie dobrze* (*All Will Be Well*, 2007), is a road movie with religion in the background, directed by Tomasz Wiszniewski (1958–2016). Its story of redemption introduces a twelve-year-old boy, Paweł (Adam Werstak), who trains as a long-distance runner and tries to save his terminally ill mother. Paweł, whose alcoholic father died two years earlier and whose older brother is mentally handicapped, runs to the holy shrine of the Black Madonna of Częstochowa to ask her for mercy so that his mother is cured of cancer. He crosses 230 miles from his small town in Pomerania (northern Poland) to Częstochowa, accompanied by his recovering alcoholic teacher and coach (Robert Więckiewicz). The boy's effort gets media coverage, resulting in another chance for his mother: she will have an added surgery. For both characters, the pilgrimage to Częstochowa becomes a transformational journey. The film features a developing bond between the two and becomes a story of fighting an addiction. For the coach, this journey offers a chance to escape his professional problems caused by his alcoholism. Despite its premise, *All Will Be Well* is not a religious film but, perhaps, a commentary on the shallow nature of Polish Catholicism. It is an open-ended, genre-defying film with a distinct visual style relying on medium close ups to register emotions (Jarosław Szoda's cinematography).[92]

Two very different films that have been made in recent years both offer an unflattering portrayal of the Polish reality: Tomasz Wasilewski's *Zjednoczone stany miłości* (*United States of Love*, 2016, Poland–Sweden) and Agnieszka Holland's *Pokot* (*Spoor*, aka *Game Count*, 2017, Poland–Czech Republic–Germany–Sweden). After making *Płynące wieżowce* (*Floating Skyscrapers*, 2013), a contemporary coming-out drama, heralded as the first Polish film to feature an openly gay protagonist, Wasilewski's third film, *United States of Love*, received much critical attention. Set after the transition to democracy, the film portrays a drab landscape in which four women, whose stories intersect, yearn for unattainable romantic liaisons. Their feelings (or fixations), however, are doomed from the start.

Wasilewski's film looks like a compact version of Kieślowski's *Decalogue*, with interconnected stories of a joyless young mother, Agata (Julia Kijowska); a cold school principal, Iza (Magdalena Cielecka); her younger sister, Marzena (Marta Nieradkiewicz); and an older woman, Renata (Dorota Kolak), who is fixated on Marzena. Jonathan Romney calls it "a short film about anguish," and "an intricately constructed puzzlebox drama."[93] The Romanian cinematographer Oleg Mutu (who also worked on award-winning films by Cristi Puiu and Cristian Mungiu) contributes to the cold visual style. He creates an inhospitable, washed-out (almost black-and-white) landscape in this "bleak picture of the human condition, shot in appropriately cadaverous tones."[94] Rightly pointing out some shortcomings of the screenplay (which, interestingly, was awarded the Silver Bear at the Berlin International Film Festival), several critics emphasized the ironic and cynical portrayal of the post-1989 reality.

Agnieszka Holland's *Spoor* offers another comment on the Polish reality. It is an adaptation of a popular novel by Olga Tokarczuk, one of Poland's most popular and critically acclaimed writers.⁹⁵ Like the novel, Holland's multigenre film follows the conventions of a detective story. Its main character, Janina Duszejko (Agnieszka Mandat), a retired civil engineer who used to build bridges in the Middle East, now teaches part time and lives in a secluded village in a picturesque part of Poland, the Kłodzko Valley near the Czech-Polish border (the Sudeten mountain range). This eccentric older woman, interested in environmental issues and astrology, conducts her own investigation into the mysterious deaths of several local hunters and poachers. She is a militant animal rights activist willing to avenge wild animals by killing hunters and those who kill or mistreat animals.

Holland's film starts as a murder mystery but changes into a detective story and ecological thriller with magic realist elements, eventually leaving the viewer wondering about its multilayered construct, which is full of red herrings and obscure plots, undeveloped characters, and an unreliable narrator. The film's cinematography displays stylish shots of wintry landscapes and nature. Though not intended as a political film, according to several commentaries by Holland, *Spoor* nonetheless remarks on the divided political spectrum in Poland. An observation voiced by one of the film's characters, a Czech entomologist, summarizes it aptly: "Mushroom picking in the forest is the only thing that brings Poles together."

A growing number of realistic films focus on the issue of emigration, thus reflecting problems that many Polish families face. With the total population of Poland at 38.4 million, almost 2.4 million Poles stayed temporarily outside Poland in 2015, most them in EU countries. That number increased from one million since Poland's accession to the European Union in 2004.⁹⁶ Popular television series, such as *Londyńczycy* (*Londoners*, 2008, thirteen episodes), show Polish immigrants and temporary workers in London. Films such as *Pomiędzy słowami* (*Beyond Words*, Poland–The Netherlands, 2017), directed by the Polish-Dutch filmmaker Urszula Antoniak, deal with maintaining the Polish identity abroad while blending into the social fabric of a chosen homeland. Impeccably shot in black and white by Lennert Hillege, *Beyond Words* revolves around Michael/Michał (Jakub Gierszał), a young Polish lawyer in Berlin who is successfully assimilated, yet emotionally withdrawn. An unexpected visit by his estranged, presumed dead Polish father (Andrzej Chyra) forces him to rethink his status in his adoptive country and his links with Poland.

Other films deal with the impact of temporary economic migration on family life and with the issue of illegal immigration. They include, among others, *Jutro będzie lepiej* (*Tomorrow Will Be Better*, 2011, Dorota Kędzierzawska), about three young boys from Ukraine who move to Poland, and *Obce niebo* (*Strange Heaven*, 2015, Dariusz Gajewski), about a Polish family living in Sweden. *Dzikie róże* (*Wild Roses*, 2017, Anna Jadowska) deals with a marital crisis involving a husband working in Norway and his young wife Ewa (Marta Nieradkiewicz) who has an affair with a teenage boy during his absence. *Moja krew* (*My Flesh, My Blood*, 2009, Marcin Wrona) portrays a terminally ill Polish boxer (Eryk Lubos) who wants to father a child with his Vietnamese girlfriend, an illegal immigrant in Poland. This is arguably the first narrative film that focuses on immigration to Poland, an unexplored territory in Polish cinema. Perhaps the most accomplished in this group is the 2017 winner of the Gdynia Film Festival, *Cicha noc* (*Silent Night*), Piotr Domalewski's feature debut. Set in northeastern Poland, the film tells the story of a Polish economic migrant in Holland (Dawid Ogrodnik, Best Actor Award in Gdynia), who returns unexpectedly to spend Christmas Eve with his family. This tragicomic film deals with the impact of emigration on family life, resulting in broken family bonds.

An unusual film in the Polish context is *Ptaki śpiewają w Kigali* (*Birds Are Singing in Kigali*, 2017), directed by Joanna Kos-Krauze and Krzysztof Krauze (who died at the beginning of filming in December 2014), which is advertised as the first Polish film about refugees. It deals with the Rwandan genocide and revolves around two women: a Rwandan woman who survived the genocide, Claudine (Elaine Umuhire), and a Polish woman, Anna (Jowita Budnik), an ornithologist who used to work in Rwanda and now assists Claudine. *Birds Are Singing in Kigali* is a formalistic film that offers a universal story about coming to terms with a traumatic event, but the focus is on the trauma rather than the tragedy itself. The Krauzes employ art house devices as if to comment on the process of memory, for example, by inserting elongated images of vultures indulging on carrions. Their ambitious film has been appreciated for its noble intentions, but unable to capture the much-needed emotions.

A Note on Documentary and Animation

Recent Polish documentaries often garner critical attention and win prizes at film festivals. For example, Marcel Łoziński's *Poste Restante* won the European Film Award in 2009 and Bartosz Konopka's short documentary *Królik po berlińsku* (*Rabbit á la Berlin*, 2009), an unusual take on the history of the Berlin Wall, was nominated for the 2010 Academy Award for Best Documentary. Social documentaries by Ewa Borzęcka, *Arizona* (1997) and *Oni* (*They*, 1999), which picture problems facing the Polish poor in adapting to the new capitalist reality, find their continuation in many contemporary documentaries. Very personal, almost exhibitionist documentaries by Marcin Koszałka (cinematographer and director) have won awards and provoked discussions, among them *Takiego pięknego syna urodziłam* (*Such a Nice Boy I Gave Birth To*, 1999), *Istnienie* (*The Existence*, 2007), and *Deklaracja nieśmiertelności* (*The Declaration of Immortality*, 2010). Paweł Łoziński's multi-award-winning documentary about a difficult mother-daughter relationship, *Nawet nie wiesz jak bardzo cię kocham* (*You Have No Idea How I Love You*, 2016), covers similar territory.

As expected, the bulk of recent Polish documentaries deal with various aspects of Polish history, often resulting in films that gain international acclaim. For example, in *Po-lin: Okruchy pamięci* (*Po-lin*, 2008) Jolanta Dylewska uses amateur family films made in the 1930s in Polish shtetls and Polish towns with a sizeable Jewish population by the visiting American relatives of Polish Jews. Dylewska talks to the Polish inhabitants of towns featured in the footage and identifies several people featured in the archival materials. As a result, by focusing on the everyday, unhurried rhythm of prewar Jewish life in Poland, Dylewska shows history with a human face.

The best-known examples of recent Polish documentaries focus on everyday issues: relationships, social issues, aging, and death in the family. *Bracia* (*Brothers*, 2015, Wojciech Staroń), tells the story of two older men: brothers who returned to Poland after living for several years in Siberia and Kazakhstan. Staroń makes the film about brotherly love and help, the passing of time, and aging with dignity. Another documentary, *Joanna* (2013, Aneta Kopacz), is an intimate, Oscar-nominated film about the last months of a young mother dying of cancer. *Komunia* (*Communion*, 2015, Anna Zamecka), the winner at Locarno and other festivals, tells the story of the fourteen-year-old girl Ola who must grow up quickly because she has undependable parents. Ola takes care of her younger, autistic brother for whom she prepares a communion celebration. The paradocumentary *Wszystkie nieprzespane noce* (*All These Sleepless Nights* (2015, Michał Marczak), which won the Best Director Award at the Sundance Film Festival, offers a common generational portrait of Warsaw youth.

Contemporary Polish animated filmmakers draw on the visual language of their predecessors to produce sophisticated and challenging animation. One of the leading representatives, Piotr Dumała (1956–), gained international fame for his unique stories inspired by Franz Kafka and Fyodor Dostoevsky, such as *Łagodna* (*Gentle Spirit*, 1985), *Franz Kafka* (1991), and *Zbrodnia i kara* (*Crime and Punishment*, 2000), and continues his career with films such as *Hipopotamy* (*Hippos*, 2014). A member of the younger generation, Tomasz Bagiński (1976–), was nominated for an Oscar in 2002 for his computer-generated fantasy *Katedra* (*The Cathedral*) and received acclaim, including a BAFTA award, for *Sztuka spadania* (*Fallen Art*, 2004) and *Kinematograf* (*The Kinematograph*, 2009). In 2008, the model animation *Peter & the Wolf* (2006, Suzie Templeton, Poland-UK-Norway-Mexico) received the Academy Award for Best Animated Short Film. Platige Image, the film studio that produced Bagiński's films, also enabled Damian Nenow to make his award-winning *Paths of Hate* (2010).

Arguably, the best-known recent animated work is the Polish-English coproduction *Twój Vincent* (*Loving Vincent*, 2017, Dorota Kobiela and Hugh Welchman). This Oscar-nominated, feature-length animation is the first to recreate the visual world of Vincent van Gogh on screen: his paintings are brought to life. Relying on the flashback structure, *Loving Vincent* offers a detective-like story in oil-painted animation, which refers to the tragic death of Van Gogh.

* * *

Since the foundation of the Polish Film Institute in 2005, the local film industry has produced an impressive number of first-rate films. It has become better known internationally, as evidenced by a wider distribution of Polish films abroad and several prizes at international film festivals, including the 2015 Oscar for *Ida*. In addition, local cinema has been increasingly popular among Polish viewers. Since 2005, when not a single Polish film appeared among the top ten at the box office, four or five Polish films have been among the top ten every year. For example, there were four Polish films in the top ten in 2008 (the comedy *Ladies* on top of the list), four in 2011 (the romantic comedy *Letters to Santa* as the most successful), and local films dominating the box office in 2016 and 2017.[97]

Film debuts usually indicate the rank and health of any national cinema. If this is the case, then the numbers at the 2017 Gdynia Film Festival are encouraging indeed. First-time filmmakers have made six of the sixteen films shown in the main competition, and a debut film by Piotr Domalewski, *Silent Night*, won the Golden Lion. In 2016, the main award went to another emerging director, Jan P. Matuszyński, for *The Last Family*.

Polish cinema has entered a new stage. With the passing of Andrzej Wajda in 2016, and with several classic Polish directors no longer making films, the time has come for younger filmmakers, who spent their formative years in the transition to democracy, to pursue new vistas in local cinema and to offer different perspectives on Polish history and present-day realities. Judging by the critical reception of Polish films and their box office figures, local audiences anticipate seeing stylistically innovative works that incorporate new trends in world cinema yet nurture the local idiom.

Notes

1. *Film Production Guide: Poland 2010* (Warsaw: Polish Film Institute, 2010): 32.
2. "Ustawa z dnia 30 czerwca 2005 r. o kinematografii," Dz.U. 2005 nr 132 poz 1111. ISAP (Internetwoy System Aktów Prawnych), http://isap.sejm.gov.pl/DetailsServlet?id=WDU20051321111.
3. *Film Production Guide: Poland 2010*, 29.
4. Tadeusz Kowalski, ed., "Raport o stanie kultury: Kinematografia—W kierunku rynku i Europy" (Warsaw: Ministerstwo Kultury i Dziedzictwa Narodowego, 2009), 9. http://www.kongreskultury.pl/library/File/RoSK%20kinematografia/kinematografia_kowalski.pdf.
5. *Polskie Filmy 2016* (Warsaw: Polish Film Institute, 2016), 183.
6. *Film Production Guide: Poland 2010*, 30. The first multiplex cinema was built in Warsaw in 1996.
7. Tadeusz Miczka, "Raport o stanie polskiej kinematografii" (Warsaw: Ministerstwo Kultury i Dziedzictwa Narodowego, 2009), http://www.kongreskultury.pl/library/File/RaportKinema/kinematografia_raport_w.pelna.pdf.
8. For example, from 2006 to 2009 as many as thirty Polish films were international coproductions. *Film Production Guide: Poland 2010*, 33.
9. *Film Production Guide: Poland 2010*, 99.
10. "Rynek filmowy: Polskie kino historyczne" (Warsaw: Polish Film Institute), http://www.pisf.pl/rynek-filmowy/polskie-kino-historyczne-2005-2015 (accessed 15 October 2017).
11. James Mark, *The Unfinished Revolution: Making Sense of the Communist Past in Central-Eastern Europe* (New Haven, CT: Yale University Press, 2010), 47.
12. Ibid, 50–58. The ruling party Prawo i Sprawiedliwość (PiS) was founded in 2001 by twin brothers Lech and Jarosław Kaczyński. PiS formed the government from 2005 to 2007. It has been in power since November 2015. Lech Kaczyński was the Polish president from 2005 to 2010.

13. See a collection of significant documents pertaining to the tragedy, Anna M. Cienciala, Natalia S. Lebedeva, and Wojciech Materski, eds., *Katyń: A Crime Without Punishment* (New Haven, CT: Yale University Press, 2007).
14. Andrzej Mularczyk, *Katyń. Post mortem. Powieść filmowa* (Warsaw: Muza, 2007).
15. Nick Hodge and Marta Urbańska, "Andrzej Wajda on *Katyń*: The Full Transcript," *Krakow Post* (23 June 2009), http://www.krakowpost.com/article/1388
16. Geoffrey Mcnab, "The Bloodshed Had to Be Shown," *The Guardian* (1 May 2008), http://www.guardian.co.uk/film/2008/may/02/1.
17. A. O. Scott, "Bearing Witness to Poland's Pain: *Katyń*," *New York Times* (17 February 2009) http://www.nytimes.com/2009/02/19/arts/19iht-18katy.20301236.html.
18. Polish President Bronisław Komorowski attended the premiere of Hoffman's film. Given its comparatively high budget, the film's box office (1.5 million viewers) was disappointing. Website of the Polish Ministry of Culture and National Heritage (Ministerstwo Kultury i Dziedzictwa Narodowego) http://www.mkidn.gov.pl/pages/posts/premiera-filmu—1920-bitwa-warszawskardquo-2324.php (accessed 15 May 2017).
19. *Influence* had only 62,610 viewers. PISF, Box Office, Polskie premiery, http://www.pisf.pl/rynek-filmowy/box-office/filmy-polskie?cat=11507 (accessed 14 November 2017).
20. Jan Komasa is a graduate of the Łódź Film School. He started his career as the coauthor of three-part *Oda do radości* (*Ode to Joy*, 2005, with Anna Kazejak-Dawid and Maciej Migas). His first feature was *Sala samobójców* (*The Suicide Room*, 2011), a film about a sensitive but troubled teenager and the world of virtual reality.
21. Tadeusz Sobolewski, "O której skończy się powstanie?" *Gazeta Wyborcza* 176 (2014): 12. See also Sobolewski, "Przeżyj sobie powstanie," *Gazeta Wyborcza* 218 (2014): 20–21.
22. The official page of *Warsaw Uprising* (2014). http://warsawrising-thefilm.com.
23. Robert Gliński directed *Stones for the Rampart* after making two realistic films, *Benek* and *Świnki* (*Piggies*, 2009). Gliński's earlier film, *Wróżby kumaka*, aka *Unkenrufe* (*The Call of the Toad*, 2005), the Polish-German coproduction dealing with reconciliation between the two nations, is based on Günter Grass's novel set in Gdańsk. It tells a story of a mature love between a Polish woman and a German man who create the Polish-German Cemetery Society.
24. Jan T. Gross, *Neighbors: The Destruction of the Jewish Community in Jedwabne* (Princeton, NJ: Princeton University Press, 2001).
25. Jan T. Gross, *Sąsiedzi: Historia zagłady żydowskiego miasteczka* (Sejny: Fundacja Pogranicze, 2000). For debates in Poland on Gross's book, see Antony Polonsky and Joanna B. Michlic, eds., *The Neighbors Respond: The Controversy over the Jedwabne Massacre in Poland* (Princeton, NJ: Princeton University Press, 2003); also several essays in Dorota Glowacka and Joanna Zylinska, eds., *Imaginary Neighbors: Mediating Polish-Jewish Relations after the Holocaust* (Lincoln: University of Nebraska Press, 2007).

26. Gross acknowledged that his research about the "Jedwabne controversy" owes its inspiration to Agnieszka Arnold's documentary *Sąsiedzi* (*Neighbors*, 2001). Arnold started the work on her documentary in 1998 and allowed Gross to see the footage from Jedwabne.
27. Jan Gross and Irena Grudzinska-Gross, *Golden Harvest: Events at the Periphery of the Holocaust* (Oxford: Oxford University Press, 2012).
28. Andrzej Stasiuk, "The Gold Harvest," trans. Julia Sherwood, *Central European Forum Salon* (11 February 2011), http://salon.eu.sk/en/archiv/1911.
29. Tadeusz Słobodzianek, "Tadeusz Słobodzianek o *Naszej klasie*," Warsaw: Teatr Dramatyczny, http://teatrdramatyczny.pl/index.php?option=com_content&view =article&id=850:tadeusz-sobodzianek-o-qnaszej-klasieq&catid=65&Itemid=251 (accessed 12 November 2017). Słobodzianek's play, *Nasza klasa* (*Our Class*), won the prestigious Polish prize, the Nike Literary Award.
30. Barbara Hollender, "O pogromie bez niedopowiedzeń," *Rzeczpospolita* 110 (12–13 May 2012): A12. The film's coproducer, Dariusz Jabłoński, explains that foreign coproducers (Russian-Slovak-Dutch) later supported the project because they did not consider its subject to be a uniquely Polish phenomenon.
31. For a detailed analysis of the Polish reception of Pasikowski's *Aftermath*, see Magdalena Nowicka, "Polskość jako przedmiot sporu: Przykład kontrowersji wokół filmu *Pokłosie* w reż—Władysława Pasikowskiego," *Przegląd Socjologiczny* 1 (2015): 183–210; Piotr Forecki, "*Pokłosie*, poGrossie i kibice polskości," *Studia Litteraria Historica* 2 (2013): 211–35.
32. Ronnie Scheib, "Film Review: *Aftermath*," *Variety* (1 November 2013), http://variety.com/2013/film/reviews/aftermath-review-1200783281.
33. "Wieś to Jedwabne, miasto to Żegota"; quoted from Forecki, "*Pokłosie*, poGrossie i kibice polskości," 220.
34. Screenwriter and director Marcin Wrona (1973–2015) started his career in cinema with *Moja krew* (*My Flesh My Blood*, 2009) and *Chrzest* (*The Christening*, 2010).
35. For example, Simon Abrams writes: "*Demon* ranks up there with *The Witch* and *The Babadook* as one of the best recent horror films." Simon Abrams, "Demon," rogerebert.com (9 September 2016), http://www.rogerebert.com/reviews/demon-2016.
36. *Merriam-Webster Dictionary*, https://www.merriam-webster.com/dictionary/dybbuk (accessed 29 October 2017).
37. Terry Gross, "'Ida' Director Made Film to 'Recover the Poland' of His Childhood" [Conversation with Paweł Pawlikowski on *Fresh Air*], NPR (12 February 2015), http://www.npr.org/2015/02/12/385742784/ida-director-made-film-to-recover-the-poland-of-his-childhood.
38. Ibid.
39. Megan Ratner, "Displaced Persons: *Ida*'s Window on Vanished Lives," *Film Quarterly* 67, no. 3 (2014): 34.

40. See, e.g., David Denby, "*Ida*: A Film Masterpiece," *The New Yorker* (27 May 2014), https://www.newyorker.com/culture/culture-desk/ida-a-film-masterpiece. Denby calls *Ida* a "compact masterpiece."
41. Glowacka and Zylinska, eds., *Imaginary Neighbors*, 4. Protests against *Ida*, launched by Poland's nationalist groups after the film was nominated for Academy Awards, were widely reported by the press. See, e.g., Andrew Pulver, "Polish Nationalists Launch Petition against Oscar-Nominated film *Ida*," *The Guardian* (22 January 2015), https://www.theguardian.com/film/2015/jan/22/ida-oscars-2015-film-polish-nationalists-petition.
42. Polish Film Institute, Box Office, http://www.pisf.pl/rynek-filmowy/box-office/table:polskie-premiery-2013 (accessed 20 September 2017). For comparison, the highest-grossing film released in 2013, Wojciech Smarzowski's *Traffic Department*, had 1,025,407 viewers. It was followed by Andrzej Wajda's *Walesa: Man of Hope* with 970,529 viewers.
43. Robert Marshall, *In the Sewers of Lvov* (London: William Collins, 1990). Earlier, in 2003, Agnieszka Holland directed a Canadian-German-Polish coproduction, *Julia Walking Home* (aka *The Healer*), which received mixed reviews. Recently, she directed *Copying Beethoven* (2006, US), *Janosik: Prawdziwa historia* (*Janosik: A True Story*, codirected with her daughter, Katarzyna Adamik, 2009, Polish-Slovak-Czech), and *Hořici Keř* (*Burning Bush*, 2013, TV, Czech Republic). From 2008 to 2012, Holland was the president of the Polish Film Academy. Since December 2013, she has been chairing the European Film Academy (EFA).
44. Jolanta Dylewska also written, photographed, and directed two classic Polish documentaries about the Holocaust, *Chronicle of the Warsaw Ghetto Uprising according to Marek Edelman* (1993) and *Po-lin* (2008).
45. Timothy Snyder, "The Overwhelming Realism of *In Darkness*," *The New Yorker* (22 February 2012), https://www.newyorker.com/culture/culture-desk/the-overwhelming-realism-of-in-darkness.
46. Robert Więckiewicz's (1967–) breakthrough came in 2004 with his starring role of an art thief in Juliusz Machulski's heist film *Vinci*. His real break came three years later, in 2007, when he appeared in Tomasz Wiszniewski's road movie *All Will Be Well*, where he played the leading role of a recovering alcoholic teacher (Best Actor Award at the Gdynia Film Festival and the Polish Film Award). He became known for his roles in films set in the communist past, including Wojciech Smarzowski's *The Dark House*, Jan Kidawa-Błoński's *Rosebud*, and Andrzej Wajda's *Walesa: Man of Hope*.
47. Larry Rohter, "In the Sewers with *In Darkness*," *New York Times* (3 February 2012), https://carpetbagger.blogs.nytimes.com/2012/02/03/in-the-sewers-with-in-darkness/?scp=3&sq=in%20darkness&st=cse.
48. See Elżbieta Ostrowska, "'I Will Wash It Out': Holocaust Reconciliation in Agnieszka Holland's 2011 Film *In Darkness*," *Holocaust and Genocide Studies* 29, no. 1 (2015): 57–75.

49. David Edelstein, "Schindler in the Sewers," *New York Magazine* (6 February 2012), http://nymag.com/movies/reviews/in-darkness-rampart-edelstein-2012-2.
50. Snyder, "The Overwhelming Realism of *In Darkness*."
51. Several Polish documentaries dealt with the Smolensk tragedy. In 2016, Antoni Krauze (1940–2018) made the controversial and uneven docudrama *Smoleńsk* (*Smolensk*).
52. Similar story, although less noteworthy, is narrated in *Historia Roja* (*The Story of Roj*, 2016, Jerzy Zalewski), about an anticommunist partisan (member of the National Armed Forces, NSZ) and his unit fighting the communist regime until 1951.
53. Tadeusz Sobolewski, "*Generał Nil*: Film jak salwa honorowa dla generała Fieldorfa," *Gazeta Wyborcza* (17 kwietnia 2009), http://wyborcza.pl/1,75410,6507630,_General_Nil____film_jak_salwa_honorowa_dla_generala.html.
54. See, e.g., Konstanty R. Piekarski, *Escaping Hell: The Story of a Polish Underground Officer in Auschwitz and Buchenwald* (Toronto: Dundurn Press, 1989). See also Polish docudrama *Pilecki* (2015, Mirosław Krzyszkowski).
55. Belén Vidal, "Introduction: The Biopic and Its Critical Contexts," in *The Biopic in Contemporary Film Culture*, ed. Tom Brown and Belén Vidal (New York: Routledge, 2014), 2.
56. Interestingly, in 2009 Wajda received the Alfred Bauer Prize at the Berlin Film Festival for *Tatarak* (*Sweet Rush*, 2009), his fourth adaptation of the works of Jarosław Iwaszkiewicz. The prize is given to filmmakers who open new perspectives on cinematic art.
57. Michał Oleszczyk, "Andrzej Wajda: The Searcher," *Criterion Collection* (6 March 2017), https://www.criterion.com/current/posts/4450-andrzej-wajda-the-searcher.
58. Andrzej Wajda, "Nie tracąc nadziei: z Andrzejem Wajdą rozmawia Tadeusz Lubelski," *Kino* 10 (2013): 15. Wajda comments that the inclusion of the documentary footage was necessary not only for financial reasons (the lack of resources to reenact certain historical events) but also in order to render the past events truthfully.
59. Answering the question why he makes films referring to difficult historical subjects, *Aftermath* and now *Jack Strong*, Pasikowski answers, "I think that it wasn't me, but the producers who butchered romantic comedies and adapted all compulsory school readings, discovered a fondness for history." Joanna Poros, "Cold War Spy Jack Strong: Interview with the Director," *Culture.pl* (28 January 2014), http://culture.pl/en/article/cold-war-spy-jack-strong-interview-with-the-director.
60. Biopics of Pope John Paul II enjoyed popular success in Poland—three of them are among top ten box office hits of 2005–2006.
61. Maria Sadowska (1976–), the 2002 graduate of the Łódź Film School, is also an accomplished singer, composer, and song writer who moves between jazz, electronic music, and pop (she released her first album in 1995). In 2013, she made her full-length debut film, *Dzień kobiet* (*Women's Day*).

62. Michalina Wisłocka, *Sztuka kochania* (Warsaw: Iskry, 1978). English edition, *A Practical Guide to Marital Bliss* (Worcester: M & A Publishers, 1987).
63. Cinematographers Michał Sobociński (1987–) and Piotr Sobociński Jr. (1983–) come from a family of internationally well-known cinematographers. The sons of the actor Hanna Mikuć and the cinematographer Piotr Sobociński (1958–2001). Their father worked, among others, on two parts (2 and 9) of Krzysztof Kieślowski's *Decalogue* and *Three Colours: Red* (for which he received an Oscar nomination). Later he worked on several big-budget Hollywood films, including *Marvin's Room* (Jerry Zaks, 1996), *Ransom* (1996, Ron Howard), and *Twilight* (1998, Robert Benton). He died prematurely during the production of *Trapped* (2002, Luis Mandoki), released after his death. Their grandfather, Witold Sobociński (1929–), is one of the most esteemed Polish cinematographers. His credits include Wajda's *The Wedding* and *The Promised Land*, Polański's *Frantic*, Andrzej Żuławski's *The Third Part of the Night*, and Zanussi's *Family Life*, among others.
64. The audiovisual footage recorded over the years by Beksiński and other materials are employed in a recent documentary by Marcin Borchardt, *Beksińscy: Album wideofoniczny* (*The Beksinskis: A Sound and Picture Album*, 2017).
65. Jay Weissberg, "The Last Family," *Variety* (8 August 2016), http://variety.com/2016/film/reviews/the-last-family-review-1201832466.
66. Thomas Anessi, "Moving Ahead into the Past: Historical Contexts in Recent Polish Cinema," *Images* 11, no. 20 (2012): 21.
67. Maria Todorova, "Introduction: From Utopia to Propaganda and Back," in *Post-Communist Nostalgia*, ed. Maria Todorova and Zsuzsa Gille (New York: Berghahn Books, 2010), 1.
68. For an overview, see Monika Prusik and Maria Lewicka, "Nostalgia for Communist Times and Autobiographical Memory: Negative Present or Positive Past?" *Political Psychology* 37, no. 5 (2016): 677–93.
69. Ibid., 678. Grzegorz Osiecki, "Europa mo muerte! Polacy jednoznacznie za Unią," *Dziennik Gazeta Prawna* (14 March 2017), http://www.gazetaprawna.pl/artykuly/1027016,europa-o-muerte-polacy-jednoznacznie-za-unia.html.
70. Maciej Pieprzyca, screenwriter-director born in 1964 in Katowice, started his career with a series of documentaries, including *Przez nokaut* (*By Knockout*, 1995), about a Polish boxing champion Leszek Błażyński. Pieprzyca continued his career with two popular television films, *Inferno* (2001) and *Barbórka* (*The Feast of St. Barbara*, 2005), a comedy set in industrial Silesia. The lighthearted humor in the latter and present-day realities are also present in his big-screen debut, *Drzazgi* (*Splinters*, 2008), a modern coming-of-age story.
71. The American Film Institute's definition quoted in Leger Grindon, *The Hollywood Romantic Comedy: Conventions, History, Controversies* (Malden, MA: Blackwell, 2011), 1.
72. *Polskie Filmy 2016*, 181.
73. In terms of the box office, among films released after 1990, *Letters to Santa* is at number 8 with more than 2.5 million viewers and *Planet Single* at number 15 with

1.9 million (see Appendix B). The box office success of *Letters to Santa* resulted in a sequel, which was directed by Maciej Dejczer in 2015 (number 5, with almost three million viewers). Another successful sequel, directed by Tomasz Konecki, was released in November 2017 (number 4).

74. *The Criterion Collection*, "Synopsis," https://www.criterion.com/films/29061-the-lure (accessed 6 November 2017).
75. Angela Lovell, "*The Lure*: One Is Silver and the Other Gold," *The Criterion Collection* (10 October 2017), https://www.criterion.com/current/posts/5030-the-lure-one-is-silver-and-the-other-gold.
76. Michał Oleszczyk in Nikolaj Nikitin, "Poland Grows Filmmakers Catering to Audiences with Mainstream Hits," *Variety* (22 May 2017), http://variety.com/2017/film/spotlight/poland-grows-filmmakers-catering-to-audiences-with-mainstream-hits-1202434704.
77. A. O. Scott, "*11 Minutes*, a Whirl of Intersecting Tales Heading toward Combustion," *New York Times* (7 April 2016), https://www.nytimes.com/2016/04/08/movies/11-minutes-review.html.
78. Peter Debruge, "Berlin Film Review: *Body*," *Variety* (9 February 2015), http://variety.com/2015/film/festivals/berlin-film-review-body-1201428455.
79. Marian Dziędziel (1947–) has also appeared in other films by Smarzowski, playing dynamic blue-collar characters. Such strong plebeian characters became his specialty, and it would be difficult to imagine contemporary Polish cinema without Dziędziel's commanding presence and the way he uses the vernacular (he was born in Silesia).
80. Tadeusz Sobolewski, "Smarzowski zrobił polskie *Fargo*," *Gazeta Wyborcza* (18 September 2009), http://wyborcza.pl/1,75410,7051411,Smarzowski_zrobil_polskie__Fargo__.html.
81. The film received only one major award, for best actor (Marcin Dorociński). Jerzy Skolimowski's *Essential Killing* received top awards.
82. Tadeusz Sobolewski, "Wybitny film *Róża*: Pole minowe historii," *Gazeta Wyborcza* (2 February 2012), http://wyborcza.pl/1,75410,11073235,Wybitny_film__Roza___Pole_minowe_historii.html.
83. Izabela Kalinowska, "From Political Engagement to Politics of Abjection in Polish Auteur Cinema: The Case of Wojtek Smarzowski," in *The Global Auteur: The Politics of Authorship in 21st Century Cinema*, ed. Seung-Hoon Jeong and Jeremi Szaniawski (London: Bloomsbury Academic, 2016), 129.
84. Alissa Simon, "Rose," *Variety* (16 June 2011), http://variety.com/2011/film/markets-festivals/rose-1117945460.
85. Ewa Siemaszko, "Bilans zbrodni," *Biuletyn IPN* 1–2 (2009): 93.
86. Grzegorz Motyka, *Od rzezi wołyńskiej do akcji "Wisła": Konflikt polsko-ukraiński 1943–1947* (Kraków: Wydawnictwo Literackie, 2011), 448.
87. "Narodowy Dzień Pamięci Ofiar Ludobójstwa dokonanego przez ukraińskich nacjonalistów na obywatelach II Rzeczypospolitej Polskiej." On Sunday, 11 July 1943

(known as Bloody Sunday), with Poles attending Sunday mass at Catholic churches, around one hundred Polish settlements on territories occupied by Nazi Germany were attacked by the Ukrainian nationalists. See Motyka, *Od rzezi wołyńskiej do akcji "Wisła,"* 137–41. The action of the Polish parliament, calling the Volhynian massacre a genocide, was harshly criticized by the Ukrainian parliament for politicizing the Polish-Ukrainian history.

88. Timothy Snyder, *Bloodlands: Europe between Hitler and Stalin* (New York: Basics Books, 2010).
89. Timothy Snyder, *The Reconstruction of Nations: Poland, Ukraine, Lithuania, Belarus, 1569–1999* (New Haven, CT: Yale University Press, 2003), 169.
90. "Unemployment Rate 1990–2017," Central Statistical Office of Poland, Unemployment: https://stat.gov.pl/en/topics/labour-market/registered-unemployment/unemployment-rate-1990-2017,3,1.html (accessed 30 November 2017). The unemployment figures are quoted from September each year.
91. The theme of prostitution present in the 2010 film *Ewa* (the unemployed miner's wife is forced into prostitution) also reappears in Robert Gliński's *Piggies* about teenage boys working as prostitutes near the German border.
92. Cinematographer Jarosław Szoda later codirected with Bolesław Pawica *Handlarz cudów* (*Miracle Seller*, 2010, Poland-Sweden), a narrative film about another recovering alcoholic, this time on a journey to Lourdes, France. His life changes after an accidental meeting with two young refuges searching for their father in France.
93. Jonathan Romney, "*United States of Love*: Berlin Review," *ScreenDaily* (19 February 2016), https://www.screendaily.com/reviews/united-states-of-love-berlin-review/5100592.article.
94. Michael Brooke, "United States of Love," *Sight & Sound* 26, no. 12 (2016): 62.
95. Olga Tokarczuk, *Prowadź pług przez kości umarłych* (Kraków: Wydawnictwo Literackie, 2009).
96. "Informacja o rozmiarach i kierunkach emigracji z Polski w latach 2004–2015," Główny Urząd Statystyczny, Portal Informacyjny (Warsaw 2016): 3, https://stat.gov.pl/obszary-tematyczne/ludnosc/migracje-zagraniczne-ludnosci/informacja-o-rozmiarach-i-kierunkach-emigracji-z-polski-w-latach-20042015,2,9.html.
97. "Poland Yearly Box Office," Box Office Mojo, http://www.boxofficemojo.com/intl/poland/yearly/?yr=2017&p=.htm (accessed 5 December 2017).

APPENDIX A

The Twenty-Five Biggest Polish Box Office Hits on Polish Screens from 1945 to 1989

1. *The Teutonic Knights* (*Krzyżacy*, 1960, Aleksander Ford), 33,315,695 viewers
2. *In Desert and Wilderness* (*W pustyni i w puszczy*, 1973, Władysław Ślesicki), 30,089,874
3. *The Deluge* (*Potop*, 2 parts, 1974, Jerzy Hoffman), 27,615,921
4. *Nights and Days* (*Noce i dnie*, 1975, Jerzy Antczak), 22,350,078
5. *Forbidden Songs* (*Zakazane piosenki*, 1947, Leonard Buczkowski), 15,235,445
6. *Mr. Kleks' Academy* (*Akademia pana Kleksa*, 2 parts, 1984, children's film, Krzysztof Gradowski), 14,094,014
7. *Sex Mission* (*Seksmisja*, 1984, Juliusz Machulski), 11,164,329
8. *Pan Michael* (*Pan Wołodyjowski*, 1969, Jerzy Hoffman), 10,934,458
9. *The Leper* (*Trędowata*, 1976, Jerzy Hoffman), 9,834,145
10. *Pharaoh* (*Faraon*, 1966, Jerzy Kawalerowicz), 9,453,934
11. *Love It or Leave It* (*Kochaj albo rzuć*, 1977, Sylwester Chęciński), 9,384,135
12. *Treasure* (*Skarb*, 1949, Leonard Buczkowski), 9,312,596
13. *Big Deal* (*Nie ma mocnych*, 1974, Sylwester Chęciński), 8,695,942
14. *The Travels of Mr. Kleks* (*Podróże pana Kleksa*, 2 parts, 1986, children's film, Krzysztof Gradowski), 8,678,791
15. *How I Unleashed World War II* (*Jak rozpętałem II wojnę światową*, 3 parts, 1970, Tadeusz Chmielewski), 8,485,163
16. *The Great Journey of Bolek and Lolek* (*Wielka podróż Bolka i Lolka*, 1977, children's film, Władysław Nehrebecki and Stanisław Dülz), 8,442,005
17. *Four Tankmen and a Dog* (*Czterej pancerni i pies*, 4 parts, 1968, Konrad Nałęcki), 8,343,912
18. *Argument about Basia* (*Awantura o Basię*, 1959, children's film, Maria Kaniewska), 8,234,616
19. *Border Street* (*Ulica Graniczna*, 1949, Aleksander Ford), 8,012,859
20. *Devil's Ravine* (*Czarci żleb*, 1950, Aldo Vergano and Tadeusz Kański), 8,012,748
21. *The Story of Sin* (*Dzieje grzechu*, 1975, Walerian Borowczyk), 7,972,988
22. *Hubal* (1973, Bohdan Poręba), 7,964,982
23. *The Last Stage* (*Ostatni etap*, 1948, Wanda Jakubowska), 7,862,655
24. *Ashes* (*Popioły*, 1965, Andrzej Wajda), 7,707,170

25. *The Promised Land* (*Ziemia obiecana*, 1975, Andrzej Wajda), 7,312,407

Source: Krzysztof Kucharski, "100 filmów o największej frekwencji do 31.12.2000," in *Kino Plus: Film i dystrybucja kinowa w Polsce w latach 1990–2000* (Toruń: Oficyna Wydawnicza Kucharski, 2002), 388.

APPENDIX B
The Forty Biggest Polish Box Office Hits on Polish Screens from 1990 to 2017

1. *With Fire and Sword* (*Ogniem i mieczem*, 1999, Jerzy Hoffman), 7,151,354 viewers
2. *Pan Tadeusz* (1999, Andrzej Wajda), 6,168,344
3. *Quo Vadis* (2001, Jerzy Kawalerowicz), 4,300,351
4. *Letters to Santa 3* (*Listy do M. 3*, 2017, Tomasz Konecki), 3,007,210
5. *Letters to Santa 2* (*Listy do M. 2*, 2015, Maciej Dejczer), 2,968,392
6. *Pitbull: Tough Women* (*Pitbull: Niebezpieczne kobiety*, 2016, Patryk Vega), 2,873,302
7. *Katyń* (2007, Andrzej Wajda), 2,770,313
8. *Letters to Santa* (*Listy do M.*, 2011, Mitja Okorn), 2,560,734
9. *Ladies* (*Lejdis*, 2008, Tomasz Konecki), 2,530, 660
10. *Botox* (*Botoks*, 2017, Patryk Vega), 2,314,882
11. *Gods* (*Bogowie*, 2014, Łukasz Palkowski), 2,265,468
12. *In Desert and Wilderness* (*W pustyni i w puszczy*, 2001, Gavin Hood), 2,227,228
13. *Kiler* (1997, Juliusz Machulski), 2,200,945
14. *Revenge* (*Zemsta*, 2002, Andrzej Wajda), 1,976,984
15. *Planet Single* (*Planeta Singli*, 2016, Mitja Okorn), 1,926,090
16. *The Art of Loving: The Story of Michalina Wisłocka* (*Sztuka kochania Michaliny Wisłockiej*, 2017, Maria Sadowska), 1,804,114
17. *Warsaw '44* (*Miasto '44*, 2014, Jan Komasa), 1,753,255
18. *Early Spring* (*Przedwiośnie*, 2001, Filip Bajon), 1,743,933
19. *Oh, Charles 2* (*Och, Karol 2*, 2011, Piotr Wereśniak), 1,708,905
20. *Just Love Me* (*Tylko mnie kochaj*, 2006, Ryszard Zatorski), 1,669,638
21. *Never ever!* (*Nigdy w życiu!* 2004, Ryszard Zatorski), 1,625,485
22. *The Battle of Warsaw 1920* (*1920 Bitwa Warszawska*, 2011, Jerzy Hoffman), 1,521,180
23. *You Are God* (*Jesteś bogiem*, 2012, Leszek Dawid), 1,445,616
24. *Volhynia* (aka *Hatred, Wołyń*, 2016, Wojciech Smarzowski), 1,449,228
25. *Pitbull: New Order* (*Pitbull: Nowe porządki*, 2016, Patryk Vega), 1,433,466
26. *Don't Lie, Honey* (*Nie kłam kochanie*, 2008, Piotr Wereśniak), 1,400,287
27. *Testosterone* (*Testosteron*, 2007, Tomasz Konecki, Andrzej Saramonowicz), 1,361,228
28. *Love and Dance* (*Kochaj i tańcz*, 2009, Bruce Parramore), 1,336,552
29. *Freedom Is within Us: Popiełuszko* (*Popiełuszko, wolność jest w nas*, 2009, Rafał Wieczyński), 1,312,230

30. *The Pianist* (*Pianista*, 2002, Roman Polański), 1,252,390
31. *In Darkness* (*W ciemności*, 2012, Agnieszka Holland), 1,200,477
32. *Jack Strong* (2014, Władysław Pasikowski), 1,180,010
33. *Why Not!* (*Dlaczego nie!* 2007, Ryszard Zatorski), 1,152,693
34. *Seven Things You Don't Know about Guys* (*7 rzeczy, których nie wiecie o facetach*, 2016, Kinga Lewińska), 1,144,532
35. *Testimony* (*Świadectwo*, 2008, Paweł Pitera), 1,040,616
36. *Traffic Police* (*Drogówka*, 2013, Wojciech Smarzowski), 1,025,395
37. *Maiden Vows* (*Śluby panieńskie*, 2010, Filip Bajon), 1,002,141
38. *Wałęsa: Man of Hope* (*Wałęsa: Człowiek z nadziei*, 2013, Andrzej Wajda), 970,520
39. *The Crown Witness* (*Świadek koronny*, 2007, Jarosław Sypniewski), 959,697
40. *Hunk* (*Ciacho*, 2010, Patryk Vega), 956,395

Compiled by the author with the help of the following sources:
- Krzysztof Kucharski, "100 filmów o największej frekwencji do 31.12.2000," in *Kino Plus: Film i dystrybucja kinowa w Polsce w latach 1990–2000* (Toruń: Oficyna Wydawnicza Kucharski, 2002), 388–90.
- Box office figures provided by the Polish Film Institute (PISF): http://www.pisf.pl/rynek-filmowy/box-office/filmy-polskie.
- "Top 20: Domestic Films 1990–2016," in *New Polish Films 2017* (Warsaw PISF, 2017).

Selected Filmography

Asterisks indicate films that are lost. Dates shown are the years of release. If a premiere was significantly delayed, the production year is given first, and the release date follows in brackets.

1902 *Powrót birbanta* (*The Return of a Merry Fellow*), directed by Kazimierz Prószyński*
1908 *Antoś pierwszy raz w Warszawie* (*Antoś for the First Time in Warsaw*), Jerzy Meyer*
  Pruska kultura (*Prussian Culture*), Mordechai Towbin
1911 *Der Wilder Foter* (*The Savage Father*), Marek Arnsztejn (in Yiddish)
  Dzieje grzechu (*The Story of Sin*), Antoni Bednarczyk*
  Meir Ezofowicz, Józef Ostoja-Sulnicki (with Aleksander Hertz, *fragments)
  Sąd Boży (*God's Trial*), Stanisław Knake-Zawadzki*
1912 *Krwawa dola* (*Bloody Fate*), Władysław Paliński*
1913 *Kościuszko pod Racławicami* (*Kościuszko at Racławice*), Orland (*fragments)
  Wykolejeni (*Human Wrecks*, aka *The Led Astray*), Kazimierz Kamiński and Aleksander Hertz*
1914 *Niewolnica zmysłów* (*Slave of Sin*, aka *Love and Passion*), Jan Pawłowski
1915 *Żona* (*Wife*), Jan Pawłowski*
1916 *Ochrana warszawska i jej tajemnice* (*The Secrets of the Warsaw Police*), Aleksander Hertz
1917 *Bestia* (*The Polish Dancer*), Aleksander Hertz
  Carat i jego sługi (*The Tsarist Regime and Its Servants*), Aleksander Hertz*
1919 *Blanc et noir*, Eugeniusz Modzelewski*
1920 *Bohaterstwo polskiego skauta* (*The Heroism of a Polish Boy Scout*), Ryszard Bolesławski*
  Dla ciebie, Polsko (*For You, Poland*), Antoni Bednarczyk
  Tamara (aka *Obrońcy Lwowa*, *The Defenders of Lvov*), Nina Niovilla*
1921 *Cud nad Wisłą* (*Miracle on the Vistula*), Ryszard Bolesławski
  Idziem do Ciebie Polsko, matko nasza (*We Come to You, Poland, Our Mother*), Nina Niovilla*
  Ludzie bez jutra (*People with No Tomorrow*), Aleksander Hertz
1922 *Rok 1863* (*The Year 1863*), Edward Puchalski
  Tajemnica przystanku tramwajowego (*The Tram Stop Mystery*), Jan Kucharski*
1923 *Bartek zwycięzca* (*Bartek, the Victor*), Edward Puchalski

Niewolnica miłości (The Slave of Love), Jan Kucharski*
Otchłań pokuty (The Abyss of Repentance), Wiktor Biegański*
Syn szatana (Satan's Son), Bruno Bredschneider*
1924 *O czym się nie mówi* (The Unspeakable), Edward Puchalski*
Tkies Kaf (The Vow, aka The Handshake, 1924), Zygmunt Turkow (in Yiddish)*
1925 *Iwonka*, Emil Chaberski (*fragments)
Der Lamedvovnik (One of the Thirty-Six), Henryk Szaro (in Yiddish)
Wampiry Warszawy (The Vampires of Warsaw), Wiktor Biegański*
1926 *Czerwony błazen* (Red Jester), Henryk Szaro*
Trędowata (The Leper), Edward Puchalski and Józef Węgrzyn*
1927 *Kochanka Szamoty* (Szamota's Lover), Leon Trystan*
Mogiła nieznanego żołnierza (The Tomb of the Unknown Soldier), Ryszard Ordyński
Zew morza (The Call of the Sea), Henryk Szaro
Ziemia obiecana (The Promised Land), Aleksander Hertz and Zbigniew Gniazdowski*
1928 *Huragan* (The Hurricane), Józef Lejtes
Kropka nad i (The Final Touch), Juliusz Gardan*
Pan Tadeusz, Ryszard Ordyński
Szaleńcy (Daredevils), Leonard Buczkowski
1929 *In di Poylishe Velder* (In Polish Woods), Jonas Turkow (in Yiddish)*
Kobieta, która grzechu pragnie (The Woman Who Desires Sin), Wiktor Biegański*
Mocny człowiek (A Strong Man), Henryk Szaro
Policmajster Tagiejew (The Police Chief Tagiejew), Juliusz Gardan
1930 *Janko Muzykant* (Johnny the Musician), Ryszard Ordyński
Kult ciała (The Cult of the Body), Michał Waszyński
Moralność pani Dulskiej (The Morality of Mrs. Dulska), Bolesław Newolin
Niebezpieczny romans (A Dangerous Love Affair), Michał Waszyński
Na Sybir (To Siberia), Henryk Szaro
1931 *Cham* (The Boor), Jan Nowina-Przybylski
Dziesięciu z Pawiaka (The Ten from the Pawiak Prison), Ryszard Ordyński
Krwawy wschód (Bloody East), Jan Nowina-Przybylski
Serce na ulicy (A Heart on the Street), Juliusz Gardan
1932 *Biały ślad* (White Trail), Adam Krzeptowski
Dzikie pola (Wild Fields), Józef Lejtes*
Legion ulicy (The Legion of the Street), Aleksander Ford*
Księżna Łowicka (The Princess of Łowicz, aka November Night), Janusz Warnecki and Mieczysław Krawicz
1933 *Dzieje grzechu* (The Story of Sin), Henryk Szaro
Każdemu wolno kochać (Anybody Can Love), Mieczysław Krawicz and Janusz Warnecki
Pod Twoją obronę (Under Your Protection), Edward Puchalski (in reality: Józef Lejtes)

Sabra, Aleksander Ford
Przybłęda (The Vagabond), Jan Nowina-Przybylski
Wyrok życia (Life Sentence), Juliusz Gardan
1934 *Co mój mąż robi w nocy (What Is My Husband Doing at Night?)*, Michał Waszyński
Córka generała Pankratowa (General Pankratov's Daughter), Mieczysław Znamierowski (in reality Józef Lejtes)
Czy Lucyna to dziewczyna? (Is Lucyna a Girl?), Juliusz Gardan
Młody las (The Young Forest), Józef Lejtes
1935 *ABC miłości (ABC of Love)*, Michał Waszyński
Antek Policmajster (Antek, the Police Chief), Michał Waszyński
Rapsodia Bałtyku (The Baltic Rhapsody), Leonard Buczkowski
1936 *Al Chet (For the Sins)*, Aleksander Marten (in Yiddish)
Barbara Radziwiłłówna (Love or a Kingdom), Józef Lejtes
Bohaterowie Sybiru (The Heroes of Siberia), Michał Waszyński
Róża (The Rose, aka Red Rose), Józef Lejtes
Trędowata (The Leper), Juliusz Gardan
Yidl mitn Fidl (Yiddle with His Fiddle), Jan Nowina-Przybylski and Joseph Green (in Yiddish)
1937 *Der Dibuk (The Dybbuk)*, Michał Waszyński (in Yiddish)
Dziewczęta z Nowolipek (The Girls of Nowolipki), Józef Lejtes
Znachor (The Quack), Michał Waszyński
1938 *A Briwele der Mamen (A Little Letter to Mother)*, Leon Trystan with Joseph Green (in Yiddish)
Granica (The Line), Józef Lejtes
Ludzie Wisły (The People of the Vistula), Aleksander Ford and Jerzy Zarzycki
Profesor Wilczur (Professor Wilczur), Michał Waszyński
Strachy (The Ghosts, aka Anxiety, aka The Creeps), Eugeniusz Cękalski and Karol Szołowski
Wrzos (Heather), Juliusz Gardan
Zapomniana melodia (Forgotten Melody), Konrad Tom and Jan Fethke
1939 *Czarne diamenty (Black Diamonds, premiere in 1981)*, Jerzy Gabryelski
Kłamstwo Krystyny (Krystyna's Lie), Henryk Szaro
O czym się nie mówi (What You Do Not Talk About), Mieczysław Krawicz
Nad Niemnem (On the Niemen River), Wanda Jakubowska* (no premiere, lost during World War II)
1944 *Majdanek – Cmentarzysko Europy (Majdanek, the Cemetery of Europe)*, Aleksander Ford (documentary)
1946 *Dwie godziny (Two Hours, released in 1957)*, Stanisław Wohl and Józef Wyszomirski
Wielka droga (The Long Road, aka The Great Road), Michał Waszyński (made in Italy, not shown in postwar Poland, big-screen Polish premiere in 2013)
1947 *Jasne Łany (Bright Fields)*, Eugeniusz Cękalski
Zakazane piosenki (Forbidden Songs), Leonard Buczkowski

1948 *Ostatni etap* (*The Last Stage*, aka *The Last Stop*), Wanda Jakubowska
Unzere Kinder (*Our Children*), Natan Gross (in Yiddish)
1949 *Skarb* (*Treasure*), Leonard Buczkowski
Ulica Graniczna (*Border Street*), Aleksander Ford
1950 *Czarci żleb* (*Devil's Ravine*), Aldo Vergano and Tadeusz Kański
Dom na pustkowiu (*House in the Wilderness*), Jan Rybkowski
Miasto nieujarzmione (*The Unvanquished City*), Jerzy Zarzycki
1951 *Warszawska premiera* (*Warsaw Premiere*), Jan Rybkowski
1952 *Gromada* (*The Village Mill*), Jerzy Kawalerowicz
Młodość Szopena (*The Youth of Chopin*), Aleksander Ford
1953 *Sprawa do załatwienia* (*A Matter to Be Settled*), Jan Rybkowski and Jan Fethke
1954 *Celuloza* (*A Night of Remembrance*), Jerzy Kawalerowicz
Piątka z ulicy Barskiej (*Five Boys from Barska Street*), Aleksander Ford
Pod Gwiazdą Frygijską (*Under the Phrygian Star*), Jerzy Kawalerowicz
Przygoda na Mariensztacie (*An Adventure at Marienstadt*), Leonard Buczkowski
Trudna miłość (*Difficult Love*), Stanisław Różewicz
1955 *Błękitny krzyż* (*The Blue Cross*, aka *The Men of the Blue Cross*), Andrzej Munk
Godziny nadziei (*The Hours of Hope*), Jan Rybkowski
Irena do domu! (*Irena, Go Home!*), Jan Fethke
Pokolenie (*A Generation*), Andrzej Wajda
1956 *Cień* (*The Shadow*), Jerzy Kawalerowicz
Sprawa pilota Maresza (*The Case of Pilot Maresz*), Leonard Buczkowski
1957 *Człowiek na torze* (*Man on the Tracks*), Andrzej Munk
Kanał (*Kanal*), Andrzej Wajda
Koniec nocy (*The End of the Night*), Julian Dziedina, Paweł Komorowski, and Walentyna Uszycka
Prawdziwy koniec wielkiej wojny (*The True End of the Great War*), Jerzy Kawalerowicz
Trzy kobiety (*Three Women*), Stanisław Różewicz
Zagubione uczucia (*Lost Feelings*), Jerzy Zarzycki
Zimowy zmierzch (*Winter Twilight*), Stanisław Lenartowicz
1958 *Dezerter* (*The Deserter*), Witold Lesiewicz
Eroica, Andrzej Munk
Ewa chce spać (*Ewa Wants to Sleep*), Tadeusz Chmielewski
Ostatni dzień lata (*The Last Day of Summer*), Tadeusz Konwicki
Pętla (*The Noose*), Wojciech J. Has
Pigułki dla Aurelii (*Pills for Aurelia*), Stanisław Lenartowicz
Popiół i diament (*Ashes and Diamonds*), Andrzej Wajda
Pożegnania (*Farewells*, aka *Lydia Ate the Apple*), Wojciech J. Has
Wolne miasto (*Free City*), Stanisław Różewicz
1959 *Baza ludzi umarłych* (*Damned Roads*), Czesław Petelski
Krzyż Walecznych (*Cross of Valor*), Kazimierz Kutz
Lotna (*Speed*), Andrzej Wajda

Orzeł (The Submarine "Eagle"), Leonard Buczkowski
Pociąg (Night Train, aka *Baltic Express)*, Jerzy Kawalerowicz
Zamach (Answer to Violence), Jerzy Passendorfer
1960 *Krzyżacy (Teutonic Knights,* aka *Black Cross)*, Aleksander Ford
Lunatycy (Moonwalkers), Bohdan Poręba
Małe dramaty (Small Dramas), Janusz Nasfeter
Miasteczko (Small Town), Romuald Drobaczyński, Julian Dziedzina, and Janusz Łęski
Niewinni czarodzieje (Innocent Sorcerers), Andrzej Wajda
Nikt nie woła (Nobody Is Calling), Kazimierz Kutz
Rok pierwszy (First Year), Witold Lesiewicz
Zezowate szczęście (Bad Luck, aka *Cockeyed Luck)*, Andrzej Munk
1961 *Dotknięcie nocy (The Touch of the Night)*, Stanisław Bareja
Kwiecień (April), Witold Lesiewicz
Ludzie z pociągu (People from the Train), Kazimierz Kutz
Matka Joanna od Aniołów (Mother Joan of the Angels), Jerzy Kawalerowicz
Ogniomistrz Kaleń (Sergeant Major Kaleń), Ewa and Czesław Petelski
Samson, Andrzej Wajda
Świadectwo urodzenia (The Birth Certificate), Stanisław Różewicz
Zaduszki (All Souls Day), Tadeusz Konwicki
1962 *Głos z tamtego świata (The Voice from Beyond)*, Stanisław Różewicz
Mój stary (My Old Man), Janusz Nasfeter
Nóż w wodzie (Knife in the Water), Roman Polański
Odwiedziny prezydenta (The Visit of the President), Jan Batory
O dwóch takich, co ukradli księżyc (The Two Who Stole the Moon), Jan Batory
1963 *Gangsterzy i filantropi (Gangsters and Philanthropists)*, Jerzy Hoffman and Edward Skórzewski
Jak być kochaną (How to Be Loved), Wojciech J. Has
Milczenie (Silence), Kazimierz Kutz
Pasażerka (The Passenger), Andrzej Munk
Zbrodniarz i panna (The Criminal and the Maiden), Janusz Nasfeter
1964 *Gdzie jest generał? (Where Is the General?)*, Tadeusz Chmielewski
Koniec naszego świata (The End of Our World), Wanda Jakubowska
Naganiacz (The Beater, aka *Men Hunters)*, Ewa and Czesław Petelski
Prawo i pięść (The Law and the Fist), Jerzy Hoffman and Edward Skórzewski
Ranny w lesie (Wounded in the Forest), Janusz Nasfeter
Żona dla Australijczyka (A Wife for an Australian), Stanisław Bareja
1965 *Popioły (Ashes)*, Andrzej Wajda
Rękopis znaleziony w Saragossie (The Saragossa Manuscript), Wojciech J. Has
Rysopis (Identification Marks: None), Jerzy Skolimowski
Salto (Somersault), Tadeusz Konwicki
Walkower (Walkover), Jerzy Skolimowski

        Życie raz jeszcze (*Life Once Again*), Janusz Morgenstern
1966 *Bariera* (*The Barrier*), Jerzy Skolimowski
        Faraon (*Pharaoh*), Jerzy Kawalerowicz
        Ktokolwiek wie (*Whoever Knows*), Kazimierz Kutz
        Niekochana (*Unloved*), Janusz Nasfeter
        Potem nastąpi cisza (*Then There Will Be Silence*), Janusz Morgenstern
        Szyfry (*Cyphers*, aka *Codes*), Wojciech J. Has
1967 *Chudy i inni* (*Skinny and Others*), Henryk Kluba
        Długa noc (*The Long Night*, released in 1989), Janusz Nasfeter
        Kontrybucja (*Contribution*), Jan Łomnicki
        Ręce do góry (*Hands Up*, released in 1985), Jerzy Skolimowski
        Powrót na ziemię (*Return to Earth*), Stanisław Jędryka
        Sami swoi (*All among Ourselves*), Sylwester Chęciński
        Słońce wschodzi raz na dzień (*The Sun Rises Once a Day*, released in 1972), Henryk Kluba
        Stajnia na Salwatorze (*Stall on Salvador*), Paweł Komorowski
        Westerplatte, Stanisław Różewicz
1968 *Julia, Anna, Genowefa*, Anna Sokołowska
        Lalka (*The Doll*), Wojciech J. Has
        Wilcze echa (*Wolves' Echoes*), Aleksander Ścibor-Rylski
        Wycieczka w nieznane (*A Journey into the Unknown*), Jerzy Ziarnik
        Żywot Mateusza (*The Life of Matthew*), Witold Leszczyński
1969 *Molo* (*Jetty*), Wojciech Solarz
        Kierunek Berlin (*Heading for Berlin*), Jerzy Passendorfer
        Pan Wołodyjowski (*Pan Michael*, aka *Colonel Wolodyjowski*), Jerzy Hoffman
        Polowanie na muchy (*Hunting Flies*), Andrzej Wajda
        Ruchome piaski (*Shifting Sands*), Władysław Ślesicki
        Struktura kryształu (*The Structure of Crystals*), Krzysztof Zanussi
        Wniebowstąpienie (*Ascension Day*), Jan Rybkowski
        Wszystko na sprzedaż (*Everything for Sale*), Andrzej Wajda
        Zbrodniarz, który ukradł zbrodnię (*The Criminal Who Stole a Crime*), Janusz Majewski
1970 *Abel, twój brat* (*Abel, Your Brother*), Janusz Nasfeter
        Brzezina (*Birchwood*), Andrzej Wajda
        Jak rozpętałem II wojnę światową (*How I Unleashed World War II*), Tadeusz Chmielewski
        Jarzębina czerwona (*The Rowan Tree*), Ewa and Czesław Petelski
        Krajobraz po bitwie (*Landscape after Battle*), Andrzej Wajda
        Rejs (*The Cruise*), Marek Piwowski
        Sól ziemi czarnej (*Salt of the Black Earth*), Kazimierz Kutz
1971 *Kardiogram* (*Cardiogram*), Roman Załuski
        Nie lubię poniedziałku (*I Hate Mondays*), Tadeusz Chmielewski
        Trąd (*Leprosy*), Andrzej Trzos-Rastawiecki

Twarz anioła (The Face of an Angel), Zbigniew Chmielewski
Życie rodzinne (Family Life), Krzysztof Zanussi
1972 *Anatomia miłości (Anatomy of Love, 1972)*, Roman Załuski
Jak daleko stąd, jak blisko (How Far from Here, How Near), Tadeusz Konwicki
Ocalenie (Deliverance), Edward Żebrowski
Perła w koronie (The Pearl in the Crown), Kazimierz Kutz
Trzeba zabić tę miłość (Kill That Love), Janusz Morgenstern
Trzecia część nocy (The Third Part of the Night), Andrzej Żuławski
Uciec jak najbliżej (Escape as Near as Possible), Janusz Zaorski
1973 *Chłopi (Peasants)*, Jan Rybkowski
Hubal, Bohdan Poręba
Iluminacja (Illumination), Krzysztof Zanussi
Na wylot (Through and Through, aka Clear Through), Grzegorz Królikiewicz
Palec Boży (God's Finger), Antoni Krauze
Sanatorium pod Klepsydrą (The Hourglass Sanatorium, aka The Sandglass), Wojciech J. Has
W pustyni i w puszczy (In Desert and Wilderness), Władysław Ślesicki
Wesele (The Wedding), Andrzej Wajda
Zazdrość i medycyna (Jealousy and Medicine), Janusz Majewski
1974 *Ciemna rzeka (Dark River)*, Sylwester Szyszko
Nie ma mocnych (Big Deal), Sylwester Chęciński
Potop (The Deluge), Jerzy Hoffman
Zapamiętaj imię swoje (Remember Your Name, Poland, Soviet Union), Sergei Kolosov
Zapis zbrodni (Record of Crime), Andrzej Trzos-Rastawiecki
1975 *Bilans kwartalny (A Woman's Decision, aka Balance Sheet)*, Krzysztof Zanussi
Dzieje grzechu (The Story of Sin), Walerian Borowczyk
Noce i dnie (Nights and Days), Jerzy Antczak
Zaklęte rewiry (Hotel Pacific), Janusz Majewski
Personel (Personnel), Krzysztof Kieślowski
Ziemia obiecana (The Promised Land), Andrzej Wajda
1976 *Con Amore*, Jan Batory
Blizna (The Scar), Krzysztof Kieślowski
Przepraszam, czy tu biją (Foul Play), Marek Piwowski
Spokój (Calm, released in 1980), Krzysztof Kieślowski
Zofia, Ryszard Czekała
1977 *Barwy ochronne (Camouflage)*, Krzysztof Zanussi
Człowiek z marmuru (Man of Marble), Andrzej Wajda
Indeks (Index, released in 1981), Janusz Kijowski
Kochaj albo rzuć (Love It or Leave It), Sylwester Chęciński
Sprawa Gorgonowej (The Gorgon Affair), Janusz Majewski
Śmierć Prezydenta (Death of a President), Jerzy Kawalerowicz

1978 *Akcja pod Arsenałem (Operation Arsenal)*, Jan Łomnicki
Bez znieczulenia (Rough Treatment, aka *Without Anesthesia)*, Andrzej Wajda
Co mi zrobisz jak mnie złapiesz (What Will You Do With Me When You Catch Me), Stanisław Bareja
Gdziekolwiek jesteś, Panie Prezydencie (Wherever You Are, Mr. President), Andrzej Trzos-Rastawiecki
Spirala (Spiral), Krzysztof Zanussi
Tańczący jastrząb (Dancing Hawk), Grzegorz Królikiewicz
Wodzirej (Top Dog), Feliks Falk
Wśród nocnej ciszy (Silent Night, aka *In the Still of the Night)*, Tadeusz Chmielewski
1979 *Aktorzy prowincjonalni (Provincial Actors)*, Agnieszka Holland
Amator (Camera Buff), Krzysztof Kieślowski
Aria dla atlety (Aria for an Athlete), Filip Bajon
Lekcja martwego języka (The Lesson of a Dead Language), Janusz Majewski
Panny z Wilka (The Maids of Wilko, Poland, France), Andrzej Wajda
Szpital Przemienienia (The Hospital of Transfiguration), Edward Żebrowski
Zmory (Nightmares), Wojciech Marczewski
1980 *Bez miłości (Without Love)*, Barbara Sass
Constans (The Constant Factor), Krzysztof Zanussi
Dyrygent (The Conductor), Andrzej Wajda
Golem, Piotr Szulkin
Grzeszny żywot Franciszka Buły (The Sinful Life of Franciszek Buła), Janusz Kidawa
Kontrakt (Contract), Krzysztof Zanussi
Paciorki jednego różańca (The Beads of One Rosary), Kazimierz Kutz
Tango, Zbigniew Rybczyński (experimental short film)
1981 *Człowiek z żelaza (Man of Iron)*, Andrzej Wajda
Dreszcze (Shivers), Wojciech Marczewski
Dziecinne pytania (Child's Questions), Janusz Zaorski
Gorączka (Fever), Agnieszka Holland
Kobieta samotna (A Woman Alone, released in 1988), Agnieszka Holland
Miś (Teddy Bear), Stanisław Bareja
Niech cię odleci mara (The Haunted, released in 1983), Andrzej Barański
Przypadek (Blind Chance, released in 1987), Krzysztof Kieślowski
Wizja lokalna 1901 (Inspection at the Scene of the Crime, 1901), Filip Bajon
Wielki bieg (The Big Run, released in 1987), Jerzy Domaradzki
1982 *Debiutantka (Debutante)*, Barbara Sass
Konopielka, Witold Leszczyński
Matka Królów (The Mother of Kings, released in 1987), Janusz Zaorski
Przesłuchanie (Interrogation, released in 1989), Ryszard Bugajski
Ryś (Lynx), Stanisław Różewicz
Vabank (Va Banque), Juliusz Machulski
1983 *Austeria (The Inn)*, Jerzy Kawalerowicz

SELECTED FILMOGRAPHY · 439

     Danton (Poland, France), Andrzej Wajda
     Krzyk (*The Shout*), Barbara Sass
     Prognoza pogody (*Weather Forecast*), Antoni Krauze
     Wielki Szu (*The Big Rook*), Sylwester Chęciński
1984 *Akademia pana Kleksa* (*Mr. Blot's Academy*), Krzysztof Gradowski
     Cztery pory roku (*Four Seasons*), Andrzej Kondratiuk
     Kartka z podróży (*A Postcard from the Journey*), Waldemar Dziki
     Nie było słońca tej wiosny (*There Was No Sun That Spring*), Juliusz Janicki
     Seksmisja (*Sex Mission*), Juliusz Machulski
1985 *Bez końca* (*No End*), Krzysztof Kieślowski
     Kobieta w kapeluszu (*A Woman with a Hat*), Stanisław Różewicz
     Kobieta z prowincji (*Woman from the Provinces*, aka *Life's Little Comforts*), Andrzej Barański
     Nadzór (*Custody*), Wiesław Saniewski
     Rok spokojnego słońca (*Year of the Quiet Sun*, Poland–West Germany–US), Krzysztof Zanussi
     Yesterday, Radosław Piwowarski
1986 *C.K. Dezerterzy* (*Deserters*, Poland–Hungary), Janusz Majewski
     Cudzoziemka (*Foreigner*), Ryszard Ber
     Dziewczęta z Nowolipek (*The Girls of Nowolipki*), Barbara Sass
     Jezioro Bodeńskie (*Sons and Comrades*, aka *Bodensee*), Janusz Zaorski
     Kronika wypadków miłosnych (*Chronicle of Amorous Accidents*), Andrzej Wajda
     Rajska jabłoń (*Crabapple Tree*), Barbara Sass
     W cieniu nienawiści (*In the Shadow of Hatred*), Wojciech Żółtowski
1987 *Magnat* (*The Magnate*), Filip Bajon
     Nad Niemnem (*On the Niemen River*), Zbigniew Kuźmiński
     Pociąg do Hollywood (*Train to Hollywood*), Radosław Piwowarski
     W zawieszeniu (*Suspended*), Waldemar Krzystek
1988 *Dotknięci* (*The Touched*), Wiesław Saniewski
     Dekalog (*Decalogue*), Krzysztof Kieślowski (ten-part series of television films)
     Krótki film o miłości (*A Short Film about Love*), Krzysztof Kieślowski
     Krótki film o zabijaniu (*A Short Film about Killing*), Krzysztof Kieślowski
     Łuk Erosa (*Cupid's Bow*), Jerzy Domaradzki
1989 *Deja vu* (*Déjà Vu*, Poland–Soviet Union), Juliusz Machulski
     Kornblumenblau, Leszek Wosiewicz
     Łabędzi śpiew (*The Swan's Song*), Robert Gliński
     Stan posiadania (*Inventory*), Krzysztof Zanussi
     300 mil do nieba (*300 Miles to Heaven*), Maciej Dejczer
1990 *Historia niemoralna* (*An Immoral Story*), Barbara Sass
     Korczak, Andrzej Wajda (Poland–Germany)
     Kramarz (*The Peddler*), Andrzej Barański
     Marcowe migdały (*March Almonds*), Radosław Piwowarski

        Ucieczka z kina "Wolność" (*Escape from the "Liberty" Cinema*), Wojciech Marczewski
1991 *Femina*, Piotr Szulkin
        Jeszcze tylko ten las (*Just Beyond this Forest*), Jan Łomnicki
        Kroll, Władysław Pasikowski
        Podwójne życie Weroniki (*The Double Life of Veronique*, Poland-France), Krzysztof Kieślowski
        Pogrzeb kartofla (*The Burial of a Potato*), Jan Jakub Kolski
        Śmierć dziecioroba (*Death of a Childmaker*), Wojciech Nowak
        Życie za życie: Maksymilian Kolbe (*Life for Life: Maximilian Kolbe*, 1991, Poland-Germany), Krzysztof Zanussi
1992 *Dotknięcie ręki* (*The Silent Touch*, Poland-UK-Denmark), Krzysztof Zanussi
        Pierścionek z orłem w koronie (*The Ring with a Crowned Eagle*), Andrzej Wajda
        Psy (*The Pigs*), Władysław Pasikowski
        Rozmowy kontrolowane (*Controlled Conversations*, aka *Calls Controlled*), Sylwester Chęciński
        Tragarz puchu (*Warszawa. Année 5703*, Poland-France-Germany), Janusz Kijowski
        Wszystko co najważniejsze (*All That Really Matters*), Robert Gliński
1993 *Cynga* (*Scurvy*), Leszek Wosiewicz
        Jańcio Wodnik (*Johnnie the Aquarius*), Jan Jakub Kolski
        Kolejność uczuć (*The Sequence of Feelings*), Radosław Piwowarski
        Pożegnanie z Marią (*Farewell to Maria*), Filip Zylber
        Przypadek Pekosińskiego (*The Case of Pekosiński*), Grzegorz Królikiewicz
        Rozmowa z człowiekiem z szafy (*Conversation with a Person in a Wardrobe*), Mariusz Grzegorzek
        Szwadron (*Squadron*, Poland-Belgium-France-Ukraine), Juliusz Machulski
        Trzy Kolory: Niebieski (*Three Colours: Blue*, Poland-France-Switzerland), Krzysztof Kieślowski
1994 *Pamiętnik znaleziony w garbie* (*Diary in Marble*, aka *Memoirs Found in a Hunched Back*), Jan Kidawa-Błoński
        Psy 2: Ostatnia krew (*The Pigs 2: The Last Blood*), Władysław Pasikowski
        Śmierć jak kromka chleba (*Death as a Slice of Bread*), Kazimierz Kutz
        Trzy kolory: Biały (*Three Colours: White*, Poland-France), Krzysztof Kieślowski
        Trzy kolory: Czerwony (*Three Colours: Red*, Poland-France-Switzerland), Krzysztof Kieślowski
        Wrony (*Crows*), Dorota Kędzierzawska
        Zawrócony (*The Turned Back*), Kazimierz Kutz
1995 *Faustyna* (*Faustina*), Jerzy Łukaszewicz
        Girl Guide, Juliusz Machulski
        Tato (*Daddy*), Maciej Ślesicki
        Pokuszenie (*Temptation*), Barbara Sass
        Wrzeciono czasu (*The Spinning Wheel of Time*), Andrzej Kondratiuk
1996 *Cwał* (*In Full Gallop*), Krzysztof Zanussi

Debora (Deborah), Ryszard Brylski
Dzieci i ryby (Seen but Not Heard), Jacek Bromski
Gry uliczne (Street Games), Krzysztof Krauze
Odwiedź mnie we śnie (Visit Me in My Dream), Teresa Kotlarczyk
Pułkownik Kwiatkowski (Colonel Kwiatkowski), Kazimierz Kutz
Spis cudzołożnic (The List of Adulteresses), Jerzy Stuhr
Wielki Tydzień (Holy Week), Andrzej Wajda
1997 *Farba (Paint)* Michał Rosa
Historie miłosne (Love Stories), Jerzy Stuhr
Kiler, Juliusz Machulski
Kroniki domowe (Family Events), Leszek Wosiewicz
1998 *Historia kina w Popielawach (The History of Cinema Theater in Popielawy)*, Jan Jakub Kolski
Nic (Nothing), Dorota Kędzierzawska
Poniedziałek (Monday), Witold Adamek
Zabić Sekala (To Kill Sekal, Poland–Czech Republic), Vladimir Michálek
1999 *Dług (Debt)*, Krzysztof Krauze
Ogniem i mieczem (With Fire and Sword), Jerzy Hoffman
Pan Tadeusz, Andrzej Wajda
Prawo ojca (Father's Law), Marek Kondrat
Tydzień z życia mężczyzny (A Week in the Life of a Man), Jerzy Stuhr
Wojaczek, Lech Majewski
2000 *Daleko od okna (Keep Away from the Window, aka Far from the Window)*, Jan Jakub Kolski
Duże zwierzę (The Big Animal), Jerzy Stuhr
Prymas: Trzy lata z tysiąclecia (The Primate: Three Years Out of the Millennium), Teresa Kotlarczyk
Życie jako śmiertelna choroba przenoszona drogą płciową (Life as a Fatal Sexually Transmitted Disease), Krzysztof Zanussi
2001 *Angelus*, Lech Majewski
Boże skrawki (Edges of the Lord, Poland–US), Yurek Bogayevicz
Cisza (Silence), Michał Rosa
Cześć Tereska (Hi, Tereska), Robert Gliński
Quo Vadis, Jerzy Kawalerowicz
Sezon na leszcza (Sucker Season), Bogusław Linda
Stacja (Station), Piotr Wereśniak
2002 *Dzień świra (The Day of the Wacko)*, Marek Koterski
Edi, Piotr Trzaskalski
Głośniej od bomb (Louder than Bombs), Przemysław Wojcieszek
Moje pieczone kurczaki (My Roast Chicken), Iwona Siekierzyńska (television film)
Pianista (The Pianist, France–Poland–Germany–UK), Roman Polański
2003 *Pogoda na jutro (Tomorrow's Weather)*, Jerzy Stuhr

Pornografia (Pornography), Jan Jakub Kolski
Superprodukcja (Super Production), Juliusz Machulski
Warszawa (Warsaw), Dariusz Gajewski
Zmruż oczy (Squint Your Eyes), Andrzej Jakimowski
2004 *Mój Nikifor (My Nikifor)*, Krzysztof Krauze
Pręgi (The Welts), Magdalena Piekorz
Trzeci (The Third), Jan Hryniak
Vinci, Juliusz Machulski
Wesele (The Wedding), Wojciech Smarzowski
2005 *Jestem (I Am)*, Dorota Kędzierzawska
Komornik (The Debt Collector), Feliks Falk
Persona Non Grata, Krzysztof Zanussi
Pittbul, Patryk Vega
Rozdroże Cafe (The Crossroads Café), Leszek Wosiewicz
Skazany na bluesa (Destined for Blues), Jan Kidawa-Błoński
W dół kolorowym wzgórzem (Down the Colorful Hill), Przemysław Wojcieszek
2006 *Bezmiar sprawiedliwości (Immensity of Justice)*, Wiesław Saniewski
Co słonko widziało (What the Sun Has Seen), Michał Rosa
Plac Zbawiciela (Savior Square), Krzysztof Krauze and Joanna Kos-Krauze
Statyści (Movie Extras), Michał Kwieciński
Z odzysku (Retrieval), Sławomir Fabicki
2007 *Katyń*, Andrzej Wajda
Rezerwat (The Reserve), Łukasz Palkowski
Pora umierać (Time to Die), Dorota Kędzierzawska
Świadek koronny (The Crown Witness), Jarosław Sypniewski
Szklane usta (Glass Lips), Lech Majewski
Sztuczki (Tricks), Andrzej Jakimowski
Wszystko będzie dobrze (All Will Be Well), Tomasz Wiszniewski
2008 *Cztery noce z Anną (Four Nights with Anna*, Poland-France), Jerzy Skolimowski
Ile waży koń trojański? (How Much Does the Trojan Horse Weigh?), Juliusz Machulski
Mała Moskwa (Little Moscow), Waldemar Krzystek
Po-lin: Okruchy pamięci (Po-lin), Jolanta Dylewska (documentary)
Rysa (Scratch), Michał Rosa
Senność (Drowsiness), Magdalena Piekorz
33 sceny z życia (33 Scenes from Life, Poland-Germany), Małgorzata Szumowska
2009 *Drzazgi (Splinters)*, Maciej Pieprzyca
Dom zły (The Dark House), Wojciech Smarzowski
Generał Nil (General Nil), Ryszard Bugajski
Moja krew (My Flesh, My Blood), Marcin Wrona
Popiełuszko, wolność jest w nas (Freedom Is within Us: Popiełuszko), Rafał Wieczyński
Rewers (The Reverse), Borys Lankosz
Tatarak (Sweet Rush), Andrzej Wajda

Wojna polsko-ruska (Snow White and Russian Red), Xawery Żuławski
Zero, Paweł Borowski
2010 Chrzest (The Christening), Marcin Wrona
Essential Killing (Poland-Norway-Hungary-Ireland), Jerzy Skolimowski
Erratum, Marek Lechki
Joanna, Feliks Falk
Lincz (Lynching), Krzysztof Łukaszewicz
Made in Poland, Przemysław Wojcieszek
Matka Teresa od kotów (Mother Teresa of Cats), Paweł Sala
Różyczka (Rosebud), Jan Kidawa-Błoński
Trzy minuty: 21:37 (Three Minutes: 9:37 p.m.), Maciej Ślesicki
2011 Czarny czwartek: Janek Wiśniewski padł (Black Thursday), Antoni Krauze
Daas, Adrian Panek
Kret (The Mole, Poland-France), Rafael Lewandowski
Lęk wysokości (Fear of Falling), Bartosz Konopka
Listy do M. (Letters to Santa), Mitja Okorn
Młyn i krzyż (The Mill and the Cross, Poland-Sweden), Lech Majewski
Róża (Rose), Wojciech Smarzowski
Sala samobójców (The Suicide Room), Jan Komasa
Jutro będzie lepiej (Tomorrow Will Be Better), Dorota Kędzierzawska
Wymyk (Courage), Greg Zglinski
2012 Dziewczyna z szafy (The Girl from the Wardrobe), Bodo Kox
Jesteś Bogiem (You Are God), Leszek Dawid
Księstwo (Heritage), Andrzej Barański
Obława (Manhunt), Marcin Krzyształowicz
Pokłosie (Aftermath, Poland–The Netherlands–Russia–Slovak Republic), Władysław Pasikowski
W ciemności (In Darkness, Poland-Canada-Germany), Agnieszka Holland
2013 Bilet na księżyc (One Way Ticket to the Moon), Jacek Bromski
Chce się żyć (Life Feels Good), Maciej Pieprzyca
Ida (Poland-Denmark), Paweł Pawlikowski
Imagine (Poland-France-Portugal), Andrzej Jakimowski
Miłość (Loving), Sławomir Fabicki
Papusza, Joanna Kos-Krauze and Krzysztof Krauze
Układ zamknięty (The Closed Circuit), Ryszard Bugajski
Wałęsa: Człowiek z nadziei (Wałęsa: Man of Hope), Andrzej Wajda
2014 Bogowie (Gods), Łukasz Palkowski
Jack Strong, Władysław Pasikowski
Fotograf (The Photographer), Waldemar Krzystek
Kamienie na szaniec (Stones for the Rampart), Robert Gliński
Miasto 44 (Warsaw '44), Jan Komasa
Onirica (Field of Dogs), Lech Majewski

Pod Mocnym Aniołem (The Mighty Angel), Wojciech Smarzowski
Powstanie Warszawskie (Warsaw Uprising), Jan Komasa (fictionalized documentary)
2015 11 minut (11 Minutes, Poland-Ireland), Jerzy Skolimowski
Body/Ciało, Małgorzata Szumowska
Chemia (Chemo), Bartosz Prokopowicz
Córki dancingu (The Lure), Agnieszka Smoczyńska
Czerwony pająk (Red Spider), Marcin Koszałka
Demon (Poland-Israel), Marcin Wrona
Intruz (The Here After, Poland-Sweden-France), Magnus von Horn
Moje córki krowy (These Daughters of Mine), Kinga Dębska
Wszystkie nieprzespane noce (All These Sleepless Nights), Michał Marczak
Ziarno prawdy (A Grain of Truth), Borys Lankosz
2016 Baby Bump, Kuba Czekaj
Jestem mordercą (I'm a Killer), Maciej Pieprzyca
Kamper, Łukasz Grzegorzek
Letnie przesilenie (Summer Solstice, Poland-Germany), Michał Rogalski
Ostatnia rodzina (The Last Family), Jan P. Matuszyński
Planeta Singli (Planet Single), Mitja Okorn
Powidoki (Afterimage), Andrzej Wajda
Wołyń (Volhynia, aka Hatred), Wojciech Smarzowski
#WszystkoGra (Game On), Agnieszka Glińska
Zjednoczone stany miłości (United States of Love, Poland-Sweden), Tomasz Wasilewski
2017 Cicha noc (Silent Night), Piotr Domalewski
Człowiek z magicznym pudełkiem (The Man with the Magic Box), Bodo Kox
Dzikie róże (Wild Roses), Anna Jadowska
Najlepszy (The Fastest), Łukasz Palkowski
Pokot (Spoor, aka Game Count, Poland–Czech Republic–Germany–Sweden), Agnieszka Holland
Ptaki śpiewają w Kigali (Birds Are Singing in Kigali), Joanna Kos-Krauze, Krzysztof Krauze
Pomiędzy słowami (Beyond Words, Poland-The Netherlands), Urszula Antoniak
Sztuka kochania: Historia Michaliny Wisłockiej (The Art of Loving), Maria Sadowska
Twój Vincent (Loving Vincent, Poland-UK), Dorota Kobiela and Hugh Welchman
Wyklęty (Cursed, aka The Damned), Konrad Łęcki
Zgoda (The Reconciliation), Maciej Sobieszczański

Selected Bibliography

Adamczak, Marcin. *Globalne Hollywood, filmowa Europa i polskie kino po 1989 roku.* Gdańsk: słowo/obraz terytoria, 2010.

———. "Między poetyką kulturową a kulturą produkcji: Społeczny kontekst realizacji pierwszych filmów Andrzeja Wajdy." *Images* 13, no. 22 (2013): 73–90.

Adamczak, Marcin, Marcin Malatyński, and Piotr Marecki, eds. *Restart zespołów filmowych / Film Units: Restart.* Kraków and Łódź: Korporacja Ha!art and Łódź Film School, 2012.

Andrew, Geoff. *The "Three Colours" Trilogy.* London: BFI Modern Classics, 1998.

Anessi, Thomas. "Moving Ahead into the Past: Historical Contexts in Recent Polish Cinema." *Images* 11, no. 20 (2012): 5–22.

Armata, Jerzy, and Anna Wróblewska. *Polski film dla dzieci i młodzieży.* Warsaw: Fundacja Kino, 2014.

Armatys, Barbara, Leszek Armatys, and Wiesław Stradomski. *Historia filmu polskiego 1930–1939.* Vol. 2. Warsaw: Wydawnictwa Artystyczne i Filmowe, 1988.

Armatys, Leszek, and Wiesław Stradomski. *Od Niewolnicy zmysłów do Czarnych diamentów: Szkice o polskich filmach z lat 1914–1939.* Warsaw: COMUK, 1988.

Avisar, Ilan. *Screening the Holocaust: Cinema's Images of the Unimaginable.* Bloomington: Indiana University Press, 1988.

Badowska, Eva, and Francesca Parmeggiani, eds. *Of Elephants and Toothaches: Ethics, Politics, and Religion in Krzysztof Kieślowski's Decalogue.* New York: Fordham University Press, 2016.

Balázs, Béla. "The Last Stop." In "Béla Balázs on Wanda Jakubowska's *The Last Stop*: Three Texts," trans. Stuart Liebman and Zsuzsa Berger. *Slavic and East European Performance* 16, no. 3 (1996): 64–70.

Ballester, César. "Subjectivism, Uncertainty and Individuality: Munk's *Człowiek na torze / Man on the Tracks* (1956) and Its Influence on the Czechoslovak New Wave." *Studies in Eastern European Cinema* 2, no. 1 (2011): 61–73.

Balski, Grzegorz, ed. *Directory of Eastern European Film-Makers and Films.* Westport, CT: Greenwood Press, 1992.

Banaszkiewicz, Władysław. "Pola Negri: Początki kariery i legendy." *Kwartalnik Filmowy* 1 (1960): 37–80.

Banaszkiewicz, Władysław, and Witold Witczak. *Historia filmu polskiego 1895–1929.* Vol. 1. Warsaw: Wydawnictwa Artystyczne i Filmowe, 1989.

Baniewicz, Elżbieta. *Kazimierz Kutz: Z dołu widać inaczej.* Warsaw: Wydawnictwa Artystyczne i Filmowe, 1994.

Baron, Lawrence. "Cinema in the Crossfire of Jewish-Polish Polemics: Wajda's *Korczak* and Polanski's *The Pianist*." In *Rethinking Poles and Jews: Troubled Past, Brighter Future*, edited by Robert Cherry and Annamaria Orla-Bukowska, 43–53. Lanham, MD: Rowman & Littlefield, 2007.

Bartov, Omer. *The "Jew" in Cinema: From* The Golem *to* Don't Touch My Holocaust. Bloomington: Indiana University Press, 2005.

Baugh, Lloyd. "Cinematographic Variations on the Christ-Event: Three Film Texts by Krzysztof Kieślowski—Part One: *A Short Film about Love*." *Gregorianum* 84, no. 3 (2003): 551–83.

———. "Cinematographic Variations on the Christ-Event: Three Film Texts by Krzysztof Kieślowski—Part Two: *Decalogue Six* and the Script." *Gregorianum* 84, no. 4 (2003): 919–46.

Bernard, Renata, and Steven Woodward. *Krzysztof Kieślowski: Interviews*. Jackson: University Press of Mississippi, 2016.

Bickley, Daniel. "The Cinema of Moral Dissent: A Report from the Gdańsk Film Festival." *Cineaste* 11, no. 1 (1980–1981): 10–15.

Biel, Urszula. *Śląskie kina między wojnami, czyli przyjemność upolityczniona*. Katowice: Śląsk, 2002.

Biskupski, M. B. B. *Hollywood's War with Poland 1939–1945*. Lexington: University Press of Kentucky, 2010.

Blankenship, Janelle, and Tobias Nagl, eds. *European Visions: Small Cinemas in Transition*. Bielefeld: Transcript, 2015.

Blumenfeld, Samuel. *L'homme qui voulait être prince: Les vies imaginaires de Michal Waszinski*. Paris: Grasset & Fasquelle, 2006.

Bobowski, Sławomir. *Dyskurs filmowy Zanussiego*. Wrocław: Towarzystwo Przyjaciół Polonistyki Wrocławskiej, 1996.

———. *W poszukiwaniu siebie: Twórczość filmowa Agnieszki Holland*. Wrocław: Wydawnictwo Uniwersytetu Wrocławskiego, 2001.

Bocheńska, Jadwiga. *Polska myśl filmowa: Antologia tekstów z lat 1898–1939*. Wrocław: Ossolineum, 1975.

———. *Polska myśl filmowa do roku 1939*. Wrocław: Ossolineum, 1974.

Bondejberg, Ib. "Confronting the Past: Trauma, History and Memory in Wajda's Film." *Images* 11, no. 20 (2012): 37–52.

Bren, Frank. *World Cinema 1: Poland*. London: Flicks Books, 1986.

Brouwer, Sander, ed. *Contested Interpretations of the Past in Polish, Russian, and Ukrainian Film: Screen as Battlefield*. Leiden and Boston: Brill and Rodopi, 2016.

Caputo, Davide. *Polanski and Perception*. Bristol: Intellect, 2012.

Chyb, Dariusz. "Inspiracje malarskie w filmach Andrzeja Wajdy." *Kwartalnik Filmowy* 15–16 (1996): 144–86.

Ciechowicz, Jan, and Tadeusz Szczepański, eds. *Zbigniew Cybulski: Aktor XX wieku*. Gdańsk: University of Gdańsk Press, 1997.

Cieśliński, Marek. *Piękniej niż w życiu: Polska Kronika Filmowa 1944–1994*. Warsaw: Trio, 2006.
Coates, Paul. "'Choose the Impossible': Wojciech Has Reframes Prus's *Lalka*." *Studies in Eastern European Cinema* 4, no. 1 (2013): 79–94.
———. "Człowiek z marmuru/Man of Marble." In Hames, *The Cinema of Central Europe*, 181–89.
———. "Forms of the Polish Intellectual's Self-Criticism: Revisiting *Ashes and Diamonds* with Andrzejewski and Wajda." *Canadian Slavonic Papers* 38, nos. 3–4 (1996): 287–303.
———. "Karol Irzykowski: Apologist of the Inauthentic Art." *New German Critique* 42 (1987): 113–15.
———. "Kieślowski and the Antipolitics of Color: A Reading of the 'Three Colors Trilogy.'" *Cinema Journal* 41, no. 2 (2002): 41–66.
———. ed. *Lucid Dreams: The Films of Krzysztof Kieślowski*. London: Flicks Books, 1999.
———. "Notes on Polish Cinema, Nationalism and Wajda's *Holy Week*." In *Cinema and Nation*, edited by Mette Hjort and Scott MacKenzie, 189–202. London: Routledge, 2000.
———. "Nóż w wodzie / Knife in the Water." In Hames, *The Cinema of Central Europe*, 77–85.
———. "Observing the Observer: Andrzej Wajda's Holy Week (1995)." *Canadian Slavonic Papers* 42, nos. 1–2 (2000): 25–33.
———. "Politics of Memory, Ghosts of Defeat: Kieślowski's *No End*." *The Polish Review* 33, no. 3 (1988): 343–46.
———. *The Red and the White: The Cinema of People's Poland*. London: Wallflower Press, 2005.
———. "The Sense of an Ending: Reflections on Kieślowski's Trilogy." *Film Quarterly* 50, no. 2 (1996–1997): 19–27.
———. *The Story of the Lost Reflection: The Alienation of the Image in Western and Polish Cinema*. London: Verso, 1985.
———. "Walls and Frontiers: Polish Cinema's Portrayal of Polish-Jewish Relations." *Polin: Studies in Polish Jewry* 10 (1997): 221–46.
Cowie, Peter. "Wajda Redux." *Sight and Sound* 49, no. 1 (1979–1980): 32–34.
Cronin, Paul, ed. *Roman Polanski: Interviews*. Jackson: University Press of Mississippi, 2005.
Dabert, Dobrochna. *Kino moralnego niepokoju: Wokół wybranych problemów poetyki i etyki*. Poznań: Wydawnictwo Naukowe Uniwersytetu im. Adama Mickiewicza, 2003.
Dipont, Małgorzata, and Stanisław Zawiśliński. *Faraon kina*. Warsaw: Skorpion, 1997.
Dondziłło, Czesław. *Młode kino polskie lat siedemdziesiątych*. Warsaw: Młodzieżowa Agencja Wydawnicza, 1985.
Dyer, Richard, and Ginette Vincendeau, eds. *Popular European Cinema*. London: Routledge, 1992.
Dziewoński, Edward. *W życiu jak w teatrze*. Warsaw: Czytelnik, 1987.

Dziewoński, Roman. *Dodek Dymsza*. Warsaw: LTW, 2011.
Eagle, Herbert. "Andrzej Wajda: Film Language and the Artist's Truth." *Cross Currents: A Yearbook of Central European Culture* 1 (1982): 339–53.
———. "Exile and Emigration in the Films of Roman Polanski." In Stephan, *Living in Translation*, 289–312.
———. "Polanski." In Goulding, *Five Filmmakers*, 92–155.
Ebbrecht-Hartmann, Tobias. "Locked Doors and Hidden Graves: Searching the Past in *Pokłosie*, *Sarah's Key* and *Ida*." In *Holocaust Cinema in the Twenty-First Century: Memory, Images and the Ethics of Representation*, edited by Oleksandr Kobrynskyy and Gerd Bayer, 141–60. New York: Columbia University Press 2015.
Eberhardt, Konrad. *Zbigniew Cybulski*. Warsaw: Wydawnictwa Artystyczne i Filmowe, 1976.
———. *Wojciech Has*. Warsaw: Wydawnictwa Artystyczne i Filmowe, 1967.
Ehrenstein, David. *Masters of Cinema: Roman Polanski*. London: Phaidon Press, 2012.
Eidsvik, Charles. "Kieślowski's 'Short Films.'" *Film Quarterly* 44, no. 1 (1990): 50–55.
Falkowska, Janina. "Agnieszka Holland, Barbara Sass and Dorota Kędzierzawska in the World of Male Polish Filmmaking." In *Women Filmmakers: Refocusing*, edited by Jacqueline Levitin, Judith Plessis, and Valerie Raoul, 96–108. Vancouver: University of British Columbia Press, 2003.
———. *Andrzej Wajda: History, Politics, and Nostalgia in Polish Cinema*. New York: Berghahn Books, 2007.
———. "New Cinema of Nostalgia in Poland." In *Small Cinemas in Global Markets: Genres, Identities, Narratives*, edited by Lenuta Giukin, Janina Falkowska, and David Desser, 17–30. London: Lexington Books, 2015.
———. *The Political Films of Andrzej Wajda: Dialogism in* Man of Marble, Man of Iron, *and* Danton. New York: Berghahn Books, 1996.
———. "'The Political' in the Films of Andrzej Wajda and Krzysztof Kieślowski." *Cinema Journal* 34, no. 2 (1995): 37–50.
———. "*Popiół i diament*/Ashes and Diamonds." In Hames, *The Cinema of Central Europe*, 65–74.
Falkowska, Janina, and Marek Haltof, eds. *The New Polish Cinema*. London: Flicks Books, 2003.
Figielski, Łukasz, and Bartosz Michalak. *Prywatna historia kina polskiego*. Gdańsk: słowo/obraz terytoria, 2006.
Ford, Charles, and Robert Hammond. *Polish Film: A Twentieth Century History*. Jefferson, NC: McFarland, 2005.
Forecki, Piotr. "*Pokłosie*, poGrossie i kibice polskości." *Studia Litteraria Historica* 2 (2013): 211–35.
Fox, Geoffrey. "Men of Wajda." *Film Criticism* 6, no. 1 (1981): 3–9.
Fredericksen, Don, and Marek Hendrykowski. *Wajda's Kanal*. Poznań: Wydawnictwo Naukowe Uniwersytetu im. Adama Mickiewicza, 2007.
Fuksiewicz, Jacek. *Film and Television in Poland*. Warsaw: Interpress, 1976.

———. *Tadeusz Konwicki*. Warsaw: Wydawnictwa Artystyczne i Filmowe, 1967.
Gajewski, Arkadiusz. *Polski film sensacyjno-kryminalny (1960–1980)*. Warsaw: Trio, 2008.
Garbowski, Christopher. "The Glorious Dead and Sacred Communities in Spielberg's *Saving Private Ryan* and Wajda's *Katyń*." *Religion and the Arts* 18 (2014): 373–98.
———. "Kieślowski's Seeing I/Eye." *The Polish Review* 15, no. 1 (1995): 53–60.
———. "Krzysztof Kieślowski's *Decalogue*: Presenting Religious Topics on Television." *The Polish Review* 37, no. 3 (1992): 327–34.
———. *Krzysztof Kieślowski's Decalogue Series: The Problem of the Protagonists and Their Self-Transcendence*. New York: Columbia University Press.
Gębicka, Ewa. *Między państwowym mecenatem a rynkiem: Polska kinematografia po 1989 roku w kontekście transformacji ustrojowej*. Katowice: Wydawnictwo Uniwersytetu Śląskiego, 2006.
———. "Nie strzelać do Czapajewa! Jak po wojnie przyjmowano filmy radzieckie w Polsce." *Kwartalnik Filmowy* 2 (1993): 94–107.
Gierszewska, Barbara. *Czasopiśmiennictwo filmowe w Polsce do 1939 roku*. Kielce: Wyższa Szkoła Pedagogiczna, 1995.
———. *Kino i film we Lwowie do 1939 roku*. Kielce: Wydawnictwo Akademii Świętokrzyskiej, 2006.
———. ed. *Mniszkówna i co dalej w polskim kinie? Wybór tekstów z czasopism filmowych dwudziestolecia międzywojennego*. Kielce: Wydawnictwo Akademii Świętokrzyskiej, 2001.
———. ed. *Polski film fabularny 1918–1989: Recenzje*. Kraków: Księgarnia Akademicka, 2012.
Giza, Barbara. *Między literaturą a filmem: O scenariuszach filmowych Tadeusza Konwickiego*. Warsaw: Trio, 2007.
———. *Stawiński i wojna: Reprezentacje doświadczenia jako podróż autobiograficzna*. Warsaw: Wyższa Szkoła Psychologii Społecznej / Trio, 2012.
Giżycki, Marcin. *Awangarda wobec kina: Film w kręgu polskiej awangardy artystycznej dwudziestolecia międzywojennego*. Warsaw: Małe Wydawnictwo, 1996.
———. *Walka o film artystyczny w międzywojennej Polsce*. Warsaw: Państwowe Wydawnictwo Naukowe, 1989.
Giżycki, Marcin, and Bogusław Żmudziński, eds. *Polski film animowany*. Warsaw: Polskie Wydawnictwo Audiowizualne, 2008.
Głowa, Jadwiga, ed. *Zooming in on History's Turning Points: Documentaries in the 1990s in Central and Eastern Europe*. Conference papers in Polish and English translations. Kraków: Uniwersytet Jagielloński, 1999.
———. "How to Be Loved." *MovEast* 3 (1993–1994): 128–143.
Głowiński, Michał. *Rytuał i demagogia: Trzynaście szkiców o sztuce zdegradowanej*. Warsaw: Open, 1992.
Goban-Klas, Tomasz. *The Orchestration of the Media: The Politics of Mass Communications in Communist Poland and the Aftermath*. Boulder, CO: Westview Press, 1994.

Goddard, Michael. "The Impossible Polish New Wave and Its Accursed Émigré Auteurs: Borowczyk, Polański, Skolimowski, and Żuławski." In Imre, *A Companion to Eastern European Cinemas*, 291–310.

———. "Rękopis znaleziony w Saragossie/The Saragossa Manuscript." In Hames, *The Cinema of Central Europe*, 87–95.

Godzic, Wiesław. "Metafora polityczna: *Człowiek z marmuru* Andrzeja Wajdy." In Helman and Miczka, *Analizy i interpretacje*, 106–21.

Goldberg, Judith N. *Laughter through Tears: The Yiddish Cinema*. East Brunswick, NJ: Fairleigh Dickinson University Press, 1983.

Goldman, Eric A. *Visions, Images, and Dreams: Yiddish Film Past and Present*. Ann Arbor, MI: UMI Research Press, 1983.

Goulding, Daniel J., ed. *Five Filmmakers*. Bloomington: Indiana University Press, 1994.

———, ed. *Post New Wave Cinema in the Soviet Union and Eastern Europe*. Bloomington: Indiana University Press, 1989.

Greenberg, James. *Roman Polanski: A Retrospective*. New York: Harry N. Adams, 2013.

Grodź, Iwona. *Jerzy Skolimowski*. Warsaw: Wydawnictwo Więź, 2010.

———. *Zaszyfrowane w obrazie: O filmach Wojciecha Jerzego Hasa*. Gdańsk: słowo/obraz terytoria, 2009.

Gross, Jan T. *Neighbors: The Destruction of the Jewish Community in Jedwabne*. Princeton, NJ: Princeton University Press, 2001.

Gross, Natan. *Film żydowski w Polsce*. Kraków: Rabid, 2002.

Guerin, Frances. "Reframing the Photographer and His Photographs: *Photographer* (1995)." *Film and History* 32, no. 1 (2002): 43–54.

Guść, Iwona. "Polish Film Culture in Transition: On the 'Private Films' of Andrzej Kondratiuk (1985–1996)." In Blankenship and Nagl, *European Visions*, 299–316.

Guzek, Mariusz. *Co wspólnego z wojną ma kinematograf? Kultura filmowa na ziemiach polskich w latach 1914–1918*. Bydgoszcz: Wydawnictwo Uniwersytetu Kazimierza Wielkiego, 2014.

———. *Filmowa Bydgoszcz 1896–1939*. Toruń: Dom Wydawniczy Duet, 2004.

Gwóźdź, Andrzej, ed. *Filmowcy i kiniarze: Z dziejów X muzy na Górnym Śląsku*. Kraków: Rabid, 2004.

———, ed. *Filmowe światy: Z dziejów X muzy na Górnym Śląsku*. Katowice: Śląsk, 1998.

———, ed. *Historie celuloidem podszyte: Z dziejów X muzy na Górnym Śląsku i w Zagłębiu Dąbrowskim*. Kraków: Rabid, 2005.

———. *Kina i okolice: Z dziejów X muzy na Śląsku*. Katowice: Wydawnictwo Naukowe Śląsk, 2008.

———, ed. *Kino Kieślowskiego, kino po Kieślowskim*. Warsaw: Skorpion, 2006.

———, ed. *Kutzowisko. O twórczości filmowej, teatralnej i telewizyjnej Kazimierza Kutza*. Katowice: Wydawnictwo "Książnica," 2000.

———, ed. *Kutzowisko 2*. Katowice: Wydawnictwo Naukowe Śląsk, 2009.

———, ed. *Nie tylko filmy, nie same kina ... Z dziejów X muzy na Górnym Śląsku i Zagłębiu Dąbrowskim*. Katowice: Śląsk, 1996.

———, ed. *Odkrywanie prowincji: Z dziejów X muzy na Górnym Śląsku*. Kraków: Rabid, 2002.
Halle, Randall. *The Europeanization of Cinema: Interzones and Imaginative Communities*. Champaign: University of Illinois Press, 2014.
Haltof, Marek. "Adapting the National Literary Canon: Polish Heritage Cinema." *Canadian Revue of Comparative Literature / Revue Canadienne de Littérature Comparée* 34, no. 3 (2007): 298–306.
———. "'Amerykańskie kino polskie': *Psy* (1992), pozytywna wtórność i polityczny przekaz." In Zwierzchowski and Mazur, *Polskie kino popularne*, 177–86.
———. *The Cinema of Krzysztof Kieślowski: Variations on Destiny and Chance*. London: Wallflower Press, 2004.
———. "A Fistful of Dollars: Polish Cinema after 1989 Freedom Shock." *Film Quarterly* 48, no. 3 (1995): 15–25.
———. "Everything for Sale: Polish National Cinema after 1989." *Canadian Slavonic Papers* 39, no. 1 (1997): 137–52.
———. "Film Theory in Poland before World War II." *Canadian Slavonic Papers* 40, nos. 1–2 (1998): 67–78.
———. *Historical Dictionary of Polish Cinema*. 2nd ed. Lanham, MD: Rowman & Littlefield, 2015.
———. *Polish Film and the Holocaust: Politics and Memory*. New York: Berghahn Books, 2012.
———. "Return to Auschwitz: Wanda Jakubowska's *The Last Stage* (1948)." *The Polish Review* 55, no. 1 (2010): 7–34.
———. *Screening Auschwitz: Wanda Jakubowska's* The Last Stage *and the Politics of Commemoration*. Evanston, IL: Northwestern University Press, 2018.
———. "Screening the Unrepresented World: Kieślowski's Early Film-Essays" (Personnel, The Scar, and The Calm)." *The Polish Review* 48, no. 4 (2003): 463–79.
———. "Still Alive: Krzysztof Kieślowski's Influence on Post-Communist Polish Cinema." In Woodward, *After Kieślowski*, 19–33.
———. "The Representation of Stalinism in Polish Cinema." *Canadian Slavonic Papers* 42, nos. 1–2 (2000): 47–61.
Hames, Peter, ed. *The Cinema of Central Europe*. London: Wallflower Press, 2005.
Hauser, Ewa. "Reconstruction of National Identity: Poles and Ukrainians among Others in Jerzy Hoffman's *With Fire and Sword*." *The Polish Review* 45, no. 3 (2000): 305–17.
Helman, Alicja. "Andrzej Munk: Cockeyed Luck." *MovEast* 2 (1992): 96–107.
———. *Dwadzieścia lat filmu polskiego: Film fabularny 1947–1967*. Warsaw: Wydawnictwa Artystyczne i Filmowe, 1969.
———. "*Jak daleko stąd, jak blisko*: Analiza kilku wybranych motywów." *Kino* 4 (1972): 17–21.
———. "The Masters Are Tired." *Canadian Slavonic Papers* 42, nos. 1–2 (2000): 99–111.
———. "Polish Film Theory." In *The Jagiellonian University Film Studies*, edited by Wiesław Godzic, 9–40. Kraków: Universitas, 1996.
———. "Women in Kieślowski's Late Films." In Cox, *Lucid Dreams*, 116–35.

Helman, Alicja, and Alina Madej, eds. *Film polski wobec innych sztuk*. Katowice: Wydawnictwo Uniwersytetu Śląskiego, 1979.
Helman, Alicja, and Tadeusz Miczka, eds. *Analizy i interpretacje: Film polski*. Katowice: Wydawnictwo Uniwersytetu Śląskiego, 1984.
Hendrykowska, Małgorzata. *Film polski wobec wojny i okupacji: Tematy, motywy, pytania*. Poznań: Wydawnictwo Naukowe Uniwersytetu im. Adama Mickiewicza, 2011.
———. "From the Phonograph to the Kinetophone." *Film History* 11, no. 4 (1999): 444–48.
———. *Historia polskiego filmu dokumentalnego (1896–1944)*. Poznań: Wydawnictwo Naukowe Uniwersytetu im. Adama Mickiewicza, 2015.
———, ed. *Historia polskiego filmu dokumentalnego (1945–2014)*. Poznań: Wydawnictwo Naukowe UAM, 2015.
———, ed. *Klucze do rzeczywistości: Szkice i rozmowy o polskim filmie dokumentalnym po roku 1989*. Poznań: Wydawnictwo Naukowe Uniwersytetu im. Adama Mickiewicza, 2005.
———. *Kronika kinematografii polskiej 1895–1997*. 2nd ed. Poznań: Ars Nova, 2012. First published 1999.
———. "Meandry i paradoksy międzywojennej cenzury filmowej w Polsce." *Images* 18, no. 27 (2016): 63–86.
———. *Śladami tamtych cieni: Film w kulturze polskiej przełomu stuleci 1895–1914*. Poznań: Oficyna Wydawnicza Book Service, 1993.
———. *Smosarska*. Poznań: Wydawnictwo Naukowe Uniwersytetu im. Adama Mickiewicza, 2007.
———. "Was the Cinema Fairground Entertainment? The Birth and Role of Popular Cinema in the Polish Territories up to 1908." In Dyer and Vincendeau, *Popular European Cinema*, 112–26.
———, ed. *Widziane po latach: Analizy i interpretacje filmu polskiego*. Poznań: Wydawnictwo Poznańskiego Towarzystwa Przyjaciół Nauk, 2000.
Hendrykowska, Małgorzata, and Marek Hendrykowski. *Film w Poznaniu i Wielkopolsce 1896–1996*. Poznań: Ars Nova, 1997.
———. "The First Polish Feature Film: *Les Martyrs de la Pologne / The Prussian Culture* (1908)." *Images* 6, nos. 11–12 (2008): 5–25.
Hendrykowski, Marek, ed. *Andrzej Kondratiuk*. Poznań: Apeks, 1996.
———, ed. *Debiuty polskiego kina*. Konin: Wydawnictwo Przegląd Koniński. 1998.
———. "Etiudy Romana Polańskiego." *Images* 9, nos. 17–18 (2011): 159–98.
———. "Kazimierz Prószyński and the Origins of Polish Cinematography. In *Celebrating 1895: The Centenary of Cinema*, edited by John Fullerton, 13–18. London: John Libbey, 1998.
———. *Marcel Łoziński*. Warsaw: Wydawnictwo Więź, 2008.
———. *Munk's Eroica*. Translated by Richard Reisner. Poznań: Wydawnictwo Naukowe Uniwersytetu im. Adama Mickiewicza, 2011.
———. *Morgenstern*. Poznań: Wydawnictwo Naukowe Uniwersytetu im. Adama Mickiewicza, 2012.

---. *Polański's Knife in the Water*. Translated by Mikołaj Jazdon. Poznań: Wydawnictwo Naukowe Uniwersytetu im. Adama Mickiewicza, 2005.

---. *Stanisław Różewicz*. Poznań: Ars Nova, 1999.

---. *Wajda's Ashes and Diamonds*. Translated by Peter Langer. Poznań: Wydawnictwo Naukowe Uniwersytetu im. Adama Mickiewicza, 2009.

---, ed. *Wojciech Wiszniewski*. Poznań: Wydawnictwo Naukowe Uniwersytetu im. Adama Mickiewicza, 2006.

Hoberman, J. *Bridge of Light: Yiddish Film between Two Worlds*. New York: Museum of Modern Art and Schocken Books, 1991.

Hodge, Nick, and Marta Urbańska. "Andrzej Wajda on *Katyń*: The Full Transcript." *Krakow Post*, 23 June 2009. http://www.krakowpost.com/article/1388.

Hollender, Barbara. *Od Wajdy do Komasy*. Warsaw: Prószyński i S-ka, 2014.

Hollender, Barbara, and Zofia Turowska, eds. *Zespół TOR*. Warsaw: Wydawnictwo Prószyński i S-ka, 2000.

Holoubek, Gustaw. *Wspomnienia z niepamięci*. Warsaw: Marginesy, 2009.

Hopfinger, Maryla. "Adaptacje utworów literackich w polskim filmie okresu powojennego." In *Problemy socjologii literatury*, edited by Janusz Sławiński, 467–89. Wrocław: Ossolineum, 1971.

Horton, Andrew James. "Tales of Hoffman." *Central Europe Review* 3, no. 14 (23 April 2001). http://www.ce-review.org/01/14/kinoeye14_horton.html.

Imre, Anikó, ed. *A Companion to Eastern European Cinemas*. Oxford: Wiley-Blackwell, 2012.

Insdorf, Annette. *Double Lives, Second Chances: The Cinema of Krzysztof Kieslowski*. New York: Hyperion, 1999.

---. *Indelible Shadows: Film and the Holocaust*. Cambridge: Cambridge University Press, 2003.

---. *Intimations: The Cinema of Wojciech Has*. Evanston, IL: Northwestern University Press, 2017.

Iordanova, Dina. *Cinema of the Other Europe: The Industry and Artistry of East Central European Film*. London: Wallflower Press, 2003.

Irzykowski, Karol. *X Muza: Zagadnienia estetyczne kina*. Kraków: Krakowska Spółka Wydawnicza, 1924 [reprints: 1957, 1960, 1977, 1982].

Izod, John, and Joanna Dovalis. "Grieving, Therapy, Cinema, and Kieslowski's *Trois Couleurs: Blue*." *The San Francisco Jung Institute Library Journal* 25, no. 3 (2006): 49–73.

Jackiewicz, Aleksander. *Film jako powieść XX wieku*. Warsaw: Wydawnictwa Artystyczne i Filmowe, 1968.

---. *Moja filmoteka: Kino polskie*. Warsaw: Wydawnictwa Artystyczne i Filmowe, 1983.

---. "Powrót Kordiana: Tradycja romantyczna w kinie polskim." *Kwartalnik Filmowy* 4 (1961): 23–37.

Jagielski, Sebastian. *Maskarady męskości: Pragnienie homospołeczne w polskim kinie fabularnym*. Kraków: Universitas, 2013.

Jagielski, Sebastian, and Magdalena Podsiadło, eds. *Kino polskie jako kino transnarodowe.* Kraków: Universitas, 2017.
Jakubowska, Małgorzata. *Kryształy czasu: Kino Wojciecha Jerzego Hasa.* Łódź: Wydawnictwo Uniwersytetu Łódzkiego, 2013.
———. *Laboratorium czasu: Sanatorium pod klepsydrą Wojciecha Jerzego Hasa.* Łódź: Łódź Film School, 2010.
Jakubowska, Małgorzata, Kamila Żyto, and Anna M. Zarychta, eds. *Filmowe ogrody Wojciecha Jerzego Hasa.* Łódź: Łódź Film School, 2011.
Jakubowska, Wanda. "Kilka wspomnień o powstaniu scenariusza (na marginesie filmu *Ostatni etap*)." *Kwartalnik Filmowy* 1 (1951): 40–47.
Janicka Bożena, and Andrzej Kołodyński, eds. *Chełmska 21: 50 lat Wytwórni Filmów Dokumentalnych i Fabularnych w Warszawie.* Bilingual publication. Warsaw: WFDiF, 2000.
Janicki, Stanisław. *Aleksander Ford.* Warsaw: Wydawnictwa Artystyczne i Filmowe, 1967.
———. *Film polski od A do Z.* Warsaw: Wydawnictwa Artystyczne i Filmowe, 1973.
———. *Polscy twórcy filmowi o sobie.* Warsaw: Wydawnictwa Artystyczne i Filmowe, 1962.
———. *Polskie filmy fabularne 1902–1988.* Warsaw: Wydawnictwa Artystyczne i Filmowe, 1990.
Jankun-Dopartowa, Mariola. *Gorzkie Kino Agnieszki Holland.* Gdańsk: słowo/obraz terytoria, 2000.
———. *Labirynt Polańskiego.* Kraków: Rabid, 2000.
———. "*Rysopis* jako duchowa biografia pokolenia." *Kwartalnik Filmowy* 17 (1997): 98–104.
———. "Trójkolorowy transparent: Vive le chaos!" *Kino* 6 (1995): 4–7.
Jankun-Dopartowa, Mariola, and Mirosław Przylipiak, eds. *Człowiek z ekranu: Z antropologii postaci filmowej.* Kraków: Arcana, 1996.
Jaworski, Adam. "Talk and Silence in *The Interrrogation*." *Language and Literature* 7, no. 2 (1998): 99–122.
Jazdon, Mikołaj. *Dokumenty Kieślowskiego.* Poznań: Wydawnictwo Poznańskie, 2002.
———. *Kino dokumentalne Kazimierza Karabasza.* Poznań: Wydawnictwo Naukowe Uniwersytetu im. Adama Mickiewicza, 2009.
———. "Ograniczony punkt widzenia: Filmowy obraz powstania w getcie warszawskim." *Kwartalnik Historii Żydów* 2 (2004): 225–32.
———. *Polskie kino niezależne.* Poznań: Wojewódzka Biblioteka Pedagogiczna, 2005.
———. "Starring: Photos—On Polish Iconographic Films Made from Photos." Special issue in English on "Polish Film Scholars on Polish Cinema," *Kwartalnik Filmowy* (2013): 140–58.
Jazdon, Mikołaj, and Katarzyna Mąka-Malatyńska, eds. *Zobaczyć siebie: Polski film dokumentalny przełomu wieków.* Poznań: Centrum Kultury Zamek, 2011.
Jewsiewicki, Władysław. *Filmowcy polscy na frontach drugiej wojny światowej.* Warsaw: Wydawnictwa Artystyczne i Filmowe, 1972.
———. *Materiały do dziejów filmu w Polsce.* Warsaw: Państwowe Wydawnictwo Naukowe, 1952.

———. *Polska kinematografia w okresie filmu dźwiękowego (1930–1939)*. Łódź: Ossolineum, 1967.
———. *Polska kinematografia w okresie filmu niemego (1895–1929/1930)*. Łódź: Ossolineum, 1966.
Kalinowska, Izabela. "Cinema of Hard Times: Individuals, Families and Society in Polish Contemporary Films." *Canadian Slavonic Papers* 46, nos. 3–4 (2004): 401–16.
———. "From Orientalism to Surrealism: Wojciech Jerzy Has Interprets Jan Potocki." *Studies in Eastern European Cinema* 4, no. 1 (2013): 47–62.
———. "From Political Engagement to Politics of Abjection in Polish Auteur Cinema: The Case of Wojtek Smarzowski." In *The Global Auteur: The Politics of Authorship in 21st Century Cinema*, edited by Seung-Hoon Jeong and Jeremi Szaniawski, 115–32. London: Bloomsbury Academic, 2016.
———. "Original Journeys in Polish Cinema during the Second Half of the 1990s." *The Polish Review* 47, no. 2 (2002): 133–43.
Kaniecki, Przemysław, and Jerzy Speina, eds. *Konwicki*. Toruń: Wydawnictwo Naukowe Uniwersytetu im. Mikołaja Kopernika, 2008.
Karpiński, Maciej. *The Theatre of Andrzej Wajda*. Cambridge: Cambridge University Press, 1989.
Katafiasz, Olga. *To, co ulepsza: Tradycja i współczesność w filmach Andrzeja Wajdy*. Kraków: Rupella, 2009.
Kawalerowicz, Jerzy. *Więcej niż kino*. Warsaw: Skorpion, 2001.
Kehr, Dave. "To Save the World: Kieślowski's *Three Colours* Trilogy." *Film Comment* 30, no. 6 (1994): 10–20.
Kenez, Peter. *Cinema and Soviet Society, 1917–1953*. Cambridge: Cambridge University Press, 1992.
Kerner, Aaron. *Film and the Holocaust: New Perspectives on Dramas, Documentaries, and Experimental Films*. London: Continuum, 2011.
Kickasola, Joseph G. *The Films of Krzysztof Kieslowski: The Liminal Image*. New York: Continuum, 2004.
Kieślowski, Krzysztof. "In Depth Rather than Breadth." *Polish Perspectives* 24, nos. 6–7 (1981): 67–70.
Kieślowski, Krzysztof, and Krzysztof Piesiewicz. *Decalogue: The Ten Commandments*. Translated by Phil Cavendish and Suzannah Bluh. London: Faber & Faber, 1991.
———. *Three Colours Trilogy: Blue, White, Red*. Translated by Danusia Stok. London: Faber & Faber, 1998.
Klejsa, Konrad. "Stanisław Bareja: Nadrealizm socjalistyczny." In Stachówna and Żmudziński, *Autorzy kina polskiego*, 79–128.
Klejsa, Konrad, and Ewelina Nurczyńska-Fidelska, eds. *Kino polskie: Reinterpretacje. Historia—Ideologia—Polityka*. Kraków: Rabid, 2008.
Klejsa, Konrad, Schamma Schahadat, and Margarete Wach, eds. *Der Polnische Film: Von seinen Anfängen bis zur Gegenwart*. Marburg: Schüren Verlag, 2013.
Klich, Aleksandra. *Cały ten Kutz: Biografia niepokorna*. Kraków: Znak, 2009.

Kluszczyński, Ryszard W. *Obrazy na wolności: Studia z historii sztuk medialnych w Polsce*. Warsaw: Instytut Kultury, 1998.

Koczarowska-Różycka, Natasza. *Inne spojrzenie: Wyobrażenia historii w filmach Wojciecha Jerzego Hasa, Jana Jakuba Kolskiego, Filipa Bajona i Anny Jadowskiej—Studium przypadków*. Łódź: Łódź Film School, 2013.

Konigsberg, Ira. "*Our Children* and the Limits of Cinema: Early Jewish Responses to the Holocaust." *Film Quarterly* 52, no. 1 (1998): 7–19.

Konwicki, Tadeusz. *Moonrise, Moonset*. Translated by Richard Lourie. New York: Farrar, Straus, & Giroux, 1987.

Konwicki, Tadeusz, Katarzyna Bielas, and Jacek Szczerba. *Pamiętam, że było gorąco: Rozmowa z Tadeuszem Konwickim*. Kraków: Znak, 2001.

Kornacki, Krzysztof. *Kino polskie wobec katolicyzmu (1945–1970)*. Gdańsk: słowo/obraz terytoria, 2005.

———. *"Popiół i diament" Andrzeja Wajdy*. Gdańsk: słowo/obraz terytoria, 2011.

Kornatowska, Maria. *Agnieszka Holland: Magia i pieniądze*. Kraków: Znak, 2002.

———. *Eros i film*. Łódź: Krajowa Agencja Wydawnicza, 1986.

———. *Wodzireje i amatorzy*. Warsaw: Wydawnictwa Artystyczne i Filmowe, 1990.

Kossakowski, Andrzej. *Polski film animowany 1945–1974*. Wrocław: Ossolineum, 1977.

Kotowski, Mariusz. *Pola Negri: Hollywood's First Femme Fatale*. Lexington: University of Kentucky Press, 2014.

Kowalska, Jolanta. *Kazimierz-Junosza-Stępowski*. Warsaw: Oficyna Wydawnicza Errata, 2000.

Krakus, Anna. "The Abuses, and Uses, of Film Censorship: An Interview with Andrzej Wajda." *Cineaste* 39, no. 3 (2014): 3–9.

Krubski, Krzysztof, Marek Miller, Zofia Turowska, and Waldemar Wiśniewski, eds. *Filmówka*. Warsaw: Tenten, 1998.

Kuc, Kamila. *Visions of Avant-Garde Film: Polish Cinematic Experiments from Expressionism to Constructivism*. Bloomington: Indiana University Press, 2016.

Kuc, Kamila, Kuba Mikurda, and Michał Oleszczyk, eds. *Boro, l'île d'amour: The Films of Walerian Borowczyk*. New York: Berghahn Books, 2015.

Kuc, Kamila, and Michael O'Pray, eds. *The Struggle for Form: Perspectives on Polish Avant-Garde Film, 1916–1989*. London: Wallflower Press, 2014.

Kucharski, Krzysztof. *Kino plus: Film i dystrybucja kinowa w Polsce w latach 1990–2000*. Toruń: Oficyna Wydawnicza Kucharski, 2002.

Kulesza, Marek. *Ryszard Bolesławski: Umrzeć w Hollywood*. Warsaw: Państwowy Instytut Wydawniczy, 1989.

Kulig, Agnieszka. *Etyka "bez końca": Twórczość filmowa Krzysztofa Kieślowskiego wobec problemów etycznych*. Poznań: Wydawnictwo Poznańskie, 2009.

Kunicki, Mikołaj. "Heroism, Raison d'état, and National Communism: Red Nationalism in the Cinema of People's Poland." *Contemporary European History* 21, no. 2 (2012): 235–56.

Kurpiewski, Piotr. *Historia na ekranie Polski Ludowej*. Gdańsk: Wydawnictwo Uniwersytetu Gdańskiego, 2017.
Kurz, Iwona. "'Ten obraz jest trochę straszliwy': Historia pewnego filmu, czyli naród polski twarzą w twarz z Żydem." *Zagłada Żydów: Studia i Materiały* 4 (2008): 466–83.
———. *Twarze w tłumie: Wizerunki bohaterów wyobraźni zbiorowej w kulturze polskiej lat 1955–1969*. Warsaw: Świat Literacki, 2005.
Kuśmierczyk, Seweryn. *Wyprawa bohatera w polskim filmie fabularnym*. Warsaw: Czuły Barbarzyńca Press, 2014.
Kwiatkowska, Paulina. "The Structures of Memory: The Images of Space-Time in Andrzej Munk's Film *Passenger*." Special issue in English on "Polish Film Scholars on Polish Cinema," *Kwartalnik Filmowy* (2013): 6–30.
Lebecka, Magda. *Lech Majewski*. Kraków: Wydawnictwo Więź, 2010.
Lemann-Zajiček, Jolanta. *Eugeniusz Cękalski*. Łódź: Muzeum Kinematografii, 1996.
———. *Kino i polityka: Polski film dokumentalny 1945–1949*. Łódź: Łódź Film School, 2003.
———, ed. *Państwowa Wyższa Szkoła Filmowa, Telewizyjna i Teatralna im. Leona Schillera w Łodzi 1948–1998*. Łódź: Łódź Film School, 1998.
———, ed. *Polska kultura filmowa do 1939 roku*. Łódź: Łódź Film School, 2003.
Lewandowski, Jan F. *Kino na pograniczu: Wędrówki po dziejach filmu na Górnym Śląsku*. Katowice: Śląsk, 1998.
———. *Kino śląskie*. Katowice: Wydawnictwo Naukowe Śląsk, 2012.
———. *Historia Śląska według Kutza*. Katowice: Śląsk, 2004.
———. *100 filmów polskich*. Katowice: Videograf II, 1997.
Lewis, Clifford, and Carroll Britch. "Andrzej Wajda's War Trilogy: A Retrospective." *Film Criticism* 10, no. 3 (1986): 22–35.
Liebman, Stuart. "The Art of Memory: Andrzej Wajda's War Trilogy." *Cineaste* 32, no. 1 (2006): 42–47.
———. "Documenting the Liberation of the Camps: The Case of Aleksander Ford's *Vernichtungslager Majdanek—Cmentarzysko Europy* (1944)." In *Lessons and Legacies VII: The Holocaust in International Perspective*, edited by Dagmar Herzog, 333–51. Evanston, IL: Northwestern University Press, 2006.
———. "'I Was Always in the Epicenter of Whatever Was Going On ...' An Interview with Wanda Jakubowska." *Slavic and East European Performance* 17, no. 3 (1997): 16–30.
———. "The Majdanek Trial: The Holocaust on Trial on Film—Kazimierz Czyński's *Swastyka i szubienica* (1945)." In *The Scene of the Mass Crime: History, Film, and International Tribunals*, edited by Christian Delage and Peter Goodrich, 113–28. London: Routledge, 2013.
———. "On Andrzej Munk." *Cineaste* 32, no. 2 (2007): 62–66.
———. "Pages from the Past: Wanda Jakubowska's *The Last Stop (Ostatni etap)*." *Slavic and East European Performance* 16, no. 3 (1996): 56–63.
Liebman, Stuart, and Leonard Quart. "Lost and Found: Wanda Jakubowska's *The Last Stop*." *Cineaste* 22, no. 4 (1997): 43–45.

Lis, Marek, and Michał Legan, eds. *Kieślowski czyta Dekalog*. Opole: Wydawnictwo Uniwersytetu Opolskiego, 2014.
Litka. Piotr. "Polacy i Żydzi w *Ulicy Granicznej*." *Kwartalnik Filmowy* 29–30 (2000): 60–74.
Loewy, Hanno. "The Mother of All Holocaust Films? Wanda Jakubowska's Auschwitz Trilogy." *Historical Journal of Film, Radio and Television* 24, no. 2 (2004): 179–204.
Liehm, Mira, and Antonin J. Liehm. *The Most Important Art: Soviet and Eastern European Film after 1945*. Berkeley: University of California Press, 1977.
Lovell, Angela. "*The Lure*: One Is Silver and the Other Gold." *Criterion Collection*, 10 October 2017. https://www.criterion.com/current/posts/5030-the-lure-one-is-silver-and-the-other-gold.
Lubelski, Tadeusz. *Historia kina polskiego 1895–2014*. Kraków: Universitas, 2015.
———. *Historia niebyła kina PRL*. Kraków: Wydawnictwo Znak, 2012.
———, ed. *Kino Krzysztofa Kieślowskiego*. Kraków: Universitas, 1997.
———, ed. *Od Mickiewicza do Masłowskiej: Adaptacje filmowe literatury polskiej*. Kraków: Universitas, 2014.
———. *Poetyka powieści i filmów Tadeusza Konwickiego*. Wrocław: Wydawnictwo Uniwersytetu Wrocławskiego, 1984.
———. "Polska Szkoła Filmowa na tle rodzimego kina." In *Historia kina, tom 2: Kino klasyczne*, edited by Tadeusz Lubelski, Iwona Sowińska, and Rafał Syska, 935–92. Kraków: Universitas, 2011.
———. *Strategie autorskie w polskim filmie fabularnym lat 1945–1961*. Kraków: Wydawnictwo Uniwersytetu Jagiellońskiego, 1992.
———. *Wajda: Portret mistrza w kilku odsłonach*. Wrocław: Wydawnictwo Dolnośląskie, 2006.
———, ed. *Zdjęcia: Jerzy Lipman*. Warsaw: Wydawnictwa Artystyczne i Filmowe, 2005.
Lubelski, Tadeusz, and Konrad J. Zarębski, eds. *Historia kina polskiego*. Warsaw: Fundacja Kino, 2006.
Lubelski, Tadeusz, and Maciej Stroiński, eds. *Kino polskie jako kino narodowe*. Kraków: Korporacja Ha!art, 2009.
Łuczak, Maciej. *Miś, czyli rzecz o Stanisławie Barei*. Warsaw: Prószyński i S-ka, 2002.
Łysak, Tomasz. *Od kroniki do filmu posttraumatycznego: Filmy dokumentalne o Zagładzie*. Warsaw: Instytut Badań Literackich PAN, 2016.
———. "On the Impossibility of Believing in the Documentary: Dariusz Jabłoński's *Photographer*." Special issue in English on "Polish Film Scholars on Polish Cinema," *Kwartalnik Filmowy* (2013): 128–39.
———. "Reconstruction or Creation? The Liberation of a Concentration Camp in Andrzej Wajda's *Landscape after Battle*." *Slovo* 25, no. 1 (2013): 31–47.
Madej, Alina. "Wanda Jakubowska: Jak powstawał *Ostatni etap*." *Kino* 5 (1998): 13–17.
———. *Kino, władza, publiczność: Kinematografia polska w latach 1944–1949*. Bielsko-Biala: Wydawnictwo "Prasa Beskidzka," 2002.
———. *Mitologie i konwencje: O polskim kinie fabularnym dwudziestolecia międzywojennego*. Kraków: Universitas, 1994.

Madej, Alina, and Jakub Zajdel. *Śmierć jak kromka chleba: Historia jednego filmu*. Warsaw: PAN-Instytut Sztuki, 1994.
Majer, Artur. *Kino Juliusza Machulskiego*. Bielsko-Biała: Wydawnictwo Kwieciński, 2014.
Mąka-Malatyńska, Katarzyna. *Agnieszka Holland*. Warsaw: Wydawnictwo Więź, 2009.
———. *Holland's Europa, Europa*. Translated by Daniel Polsby. Poznań: Wydawnictwo Naukowe Uniwersytetu im. Adama Mickiewicza, 2007.
———. *Widok z tej strony: Przedstawienia Holocaustu w polskim filmie*. Poznań: Wydawnictwo Naukowe Uniwersytetu im. Adama Mickiewicza, 2012.
Malatyńska, Maria. "Siedmioramiennie." An interview with Andrzej Wajda. *Tygodnik Powszechny* 9 (1996): 7.
Marciniak, Katarzyna. "Second World-ness and Transnational Feminist Practices: Agnieszka Holland's *Kobieta samotna (A Woman Alone)*." In *East European Cinemas*, edited by Anikó Imre, 3–20. New York: Routledge, 2005.
Marczak, Mariola. *Niepokój i tęsknota. Kino wobec wartości: O filmach Krzysztofa Zanussiego*. Olsztyn: Wydawnictwo Uniwersytetu Warmińsko-Mazurskiego, 2011.
Marecki, Piotr. *Kino niezależne w Polsce 1989–2009: Historia mówiona*. Warsaw: Wydawnictwo Krytyki Politycznej, 2009.
Marecki, Piotr, Aniela Pilarska, and Kaja Puto, eds. *Literatura i kino: Polska po 1989 roku*. Kraków: Ha!art, 2013.
Mark, James. *The Unfinished Revolution: Making Sense of the Communist Past in Central-Eastern Europe*. New Haven, CT: Yale University Press, 2010.
Maron, Marcin. *Dramat czasu i wyobraźni: Filmy Wojciecha J. Hasa*. Kraków: Universitas, 2010.
———. "Head of Medusa, or Realism in Films of the Cinema of Moral Anxiety." Special issue in English on "Polish Film Scholars on Polish Cinema," *Kwartalnik Filmowy* (2013): 231–56.
Marszałek, Rafał. "Film fabularny." In Marszałek, *Historia filmu polskiego 1968–1972*, 15–176.
———. *Filmowa pop-historia*. Kraków: Wydawnictwo Literackie, 1984.
———. "Kapelusz i chustka." In Palczewska and Benedyktynowicz, *Film i kontekst*, 35–55.
———. *Kino rzeczy znalezionych*. Gdańsk: słowo/obraz terytoria, 2006.
———. *Polska wojna w obcym filmie*. Wrocław: Ossolineum, 1976.
Marszałek, Rafał, ed. *Historia filmu polskiego 1962–1967*. Vol. 5. Warsaw: Wydawnictwa Artystyczne i Filmowe, 1985.
———, ed. *Historia filmu polskiego 1968–1972*. Vol. 6. Warsaw: Wydawnictwa Artystyczne i Filmowe, 1994.
Maśnicki, Jerzy, and Kamil Stepan. *Pleograf: Słownik biograficzny filmu polskiego 1896–1939*. Kraków: Staromiejska Oficyna Wydawnicza, 1996. No page numbers available.
Maszewska-Łupiniak, Monika. *Rzeczywistość filmowa Stanisława Różewicza*. Kraków: Wydawnictwo Uniwersytetu Jagiellońskiego, 2009.
———. "War Beading Up into a Red Dot: Autobiographical Discourse in Andrzej Żuławski's *The Third Part of the Night*." Special issue in English on "Polish Film Scholars on Polish Cinema," *Kwartalnik Filmowy* (2013): 95–108.

Matuszewski, Bolesław. *A New Source of History / Animated Photography: What It Is, What It Should Be*. Translated by Ryszard Drzewiecki. Warsaw: Filmoteka Narodowa, 1999. First published 1898 (Paris).
Mazierska, Ewa. "In the Land of Noble Knights and Mute Princesses: Polish Heritage Cinema." *Historical Journal of Film, Radio and Television* 21, no. 2 (2001): 167–82.
———. *Jerzy Skolimowski: The Cinema of a Nonconformist*. New York: Berghahn Books, 2010.
———. *Masculinities in Polish, Czech and Slovak Cinema: Black Peters and Men of Marble*. New York: Berghahn Books, 2008.
———. *Poland Daily: Economy, Work, Consumption and Social Class in Polish Cinema*. New York: Berghahn Books, 2017.
———. *Polish Postcommunist Cinema*. Oxford: Peter Lang, 2007.
———. "Searching for Survival and Meaning: Polish Film after 1989." In *Cinemas in Transition in Central and Eastern Europe after 1989*, edited by Catherine Portuges and Peter Hames, 135–60. Philadelphia, PA: Temple University Press, 2013.
Mazierska, Ewa, and Elżbieta Ostrowska. *Women in Polish Cinema*. New York: Berghahn Books, 2006.
Mazierska, Ewa, and Michael Goddard, eds. *Polish Cinema in a Transnational Context*. Rochester, NY: University of Rochester Press, 2014.
Mazur, Daria. "Paradoks i topika judajska: *Austeria* Jerzego Kawalerowicza." In *Gefilte film: Wątki żydowskie w kinie*, edited by Joanna Preizner, 145–68. Kraków: Azolem Alejchem, 2008.
———. *Waszyński's The Dybbuk*. Translated by Maciej Smoczynski. Poznań: Wydawnictwo Naukowe Uniwersytetu im. Adama Mickiewicza, 2009.
McArthur, Colin, ed. *Andrzej Wajda*. London: British Film Institute, 1970.
Michalewicz, Kazimierz S. *Polskie rodowody filmu: Narodziny masowego zjawiska*. Warsaw: Polska Agencja Ekologiczna, 1998.
Michałek, Bolesław. *The Cinema of Andrzej Wajda*. London: Tantivy Press, 1973.
———. *Szkice o filmie polskim*. Warsaw: Wydawnictwa Artystyczne i Filmowe, 1960.
Michałek, Bolesław, and Frank Turaj. *The Modern Cinema of Poland*. Bloomington: Indiana University Press, 1988.
Miczka, Tadeusz. "Cinema as Optic Poetry: On Attempts to Futurize the Cinematograph in Poland of the 1920s and 1930s." *Canadian Slavonic Papers* 40, no. 1 (1998): 1–15.
———. "Cinema under Political Pressure: A Brief Outline of Authorial Roles in Polish Post-war Feature Film 1945–1995." *Kinema* 4 (1995): 32–48.
———. *Inspiracje plastyczne w twórczości filmowej i telewizyjnej Andrzeja Wajdy*. Katowice: Wydawnictwo Uniwersytetu Śląskiego, 1987.
———. "Kino polskie po reformie (2005–2010)." *Postscriptum Polonistyczne* 1, no. 5 (2010): 65–85.
———. *O śmierci na ekranie*. Katowice: Wydawnictwo Naukowe Śląsk, 2013.

———. "Raport o stanie polskiej kinematografii." Warsaw: Ministerstwo Kultury i Dziedzictwa Narodowego, 2009. http://www.kongreskultury.pl/library/File/RaportKinema/kinematografia_raport_w.pelna.pdf.

———. "'We Live in the World Lacking Idea on Itself': Krzysztof Kieślowski's Art of Film." *Kinema* 7 (1997): 23-47.

Miczka, Tadeusz, and Alina Madej. *Syndrom konformizmu? Kino polskie lat sześćdziesiątych.* Katowice: Wydawnictwo Uniwersytetu Śląskiego, 1994.

Mikurda, Kuba, and Kamila Wielebska, eds. *Dzieje grzechu: Surrealism w kinie polskim.* Kraków: Korporacja Ha!art, 2010.

Miller-Klejsa, Anna, and Monika Woźniak, eds. *Polsko-włoskie kontakty filmowe: Topika, koprodukcje, recepcja.* Łódź: Łódź Film School, 2014.

Misiak, Anna. Misiak, Anna. "Don't Look East: National Sentiments in Andrzej Wajda's Contemporary Film Epics." *Journal of Film and Video* 65, no. 3 (2013): 26-39.

———. *Kinematograf kontrolowany: Cenzura filmowa w kraju socjalistycznym i demokratycznym—Analiza socjologiczna.* Kraków: Universitas, 2006.

———. "Our Own Courtyard: Post-traumatic Polish Cinema." *New Cinemas: Journal of Contemporary Film* 7, no. 3 (2009): 237-56.

———. "Politically Involved Filmmaker: Aleksander Ford and Film Censorship in Poland after 1945." *Kinema* 20 (2003): 19-31.

Morrison, James. *Roman Polanski.* Champaign: University of Illinois Press, 2007.

Morstin-Popławska, Agnieszka. *Jak daleko stąd do raju? Religia jako pamięć w polskim filmie fabularnym.* Kraków: Universitas, 2010.

Możejko, Edward. *Der socialistische Realismus: Theorie, Entwicklung und Versagen einer Literaturmethode.* Bonn: Bouvier Verlag Herbert Grundmann, 1977.

Mroz, Matilda. "Displacement, Suffering and Mourning: Post-war Landscapes in Contemporary Polish Cinema." In Brouwer, *Contested Interpretations of the Past in Polish, Russian, and Ukrainian Film*, 59-76.

———. "The Monument and the Sewer: Memory and Death in Wajda's Kanal (1957)." *Historical Journal of Film, Radio and Television* 34, no. 4 (2014): 528-45.

———. "Neighbours: Polish-Jewish Relations in Contemporary Polish Visual Culture." In *Holocaust Intersections: Genocide and Visual Culture at the New Millenium*, edited by Axel Bangert, Robert S. C. Gordon, and Libby Saxton, 132-47. Oxford: Legenda, 2013.

Mruklik, Barbara. *Andrzej Wajda.* Warsaw: Wydawnictwa Artystyczne i Filmowe, 1969.

———. "Film fabularny." In Toeplitz, *Historia filmu polskiego 1939-1956*, 144-66, 223-59, and 247-65.

———. "Wierność sobie. Rozmowa z Wandą Jakubowską." *Kino* 5 (1985): 4-9 and 20-21.

Negri, Pola. *Memoirs of a Star.* New York: Doubleday, 1970.

Nowicka, Magdalena. "Polskość jako przedmiot sporu: Przykład kontrowersji wokół filmu Pokłosie w reż. Władysława Pasikowskiego." *Przegląd Socjologiczny* 1 (2015): 183-210.

Nurczyńska-Fidelska, Ewelina. *Andrzej Munk.* Kraków: Wydawnictwo Literackie, 1982.

———. *Czas i przesłona. O Filipie Bajonie i jego twórczości.* Kraków: Wydawnictwo Rabid, 2003.

———, ed. *Kino polskie w trzynastu sekwencjach*. Kraków: Wydawnictwo Rabid, 2005.
———. *Polska klasyka literacka według Andrzeja Wajdy*. Katowice: Śląsk, 1998. Expanded edition published 2010 by Wydawnictwo Uniwersytetu Łódzkiego (Łódź).
Nurczyńska-Fidelska, Ewelina, and Bronisława Stolarska, eds. *"Szkoła polska": Powroty*. Łódź: Wydawnictwo Uniwersytetu Łódzkiego, 1998.
Nurczyńska-Fidelska, Ewelina, and Piotr Sitarski, eds. *Filmowy świat Andrzeja Wajdy*. Kraków: Universitas, 2003.
Oleszczyk, Michał. "Andrzej Wajda: The Searcher." *Criterion Collection*, 6 March 2017. https://www.criterion.com/current/posts/4450-andrzej-wajda-the-searcher.
Orr, John, and Elżbieta Ostrowska, eds. *The Cinema of Andrzej Wajda: The Art of Irony and Defiance*. London: Wallflower Press, 2003.
———. *The Cinema of Roman Polanski: Dark Spaces of the World*. London: Wallflower Press, 2006.
Osadnik, Wacław. "Possible Worlds in Krzysztof Kieślowski's *Decalogue*." *Canadian Revue of Comparative Literature / Revue Canadienne de Littérature Comparée* 34, no. 3 (2007): 345–51.
Ossowska-Zwierzchowska, Aldona. *Wizerunek nauczyciela w polskim filmie fabularnym w latach 1945–1989*. Toruń: Wydawnictwo Naukowe Uniwersytetu im. Adama Mickiewicza, 2013.
Ostrowska, Dorota. "An Alternative Model of Film Production: Film Units in Poland after World War Two." In Imre, *A Companion to Eastern European Cinemas*, 453–65.
Ostrowska, Elżbieta. "Filmic Representations of the 'Polish Mother' in Post–Second World War Polish Cinema." *European Journal of Women Studies* 5, nos. 3–4 (1998): 419–35.
———. "Invisible Deaths: Polish Cinema's Representation of Women in World War II." In *Embracing Arms: Cultural Representation of Slavic and Balkan Women in War*, edited by Helena Goscilo and Yana Hashamova, 29–58. Budapest: Central University Press, 2012.
———. "'I Will Wash It Out': Holocaust Reconciliation in Agnieszka Holland's 2011 Film *In Darkness*." *Holocaust and Genocide Studies* 29, no. 1 (2015): 57–75.
———. "*Katyń* Andrzeja Wajdy: Melodramatyczny afekt i historia." *Pleograf: Kwartalnik Akademii Polskiego Filmu* 1 (2016). http://akademiapolskiegofilmu.pl/pl/historia-polskiego-filmu/pleograf/andrzej-wajda/1/katyn-andrzeja-wajdy-melodramatyczny-afekt-i-historia.
———. "Krystyna Janda: The Contradictions of Polish Stardom." In *Poles Apart: Women in Modern Polish Culture*, edited by Helena Gościło and Beth Holmgren, 37–64. Bloomington: Indiana University Press, 2006.
———. "Obraz Matki Polki w kinie polskim: Mit czy stereotyp?" *Kwartalnik Filmowy* 17 (1997): 131–40.
———, ed. "Polish Cinema." Special issue, *KinoKultura*. www.kinokultura.com/specials/2/polish.shtml.

———. "The Polish Femme Fatale: Ideological Demand versus Visual Pleasure." *Canadian Revue of Comparative Literature / Revue Canadienne de Littérature Comparée* 34, no. 3 (2007): 307–15.
———. "Postcolonial Fantasies: Imagining the Balkans—The Polish Popular Cinema of Władysław Pasikowski." In *Postcolonial Approaches to Eastern European Cinema: Portraying Neighbours on Screen*, edited by Ewa Mazierska, Lars Kristensen, and Eva Näripea, 175–200. London: I. B. Tauris, 2013.
Otto, Wojciech. *Literatura i film w kulturze polskiej dwudziestolecia międzywojennego*. Poznań: Wydawnictwo Poznańskiego Towarzystwa Przyjaciół Nauk, 2007.
———. *Obrazy niepełnosprawności w polskim filmie*. Poznań: Wydawnictwo Naukowe Uniwersytetu im. Adama Mickiewicza. 2012.
Ozimek, Stanisław. *Film polski w wojennej potrzebie*. Warsaw: Państwowy Instytut Wydawniczy, 1974.
———. "Konfrontacje z Wielką Wojną." In Toeplitz, *Historia filmu polskiego 1957–1961*, 11–128.
———. "Od wojny w dzień powszedni." In Toeplitz, *Historia filmu polskiego 1957–1961*, 129–98.
———. "Spojrzenie na 'szkołę polską.'" In Toeplitz, *Historia filmu polskiego 1957–1961*, 199–212.
———. "The Polish Newsreel in 1945: The Bitter Victory." In *Hitler's Fall: The Newsreel Witness*, edited by K. R. M. Short and Stephan Dolezel, 70–79. London: Croom Helm, 1988.
Pakier, Małgorzata. *The Construction of European Holocaust Memory: German and Polish Cinema after 1989*. Frankfurt: Peter Lang, 2013.
Palczewska, Danuta, and Zbigniew Benedyktowicz, eds. *Film i kontekst*. Wrocław: Ossolineum, 1988.
Palczewska, Danuta. *Współczesna polska myśl filmowa*. Wrocław: Ossolineum, 1981.
Paul, David. "Andrzej Wajda's War Trilogy." *Cineaste* 20, no. 4 (1994): 52–54.
———. *Politics, Art and Commitment in East European Cinema*. New York: St. Martin's Press, 1983.
Paul, David, and Sylvia Glover. "The Difficulty of Moral Choice: Zanussi's *Contract* and *The Constant Factor*." *Film Quarterly* 37, no. 2 (1983–1984): 19–26.
Petrie, Graham, and Ruth Dwyer. *Before the Wall Came Down: Soviet and East European Filmmakers in the West*. New York: University Press of America, 1990.
Pietrasik, Zdzisław. "Andrzej Wajda: Na moich warunkach." An interview with Andrzej Wajda. *Polityka* 10 (1996): 45–48.
———. "Broń się: Najbardziej lubimy oglądać amerykańskie filmy polskie." *Polityka* 15 (1997): 72–73.
———. "Brudny Marek: Samotny mściciel w polskich realiach." *Polityka* 6 (2000): 44–45.
Pirie, Donald, Jekaterina Young, and Christopher Carrell, eds. *Polish Realities: The Arts in Poland 1980–1989*. Glasgow: Third Eye Centre, 1990.
Piwowarska, Barbara, and Łukasz Ronduda, eds. *Polish New Wave: The History of a Phenomenon that Never Existed / Polska Nowa Fala: Historia zjawiska, którego nie było*. Warsaw: Adam Mickiewicz Institute, 2008.

Płażewski, Jerzy, Grzegorz Balski, and Jan Słodowski. *Wajda Films*. 2 vols. Warsaw: Wydawnictwa Artystyczne i Filmowe, 1996.
Polański, Roman. *Polanski: Three Film Scripts*. New York: Harper & Row, 1975.
———. *Roman by Polanski*. New York: William Morrow, 1984.
Polonsky, Antony, and Joanna B. Michlic, eds. *The Neighbors Respond: The Controversy over the Jedwabne Massacre in Poland*. Princeton, NJ: Princeton University Press, 2003.
Powell, Larson. "The Moral Microhistory of Post-Communism: Zanussi's *Weekend Stories*." In Blankenship and Nagl, *European Visions*, 285–98.
Preizner, Joanna. *Kamienie na macewie: Holocaust w polskim kinie*. Kraków: Austeria, 2012.
Pryzwan, Mariola, ed. *"Cześć, starenia!" Zbyszek Cybulski we wspomnieniach*. Warsaw: MK, 1994.
Przylipiak, Mirosław. "Dekalog / The Decalogue." In Hames, *The Cinema of Central Europe*, 225–34.
———. "Exploring *Assassination in Gibraltar* by Anna Jadowska in the Context of Dominant Tendencies in Contemporary Polish Cinema." *Studies in Eastern European Cinema* 1, no. 2 (2010): 139–52
———. *Kino stylu zerowego*. Gdańsk: Gdańskie Wydawnictwo Psychologiczne, 2017.
———. *Poetyka kina dokumentalnego*. Gdańsk: Wydawnictwo Uniwersytetu Gdańskiego, 2000.
———. "Polish Documentary Film after 1989." In Falkowska and Haltof, *The New Polish Cinema*, 143–64.
Radkiewicz, Małgorzata. *"Młode wilki" polskiego kina: Kategoria gender a debiuty lat 90*. Kraków: Wydawnictwo Uniwersytetu Jagiellońskiego, 2006.
———. *Modernistyki o kinie: Kobiety w polskiej krytyce i publicystyce filmowej 1918–1939*. Kraków: Korporacja Ha!art, 2016.
Ratner, Megan. "Action Is a Most Dangerous Thing: Interview with Agnieszka Holland." *Film Quarterly* 67, no. 3 (2014): 9–16.
———. "Displaced Persons: *Ida*'s Window on Vanished Lives." *Film Quarterly* 67, no. 3 (2014): 30–34.
Rek, Jan. *Kino Jerzego Kawalerowicz i jego konteksty*. Łódź: Wydawnictwo Uniwersytetu Łódzkiego, 2008.
Reyland, Nicholas W. *Zbigniew Preisner's Three Colors Trilogy: Blue, White, Red*. Lanham, MD: Scarecrow Press, 2012.
Rogerson, Edward. "Polish Cinema: An Internal Exile." *Sight and Sound* 55, no. 3 (1986): 195–97.
Rogowski, Grzegorz. *Skazane na zapomnienie: Polskie aktorki filmowe na emigracji*. Warsaw: Muza, 2017.
Rutkowska, Teresa. "*Panny z Wilka*: Pięć nieszczęśliwych kobiet z Wenus i zmęczony mężczyzna z Marsa." *Kwartalnik Filmowy* 18 (1997): 141–52.
Safran, Gabriella. "Dancing with Death and Salvaging Jewish Culture in *Austeria* and *The Dybbuk*." *Slavic Review* 59, no. 4 (2000): 761–81.

Saryusz-Wolska, Magdalena. "The Transformation of National Memory in Polish Postwar Cinema." *Studia Universitatis Cibiniensis* 11 (2014): 201–14.
Sitkiewicz, Paweł. *Polska szkoła animacji*. Gdańsk: słowo/obraz terytoria, 2011.
Skaff, Sheila. *Studying Ida*. Leighton Buzzard: Auteur Publishing, 2018.
———. *The Law of the Looking Glass: Cinema in Poland, 1896–1939*. Athens: Ohio University Press, 2008.
Skotarczak, Dorota. *Obraz społeczeństwa PRL w komedii filmowej*. Poznań: Wydawnictwo Naukowe Uniwersytetu im. Adama Mickiewicza, 2004.
Skrodzka, Aga. "Clandestine Human and Cinematic Passages in the United Europe: The Polish Plumber and Kieślowski's Hairdresser." *Studies in Eastern European Cinema* 2, no. 1 (2011): 75–90.
———. "History from Inside Out: The Vernacular Cinema of Jan Jakub Kolski." *Kinokultura* (2005). www.kinokultura.com/specials/2/skrodzka.shtml.
———. *Magic Realist Cinema in East Central Europe*. Edinburgh: Edinburgh University Press, 2012.
———. "Woman's Body and Her Pleasure in the Celluloid Erotica of Walerian Borowczyk." *Studies in European Cinema* 8, no. 1 (2011): 67–79.
Skwara, Anita. "Film Stars Do Not Shine in the Sky over Poland: The Absence of Popular Cinema in Poland." In Dyer and Vincendeau, *Popular European Cinema*, 220–31.
Słodowski, Jan, ed. *Leksykon polskich filmów fabularnych*. Warsaw: Wiedza i Życie, 1996.
Snyder, Timothy. *Bloodlands: Europe between Hitler and Stalin*. New York: Basics Books, 2010.
———. *The Reconstruction of Nations: Poland, Ukraine, Lithuania, Belarus, 1569–1999*. New Haven, CT: Yale University Press, 2003.
Sobański, Oskar. *Polish Feature Films: A Reference Guide 1945–1985*. West Cornwall: Locust Hill, 1987.
Sobolewski, Tadeusz. *Dziecko Peerelu. Esej. Dziennik*. Warsaw: Wydawnictwo Sic!, 2000.
———. "Peace and Rebellion." In *Polish Cinema in Ten Takes*, edited by Ewelina Nurczyńska-Fidelska and Zbigniew Batko, 123–37. Łódź: Łódzkie Towarzystwo Naukowe, 1995.
Sobotka, Kazimierz, ed. *Film polski: Twórcy i mity*. Łódź: Łódzki Dom Kultury, 1987.
———. "Robotnik na ekranie, czyli o tak zwanym 'filmie produkcyjnym.'" In Stolarska, *Szkice o filmie polskim*, 25–70.
Sokołowski, Marek, ed. *Arystokratyzm ducha: Kino Krzysztofa Zanussiego*. Warsaw: Wydawnictwo WSP TWP, 2009.
Sosnowski, Alexandra. "Cinema in Transition: The Polish Film Today." *Journal of Popular Film and Television* 24, no. 1 (1996): 10–16.
———. "Polish Cinema Today: A New Order in the Production, Distribution and Exhibition of Film." *The Polish Review* 15, no. 1 (1995): 315–29.
Sowińska, Iwona. *Chopin idzie do kina*. Kraków: Universitas, 2013.
———. *Polska muzyka filmowa 1945–1968*. Katowice: Wydawnictwo Uniwersytetu Śląskiego, 2006.

Spalińska-Mazur, Joanna. *Inwencje i kontynuacje: Polski autorski film animowany w latach 1980–1990*. Opole: Wydawnictwo Uniwersytetu Opolskiego, 2009.
Stachówna, Grażyna, ed. *Kobieta z kamerą*. Kraków: Wydawnictwo Uniwersytetu Jagiellońskiego, 1998.
———. *Roman Polański i jego filmy*. Warsaw: Państwowe Wydawnictwo Naukowe, 1994.
———. "Równanie szeregów: Bohaterowie filmów socrealistycznych (1949–1955)." In Jankun-Dopartowa and Przylipiak, *Człowiek z ekranu: Z antropologii postaci filmowej*, 7–28.
———. "A Wormwood Wreath: Polish Women's Cinema." In Falkowska and Haltof, *The New Polish Cinema*, 98–115.
Stachówna, Grażyna, and Joanna Wojnicka, eds. *Autorzy kina polskiego*. Kraków: Rabid, 2004.
Stachówna, Grażyna, and Bogusław Żmudziński, eds. *Autorzy kina polskiego, tom 2*. Kraków: Wydawnictwo Uniwersytetu Jagiellońskiego, 2007.
———, eds. *Autorzy kina polskiego, tom 3*. Kraków: Wydawnictwo Uniwersytetu Jagiellońskiego, 2007.
Stalnaker, Maria T. "Agnieszka Holland Reads Hollywood." In Stephan, *Living in Translation*, 313–30.
Stawiński, Jerzy Stefan. *Notatki scenarzysty*. Warsaw: Czytelnik, 1988.
Stawiński, Jerzy Stefan, and Barbara Giza. *Do filmu trafiłem przypadkiem: Z Jerzym Stefanem Stawińskim rozmawia Barbara Giza*. Warsaw: Trio, 2007.
Stephan, Halin, ed. *Living in Translation: Polish Writers in America*. Amsterdam: Rodopi, 2003.
Stevenson, Michael. "*The Pianist* and Its Contexts: Polanski's Narration of Holocaust Evasion and Survival." In Orr and Ostrowska, *The Cinema of Roman Polanski: Dark Spaces of the World*, 146–57.
Stok, Danusia, ed. *Kieślowski on Kieślowski*. London: Faber & Faber, 1993.
Stolarska, Bronisława, ed. *Szkice o kinie polskim*. Łódź: Łódzki Dom Kultury, 1985.
Świdziński, Wojciech. *Co było grane? Film zagraniczny w Polsce w latach 1918–1929 na przykładzie Warszawy*. Warsaw: Instytut Sztuki PAN, 2015.
Szarota, Tomasz. *Karuzela na Placu Krasińskich: Studia i szkice z lat wojny i okupacji*. Warsaw: Oficyna Wydawnicza Rytm, 2007.
Szczepański, Tadeusz. "Kieślowski wobec Bergmana, czyli Tam, gdzie spotykają się równoległe." In Lubelski, *Kino Krzysztofa Kieślowskiego*, 163–71.
Szpulak, Andrzej. *Filmy Wojciecha Maczewskiego*. Poznań: Wydawnictwo Naukowe Uniwersytetu im. Adama Mickiewicza, 2009.
———. *Kino wśród mitów: O filmach śląskich Kazimierza Kutza*. Gniezno: Collegium Europaenum Gnesnense, 2004.
———. *Róża*. Poznań: Wydawnictwo Naukowe Uniwersytetu im. Adama Mickiewicza, 2016.
Taborska, Agnieszka, Marcin Giżycki, Jonathan L. Owen, and Kamila Kuc. *A Story of Sin: Surrealism in Polish Cinema*. Kraków: Korporacja Ha!art, 2010.

Talarczyk-Gubała, Monika. *Biały mazur: Kino kobiet w polskiej kinematografii*. Poznań: Galeria Miejska Arsenał, 2013.
———. *PRL się śmieje: Polska komedia filmowa lat 1945–1989*. Warsaw: Trio, 2007.
———. *Wanda Jakubowska: Od nowa*. Warsaw: Wydawnictwo Krytyki Politycznej, 2015.
———. *Wszystko o Ewie: Filmy Barbary Sass a kino kobiet w drugiej połowie XX wieku*. Szczecin: Wydawnictwo Uniwersytetu Szczecińskiego, 2013.
Taras, Katarzyna. *"Egoista" czy Edi? Bohaterowie najnowszych polskich filmów—Rekonesans*. Warsaw: Wydawnictwo Uniwersytetu Kardynała Stefana Wyszyńskiego, 2007.
Thompson, Kristin. *Exporting Entertainment: America and the World Film Market, 1907–1934*. London: British Film Institute, 1985.
Tibbets, John C. "An Interview with Agnieszka Holland: The Politics of Ambiguity." *Quarterly Review of Film and Video* 25, no. 2 (2008): 132–43.
Toeplitz, Jerzy, ed. *Historia filmu polskiego 1939–1956*. Vol. 3. Warsaw: Wydawnictwa Artystyczne i Filmowe, 1974.
———. *Historia filmu polskiego 1957–1961*. Vol. 4. Warsaw: Wydawnictwa Artystyczne i Filmowe, 1980.
Toeplitz, Krzysztof-Teodor. "Jerzy Skolimowski: Portrait of a Debutant Director." Translated by Wanda Tomczykowska. *Film Quarterly* 21, no. 1 (1967): 25–31.
———. "The Films of Wojciech Has." *Film Quarterly* 18, no. 2 (1964): 2–6.
Trzynadlowski, Jan, ed. *Polska Szkoła Filmowa: Poetyka i tradycja*. Wrocław: Ossolineum, 1976.
Turaj, Frank. "Poland: The Cinema of Moral Concern." In *Post New Wave Cinema in the Soviet Union and Eastern Europe*, edited by Daniel J. Goulding, 143–71. Bloomington: Indiana University Press, 1989.
Turim Maureen. "Remembering and Deconstructing: The Historical Flashback in *Man of Marble* and *Man of Iron*. In Orr and Ostrowska, *The Cinema of Andrzej Wajda*, 93–102.
———. "On the Charge of Memory: Auschwitz, Trauma and Representation." *Arcadia: International Journal for Literary Studies* 45, no. 2 (2011): 297–306.
Wach, Margarete, ed. *Nouvelle Vague Polonaise? Auf der Suche nach einen flüchtigen Phänomen der Filmgeschichte*. Marburg: Schüren, 2015.
Wajda, Andrzej. *Ashes and Diamonds, Kanal, A Generation: Three Films*. London: Lorrimer, 1973.
———. *Double Vision: My Life in Film*. New York: Holt, 1989.
———. *Wajda—Filmy*. Warsaw: Wydawnictwa Artystyczne i Filmowe, 1996.
Wajda, Katarzyna. "Gdy biedni Polacy nie tylko patrzą na getto: *Wielki Tydzień* Andrzeja Wajdy." *Kwartalnik Filmowy* 34 (2001): 78–101.
Walden, Joshua S. "Leaving Kazimierz: Comedy and Realism in the Yiddish Film Musical *Yidl mitn Fidl*." *Music, Sound, and the Moving Image* 3, no. 2 (2009): 159–93.
Walker, Michael. "Jerzy Skolimowski." In *Second Wave*, 34–62. London: Studio Vista, 1970.
Warchoł, Tomasz. "Polish Cinema: The End of a Beginning." *Sight and Sound* 55, no. 3 (1986): 190–94.

Wasilewski, Piotr. *Świadectwa metryk: Polskie kino młodych w latach osiemdziesiątych*. Kraków: Oficyna Obecnych, 1990.
Weiner, Steve. "Jan Lenica and Landscape." *Film Quarterly* 45, no. 4 (1992): 2–16.
Werner, Andrzej. "Film fabularny." In Marszałek, *Historia filmu polskiego 1962–1967*, 19–117.
Wertenstein, Wanda. *Wajda mówi o sobie: Wywiady i teksty*. Kraków: Wydawnictwo Literackie, 1991.
———. *Zespół filmowy X*. Warsaw: Wydawnictwo "Officina," 1991.
Wierski, Dominik. *Sport w polskim kinie 1944–1989*. Gdańsk: Wydawnictwo Naukowe Katedra, 2014.
Wilson, Emma. *Memory and Survival: The French Cinema of Krzysztof Kieślowski*. Oxford: European Humanities Research Centre, University of Oxford, 2000.
———. "Three Colours: *Blue*—Kieślowski, Colour and the Postmodern Subject." *Screen* 39, no. 4 (1998): 349–63.
Winchell, James. "Metaphysics of Post-nationalism: La Double Vie de Krzysztof Kieślowski." *Contemporary French Civilization* 22, no. 2 (1998): 240–63.
Witek, Piotr. "Andrzej Wajda as Historian." In *A Companion to Historical Film*, edited by Robert A. Rosenstone and Constantin Parvulescu, 154–75. Malden, MA: Wiley-Blackwell, 2013.
———. *Andrzej Wajda jako historyk: Metodologiczne stadium z historii wizualnej*. Lublin: Marie Curie Skłodowska University, 2016.
Włodarczyk, Wojciech. *Socrealism: Sztuka polska w latach 1950–1954*. Kraków: Wydawnictwo Literackie, 1991.
Wolański, Ryszard. *Aleksander Żabczyński: "Jak drogie są wspomnienia."* Poznań: Rebis, 2015.
———. *Tola Mankiewiczówna: "Jak za dawnych lat."* Poznań: Rebis, 2013.
Woodward, Steven, ed. *After Kieślowski: The Legacy of Krzysztof Kieślowski*. Detroit: Wayne State University Press, 2009.
Wróbel, Marta. "*Ostatni etap* Wandy Jakubowskiej jako pierwszy etap polskiego kina ideologicznego." *Kwartalnik Filmowy* 43 (2003): 6–19.
Wróblewska, Anna. *Rynek filmowy w Polsce*. Wydawnictwo Wojciech Marzec, 2014.
Wynot, Edward D., Jr., *Warsaw between the World Wars: Profile of the Capital City in a Developing Land, 1918–1939*. New York: Columbia University Press, 1983.
Wyżyński, Adam. "Ostatnie lata Eugeniusza Bodo." *Kino* 6 (1996): 15.
Uszyński, Jerzy. "Jerzy Skolimowski o sobie: Całe życie jak na dłoni." *Film na Świecie* 373 (1990): 3–47.
Zajiček, Edward. *Film polski: Ekonomika i organizacja produkcji*. Warsaw: Państwowe Wydawnictwo Naukowe, 1983.
———, ed. *Encyklopedia kultury polskiej XX wieku: Film i kinematografia*. Warsaw: Instytut Kultury and Komitet Kinematografii, 1994.
———. *Poza ekranem: Kinematografia polska, 1896–2005*. Warsaw: Stowarzyszenie Filmowców Polskich, 2009.

———. *Poza ekranem: Kinematografia polska, 1918–1991*. Warsaw: Filmoteka Narodowa and Wydawnictwa Artystyczne i Filmowe, 1992.
———. *Zarys historii gospodarczej kinematografii polskiej: Tom I—Kinematografia wolnorynkowa 1896–1939*. Łódź: Wyższa Szkoła Filmowa, Telewizyjna i Teatralna, 2015.
Zanussi, Krzysztof. *In Full Gallop and Six Other Screenplays*. Translated by Charles S. Kraszewski. Lehman, PA: Libella Veritatis, 2001.
Zawojski, Piotr. "Nomada ze stałym adresem: Lech Majewski." *Postscriptum* 1–2 (2003): 88–97.
———. "Poezja kamerą (za)pisana: Od *Wojaczka* do *Krwi poety* i *Szklanych ust* Lecha Majewskiego." In *Sztuka obrazu i obrazowania w epoce nowych mediów* by Piotr Zawojski, 118–42. Warsaw: Oficyna Naukowa, 2012.
Żelasko, Justyna. *Przygoda w pociągu: Początki polskiego modernizmu filmowego (Has, Kawalerowicz, Konwicki, Kutz, Munk)*. Kraków: Ha!art, 2015.
Žižek, Slavoj. "Chance and Repetition in Kieślowski's Films." *Paragraph: A Journal of Modern Critical Theory* 24, no 2 (2001): 23–39.
———. *The Fright of Real Tears: Krzysztof Kieślowski between Theory and Post-theory*. London: British Film Institute, 2001.
Żmudziński, Bogusław, ed. *Roman Polański*. Kraków: Instytut Francuski, 1995.
Zwierzchowski, Piotr. *Kino nowej pamięci: Obraz II wojny światowej w kinie polskim lat 60*. Bydgoszcz: Wydawnictwo Uniwersytetu Kazimierza Wielkiego, 2013.
———. *Munk's Bad Luck*. Translated by Maciej Smoczyński. Poznań: Wydawnictwo Naukowe Uniwersytetu im. Adama Mickiewicza, 2009.
———. *Pęknięty monolit: Konteksty polskiego kina socrealistycznego*. Bydgoszcz: Wydawnictwo Uniwersytetu Kazimierza Wielkiego, 2005.
———. *Zapomniani bohaterowie: O bohaterach filmowych polskiego socrealizmu*. Warsaw: Wydawnictwo Trio, 2000.
Zwierzchowski, Piotr, and Daria Mazur, eds. *Kino polskie po roku 1989*. Bydgoszcz: Wydawnictwo Uniwersytetu Kazimierza Wielkiego, 2007.
———. *Kino polskie wobec umierania i śmierci*. Bydgoszcz: Wydawnictwo Uniwersytetu Kazimierza Wielkiego, 2005.
———. *Polskie kino popularne*. Bydgoszcz: Wydawnictwo Uniwersytetu Kazimierza Wielkiego, 2011.
Zwierzchowski, Piotr, Daria Mazur, and Mariusz Guzek, eds. *Kino polskie wobec II wojny światowej*. Bydgoszcz: Wydawnictwo Uniwersytetu Kazimierza Wielkiego, 2011.
Zwierzchowski, Piotr, and Dominik Wierski, eds. *Kino, którego nie ma*. Bydgoszcz: Wydawnictwo Uniwersytetu Kazimierza Wielkiego, 2013.
Zwierzchowski, Piotr, and Krzysztof Kornacki. "Metodologiczne problem badania kina PRL-u." *Kwartalnik Filmowy* 85 (2014): 28–39.

Index of Names

A

Abuladze, Tengiz, 289
Adamczyk, Piotr, 391
Adamek, Bożena, 266, 318
Adamek, Witold, 270, 441
Adamik, Kasia, 413, 422
Alexandrov, Grigori, 78
Allen, Woody, 284
Altenloh, Emilie, 30
Anczyc, Władysław Ludwik, 13
Anders, Anna Maria, 73
Anders, Władysław, 72–73
Andersen, Hans Christian, 399
Anderson, Benedict, 6
Andrejew, Piotr, 221–22, 231, 236, 253
Andrew, Geoff, 238
Andrzejewska, Jadwiga, 54–56, 60, 72–74
Andrzejewski, Jerzy, 79, 119, 121, 132, 137, 299, 312
Anessi, Thomas, 393
Angel-Engelówna, Stanisława, 44, 57
Ankwicz, Krystyna, 55
An-sky, S. (Shloyme Zanvil Rappoport), 62
Antczak, Jerzy, 173, 179, 215, 302
Antkowiak, Andrzej, 188
Antoniak, Urszula, 415
Antonioni, Michelangelo, 138, 203
Antonisz, Julian Józef, 253
Anweiler, Mieczysław, 332
Arnheim, Rudolf, 32
Arnold, Agnieszka, 252n55, 421n26
Arnsztejn, Marek, 14, 71, 431
Assböck, Joachim Paul, 380
Auerbach, Rachela, 88

B

Bacon, Lloyd, 41
Bacsó, Péter, 132, 289
Baczyński, Krzysztof Kamil, 119
Bagiński, Tomasz, 418
Bajerski, Adam, 403
Bajon, Filip, 241, 247, 275, 283, 291–92, 316, 335n35, 341–43, 366n6
Baka, Mirosław, 269
Balázs, Béla, 31–32, 88
Ballester, César, 110
Barańska, Jadwiga, 179
Barański, Andrzej, 241–42, 244, 257, 261, 278, 318–20, 322, 401
Barciś, Artur, 268, 356
Barczyk, Łukasz, 376
Bareja, Stanisław, 208, 210–11, 246, 252n55, 317
Barnet, Boris, 307
Barszczewska, Elżbieta, 56–57
Bartkowiak, Andrzej, 5
Bartólewska, Iwona, 290
Bartówna, Wanda, 85
Batory, Jan, 149, 208, 248
Battiato, Giacomo, 391
Bauer, Yevgeni, 27
Beckett, Samuel, 191
Bednarczyk, Antoni, 23
Beksiński, Zdzisław, 393–94, 424n64
Belmont, Leon, 31
Benita, Ina, 44–46, 52, 61, 71–72
Ber, Ryszard, 208, 215n25, 261–62, 322
Berestowski, Wadim, 118
Bergman, Ingmar, 131, 195, 269, 273n28, 327
Bergson, Henri, 32
Berman, Jakub, 97
Biedrzyńska, Adrianna, 316
Biegański, Wiktor, 27, 38n62
Bierut, Bolesław, 96, 116, 295
Bilewski, Bogusz, 127
Bilov, Dimitri, 390
Bińczycki, Jerzy, 179, 205
Binoche, Juliette, 327, 339n84, 404
Błaszczyk, Ewa, 256
Błęcka-Kolska, Grażyna, 320
Bloem, Walter, 29
Błoński, Jan, 296–97

Bluteau, Lothaire, 282
Bocheńska, Jadwiga, 32
Bochniak, Maciej, 399
Boczarska, Magdalena, 392, 397
Bodo, Eugeniusz, 51–52, 59–60, 65n9, 66n17, 71, 91n7
Bogayevicz, Yurek, 349–50, 367n26
Bogda, Maria, 27, 48, 53, 56, 67n36
Bogdańska, Renata, 72–73
Boguszewska, Helena, 61
Bohdziewicz, Antoni, 115, 120, 162n29
Bohosiewicz, Sonia, 342, 392
Bolesławski, Ryszard, 19, 23, 36n34
Bolesto, Robert, 393, 399
Borchardt, Marcin, 424n64
Borcuch, Jacek, 357
Borowczyk, Walerian, 122, 150, 167n89, 180
Borowski, Paweł, 403
Borowski, Tadeusz (writer), 144, 181, 200, 285–86, 301–2, 352
Borowski, Tadeusz, 200
Borzęcka, Ewa, 417,
Bossak, Jerzy, 58, 74, 77, 81–83, 120, 151, 167n85, 305
Boukołowski, Henryk, 137, 138
Boym, Svetlana, 290
Braciak, Jacek, 362
Bradecki, Tadeusz, 234
Brandys, Kazimierz, 128, 145, 255
Bratny, Roman, 121, 161n11
Braun Ewa, 298
Braunek, Małgorzata, 179, 188–89, 198
Bredschneider, Bruno, 25
Bresson, Robert, 385
Brezhnev, Leonid, 390
Brik, Lili, 307
Brik, Osip, 307
Brodniewicz, Franciszek, 50, 57, 71
Brodzisz, Adam, 27, 47–49, 56, 66n17, 66n18, 67n36
Bromski, Jacek, 297, 303, 318, 362, 394–95
Broniewski, Władysław, 59
Brooks, Louise, 55
Bruczówna, Halina, 37n37
Bruno, Giordano, 297
Bruno, Leon, 26

Brylska, Barbara, 201
Brylski, Ryszard, 297, 301
Brystiger, Julia, 388
Brzozowski, Stanisław, 31
Buchowetzki, Dimitri, 25
Buczkowski, Leonard, 38n59, 76–77, 81, 90, 100–1, 140
Budnik, Jowita, 392, 411, 416
Bugajski, Ryszard, 236, 241–43, 252n50, 254–55, 275, 387
Bugdoł, Bernard, 174
Bukowski, Marek, 357
Buñuel, Luis, 136, 191
Burian, Vlasta, 52
Buzek, Agata, 378

C

Carré, Le, John, 390
Cękalski, Eugeniusz, 59–60, 74, 98, 99
Celińska, Stanisława, 182, 375
Cembrzyńska, Iga, 319, 338n78
Chaberski, Emil, 20
Chagall, Marc, 178, 348
Chaplin, Charlie, 22
Chęciński, Sylwester, 120, 209–10, 219n93, 260, 317
Chekhov, Anton, 245, 262
Chiaureli, Mikheil, 93n25
Chmara, Gregori, 25
Chmielewski, Tadeusz, 38n59, 118, 152–53, 171, 210, 248, 275, 341
Chmielewski, Zbigniew, 187, 224
Chochlew, Paweł, 216n46
Chodakowski, Andrzej, 237
Chołodowski, Waldemar, 247
Chopin, Fryderyk, 102, 351
Choromański, Michał, 200
Chutnik, Sylwia, 383
Chwalibóg, Maria, 239
Chyra, Andrzej, 365, 374, 404, 411, 415
Cielecka, Magdalena, 293, 356, 374, 414
Ciepielewska, Anna, 147
Cieślak, Bronisław, 209
Cimino, Michael, 307, 409
Clair, René, 152–53
Clift, Montgomery, 135

INDEX OF NAMES · 473

Clouzot, Henri-George, 163n35
Cnota, Jerzy, 205-6
Coates, Paul, 31, 136, 141, 145, 165n63, 169n115, 181, 195
Coen, Joel and Ethan, 407
Conrad, Joseph, 216n35
Corelli, Arcangelo, 198
Curtis, Richard, 398
Ćwikiel, Agnieszka, 209
Ćwiklińska, Mieczysława, 44, 53, 59, 65n11
Cybulski, Mieczysław, 44, 49, 55
Cybulski, Zbigniew, 124, 133-35, 154, 158, 177, 180-81, 187, 208, 313
Cyganiewicz, Zbyszko, 247
Czechowicz, Mieczysław, 210
Czekała, Ryszard, 248, 253n62
Czerniakow, Adam, 299
Czeszko, Bohdan, 119, 123
Czop, Ireneusz, 381
Czyński, Kazimierz, 66n19, 82
Czyżewska, Elżbieta, 143, 180, 192, 212

D

Dąbal, Wit, 265
Dąbrowska, Maria, 179
Dafoe, Willem, 349
Dal, Jerzy, 46
Dałkowska, Ewa, 233, 246, 261
Dancewicz, Renata, 301
Daniłowski, Władysław, 66n25
Danton, Georges-Jacques, 264
Dawid, Leszek, 371, 399
Dean, James, 135, 358
Debruge, Peter, 405
Dederko, Henryk, 362
Dejczer, Maciej, 256, 285, 425n73
Dejmek, Kazimierz, 99
Dękierowski, Stefan, 70
Delluc, Louis, 30
Delpy, Julie, 300, 328
Demarczyk, Ewa, 194
DeMille, Cecil B., 22
Depardieu, Gerard, 264
Długołęcka, Grażyna, 180
Dmochowski, Mariusz, 178, 200
Dobrowolska, Gosia, 5, 354

Dobrowolski, Ireneusz, 378
Dołęga-Mostowicz, Tadeusz, 57, 362
Domalewski, Piotr, 416, 418
Domaradzki, Jerzy, 241, 251n29, 255, 260, 275
Donskoi, Mark, 78, 87, 106, 113n27
Dorociński, Marcin, 390, 399, 407, 412, 425n81
Dostoevsky, Fyodor, 314, 418
Drapińska, Barbara, 87
Drążewski, Marek, 368n27, 368n30
Dreyer, Carl Theodor, 385
Dumała, Piotr, 253n62, 417
Dunowska, Hanna, 296
Durbin, Deanna, 54
Duriasz, Józef, 187
Duszyński, Jerzy, 90
Dutkiewicz, Maciej, 306, 359
Dybowski, Wacław, 216n42
Dygat, Stanisław, 121, 262
Dylewska, Jolanta, 304-5, 357, 385, 417, 422n44
Dymna, Anna, 324
Dymny Wiesław, 201
Dymsza, Adolf, 52-53, 67n26, 67n28, 72, 76, 90, 101, 112n15
Dziędziel, Marian, 396, 405-7, 425n79
Dziedzina, Julian, 181, 162n29
Dziewoński, Edward, 86, 131
Dziewoński, Roman, 67n26, 86
Dzigan, Shimon, 83-84
Dziki, Waldemar, 256, 265, 341, 262
Dziwisz, Stanisław, 391

E

Eastwood, Clint, 314
Eberhardt, Konrad, 178, 180
Edelman, Marek, 305, 337n61, 385
Edelman, Paweł, 310, 350, 354, 368n28, 373, 390
Edison, Thomas, 9
Eichlerówna, Irena, 55, 94n36
Eisenstein, Sergei, 22, 32, 37n52, 78, 177
Ellstein, Abraham, 64
Englert, Jan, 205-6, 374
Epstein, Jean, 30-31

F

Fäberböck, Max, 408
Fabicki, Sławomir, 412

INDEX OF NAMES

Falk, Feliks, 221, 231, 234, 241, 281, 283, 309, 379–80, 411
Falkowska, Janina, 229
Fallaci, Oriana, 389
Fanck, Arnold, 45
Feldman, Krystyna, 365
Fellini, Federico, 181, 228
Fenigsten, Felicja and Leon, 43
Ferency, Adam, 242–43
Fertacz, Kacper, 393
Fertner, Antoni, 5, 11, 33n5, 44, 52, 54, 65n11
Fethke, Jan, 53–54, 67n30, 69, 88, 101
Fetting, Edmund, 142
Ficowski, Jerzy, 393
Fidyk, Andrzej, 291
Fieldorf, Emil, 384, 387–88
Figura, Katarzyna, 260, 360
Fijewski, Tadeusz, 153, 178
Filipski, Ryszard, 185, 198, 208, 245
Finkelstein, Henryk, 15–16, 43
Flaherty, Robert, 151
Flanz, Marta, 42
Forbert, Adolf, 82–83, 101
Forbert, Leo, 15, 43
Forbert, Władysław, 82–83
Ford, Aleksander, 46, 58–59, 60, 67n42, 68n45, 74, 76–79, 81, 84, 88–89, 93n32, 95n48, 102, 105–6, 118, 120, 122, 132, 152, 158, 169n110, 169n111, 170, 178, 191
Ford, John, 64
Forman, Miloš, 200–11, 256
Fostel, Symcha, 63
Fredericksen, Don, 131
Frenkiel, Mieczysław, 47
Frenkiel, Tadeusz, 71
Frič, Martin, 52
Fronczewski, Piotr, 196
Fudalej, Beata, 299, 342
Fürmann, Benno, 387

G

Gábor, Pál, 289
Gad, Urban, 14
Gajcy, Tadeusz, 119
Gajos, Janusz, 186, 242, 284, 347, 405
Gałczyński, Konstanty Ildefons, 59
Gallo, Vincent, 402
Gallone, Soava, 16
Gancarczyk, Roman, 365
Gardan, Juliusz, 25, 27, 43, 46–47, 52, 55, 57, 71
Garlicki, Piotr, 231
Gąsiorowska, Roma, 399
Gąssowski, Tomasz, 403
Gębicka, Ewa, 93n25
Gębski, Józef, 291, 374
Gielgud, John, 74, 235
Gierek, Edward, 171, 220, 224, 234
Giersz, Witold, 150
Gierszał, Jakub, 392, 415
Gietner, Aleksandra, 358
Ginzberg, Samuel (Shmuel), 15
Gish, Lillian, 20
Giżycki, Marcin, 28
Gleisner, Henryk and Leopold, 43
Glińska, Agnieszka, 399
Gliński, Robert, 241, 279, 284, 294, 297, 342, 358, 378, 412, 420n23, 426n91
Gliński, Wieńczysław, 130, 208
Globisz, Krzysztof, 270
Głowacki, Janusz, 201–2, 211, 289
Gniazdowski, Zbigniew, 26
Godard, Jean-Luc, 31, 191
Godzic, Wiesław, 113n24
Goetel, Ferdynand, 66n18
Gogol, Nikolai, 52
Gojawiczyńska, Pola, 56, 262
Gołas, Wiesław, 140, 208, 210
Gold, Daniel M., 363
Goldman, Eric A., 64, 70
Goldszmit, Henryk. See Janusz Korczak
Gołębiewski, Henryk, 362
Gombrowicz, Witold, 179, 348–49
Gomułka, Władysław, 113n39, 116, 156, 159, 170–71, 191, 211, 242
Gordin, Jacob, 14
Gorki, Maxim, 106, 113n27
Goskind, Izak, 83–84
Goskind, Saul, 59, 83–84
Gothár, Péter, 289
Grabowska, Urszula, 380
Gradowski, Krzysztof, 261
Green, Joseph, 30, 62–64, 83

Greengrass, Paul, 376
Griffith, D.W., 21–22, 24
Grochowska, Agnieszka, 389
Gross, Jan T., 379–82, 420n25
Gross, Natan, 83–84
Grossówna, Helena, 53–54
Grottger, Artur, 22, 24, 141
Gruza, Jerzy, 173, 224
Gryczełowska, Krystyna, 173
Grynberg, Henryk, 304, 337n59, 384
Grzegorzek, Mariusz, 318
Grzelecki, Stanisław, 127
Guazzoni, Enrico, 13
Guzek, Mariusz, 34n7, 35n26, 46

H
Häfker, Hermann, 30
Hager, Ludwik, 120, 170
Haggis, Paul, 403
Hall, Conrad, 277
Halladin, Danuta, 173
Halle, Randall, 4
Halotta, Augustyn, 207
Hańcza, Władysław, 80, 101, 210
Hanin, Ryszarda, 302
Haniszewski, Mirosław, 395–96
Harasimowicz, Cezary, 285
Harris, Ed, 301
Hart, William S., 22
Has, Wojciech J., 78, 117, 120, 122, 126–27, 159, 163n41, 177, 215n25, 262, 342
Hauer, Rutger, 363–64
Hauser, Ewa, 346
Hayward, Susan, 6
Helman, Alicja, 142, 155, 210, 263
Hen, Józef, 119, 136, 165n64
Hendrykowska, Małgorzata, 33n6, 54
Hendrykowski, Marek, 33n6, 118–19
Herdegen, Leszek, 139, 176
Herszfinkel, Maurycy, 42
Hertz, Aleksander, 14–17, 26, 34n9, 35n28, 43
Higson, Andrew, 345–46
Hill, George Roy, 259
Hillege, Lennert, 415
Himilsbach, Jan, 202, 211–12
Hirszbejn, Maria, 43, 71

Hitchcock, Alfred, 107, 154, 270, 402
Hłasko, Marek, 119, 136, 158
Hoberman, J., 34n8, 64
Hoffman, Jerzy, 66n20, 125, 151–52, 171–72, 278–79, 181, 190, 215n26, 260, 264, 272n19, 275, 343, 346–47, 376, 420n18
Hogg, James, 263
Holender, Adam, 5
Holland, Agnieszka, 221, 232–33, 235–36, 238, 242, 254–55, 259, 266, 271n1, 275, 294, 297–99, 313, 322, 335n43, 379, 385–87, 391, 414–15, 422n43
Hollender, Barbara, 343
Holoubek, Gustaw, 101, 127, 163n38, 190, 212
Hołuj, Tadeusz, 144, 166n80
Holzapfel, Rudolf, 30, 32
Hood, Gavin, 343
Horton, Andrew James, 354, 364
Howard, Leslie, 74
Hřebejk, Jan, 349
Hryniak, Jan, 355–56
Hübner, Zygmunt, 185, 208
Hudziec, Tomasz, 241
Huelle, Paweł, 347
Huk, Tadeusz, 232

I
Idziak, Sławomir, 235, 258, 270, 326, 328, 376
Iñárritu, Alejandro G., 403
Insdorf, Annette, 178
Iordanova, Dina, 343
Irwin-Zarecka, Iwona, 265
Irzykowski, Karol, 30–33, 39n73, 40n88
Iwaszkiewicz, Jarosław, 155, 181, 244
Iżewska, Teresa, 126, 130, 168n98

J
Jabłoński, Dariusz, 277, 304–5, 341, 421n30
Jackiewicz, Aleksander, 115, 117, 186, 191, 195, 197
Jacob, Irène, 325–26, 329
Jadowska, Anna, 357, 416
Jaehne, Karen, 266
Jagiełło, Władysław, 152
Jahoda, Mieczysław, 127, 152
Jakimowska, Ewa, 403
Jakimowski, Andrzej, 342, 366, 403–4

Jakubik, Arkadiusz, 396, 407, 410, 413
Jakubowska, Wanda, 70, 84–86, 87–89, 94n46, 95n48, 95n49, 101–2, 112n17, 120, 122, 141, 143–45, 148, 187, 191, 265–66
Jamróz, Katarzyna, 302
Jancsó, Miklós, 204
Janczar, Tadeusz, 101, 106, 124
Janda, Krystyna, 229, 235, 237–38, 242–43, 278, 282, 290, 397
Janicka, Jagna, 394
Janicki, Juliusz, 266
Janicki, Stanisław, 91n7, 213n2
Janiczek, Arkadiusz, 412
Janion, Maria, 119
Jankowska-Cieślak, Jadwiga, 201–2, 396
Jankowski, Grzegorz, 399
Jankun-Dopartowa, Mariola, 222
Jannings, Emil, 42
Jaracz, Stefan, 71
Jaraczówna, Hanna, 57
Jarman, Derek, 277
Jarmusch, Jim, 277
Jaroszewicz, Andrzej, 342
Jaruzelski, Wojciech, 220, 249, 255, 264–65, 274
Jasienica, Paweł, 397
Jasny, Vojtěch, 289
Jędryka, Stanisław, 159, 362
Jentsch, Julia, 404
Jesionowski, Jerzy, 171
Jireš, Jaromir, 289
John Paul II, 220, 282–83, 391, 423n60
Jolson, Al, 41
Junak, Tadeusz, 247
Jungingen, Ulrich von, 152
Junosza-Stępowski, Kazimierz, 10–11, 42, 50, 57, 70–71, 91n6
Jurga, Andrzej, 236

K

Kac, Emil, 43
Kacyzne, Alter, 71
Kaczor, Kazimierz, 245, 260
Kaczyński, Jarosław, 149, 419n12
Kaczyński, Lech, 149, 387, 419n12
Kaden, Danny, 71
Kafka, Franz, 150, 230, 418

Kalinowska, Izabela, 408
Kamień, Adam, 285
Kamieńska, Irena, 223
Kamińska, Ester-Rokhl, 15
Kamińska, Ida, 15, 35n20, 200, 302
Kamiński, Aleksander, 378
Kamiński, Izak, 14
Kaminski, Janusz, 5, 298
Kamiński, Kazimierz, 14
Kamykowski, Bolesław, 218n82
Kania, Stanisław, 220
Kaniewska, Maria, 86, 99, 103, 112n12, 120
Kański, Tadeusz, 101
Kaper, Bronisław, 76, 92n16
Kapuściński, Ryszard, 175
Kar, Alma, 55
Karabasz, Kazimierz, 122, 125, 151, 173
Karewicz, Emil, 126, 130, 214n11
Karwowska, Hanka, 59–60
Karwowski, Łukasz, 398
Kasprzyk, Marek, 322
Kataszek, Szymon, 71
Kawalec, Julian, 248
Kawalerowicz, Jerzy, 78, 99, 105–7, 117–18, 120, 141–42, 153–56, 171–72, 176–77, 191, 245, 264–65, 275, 281, 342–43
Kawin, Bruce F., 328
Kaźmierczak, Wacław, 82–83, 151
Kędzierski, Paweł, 232
Kędzierzawska, Dorota, 323, 415
Kerner, Aaron, 95n50
Kęstowicz, Zygmunt, 126
Khanzhonkov, Alexandr, 11, 16, 27
Kidawa, Janusz, 248, 255
Kidawa-Błoński, Jan, 292, 335n34, 342, 379, 397, 399
Kielar, Wieslaw, 166n80
Kieślowski, Krzysztof, 1, 6, 173, 214n12, 220–28, 232, 239–40, 250n11, 255–56, 259, 267–70, 271n6, 275, 277, 280, 313, 324–32, 352–57, 376, 398, 402, 405, 414
Kijowicz, Mirosław, 150
Kijowska, Julia, 412
Kijowski, Jakub, 400
Kijowski, Janusz, 221, 234, 283, 297, 301
Kilar, Wojciech, 138, 195, 203, 282, 354

INDEX OF NAMES · 477

Klata, Wojciech, 285
Klijnstra, Redbad, 286
Klimov, Elem, 408
Kłosiński, Edward, 233, 245
Kłosowski, Roman, 126, 319
Kluba, Henryk, 191, 201, 218n77
Knake-Zawadzki, Stanisław, 12
Kobiela, Bogumił, 131, 134, 180
Kobiela, Dorota, 418
Kolak, Dorota, 413–14
Kolbe, Maksymilian, 282–83
Kołodziej, Marian, 166n80
Kolski, Jan Jakub, 278, 297–98, 318, 320–22, 333, 335n44, 342, 348–49, 401
Komasa, Jan, 377–78, 420n20
Komeda, Krzysztof, 144, 153, 157, 190, 193
Komorowska, Maja, 196, 257–58, 282, 293, 374
Komorowski, Paweł, 186, 209
Kon, Henoch, 62
Kondrat, Marek, 200, 293, 316, 356, 359–61, 269n42
Kondratiuk, Andrzej, 212, 318–19, 338n78
Kondratiuk, Janusz, 339n78
Konecki, Tomasz, 360, 397
Konic, Andrzej, 172
Konieczna, Aleksandra, 393–94
Konopka, Bartosz, 416
Konwicki, Tadeusz, 118, 120–21, 127, 135, 138, 141–42, 159, 176, 212, 255, 262
Kopacz, Aneta, 417
Korczak, Janusz, 79, 93n32, 298–99, 303, 251
Kordecki Augustyn, 50
Kornacki, Jerzy, 61
Kornacki, Krzysztof, 170
Kornatowska, Maria, 235, 236
Kornhauser, Julian, 220
Korsakówna, Lidia, 100
Koryncka-Gruz, Natalia, 363
Korzyński, Andrzej, 189
Kościukiewicz, Mateusz, 395
Kościuszko, Tadeusz, 13, 51, 74
Kosinski, Jerzy, 298
Kosiński, Ryszard, 171
Kos-Krauze, Joanna, 392, 411, 416
Kośmicki, Łukasz, 286
Kossak, Wojciech, 141

Kostenko, Andrzej, 198
Koszałka, Marcin, 395, 417
Kot, Tomasz, 392, 399
Koterski, Marek, 278, 317–18, 360–61
Kotlarczyk, Teresa, 322–23, 347
Kovács, András, 289
Kovács, Lászlo, 278
Kowalska, Faustyna, 283
Kowalska, Kasia, 359
Kowalski, Wacław, 210
Kowalski, Władysław, 202, 265
Kowolik, Łucja, 206
Kox, Bodo, 357, 401
Kozintsev, Grigori, 106
Kozłowski, Maciej, 266
Krafftówna, Barbara, 128
Krakowska, Emilia, 182
Krall, Hanna, 348
Kraszewski, Józef Ignacy, 343
Krauze, Antoni, 201, 209, 218n78, 262, 309, 375–76, 422n51
Krauze, Krzysztof, 285–87, 333, 342, 361–62, 365, 392, 411, 416
Krawczyk, Bernard, 206
Krawicz, Mieczysław, 44, 71, 397
Kreczmar, Jan, 196
Kretschmann, Thomas, 351
Kriuczkov, Siergiej, 390
Królikiewicz, Grzegorz, 199, 218n75, 248, 257, 284, 291–92
Królikowski, Rafał, 356
Krukówna, Agnieszka, 332
Krukowski, Kazimierz, 51
Krynicki, Nikifor, 365
Krzeptowski, Adam, 45
Krzystek, Waldemar, 255–56, 283, 289–90, 362, 380, 395, 397
Krzyształowicz, Marcin, 376
Krzyżewska, Ewa, 134, 142, 200, 208
Kuc, Dariusz, 302
Kucharski, Jan, 23
Kucia, Jerzy, 253n62
Kukliński, Ryszard, 390
Kulej, Jerzy, 209
Kuleshov Lev, 307
Kulesza, Agata, 355, 383–84, 404, 407

Kulikov, Viktor, 390
Kuncewiczowa, Maria, 262
Kundera, Milan, 4
Kurnakowicz, Jan, 101
Kurosawa, Akira, 109, 191
Kuśniewicz, Andrzej, 246
Kutz, Kazimierz, 4, 78, 115, 117–18, 120, 132, 136–37, 139, 156, 171, 186, 190, 219n87, 225, 237, 256, 280, 285, 287–88, 291, 293–94, 308, 342, 371
Kuźmiński, Zbigniew, 363
Kwiatkowska, Barbara, 153
Kwiatkowska, Irena, 210
Kwieciński, Michał, 398

L

Łabacz, Michalina, 409–10
Łabonarska, Halina, 232
Lambert, Christopher, 391
Land, Bolesław, 42
Lang, Fritz, 25, 38n60
Lang, Krzysztof, 395, 398
Lange, Konrad, 30, 32
Lankosz, Borys, 396
Lanzmann, Claude, 296, 299
Łapicki, Andrzej, 99, 180, 200, 208, 212
Laskowski, Jan, 154
Latałło, Stanisław, 197
Lawton, Anna, 289
Łazarkiewicz, Magdalena, 256, 322–23
Łazarkiewicz, Piotr, 256, 323
Lebiedziński, Piotr, 9
Lechki, Marek, 355
Łęcki, Konrad, 387
Leconte, Patrice, 270
Leigh, Mike, 412
Lejtes, Józef, 23–24, 27, 47, 50–51, 56–57, 66n22, 72, 76, 92n10, 262
Lenar, Piotr, 320
Lenartowicz, Stanisław, 68n44, 117–18, 120, 127, 138–39
Lenczewski, Ryszard, 385
Lenczewski, Władysław, 23
Lengren, Tomasz, 231, 236, 251n27
Lenica, Jan, 122, 150
Leone, Segio, 327

Lesiewicz, Witold, 139, 146, 177
Leszczyński, Witold, 197, 262–63, 320, 357
Lewandowski, Rafael, 396
Libkow, Marek, 43
Liebman, Stuart, 81–82, 149
Liehm Antonin J. and Mira, 98
Liliana, Lili, 62
Linda, Bogusław, 239, 255, 292, 310–15, 341, 357, 360, 389
Linde-Lubaszenko, Edward, 360, 203
Linkowski, Grzegorz, 385
Lipiec, Grzegorz, 357
Lipińska, Dela, 42
Lipiński, Stanisław, 61, 72–73
Lipman, Jerzy, 106–7, 129, 144, 157, 164n48, 170, 175, 213n3
Lipowski, Nachum, 14
Łomakowski, Andrzej, 55
Łomnicki, Jan, 67n28, 186, 245, 297, 302–3, 316, 378
Łomnicki, Tadeusz, 123–24, 126, 144, 146, 153, 179, 245
Lorenc, Michał, 311
Lorit, Jean-Pierre, 329
Loth, Stanisław, 206
Lovel, Angela, 400
Łoziński, Marcel, 222–23, 231, 290, 331, 374, 416
Łoziński, Paweł, 304–5, 331, 384, 417
Lubaszenko, Olaf, 270, 273n29, 292, 309, 356, 360
Lubelski, Tadeusz, 90, 111, 302
Lubitsch, Ernst, 18
Lubos, Eryk, 416
Lucas, George, 101
Łukaszewicz, Jerzy, 283
Łukaszewicz, Krzysztof, 412
Łukaszewicz, Olgierd, 182, 205–6, 246, 259, 301, 388
Lumière, Louis and Auguste, 9, 28–29
Łuszczak, Sylwia, 358

M

Machowski, Ignacy, 134
Machulski, Jan, 259
Machulski, Juliusz, 222, 259–61, 275, 278, 306–8, 316, 341, 356, 360, 399

INDEX OF NAMES · 479

Maćkowiak, Rafał, 358
Macnab, Geoffrey, 375
Madej, Alina, 9, 24, 50, 93n31
Majchrzak, Krzysztof, 247, 263, 349
Majdrowicz, Maria, 25
Majewski, Janusz, 171, 191, 199, 200, 208, 246, 261, 399
Majewski, Lech, 357, 363–64, 369n45, 371
Makk, Károly, 289
Maklakiewicz, Zdzisław, 211–12
Makowska, Helena, 16
Malajkat, Wojciech, 299
Malanowicz, Zygmunt, 157
Malczewski, Jacek, 183
Malicka, Maria, 194
Mamona, Maria, 388
Mandat, Agnieszka, 415
Mankiewicz, Joseph L., 73, 171
Mankiewiczówna, Tola, 51
Mann, Anthony, 73
Mara, Mia (Lya), 16
Marcinkowska, Zofia, 137–38
Marczak, Michał, 417
Marczewska, Teresa, 241
Marczewski, Wojciech, 241–42, 244–45, 247, 254–55, 284, 334n22, 341, 347
Marek, Andrzej, 71
Marisówna, Janina, 86
Mark, James, 372
Marker, Chris, 150
Marshall, Robert, 385
Marszałek, Rafał, 104–5, 131, 191, 195, 204
Marten, Aleksander, 71
Marx, Groucho, 52
Marx, Karl, 242
Maslennikov, Oleg, 390
Maszewska-Łupiniak, Monika, 189
Matejko, Jan, 24
Matuszewski, Bolesław, 9, 28–29, 38n66
Matuszyński, Jan P., 393, 418
Matwiejczyk, Piotr, 357
Mayakovsky, Vladimir, 307
Mazierska, Ewa, 344–45
Mazowiecki, Tadeusz, 274
Mazurek, Marta, 399, 400
Mead Gary [Gustaw Moszcz], 244

Menzel, Jiří, 289, 319
Merimée, Prosper, 200
Merlin, Serge, 145
Mészáros, Márta, 289, 223–24
Meyer, Jerzy, 11
Meyrink, Gustav, 247
Michałek, Bolesław, 154, 171, 180, 183, 254
Michalek, Vládimir, 306
Michnikowski, Wiesław, 210
Mickiewicz, Adam, 26
Miczka, Tadeusz, 118
Mierzejewski, Bolesław, 20
Migowa, Jadwiga, 71
Mikhalkov, Nikita, 365
Mikołajewski, Adam, 104
Mikuć, Hanna, 261, 424n63
Mikulski, Stanisław, 172, 214n10
Milewska, Anna, 197
Miłosz, Czesław, 79, 255, 297
Miłoszewski, Zygmunt, 396
Milski, Stanisław, 134
Mniszkówna, Helena, 21, 57
Moczar, Mieczysław, 190
Modrzyńska, Urszula, 123, 168n98
Monastyrski, Boris, 87
Moniuszko, Stanisław, 112n18, 13
Monroe, Marilyn, 260
Morgenstern, Janusz, 78, 120, 143–44, 153, 166n77, 172, 181, 190, 201–2, 245, 265,
Motyka, Grzegorz, 409
Mrożewski, Zdzisław, 245
Mucha, Stanisław, 353
Mularczyk, Andrzej, 374, 210
Mungiu, Cristian, 414
Munk, Andrzej, 78, 98, 107–10, 115, 117–20, 129, 131–32, 136, 143, 146–49, 159, 161n13, 164n53, 164n55, 166n84, 167n85, 191, 317, 377
Münsterberg, Hugo, 32
Murnau. F. W., 55
Mutu, Oleg, 414
Myśliwski, Wiesław, 322
Mysłowicz, Jan, 195

N

Nakonieczna, Zofia, 92n17
Nałęcki, Konrad, 172

Nałkowska, Zofia, 56–57
Narutowicz, Gabriel, 245
Nasfeter, Janusz, 120, 149, 181, 187–88, 208, 212, 362
Negri, Pola, 16–18, 36n31, 36n32, 54
Neverly, Igor, 106
Newell, Mike, 398
Newolin, Bolesław, 42
Ney, Nora, 27, 50
Nieborowska, Anna, 199
Nielsen, Asta, 14, 17, 20, 37n37
Niemczyk, Leon, 126, 154, 157
Niemczyk, Wojciech, 387
Niemirski, Alfred, 54
Nieradkiewicz, Marta, 414, 416
Niovilla, Nina, 23, 38n55
Niwiński, Władysław, 245
Nolan, Christopher, 403
Norris, Chuck, 280
Norris, Stefan, 62
Nowak, Jerzy, 226, 331
Nowak, Józef, 106
Nowak, Wojciech, 322
Nowakowski, Przemysław, 374
Nowicki, Jan, 178, 193, 210, 247–48
Nowicki, Marek, 261, 362
Nowina-Przybylski, Jan, 45, 49–50, 55, 63–64
Nurczyńska-Fidelska, Ewelina, 108, 110, 119, 125–26, 129, 183, 216n35
Nykvist, Sven, 277

O

Ogiński, Michał K., 136
Ogrodnik, Dawid, 393–94, 413, 416
Okorn, Mitja, 397–98
Olbrychski, Daniel, 179–84, 196, 205, 215n33, 245, 313, 316
Oleszczyk, Michał, 389, 402
Olszańska, Michalina, 399, 400
Ondříček, Miroslav, 200
Opaliński, Kazimierz, 108–9
Opania, Bartosz, 353
Opania, Marian, 201, 237
Opatoshu, Joseph, 15
Ordyński, Ryszard, 18, 24, 26, 36n31, 42, 47–48, 56, 91n10

Orland, 13
Orłoś, Kazimierz, 355
Orzeszkowa, Eliza, 9, 12, 55, 69, 262
Osment, Joel, 399
Ossowski, Albin, 73
Ostaszewska, Maja, 390, 405
Ostoja-Sulnicki, Józef, 12
Ostrowska, Elżbieta, 346
Ozimek, Stanisław, 117

P

Pabst, Georg Wilhelm, 25, 55
Pacuła, Joanna, 5
Pakula, Alan, 87
Paliński, Władysław, 13
Palkowski, Łukasz, 391–92
Panek, Adrian, 376
Parajanov, Sergei, 204
Pasikowski, Władysław, 278, 306, 309–14, 357, 372, 374, 379, 381, 390, 423n59
Passendorfer, Jerzy, 139, 165n68, 171, 186, 190
Paul, David, 289
Pawlicki, Antoni, 412
Pawlik, Bronisław, 146, 316
Pawlikowski, Adam, 133–34
Pawlikowski, Paweł, 1, 5, 379, 383–85
Pawłowski, Jan, 17, 35n28
Pazura, Cezary, 306, 311–13, 315, 317, 360, 362
Pec-Ślesicka, Barbara, 254
Peiper, Tadeusz, 31
Penderecki, Krzysztof, 373
Perski, Ludwik, 74
Petelska, Ewa, 120, 139, 143, 156, 163n34, 163n44, 165n67, 186
Petelski, Czesław, 107, 120, 126, 139, 143, 156, 163n34, 163n44, 165n67, 171, 186
Petersburski, Jerzy, 66n25
Petrycki, Jacek, 239, 242, 276
Pichelski, Jerzy, 57, 61
Picon, Molly, 63–64, 83
Pieczka, Franciszek, 197, 206, 223, 264–65, 298, 320–21
Piekorz, Magdalena, 365, 371
Piekutowski, Andrzej, 187
Pieprzyca, Maciej, 355, 395–96, 413, 424n70
Piesiewicz, Krzysztof, 332, 353–54, 267–68

INDEX OF NAMES · 481

Pietrasik, Zdzisław, 308, 343, 359
Pilch, Jerzy, 409
Pilecki, Witold, 388
Piłsudski, Józef, 23–24, 38n54, 48–49, 245
Piwowarski, Radosław, 260, 297, 303–4, 308, 316
Piwowski, Marek, 174, 196, 209, 211–12, 317
Płażewski, Jerzy, 109, 280, 291, 293
Pogorzelska, Zula, 51
Polański, Roman, 1, 5, 80, 82, 122, 124, 153, 156–57, 159, 168n107, 169n114, 191, 342, 349–52, 355–56, 361n25, 407
Polony, Anna, 397
Poniedziałek, Jacek, 356
Popiełuszko, Jerzy, 390–91
Popławski, Jan and Józef, 9, 11
Poręba, Bohdan, 125, 160, 162n30, 185, 245, 252n53, 275
Posmysz-Piasecka, Zofia, 146, 166n84
Potocki, Jan, 177
Powell, Larson, 281
Pratley, Gerald, 254
Preis, Kinga, 353, 368n35, 400, 402, 407
Preisner, Zbigniew, 267, 270, 326–28
Pritulak, Małgorzata, 197
Probosz, Marek, 244
Prószyński, Kazimierz, 11, 33n4, 71
Prucnal, Anna, 316
Prus, Bolesław, 9, 172, 176, 178
Przybora, Jeremi, 210
Przybył, Hieronim, 173, 211
Przybyszewska, Stanisława, 264
Przybyszewski, Stanisław, 25
Przylipiak, Mirosław, 174, 292
Przymanowski, Janusz, 172
Pszoniak, Wojciech, 184, 264, 298, 362
Ptak, Krzysztof, 392
Puchalski, Edward, 4, 16–17, 19–20, 24, 50, 56
Pudovkin, Vsevolod, 22, 32
Puiu, Cristi, 414
Pyjas, Stanisław, 286
Pyrkosz, Witold, 259, 262
Pytlasiński, Władysław, 23

R
Radziwiłowicz, Jerzy, 228, 237–38, 264, 267, 290, 381

Rak, Krzysztof, 391
Ramlau, Andrzej, 342
Rappoport, Shloyme Zanvil. See An-sky
Ratner, Megan, 385
Redliński, Edward, 316, 363
Reich, Aleksander, 71
Reinhardt, Max, 18, 62
Reinhart, Artur, 323
Reinl, Harald, 171
Religa, Zbigniew, 391–92
Renée, Renata, 24
Resnais, Alain, 87, 327
Reymont, Władysław Stanisław, 26, 173, 181, 184–85
Riedel, Ryszard, 399
Riefenstahl, Leni, 45
Ringelblum, Emmanuel, 83, 88
Robespierre, Maximilien, 264
Rodziewiczówna, Maria, 57
Rokossowski, Konstanty, 111n1
Romantowska, Anna, 318
Rosa, Michał, 332
Rosen, Józef, 71
Rotmil, Jacek, 62, 71
Rotunno, Giuseppe, 277
Różewicz, Stanisław, 118, 120, 122, 140–41, 143, 160, 165n73, 171, 185–86, 261, 264, 272n18
Różewicz, Tadeusz, 166n73, 170
Rudnicki, Adolf, 212
Russell, Ken, 155
Rybczyński, Zbigniew, 253n61, 257, 307
Rybkowski, Jan, 98, 101, 105, 120, 153, 167n95, 171, 173, 188, 362
Rywin, Lew, 277, 341

S
Sądek, Napoleon, 53
Sadowska, Maria, 391, 423n61
Safran, Gabriella, 266
Sala, Paweł, 403
Samberg, Ajzyk, 71
Samborski, Bogusław, 42, 37, 91n5
Samosiuk, Zygmunt, 182, 245, 248
Saniewski, Wiesław, 256–57
Saniternik, Mariusz, 320
Saramonowicz, Andrzej, 360, 397

Sass, Barbara, 222, 232, 262, 285, 291–92, 316, 322–24, 347
Sawan, Zbigniew, 24
Schiff, Stephen, 230
Schiller, Leon, 70
Schnabel, Julian, 413
Schneider, Gerda, 84
Schulz, Bruno, 118
Schumacher, Israel, 83
Schygulla, Hanna, 300
Ścibor-Rylski, Aleksander, 171, 190, 228
Scorsese, Martin, 1, 307, 402
Scott, A. O., 403
Segda, Dorota, 283
Sekuła, Andrzej, 5
Sempoliński, Ludwik, 44, 90
Sendler, Irena, 266, 273n27
Seweryn, Andrzej, 184, 233, 235, 347, 393–94, 397
Seweryn, Maria, 316
Siegel, Don, 359
Siekierzyńska, Iwona, 355
Sielański, Stanisław, 44, 54
Siemaszko, Ewa, 409
Siemion, Wojciech, 140, 165n68
Sienkiewicz, Henryk, 12–13, 23, 26, 50, 56, 66n20, 74, 150, 152, 172, 178–79, 181, 343–46
Sienkiewicz, Joanna, 263
Sikora, Adam, 363, 402, 412
Siwkiewicz, Piotr, 303
Skaff, Sheila, 12–13, 34n9, 38n52, 43
Skalski, Jacek, 275, 306
Skarżanka, Hanna, 257
Skolimowski, Jerzy, 159, 171, 191–94, 199, 323, 402–3
Skolimowski, Lech, 144
Skórzewski, Edward, 125, 151, 190
Skrzepiński, Jerzy, 177
Skwara, Anita, 280, 306
Śląska, Aleksandra, 86, 105, 147–48, 200
Ślesicki, Maciej, 306, 315, 341, 360, 403
Ślesicki, Władysław, 122, 125, 151–52, 179, 198
Słobodzianek, Tadeusz, 380
Smarzowski, Wojciech, 342, 359, 366, 405–11
Smoczyńska, Agnieszka, 399–400
Smosarska, Jadwiga, 16–20, 47, 51–52, 92n10
Snyder, Timothy, 386–87, 409–10

Sobieszczański, Maciej, 376
Sobociński, Michał, 392, 424n 63
Sobociński, Piotr, 268, 424n63
Sobociński, Piotr, Jr., 392, 410, 424n63
Sobociński, Witold, 189, 277, 424n63
Sobolewski, Tadeusz, 175, 257, 279, 325, 330, 377, 388, 407–8
Sobotka, Kazimierz, 103, 105
Sokołowska, Anna, 187
Sokorski, Włodzimierz, 98
Solarz, Wojciech, 198
Solski, Ludwik, 54
Sonnenfeld, Barry, 399
Sørensen, Bjørn, 230
Spielberg, Steven, 87, 297
Stachówna, Grażyna, 98, 105, 330
Stachura, Edward, 262–63
Stakhanov, Alexei, 98, 104, 112n11, 174
Stalin, Joseph, 78, 85, 96–97, 101, 116, 194, 241, 284, 289, 294–95, 374,
Stalińska, Dorota, 232
Stankiewicz, Ewa, 357
Stańko, Tomasz, 301
Starewicz, Władysław (Ladislas Starevich), 5, 16
Staroń, Wojciech, 392, 417
Starski, Allan, 298
Starski, Ludwik, 54, 72, 79, 81, 88, 101, 120
Starzyński, Stefan, 245
Stasiuk, Andrzej, 380
Stawiński, Jerzy Stefan, 110, 119–20, 129, 131, 161n15, 164n47, 164n55
Steinwurzel, Seweryn, 15, 50, 72–73
Stenka, Danuta, 223, 375
Štepánek, Emil, 42
Steranko, Artur, 402
Stern, Anatol, 120
Stoor, Mieczysław, 181
Storaro, Vittorio, 277
Strassburger, Karol, 245
Straszna, Marta, 207
Stroiński, Krzysztof, 318, 396
Strug, Andrzej, 238
Stryjkowski, Julian, 265
Strzemiński, Władysław, 388–89
Studlar, Gaylyn, 327

INDEX OF NAMES · 483

Stuhr, Jerzy, 225–26, 231, 233, 236, 259, 307–8, 329, 331, 354–55, 365
Stuhr, Maciej, 360, 381, 398, 404, 406
Sucharski, Henryk, 185
Sulik, Bolesław, 124
Sumerski, Kazimierz, 99
Suvorov, Victor, 309
Suwała, Justyna, 405
Świdwiński, Aleksander, 82
Świerczewski, Karol, 101, 112n16
Sygietyński, Tadeusz, 101
Sym, Igo, 70
Szaflarska, Danuta, 90, 138, 302
Szapołowska, Grażyna, 267, 270
Szaro, Henryk, 24–27, 43, 47, 54, 71
Szczechura, Daniel, 150
Szczepanik, Jan, 9
Szczepański, Jan, 209
Szczepański, Jan Józef, 283
Szczepański, Tadeusz, 330
Szczerbic, Joanna, 193
Szelburg-Zarembina, Ewa, 80
Szlachtycz, Stefan, 336n54
Szmagier, Krzysztof, 209
Szmidt, Jarosław, 391
Szmidt, Tadeusz, 100
Szoda, Jarosław, 414, 426n92
Szołajski, Konrad, 290, 317
Szołowski, Karol, 59–60, 70
Szpilman, Władysław, 79–80, 82, 350–2, 367n27
Sztwiertnia, Jerzy, 91n6
Szulkin, Piotr, 223, 247–48, 253n60, 295, 312, 314
Szumacher, Israel, 83–84
Szumowska, Małgorzata, 365, 404–6
Szyc, Borys, 396
Szyma, Tadeusz, 148
Szyszko Sylwester, 190

T

Tanović, Danis, 353
Tarantino, Quentin, 357
Tatarkiewicz, Władysław, 196
Tati, Jacques, 211
Teleszyński, Leszek, 188
Templeton, Suzie, 418
Terlecki, Władysław, 263

Tesarz, Jan, 269
Themerson, Franciszka and Stefan, 74, 76, 92n13
Thompson, Kristin, 22
Tiran, Itay, 382–83
Tischner, Józef, 96, 279
Titkow, Andrzej, 174, 342
Tkacz, Kamil, 413
Toeplitz, Jerzy, 58, 121
Toeplitz, Krzysztof Teodor, 120, 128, 227
Tokarczuk, Olga, 414
Tom, Konrad, 51, 53, 64, 72
Tomiak, Arkadiusz, 348, 401
Towbin, Mordechai, 11, 15
Trauberg, Leonid, 106
Trintignant, Jean-Louis, 329
Tristan, Frédèric, 263
Truffaut, François, 181
Trystan, Leon, 30–31, 54, 64, 71, 397
Trzaskalski, Piotr, 362
Trzebuchowska, Agata, 383–84
Trzeciak, Franciszek, 199, 238, 248
Trzos-Rastawiecki, Andrzej, 201, 245
Turaj, Frank, 154, 171, 241
Turek, Jerzy, 136
Turkow, Jonas, 15
Turkow, Zygmunt, 15, 43
Tuzar, Jaroslav, 88
Tykwer, Tom, 353
Tym, Stanisław, 211, 317
Tyszkiewicz, Beata, 178, 180

U

Ucicky, Gustav, 70
Ukniewska, Maria, 59–60, 68n44
Ulewicz, Wacław, 240
Umecka, Jolanta, 157
Umuhire, Elaine, 416
Urbański, Artur, 355
Ursel, Marian, 141

V

Van Gogh, Vincent, 418
Vasilyev, Georgi and Sergey, 140
Vasylyk, Vasili, 409
Vega, Patryk, 401–2
Vergano, Aldo, 101

Vesaas, Tarjei, 197
Vidal, Belén, 388
Vigo, Jean, 61
Villquist, Ingmar, 412
Vitrotti, Giovanni, 42
Vivaldi, Antonio, 181
Vláčil, František, 408
Voit, Mieczysław, 155
Von Sydow, Max, 282

W

Wajda, Andrzej, 1, 78, 98, 101, 106, 117–20, 123–25, 127, 129–38, 140–41, 143, 145, 153, 160n7, 162n24, 171, 175, 180–87, 191, 200, 211, 216n34, 221, 227–30, 232–33, 235, 237–38, 241–42, 244–45, 254–56, 262–64, 268, 271n2, 278–81, 287, 290–91, 293–94, 297–99, 300–3, 312–13, 317, 323, 325, 335n36, 338n71, 342–43, 345–47, 372–75, 377, 388–89, 405, 419, 423n56, 423n58
Wajda, Jakub, 374
Wajs, Bronisława, 392
Walczewski, Marek, 148, 198, 245
Wałęsa, Danuta, 389
Wałęsa, Lech, 220, 225, 237, 264, 274, 389–90
Walker, Michael, 194
Waltz, Christoph, 283
Warnecki, Janusz, 43
Wars, Henryk, 50–51, 54, 66n25, 72–74, 76
Wasilewski, Tomasz, 414
Wasowski, Jerzy, 210
Waszyński, Michał, 27, 38n64, 42–43, 46, 48, 52–55, 62, 72–73, 76
Weber, Kurt, 126, 150, 170, 213n3
Wegener, Paul, 25
Węgrzyn, Józef, 19–20, 59–60
Weigl, Rudolf, 189, 217n54
Weksler-Waszkinel, Romuald Jakub, 385
Welchman, Hugh, 418
Welles, Orson, 73, 78, 229, 248
Wells, H.G., 248
Wencel, Ewa, 411
Wereśniak, Piotr, 360, 397
Werner, Andrzej, 128
Werstak, Adam, 413
Wexler, Haskell, 277

Więckiewicz, Robert, 360, 386, 389–90, 396, 407, 409, 414, 422n46
Wieczyński, Rafał, 332, 391
Wiene, Robert, 23, 25
Wilczówna, Janina, 92n17
Wilhelmi, Roman, 223, 248, 260, 362
Wilson, Lambert, 300
Wilson, Scott, 282, 257–58
Winiewicz, Krzysztof, 147
Winnicka, Ernestyna, 266
Winnicka, Lucyna, 142, 154–55
Wionczek, Roman, 255
Wisłocka, Michalina, 391–92
Wiszniewska, Tamara, 57
Wiszniewski, Tomasz, 373, 413
Wiszniewski, Wojciech, 173–74, 212, 214n15, 250n18, 257
Włast, Andrzej, 15
Włodarczyk, Wojciech, 111
Wohl, Stanisław, 58–59, 61, 74, 76, 80, 82
Wojaczek, Rafał, 363
Wojciechowski, Karol, 13
Wojciechowski, Krzysztof, 174, 223, 250n12
Wojciechowski, Piotr, 128
Wojcieszek, Przemysław, 357–58, 379
Wójcik, Jerzy, 129, 137, 145, 164n48, 177
Wójcik, Magda Teresa, 255
Wójcik, Wojciech, 260, 306, 309, 342, 347, 360
Wojtyła, Karol. See John Paul II
Wolińska-Brus, Helena, 384
Wołłejko, Czesław, 102
Wolski, Dariusz, 5
Worcell, Henryk, 200
Woronowicz, Adam, 391
Woroszylski, Wiktor, 146
Wosiewicz, Leszek, 144, 285–86, 291, 294, 297, 378, 412
Woszczerowicz, Jacek, 59–60, 80, 101
Wrona, Marcin, 379, 383, 416, 421n34
Wrzesińska, Barbara, 195
Wyler, William, 73
Wylężałek, Łukasz, 362
Wysocka, Stanisława, 44, 61
Wyspiański, Stanisław, 9, 12, 181, 191, 232, 405
Wyszomirski, Józef, 80
Wyszyński, Stefan, 113n29, 156, 292, 347

INDEX OF NAMES · 485

Wywerka, Albert, 46, 55, 62

Z

Żabczyński, Aleksander, 42, 51, 53–54, 76
Ząbkowska, Małgorzata, 225
Zacharewicz, Witold, 71
Zaczyk, Stanisław, 139
Zadrzyński, Łukasz, 362
Zagajewski, Adam, 207–8, 220
Zahorska, Stefania, 37n52
Zajączkowski, Andrzej, 237
Żal, Łukasz, 385
Zaleski, Krzysztof, 234
Załuski, Roman, 224–25, 261, 200
Zamachowski, Zbigniew, 288, 323, 328, 360, 404
Zamecka, Anna, 417
Żamojda, Jarosław, 306, 359
Zanussi, Krzysztof, 171, 173, 191, 194–97, 199, 221
   227–28, 230–31, 234, 240, 248, 256–59,
   271n9, 275, 278, 280–83, 291, 293, 325, 332,
   241–42, 364–65, 369n48, 408
Zaorski, Janusz, 201, 221–22, 233, 241, 255, 260,
   262, 295, 316, 376
Zapasiewicz, Zbigniew, 196–97, 231, 237, 260,
   364–65
Zapolska, Gabriela, 12, 25, 42, 44
Żarnecki, Andrzej, 195
Zarzycki, Jerzy, 46, 58–59, 61, 69, 79–80, 107–8,
   113n30, 118, 120, 125, 143
Zastrzeżyński, Wacław, 133
Zatorski, Ryszard, 397
Zawadzka, Magdalena, 179
Zdort, Wiesław, 203–4, 282–93
Żebrowski, Edward, 197, 238
Zegadłowicz, Emil, 244
Żelichowska, Lena, 57
Zelnik, Jerzy, 176–77
Zeman, Boživoj, 94n36
Żentara, Edward, 282–83
Żeromski, Stefan, 24, 26, 50, 175, 180, 275, 343
Zhdanov, Andrei, 96
Ziarnik, Jerzy, 151, 173, 198–99
Zieliński, Jerzy, 244, 253n58
Zieliński, Stanisław, 171
Ziemann, Sonja, 159
Ziembiński, Włodzimierz, 127

Zimetbaum, Mala, 87
Zimowski, Rafał, 285
Żmijewski, Artur, 282, 313
Znamierowski, Mieczysław, 50, 66n22
Znicz, Michał, 54, 71
Żółtowski, Wojciech, 266
Zsigmond, Vilmos, 277
Zucker, Jerry, 323
Żuławski, Andrzej, 145, 171, 188–89, 378
Żuławski, Mirosław, 188
Żulewska, Agnieszka, 383
Zwierzchowski, Piotr, 186
Żydowicz, Marek, 277
Zygadło, Tomasz, 174, 223, 336
Zylber, Filip, 297, 301–2, 362
Zylinska, Joanna, 385

Index of Film Titles

A

Abbot Kordecki: The Defender of Częstochowa (Przeor Kordecki – obrońca Częstochowy, 1934), 50
ABC of Love (ABC miłości, 1935), 53
Abel, Your Brother, (Abel, twój brat, 1970), 212
Abyss of Repentance, The (Otchłań pokuty, 1922), 27
According to the Decrees of Providence (Wedle wyroków Twoich, 1983), 264, 272n19
Achte Wochentag, Der. See Eighth Day of the Week
Addams Family, The (1991), 399
Adelheid (1969), 408
Adventure at Marienstadt, An (Przygoda na Mariensztacie, 1954), 100–1, 103–5, 230, 251n22
Adventure of a Good Citizen, The (Przygoda człowieka poczciwego, 1937), 92n13
Adventures of the Police Dog Cywil, The (Przygody psa Cywila, 1970), 209
Afterimage (Powidoki, 2016), 388–89
Aftermath (Pokłosie, 2012), 279, 381
After the Fall (Po upadku, 1990), 283
Alexander Nevsky (1938), 78
All among Ourselves (Sami swoi, 1967), 210
All My Good Countrymen (Všichni dobři rodáci, 1969), 289
All Souls Day (Zaduszki, 1961), 142
All That Really Matters (Wszystko, co najważniejsze, 1992), 297, 284
All These Sleepless Nights (Wszystkie nieprzespane noce, 2015), 417
All Will Be Well (Wszystko będzie dobrze, 2007), 413–14
Alone among His Own (Sam pośród swoich, 1985), 260
Ambulance (Ambulans, 1961), 143–44, 166n77
Among People (Wśród ludzi, 1963), 151
Anatomy of Love (Anatomia miłości, 1972), 201
And a Warm Heart (Serce na dłoni, 2008), 369n48
Angel in the Wardrobe, An (Anioł w szafie, 1988), 272n18
Angelus (2001), 357, 363
Angi Vera (1978), 289
Angry Harvest (Bittere Ernte, 1985), 266, 297
Anna (1987), 349
Anna and the Vampire (Anna i wampir, 1982), 255
Another Way (Egymásra nézve, 1982), 289
Answer to Violence (Zamach, 1959), 139
Ant and the Grasshopper, The (1911), 16
Antek the Police Chief (Antek Policmajster, 1935), 52
Antoś for the First Time in Warsaw (Antoś pierwszy raz w Warszawie, 1908), 11
Anxiety. See The Ghosts
Anybody Can Love (Każdemu wolno kochać, 1933), 43, 52
April (Kwiecień, 1961), 139
Aquarium, The (Akwarium, 1995), 309
Arabella (1917), 35n30
Aria for an Athlete (Aria dla atlety, 1979), 247, 316
Arizona (1997), 417
Armchair, The (Fotel, 1963), 150
Art of Loving: The Story of Michalina Wisłocka, The (Sztuka kochania: Historia Michaliny Wisłockiej, 2017), 391–92
Ascended, The (Wniebowzięci, 1973), 212, 319
Ascension Day (Wniebowstąpienie, 1969), 188
Ashes (Popioły, 1965), 175
Ashes and Diamonds (Popiół i diament, 1958), 101, 117, 125, 132–37, 160, 180, 183, 187, 200, 208, 279–80, 293, 312, 375
Astronauts (Les Astronautes, 1959), 150
Atalante, L' (1934), 61
Attention, Hooligans! (Uwaga, chuligani! 1955), 126

INDEX OF FILM TITLES · 487

August's Sky: 63 Days of Glory (Sierpniowe niebo: 63 dni chwały, 2013), 378
Austeria (1983), 265–66, 272n23
Awatar, or the Exchange of Souls (Awatar, czyli zamiana dusz, 1967), 200
AWOL (Samowolka, 1993), 209
Axiliad (Siekierezada, 1986), 262–63

B

Bachelor's Life Abroad, A (Kawalerskie życie na obczyźnie, 1992), 319
Bad Luck (Zezowate szczęście, 1960), 117–19, 131–32, 148, 164n55
Bajland (2000), 362
Balance Sheet. *See* A Woman's Decision
Ball at the Koluszki Railway Station (Bal na dworcu w Koluszkach, 1990), 283
Baltic Express. *See* Night Train
Baltic Rhapsody, The (Rapsodia Bałtyku, 1935), 48–49, 66n19
Barbara and Jan (Barbara i Jan, 1965), 173
Barbara Radziwiłłówna. *See* Love or a Kingdom
Barefoot Contessa, The (1954), 73
Bareism (Bareizm, 1997), 252n55
Baritone, The (Baryton, 1985), 260
Barrier, The (Bariera, 1966), 192–94
Bartek the Victor (Bartek zwycięzca, 1923), 23
Battle of the Stag Beetles (1910), 16
Battle of Warsaw 1920 (1920 Bitwa Warszawska, 2011), 376
Battleship Potemkin (1925), 22, 97, 307
Beads of One Rosary, The (Paciorki jednego różańca, 1980), 203, 207, 237
Bear, The (Lokis, 1970), 200
Beast, The (Bestia, 1979), 251n29
Beater, The (Naganiacz, 1964), 143, 146
Beautiful Lukanida, The (1910), 16
Beauty of Life, The (Uroda życia, 1930), 27
Before the Leaves Fall (Zanim opadną liście, 1964), 151
Beksinskis, The: A Sound and Picture Album (Beksińscy: Album wideofoniczny (2017), 424n64
Bellissima (2001), 355
Benek (2007), 412
Beyond Words (Pomiędzy słowami, 2017), 415

Big Animal, The (Duże zwierzę, 2006), 354
Big Deal (Nie ma mocnych, 1974), 210
Big Giveaway, The (Wielka wsypa, 1993), 316
Big Rook, The (Wielki Szu, 1983), 260
Big Run, The (Wielki bieg, 1981), 241, 255, 275
Billboard (1998), 363
Birchwood (Brzezina, 1970), 181–83, 244
Birds Are Singing in Kigali (Ptaki śpiewają w Kigali, 2017), 416
Birth Certificate, The (Świadectwo urodzenia, 1961), 122, 140, 143, 349
Birthplace (Miejsce urodzenia, 1992), 304, 384
Bitter Moon (1992), 109n91
Bittersweet (Słodko-gorzki, 1996), 278
Black Cross. *See* Teutonic Knights
Black Dress, The (Czarna suknia, 1967), 200
Black Pearl (Czarna perła, 1934), 54
Black Peter (Černy Petr, 1963), 223
Black Thursday (Czarny czwartek: Janek Wiśniewski padł, 2011), 275–76
Blanc et noir (1919), 25
Blanche (1972), 180
Blind Chance (Przypadek, 1981), 239–40, 252n46, 255, 267, 275, 313, 325
Blind Man's Bluff (Ciuciubabka, 1977), 260
Blok.pl (2001), 357
Bloody East (Krwawy Wschód, 1931), 49
Bloody Fate (Krwawa dola, 1912), 13
Bloody Sunday (2002), 376
Bluebeard (Blaubart, 1984), 271n9
Blue Cross, The (Błękitny krzyż, 1955), 98
Blue Light, The (Das blaue Licht, 1932), 45
Blue Note (La note bleue, 1991), 189
Bodensee. *See* Sons and Comrades
Body (Ciało, 2003), 360
Body (Body/Ciało, 2015), 405
Bolek and Lolek (Bolek i Lolek, 1936), 53
Bolesław the Bold (Bolesław Śmiały, 1972), 177
Boor, The (Cham, 1931), 55
Border Street (Ulica Graniczna, 1949), 84, 88–89, 97, 301
Boris Godunov (1990), 189
Botox (Botoks, 2017), 402
Boys Don't Cry (Chłopaki nie płaczą, 2000), 356
Boxer, The (Bokser, 1966), 181
Bridget Jones Diary (2001), 344

Bright Fields (Jasne Łany, 1947), 99
Brother of Our God, The (Brat naszego Boga, 1997), 281
Brothers (Bracia, 2015), 417
Burial of a Potato, The (Pogrzeb kartofla, 1991), 297–98, 320–22, 335n44
Bus Leaves at 6:20, The (Autobus odjeżdża 6.20, 1954), 105
Butterflies (Motyle, 1973), 212
By Knockout (Przez nokaut, 1995), 424n70

C

Cabaret of Elderly Gentlemen (Kabaret Starszych Panów), 210
Call of the Toad, The (Wróżby kumaka, 2005), 420n23
Calling Mr. Smith (1943), 74
Calm (Spokój, 1976), 223, 225, 236, 267
Camera Buff (Amator, 1979), 221, 225–28, 236, 325, 355
Camouflage (Barwy ochronne, 1977), 195, 221–22, 228, 230–31, 236
Cardiogram (Kardiogram, 1971), 200
Captain Sowa Investigates (Kapitan Sowa na tropie, 1965), 208
Career of Nikoś Dyzma, The (Kariera Nikosia Dyzmy, 2002), 362
Carmen (1918), 18
Case of Pekosiński, The (Przypadek Pekosińskiego, 1993), 284, 291
Cast Away (2000), 343
Catamount Killing, The (1974), 259
Chance, The (Szansa, 1980), 221
Chapaev (1934), 140
Cheap Money (Tanie pieniądze, 1986), 251n27
Child's Questions (Dziecinne pytania, 1981), 222, 233–34
Children Must Laugh (Mir kumen on, Droga młodych, 1936), 59
Children of the Ramp (Dzieci rampy, 1963), 187
Christening, The (Chrzest, 2010), 421n34
Chronicle of Amorous Accidents (Kronika wypadków miłosnych, 1986), 262
Chronicle of the Warsaw Ghetto Uprising According to Marek Edelman (Kronika powstania w getcie warszawskim według Marka Edelmana, 1993), 304–5
Citizen Kane (1941), 78, 109, 174
Citizen P. (Obywatel Piszczyk, 1989), 164n55
Clear Through. *See* Through and Through
Cleopatra (1963), 171
Clinch (Klincz, 1979), 222, 231, 236
Closed Circuit, The (Układ zamknięty, 2013), 412
Cockeyed Luck. *See* Bad Luck
Colonel Kwiatkowski (Pułkownik Kwiatkowski, 1996), 285, 287, 291, 293
Colonel Wolodyjowski. *See* Pan Michael
Colored Stockings (Kolorowe pończochy, 1960), 149
Color of Pomegranates, The (Sayat-nova, 1969), 204
Columbuses (Kolumbowie, 1970), 377
Come and See (Idi i smotri, 1985), 408
Communion (Komunia, 2015), 417
Con Amore (1976), 248
Conductor, The (Dyrygent, 1980), 222, 235
Constant Factor, The (Constans, 1980), 234
Contract (Kontrakt, 1980), 234
Contribution (Kontrybucja, 1967), 186
Controlled Conversations (Rozmowy kontrolowane, 1992), 317
Conversation with a Person in a Wardrobe (Rozmowa z człowiekiem z szafy, 1993), 318
Corkscrew (Korkociąg, 1971), 174
Corner of Brzeska and Capri, The (Róg Brzeskiej i Capri, 1980), 223
Countess Cosel (Hrabina Cosel, 1968), 173
Courageous Heart of Irena Sendler, The (2009), 273n27
Coup d'état (Zamach stanu, 1980), 245
Crabapple Tree (Rajska jabłoń, 1986), 262
Crash (2004), 403
Creeps, The. *See* The Ghosts
Crime and Punishment (Raskolnikow, 1923), 25
Crime and Punishment (Zbrodnia i kara, 2000), 418
Criminal and the Maiden, The (Zbrodniarz i panna, 1963), 208, 212
Criminal Who Stole a Crime, The (Zbrodniarz, który ukradł zbrodnię, 1969), 200, 208

INDEX OF FILM TITLES · 489

Cross of Valor (Krzyż Walecznych, 1959), 136–37, 139, 294
Crossroads Café, The (Rozdroże Cafe, 2005), 412
Crows (Wrony, 1994), 322
Cruise, The (Rejs, 1970), 211, 317
Cult of the Body, The (Kult ciała, 1930), 43
Cupid's Bow (Łuk Erosa, 1988), 260
Cure for Love, A (Lekarstwo na miłość, 1966), 208
Cursed (Wyklęty, 2017), 387
Custody (Nadzór, 1985), 256
Cyphers (Szyfry, 1966), 159

D

Daas (2011), 376
Daddy (Tato, 1995), 306, 315
Damned, The. *See* Cursed
Damned Roads (Baza ludzi umarłych, 1959), 126, 139, 163n34
Dancing Hawk (Tańczący jastrząb, 1978), 248, 257
Dangerous Love Affair, A (Niebezpieczny romans, 1930), 42
Danton (1983), 263–64, 313
Daredevils (Szaleńcy, 1928/1934), 24, 26
Dark House, The (Dom zły, 2009), 406–7, 409
Dark Eyes. *See* Hanka
Dark River (Ciemna rzeka, 1974), 190
Daughter or a Son, A (Córka albo syn), 260
Day for Night (La nuit américaine, 1973), 181
Day of the Wacko, The (Dzień świra, 2002), 360–61, 369n43
Daze (Oszołomienie, 1989), 91n6
Dead Echo (Zamarłe echo, 1934), 45
Dead Track (Ślepy tor, 1947), 94n36
Death as a Slice of Bread (Śmierć jak kromka chleba, 1994), 287–88
Death of Cavalry Captain Pilecki, The (Śmierć Rotmistrza Pileckiego, 2006), 388
Death of a President (Śmierć Prezydenta, 1977), 245
Death of a Provincial, The (Śmierć Prowincjała, 1965), 173, 194, 364
Death of a Childmaker (Śmierć dziecioroba, 1991), 322

Deborah (Debora, 1995), 297, 301
Debt (Dług, 1999), 342, 361
Debt Collector, The (Komornik, 2005), 411
Debutante (Debiutantka, 1982), 324, 332
Decalogue (Dekalog, 1988), 239, 267–70, 273n28, 285, 330–32, 356–57, 398, 414
Declaration of Immortality, The (Deklaracja nieśmiertelności, 2010), 417
Deer Hunter, The (1970), 409
Defenders of Lvov, The (Tamara, aka Obrońcy Lwowa, 1919), 23
Déjà Vu (Deja vu, 1989), 307–8
Deliverance (Ocalenie, 1972), 197
Deluge, The (Potop, 1974), 152, 178–79, 181
Demon (2015), 379, 382–83
Departure (Odjazd, 1992), 323
Deserter, The (Dezerter, 1958), 139
Deserters (C.K. Dezerterzy, 1986), 261
Destined for Blues (Skazany na bluesa, 2005), 399
Developmentally Challenged (Nienormalni, 1990), 334n30
Devil (Diabeł, 1972/1988), 189
Devil's Ravine (Czarci żleb, 1950), 101
Devils, The (1971), 155
Devils, Devils (Diabły, diabły, 1991), 322
Diamonds of Mrs. Zuza, The (Brylanty pani Zuzy, 1972), 209
Diary for My Children (Napló gyermekeimnek, 1982), 289
Diary for My Loves (Napló szerelmeimnek, 1987), 289
Diary in Marble (Pamiętnik znaleziony w garbie, 1994), 292
Diary of Anne Frank, The (1959), 87
Difficult Love (Trudna miłość, 1954), 104–5
Dignity (Godność, 1984), 255
Directors (Dyrektorzy, 1975), 224
Dirty Harry (1972), 314, 359
Disco Daughters, The. *See* The Lure
Disco Polo (2015), 399
Dismissed from Life (Zwolnieni z życia, 1991), 283
Divided We Fall (Musimé si pomahát, 2000), 349
Diving Bell and the Butterfly, The (2007), 413

Dodek at the Front (Dodek na froncie, 1936), 52
Doll, The (Lalka, 1968), 178
Doll, The (Lalka, 1977), 215n25
Don't Lie, Honey (Nie kłam kochanie, 2008), 397
Down the Colorful Hill (W dół kolorowym wzgórzem, 2005), 358
Double Life of Véronique, The (Podwójne życie Weroniki, 1991), 324–27, 329, 354
Drama of the St. Mary's Church Tower, The (Dramat Wieży Mariackiej, 1913), 26
Dr. Jekyll and Mr. Hyde (1931), 45
Dr. Korczak, the Martyr (Sie Sind Frei, Doktor Korczak, 1974), 93n32
Dr. Mabuse, der Spieler (1922),
Drowsiness (Senność, 2008), 371
Duke Michorowski (Ordynat Michorowski, 37n39
Dybbuk, The (Der Dibuk, 1937), 62, 68n47

E

$E=mc^2$ (2002), 360
Earlobe (Małżowina, 1998), 405
Early Spring (Przedwiośnie, 2001), 343
Eccentrics, the Sunny Side of the Street (Ekscentrycy, czyli po słonecznej stronie ulicy, 2016), 399
Echo (1964), 166n73
Edges of the Lord (Boże skrawki, 2001), 349–50, 367n26
Edi (2002), 362
8 1/2 (Otto e mezzo, 1963), 181
Eighth Day of the Week, The (Ósmy dzień tygodnia, 1958, 1983), 158, 169n110
El Cid (1961), 74
Elementary School (Szkoła podstawowa, 1971), 174
11 Minutes (11 minut, 2015), 403
Elles (Sponsoring, 2012), 404
End of the Game, The (Koniec gry, 1991), 281, 283
End of the Night, The (Koniec nocy, 1957), 126, 158, 162n28, 162n29
End of Our World, The (Koniec naszego świata, 1964), 143–44, 164n29

End of the World, The (Koniec świata, 1988), 322
Enter the Dragon (1973), 255
Eroica (1958), 117, 119, 129, 131, 148, 317
Escape as Near as Possible (Uciec jak najbliżej, 1972), 201
Escape from the "Liberty" Cinema (Ucieczka z kina "Wolność", 1990), 284
Essential Killing (2010), 402
Eugeniusz Bodo: For Crimes Not Committed (Za winy niepopełnione: Eugeniusz Bodo, 1997), 91n7
Europa, Europa (1991), 294, 297, 335n43, 385
Ewa Wants to Sleep (Ewa chce spać, 1958), 118, 122, 152
Everything for Sale (Wszystko na sprzedaż, 1969), 180–81, 227
Ewa (2010), 412
Executor (Egzekutor, 1999), 362
Existence, The (Istnienie, 2007), 417
Expecting Love (Mała wielka miłość, 2008), 398
Extradition, The (Ekstradycja, 1995–1996), 309, 359
Eyes of the Mummy Ma, The (The Augen der Mumie Ma, 1918), 19

F

Fabulous Journey of Balthazar Kober, The (Niezwykła podróż Baltazara Kobera, 1988), 263
Face of an Angel, The (Twarz anioła, 1971), 187
Face to Face (Twarzą w twarz, 1968), 173
Faithfulness (La fidélité, 2000), 189
Faithful River (Wierna rzeka, 1936), 38n59
Faithful River (Wierna rzeka, 1983), 275
Fall of the Roman Empire, The (1964), 73
Fallen Art (Sztuka spadania, 2004), 418
Family Events (Kroniki domowe, 1997), 291, 294
Family Life (Życie rodzinne, 1971), 196
Family of Man, The (Rodzina człowiecza, 1966), 151
Far from the Other (Daleko od siebie, 1996), 281
Far Is the Road (Daleka jest droga, 1963), 163n30
Farewells (Pożegnania, 1958), 128
Farewell to Maria (Pożegnanie z Marią, 1993), 297, 301–2

Fargo (1996), 407
Fast Lane (Młode wilki, 1995), 306, 308, 314, 359
Fast Lane 1/2 (Młode wilki 1/2, 1998), 359
Fastest, The (Najlepszy), 392
Father's Law (Prawo ojca, 1999), 359–60
Faustina (Faustyna, 1995), 283
Fear (Strach, 1975), 209
The Feast of St. Barbara (Barbórka, 2005), 425n70
Female Workers (Robotnice, 1980), 223
Femina (1991), 295, 314
Fever (Gorączka, 1981), 313, 338
Few People, a Little Time, A (Parę osób, mały czas, 2007), 401
Film Found in Katyń, The (Film znaleziony w Katyniu, 1992), 290, 374
Final Touch, The (Kropka nad i, 1928), 25
First Love (Pierwsza miłość, 1974), 173
First Million (Pierwszy million, 2000), 362
First Textbook, The (Elementarz, 1976), 174
First Year (Rok pierwszy, 1960), 93–94
Five Boys from Barska Street (Piątka z ulicy Barskiej, 1954), 105–6, 123
Flames (Płomienie, 1979), 248
Flight of the Spruce Goose (1985), 363
Floating Skyscrapers (Płynące wieżowce, 2013), 414
Flood, The (Powódź, 1947), 83
Forbidden Songs (Zakazane piosenki, 1947), 76, 81, 90, 97, 106
For Crimes Not Committed (Za winy nie popełnione, 1938), 91n7
Foreign Body, The (Obce ciało, 2014), 369n48
Foreigner (Cudzoziemka, 1986), 262
Forgotten Melody (Zapomniana melodia, 1938), 53–54, 66n25, 397
For the Sin (Al Chet, 1936), 62
Forty-Year-Old, The (Czterdziestolatek, 1974–1976), 224
For What? (Za co? 1996), 278, 281
For You, Poland (Dla Ciebie, Polsko, 1920), 23
Foul Play (Przepraszam, czy tu biją, 1976), 210
Four Nights with Anna (Cztery noce z Anną, 2008), 402
Four Seasons (Cztery pory roku, 1984), 319

Four Tankmen and a Dog (Czterej pancerni i pies, 1966–1967), 172
Four Weddings and a Funeral (1994), 398
Fourth Dimension, The (1988), 257
Frankenstein (1931), 45
Franz Kafka (1991), 418
Free City (Wolne miasto, 1958), 118, 140
Freedom Is within Us: Popiełuszko (Popiełuszko, wolność jest w nas, 2009), 390–91
Freelancer, The (Wolny strzelec, 1981), 256
From a Far Country: Pope John II (Z dalekiego kraju, 1981), 282
From Day to Day (Z dnia na dzień, 1929), 47
From Nowhere to Nowhere (Znikąd donikąd, 1975), 190
From the City of Łódź (Z miasta Łodzi, 1969), 173
From the Point of View of the Night Porter (Z punktu widzenia nocnego portiera, 1977), 223
Full Moon (Pełnia, 1979), 319
Fury Is a Woman. *See* Siberian Lady Macbeth

G

Ga, Ga: Glory to the Heroes (Ga, ga: Chwała bohaterom, 1986), 263n60
Gallows in the Stutthof Concentration Camp, The (Szubienice w Sztutthofie, 1946), 82
Game On (#WszystkoGra, 2016), 399
Gates to Paradise (1967), 159
Garden of Earthly Delights, The (2003), 363
General Nil (Generał Nil, 2009),
General Pankratov's Daughter (Córka generała Pankratowa, 1934), 50, 66n22
Generation, A (Pokolenie, 1955), 98, 105–6, 115, 117, 123–24, 135, 143, 145, 162n24, 183, 326n53
Gentle Spirit (Łagodna, 1985), 418
Ghost (1990), 323
Ghosts, The (Strachy, 1938), 59–61
Ghosts, The (Strachy, 1979), 68n44
Girl Guide (1996), 278, 307–8
Girl from the Wardrobe, The (Dziewczyna z szafy, 2012), 401
Girls of Nowolipki, The (Dziewczęta z Nowolipek, 1937), 56

Girls of Nowolipki, The (Dziewczęta z Nowolipek, 1986), 324, 362
Glass Lips (Szklane usta, 2007), 363
God's Finger (Palec Boży, 1973), 201
God's Trial (Sąd Boży, 1911), 12
God's Punishment (Gots Sztrof, 1913), 14
Gods (Bogowie, 2014), 391–92
Gold (Złoto, 1961), 128
Golem (1980), 247–48
Gone with the Wind (1939), 346
Goodbye to the Past (Rozstanie, 1961), 128
Gorgon's Affair, The (Sprawa Gorgonowej, 1977), 246
Gospel According to Harry, The (1992), 363
Goto, Island of Love (Goto, l'île d'amour, 1969), 180
Grain of Truth, A (Ziarno prawdy, 2015), 396
Great Road, The. *See* The Long Road
Guards, The (Czaty, 1920), 38n55

H

Halka (1913), 13
Hanka (1934), 46
Hands Up (Ręce do gory, 1967), 196
Hans Kloss: More than Death at Stake (Hans Kloss: Stawka większa niż śmierć, 2012), 214n11
Happy Aphonia (Afonia i pszczoły, 2009), 401
Happy Man (Szczęśliwy człowiek, 2000), 404
Hat of Mr. Anatol, The (Kapelusz pana Anatola, 1957), 153
Hatred. *See* Volhynia
Haunted, The (Niech cię odleci mara, 1981), 241, 243–44
Heading for Berlin (Kierunek Berlin, 1969), 186
Heart on the Street, A (Serce na ulicy, 1931), 46
Heat (Upał, 1964), 210
Heather (Wrzos, 1938), 57
Heaven (2002), 353
Heimkehr (1941). *See* Return Home
He Left on a Bright, Sunny Day (Wyszedł w jasny, pogodny dzień, 1971), 174
Hell (L'enfer, 2005), 353
Heritage (Księstwo, 2012), 401
Heroes of Siberia, The (Bohaterowie Sybiru, 1936), 48

Heroism of a Polish Boy Scout, The (Bohaterstwo polskiego skauta, 1920), 23
Hi, Tereska (Cześć, Tereska, 2001), 359, 411
Hippos (Hipopotamy, 2014), 418
His Excellency, the Chauffeur (Jaśnie pan szofer, 1935), 52
His Excellency, the Shop Assistant (Jego ekscelencja subiekt, 1933), 52
His Name Is Błażej Rejdak (Nazywa się Błażej Rejdak, 1968), 173
History of Cinema Theater in Popielawy, The (Historia kina w Popielawach, 1998), 320, 342
Hole in the Ground, The (Dziura w ziemi, 1970), 319
Holy Week (Wielki Tydzień, 1996), 278, 281, 297, 299, 300, 302
Hope (Nadzieja, 2007), 353
Hospital of Transfiguration, The (Szpital Przemienienia, 1979), 197
Hot Thursday (Gorący czwartek, 1993), 322
Hotel Pacific (Zaklęte rewiry, 1975), 200
Hourglass Sanatorium, The (Sanatorium pod Klepsydrą, 1973), 177–78
House (Dom, 1958), 150
House of Fools, The (Dom wariatów, 1984), 360
Hours of Hope, The (Godziny nadziei, 1955), 98
How Are We to Live? (Jak żyć? 1977), 222, 231
How Far from Here, How Near (Jak daleko stąd, jak blisko, 1972), 212
How I Unleashed World War II (Jak rozpętałem II wojnę światową, 1970), 210
How It Is Done (Jak to się robi, 1974), 212
How Much Does the Trojan Horse Weigh? (Ile waży koń trojański? 2008), 399
How to Be Loved (Jak być kochaną, 1963), 122, 128
Hubal (1973), 104, 185
Human Wrecks (Wykolejeni, 1913), 14
Hunting Flies (Polowanie na muchy, 1969), 211
Hurricane, The (Huragan, 1928), 23–24

I

I Am (Jestem, 2005), 322
I Am Burning! (Ja gorę! 1968), 200
I'm a Killer (Jestem mordercą, 2016), 395–96

INDEX OF FILM TITLES · **493**

I'm So-So (1995), 220
Ida (2013), 1, 5, 379, 383–85, 418
Identification Marks (Znaki szczególne, 1976), 224
Identification Marks: None (Rysopis, 1965), 192
Idol, The (Bożyszcze, 1923), 27
I Hate Mondays (Nie lubię poniedziałku, 1971), 210
I Have Sinned. *See* For the Sin
I Love You (Ajlawju, 1999), 360
Illumination (Iluminacja, 1973), 195–97, 218n72, 240
Imagine (2013), 404
Immoral Stories (Contes immoraux, 1974), 180
Immoral Story, An (Historia niemoralna, 1990), 324
Imperative (1982), 259
In Broad Daylight (W biały dzień, 1981), 238
In Darkness (W ciemności, 2012), 379, 385–87, 400
In Desert and Wilderness (W pustyni i w puszczy, 1973), 152, 179
In Desert and Wilderness (W pustyni i w puszczy, 2001), 343
Index (Indeks, 1977), 221, 234
In Hiding (W ukryciu, 2013), 379
In the Name of... (W imię..., 2013), 404
Inferno (2001), 355
Influence (Hiszpanka, 2015), 376–77
In Full Gallop (Cwał, 1996), 281, 291, 293, 278
In Such a Small town (W takim niedużym mieście, 1971), 174
Inn, The. *See* Austeria
Innocent Sorcerers (Niewinni czarodzieje, 1960), 153, 192
In Polish Woods (In di Poylishe Velder, 1929), 15, 24
Inspection at the Scene of the Crime, 1901 (Wizja lokalna 1901, 1981), 247
Inspection of Mr. Anatol, The (Inspekcja pana Anatola, 1959), 167n95
Interrogation (Przesłuchanie, 1982), 236, 242–43, 255–56, 275, 291, 295, 388
In the Shadow of Hatred (W cieniu nienawiści, 1986), 266
In the Still of the Night. *See* Silent Night

Inventory (Stan posiadania, 1989), 282
Invitation, The (Zaproszenie, 1985), 266
Irena, Go Home! (Irena do domu!, 1955), 101
Is Lucyna a Girl? (Czy Lucyna to dziewczyna? 1934), 52, 397
It Looks Pretty from a Distance (Z daleka widok jest piękny, 2012), 379, 382
It's Better to Be Beautiful and Rich (Lepiej być piękną i bogatą, 1993), 316
I Will Stand on My Guard (Na straży swej stać będę, 1983), 219n87
Iwonka (1925), 20

J

Jack Strong (2014), 390
Jadzia (1936), 397
Jealousy and Medicine (Zazdrość i medycyna, 1973), 200
Jetty (Molo, 1969), 198
Joanna (2010), 379–80
Joanna (2013), 417
John Heart (Jan Serce, 1982), 260
John Paul II: I Looked for You (Jan Paweł II: Szukałem was..., 2011), 391
John Paul II: The Testimony (Świadectwo, 2008), 391
Johnnie the Aquarius (Jańcio Wodnik, 1993), 320–21
Johnny the Musician (Janko Muzykant, 1930), 56
Joke, The (Žert, 1968), 289
Jowita (1967), 181
Joyless Street, The (Die freudlose Gasse, 1925), 25
Julia, Anna, Genowefa (1968), 187
Just Beyond this Forest (Jeszcze tylko ten las, 1991), 297, 302–3

K

Kafka (1992), 257
Kanal (Kanał, 1957), 117, 119, 122, 129–31, 164n47, 183, 301, 377
Karate Polish Style (Karate po polsku, 1983), 260
Karol: A Man Who Became Pope (Karol: Człowiek, który został papieżem, 2005), 191

Karol: The Pope, the Man (Karol: Papież, który pozostał człowiekiem, 2006), 391
Katyń (2007, Gębski), 374
Katyń (2007, Wajda), 372–75
Katyń Forest, The (Las Katyński, 1991), 290
Katyń Massacre, The (Zbrodnia katyńska, 1991), 374
Katyń: The Truth and the Lie about the Crime (Katyń: Prawda i kłamstwo o zbrodni, 2005), 374
Katyń Woods (Las katyński, 1990), 374
Keep Away from the Window (Daleko od okna, 2000), 348–49
Kidnapping of Agata, The (Uprowadzenie Agaty, 1993), 317
Kiler (1997), 306
Kiler 2 (Kiler-ów 2-óch, 1999), 306
Kill That Love (Trzeba zabić tę miłość, 1972), 201–2
Kill Them All (Zabij ich wszystkich, 1999), 357
Kinematograph, The (Kinematograf, 2009), 418
Klezmer (2015), 379
Knife in the Water (Nóż w wodzie, 1962), 122, 156–57, 159, 168n104, 192, 350, 355, 407
Knight, The (Rycerz, 1980), 363
Konopielka (1982), 263, 320
Korczak (1990), 297–98
Kornblumenblau (1989), 144, 285–86, 294, 297
Kościuszko at Racławice (Kościuszko pod Racławicami, 1913), 13
Kościuszko at Racławice (Kościuszko pod Racławicami, 1938), 51
Kroll (1991), 306, 309–10
Kung-fu (1980), 221, 234–35

L

Labyrinth (Labirynt, 1963), 150
Ladies (Lejdis, 2008), 397–98, 418
Land, The (Ziemia, 1971), 174
Landscape after Battle (Krajobraz po bitwie, 1970), 181, 183
Larks on a String (Skřivánci na niti, 1969), 289
Last Bell, The (Ostatni dzwonek, 1989), 322
Last Day of Summer, The (Ostatni dzień lata, 1958), 138, 142
Last Days, The (Ostatnie dni, 1969), 165n68

Last Family, The (Ostatnia rodzina, 2016), 392–93, 418
Last Ferry, The (Ostatni prom, 1989), 283
Last Mission, The (Ostatnia misja, 2000), 360
Last Resort (2000), 383
Last Ride, The (Ostatni kurs, 1963), 208
Last Stage, The (Ostatni etap, 1948), 84–88, 97, 141, 144, 148
Last Stop, The. See The Last Stage
Lava: The Story of Forefathers (Lawa: Opowieść o Dziadach, 1989), 337n58
Law and the Fist, The (Prawo i pięść, 1964), 190
Led Astray, The. See Human Wrecks
Legion of the Street, The (Legion ulicy, 1932), 58
Leper, The (Trędowata, 1926), 19–20
Leper, The (Trędowata, 1936), 57
Leper, The (Trędowata, 1976), 37n39
Leprosy (Trąd, 1971), 201
Lesson of a Dead Language, The (Lekcja martwego języka, 1979), 246
Letters to Santa (Listy do M., 2011), 418, 424n73, 397–98
Let Us Love (Kochajmy się, 1974), 223
Life as a Fatal Sexually Transmitted Disease (Życie jako śmiertelna choroba przenoszona drogą płciową, 2000), 342, 364
Life Feels Good (Chce się żyć, 2013), 413
Life for Life: Maximilian Kolbe (Życie za życie: Maksymilian Kolbe, 1990), 281–83
Life of Matthew, The (Żywot Mateusza, 1968), 198, 263, 320
Life Once Again (Życie raz jeszcze, 1965), 324n24
Life Sentence (Wyrok życia, 1933), 55
Life's Little Comforts. See Woman from the Provinces
Lightship, The (1985), 144
Like a Drug (Jak narkotyk, 1999), 324
Line, The (Granica, 1938), 56–57
List of Adulteresses, The (Spis cudzołożnic, 1984), 331
Listen to My Cry (Usłyszcie mój krzyk, 1991), 334n30
Little Letter to Mother, A (A Brivele der Mamen, 1938), 30, 64

INDEX OF FILM TITLES · 495

Little Moscow (Mała Moskwa, 2008), 397
Little Western (Mały western, 1960), 150
Lodger, The (Sublokator, 1967), 200
Londoners (Londyńczycy, 2008), 418
Lonely Together (Samotność we dwoje, 1969), 166n73
Long Night, The (Długa noc, 1967), 187
Long Road, The (Wielka droga, 1946), 72–73
Lost Feelings (Zagubione uczucia, 1957), 107–8, 125–26
Lotna. *See* Speed
Louder than Bombs (Głośniej od bomb, 2002), 357–58
Love Actually (2003), 398
Love and Passion. *See* Slave of Sin
Love at Twenty (1962), 159
Love It or Leave It (Kochaj albo rzuć, 1977), 210, 219n93
Love or a Kingdom (Barbara Radziwiłłówna, 1936), 51
Love Requited (Nagrodzone uczucia, 1957), 150
Love Stories (Historie miłosne, 1997), 331
Love Through Fire and Blood (Miłość przez ogień i krew, 1924), 23
Loved and Hated: The Tragedy of Life and Death of the Maker of *The Teutonic Knights* (Kochany i znienawidzony. Dramat życia i śmierci twórcy *Krzyżaków*, 2002), 213n2
Loving (Miłość, 2013), 412
Loving Vincent (Twój Vincent, 2017), 418
Lullaby Killer (Ach śpij kochanie, 2017), 395
Lure, The (Córki dancingu, 2015), 399, 400
Lydia Ate the Apple. *See* Farewells
Lynching (Lincz, 2010), 412

M

Machine, The (Maszyna 1961), 150
Madame DuBarry. *See* Passion
Mad Love (L'amour braque, 1985), 189
Magnate, The (Magnat, 1987), 247, 316
Maiden Vows (Śluby panieńskie, 2010), 366n6
Maidens and Widows (Panny i wdowy, 1991), 315
Maids of Wilko, The (Panny z Wilka, 1979), 244–45
Majdanek, the Cemetery of Europe (Majdanek – Cmentarzysko Europy, 1944), 81

Mammals (Ssaki, 1962), 157
Manhole, The (Kratka, 1996), 331
Manhunt (Obława, 2012), 376
Man of... (Człowiek z…, 1993), 317
Man of Iron (Człowiek z żelaza, 1981), 237–38, 253n60, 255, 257, 268, 312–13, 317, 389–90
Man of Marble (Człowiek z marmuru, 1977), 228–30, 238, 241, 287, 290, 317, 389
Man on the Tracks (Człowiek na torze, 1957), 107–9, 119
Man Thing, A (Męska sprawa, 2001), 412
Man with the Magic Box, The (Człowiek z magicznym pudełkiem, 2017), 401
March Almonds (Marcowe migdały, 1990), 297, 303–4
Marriageable Girls (Dziewczyny do wzięcia, 1972), 338n78
Masked Spy, The (Szpieg w masce, 1933), 66n25
Matilda's Birthday (Urodziny Matyldy, 1975), 162n15
Matter to Be Settled, A (Sprawa do załatwienia, 1953), 101
Meetings in the Twilight (Spotkania w mroku, 1960), 143
Meir Ezofowicz (1911), 12–13, 34n8
Memento (2000), 403
Memoirs Found in a Hunched Back. *See* Diary in Marble
Memoirs of a Sinner (Osobisty pamiętnik grzesznika przez niego samego spisany, 1986), 263
Microphone for Everybody (Mikrofon dla wszystkich, 1976), 223
Microphone Test, The (Próba mikrofonu, 1980), 223
Mighty Angel, The (Pod Mocnym Aniołem, 2014), 409
Mill and the Cross, The (Młyn i krzyż, 2011), 363–64, 371
Million, Le (1931), 153
Miracle on the Vistula (Cud nad Wisłą, 1921), 19, 23
Miracle Seller (Handlarz cudów, 2010), 426n92
Miraculous Place (Cudowne miejsce, 1994), 320
Miss Nobody (Panna Nikt, 1996), 281
Mole, The (Kret, 2011), 396

Monidło (1970), 218n78
Monsieur Hire (1988), 270
Moonlighting (1982), 194
Moonwalkers (Lunatycy, 1960), 125–26
Morality of Mrs. Dulska, The (Moralność pani Dulskiej, 1930), 42
More than Life at Stake (Stawka większa niż życie, 1965–67), 172
Morning of Coyote, The (Poranek Kojota, 2001), 360
Moth, The (Ćma, 1980), 223
Mother (Pudovkin, 1926), 22
Mother Joan of the Angels (Matka Joanna od Aniołów, 1961), 118, 122, 153–56
Mother of Kings, The (Matka Królów, 1982/1987), 241, 255, 275, 295, 313
Mother's Heart (Serce matki, 1938), 46,
Mother Teresa of Cats (Matka Teresa od kotów, 2010), 403
Mountains at Dusk (Góry o zmierzchu, 1970), 196
Movie Extras (Statyści, 2006), 398
Mr. Anatol Seeks a Million (Pan Anatol szuka miliona, 1959), 167n95
Mr. Blot's Academy (Akademia pana Kleksa, 1984), 260
Mr. Dodek (Pan Dodek, 1970), 67n28
Mutiny of Blood and Iron, The (Bunt krwi i żelaza, 1927), 30
My Flesh, My Blood (Moja krew, 2009), 416
My Nikifor (Mój Nikifor, 2004), 342, 365
My Old Man (Mój stary, 1962), 149
My Roast Chicken (Moje pieczone kurczaki, 2002), 355
Mystery of a Doctor, The (Tajemnica lekarza, 1930), 42
Mystery of Ujazdowskie Avenue, The (Tajemnica Alei Ujazdowskich, 1917), 35n30
My Street (Moja ulica, 1965), 173
My Summer of Love (2004), 283
My Town (Moje miasto, 2002), 355

N

Nation in Exile, A. *See* The White Eagle
Never Ever! (Nigdy w życiu! 2004), 397
New Janko Musician, The (Nowy Janko Muzykant, 1960), 150
Next Door (Za ścianą, 1971), 196, 236
Night and Fog (Nuit et Brouillard, 1955), 87
Night Graffiti (Nocne graffiti, 1997), 306, 308, 359
Nightmare, A (Gehenna (1938), 46
Nightmares (Zmory, 1979), 242, 244, 247, 284
Night of Remembrance, A (Celuloza, 1954), 105–6, 123
Nights and Days (Noce i dnie, 1975), 179
Night Train (Pociąg, 1959), 153–56
Nightwatching (2007), 371
Nikodem Dyzma (1956), 67n28
1968: Happy New Year (1968: Szczęśliwego Nowego Roku, 1993), 297, 303
Nobody Is Calling (Nikt nie woła, 1960), 118, 132, 136–38, 158
No End (Bez końca, 1985), 267–68
No Mercy (Nie ma zmiłuj, 2000), 362
No More Divorces (Rozwodów nie będzie, 1964), 161n15
Noose, The (Pętla, 1958), 126–28
Not Far from Warsaw (Niedaleko Warszawy, 1954), 99, 103–4, 112n12
Nothing (Nic, 1998), 322
Nothing Funny (Nic śmiesznego, 1996), 278, 317–18, 360
Not One Stone Upon Another (Kamień na kamieniu, 1995), 322

O

O-bi, o-ba: End of Civilization (O-bi, o-ba: Koniec cywilizacji, 1985), 253n60
Ode to Joy (Oda do radości, 2005), 420n20
Office, The (Urząd, 1966), 173, 214n12
Office, The (Urząd, 1969), 168n102
Offsiders, The (Boisko bezdomnych, 2008), 413
Oh, Charles (Och, Karol, 1985), 261
Old Tale, The (Stara baśń, 2003), 215n33, 243
Once Upon a Time (Był sobie raz, 1957), 150
Once Upon a Time in November (Pewnego razu w listopadzie, 2017), 404
Once Upon a Time in Warsaw (Był sobie dzieciak, 2013), 378
One Flew over the Cuckoo's Nest (1975), 256

One of the Thirty-six (Der Lamedvovnik, 1925), 24
One Room Tenants. *See* Shared Room
One Way Ticket to the Moon (Bilet na księżyc, 2013), 394–95
Only Fear (Tylko strach, 1993), 324
Only the Dead Will Answer (Tylko umarły odpowie, 1969), 209
On the Niemen River (Nad Niemnem, 1939), 70
On the Niemen River (Nad Niemnem, 1987), 262
On the Silver Globe (Na srebrnym globie, 1977/1989), 189
Operation Arsenal (Akcja pod Arsenałem, 1978), 245
Operation Samum (Operacja Samum, 1999), 306
Orchestra, The (1990), 257
Ordinary Day of Szmidt, the Gestapo Man, An (Powszedni dzień gestapowca Szmidta, 1963), 151
Orphans of the Storm (1921), 21
Othello (1950), 73
Our Chidren (Unzere Kinder, 1948), 83–84, 94n44
Outbreak, The (Zaraza, 1972), 200

P

Paint (Farba, 1997), 332
Palace, The (Pałac, 1980), 247
Pandora's Box (1929), 55
Pan Michael (Pan Wołodyjowski, 1969), 66n20, 172, 178–79
Pan Tadeusz (1928), 26
Pan Tadeusz (1999), 343–47
Paper Marriage (Papierowe małżeństwo, 1992), 397–98
Papusza (2013), 392
Parade, The (Defilada, 1989), 291
Paradigm (1985), 251n34, 259
Partings. *See* Goodbye to the Past
Pass Mark (Zaliczenie, 1968), 173
Passenger, The (Pasażerka, 1963), 143, 146–48, 159, 165n55, 166n84
Passion (Madame DuBarry, 1919), 18
Paths of Hate (2010), 418

Pearl Harbour (2001), 343
Pearl in the Crown, The (Perła w koronie, 1972), 203, 205–6
Peasant Diaries (Pamiętniki chłopów, 1953), 161n13
Peasants (Chłopi, 1973), 173
Peddler, The (Kramarz, 1990), 319–20
Penguin (Pingwin, 1965), 161n15
People from Nowhere (Ludzie z pustego obszaru, 1957), 125
People from the Train (Ludzie z pociągu, 1961), 138
People of the Vistula, The (Ludzie Wisły, 1938), 46, 59, 61
Perfect Afternoon, A (Doskonałe popołudnie, 2005), 358
Persona non grata (2005), 365
Personnel (Personel, 1975), 212, 222–23, 232, 236, 250n11, 255, 259
Peter & the Wolf (2008), 418
Phantom (Widziadło, 1984), 261
Pharaoh (Faraon, 1966), 172, 176–77
Photograph, The (Zdjęcie, 1968), 173
Photographer (Fotoamator, 1998), 304–5
Photographer, The (Fotograf, 2014), 395–97
Pigs, The (Psy, 1992), 306, 308, 310–15, 338n71, 33n74, 359, 372
Pigs 2: The Last Blood, The (Psy 2: Ostatnia krew, 1994), 313–14
Pills for Aurelia (Pigułki dla Aurelii, 1958), 118, 139
Pip (Pestka, 1995), 278
Pitbull (2005), 359, 401–2
Pitbull: New Order (Pitbull: Nowe porządki, 2016), 401–2
Pitbull: Tough Women (Pitbull: Niebezpieczne kobiety, 2016), 401–2
Place on Earth, A (Miejsce na ziemi, 1960), 166n73
Planet Single (Planeta Singli, 2016), 397–98, 424n73
Planet Tailor, The (Planeta krawiec, 1984), 251n29
Plate Player, The (Grający z talerza, 1995), 320–21
Players (Gracze, 1996), 252n50
Pograbek (1992), 320

Police Chief Tagiejew, The (Policmajster Tagiejew, 1929), 25, 46
Po-lin (Po-lin. Okruchy pamięci, 2008), 417
Polish Dancer, The (Bestia, 1917), 17
Polish Newsreel (Polska Kronika Filmowa), 82–83
Polish Shit (Polskie gówno, 2015), 399
Polish Ways (Polskie drogi, 1976–77), 245
Polonia Restituta (1981), 245
Pornography (Pornografia, 2003), 189
Possession (1981), 189
Postcard from the Journey, A (Kartka z podróży, 1984), 256, 264–65
Poste Restante (2009), 416
Primate: Three Years Out of the Millennium, The (Prymas: Trzy lata z tysiąclecia, 2000), 347
Prisoner of Europe, The (Jeniec Europy, 1989), 281
Prisoner of Rio, The (1988), 363
Private Fleischer's Photo Album (Album Fleischera, 1963), 199
Private Investigation (Prywatne śledztwo, 1987), 260
Private Town, The (Miasto prywatne, 1993), 306, 314
Professor Wilczur (Profesor Wilczur, 1938), 57
Professor Wilczur's Last Will (Testament Profesora Wilczura, 1939/1942), 57
Promised Land, The (Ziemia obiecana, 1927), 26
Promised Land, The (Ziemia obiecana, 1975), 181, 184, 216n34
Provincial Actors (Aktorzy prowincjonalni, 1979), 221, 232, 236
Prussian Culture (Pruska kultura, 1908), 11, 33n6
Public Woman, The (La femme publique, 1984), 189
Purim Player, The (Der Purimshpiler, 1937), 64
Purple Rose of Cairo, The (1985), 284

Q

Quack, The (Znachor, 1937), 57
Quack (Znachor, 1982), 260
Quiet American, The (1958), 73
Quo Vadis? (1913), 13
Quo Vadis (2001), 343, 366n5

R

Rabbit á la Berlin (Królik po berlińsku, 2009), 416
Rafts Are Floating (Płyną tratwy, 1962), 151
Railwayman's Pledge (Kolejarskie słowo, 1953), 114n36
Rainbow, The (Raduga, 1944), 78, 87
Rainy July (Deszczowy lipiec, 1958), 168n98
Rainy Soldier, The (Deszczowy żołnierz, 1996), 257
Rancho Texas (1959), 118
Rashomon (1950), 109
Rassenschande (Kiedy miłość była zbrodnią, 1968), 188
Rear Window (1954), 270
Rebus (1977), 223
Reconciliation, The (Zgoda, 2017), 376
Record of Crime (Zapis zbrodni, 1974), 201
Red and Black (Czerwone i czarne, 1963), 150
Red Jester (Czerwony błazen, 1926), 26
Red Spider (Czerwony pająk, 2015), 395
Reformatory, The (Zakład, 1990), 323
Reich (2001), 357
Remember Your Name (Zapamiętaj imię swoje, 1974), 187
Repentance (Pokajanie, 1987), 289
Repulsion (1965), 351
Requiem (2001), 357
Requiem for 500,000 (Requiem dla 500 000, 1963), 151, 305
Reserve, The (Rezerwat), 392
Respectable Sins (Zacne grzechy, 1963), 168n102
Retrieval (Z odzysku, 2006), 412
Return Home (Heimkehr, 1941), 70, 91n5
Return of a Merry Fellow, The (Powrót birbanta, 1902), 11
Return to Earth (Powrót na ziemię, 1967), 159
Revenge (Zemsta, 2002), 343, 345
Reverse, The (Rewers, 2009), 396
Revisited (Rewizyta, 2009), 369n48
Righteous, The (Sprawiedliwi, 2010), 380
Ring with a Crowned Eagle, The (Pierścionek z orłem w koronie, 1993), 169n115, 281, 291, 293, 335n36
Road West, The (Droga na zachód, 1961), 162n30

INDEX OF FILM TITLES · 499

Robbery (Skok, 1969), 203
Roll Call, The (Apel, 1970), 253n62
Roman Holiday (1953), 73
Rome, Open City (Roma città aperta, 1945), 78
Room No. 13 (Pokój nr 13, 1917), 35n30
Rose, The (Róża, 1936), 50
Rose (Róża, 2012), 407–8
Rosebud (Różyczka, 2010), 397
Rosemary's Baby (1968), 169n114
Rough Treatment (Bez znieczulenia, 1978), 221–22, 232–33, 236
Rowan Tree, The (Jarzębina czerwona, 1970), 186
Run Lola Run (Lola rennt, 1998), 403

S

Sabra (1933), 59, 67n42
Sabre from the Commander, The (Szabla od komendanta, 1995), 320–21
Salt of the Black Earth (Sól ziemi czarnej, 1970), 203–6
Samson (1961), 143, 145
Sandglass, The. *See* The Hourglass Sanatorium
Sara (1997), 306
Saragossa Manuscript, The (Rękopis znaleziony w Saragossie, 1965), 177
Satan's Son (Syn szatana, 1923), 25
Savage Father, The (Der Wilder Foter, 1911), 14
Savior Square (Plac Zbawiciela), 411
Scar, The (Blizna, 1976), 223–25, 236, 240
Scenes of Battle (Barwy walki, 1965), 190
Schindler's List (1993), 87, 297, 302
Scratch (Rysa, 2008), 396
Screen Tests (Zdjęcia próbne, 1977), 232
Scribbler, The (Pismak, 1985), 262–63
Scurvy (Cynga, 1993), 291, 294–95
Season of Dead Birds, The (Sezon na bażanty, 1986), 256
Secret (Sekret, 2012), 379
Secret of Westerplatte, The (Tajemnica Westerplatte, 2013), 216n46
Secret Service 1944–1956 (Bezpieka 1944–1956, 1997), 291
Secrets of the Warsaw Police, The (Ochrana warszawska i jej tajemnice, 1916), 12
Seduced Woman, A (Uwiedziona, 1931), 54

Seen but Not Heard (Dzieci i ryby, 1996), 318
See You Tomorrow (Do widzenia, do jutra, 1960), 153
Sensitive Spots (Czułe miejsca, 1981), 253n60
Sequence of Feelings, The (Kolejność uczuć, 1993), 308, 316, 398
Sergeant Major Kaleń (Ogniomistrz Kaleń, 1961), 139–40
Sex Mission (Seksmisja, 1984), 259–60
Seychelles (Seszele, 1989), 313
Shadow, The (Cień, 1956), 107
Shadow Line, The (Smuga cienia, 1976), 216n35
Shared Room (Wspólny pokój, 1960), 128
Shelter (Meta, 1971), 218n78, 250n14
She-Shaman (Szamanka, 1996), 189, 278
Shifting Sands (Ruchome piaski, 1971), 198
Shilly Shally (Wahadełko, 1981), 241
Shivers (Dreszcze, 1981), 241–42, 255, 284, 291, 295
Shoah (1985), 266, 296
Shop on Main Street, The (Obchod na korze, 1965), 302
Short Film About Killing, A (Krótki film o zabijaniu, 1988), 268–70, 313
Short Film About Love, A (Krótki film o miłości, 1988), 268, 270, 273n29
Short Working Day (Krótki dzień pracy, 1981), 240
Shout, The (1978), 194
Shout, The (Krzyk, 1983), 232, 324
Show (2003), 360
Shrek (2001), 343
Siberian Lady Macbeth (Sibirska Ledi Makbet, 1962), 159
Siberian Exile (Syberiada polska, 2013), 376
Silence (Cisza, 2001), 353–54
Silence (Milczenie, 1963), 203
Silence, The (Tystnaden, 1963), 269
Silent Night (Wśród nocnej ciszy, 1978), 248
Silent Night (Cicha noc, 2017), 416
Silent Touch, The (Dotknięcie ręki, 1992), 281–82
Sinful Life of Franciszek Buła, The (Grzeszny żywot Franciszka Buły, 1980), 248
Singing Fool, The (1928), 41
Skinny and Others (Chudy i inni, 1967), 201
Sky of Stone, A (Kamienne niebo, 1959), 163n44

Slave of Love, The (Niewolnica miłości, 1923), 16, 20
Slave of Sin, The (Niewolnica zmysłów, 1914), 17
Small Dramas (Małe dramaty, 1960), 149
Small Town (Miasteczko, 1960), 125–26
Smolensk (Smoleńsk, 2016), 423n51
Snug as a Bug in a Rug (U pana Boga za piecem, 1998), 318
Soccer Poker (Piłkarski poker, 1989), 260
Soldier of the Queen of Madagascar, The (Żołnierz królowej Madagaskaru, 1940), 60
Soldier of Victory, The (Żołnierz zwycięstwa, 1953), 101, 112n16
Somersault (Salto, 1965), 159
Sons and Comrades (Jezioro Bodeńskie, 1986), 260, 262
Sophie's Choice (1982), 87
Sound of the Desert, The (Głos pustyni, 1932), 54
Souls in Slavery (Dusze w niewoli, 1930), 54
Souvenir from Calvary, A (Pamiątka z Kalwarii, 1958), 151
Speed (Lotna, 1959), 117, 140–41, 183, 185
Spider Women (Pajęczarki, 1992), 316
Spinning Wheel of Time, The (Wrzeciono czasu, 1995), 318–19, 338n78
Spiral (Spirala, 1978), 248
Splinters (Drzazgi, 2008), 424n70
Spoor (Pokot, 2017), 414–15
Squadron (Szwadron, 1993), 307
Squint Your Eyes (Zmruż oczy, 2003), 342, 366, 404
Stalking Season, The. *See* The Season of Dead Birds
Stall on Salvador (Stajnia na Salwatorze, 1967), 159, 186
Star Wars (1977), 101
State of Fear, The (Stan strachu, 1990), 284
Station (Stacja, 2001), 360
Steps (1987), 257, 308
Sting, The (1973), 259
Sting (Sztos, 1997), 360
Stones for the Rampart (Kamienie na szaniec, 2014), 378
Story of a Certain Love, The (Historia pewnej miłości, 1974, 1982), 212

Story of a Man Who Produced 552 Percent of the Norm, The (Opowieść o człowieku, który wykonał 552% normy, 1973), 174, 259n18
Story of Prophet Elijah of Wierszalin, The (Historia o proroku Eliaszu z Wierszalina, 1997), 250n12
Story of Roj, The (Historia Roja, 2016), 423n52
Story of Sin, The (Dzieje grzechu, 1911), 12
Story of Sin, The (Dzieje grzechu, 1933), 54
Story of Sin, The (Dzieje grzechu, 1975), 180
Story of the Kowalskis, The (Historia Kowalskich, 2009), 380
Strange Heaven (Obce niebo, 2015), 416
Stranger (Der Unbekanter, 1913), 14
Stranger (Ono, 2004), 404
Stranger Must Fly, The (Obcy musi fruwać, 1993), 257
Street Boys (Poznań 56, 1996), 291, 293
Street Games (Gry uliczne, 1996), 285–87
Strike (2006), 371
Strong Man, A (Mocny człowiek, 1929), 25
Structure of Crystals, The (Struktura kryształu, 1969), 195–96, 240
Stud Farm, The (Ménezgazda, 1978), 289
Stupor (Amok, 1999), 362
Submarine "Eagle," The (Orzeł, 1959), 140
Success is the Best Revenge (1984), 194
Such a Nice Boy I Gave Birth To (Takiego pięknego syna urodziłam, 1999), 417
Sucker Season (Sezon na leszcza, 2001), 357
Suicide Room, The (Sala samobójców, 2011), 420n20
Summer Solstice (Letnie przesilenie, 2016), 379
Sumurun (1920), 18, 36n31
Sunday Musicians, The (Muzykanci, 1960), 151
Sunday Pranks (Niedzielne igraszki, 1983), 241, 294
Sundial, The (Słoneczny zegar, 1997), 318–19
Sunrise (1927), 55
Sun Rises Once a Day, The (Słońce wschodzi raz na dzień, 1967), 201
Super Production (Superprodukcja, 2003), 356
Suspended (W zawieszeniu, 1987), 289–90, 295
Swan's Song, The (Łabędzi śpiew, 1989), 278

INDEX OF FILM TITLES · 501

Swastika and Gallows (Swastyka i szubienica, 1945), 82
Sweet Rush (Tatarak, 2009), 423n56
Szamota's Lover (Kochanka Szamoty, 1927), 30

T

Tango (1980), 253n61, 257
Tapes of Horror (Taśmy grozy, 2002), 401
Teddy Bear (Miś, 1981), 246
Temptation (Pokuszenie, 1995), 285, 291–92, 295, 324, 347
Ten from the Pawiak Prison, The (Dziesięciu z Pawiaka, 1931), 48, 66n18
Tenant, The (Le Locataire, 1976), 109n.91, 351
Terrible Dream of Dzidziuś Górkiewicz, The (Straszny sen Dzidziusia Górkiewicza, 1993), 164n55
Testosterone (Testosteron, 2007), 397–98
Teutonic Knights (Krzyżacy, 1960), 118, 152, 178
Thais (1984), 261
That Life Makes Sense... (...Że życie ma sens..., 2001), 357
Then There Will Be Silence (Potem nastąpi cisza, 1966), 190
There and Back (Tam i z powrotem, 2002), 348
There Was Jazz (Był jazz, 1981), 241
There Was No Sun That Spring (Nie było słońca tej wiosny, 1984), 266
They (Oni, 1999), 417
Third, The (Trzeci, 2004), 355–56
Third Part of the Night, The (Trzecia część nocy, 1972), 188–89
33 Scenes from Life (33 sceny z życia, 2008), 404
Three Colours: Blue (Trois couleurs: Bleu, 1993), 324, 327–28, 330–31, 339n84
Three Colours: Red (Trois couleurs: Rouge, 1994), 324, 329–31, 339n84
Three Colours: White (Trois couleurs: Blanc, 1994), 324, 328–29, 330–31, 339n84, 356
300 Miles to Heaven (300 mil do nieba, 1989), 285
Three Minutes 9:37 p.m. (Trzy minuty 21:37, 2010), 403
Three of Hearts (1992), 349
Three Women (Trzy kobiety, 1957), 141

Thou, Who Shines in the Gate (Ty, co w Ostrej świecisz Bramie, 1937), 50
Through and Through (Na wylot, 1973), 199
Time of Honor (Czas honoru, 2008), 380
Time Stands Still (Megáll az idö, 1981), 289
Tin Drum (Die Blechtrommel, 1979), 216n33
To Happiness through Tears (Przez łzy do szczęścia, 1939/1943), 54, 69
To Kill a Beaver (Zabić bobra, 2014), 401
To Kill a Priest (1988), 391
To Kill at the End (Zabić na końcu, 1990), 306
To Kill Sekal (Zabić Sekala, 1998), 306
Tomb of the Unknown Soldier, The (Mogiła nieznanego żołnierza, 1927), 24
Tomorrow Will be Better (Jutro będzie lepiej, 2011), 415
Tomorrow's Weather (Pogoda na jutro, 2003), 354
Top Dog (Wodzirej, 1978), 221–22, 231–32, 236
Torrents of Spring (1989), 194
To Siberia (Na Sybir, 1930), 47
Touch Me, (Dotknij mnie, 2003), 357
Touched, The (Dotknięci, 1988), 256
Toy, The (Zabawka, 1933), 55
Traffic Department (Drogówka, 2013), 359, 408–9, 422n42
Train to Hollywood (Pociąg do Hollywood, 1987), 260
Tramps, The (Włóczęgi, 1939), 27
Tram Stop Mystery, The (Tajemnica przystanku tramwajowego, 1922), 16, 20
Treasure (Skarb, 1949), 90, 97, 152, 210
Tricks (Sztuczki, 2007), 404
True End of the Great War, The (Prawdziwy koniec wielkiej wojny, 1957), 118, 142, 164n48
Truly Short Film about Love, Killing and One More Commandment, A (Naprawdę krótki film o miłości, zabijaniu i jeszcze jednym orzykazaniu, 1993), 332
Trumpeter's Monologue, The (Monolog trębacza, 1965), 319
Tsarist Regime and Its Servants, The (Carat i jego sługi, 1917), 12, 16
Turned Back, The (Zawróceny, 1994), 287–88, 308

Twelve Chairs (Dwanaście krzeseł, 1933), 52
21 Grams (2003), 403
Two Brigades (Dwie brygady, 1950), 98–99
Two Hours (Dwie godziny, 1946), 80, 94n36
Two Men and a Wardrobe (Dwaj ludzie z szafą, 1958), 157
Two Moons (Dwa księżyce, 1993), 319
Two Who Did Not Steal Anything, The (O dwóch takich, co nic nie ukradli, 1999), 362
Two Who Stole the Moon, The (O dwóch takich co ukradli księżyc, 1962), 149

U

Under the Banner of Love (Pod banderą miłości, 1929), 27, 66n19
Under the Phrygian Star (Pod gwiazdą frygijską, 1954), 105–6, 123
Under This Same Sky (Pod jednym niebem, 1955), 150
Under Your Protection (Pod Twoją obronę, 1933), 56
Uneventful Story, An (Nieciekawa historia, 1983), 262
Unfinished Journey (1943), 74
United States of Love (Zjednoczone stany miłości, 2016), 414
Unloved (Niekochana, 1966), 188, 212
Unspeakable, The. *See* What You Do Not Talk About
Unthinkable, The (O czym się nie myśli, 1926), 17
Unusually Quiet Man, An (Niespotykanie spokojny człowiek, 1975), 252n55
Unvanquished City, The (Miasto nieujarzmione, 1950), 79–80
Upstairs (Piętro wyżej, 1937), 397

V

Va Banque (Vabank, 1982), 259, 306
Va Banque II (Vabank II, czyli riposta, 1985), 259
Vagabond, The (Przybłęda, 1933), 45–46
Valley of Issa, The (Dolina Issy, 1982), 255
Vampires of Warsaw, The (Wampiry Warszawy, 1925), 27
Village Mill, The (Gromada, 1952), 99, 106
Vilna Legend, A. *See* The Vow (1937)

Vinci (2004), 360
Visit Me in My Dream (Odwiedź mnie we śnie, 1996), 323
Visit of the President, The (Odwiedziny prezydenta, 1962), 149
Voice, The (Głos, 1992), 338n78
Voice from Beyond, The (Głos z tamtego świata, 1962), 166n73
Voice from the Heart (Głos serca, 1931), 42
Volga-Volga (1937), 78
Volhynia (Wołyń, 2016), 409–14
Volta (2017), 399
Vow, The (Tkies Kaf, 1924), 15, 35n30
Vow, The (Tkies Kaf, 1937), 35n20
Vow, The (Pitsi, 1946), 93n25

W

Wacuś (1935), 53
Walesa: Man of Hope (Wałęsa. Człowiek z nadziei, 2013), 388–89
Walk in the Old Town, A (Spacerek staromiejski, 1958), 164n53
Walkover (Walkower, 1965), 192–93
Walpurgis Night (Noc Walpurgi, 2015), 379
Wanda Gościmińska, the Textile Worker (Wanda Gościmińska – włókniarka, 1975/1981), 173, 257
Wanted (Poszukiwany, poszukiwana, 1972), 246
War at Home (Wojna domowa, 1965–66), 173
War Demons According to Goya, The (Demony wojny według Goyi, 1998), 306
War of the Worlds: Next Century (Wojna światów: następne stulecie, 1981), 248
Warsaw (Warszawa, 2003), 365, 404
Warsaw '44 (Miasto 44, 2014), 377
Warsaw Premiere (Warszawska premiera, 1951), 112n18
Warsaw Robinson, The (Robinson warszawski, 1949), 79
Warsaw Uprising (Powstanie Warszawskie, 2014), 377–78
Warszawa. Année 5703 (Tragarz puchu, 1992), 297, 300–1, 336n54
Washington Square (1997), 271n1
Ways in the Night (Wege in der Nacht, 1979), 271n9

INDEX OF FILM TITLES · 503

We Are All Christs (Wszyscy jesteśmy Chrystusami, 2006), 369n42
We Are Still Alive (Mir Lebn Geblibene, 1947), 83
We Come to You, Poland, Our Mother (Idziem do ciebie Polsko, matko nasza, 1921), 38n55
Weather Forecast (Prognoza pogody, 1983), 262
Wedding, The (Wesele, 1973), 181, 183
Wedding, The (Wesele, 2004), 342, 366, 405–6
Week in the Life of a Man, A (Tydzień z życia mężczyzny, 1999), 354
Weekend Stories (Opowieści weekendowe, 1996–2000), 281, 331
Weekend with a Girl (Weekend z dziewczyną, 1968), 212
Weiser (2001), 347
Welts, The (Pręgi, 2004), 365
Westerplatte (1967), 160, 185
We Will not Give up Our Land (Nie damy ziemi skąd nasz ród, 1920), 23
What the Sun Has Seen (Co słonko widziało, 2006), 412
What You Do Not Talk About (O czym się nie mówi, 1939), 44, 46
What Will You Do With Me When You Catch Me (Co mi zrobisz jak mnie złapiesz, 1978), 246
When Angels Fall (Gdy spadają anioły, 1959), 157
When a Wife Cuckolds Her Husband. *See* The Woman Who Desires Sin
When Love Was a Crime. *See* Rassenschande
Where Is the General? (Gdzie jest generał? 1964), 210
Where Is the Third King (Gdzie jest trzeci król, 1967), 208
Where the Devil Says Good Night (Gdzie diabeł mówi dobranoc, 1957), 125
Where the Water Is Clear and the Grass Is Green (Gdzie woda czysta i trawa zielona, 1977), 252n53
Wherever You Are (Gdzieśkolwiek jest, jeśliś jest, 1989), 281–82
Wherever You Are, Mr. President (Gdziekolwiek jesteś, Panie Prezydencie, 1978), 245
White Bear (Biały niedźwiedź, 1959), 118, 143, 146
White Eagle, The (1941), 74
White Marriage (Białe małżeństwo, 1993), 323
White Poison (Biała trucizna, 1932), 54
White Trail (Biały ślad, 1932), 45
Whoever Knows (Ktokolwiek wie, 1966), 203
Wife (Żona, 1915), 17
Wife for an Australian, A (Żona dla Australijczyka, 1964), 211, 397
Wild Fields (Dzikie pola, 1932), 50
Wild Horses (Tarpany, 1962), 202
Wild Roses (Dzikie róże, 2017), 416
Wind from the Sea, The (Wiatr of morza, 1930), 66n19
Window (Okno, 1981/1983), 260
Winnetou (Apache Gold, 1965), 171
Winter Twilight (Zimowy zmierzch, 1957), 118, 126–27, 138, 158
With Fire and Sword (Ogniem i mieczem, 1999), 345–47
Without Anesthesia. *See* Rough Treatment
Without Love (Bez miłości, 1980), 222, 232, 323–24
Witness, The, (A tanú, 1969), 132, 289
Władysław Szpilman 1911–2000: In His Own Words (Władysław Szpilman 1911–2000, własnymi słowami, 1994), 368n27
Wojaczek (1999), 363
Wolves' Echoes (Wilcze echa, 1968), 190
Woman Alone, A (Kobieta samotna, 1981), 238–39, 255, 275, 313
Woman from the Provinces (Kobieta z prowincji, 1985), 319, 401
Woman Who Desires Sin, The (Kobieta, która grzechu pragnie, 1929), 27
Woman with a Hat, A (Kobieta w kapeluszu, 1985), 261
Women's Day (Dzień kobiet, 2013), 423n61
Woman's Decision, A. (Bilans kwartalny, 1975), 196
Women's Republic (Rzeczpospolita babska, 1969), 211
Wooden Rosary (Drewniany różaniec, 1965), 156
Word on Wincenty Pstrowski, A (Słowo o Wincentym Pstrowskim, 1973), 250n18
Workers 1980 (Workers '80, 1981), 237

Workers 1971: Nothing About Us Without Us (Robotnicy '71. Nic o nas bez nas, 1972), 252n43
Working Women (Kobiety pracujące, 1978), 223
Wounded in the Forest (Ranny w lesie, 1964), 181
Write and Fight. *See* The Scribbler

Y

Year 1863 (Rok 1863, 1922), 24, 38n59
Year of Franek W., A (Rok Franka W., 1967), 173
Year of the Quiet Sun (Rok spokojnego słońca, 1985), 257–58, 408
Yesterday (1985), 260–61
Yiddle with His Fiddle (Yidl mitn Fidl, 1936), 63–64, 83
You Are God (Jesteś Bogiem, 2012), 371, 399
You have No Idea How I Love You (Nawet nie wiesz jak bardzo cię kocham, 2016), 417
Young Eagle (Orlę, 1927), 25
Young Forest, The (Młody las, 1934), 47, 50–51
Youth of Chopin, The (Młodość Chopina, 1952), 102, 112n18

Z

Zabriskie Point (1969), 202
Zero (2009), 403
07 Report (07 zgłoś się, 1976–1987), 209
Zofia (1976), 248

www.ingramcontent.com/pod-product-compliance
Lightning Source LLC
Chambersburg PA
CBHW072140100526
44589CB00015B/2015